LORD *of* *the* BANQUET

LORD *of*
the BANQUET

The Literary and Theological
Significance of the Lukan Travel Narrative

DAVID P. MOESSNER

FORTRESS PRESS   MINNEAPOLIS

LORD OF THE BANQUET
The Literary and Theological Significance of the Lukan Travel Narrative

Library of Congress Cataloging-in-Publication Data

Moessner, David P., date
    Lord of the banquet: The literary and theological significance
    of the Lukan travel narrative.

    Bibliography: p.
    Includes indexes.
    1. Bible. N.T. Luke IX, 51–XIX, 44—Criticism,
interpretation, etc.   2. Jesus Christ—Journeys.
I. Title.
BS2595.2.M62   1989   226.4'06   88–45245
ISBN 0-8006-0893-3

Manufactured in the United States of America   AF 1–893

93   92   91   90   89   1   2   3   4   5   6   7   8   9   10

To Jeanne
יחננה

Contents

† For a list of passages treated, see Index I.

Preface

The problems concerning form and content in the central "travel" section of the Gospel of Luke appear insoluble. The journeying and teaching of Jesus seem hopelessly confused. But as the title suggests, this study finds a decisive clue to solving this puzzle in the many references to Jesus' eating and drinking. And as the subtitle indicates, the following pages purport to set the longest narrative portion (nearly 40 percent) of the Third Gospel within its even larger frame in order to illuminate its significance for the overall story and theology of Luke-Acts.

Such an objective is obviously daunting. We shall have to sift and analyze and align the many tradition units in Luke 9:51—19:44 from different angles and perspectives; repetition of insights and conclusions will be unavoidable. Those less eager to descend into the crooks and crevasses of the tortuous terrain of Luke's "journey" are urged to proceed immediately from Part II to the Conclusion of Part III where the movements and words of Jesus have been charted into a coherent and dynamic plot. But it is only as we approach the difficulties from as many divergent vantage points as possible that we minimalize unwarranted interpretations and superficial solutions.

This study was first accepted as a dissertation for the degree of Doctor of Theology by the Theology Faculty of the University of Basel on August 2, 1983. I have shortened the present format considerably, especially the notes, while leaving the structure and substance of the argument intact. No attempt has been made to include all the important Lukan studies that have appeared in the meantime, though I have continued the dialogue with certain of the more recent contributions to the Central Section of Luke, particularly those from the fruitful discussions of the Luke-Acts Seminar and the Acts Group of the Society of Biblical Literature. Wherever possible I have tried to use inclusive language, though in some instances I have retained a literal rendering (e.g., "fathers") for "echo effect" and/or paronomasia within the scriptural tradition. All translations, unless specifically identified, are my own.

To thank all of those from whom I have learned and who have offered valued insights and encouragement "on the way" seems almost as insuperable as the problems confronting Luke's journey section. Gratitude must first be expressed to my parents and then to my teachers who provided unbroken years of study at Princeton University, Princeton Theological Seminary, University of Oxford, and the University of Basel. Inspiration for the present work came from my revered supervisor and friend, the late Professor Bo Reicke. It is hard to imagine one in whom the erudition of the ages and the gentleness of Spirit more closely coinhered than in the work and life of this true doctor of the church. His openness in method, pursuit of issues with ecumenical embrace, and precision in fact and expression have left indelible impressions upon all his students. Special thanks also to my "co-referent," Professor Markus Barth, whose critique was always incisive and who opened up new avenues of understanding. To Professors O. Cullmann, E. Grässer, and F. Hahn of the ATANT series, gratitude for their careful reading of the manuscript, and particularly to Professor Cullmann for his helpful suggestions and encouragement toward publication. To all those who offered invaluable insights and advice along the various stages of this effort—the late Professor G. B. Caird of Oxford, Professors B. Childs, L. Keck, and A. Malherbe of Yale, and Professor D. Gunn of Columbia Theological Seminary should be mentioned especially—let me express my thanks. I owe a special debt of gratitude for the present publication to Columbia Theological Seminary whose Dean, Professor Oscar Hussel, Presidents J. Davison Philips and now Douglas W. Oldenburg, Board of Directors, faculty, and alumni have offered critical assistance and funding. Let me thank Ann Titshaw and especially Elsie Urie for their careful retyping of the manuscript and also Ann Graham, Rick Boyette, and especially Jerry Ferrari, Sue Boardman, and Richard Deibert for their gracious assistance in proofreading and compiling of the indexes. To all my students—at Columbia Theological Seminary, Yale Divinity School, and Louisiana State University—I give my warmest thanks for the many ways that you have enriched me and for the many things that you have taught me. To Dr. John A. Hollar, Senior Editor of Fortress Press, I express my appreciation for his judicious efforts in improving style and organization; any infelicity of language that may remain must be attributed solely to me. Finally, I dedicate this work to my wife and companion, Jeanne, from whom, more than from any other, I have learned the true boundary of all biblical study: *omnia exeunt in mysteria!*

A word about the *arrows* employed throughout the book will be helpful.

An arrow represents a movement or development of plot, as defined in the introduction, and thus is a way of indicating a link between passages that is *not* simply a "piling up" or crescendoing of a particular theme as found in the usual motif analysis with its multiple citations. An asterisk (*) in Part III refers to the tradition units utilized in this study, following the divisions of K. Aland, ed., *Synopsis Quattuor Evangeliorum.* The reader is also referred to the table at the end of Part III for a cataloguing of the units in Luke 9:51—19:44, and to Index I.

The structure, then, of the following presentation is many-sided, cumulative, and intersecting. But if I may quote from a similar context the great New Testament scholar, C. H. Dodd, it is "within such an interlocking structure [that] even mere possibilities may (sometimes) come to wear a different aspect" (*Historical Tradition in the Fourth Gospel,* 423). It is hoped that the "mere possibilities" of penetrating Luke's enigmatic journey may through our investigation indeed "wear a different aspect."

David P. Moessner
Feast Day of St. Luke, 1988

Abbreviations

IB	*Interpreter's Bible*
ICC	International Critical Commentary
IDB	G. A. Buttrick, ed., *Interpreter's Dictionary of the Bible*
Int	*Interpretation*
JBL	*Journal of Biblical Literature*
JEH	*Journal of Ecclesiastical History*
JRS	*Journal of Roman Studies*
JSNT	*Journal for the Study of the New Testament*
JSS	*Journal of Semitic Studies*
KBANT	Kommentare und Beiträge zum Alten und Neuen Testament
KKNT	Kritischexegetischer Kommentar über das Neue Testament
LSJ	Liddell-Scott-Jones, *Greek-English Lexicon*
MNTC	Moffatt NT Commentary
NCB	New Century Bible
NICNT	New International Commentary on the New Testament
NIGTC	The New International Greek Testament Commentary
NovT	*Novum Testamentum*
NovTSup	Novum Testamentum, Supplements
NTAbh	Neutestamentliche Abhandlungen
NTD	Das Neue Testament Deutsch
NTS	*New Testament Studies*
OTL	Old Testament Library
PNTC	The Pelican New Testament Commentaries
PSTJ	*Perkins (School of Theology) Journal*
PVTG	Pseudepigrapha Veteris Testamenti graece
RevExp	*Review and Expositor*
RevQ	*Revue de Qumran*
RHPR	*Revue d'histoire et de philosophie religieuses*
RNT	Regensburger Neues Testament
SANT	Studien zum Alten und Neuen Testament
SBL	Society of Biblical Literature
SBLDS	SBL Dissertation Series
SBLMS	SBL Monograph Series
Scr	*Scripture*
SE	*Studia Evangelica*
SNT	Studien zum Neuen Testament
SNTSMS	Society for New Testament Studies Monograph Series
SPB	Studia Postbiblica
Str-B	(H. Strack and) P. Billerbeck, *Kommentar zum Neuen Testament*
SUNT	Studien zur Umwelt des Neuen Testaments
TDNT	G. Kittel and G. Friedrich, eds., *Theological Dictionary of the New Testament*
TSK	*Theologische Studien und Kritiken*
TZ	*Theologische Zeitschrift*
UUÅ	Uppsala universitetsårsskrift
VT	*Vetus Testamentum*

WMANT Wissenschaftliche Monographien zum Alten und Neuen Testament
ZAW   *Zeitschrift für die alttestamentliche Wissenschaft*
ZDMG   *Zeitschrift der deutschen morgenländischen Gesellschaft*
ZNW   *Zeitschrift für die neutestamentliche Wissenschaft*
ZRGG   *Zeitschrift für Religions- und Geistesgeschichte*
ZTK   *Zeitschrift für Theologie und Kirche*
ZWT   *Zeitschrift für wissenschaftliche Theologie*

COMMENTARIES AND FREQUENTLY QUOTED SHORT TITLES

Bultmann, R. *Syn. Trad.*   *Die Geschichte der synoptischen Tradition.* 3d ed. Göttingen: Vandenhoeck & Ruprecht, 1957; English ed., New York: Harper & Row, 1963.

Caird, G. B. *Luke*   Saint Luke. PNTC. Baltimore/Hardmondsworth: Penguin Books, 1963.

Conzelmann, H. *Theology*   *The Theology of St. Luke.* New York: Harper & Row, 1960; Philadelphia: Fortress Press, 1982 (German, 2d ed.: 1957).

Danby, H. *Mishnah*   *The Mishnah.* Oxford: Clarendon Press, 1933.

Danker, F. W. *Luke*   *Jesus and the New Age: According to St. Luke.* Rev. ed. Philadelphia: Fortress Press, 1988.

Ellis, E. E. *Luke*   *The Gospel of Luke.* NCB. Grand Rapids: Wm. B. Eerdmans Publishing Co., 1974.

Findlay, J. A. *Luke*   *The Gospel According to St. Luke: A Commentary.* London: SCM Press, 1937.

Fitzmyer, J. A. *Luke*   *The Gospel According to Luke.* AB. 2 vols. Garden City, N.Y.: Doubleday & Co., 1981, 1985.

Geldenhuys, N. *Luke*   *Commentary on the Gospel of Luke.* NICNT. London: Marshall, Morgan & Scott, 1950; Grand Rapids: Wm. B. Eerdmans Publishing Co., 1972.

Grundmann, W. *Lukas*   *Das Evangelium nach Lukas.* 2d ed. THKNT 3. Berlin: Evangelische Verlagsanstalt, 1961.

Keck, L. E., and Martyn, J. L., eds. *SLA*   *Studies in Luke-Acts.* Nashville: Abingdon Press, 1966; Philadelphia: Fortress Press, 1980.

Klostermann, E. *Lukas*   *Das Lukasevangelium.* 3d ed. HKNT 5. Tübingen: J. C. B. Mohr (Paul Siebeck), 1975.

Lagrange, M.-J. *Luc*   *Evangile selon Saint Luc.* 8th ed. Ebib. Paris: Gabalda, 1948.

Leaney, A. R. C. *Luke*   *The Gospel According to St. Luke.* HNTC/BNTC. New York: Harper & Row; London: A. & C. Black, 1958.

Manson, W. *Luke*   *The Gospel of Luke.* MNTC. London: Hodder & Stoughton, 1943.

Marshall, I. H. *Historian*   *Luke: Historian and Theologian.* Grand Rapids: Zondervan, 1970.

Marshall, I. H. *Luke*   *Commentary on Luke.* NIGTC. Grand Rapids: Wm. B. Eerdmans Publishing Co., 1978.

Petersen, N. R. *Literary Criticism*   *Literary Criticism for New Testament Critics.* Philadelphia: Fortress Press, 1978.

Plummer, A. *Luke*   *St. Luke.* ICC. Edinburgh: T. & T. Clark, 1922.

Rengstorf, K. H. *Lukas*   *Das Evangelium nach Lukas.* 14th ed. NTD 3. Göttingen: Vandenhoeck & Ruprecht, 1969.

Schlatter, A. *Lukas*   *Das Evangelium des Lukas: Aus seinen Quellen erklärt.* 2d ed. Stuttgart: Calwer Verlag, 1960.

Schmid, J. *Lukas*   *Das Evangelium nach Lukas.* 4th ed. RNT 3. Regensburg: Pustet, 1960.

Schmidt, K. L. *Rahmen*   *Der Rahmen der Geschichte Jesu: Literarkritische Untersuchungen zur ältesten Jesusüberlieferung.* Berlin: Trowitsch & Sohn, 1919.

Schürmann, H. *Lukas*   *Das Lukasevangelium,* vol. 1. HTKNT. Freiburg: Herder Verlag, 1969.

Schweizer, E. *Luke*   *The Good News According to Luke.* Atlanta: John Knox Press, 1984 (German: 1982).

Steck, O. H. *Israel*   *Israel und das gewaltsame Geschick der Propheten.* Neukirchen-Vluyn: Neukirchener Verlag, 1967.

Talbert, C. H. *Reading Luke*   *Reading Luke: A Literary and Theological Commentary on the Third Gospel.* New York: Crossroad, 1982.

von Rad, G. *Deuteronomy*   *Deuteronomy: A Commentary.* OTL. Philadelphia: Westminster Press, 1966.

Introduction

The Enigma
of the Central Section
of Luke (9:51—19:44)

The PROBLEM and PURPOSE of the INVESTIGATION

At Luke 9:51 it is announced that from this point on in his public activity, Jesus not only is aware of his destiny in Jerusalem but also has "resolutely determined"[1] to "journey" there to bring it to fulfillment. Immediately Luke depicts a disconcerting refusal of hospitality to Jesus and his entourage as they set out by crossing over from Galilee into Samaria. But in what follows it becomes less and less transparent what Luke is trying to describe. In 9:57–62 Jesus is still "on the way" (v. 57), and in 10:1–20 he sends out messengers to anticipate his own journey mission in various "towns and places." A journey is definitely in mind, but does Luke have a mind to convey any of the particulars of this journey? For example, is Jesus back in Galilee or still in Samaria? Which towns and places lie in his journey route toward Jerusalem?

As the story continues, the reader's hopes for possible clues are dashed: journey episodes turn into controversies with opponents and into teaching for crowds and disciples which seem to have nothing to do with a journey.[2] Here and there, of course, Luke tells his readers that a journey is still in the works, that Jesus' resolve in 9:51 has not been forgotten (10:38; 13:22, 31–33; 14:25; 17:11–12; 18:31, 35–36; 19:1, 11, 28–29, 37, 41). But aside from these occurrences primarily at the beginning and at the end of the journey, there seems little if any help in construing the increasingly confusing theater of Jesus' movements.[3] Moreover, a perusal of the contents of this entire middle portion of Luke reveals that it is essentially composed and structured on the basis of the sayings of Jesus.[4] Only two (9:51, 52–56) of the seventy-three pericopes in 9:51—19:44[5] do not contain an utterance of its central figure, while only five pericopes (apart from an introductory "travel notice") give any direct indication that

Jesus is on a journey (9:52–56; 13:31–33; 17:11–19; 18:35–43; 19:28–40).[6] Instead, we discover some of the most memorable and best-loved parables of Jesus, such as the parable of the Good Samaritan and the parable of the lost son, or unforgettable words of the Master to the poor and despised, the insignificant and marginal of society (e.g., 10:38–42 [women]; 17:11–19 [lepers]; 19:1–10 [a tax collector]). Many of these "static" traditions stem from material that is unique to Luke (his "L" source), which comprises nearly one-third of the Central Section. When combined with the fact that this section itself occupies roughly 40 percent of the entire Gospel,[7] it becomes clear that no overall grasp of the author's purpose and corresponding unity for his Gospel is possible—much less his two-volume work—without a comparable understanding of his portrayal of Jesus in 9:51—19:44. In short, unless the enigma of the "journeying" yet "still-life" sketch of Jesus is deciphered, then the whole of Luke-Acts with its journeying from Galilee to Jerusalem and from there to "the ends of the earth" remains a closed book—an enigma.

Does Luke present an ongoing journey from Galilee in 9:51 to Jesus' entry of the Temple in 19:45? If so, how does he conceive this journey to have proceeded and what is the relation of the didactic sayings traditions to this journey? Has Luke actually succeeded in presenting a focused portrait of a journeying Jesus or in the end succumbed to a blurring disparity between form and content? To answer these and other questions in order to penetrate the enigma of the Central Section—indeed a major mystery in the Lukan corpus—is the purpose of our investigation. Although many scholars render a negative verdict upon any form of coherent journey, nevertheless they ignore a number of important indicators or allusions to a journey in 9:51—19:44. A prima facie reading of this section reveals that in the frontispiece (9:51—10:24) Luke portrays Jesus and his disciples journeying as guests, depending upon homes to receive and provide them sustenance along the way. An analysis of the material in 9:51—10:24, for instance, discloses "journey hospitality" vocabulary: οἰκία (3x—10:5, 7[2x]); οἶκος (9:61; 10:5); ἐσθίω (10:7, 8); πίνω (10:7); πόλις (9:52; 10:1, 8, 10, 11, 12); κώμη (9:52, 56); ἔρχομαι (10:1);[8] εἰσέρχομαι (9:52; 10:5, 8, 10); δέχομαι (9:53; 10:8, 10); ἀποστέλλω (9:52; 10:1, 3, 16); πλατεῖα (10:10); ὁδός (9:57; 10:4). It is astonishing how frequently these journey-hospitality themes occur in the rest of the Central Section, whether in narratives about Jesus or in didactic and parabolic units in his sayings material.[9]

1. Descriptions of or allusions to a journey other than the "travel notices":[10] *(a) Parables:* 10:29–37; 11:5–8; 12:35–38, 42–48; 13:6–9; 14:15–

24; 15:3–7, 11–32; 16:19–31; 19:11–27. *(b) Sayings:* 11:9–10, 31–32; 12:49–51, 57–59; 13:29, 34–35; 14:31–32.

2. "Meal-food" imagery reflecting *hospitality: (a)* Jesus is *guest at table* in various homes:[11] 10:38–42; 11:37–54; 14:1–24; 19:1–10. *(b)* Jesus' ministry is summarily portrayed as *eating and drinking* in the context of a *journeying* theme: 13:26 (13:22; cf. v. 29); 15:1–2 (15:3–7, 11–32). *(c)* Serving a meal or receiving a guest is linked with a *journey* in parables: 10:29–37; 11:5–8; 12:35–38; 14:15–24; 15:1–7, 11–32; 16:19–31. *(d)* Salvation in the Kingdom of God is depicted as a *meal* of hospitality:[12] 12:35–38; 13:23–30; 14:12–14, 15–24; 15:1–7, 8–10, 11–32; 16:19–31; 19:1–10—all in the framework of a *journey. (e)* References to *eating and drinking* or daily sustenance could reflect a "journeying guest" background:[13] 11:3, 11–12; 12:16–21, 22–24, 29–30, 42; 16:19–20; 17:7–10.

3. A "household" with a "householder" or "steward," and "servants" where a meal may be *served* or a journeying guest *received:* 10:38–42; 12:37, 39, 42, 43, 45–47; 13:25; 14:1, 17, 21–23; 15:6, 8, 22, 25; 16:1, 2, 3, 4, 8, 27; 17:7–10; 18:29; 19:5, 9. An interesting corollary depicts unity of a "household" that can be divided or devastated: 11:17, 24–26; 12:51–53; 13:34–35; 16:13; cf. 12:39–40, 42–48; 13:23–30; 14:15–24; 15:25–32; 16:21–31.

4. Certain references to the "coming" of a "Son of Man" may be related by Luke to the *journey* to Jerusalem by Jesus: 12:40; 18:8; 19:10; cf. 11:30; 12:49–51.[14] In any case, a priori these must not be severed from a journey theme.

We will argue that it is precisely this material, by and large unnoticed in the debates concerning the form and content of the Central Section, that constitutes the organizing principle and hence the coherency of the entire section. We shall see that it is these particular traditions, a majority of them "L," which give this section its peculiar imprint. To focus these with respect to other traditions is in order to see if the still-life portrait might indeed come alive.

METHOD *and* SCOPE *of this* WORK

In 1966, W. C. van Unnik spoke of the new front emerging from the "storm center" of Luke-Acts studies. The author of this two-volume work, who is now viewed as a theologian in his own right, had grasped the significance of the delay of the Parousia by transforming the bifocal eschatological message of crisis of Jesus and the first generation of preachers into historical periods of salvation. In 1954, H. Conzelmann had marked a "turning point" in this "new look" when Luke's perspective of *Heilsgeschichte*—now in three stages, Israel-Jesus-church—was related to the different kind of crisis that this delay was causing in the

Gentile churches.[15] As Conzelmann later explained in the same volume as van Unnik's essay, Luke was a theologian of the "third generation" whose outline of historical epochs, including the distinction between the age of the apostles and that of their disciples, links the time of the apostles and the Jewish Christian community to the church of his own day via Paul, the founder of the Gentile Christian church.[16]

Hardly ten years later, C. H. Talbert noted that one could no longer speak of a solid front but must speak of "shifting sands."[17] After a survey of research he concluded: "At present, widespread agreement is difficult to find, except on the point that Conzelmann's synthesis is inadequate."[18] He had already emphasized that all of the crucial questions concerning the Gospel of Luke were now "waiting new answers."[19]

What had happened? How could an emerging front have dissipated so quickly? Talbert points out that with Conzelmann's study came a refined redaction-critical method for future scholars to emulate. And in fact this is precisely what happened. The "storm center" produced a flood of redactional-critical studies based on Conzelmann's assumption—that the main lines of Luke's theological perspectives can be discerned by examining the manner in which Luke has arranged and fused his sources, especially his use and alteration of Mark.[20] From these comparisons the critic could perceive the distinctive Lukan tendencies. But ironically instead of yielding a converging picture of Luke the theologian, this method spawned a multifractured "Luke the redactor" whose concerns and tendencies span a wide range of needs and problems in the reconstructed Lukan communities. How did this come about?

Here we shall of course not deal with the full complexity of methodological developments in Lukan studies in the past three decades. But a dissatisfaction with certain aspects of the redaction-critical method in Gospel studies in general has been in the air for some time.[21] Some of the more salient criticisms of its use include:

1. The point of departure in pursuing the unity of a particular Evangelist's theology is incompatible with this quest itself. For one of the operative principles of the method is that the present text consists essentially of various tradition units, whether individual or collected in larger clusters of oral or written sources.[22] This text-of-parts rather than the text-as-integral-whole becomes the starting point as well as the ruling conception of the "text" throughout the pursuit.[23] That is, by discovering a consistent redactional activity that transcends the various sources, the critic attempts to construct and thus discover the overall unity of the text rather than assuming that the whole of the text as it stands is a function of the author's unified composition. Thus the unity and the theology of Luke are based primarily on the resultant fusion of Mark and other

sources rather than upon the overall configuration of Luke-Acts, irrespective of its sources.[24]

2. The text is viewed primarily as a pastiche of chronological stages rather than as an integration of linear sequences.[25] For instance, the Central Section (travel narrative) is seen as a "great interpolation" or insertion[26] into an earlier configuration of Mark rather than as an organic development within the larger narrative of Luke-Acts. Hence from the outset the contribution of the Central Section to the theology of the whole is viewed from a skewed position.

3. The intention of the Evangelist is discerned through the redactional seams and threads that connect the traditional material. This intention is thus related, on the one hand, to the distinctive theological themes that these seams and threads reveal and, on the other, to the communities addressed whose needs are assumed to correspond to these themes and hence to the intention of the writer. But three major pitfalls emerge here. First, the overall purpose is conceived and based on portions of the text that do not adequately encompass the whole. What is perceived as the overriding purpose is based on what is "distinctive" to the Evangelist rather than upon what is "characteristic."[27] To assert, for example, that Luke's changes of Mark constitute a clearer picture of his overall purpose than his presentation of tradition without significant changes is arbitrary at best.[28] One could argue just the reverse: that what is important to Luke is the unaltered tradition, whereas the changes are due mainly to minor concerns. Second, the various themes gleaned from the redactional enterprise are not easily ordered in relative importance, since the quest for the unity has already been conceived upon such a narrow portion of the text.[29] Hence the intention, coordinated with those themes deemed ascendant, varies as greatly as the themes themselves, with the result that an array of occasions—even mutually contradictory—for the writing have been suggested.[30] Luke, for example, is said to address both a crisis of the delay of the Parousia and an apocalyptic fever of an imminent return.[31] In short, redaction criticism has yielded anything but a consensus on the theological unity and background for the Gospels. Third, with a requestioning of the priority of Mark, the Markan anchor of control for the distinctive divergences of both Matthew and Luke has become precarious.[32] What some have labeled distinctive for Luke may in fact be a distortion of Luke's assimilation of parallel but variant traditions of the canonical Mark. The whole edifice of redaction criticism may be resting on a cracked foundation.[33]

To summarize the main objections, redaction criticism is a key to the history or growth of the various traditions that lie behind the unified text without, however, unlocking the unity of the text itself. For this reason,

Lukan studies face the task of entering again into the world of the text in order to distinguish within Luke's own literary score the *cantus firmus* from the contrapuntal melodies and motifs. Only as the distinctive but harmonious strains of Luke's entire composition are heard with increasing clarity will Lukan studies move from shifting sands to firmer ground.

In this light, this is a modest study. It is only a preliminary study of one, though admittedly important, portion of Luke-Acts. Because the Central Section is a literary unit unparalleled in Matthew and Mark, even though about two-thirds of its tradition units find parallels in these two Gospels, any investigation of its theology must first inquire about the intrinsic narrative configuration of the section itself as well as its relation to the full narrative shape of Luke-Acts. Pointing out divergences here and there from Mark and Matthew may be illuminating in setting the section in bolder relief. But any inference of dependence upon either of these Gospels or understanding the Central Section primarily in reference to them can only give an a priori distortion of the compositional integrity of Luke-Acts and the overall section. Therefore a literary criticism is in order that does not assume or at least depend upon a Markan priority. Only as the intrinsic interplay between the form and the content in the section is perceived from the vantage point of Luke's own narrative world can one begin to understand the role that certain themes or theological purposes of the entire Central Section may play in the Evangelist's overall theology and purpose.

We therefore offer a literary-critical study of the relation of the ostensive form (a journey) to the content (primarily sayings of Jesus) in Luke 9:51—19:44. We follow no particular literary-critical model. But because of our concern for both referential (content) and poetic (form) matters,[34] we must consider "story" and "plot," especially as these have been distinguished by the Russian Formalists.[35] The sum total of all the events (e.g., healings, meals), action (e.g., journeying, teaching), and content of the sayings (e.g., hospitality meal of the Kingdom of God) in the Central Section in their causal or temporal connections represents Luke's "narrative world" or "story." The actual order in which these incidents occur in the narrative constitutes Luke's "plot." We shall examine the sequential order (plot) to see whether we can discern a coherent story.

Once a hypothesis for the conceptual world of the story in the Central Section has been formulated, we shall test it by proposing an organizing principle that has governed the overall arrangement of the traditions. To that extent we shall "plot" the story of the Jesus in 9:51—19:44. We will not present a detailed analysis of the specific sequence of each of the seventy-three pericopes of the section. Questions concerning the various Lukan "poetic devices" must be reserved for future studies.[36] Furthermore, in both the referential and the poetic tasks we restrict ourselves to Luke's narrative world. Whether Jesus actually did and said the things conceived by Luke is an issue for traditiohistorical methods which can properly be pursued after a more definitive understanding is reached of what Luke himself understands Jesus' ministry to be all about. At the same time, owing to the immensity of the section we confine ourselves primarily to the exegesis of these traditions themselves, while only comparing this section to the larger landscape of Luke-Acts at certain crucial points. Hence we offer a first step toward a deeper grasp of the overall unity and purpose of the Central Section within Luke's two volumes.

The PROCEDURE

In Part I we survey critical approaches to the form and content of the Central Section, concentrating on the "tide" produced by the "storm center" in Lukan studies. In summary we shall suggest that despite the considerable strengths and even ingenious schemes, a stubborn discrepancy between form and content prevails largely as a result of insufficient attention given to the story that Luke himself intends to tell.

Moving to our own synthesis in Part II, we propose a fourfold Exodus typology based on the calling and fate of Moses in Deuteronomy as a heuristic principle for the plotted story in 9:51—19:44. This hypothesis is grounded on an intrinsic literary investigation of the prophet as the prime character model for the narrative world of Luke-Acts; second, on an extrinsic comparison of the Moses of Deuteronomy to the prophet Jesus of Luke 9:1–50.[37] Both of these analyses reveal that 9:1–50 functions as a preview of the journey of 9:51—19:44.

Part III is the heart of the study, with evidence classified for Jesus as a prophet in 9:51—19:44. In order to provide an extrinsic literary-critical check on our hypothesis of a Deuteronomic-Exodus typology, the popular Deuteronomistic notion of the role and fate of Israel's prophets in her history as it is expressed in Palestinian Jewish literature of the intertestamental period will be brought to bear on the text. This comparison is methodologically expedient for several reasons: (1) We allow the unique prophetic figure defined by the quandary of the form and content of the Central Section to emerge first before comparing and perhaps unwittingly conforming this figure into some Mosaic mold. (2) We provide an extrinsic contemporary comparison to the figure that emerges. We thereby render it a posteriori the more probable that the figure we have focused is not primarily, at least, the product only of our own referential world read into the text. To be sure, the extrinsic comparisons are themselves products of literary narrative worlds, since various conceptions of the prophets are accessible only in textual form. Yet by adducing evidence from witnesses as diverse as Josephus and Qumran and in dialogue with the traditiohistorical results of critical scholars, we come much closer to guaranteeing that the real world of Luke's day exhibits significant bridges to Luke's narrative world. (3) Consequently we ensure that the plot we trace would have been communicable to Luke's audience; we are not imposing an alien conceptual world upon the text. By thus comparing a pervasive view of Israel's prophetic history with Luke's text—from four different but interlocking vantage points—we shall demonstrate the fundamental conformity of the Central Section to this understanding.

Part IV will then apply the extrinsic literary comparison of the Moses of Deuteronomy to the Jesus of the Central Section. Our hypothesis will be corroborated when the Deuteronomistic popular view and the fourfold typological lines are seen to converge in the plotted story. Then we will be in the position to trace the dynamic lines of the story as the drama of the New Exodus of the Prophet like Moses.

Finally, in Part V we will draw some conclusions, explore the theological implications of these Lukan studies, and suggest some further lines for research.

Notes

1. See below, Part I, n. 6.
2. See already 10:25–37. Even in 10:1–20 Jesus' address in the sending out and return of the Seventy(-two) is primarily didactic-parenetic rather than a discussion of the journey route or timetable.
3. For a definition and discussion of the travel notices in recent debate, see below, Part I, "The Dissonance of Form from Content," esp. nn. 1, 2. We shall argue in Part III that the journey indicators are integral to Luke's story and thus are not the telltale tracks of an editor anxious to maintain the semblance of a journey.
4. See below, part III.B, for fuller analysis.
5. Our pericope divisions and parallels are based on K. Aland, ed., *Synopsis Quattuor Evangeliorum* (Stuttgart: Württembergische Bibelanstalt, 1975).
6. But cf. 12:49–53, which in the *story* context indicates a partially completed journey by the *crowds* in Jesus' midst; cf. esp. Part III.A.4; III.C.11, below.
7. Reckoned in verses, 9:51—19:44 comprises 36.8 percent of the Gospel. When 9:1–50 as an introduction organic to the story of 9:51—19:44 is included (see below, Part II), then the figure is 41.2 percent. For a discussion of the length of the Central Section, see below, Part I, n. 3.
8. Πορεύομαι and compounds are not listed, since they are generally regarded as Lukan vocabulary for the journey; see D. Gill, "Observations on the Lukan Travel Narrative and Some Related Passages," *HTR* 63 (1970): 200–205.

9. For analysis, see esp. Part III.C, below.

10. Including references to a "sending" and to "following"; see esp. Part III.B and C, below.

11. For the concept and practice of hospitality in the ancient Near Eastern world, see, e.g., J. B. Mathews, "Hospitality and the New Testament Church: An Historical and Exegetical Study" (Th.D. diss., Princeton Theological Seminary, 1965), esp. 33–36. Reception into a home such as Luke 19:1–10 normally included a meal, as 10:38–42 illustrates; cf. further the commentaries, ad loc.

12. See esp. Part III.C.10, below.

13. See below, Part III.C.

14. Ibid.

15. W. C. van Unnik, "Luke-Acts, A Storm Center in Contemporary Scholarship," in Keck and Martyn, *SLA*, 15–32. In addition to H. Conzelmann's *Die Mitte der Zeit* (1954), van Unnik (pp. 22–23) points to the seminal works of E. Käsemann (1953), M. Dibelius (1951), P. Vielhauer (1950–51), and E. Haenchen (1956).

16. H. Conzelmann, "Luke's Place in the Development of Early Christianity," in Keck and Martyn, *SLA*, 298–316.

17. C. H. Talbert, "Shifting Sands: The Recent Study of the Gospel of Luke," *Int* 30 (1976): 381–95.

18. Ibid., 395.

19. Ibid., 381. In an earlier article (C. H. Talbert, "The Redaction Critical Quest for Luke the Theologian," in *Jesus and Man's Hope: Pittsburgh Festival on the Gospels, April 6–10, 1970,* 2 vols. [Pittsburgh: Pittsburgh Theological Seminary, 1970], 1:171–222), Talbert summarizes his debate with Conzelmann's eschatology and *Sitz im Leben* for Luke-Acts and presents his own alternative to the delay of the Parousia: a correction of Docetic Christology and spiritualized eschatology; cf. Talbert, *Luke and the Gnostics: An Examination of the Lucan Purpose* (Nashville: Abingdon Press, 1966), and idem, "An Anti-Gnostic Tendency in Lucan Christology," *NTS* 14 (1968): 259–71. Talbert's proposal has not won wide acceptance; cf. the methodological criticism of L. T. Johnson, "On Finding the Lukan Community, A Cautious Cautionary Essay," in *SBL Seminar Papers, 1979,* ed. P. J. Achtemeier (Missoula: Scholars Press, 1979), 1:89–91, esp. n. 22, and cf. nn. 39, 44, 47, 55. R. J. Karris ("Windows and Mirrors: Literary Criticism and Luke's *Sitz im Leben,*" in Achtemeier, *SBL Seminar Papers, 1979,* 47–48) points out that though Talbert's work on genre has proved quite fruitful for NT scholarship in general (see C. H. Talbert, *What Is a Gospel? The Genre of the Canonical Gospels* [Philadelphia: Fortress Press, 1977]), his application of genre type to Luke-Acts' purported *Sitz im Leben,* which is derived by a redactional-critical analysis, cannot be fully integrated with the literary-critical analysis which has established that genre in the first place. See further, below, Part I, n. 68.

20. For a partial listing, see below, Part I, nn. 68, 70.

21. For a survey of the development, see Petersen, *Literary Criticism,* 9–23, esp. 17–23. For the technique, see N. Perrin, *What Is Redaction Criticism?* (Philadelphia: Fortress Press, 1969); G. B. Caird, "The Study of the Gospels: III.

Redaction Criticism," *ExpTim* 87 (1975–76): 168–72; Talbert, "Shifting Sands," 392–94; and Marshall, *Historian,* 19–20.

22. Cf. Perrin, *Redaction Criticism,* 1–24; and Petersen, *Literary Criticism,* 11–17.

23. See esp. Petersen, *Literary Criticism,* 18–19.

24. See Conzelmann, on the point of departure for discerning Luke's own conception of his presentation: "We must start from a methodical comparison with his sources, in so far as these are directly available or can be reconstructed" (Conzelmann, *Theology,* 12), citing M. Dibelius, *Studies in the Acts of the Apostles* (New York: Charles Scribner's Sons, 1956). Conzelmann's use of the "two-source hypothesis" is explicit on p. 12.

25. Petersen (*Literary Criticism,* 19) clearly describes this distortion in his reference to M. Krieger's distinction between the metaphors of a text as "window" and "mirror" (*A Window to Criticism* [Princeton: Princeton University Press, 1964], 3–4): Redaction critics in determining sources look through a text (i.e., as window) in order to discern the unity of the final form rather than first treating a text as a mirror, as linear sequences of an integral whole.

26. C. C. McCown ("The Geography of Luke's Central Section," *JBL* 57 [1938]: 51–66) attributes this nomenclature to H. J. Holtzmann's and C. Weizsäcker's monumental studies of 1863 and 1864 (pp. 51–52).

27. M. D. Hooker, "Christology and Methodology," *NTS* 17 (1970–71): 480–87; Hooker uses these terms in reference to the traditiohistorical method of distinguishing "authentic" from "inauthentic" sayings in the teachings of Jesus. Cf. Talbert ("Shifting Sands," 393): "If we confine our attention to what can clearly be identified as redactional, we stand in danger of producing an eccentric picture of Lukan theology."

28. Cf. Marshall, *Historian,* 19–20. Marshall refers also to F. Schütz, *Der leidende Christus: Die angefochtene Gemeinde und das Christuskerygma der lukanischen Schriften,* BWANT 89 (Stuttgart: Kohlhammer, 1969), 19.

29. Cf., e.g., Talbert, "Shifting Sands," 390.

30. L. T. Johnson ("On Finding the Lukan Community") demonstrates the redaction-critical fallacy of *assuming* that major thematic thrusts can inevitably be related directly to some "community's" need(s). He warns of a "methodological hegemony which reduces the Gospels to cryptograms and the Evangelists to the level of tractarians" (p. 90).

31. Cf. Conzelmann, *Theology,* 95–136; Ellis, *Luke,* 58–59; and idem, *Eschatology in Luke* (Philadelphia: Fortress Press, 1972), 19. Perhaps an even more blatant contradiction is between Conzelmann and Talbert. Talbert's "spiritualized eschatology" (cf. above, n. 19) postulates a group within the Lukan community who asserted that the Parousia had already been realized in the ascension-exaltation of Christ.

32. For Matthean priority, see, e.g., W. R. Farmer, *The Synoptic Problem: A Critical Analysis* (New York: Macmillan Co., 1964); D. L. Dungan, "Mark—The Abridgement of Matthew and Luke," in *Jesus and Man's Hope,* 1:51–89; and B. Orchard and T. R. W. Longstaff, eds., *J. J. Griesbach: Synoptic and Text-Critical*

Studies, 1776–1976, SNTSMS 34 (Cambridge: Cambridge University Press, 1978). For theories of relative textual independence, see, e.g., X. Léon-Dufour, "Redaktionsgeschichte of Matthew and Literary Criticism," in *Jesus and Man's Hope,* 1:9–35, esp. 9–11; and B. Reicke, *The Roots of the Synoptic Gospels* (Philadelphia: Fortress Press, 1987). For surveys, see, e.g., R. H. Fuller, "The Synoptic Problem: After Ten Years," *PSTJ* 28 (1975): 63–68; and J. A. Fitzmyer, "The Priority of Mark and the 'Q' Source in Luke," in *Jesus and Man's Hope,* 1:131–70.

33. See, e.g., H. W. Frei's critique of historical-critical methods' confusion of the "narrative world" with the real order of events and its almost exclusive preoccupation with the latter to the reduction in meaning of the former (H. W. Frei, *The Eclipse of Biblical Narrative: A Study in Eighteenth and Nineteenth Century Hermeneutics* [New Haven: Yale University Press, 1974], esp. 124–54, 307–24). See also the comments of Petersen (*Literary Criticism,* 20–23) on Frei, and see Petersen's critique of W. Wrede's and K. L. Schmidt's analysis of Mark, arguing that they succumbed to the reductionistic or "evolutionary" fallacy by failing to take adequate account of the resulting narrative world composed by Mark from his stock of traditional sources (Schmidt) or traditional ideas (Wrede). Petersen asserts that because of the inheritance of the nineteenth century, biblical scholarship has become the "victim of an academic cultural lag" by failing to treat the text like a "mirror" (as well as a "window") as literary critics in other disciplines began to do around the beginning of this century (pp. 24–25); cf. above, n. 25.

34. The referential function of language, according to, e.g., Karl Buhler and Roman Jakobson, points to the "narrative world" or the conceptual "signified" in distinction from the "poetic" function representing the "signifier" or sign itself. For further discussion, see Petersen, *Literary Criticism,* 33–48.

35. V. Shklovsky, of the Russian Formalist group, was instrumental in developing the notion of special devices of "plot formation" *(sjužetosloženie)* and thus changed the traditional notion of plot *(sjužet)* from a set of themes or motifs to specific *compositional* concepts. Hence "plot" was distinguished from themes and actions, i.e., "narrative events," which constitute the "story" *(fabula)* or "story stuff." For surveys of the rise, rubrics, and contributions of the Russian Formalists, see S. Bann and J. E. Bowlt, eds., *Russian Formalism* (Edinburgh: Scottish Academic Press, 1973), esp. the essays of T. Todorov (pp. 6–19), R. Sherwood (pp. 26–40), and V. Shklovsky (pp. 48–72); and B. M. Ejxenbaum, "The Theory of the Formal Method," in *Readings in Russian Poetics: Formalist and Structuralist Views,* ed. L. Matejka and K. Pomorska (Cambridge: MIT Press, 1971), 3–37, esp. 15–18, 34–35. Ejxenbaum comments on Shklovsky's contribution: "The original concept of form took on the added complexity of new features of evolutionary dynamism, of incessant change" (p. 18). Our question in this study is: Does the form-content of the Central Section of Luke possibly betray a dynamic story?

36. Cf. esp. Petersen, *Literary Criticism,* 45–48. We are not concerned with the "deep" or "submerged" logical structures of the "structuralists." On structur-

alism, see D. Patte, *What Is Structural Exegesis?* (Philadelphia: Fortress Press, 1976).

37. "In all cases extrinsic criticism will consist of relating the individual text, or features of it, to other texts or to extratextual concerns, and in all cases it will presuppose intrinsic criticism" (Petersen, *Literary Criticism,* 31).

I

The Problem Expanded

*Dissonance of Form
from Content
(Luke 9:51—19:44)*

I

In the Central Section of Luke's Gospel we have observed a puzzling situation. Jesus sets out on a journey to Jerusalem, but after a few episodes we hear virtually nothing about this undertaking. We find instead a vast sea of sayings. Yet in the midst of these parables, speeches, and controversy settings we did notice that this silence appears to be broken not only by a journey-hospitality theme but not infrequently also by a Jesus who "eats and drinks." Before we forge our own path through this intriguing terrain (Parts II—V), we want to assess how modern critical scholars have worked with this puzzle.

Is there an inner coherency between a journey and the sayings of Jesus? Does Luke present a unified development or conception of the whole? We here examine recent approaches to Luke's so-called travel narrative (*Reisebericht*). Certain consensuses have begun to coalesce, and it is upon these that we wish to focus.

The DISSONANCE of FORM from CONTENT

The dilemma of any unified plot or coherent narrative for the Central Section has been comprehended from three distinct but coordinate viewing points, components of one overarching problem—dissonance of form from content. The following arguments reflect the views of critical exegetes and my engagement with them.

1. Discrepancy Between the Journey Indicators and a Journey to Jerusalem

Our problem is posed by the "travel notices"[1] or "indicators"[2] which purport a recurring if not consistent action for the main actor: 9:51, 52–

53, 56, 57; 10:1, 17, 38; 13:22, 31–33; 14:25; 17:11; 18:31, 35; 19:1, 11, 28, 41.[3] Do they congeal an apparent "characterless mass" into a continuous, coherent journey of Jesus to Jerusalem (see 9:51)? Or are they window dressing, a grasping at stylistic straws to bring cohesion to otherwise heterogeneous material?[4] Three "obstacles" with the journey indicators are often cited:[5] *(a)* their incoherent if not contradictory function as "way markers"; *(b)* their infrequency, especially in the middle of the section, and thus their inability to sustain any real sense of movement or continuous journeying; *(c)* their indefiniteness or vagueness in topographical detail with the singular sensation that the initial departure never leads to any specific locality nor ever consummates at a particular destination.

   a. The greatest problem is that at 9:51 Jesus has "determined to head"[6] for Jerusalem but at 13:31–33 still appears to be in Galilee, since the Pharisees are warning him to flee Herod. When it is pointed out that Jesus could perhaps be in Perea, also part of Herod's jurisdiction, then it is difficult to know what to do with 17:11, where Jesus is "passing between Samaria and Galilee" or "through the midst of Samaria and Galilee."[7] Since there is no indication whatever that Jesus reverses direction, there is little hope of harmonizing these notices into any kind of itinerary or even any credible general route for Jesus' travels. C. C. McCown sums up the sentiment of many modern investigators: "Luke betrays his complete ignorance or his equally complete indifference to geographical notions by concocting most confusing allusions to Jesus' movements."[8] Referring to the problematic 17:11, McCown observes: "Even if there were no problem in the difficult phrase, what can one make of a writer who brings Jesus a journey of twenty or thirty miles on the first day, puts him in Samaria, and then, after a long succession of incidents which must have occupied weeks, including the mission of the Seventy, preaching and healing in a synagogue, a dinner in the house of a Pharisee on another Sabbath, a journey through many cities and villages, not to mention much more, leaves him still between Samaria and Galilee?"[9] McCown provides his own answer: "The conclusion is inescapable . . . geography and topography serve merely as literary devices."[10]

   b. A glance at the journey indicators reveals that all but five of the twenty verses represented are located within the first two chapters and the last three,[11] that is, at the beginning and at the end of the trip to Jerusalem. And of the five, three are embedded in one unit, 13:31–33,[12] leaving only 13:22 and 14:25 as additional signposts. It is precisely the "topographical wastelands" between 10:42—13:22 and especially 14:25—17:11 which enhance the impression that any thought of geography, let alone of any movement to Jerusalem, has been all but for-gotten. In 14:25 Jesus departs from a Pharisee's dinner invitation, the locality of which remains completely nebulous, and is "accompanied" (συνπορεύομαι) by "great multitudes" in some nameless direction. He teaches the crowds, addresses the murmuring Pharisees with a number of parables, instructs his disciples with parables and sayings, responds again to the Pharisees' vindictive with seemingly isolated pronouncements on "the law and the prophets" and "divorce," tells another parable, and ad-dresses the disciples again with a catena of disjointed sayings on "tempta-tion," "forgiveness," "faith," and a parable or apothegm on "faithful service." It seems that in 17:11—"on his way to Jerusalem he was passing along between Samaria and Galilee"—the reader meets a Christ who has been "dangling" somewhere between Galilee and Jerusalem ever since the beginning in 9:51. One suspects that the few notices in this vast middle section (13:22, 31–33; 14:25) are gallant attempts by Luke to remind his readers that Jesus is progressing toward his ultimate goal of Jerusalem.[13] And though the nature of the dissonance thus produced by the addition of these journey indicators is variously perceived, yet the overriding judgment upon Luke's success in instilling some sense of a lasting journey to Jerusalem is well expressed by J. Blinzler: "His [Luke's] entire travel narrative between 9:51 and 18:14 consists in reality of only verses 9:51–56; 13:22 and 17:11 with its adjoining pericope."[14]

c. Correlative to their infrequency is their lack of specificity. Apart from *Jerusalem*, which as a destination is mentioned only in 9:51, 53; 13:22, 33–34; 17:11; 18:31;[15] 19:11,[16] 28, *Jericho* is the only other city identified (18:35–43 in v. 35; 19:1–10 in v. 1).[17] *Samaria* and *Galilee* as districts are mentioned in 17:11 and *Samaritans* in 9:52; 10:33; 17:16 and *Galileans* in 13:1, 2. *Judea* and *Judean* or *Jew* do not occur at all. That is, only three pericopes divulge any definite locality, two of them involving the same town (Jericho, 18:35–43; 19:1–10), whereas 9:52–56 does not even give the faintest clue to the general area in Samaria of its "hostile" village;[18] only from the present literary context can one assume that it lay probably not too far from the Galilee-Samaria border.[19] Such dearth of detail should strike any reader as odd if in fact a journey to Jerusalem is a concern of the author. Indeed this blank (9:57—18:35) has led many to conclude that whatever Luke's intention may have been and from wherever he might have received this material, the Central Section as it stands does not present a credible, continuous journey from Galilee to Jerusalem.[20] As K. L. Schmidt observes: "Because of the scantiness of material Luke was unable to achieve a realistic travel account."[21]

2. Discrepancy Between the Traditions
and the Journey Motif

When the Central Section is viewed apart from the explicit journey indicators, it becomes clear that the bulk of the traditions do not bear any special affinity to the journey motif.[22] The only pericopes that, exclusive of their introductory verse, treat or betray any sense of journeying are 9:52–56; 13:31–33; and 17:11–19.[23] Moreover, upon examination of the transition points it becomes evident that there are no inner links that divulge an inherent chronological sequence.[24] The only possible exception is 10:20–21, where $\dot{\epsilon}\nu$ $a\dot{v}\tau\hat{\eta}$ $\tau\hat{\eta}$ $\ddot{\omega}\rho\alpha$ follows both logically and chronologically upon the "Return of the Seventy(-two)."[25] "At that very hour" flows naturally from the "Seventy(-two)'s" exuberance and Jesus' own share in their joy as he begins in v. 21 to extol the "Father" for his gracious act of revelation to them. But other than this, many of the conjunctions appear arbitrary as well as unimaginative, even when a more precise phrase such as $\dot{\epsilon}\nu$ $a\dot{v}\tau\hat{\omega}$ $\tau\hat{\omega}$ $\kappa\alpha\iota\rho\hat{\omega}$ (13:1) is used.[26] What *time* or *season*? Where has Jesus been previous to this point? This "same time" is linked to no particular time or place at all. Indeed the use of $\kappa\alpha\iota\rho\delta s$ in 13:1 could very well stem from its use in 12:56 as a play upon the crowds' blindness to the "present time" and their stubbornness to repent "at that very [same] time." Paronomasia, catch phrases, and similar ideas and themes might well be the prevailing criteria for the juxtaposition of many pericopes.[27]

It has been suggested many times and in many different ways that the Central Section is arranged according to topic.[28] This should come as no surprise when narrative pericopes are tied to those preceding by such hollow phrases as: "And behold, a lawyer stood up" (10:25); "He was praying in a certain place" (11:1); "He was teaching in one of the synagogues" (13:10); "One Sabbath when he went to dine at the house of one of the rulers of the Pharisees" (14:1).[29] And corresponding to this imprecision are the nondescript transitions within didactic sections. For instance, in 12:1—13:9 Jesus is among the crowds, presumably somewhere between Galilee and Jerusalem, after leaving a Pharisee's dinner invitation:[30] "One from the crowd ($\tau\iota s$ $\dot{\epsilon}\kappa$ $\tauo\hat{v}$ $\ddot{o}\chi\lambdaov$) said to him" (12:13); "He said to the disciples" (12:22); "He also said to the crowds ($\ddot{o}\chi\lambda o\iota s$)" (12:54). The most specific audience transition is: "Peter said, 'Lord, are you telling this parable to us or to all?'" (12:41). Yet even here it is not clear who the "us" or the "all" are, though contextually one would probably infer the "disciples" and the "crowds."[31] Peter pops up out of a faceless throng not to emerge by name again until 18:28.[32] There is very little if any sense of an advancing party of *travelers* around Jesus who react to concrete sites, particular events, and tangible faces.[33] *Time* and *space* seem at some points to be suspended completely.[34] In short, many scholars have come to the same conclusion that analysis of the journey indicators has produced: the journey motif is a literary device to string together a mass of disparate, preeminently static material.[35] The dissonance of this *form* from its *content* is all but proof. As Conzelmann states: "The journey motif and the description of Jesus' ministry are not only not integrated with one another, they are positively incompatible, yet this very combination is a basic characteristic of Luke's account."[36]

3. Discrepancy Between Provenance and Setting of the Journey Motif

It has been argued that most of the material from 10:25—18:14 does not fit into any conceivable ministry of Jesus between Galilee and Judea. While it is possible that Jesus could have told the Good Samaritan story to a lawyer on or near the border of Samaria (10:25–37), the following are all hardly likely to have taken place in Samaria or Perea:[37] Jesus' visit with Mary and Martha (10:38–42); his meal with a Pharisee (11:37–54); the Pharisees' warning against Herod (13:31–33) and the lament over Jerusalem (13:34–35); Jesus' dining with a Pharisee on a Sabbath (14:1–24); the parables of the lost in response to the Pharisees' murmuring (15:1–32) and Jesus' reproof of them for their love of money (16:14–15); the Pharisees' question about the coming of the Kingdom (17:20–21); and the Pharisee and the publican (18:9–14).

Moreover, a number of pericopes in 9:51—19:44 are strikingly similar to incidents in the Galilean phase of Luke's account:[38] a "cripple" is healed on a Sabbath (6:6–11 — 13:10–17); Jesus teaches both his disciples and the crowds in long discourses (6:20–49 — 12:1—13:9), in which some of the logia are virtually identical (8:16 = 11:33; 8:17 = 12:2); "lepers" are healed (5:12–16 — 17:11–19); Jesus teaches on his "true mother and family" (8:19–21 — 11:27–28); parables on the "Kingdom" are related in bucolic imagery (8:4–15 — 13:18–19); and injunctions to carry a cross are posed by Jesus to his disciples and the crowds (9:23 — 14:27). The most obvious parallels are the initial rejection of Jesus (4:16–30 [Nazareth] — 9:52–56 [a Samaritan village]) and the commissioning of emissaries to proclaim the Kingdom of God and to heal (9:1–6 [the "Twelve"] — 10:1–20 [the "Seventy(-two)"]).

Note also that the dramatis personae in these two sections are much the same. A chart of the appearances of the main actors can illustrate this:

Dramatis Personae

Characters[39]	Galilean Phase (4:14—9:50)	Central Section (9:51—19:44)
1. μαθητής (αἱ)	18x (2x—John's disciples)	16x (1x—John's disciples)
2. ὄχλος (οἱ)	23x	12x
3. φαρισαῖος (οἱ)	11x (8x—in the plural)	17x (13x—in the plural)
4. γραμματεύς (εἷς)	4x	2x
5. νομικός (οἱ)	1x	5x
6. γυνή (αἷκες)	10x	11x
7. τελώνης (αι)	5x	4x
8. ἁμαρτωλός (οἱ)	9x	7x
9. χήρα (αι)	3x	2x

When these considerations are taken together it is not misleading to conclude that in the Central Section we meet the same proponents and opponents, the same kind of teaching and healing, and the same sort of controversies over Jesus' authority and ability to interpret and observe the law: e.g., "Sabbath" observance (6:1–5; 6:6–11 — 13:10–17; 14:1–6); "ritual purity" and "dietary" regulations (7:36–50 — 11:37–54); association with "tax collectors" and "sinners" (5:27–32; 7:34–35 — 15:1–2; 19:1–10).[40] The crowds, the Pharisees and the scribes, the sick and possessed—these all speckle the horizon and imbue the atmosphere with many of the same shades and feelings that Luke's readers experience in the Galilean section.[41] We shall argue, however, that compared to the Galilean phase there is a much greater dynamism in the Central Section which congeals the trip to Jerusalem into a dramatic, colorful whole. The colors are painted in starker contrasts than the softer hues of the Galilean periods (see below, Part III).

Extrinsic synoptic comparisons utilizing source and traditiohistorical categories point to the same discrepancy between provenance of the traditions and a journey outside Galilee. Using Luke's so-called Great Interpolation (9:51—18:14) as the material for comparison with its sixty-four pericopes[42] coming "before" the explicit "Perean" sections of Mark 10:1–34 = Matt. 19:1—20:19 (cf. Luke 18:15–34, and see n. 3), we discover the following:

1. *Seventeen Pericopes Common to Mark and Matthew (Non-Q)*[43]

Of the seventeen pericopes, fourteen are placed by Mark and Matthew in either Galilee or Jerusalem. Only three are located in their Perean sections: *(a)* Mark 10:1 = Matt. 19:1 (= Luke 9:51);[44] *(b)* Mark 10:31 = Matt. 19:30 (=

Luke 13:30, "the first shall be the last . . .");[45] and *(c)* Mark 10:11–12 = Matt. 19:9 (= Luke 16:18, on "divorce").[46]

2. *Twenty-four Q Pericopes*

None of the twenty-four Q parallels are located by Matthew outside Galilee or Jerusalem.[47]

3. *Twenty-three "L" Pericopes*

The approximately twenty-three "L" pericopes, which comprise over one-third of the Central Section, obviously have no direct lines of comparison with other deposits of gospel tradition, thereby making it virtually impossible to trace any earlier stages of this "L" tradition.

The suspicion is again reinforced that either Luke is not concerned at all about the placement of his travel material and/or that he himself has no idea where Jesus' ministry occurred during this period.

Has Luke constructed a believable journey between Galilee and Jerusalem? A majority of modern interpreters say no.[48] Already W. M. L. de Wette in 1846 expressed current sentiment by concluding that the Central Section is "a non-chronological and non-historical composition."[49] To sum up, both from the vantage points of the journey indicators and the traditions themselves there is in 9:51—19:44 an irresolvable tension between form and content.

Here we should note that the point of departure for most of the foregoing observations is the concern to reconstruct a general journey route in the light of 9:51 and the travel notices. When from historical-geographical considerations this has proven impossible, the conclusion frequently drawn is that these notices serve as literary devices. At the same time, these travel notices are inevitably compared to the Markan outline with the assumption that whatever Luke is doing in the Central Section per se, he is doing it in conscious conformity to the basic Markan or synoptic pattern where Jesus leaves Galilee for "Judea and beyond the Jordan" at Mark 10:1 (cf. Matt. 19:1). Even though the Lukan text cannot be juggled to present this or a similar journey with any literary or historical credibility, the Central Section is still perceived as a function of the earlier Markan outline. Thus from the outset the journey motif is viewed and focused through a bifocal a priori: *(a)* through the real historical world of the Palestine of Jesus' day;[50] and *(b)* through Mark's text. The "problem" of the Central Section is thus due to a fundamental confusion of literary and historical aims. Only fleeting attention is paid to the rest of the narrative world of Luke-Acts as the indispensable primary context for the journey motif. Of the seventeen commentators noted here (see n. 28), only two (Plummer, Grundmann) base the organization (and hence literary divisions) of the Central Section upon a journey or journey motif per se.

CHARACTERIZATIONS *of the* DISSONANCE
of the CENTRAL SECTION

In order to facilitate our survey of Luke's intention and the resulting coherency in the Central Section, we will quickly review the history of interpretation of this section, concentrating on more recent developments.

The Central Section in Critical Light

In the nineteenth century the Central Section was viewed either as a collection of sayings (drawn from a gnomology) or as an account of one or more complete or fragmentary journeys, with additional extraneous material.[51] Schleiermacher, for instance, argued that two journeys of Jesus to Jerusalem—to the Feast of Dedication and to his final Passover —had already been joined together to form the present section. While he admitted that much did not belong to either journey, he called the section *Reiseabschnitt* or *Reisebericht.*[52]

Only two decades later de Wette broke tradition by rejecting both alternatives. He labeled Schleiermacher's hypothesis "a web of improbabilities and coincidences," if for no other reason than that Luke 18:18 both stems from and conforms to the basic synoptic outline of Matthew and thus can in no way derive from a special source.[53] Attempts to harmonize with John are therefore entirely excluded. He equally eschews the gnomology proposal simply because it is unlikely that the collector would single out traditions with traces of journeying and then attach sayings that at best evince only a slight ease with the loose and rather "tortuous" thread of the journey.[54] Here, anticipating the modern consensus by about a century, de Wette puts his finger on all three of our fundamental dissonances: *(a)* the unlikelihood of several of the episodes occurring in Samaria; *(b)* the contradictory route of the journey indicators; and *(c)* the arbitrary or artificial conjunctions of many of the sayings of Jesus. He concluded that Luke encountered tradition with which he was at a loss to locate or order and therefore simply threw the material together, albeit creating the disjointed framework of a journey.[55] De Wette even anticipated redaction critics by suggesting that, for example, in 17:11 Luke may have added the phrase καὶ . . . πορεύεσθαι εἰς ᾿Ιερουσαλήμ to enhance an otherwise "confusing" journey notion.[56] Consequently de Wette still entitles the section "An Account of Jesus' Journey to Jerusalem" but with the apposite subheading, "Luke's Peculiar Account (9,51—18,14)."[57]

In K. L. Schmidt's ground-breaking monograph, *Der Rahmen der*

Geschichte Jesu (1919),[58] we discover a critical link between de Wette's approach and the conclusions of the later redaction critics. On the one hand, Schmidt's form-critical analysis demonstrated beyond doubt that Luke was dependent upon disparate traditions for his Central Section or "journey report." Though he no longer accepted J. J. Griesbach's hypothesis of Matthean priority as earlier scholars had done, the point of departure for Schmidt with a now assumed Markan priority was nevertheless essentially the same—divergence of the Central Section from the synoptic pattern. Like de Wette, Schmidt concludes that the text of 9:51—18:14 does not present a credible journey report; no satisfactory geographical thread can be untangled for a consistent historical picture. On the other hand, unlike de Wette, Schmidt shows a heightened interest in Luke's intention as editor or final compiler. Going beyond the possibility of Luke having composed one or perhaps more of the indications of a journey, on stylistic, textual, and form-critical grounds, Schmidt concludes that most of the journey notations are due to Luke.[59] For Schmidt, Luke purposely expanded the journey of Mark 10:1–34[60] into a travel narrative (*Reisebericht*) by taking traditions almost entirely void of time or place and subsuming them to a constructed geographical framework. With only the incident of the Samaritan rejection in 9:52–56 and two journey episodes in Jericho (18:35–43; 19:1–10) at his disposal, Luke has created a pattern in 9:51—19:27 strikingly different from either Mark or Matthew. By effecting a "geographical plan," the journey marks an ever-closer approach to Jerusalem. Thus from a vantage point within the text of the Gospel, Schmidt points to a Lukan literary concern[61] that transcends the insertion of 9:51—18:14 into the Markan outline. Compared to later redaction critics, Schmidt's interest in Luke's editorial activity was of course mild. Nonetheless by moving beyond de Wette, Schmidt served as an important bridge, especially for subsequent German scholarship on the Central Section. For it was soon to become axiomatic that Luke created the impression of a journey through *his* "travel narrative,"[62] even though this impression was anything but convincing. But that is another way of stating that a fundamental dissonance exists between the form and the content.

As we saw in the Introduction, the "new look" in Lukan studies spearheaded by H. Conzelmann[63] stimulated an appreciation of Luke the theologian along with a refined redactional method. Though Conzelmann built upon Schmidt's analysis of the travel notices in *The Theology of St. Luke,*[64] he parted company with Schmidt at one decisive point: It was not true that Luke promoted a geographical plan that produced an ever-increasing sensation of approaching Jerusalem. On the contrary, thinking to take Schmidt's conclusion concerning Luke's ignorance or indifference to geography to a more logical conclusion, Conzelmann argued that Luke's purpose must be sought elsewhere: in the approaching Passion, the element heightened by Mark but ironically soft-pedaled by Schmidt for Luke. Consequently it is in the very contradiction of Luke's "geographical plan" that the real intent of Luke is disclosed: "His [Luke's] intention is all the plainer because of the fact that the scheme does not harmonize with the material. This means, then, that Luke is determined to carry it out at any cost. . . . The discrepancy between the material and the scheme is the clearest indication by which we can recognize Luke's own composition and see what is his special interest."[65] Through this redactional approach to the whole of Luke-Acts, Conzelmann turned a negative discrepancy into a positive clue for the purpose of the Central Section within a larger Lukan program. The result was that the dissonance was significantly muted, in essence, by harmonizing the central piece of the Gospel upon the stage of its performance in the church rather than in the *mise en scène* of the movements of Jesus.

Conzelmann's approach seemed to solve a host of perplexing problems in Luke-Acts.[66] The easing of the discrepancy of the Central Section was perceived as a major step in the right direction in penetrating the enigma; as a theological presentation of the ministry of Jesus the journey form did not appear so anomalous after all. A torrent of studies ensued,[67] some modifying Conzelmann's theological motive,[68] others stressing a theological impetus for an aesthetical[69] or ecclesiastical-functional[70] use for the Gospel. More recently, however, Conzelmann's synthesis has waned,[71] and the tendency has again developed to disengage the journey motif almost entirely from Luke's theological aims. Now curiously approximating de Wette's analysis, this approach stresses Luke's desire to include valuable traditions without the need to place them in any coherent topological or chronological plan.[72] It would appear that interpretation has come full circle.[73] But one factor has remained constant, the focal issue of this study: Within the theater of the ministry of Jesus the Central Section displays a distinctive *dissonance of form from content*.[74]

Luke's Purpose in the Light of the Dissonance

Our historical survey has divulged two poles of interpretation of the dissonance of form from content. On the one side, some seek the resolution of this tension in a larger theological purpose for the Central Section within Luke-Acts overall. On the other, some seek to dismiss the tension as essentially irrelevant, given Luke's desire to include traditions important in their own right. In the light of these two tendencies, how, more precisely, have scholars conceived a unified purpose for the Central

Section? We shall concentrate our attention primarily on the "wake" generated by the "storm center" of the 1950s and 1960s:

APPROACH 1: Theological-Christological[75]

Luke's intention is to present a particular christological conception of Jesus' ministry within an overall plan of the history of salvation. Whether Jesus' awareness of his suffering or his suffering as a path to glory or the "way" of Jesus as the preordained "way of the Lord" or the authoritative journey of King Messiah and so forth is emphasized, the motive is the same: the journey is a viable symbol of a distinctive phase in the unfolding dynamic of the *Heilsgeschichte.* Given the theological energy of Luke-Acts, a journey framework is not so peculiar after all.

APPROACH 2: Ecclesiastical-Functional[76]

The proponents of this solution point to the predominantly didactic-parenetic character of the disparate material. Above all, Jesus is a *teacher* preparing his disciples to be the future leaders of the church as he journeys to his death in Jerusalem. Faithful following amidst suffering rejection, correction of an uncomprehending discipleship, proper orientation to the world, preparation for the Gentile mission, and so on, are all thematic thrusts programmatic to the unity of the whole. In this way Luke engages the journey motif primarily—as in approach 1—at the level of the instruction and edification of the church. In short, the Central Section coheres because it exhibits a useful parallel between Jesus' journeying and the church's present journey.

APPROACH 3: Literary-Aesthetical[77]

The amorphous mass of Luke's vast middle section betrays a distinct literary pattern. Whether already in the tradition or through Luke's literary craftsmanship, this pattern and not a "form-content" tension is constitutive of the whole; any disparity between the form of a journey with its content subsists only at a level that misses a more fundamental structure. Chiasmus, analogy to Deuteronomy, lectionary cycles, and so forth, have been suggested as the telltale templates. Thus through aesthetic reasons, pragmatic reasons, or a combination of both, cohesion is achieved essentially at the level of the use of the Central Section—whether in its initial writing or its reading—in the church. Jesus still journeys to Jerusalem, but he does so to a carefully conceived artistic pattern.

APPROACH 4: Traditional-Logical[78]

"Galilee to Jerusalem" is intrinsic to the rudimentary gospel sequence of earlier tradition. That Luke has taken advantage of this chronological fact to insert material vital to the church should strike no one as unusual. Luke's procedure in the middle part of his Gospel is in principle no different from his procedure in the Galilean phase (4:14—9:50), where Jesus is also an itinerant preacher-teacher.[79] The travel notices may imbue the section with the shades and sheen of Jesus' impending death-exaltation in Jerusalem.[80] But no overriding theological motif or plan is at work as the controlling principle throughout. Instead, a logical progression of themes, or an ordering of catchwords or phrases, or polemics with opponents, and so forth, rather than a chronological progression of Jesus' journey ministry or a period of salvation history, is the prevailing modality. The journey notices then function as a convenient scaffolding for a great mass of heterogeneous traditions. In the final analysis, the dissonance between Jesus the traveler and the content that follows is more apparent than real, more a misreading of Luke's intent and procedure than an actual problem begging solution.

Although the overlap of these approaches is clear, approaches 1 and 2 are oriented around our first pole of interpretation, while approach 4 is characteristic of the second. Approach 3 hovers between both, veering toward one or the other as the literary pattern is subsumed more to either larger theological-thematic interests or to pragmatic or functional concerns. This third approach points to the impossibility of drawing a hard-and-fast distinction between theological-christological and ecclesiastical-functional intentions or motivations.[81] Yet the first approach stresses the particular theological (e.g., christological) themes addressed to a particular ecclesial situation, whereas the second places the weight more on the practical ordering of church life guided by these various theological-christological perspectives. Approach 4 thus resembles approach 2 in its practical emphases but departs substantially by proposing no controlling or distinctive themes constitutive of the Central Section.

Approaches 1, 2, and 4 seek to mitigate the dissonance at the level of the plot of Jesus' ministry by positing a more comprehensive function, and thus coherence, for the Central Section within the overall story of Luke-Acts. In approaches 1 and 2, a "journeying teacher" seems quite natural, given Luke's penchant for the dynamic fulfillment of Israel's history which moves on into the mission of the church.[82] Approach 4 carries with it the special attraction that it appears to gain a more balanced perspective of Luke's overall literary procedure in his adherence to a normative gospel pattern. Approach 3, on the other hand, seeks a unity primarily within the literary frame of the Central Section itself. That Jesus appears to stand still in much of the "journey" is to miss Luke's dynamic skill altogether.[83]

One might question the viability of any theory that does not take Luke's plotting of his story into consideration from the ground level. This is all the more so, given Luke's express intent in his prologue (1:1-4) to relate a "connected narrative of the whole course of events that have happened among us." Whatever Luke means by this, at the very least he is intending a coherent presentation—whether logical or chronological—

at the level of his *story* of Jesus.[84] Now in 9:51, through a solemn declaration and then through intermittent echoes, the story in 9:51—19:44 has clearly taken a twist in a different direction. The journey notices have now entered into Luke's thematic and hence narrative structure. The reader thus has every right to ask where in Luke's "connected narrative of the whole course of events" Jesus' journeying is taking him as he strives to reach his goal.[85] It simply will not do to shift the form-content problem to a "higher" level.

For our literary-critical purposes, then, we must ask the representatives of approaches 1, 2, and 4 to what extent the journey motif, though dissonant from the individual traditions, nevertheless still enhances an overarching purpose for the Central Section. Given the more comprehensive program Luke is promoting, does he simply relegate the "journey" to a convenient scaffolding for disparate material (approach 4), or does this motif in some way resonate with his wider thematic schemes? Only as we probe from this angle will we be able to render a fair and more informed judgment on the adequacy of the various approaches in discerning Luke's intention and, consequently, the unity and purpose of the Central Section. For it is only as the relation of form to content is viewed within the interplay of the story of Jesus that Luke's grander schemes emerge as a genuine reflection of the narrative that he has actually composed.[86] Therefore we ask if the journey motif, whether already available in Luke's traditions or his own creation, is an integrating theme for the story Luke tells throughout Luke-Acts or is distinctive only to the Central Section. Is the journey motif intrinsic to the cohesion of the whole Lukan corpus or is it an extrinsic or external framework for a more cohesive plot for the otherwise amorphous traditions of the Central Section?

The Journey Motif in the Light of Luke's Purpose

In the light of the disparity of form and content, what role does a "journey" still play for the Central Section in the context of Luke-Acts?

APPROACH 1: Theological-Christological

The Journey Motif as External Framework

For **Hans Conzelmann** the journey motif serves primarily a christological function: to present a stage of Jesus' unfolding nature as an awareness that he must suffer.[87] From tradition Luke probably receives the idea of the necessity of both the duration and the direction of this journey;[88] but Jesus' changing of locality and his movement as a traveler are definitely not thematic concerns. That Jesus begins in Galilee and ends in Jerusalem at a prescribed time is all that Luke considers throughout, and therefore the journey framework images a changed emphasis in Jesus' ministry. The journey notices, then, function to enhance the overall framework or atmosphere, that is, to sustain the idea of a journey stage as a viable symbol of Jesus' resolved awareness of his inevitable and necessary death. In so doing, Luke expands the traditional notion of the necessity of the Passion into an entire period of Jesus' ministry so that this idea emerges and finds concrete form within the narrative itself. But Jesus' journeying from place to place, with Jerusalem as a final destination, bears no special relation to the material within this stage. For Conzelmann, in short, the "journeying Jesus" is an extrinsic Lukan scheme clearly in the interests of the christological focus within Luke's *Heilsgeschichte*.[89]

The Journey Motif as an Intrinsic Principle of Unity
Though the views of **Vincent Taylor** in *Behind the Third Gospel* antedate the "new look" of Conzelmann and others, Taylor's conception of the salvation-historical unity of the Central Section already anticipates that heightened awareness of Luke's theological program. According to Taylor, Luke had access to "good tradition" concerning a final journey, despite his ignorance of exact times and places and his placing of certain Galilean traditions in this section (e.g., 11:15–22—the "Beelzebul Controversy").[90] Luke 9:51—10:24 may even rest upon the eyewitness recollections of the "Mission of the Seventy." Taylor suggests that this closely knit section provided the model for Luke's combination of Q and "L" material in the rest of his travel narrative which, in contrast, is "loosely connected."[91] It is then possible that certain of the travel notices (e.g., 13:22; 17:11) are Luke's editorial comments to enhance the journeying theme. Yet for Taylor, the journey motif is not a narrative invention for the sake of tying loose ends together, but it is "the thread on which the story hangs. It is . . . important to recognize that St. Luke's procedure is no mere literary device. . . . In supplying us with information about a period of which Mk. has little to tell, Proto-Luke is to be trusted as an historical authority."[92] This is not to say that the journeying idea is equally strong or effective throughout. But that the travel narrative represents nearly one-third of the Gospel, giving a sense of movement from Galilee through Samaria to Jerusalem and then mirrored in reverse in the Acts, argues that "traveling" for Luke was constitutive to the gospel events themselves. In other words, the "journeying of Jesus" in the tradition strikes a deep note of resonance in the final author's modulation of the salvation history.[93] And in addition, as with Conzelmann, the motif becomes a dirge for Luke to undertone the whole of the Central Section with the ever-encroaching death of Jesus in Jerusalem.[94]

In contrast to Taylor but in line with Conzelmann, **W. C. Robinson, Jr.**, argues that the Central Section reflects Luke's creation of a travel narrative through the addition of the journey indicators. It is true that Luke is not concerned about specific geography or whether Jesus traveled through non-

Jewish territory, but yet—unlike Conzelmann—the whole of the travel narrative depicts Jesus "on the move," continually "progressing" toward his goal.[95] "Movement," "journeying" itself, along a God-given course is, as with Taylor, absolutely vital to Luke's picture.[96] Although this motif is not especially germane to the traditions of the Central Section, it is nevertheless not imposed from the "outside," perhaps by way of Mark,[97] but is intrinsic to the whole thrust of Luke-Acts: the history of salvation from the events of the Old Testament through the path of Jesus and on through the mission of the church to the final consummation of all creation is one continuous *way.*

Thus for Robinson, Taylor, and Conzelmann the Central Section as a whole is an important landscape in Luke's larger salvation-historical panorama, but only for the first two scholars is journeying itself native to that picture.

Approach 2: Ecclesiastical-Functional

The Journey Motif as External Framework

Johannes Schneider follows Conzelmann in regarding the travel notices as branding the whole of the Central Section with the sign of the cross to effect a new phase in the ministry of Jesus.[98] From 9:51 Jesus has the goal of his suffering and death ever before him, so that he no longer wanders as before. The "journey" presents then a preparatory stage to the salvation-historical events in Jerusalem which climax in the ascension. But Schneider also views Jesus' journeying from town to town within Galilee and Judea as a demonstration of Luke's interest in the universal scope of the gospel which the church is likewise to demonstrate in its life and mission.[99] However, he does not relate this emphasis directly to the universal mission of Luke-Acts as a whole or regard journeying itself as constitutive to Luke's overall plan.[100] Instead, the traditions of Jesus' journeying are convenient framework for instruction and training for the church of Luke's day. That is to say, in the numerous parables, didactic sayings, parenesis, and instruction to disciples by Jesus, Luke is engaging the journey motif primarily at another level: ecclesiology and ethics.[101] Schneider even maintains that Luke removes the definite indicators of time and place in the traditions, making Jesus' "journey" transcend all particular situations to be universally applicable. It is then this "journeying Jesus," bound for Jerusalem, who demonstrates the "boundlessness" of the ministry for the church to come.[102]

The Journey Motif as an Intrinsic Principle of Unity

Building upon a growing consensus of the travel narrative's theological-christological function, **David Gill** links the travel notices to three themes programmatic to the unity of the whole: *(a)* the necessity of suffering and death in Jerusalem; *(b)* the disciples' misunderstanding of this Passion; and *(c)* conditions of discipleship, tied both to the Passion and to the future mission of the church, which serve to correct the disciples' incomprehension.[103] Gill shows, for instance, that πορεύομαι, with its cognates, becomes a *terminus technicus* to link these motifs into a catena spanning the whole Central Section. In this way Jesus' "journeying" or progress to Jerusalem is woven into the fabric of faithful discipleship.[104] Gill shows how this same linkage—suffering of Jesus, misunderstanding, and correction of discipleship with a mission thrust—is present also in all three meal scenes at the end of the Gospel: the Last Supper (22:14–38), Emmaus (24:13–35), and the upper room (24:36–49). His conclusion: "Luke then takes this theme of discipleship and develops it, principally by his deployment of the *Reisenotizen,* into a central motif of the last two-thirds of his Gospel."[105] Gill does not stop with the Gospel only but sees the journeying-discipleship theme integrated intrinsically with Luke's overall narrative plan. Whereas the necessity of the Passion and the correction of the disciples' misunderstanding stem from Mark or basic synoptic tradition, "the connection between the Jerusalem journey and the mission is not in the sources, and it fits so well with the conception of Luke/Acts as a whole that it must be Luke's own. . . . The theme of the mission looks forward to Acts."[106] Here Gill makes explicit the parallel between Jesus' and the disciples' and the future church's "journeying": "Jesus' journey is indeed a type of the Christian life. . . . His way was the way of the cross. We too, says Luke, must go the way of the cross."[107]

In **Walter Grundmann** we meet a complete intermeshing of approaches 1 and 2 to produce a "Teacher in the face of death."[108] Though Grundmann does not see the travel narrative so much as one specific period in a series of delineated periods, as Conzelmann does, he agrees that Luke presents a particular christological stage in which the goal of death and exaltation-glorification in Jerusalem not only is announced but is ever before Jesus' eyes in fulfillment of a grand *heilsgeschichtliche* plan. As Jesus journeys to suffer, he utters teaching that is vital to the disciples' and the later church's own journey. Grundmann goes farther than Gill by stressing this "way" throughout the Gospel and Acts as a journey of suffering which only through this God-ordained means (path) leads to glory and the life of the Kingdom of God. But the intricate weaving of a journey is not limited to the theme of suffering. Grundmann envisions a "wandering, guest Prophet-Messiah" through whom God incognito visits his people. From the beginning of the public ministry in 4:42 Luke stresses a Jesus who wanders through towns, visiting homes and eating and drinking. But it is especially in the travel narrative that "this christological conception of a wanderer, who as guest receives hospitality, takes on special significance."[109] Thus Grundmann points to certain hospitality themes that are only rarely noticed in discussions of the cohesion of the Central Section.[110] But Grundmann concedes that these are limited, so that in line with critical consensus a basic tension is still marked. Yet the "journeying Jesus" is no intrusion from a Markan travel sequence or a few hints in other traditions.[111] In this way Grundmann presents a christological figure developed throughout the entire Gospel[112] to yield an organic unity for the travel narrative and to weld this wandering Messiah to the path of suffering in Acts for the church of Luke's day.

Approach 4: Traditional-Logical

By definition this orientation disavows the thematic development of the journey indicators within the larger narrative of Luke-Acts. They serve rather as convenient scaffolding.

The Journey Motif as External Framework

I. Howard Marshall argues that if a controlling theme is to be sought throughout Luke's Gospel, it is the broader development of "salvation" which enables the Evangelist in the Central Section to fill out the portrait of Jesus as teaching and instructing his disciples, defending the gospel from his opponents, and as the one who will be rejected by the Jews in Jerusalem.[113] Jesus' consciousness of the "path of suffering" in 9:51—19:27 is heightened by Luke's editing of traditional material that already contained both the journey motif and the impending death in Jerusalem.[114] Yet neither of these themes furnishes an organic unity to the whole. "It follows that the real importance of the section lies in the teaching given by Jesus. Here again, however, we land in difficulties, for the general themes of the section are hard to define, and it is even more difficult to find any kind of thread running through it."[115] Marshall is content, nonetheless, to entitle the section "Progress Towards Jerusalem," owning that the journey motif "afforded him a useful framework."[116]

Josef Blinzler does not consider the Central Section an expanded Markan outline dictated by a journey motif in Q and "L" material. Instead, the travel notices are simply Luke's stylistic creation to incorporate a great amount of material without *(a)* interrupting a continuous flow of narrative in which Jesus already in Galilee is an *itinerant* worker and without *(b)* disrupting the Markan framework of the Galilean phase.[117] As with Marshall, the journey motif possesses no closer connection to the divergent traditions in the Central Section than Jesus' travels do within the Galilean section. There has been no convincing demonstration, he contends, of any overarching or controlling theological or literary motif within the Central Section. The menagerie of themes with their kaleidoscopic arrangements is proof enough that no dominating factor has been at work.[118] For Blinzler, Luke's narrative technique is more than adequate to explain his travel notices and the consequent travel narrative.

CONCLUSIONS

The significant contributions of scholars in the first two approaches are extensive, and those highlighting an intrinsic unitive role for the journey motif especially go a long way in clarifying the raison d'être of a "journey" form at all for the large Central Section of Luke's Gospel. Whether the journey is more like a medium or underlying tone, or a distinctive theme around which other motifs cluster and take on special relevance,

Luke's interest in a coherent journeying scheme for the whole of Luke-Acts is brought out into full relief. Moreover, as the "journeying" of 9:51—19:44 is related to the "journeying" of the church, this section achieves an internal cohesion unmatched by approach 4 and a functional force more intense than approach 3.

When all of this has been said, however, we are still confronted by a disturbingly stubborn disunity at the level of Luke's story.[119] Even as the proponents of approaches 1 and 2 admit, the bulk of the traditions at the level of the plot seem to be piled up willy-nilly without regard for any plan. When it is then pointed out that the journey to the cross casts a shadow on all of the traditions, this observation amounts to a special pleading which again is not borne out at the level of the plot. The reader is confronted by the embarrassing fact that little of the didactic-parenetic material is burnished with the mark of the cross, let alone with a journey. Right in the midst of this road to death this teaching is "suspended," as it were, without the "suspense" moving through it to its denouement. The travel notices can certainly be seen to promote an overall framework or atmosphere in line with integral themes in Luke-Acts. But Gill, for instance, concedes that "not every discussion of proper discipleship has a *Reisenotiz* affixed to it" and, conversely, that much of the other material is not related to the journey theme.[120] Appeals to the use of this material in the church may explain Luke's ulterior motive for including this material in his Gospel but do not get around his own description of his procedure and intent in Luke 1:1–4. Grundmann's delineation of a wandering-hospitality theme would appear to be an extension of the journey theme to many of the diverse tradition units. But here again this observation does not go far enough. Grundmann himself despairs of this solution when he writes, "Between this data [of hospitality] and the bulk of material in the 'travel narrative' that has no direct connection with its objective, there remains a persistent tension."[121] In essence, then, approaches 1 and 2 sacrifice Luke's literary skill in his story of Jesus either to grander schemes or to practical-functional concerns.

Approach 4 is doomed from the outset: It is clearly not the case that either Luke's procedure or his plot is the same as in the Galilean ministry. The critical problems of the journey indicators notwithstanding, these notices endow the section with a journeying theme more explicit and frequent than in the earlier part of the ministry. Precisely because of the programmatic character of 9:51, recourse to a rudimentary gospel pattern may explain the origins of certain of the traditions but hardly begins to construe Luke's arrangement and development of them. This approach thus sidesteps the crux of the matter.

For the same reason, approach 3 fails to give an adequate account of the relation of the journey motif to the disparate traditions at the level of the plot. Jesus may march to Jerusalem to the beat of a larger literary pattern as Luke becomes the littérateur par excellence. But we are still faced with the uncompromising dilemma that Jesus appears to stand still in the vast "wastelands" of colorless crowds and faceless foes. Unless the journey indicators can be integrated into the larger literary pattern to explain Jesus' movement vis-à-vis his own words and deeds, every step forward by approach 3 is at the same time a step in reverse. Of the various patterns proposed, the analogy to Deuteronomy would appear to be the most promising, since a great mass of teaching is presented in the form of a journey to the Promised Land. Yet in the exposés thus far,[122] no attempt has been made to relate the peculiar tension between the teaching and the course of the journey in Deuteronomy to that of the Central Section. Rather, Jesus, the "prophet like Moses" of Deut. 18:15–19, is (so approach 2) a teacher, now delivering a "new Torah" which in sequence and substance parallels that of the "old" (Deuteronomy 1—26). A number of the parallels are indeed startlingly close; others, consisting of verbal and catchword connections without substantial similarity in either correspondence or contrast, are tenuous at best.[123] The result as before is either a functional cohesion within the edifice of the church or a literary model which at crucial joints collapses under scrutinizing stress.

All four approaches, then, lead to one conclusion: Either Luke has done a mediocre job in fulfilling his desire to give an "ordered" account or in 9:51—18:14 (19:44) he shifts his aims almost entirely for grander theological, practical, or aesthetic pursuits. To be sure, we agree with Conzelmann and others that the surest means of determining Luke's overall intention in the Central Section is at the level of the plot where the dissonance of form from content is the most acute. But can we be satisfied with an Evangelist whose literary felicity does not also include a credible picture at this level of the words and deeds of Jesus? Does Luke simply acquiesce his storytelling artistry to practical concerns?[124] Can we dismiss the "undramatic flair" of more than one-third of Luke's Gospel as merely an adherence to a normative "unpatterned" gospel pattern?

The contention of this study is that "the journey motif" is not, in the final reckoning, merely a convenient silo for a farrago of tradition. A study of the function of the journey is needed in which the journey indicators are not interpreted a priori through the double sieve of historical credibility and their variance from the Markan or synoptic outline. For even in the redactional studies of Luke's larger plan, the travel narrative is still in part conceived and to that extent defined as an alternative to or transformation of the Markan program. We need to launch a new investigation from within the story of Luke-Acts itself to see what clues Luke might provide in following his journey through the mysterious maze of 9:51—19:44. Only in this way can the hammerlock of disparity between form and content possibly be broken, a grip that in critical exegesis continues to choke the organic cohesion and hence literary function of the Central Section in Luke's great narration of the events of salvation. The truth is that the travel narrative remains an oddity in Luke-Acts. To propose a new resolution to this tension, a new solution to the problem, we now turn.

Notes

1. The "travel notices" (*Reisenotizen*) usually include the following indications that Jesus is bound for Jerusalem: 9:51, 53; 13:22, 33; 17:11. Where one concludes the Central Section determines whether 18:31; 19:11, 28; and 19:41 are also included (see below, n. 3). The list in the Introduction is not based on a supposed Lukan editorial activity, as for most uses of the phrase "travel notice." Schmidt's discussion (*Rahmen,* 259–69) set the precedent.

2. By "journey indicators" some interpreters include both the travel notices and other indications that Jesus is on a journey or journeys, namely, that he is moving from one locality to another, whether the ultimate destination is given or not; cf., e.g., the list by W. C. Robinson, Jr., *Der Weg des Herrn: Studien zur Geschichte und Eschatologie im Lukas-Evangelium; Ein Gespräch mit Hans Conzelmann* (Hamburg: Reich, 1964), 34 n. 219. "Movement" within a certain locality does not qualify as a travel indicator, e.g., 18:36, 37, 40.

3. The precise end of the Central Section depends upon whether Mark's Gospel as a written source is considered to have provided a basic outline into which Luke has inserted some extra material and where Luke intends the journey theme to come to a halt. In the first case, Markan priority dictates that Luke has followed Mark's basic outline throughout except for the "little interpolation," Luke 6:12— 8:3, and the "great interpolation," 9:51—18:14. The Central Section is thus conceived by literary and source analysis to be 9:51—18:14; cf. Luke 18:15ff. = Mark 10:13ff. Where thematic considerations are determinative, some consider the "journey to Jerusalem" to end at 19:27, since the following story of the "Entry into Jerusalem" belongs more with the final days in Jerusalem than with the trip there. For various representative judgments, see, e.g., Conzelmann, *Theology,* 73–78. Or Luke's special literary activity ends at 19:27, above all his composition of the "travel notices" of which 19:11 is the final one (so, e.g., Grundmann, *Lukas,* 198 n. 3, 365; and Schmidt, *Rahmen,* 247; and by contrast, Marshall, *Luke,* 401 [19:10 is a logical terminus]).

For our purposes the literary integrity of the Central Section vis-à-vis the text of Luke as it stands is what is important, irrespective of what sources Luke may have been indebted to in his final composition. Hence from a thematic point of view, the "journey to Jerusalem" which begins at 9:51 lasts until Jesus' arrival there, that is, up to 19:45, where Jesus enters the Temple precincts, though according to the Lukan story the journey to Jesus' "taking up" (9:51) continues to his ascension in Acts 1. For concurring divisions, see, e.g., Ellis, *Luke*, 223–24; and J. L. Resseguie, "Interpretation of Luke's Central Section (Luke 9:51— 19:44) Since 1856," *Studia Biblica et Theologica* 5 (1975): 3 n. 2. For other listings, see, e.g., J. Schneider, "Zur Analyse des lukanischen Reiseberichtes," in *Synoptische Studien,* Studies for A. Wikenhauser, ed. J. Schmid and A. Vögtle (Munich: K. Zink, 1953), 210–11; and Resseguie, "Interpretation," 3 n. 2; and for F. Schleiermacher's view, cf. below, n. 52.

4. Typical of more modern interpreters, C. C. McCown ("The Geography of Luke's Central Section," *JBL* 57 [1938]: 58) describes Luke's juxtaposing of material "which he threw together into a very loosely organized mass. . . . In all this Luke can hardly be said to live up to his reputation as a littérateur and a historian." McCown concludes, however, that Luke was interested in presenting didactic material and therefore used the journey motif as a literary device "to hold the reader's attention to the crowded mass of teachings which the section collects" (p. 65); cf. below, n. 74.

5. For clear presentations of the problems, see, e.g., J. Blinzler, "Die literarische Eigenart des sogenannten Reiseberichts im Lukasevangelium," in Schmid and Vögtle, *Synoptische Studien,* 20–52, esp. 33–41; J. Schneider, "Analyse," esp. 211–17; McCown, "Central Section," esp. 54–64; Schmidt, *Rahmen,* esp. 259– 64, 269–71; and Fitzmyer, *Luke I–IX,* 823.

6. My translation of τὸ πρόσωπον ἐστήρισεν. Literally, "set his face" (so RSV); "set his face resolutely" (NEB); "steadfastly set his face" (RV); "resolutely turn his eyes" (Marshall, *Luke,* 403); "da richtete er sein Angesicht fest darauf" (Rengstorf, *Lukas,* 128); "da richtete er sein Antlitz darauf hin" (Schmid, *Lukas,* 176); "il se détermina à prendre" (Lagrange, *Luc,* 283). Commentators are fairly unanimous in pointing to the Septuagintism here, e.g., Jer. 3:12; 21:10; Ezek. 6:2; 13:17; 14:8; Isa. 50:7. In addition to the commentaries, see C. F. Evans, "The Central Section of St. Luke's Gospel," in *Studies in the Gospels: Essays in Memory of R. H. Lightfoot,* ed. D. E. Nineham (Oxford: Basil Blackwell, 1955), 37–53, esp. 37–40, who points to the negative sense in LXX usage—"to set against," "to oppose"; P. D. M. Turner, "Two Septuagintalisms with ΣTHPIZEIN," *VT* 28 (1978): 481–82; and Schlatter, *Lukas,* 270, for Hebraic idiom.

7. διὰ μέσον Σαμαρείας καὶ Γαλιλαίας; the variant διὰ μέσου (A W Θ pl; TR) no doubt attests to the difficulty of διὰ μέσον. In BAGD the latter probably can only mean "through Samaria and Galilee." Cf. Plummer (*Luke,* 403): "It means 'through what lies between,' i.e., along the frontier, or simply, 'between.'" He goes on to assert that even if διὰ μέσου were the correct reading, it should still mean "between," as is found in Xenophon (*Anabasis* 1.4.4) or in Plato (*Leges* vii., p. 805 D); for the accusative form as a Hellenistic equivalent of the genitive, see Lagrange, *Luc,* 457. Cf. also J. Schneider, "Analyse," 212–24; Blinzler, "Eigenart," 46–52; C. C. McCown, "The Geography of Jesus' Last Journey to Jeru-

salem," *JBL* 51 (1932): 114–15; W. Gasse, "Zum Reisebericht des Lukas," *ZNW* 34 (1935): 296 n. 7 (evidence from Homer on for μέσος = "between"); E. Lohse, "Missionarisches Handeln Jesu nach dem Evangelium des Lukas," *TZ* 10 (1954): 8–9; B. Reicke, "Instruction and Discussion in the Travel Narrative," Papers presented to the International Congress on "The Four Gospels in 1957" at Christ Church, Oxford, *SE I* = TU 73 (Berlin: Akademie-Verlag, 1959), 207; D. Gill, "Observations on the Lukan Travel Narrative and Some Related Passages," *HTR* 63 (1970): 208–9; G. Ogg, "The Central Section of the Gospel According to St Luke," *NTS* 18 (1971–72): 49; M. S. Enslin, "Luke and the Samaritans," *HTR* 36 (1943): 294–97 (διὰ μέσον, an adverb phrase taking on the force of a simple preposition, i.e., "through"); R. H. Lightfoot, *Locality and Doctrine in the Gospels* (London: Hodder & Stoughton, 1938), 138–39; Conzelmann, *Theology,* 68–73 (Luke conceived Galilee and Judea as one continuous land mass, with Samaria adjoining both to the west); and K. L. Schmidt, "Der geschichtliche Wert des lukanischen Aufrisses der Geschichte Jesu," *TSK* 91 (1918): 287–88 (Luke has perhaps purposely left the topography vague).

8. McCown, "Central Section," 59 [see Intro., n. 26].

9. Ibid., 60. McCown points out that the total length of the border from Haifa to Scythopolis is only about forty miles, and the part that Jesus would have traversed (e.g., from Jenîn to Beisân) is roughly only some twelve or fifteen miles.

10. Ibid., 56.

11. See above, n. 5, esp. Blinzler, "Eigenart."

12. Luke 13:31–33, though perhaps reworked in Lukan style and including some Lukan additions, is thought by a considerable number of scholars to have at least some basis in the tradition. See e.g., Conzelmann, *Theology,* 68; Schmidt, *Rahmen,* 265–67; J. Schneider, "Analyse," 214–16; Marshall, *Luke,* 566–70; Bultmann, *Syn. Trad.,* 35, 56; and M. Black, *An Aramaic Approach to the Gospels and Acts,* 3d ed. (Oxford: Clarendon Press, 1967), 205–7.

13. See the commentaries. See also Blinzler, "Eigenart," 33–35; Schmidt, *Rahmen,* 259–69; Conzelmann, *Theology,* 60–73; Reicke, "Instruction," 206–8; W. Grundmann, "Fragen der Komposition des lukanischen Reiseberichtes," *ZNW* 50 (1959): 253–54; W. C. Robinson, Jr., "The Theological Context for Interpreting Luke's Travel Narrative (9:51ff.)," *JBL* 79 (1960): 20–22; idem, *Der Weg des Herrn,* 37–39, 52–53; Gill, "Observations," 199–200; (see Intro., n. 8); P. von der Osten-Sacken, "Zur Christologie des lukanischen Reiseberichts," *EvT* 33 (1973): 485–90; and F. Stagg, "The Journey Toward Jerusalem in Luke's Gospel," *RevExp* 64 (1967): 501.

14. Blinzler, "Eigenart," 41.

15. Jerusalem is also referred to, not as a destination, in Luke 10:30 (parable of the Good Samaritan) and 13:4 (tower of Siloam). See also n. 1, above.

16. See above, n. 3, for the literary function of 19:11.

17. Jericho is referred to as destination in the parable of the Good Samaritan (10:29–36) in v. 30!

18. εἰς κώμην Σαμαραιτῶν. For Luke's supposedly inaccurate use of κώμη and πόλις, see McCown, "Central Section," 54–55, where he contends that Luke

mistakenly uses πόλις to describe Nazareth and Bethlehem. For Conzelmann's view that Luke regards Jerusalem as a free "polis" in the Roman legal sense and therefore a relatively independent political entity, see Conzelmann, *Theology,* 69–70.

19. Cf. the commentaries and, e.g., Schmidt, "Wert," 288–90; and idem, *Rahmen,* 267–68; contra Schmidt's interpretation of v. 56 as another Samaritan village, see, e.g., Conzelmann, *Theology,* 65–66; or Gasse, "Reisebericht," 293–96. For a partial listing of other interpreters' opinions on this problem, see Blinzler, "Eigenart," 24 nn. 12 and 13 (writing in 1953, Blinzler lists thirteen authors since 1900 who take v. 56 as another Samaritan village and six since 1876 as a village outside of Samaria, presumably in Galilee, the Decapolis, or Perea).

20. It does not follow necessarily that those who understand the "travel notices" as primarily literary frameworks also conclude that therefore a credible, continuous journey has not been described; nevertheless, it is logical that most who hold to a "literary device" understanding of the travel notices take this view. All those represented in nn. 5 and 13, for instance, are of this opinion. Cf. Blinzler ("Eigenart," 36 n. 42), who reproduces L. Girard's (*L'évangile des voyages de Jésus ou la section 9,51—18,14 de Saint Luc* [Paris: J. Gabalda, 1951], 56 n. 4, 57 n. 1) lists of scholars with this approach: Protestant scholars — Reuss, de Wette, Weizsäcker, B. Weiss, Wellhausen, K. L. Schmidt, Bultmann, Sanday, Wright, Bundy, Davies, Moffatt, Cadman, Creed, McCown; Blinzler adds Wendland, Klostermann, A. Jülicher, and E. Fascher; Catholic scholars — Camerlynck, Lebreton, Bonkamp, Prat, Buzy, Ricciotti; Blinzler adds J. Schmid and J. Sickenberger.

21. Schmidt, *Rahmen,* 269, an almost exact repetition of his conclusion in "Wert," 290.

22. Contrast the Introduction and see the notable exception among recent critical treatments in Grundmann, *Lukas,* 197–200; and idem, "Fragen," 252–54.

23. So, e.g., Conzelmann, *Theology,* 62 n. 1. He even speaks of 13:31–33 not as an episode with an intrinsic "journey" theme but only as localized tradition which could motivate only the beginning of a journey, not continue the sense of a journey. He also speaks only of a change of location within 18:35–43 and 19:1–10, apparently overlooking the large caravan that is passing *through* Jericho, obviously on some kind of journey. Luke 17:12a is either overlooked altogether or is assumed to be part of the travel notice of 17:11. We have delineated *five* such pericopes indicating *some* journey by *Jesus* between 9:51—19:44 (see Introduction, "The Problem and Purpose of the Investigation").

24. E.g., Schmid, *Lukas,* 175.

25. Cf., e.g., B. M. Metzger, "Seventy or Seventy-two Disciples," *NTS* 5 (1958–59): 299–306; and S. Jellicoe, "St. Luke and the 'Seventy(-Two),'" *NTS* 6 (1959–60): 319–21. Blinzler ("Eigenart," 27–29) points to the 10:20–21 and the 10:22–23 transitions as the *only* evidence for a continuous, self-contained report; Schmidt (*Rahmen,* 258) points out that 10:23 is really superfluous within the present Lukan context and therefore reflects a conjunction already in the earlier

tradition. See Schmidt, *Rahmen,* 246ff., for still one of the clearest and fullest analyses of the pericope connections.

26. Schmidt, *Rahmen,* 259–60 (a Lukan comment); cf. Blinzler, "Eigenart," 28; and J. Schneider, "Analyse," 217.

27. E.g., Blinzler ("Eigenart," 27): "connected according to a mechanical or a topical and not according to a historical arrangement."

28. See commentaries for various topical arrangements. Cf., e.g., Grundmann ("Fragen," 259ff.; and *Lukas,* 197–200), who divides the section into three journey reports each with a special teaching section; Plummer (*Luke*) divides the journey into three parts; Fitzmyer (*Luke*) distinguishes the "Lukan Travel Account," 9:51—18:14, and the "Synoptic Travel Account," 18:15—19:27; Reicke ("Instruction," 213) sees an oscillation between "instruction" to the disciples and "discussion" with opponents and adversaries (see further, below, Part III, "Conclusion," Excursus 1); many, of course, do not delineate any topic but comment on separate pericopes or on whole chapters; see, e.g., the commentaries by Findlay, Leaney, Manson, Rengstorf, and Geldenhuys.

With great divergence in organization and no agreement on topical divisions, the question inevitably emerges: Are commentators' attempts to base an organizing principle upon any topical arrangement really endemic to the "contour" of this "journey" section?

29. For a categorization, see Schmidt, *Rahmen,* 249–53.

30. ἀριστάω, "eat a meal," "dine" (BAGD); cf. John 21:12, "eat breakfast."

31. See below, Part III.C.10.

32. Schmidt (*Rahmen,* 257–58) considers the audience changes between the disciples and crowds and opponents to have been established already within the tradition Luke takes over. Otherwise it is impossible to explain the arbitrary distribution of dominical logia among both the crowds and the disciples; those directed to opponents have an intrinsic connection to the challenge put forward. Thus they too were given to Luke in the tradition (for specific transitions, see Schmidt's charts, *Rahmen,* 249–53). Ellis (*Luke,* 149) sees these disciple-audience changes as the feature that distinguishes the teachings of the Galilean phase from those of the Central Section. In this respect, Luke is closer to John than to Matthew or Mark.

33. Cf., e.g., Schmidt, *Rahmen,* 257.

34. E.g., esp. 16:16—17:10; cf., e.g., McCown ("Central Section," 58): "In chapters 15 and 16 Jesus stands still."

35. Cf. nn. 5, 13, 20, 33; and Blinzler, "Eigenart," 34. He quotes Ernst von Dobschütz ("Zur Erzählerkunst des Markus," *ZNW* 27 [1928]: 193) with respect to Luke's narrative technique. Cf. Ellis (*Luke,* 146): "Luke's distinction is to use the journey as a scaffolding upon which to present a different aspect of the Lord's ministry. But it is only a scaffolding." Cf. also Caird (*Luke,* 139): "The result is a somewhat artificial structure, full of topographical inconsistencies. . . . But, however that may be, his main purpose was to preserve the dramatic tension of his story by constant reminders of the crisis which lay ahead, just as John does by his repeated references to the hour which had not yet come."

36. Conzelmann, *Theology,* 67.

37. E.g., Blinzler ("Eigenart," 29–32) reckons, between 9:51—18:14, thirteen Q and twelve "L" traditions that cannot be placed into either a Perean or a Samaritan framework, including all those dealing with Pharisees and scribes. However this may be, an encounter with Pharisees in Perea should not be ruled out a priori for Luke, given Mark's or at least Matthew's assigning "On Divorce and Celibacy" (Matt. 9:3–12; Mark 10:2–12) "to the region of Judea beyond the Jordan" (Matt. 19:1; cf. Mark 10:1); cf. Klostermann, *Lukas,* 110; Grundmann, *Lukas,* 199; and Schmid, *Lukas,* 174–75.

38. Cf., e.g., Lightfoot, *Locality,* 137–39; and McCown, "Central Section," 57.

39. See a concordance on the incidence and location of these characters; and for a summary profile, see below, Part III, "Conclusion," Excursus 2.

The "Twelve" occurs only seven times in Luke (twelve times in Mark); two of these are in reference to Judas Iscariot in the Passion narrative (22:3, 47), while occurring only once in the Central Section, 18:31 (the third Passion prediction), in contrast to the remaining four times in 4:14—9:50 (6:13; 8:1; 9:1, 12).

"Laos" occurs primarily at the beginning and the end of the Gospel: 1:1—4:13 (eleven times); 19:45—24:53 (eighteen times); 4:14—9:50 (six times); 9:51—19:44 (only 18:43).

40. On ritual purity and dietary regulations, cf., e.g., *Midr.* Exod. 18:1 (65a); and *b. Ber.* 43b.

41. Typical is Klostermann (*Lukas,* 110): "Through the 'Great Interpolation' into the Markan outline, the public ministry of Jesus is substantially expanded into a 'travel narrative' at Galilee's expense."

42. See above, Introduction, n. 5.

43. Scholars differ over whether Luke used Mark as a source for the section. Most (e.g., Blinzler, Fitzmyer, W. Manson, Marshall, Reicke, Schlatter, Schmid, Rengstorf) see Luke dependent almost entirely on Q, "L," and other oral or possibly written traditions. They often point out that the alleged parallels in Mark are actually not as close as those in Matthew (see esp. Reicke, "Instruction," 208, although Reicke holds to the independence of the Gospel writers as regards written sources [see above, Introduction, n. 32]). See further, J. C. Hawkins, "Three Limitations to St. Luke's Use of St. Mark's Gospel," in *Studies in the Synoptic Problem by Members of the University of Oxford,* ed. W. Sanday (Oxford: Clarendon Press, 1911), 29–59; and B. H. Streeter, *The Four Gospels: A Study of Origins* (London: Macmillan Co., 1936), 204.

Others (e.g., Grundmann, McCown, Schneider) argue for a Markan source in at least certain passages (e.g., the "Beelzebul Controversy," 11:14–23 = Mark 3:22–27 = Matt. 12:22–30; cf., e.g., McCown, "Central Section," 57). For a thorough analysis of the triple and double tradition, see H. L. Egelkraut, *Jesus' Mission to Jerusalem: A Redaction Critical Study of the Travel Narrative in the Gospel of Luke, Lk 9:51—19:48,* European University Papers 80 (Frankfurt: Verlag Peter Lang, 1976), 62–196. Because our study is not based and does not depend—one way or the other—upon a theory of Markan priority (see above, Introduction), we are content to point out the parallels wherever they exist.

44. This discrepancy with Luke 9:51 is enough alone to throw into serious question whether Luke bases 9:51 and the travel section on Mark.

45. Cf. Matt. 20:16, presumably also the same territory unless somewhere on the western side of the Jordan in the approach to Jericho.

46. Both Mark 10:2–9 and Matt. 19:3–8 have *Pharisees* "testing" Jesus in *Perea;* see above, n. 37.

47. For those who hold to the two-source hypothesis, this observation is especially significant. But if Luke perchance writes independently of a *text* of (canonical) Mark and possesses Q material relatively independent of the Q material Matthew has used, then this point is robbed of some of its force. Reicke (in private correspondence) has pointed out that the only contextual parallels in Q are the "preaching of repentance by John the Baptist" (Matt. 3:7–10 = Luke 3:7–10—following an introduction to John) and the "temptation of Jesus" (Matt. 4:1–11 = Luke 4:1–13—immediately preceding the beginning of the Galilean ministry). This in itself argues that the Q that Luke has used was most likely not in the same shape or, at least, order as the Q that Matthew has used, if indeed we can speak of a self-contained, delimited written "source" Q at all. See also Caird, *Luke,* 18; and above, Introduction, n. 32.

48. See, e.g., above, nn. 5, 13, and recent commentators. E.g., Marshall (*Luke,* 401): "What is important is that Luke cannot have been consciously providing a geographical progress from Galilee to Jerusalem"; Talbert (*Reading Luke,* 111): "The geography cannot be satisfactorily traced. . . . This travel section is an editorial framework created by the evangelist."

49. W. M. L. de Wette, *Kurzgefasstes exegetisches Handbuch zum Neuen Testament: Kurze Erklärung der Evangelien des Lukas und Markus,* 1/2, 3d ed. (Leipzig: Weidmann'sche, 1846), 76.

50. Cf. above, Introduction, "Method and Scope of This Work," for definition of "narrative world" which is to be distinguished from the "real world," i.e., those events/actions which actually happen(ed).

51. McCown ("Central Section," 51) aligns Marsh, Eichhorn, Kuinoel, and Westcott with a "gnomology" idea and refers to Hug's term, "collectanea."

52. F. Schleiermacher, *Schriften,* Part 1 (Berlin: G. Reimer, 1817), dedicated to de Wette! Schleiermacher argued that 19:47–48 is such a distinct concluding formula for the journey motif of suffering and death announced in 9:51 that not until 19:45–46, 47–48 can a new division in the Gospel be made. Working without a Markan priority, Schleiermacher did not find the correspondence of Luke 18:15ff. with Mark 10:13ff. sufficient to warrant the notion of an earlier journey outline embedded in Mark and/or Matthew that was constitutive of Luke's source material. Indeed, because the bulk of Luke 9:51ff. is paralleled in Matthew, Matt. 19:1 should not be reckoned a definitive marker for the Lukan outline (pp. 158–59). Schleiermacher is also not impressed with the arguments from those of the "gnomology" theory, since too little about a journey is reported. He therefore insists on the conception of a *Reisebericht* (p. 161).

53. De Wette, *Lukas,* 1st ed. (1836), 76.

54. Ibid., 77.

55. Ibid., 76–77.

56. Ibid., 123.

57. Ibid., 76.

58. See above, n. 1.

59. Schmidt, *Rahmen,* 259–64, 266–67.

60. It is interesting to trace the growing dependence of Luke's "journey section" upon another Evangelist: *Schleiermacher* felt that the differences among the three Synoptists were great enough to warrant their independence vis-à-vis the journey accounts; *de Wette* considered the synoptic outline of Matthew and Mark so definitive that Luke's account had to be subsumed to that; *Schmidt* saw Luke's dependence on the *written* Gospel of Mark determinative of his literary intention in varying from the Markan journey, 10:1–34. To the present author, given the literary-critical demands of an a priori intrinsic analysis, Schleiermacher's working presupposition is the most prudent (cf. above, Introduction, n. 37).

61. Note the subtitle of Schmidt's book: *Literarkritische Untersuchungen zur ältesten Jesusüberlieferung.*

62. But see Schlatter, *Lukas,* e.g., 219–20, 268–73. He regards the travel notices and resulting schema as stemming from the combination of various sources.

63. See Conzelmann's dissertation: "Die geographischen Vorstellungen im Lukasevangelium" (Tübingen, 1950); cf. idem, "Zur Lukasanalyse," *ZTK* 49 (1952): 16–33, which highlighted some of the conclusions of the dissertations.

64. See above, Introduction, n. 24.

65. Conzelmann, *Theology,* 61–62 n. 6.

66. Cf. the alleged remark of C. H. Dodd to J. E. Yates as cited by C. H. Talbert ("Shifting Sands: The Recent Study of the Gospel of Luke," *Int* 30 [1976]: 383–84): "I suspect we shall have to give [the Lukan writings] over, so to speak, to Conzelmann."

67. We are not describing necessarily a direct dependence of one scholar upon another but an influence in scholarly exchange and growing consensuses based on those exchanges.

68. E.g.: Evans, "Central" (1955); W. C. Robinson, Jr., "Theological Context" (1960); idem, *Der Weg des Herrn* (1964); J. C. O'Neill, *The Theology of Acts in Its Historical Setting* (London: SPCK, 1961), 69–73; J. H. Davies, "The Purpose of the Central Section of St. Luke's Gospel," *SE II* = TU 87 (1964), 164–69; C. H. Talbert, *Luke and the Gnostics: An Examination of the Lucan Purpose* (Nashville: Abingdon Press, 1966); idem, "An Anti-Gnostic Tendency in Lucan Christology," *NTS* 14 (1968); idem, *Literary Patterns, Theological Themes and the Genre of Luke-Acts* (Missoula, Mont.: Scholars Press, 1974), 51–56, 118–20, 134–36; and F. Schütz, *Der leidende Christus: Die angefochtene Gemeinde und das Christuskerygma der lukanischen Schriften,* BWANT 89 (Stuttgart: Kohlhammer, 1969), 70–86.

69. See below, "Luke's Purpose in the Light of the Dissonance," Approach 3: Literary-Aesthetical.

70. J. Schneider, "Analyse" (1953); Lohse, "Missionarisches" (1954); Reicke,

"Instruction" (from 1957); Grundmann, "Fragen" (1959); H. Flender, *Heil und Geschichte in der Theologie des Lukas,* BEvT 41 (Munich: Chr. Kaiser Verlag, 1965), 69–83; Stagg, "Journey" (1967); D. Gill, "Observations" (1970); and von der Osten-Sacken, "Christologie" (1973). W. G. Kümmel (*Introduction to the New Testament,* rev. ed. [Nashville: Abingdon Press, 1965], 142), after assaying both the "theological" and the "ecclesiastical-functional" explanations for the Central Section, concludes that the only safe description of Luke's aims is the lowest common denominator of all of them: "In 9:51—19:27 the Lord who is on his way to suffer according to the will of God is equipping his disciples for carrying on his preaching after his death."

71. Cf. above, Introduction, nn. 17, 18, 19.

72. See, e.g., Ellis, *Luke,* 146–50; Marshall, *Historian,* 148–53, esp. 153; and idem, *Luke,* 400–402.

73. Cf. the "gnomology" conception, above.

74. It is necessary to assess interpretations of the Central Section by categories endemic to the critical problems themselves (namely, the overarching discrepancy of form and content) in order to make helpful distinctions in Luke's theology and aims. Otherwise, by using such categories as "the Perean Section" or "Samaritan Journey," or source theories, we lump exegetes together whose views on the significance of the "journey" differ radically.

75. E.g., Conzelmann, J. H. Davies, Evans, Fitzmyer, W. C. Robinson, Schütz, Schweizer (*Luke*), and Talbert; see above, n. 68.

76. E.g., Flender, Gill, Grundmann, Lohse, von der Osten-Sacken, Reicke, Schneider, and Stagg; see above, n. 70.

77. E.g., K. E. Bailey, *Poet and Peasant* (Grand Rapids: Wm. B. Eerdmans Publishing Co., 1976), 79–85; J. Drury, *Tradition and Design in Luke's Gospel* (Atlanta: John Knox Press, 1976), 138–64; Evans; M. D. Goulder, "The Chiastic Structure of the Lucan Journey," *SE II,* 195–202; idem, *Type and History in Acts* (London: SPCK, 1964), 138–39; A. Guilding, *The Fourth Gospel and Jewish Worship* (Oxford: Clarendon Press, 1960), 132–39, 230–31; R. Morgenthaler, *Die lukanische Geschichtsschreibung als Zeugnis,* 2 vols., ATANT 14–15 (Zurich: Zwingli Verlag, 1949), 1:156–57); and Talbert, *Patterns,* 51–56. L. T. Johnson's (*The Literary Function of Possessions in Luke-Acts,* SBLDS 39 [Missoula, Mont.: Scholars Press, 1977], 103–15) pattern of the "Prophet and the People" coheres at the level of Luke's *plotting* of the *story* and thus is not included under the rubric which, unlike Johnson, sees the dissonance of form from content as essentially subsumed to a more artistic literary pattern. Though the thesis of the present study is in fundamental agreement with Johnson's pattern, developed independently it provides a far more specific pattern purporting to resolve the tension, even of Jesus' sayings, at the story level. Cf. Johnson (*Possessions,* 106–7): "There remains a large amount of material only loosely related to the journey, if at all. . . . This is especially so for the sayings material which for the most part can be related only tenuously to the Journey motif."

78. E.g., Blinzler, "Eigenart"; and Ogg, "Central"; see commentaries of Ellis, Geldenhuys, Marshall, and Rengstorf. See also N. B. Stonehouse, *The Witness of*

Luke to Christ (London: Tyndale Press, 1951), 110–27; and V. Taylor, *Behind the Third Gospel: A Study of the Proto-Luke Hypothesis* (Oxford: Clarendon Press, 1926), 151–59, 172–75, 246–54; see above, nn. 48, 72.

79. L. Girard (*L'évangile*) does not fit neatly into our category, since he views the Central Section (9:51—18:14) to be a self-contained, independent Gospel parallel to the Synoptics and *not* fitting into the Mark 10:1ff. period. Girard's proposal has received very little currency if for no other reason than that Luke speaks of only one journey to Jerusalem following the bulk of the Galilean phase. For lists of other attempts to describe more than one journey, esp. in "harmony" with John, see Girard, *L'évangile,* 51–57; Blinzler, "Eigenart," 23–25; and Resseguie, "Interpretation," 5–11.

80. Cf. Marshall, *Luke,* 401.

81. A good example of the organic development of this second approach from the first is von der Osten-Sacken ("Christologie"), who, building principally upon Conzelmann, stresses the importance of the "ascension" in correcting a false idea of Jesus' Messiahship for the church living in the "delay" of the final advent. The church is thus instructed to conduct its life on the pattern of Jesus' journey—a road of suffering which only later leads to glory. Cf. further, e.g., Flender, *Heil und Geschichte;* O'Neill, *Theology of Acts;* and Lohse, "Missionarisches."

82. E.g., W. C. Robinson, Jr., *Der Weg des Herrn.*

83. Cf., e.g., Goulder ("Chiastic," 202) on Luke 13:34–35: "The chiasmus has as its intersection a short section. . . . We are, says St. Luke as he gives us the first lament, half way through the journey."

84. For well-balanced discussions of the issues in the Prologue and of the more recent literature, cf. Marshall, *Luke,* 39–44; and Fitzmyer, *Luke,* 1:287–302. That καθέξης (Luke 1:3) must refer to a strict chronological order is dubious if for no other reason than the lack of precise sequential and topographical detail in Luke's account. Yet a general concern for chronology does not rule out a coherent or consistently ordered development conceived within an overall continuous journey or progression. On the contrary, the "whole course of events," i.e., his story, says Luke, has through his judicious effort been "ordered," i.e., consciously plotted.

85. Cf. Schmidt (*Rahmen,* 261) on Luke 17:11: "Where are we actually?"

86. As Conzelmann (*Theology,* 9–12) expresses, though discerning Lukan intent primarily through diachronic analysis.

87. Conzelmann, "Lukasanalyse," 25.

88. See above, n. 12.

89. Conzelmann, *Theology,* 61–62 n. 6; 67.

90. Taylor, *Behind the Third Gospel,* 235.

91. Ibid.

92. Ibid., 235.

93. Taylor, speaking of the compiler of the traditions of 9:51—18:14 and the "we" sections in Acts (*Behind the Third Gospel,* 200): "It was the work of a traveller whose personal experiences have conditioned his literary methods." In "Luke, Gospel of" (s.v., *IDB*), Taylor adds that much of the material in the

Central Section would be instructive for Christian missionaries. He suggests that the order is due to Luke's closer adherence to the order in Q.

94. Taylor, *Behind the Third Gospel,* 177, 262.

95. W. C. Robinson, Jr., *Der Weg des Herrn,* 35.

96. Ibid., 67: "geography in motion."

97. Though Mark may have suggested the point at which "Luke" inserts his "travel narrative" (W. C. Robinson, Jr., *Der Weg des Herrn,* 53).

98. J. Schneider ("Analyse," 216): "The activity of Jesus now stands under a new sign."

99. Ibid., 212.

100. Jesus had a mission to fulfill in as wide an expanse as possible (J. Schneider, "Analyse," 212, 219).

101. Ibid., 219.

102. Here Schneider follows essentially the "de-eschatologizing" scheme of Conzelmann but sees Luke much more directly dependent on his sources than Conzelmann (J. Schneider, "Analyse," 218–19).

103. See above, n. 70.

104. The marks of a true disciple are especially reinforced at the *beginning,* 9:51—10:16, where the disciples' requirement for following a suffering master is conjoined to the responsibility of mission travels, and at the *end,* 19:11–27, where a despised master returns from a *journey* to find a sloven discipleship which has failed to "invest" in mission (Gill, "Observations," 201–5, 211–12).

105. Gill, "Observations," 221.

106. Ibid.

107. Ibid., 214.

108. Grundmann, *Lukas,* 200; see above, n. 70.

109. Grundmann, *Lukas,* 198; cf. idem, "Fragen," 254.

110. Cf. the Introduction, "The Problem and Purpose of the Investigation."

111. Grundmann ("Fragen") suggests that Luke got the "wandering-guest" motif from Greek mythology as, e.g., in Acts 14:11–13.

112. Jesus is the Messiah already in Luke 1—2 and remains incognito as such until his death and glorification (Grundmann, "Fragen," 255–58).

113. Marshall, *Luke,* 401; and idem, *Historian,* 91–102, 153.

114. Marshall, *Luke;* and *Historian,* 152.

115. Marshall, *Luke,* 401–2.

116. Ibid., 400–401.

117. Blinzler, "Eigenart," 33–41. According to Blinzler (p. 35 n. 41), an immovable obstacle to Conzelmann's idea of Luke transforming Mark's twofold to a threefold account is that none of the material in Luke 9:51—18:14 has a Markan foundation or antecedent (cf. also above, n. 43).

118. Ibid., 35–36 n. 41; cf. above, n. 35.

119. Cf. Marshall's cautious conclusion in 1970: "The existence of this section in Luke is hard to explain, and it is doubtful whether the various recent studies of it have adequately accounted for its nature" (Marshall, *Historian,* 149–50).

120. Gill, "Observations," 214.

121. Grundmann, *Lukas,* 199.

122. See above, n. 77.

123. Cf., e.g., Ellis, *Luke,* 147. J. W. Wenham ("Synoptic Independence and the Origin of Luke's Travel Narrative," *NTS* 27 [1980–81]: 509–10) has summed up scholarly response to Evans and Drury on Deuteronomy: "The supposed parallels are often tenuous in the extreme, e.g., . . . the command to destroy the foreigners is said to correspond *by contrast* to the parable of the Good Samaritan, the law about escaped slaves is said to correspond to the parable of the Unjust Steward. The theory is ingenious rather than plausible."

124. Despite the consensus of disparity for Luke's literary craft in the Central Section, he is still regarded — ironically — as a "master storyteller." Cf., e.g., Caird (*Luke,* 15): "He had something of the poet in his make-up and an artist's ability to depict in vivid pen-portraits the men and women who inhabit his pages"; and P. Schubert ("The Structure and Significance of Luke 24," in *Neutestamentliche Studien für Rudolf Bultmann,* ed. Walther Eltester, BZNW 21 [Berlin: A. Töpelmann, 1954], 185): "Luke is a littérateur of considerable skill and technique. His literary methods serve his theology as his theology serves them."

II

*The Preview of the Journey
of the Prophet like Moses
of Deuteronomy (Luke 9:1–50)*

II

We have concluded that in contemporary critical scholarship the Central Section remains an anomaly. Here I contend that in 9:1–50 Luke provides a preview of the journey that follows in 9:51—19:44. Through this lens the reader is able to focus the lights and shadows of the winding contour ahead as the journey of the prophet Jesus whose calling and fate both recapitulate and consummate the career of Moses in Deuteronomy. In 9:1—19:44 Luke presents nothing less than the Prophet like Moses (Deut. 18:15-19) in a New Exodus unfolding with a dramatic tension all its own.

It has long been recognized that Luke's account of Jesus' mountaintop transfiguration (9:28-36) introduces Jesus' subsequent journey in 9:51—19:44. Luke states that "Moses and Elijah . . . were speaking about his [Jesus'] exodus (ἔξοδος = departure/death) which he was about to fulfill (πληρόω) in Jerusalem" (9:31). This fulfilling is then connected to the complete fulfilling (συμπληρόω) of "the days of his taking up/death" (ἀνάλημψις) that have already begun when Jesus determines to head for that city (9:51). But it is also clear that this mountaintop discussion, led by the two prophets of a Mt. Horeb theophany,[1] is linked, on the one side, to the crowds' confusion of Jesus with John the Baptist or Elijah who "has appeared" or one of the prophets of old who "has arisen" (9:7-9, 18-19; cf. Acts 3:22), and, on the other, to the unparalleled authority of the one who is "found alone," to whom alone the disciples are to "hearken" as God's "Chosen Son" (9:35-36; cf. v. 20b). When we recall that only two of the seventy-three pericopes in 9:51—19:44 do not accommodate a saying of its central figure, we may wonder whether Luke's "journey" is not intended to present the authoritative "voice" of the mountain revelation. This all the more so, since the phrase αὐτοῦ ἀκούετε (9:35b) echoes the voice of Moses prophesying of a "prophet like me" who will utter the life-giving words of God himself (Deut. 18:15; cf. vv. 16-19). Thus Luke has prepared his readers for the journey section through his narrative markers in 9:31 and 9:51 and his "story stuff" woven with *prophets* and *fulfillment* and allusions to the OT in the narrative preceding. Prudence then would dictate that we pursue Luke's conception of a prophet and prophetic language and the role that prophetic figures play in the narrative world of his two-volume story.

LUKE'S LANGUAGE *and* LINEAGE *of the* PROPHETS

Luke alone of the Evangelists casts the entire public ministry of Jesus as the calling and fate of an eschatological prophet (4:16–30). Hence a survey of some of the leading notions of the prophetic vocation in Luke's narrative is in order.

Jesus as Prophet in Luke-Acts

Although Matthew uses προφήτης some thirty-nine times[2] as compared to thirty-one occurrences in Luke's Gospel, it is the latter writer who thrusts Jesus onto a stage of prophetic flurry and spotlights Jesus' self-proclaimed prophetic career.[3]

Jesus' Self-acclaimed Prophet Status

In the seminal account of his public activity (4:16–30), Jesus openly identifies his mission with the calling and tasks of the anointed figure of Isa. 61:1–2 (4:16–21). As Luke clearly shows by injecting the rejections of the prophets Elijah and Elisha (4:25–27) into the midst of the rejection of Jesus in v. 24 and vv. 28–30, Jesus is a prophet like one of the prophets "of old" and preeminently so as one who is spurned by his own folk (v. 29). And as Jesus later declares publicly, his own sending to Israel will consummate the tragic denouement of all her prophets (13:31–35).[4]

Public Acclamation of Jesus as Prophet

Jesus is acclaimed a "great prophet" by the crowds of Israel and by his own disciples (7:16; 9:7–9, 18–19; 24:19; Acts 3:22–24; 7:37, 52; cf. Luke 4:36–37; 5:26; 13:17); similarly this reputation is questioned (Luke 7:39).

Prophets Attending Jesus' Birth and Presentation

Introduced at the beginning of Luke 3 as the voice of Isa. 40:3–5 who "prepares the way of the Lord" (Jesus') public career (3:1–6; see 1:43, 76; 2:11), John himself receives the "word of God" like the prophets of the OT (3:2), is viewed by the masses as one of "these" prophets (20:6; 9:7–8), and is aligned and even confused with the prophet-like movement of

Jesus (9:7-9, 18-19; Acts 18:25-26; 19:1-7). Jesus must explain to the crowds what the narrator has already made clear to his readers: that John, indeed a prophet, yet is greater than all of them precisely because he is the *messenger* who "prepares the way" for Jesus' own mission (7:24-28; cf. 1:17).

Even beyond John's role, his parents are acknowledged by the people of God as channels of the prophetic word (1:22, 46-55). In a way parallel to Isaiah's vision (Isa. 6:1-13), an "angel of the Lord" appears to Zechariah in the Temple, and, after his mouth is "cleansed" (1:20-22, 63-66; cf. Isa. 6:7), prophesies (προφητεύω) of one who "will be called prophet of the Most High" (1:67-79; cf. v. 76a and Isa. 6:1) and will proclaim the coming judgment of the Lord (3:7-17; cf. Isa. 6:9-13; Luke 1:80; Acts 28:26-27). At Jesus' "presentation to the Lord" in the Temple (2:24, 27), Simeon "in the Spirit" declares Jesus to be a prophetic sign that will "be spoken against" (2:25-35; cf. v. 34 and Isa. 42:6; 49:7-8), while Anna, a prophetess, confirms Simeon's word to those "awaiting the redemption of Jerusalem" (2:36-38).

Features of the Prophets' Vocation[5]

1. *Called in a Vision and Sent by Heaven for Mission.* The "prophet" is God's *messenger* in a specific situation to effect God's will.[6] What Luke highlights is that this representative, by way of vision or audition, is admitted to and mandated by the very session of the heavenly council or presence of God:[7]

Zechariah (1:11-20, see esp. v. 19); *Mary* (1:26-38); *Judean shepherds* (2:18-20); *Jesus:* An initial commissioning (3:21-22) in which "the Holy Spirit" descends in visible form is announced at the beginning of Jesus' activity as the raison d'être of his entire mission to Israel (4:18—ἔχρισέν με . . . ἀπέσταλκέν με; cf. Acts 10:38). This *sending* as the anointed prophet (cf., e.g., 4:26, 43)[8] is confirmed through subsequent visions and auditions of testing (4:3-12) and strengthening (9:28-36; 10:18; 22:43); *Jesus' disciples:* In keeping with his "immediate" divine legitimation, Jesus gathers and *sends out* a band of disciples in executing his mission, and, curiously, in so doing, mimics the OT prophets, especially Moses and Elijah (Elisha)[9] (e.g., 9:52-56, 57-62).[10] Jesus' disciples are consequently drawn into this heavenly commission through vision and audition (9:28-36; 24:4-7).

2. *Sent to Proclaim the 'Word of the Lord.'* Prophetic speech "in" or "filled by" the Holy Spirit hails the births of John and Jesus (*Elizabeth*—1:41-42; *Zechariah*—1:67-79; *Simeon*—2:29-35; *Anna*—2:38; *Mary* (by analogy)—1:46-55). *John's* entire ministry is summed up as *"pro-*

claiming a baptism of repentance leading to the removal of sins" (3:3b, 18), and it is telling that Luke gives no direct description of any activity of John other than this preaching the "word of God" (3:2, 7–17;[11] see esp. Acts 13:24–25; 10:37b). Equally significant is that all references to John being "filled by" or "in the Holy Spirit" cease and shift to Jesus once John receives the "word of God" and Jesus subsequently comes with "all the people" to be baptized. The *preaching* of John is clear: It is Jesus, not John, who will "baptize with Holy Spirit," and Jesus will do so precisely as the one *anointed*, "the Christ" (3:15 → 16; cf. Acts 1:5; 11:16; 18:25; 19:1–7).

Jesus: All the eruptions of the prophetic Spirit in the first three chapters of Luke fulminate in the fulfillment of the Spirit "upon" Jesus (3:16; 4:1, 14, 18) as the anointed prophet of Isa. 61:1–2 (Luke 4:17–21).[12] What is punctuated in the first descriptions of Jesus' sending is the priority of *proclaiming* the powerful "word," for example:

εὐαγγελίζομαι	κηρύσσω	λόγος	ἀκούω
4:18	4:18	4:22	2:47
4:43	4:19	4:32	4:28
7:22	4:44	4:36	5:1
8:1	8:1	5:1	5:15
cf. 16:16; 20:1		6:47	6:17
Acts 10:36		8:11	6:27
		8:12	6:47
		8:13	6:49
		8:15	7:22
		8:21	7:29
		9:26	8:8
			8:10
			8:12
			8:13
			8:14
			8:15
			8:18
			8:21
			9:35

Likewise the disciples are sent out to proclaim this decisive word (9:2, 6).

3. *'Mighty Works' That Demonstrate Prophetic Authority.* Luke is careful to depict two of Jesus' miraculous deeds as mirroring the mighty deeds of the prophets Elijah and Moses. In both instances, Jesus' prophet status is authenticated in the eyes of the enthusiastic crowds (7:11–15 and vv. 16–17; 9:10–17 and vv. 18–19; cf. also the occurrences of δύναμις

and/or ἐξουσία).[13] This same response redounds to Jesus through the mighty works of his disciples (9:1–6 and vv. 7–9). But among these disciples Jesus' demonstrations of power are perceived as epiphenomena of Jesus' special anointed status, the prophet-Messiah (9:20; 19:37–38), a response not altogether discouraged by Jesus himself (7:18–23; 19:39–40; cf. 4:41!).[14]

4. *Suprapsychic Perception.* Jesus possesses the special capacity to probe the depths of the human heart to a person's thoughts or intentions (5:21–22; 6:8;[15] 7:39–47;[16] 19:5). In each case, this ability is tied to Jesus' unusual power to heal and/or the special authority of his mission. It is not surprising, then, that in 7:39 this capacity is attributed to the perspicacity of a prophet.

To sum up: however many lines Luke has used in sculpting his characters, he has certainly allowed the figure of the prophet to stand out in bold relief.[17] Jesus is the "anointed prophet" of Isaiah's prophecy. From the outset it is impossible to separate this prophetic stature from Jesus' role as "the Christ." The utterances of the prophetic Spirit in the opening chapters, summed up most clearly in John's message of 3:15–16, prepare the way for the pivotal role of the Nazareth pericope. But before we can more fully comprehend the relation of the prophetic Spirit to this prophet anointed by the Spirit, we must turn more directly to Luke's second volume.

Prophets in Acts

It is striking that whereas in the Gospel the central characters inhabiting its pages are prophets, in Acts none of Luke's primary actors is called "prophet" or acclaimed as such by others. To be sure, Barnabas and Saul are listed among a group of "prophets and teachers" at Antioch (Acts 13:1), though it is not certain how or whether the two functions are to be distinguished or distributed.[18] In any case, "prophet" is never applied directly to either character, and if either of the two roles is characteristic, it would appear to be that of "teacher" (see, e.g., 11:26; 13:12).[19] Only such peripheral figures as Agabus (11:27–28; 21:10) or Judas (15:32) or prominent OT characters such as David (2:30) are designated "prophets." Even if Jesus as exalted "Lord and Christ" (2:36) is regarded as a primary actor (cf., e.g., 1:1; 26:23), he is identified as "prophet" only twice (3:22–23; 7:37).

A look at Luke's thirty uses of the noun προφήτης will be helpful: *(a)* In two passages Jesus is the "Prophet like Moses" (Acts 3:22–23; 7:37). *(b)* Eight individuals are designated "prophets" (11:28; 13:1; 15:32), while an indeterminate number are mentioned (11:27; Philip's daughters "prophesy," 21:9; see 19:6). *(c)* Two OT prophets are named in conjunction with citations now fulfilled in the church's life (Joel—2:16–21; Isaiah—8:30–34; 28:25), while psalms can be cited as prophetic-Spirit inspiration through David now fulfilled (1:16–20; 2:25–31). Samuel is named along with "all the prophets" (3:24) and in reference to a critical period of Israel's history (13:20). In several instances quotations from prophetic books are cited simply as from "the prophet" (7:48–50), "the prophets" (13:40; 15:15), or "the book of the prophets" (7:42–43). *(d)* The greatest frequency (twelve times) refers to the sum total of the message of the Scriptures as "[all] the prophets" or "the law [of Moses]/Moses and [all] the prophets" (3:18, 21, 24, 25; 7:52; 10:43; 13:15, 27; 24:14; 26:22, 27; 28:23). In each of these references, this message is proclaimed as fulfilled in one way or another in Jesus and the community of the disciples. Additionally, in at least two instances (from 13:40 and 15:15), individual quotations are representative of the fulfilled message of *all* the prophets.

This profile of the noun, however, is misleading unless it is complemented by the equally important observation that the prominent strokes that color Jesus as the "anointed prophet" in the Gospel are repeated or paralleled in the actions of the leading characters in Acts. That Luke underscores the activity of the first disciples gathered at Pentecost by employing the verb προφητεύω[20] (2:17, 18) is warning enough that we must also investigate the actual story material through which Luke continues on from "all that Jesus began to do and teach" (1:1).

Features of the Prophets' Vocation

1. *Called in a Vision and Sent by Heaven for Mission.* If the immediacy of the heavenly council becomes the mandate for prophetic figures in the Gospel, so through visions and auditions representatives of heaven are sent out on missions in Acts. Luke relates four rudimentary visions that inaugurate decisive turns in the fulfillment of witness "to the ends of the earth." The first and seminal vision for the rest of the story, at the Feast of Pentecost, harks directly back to John the Baptist's (Luke 3:16) and Jesus' prophecy (Luke 24:49 — Acts 1:2, 4–5, 8) of the coming of the Spirit upon the disciples. And parallel to Jesus' inaugural sermon at Nazareth (Luke 4:16–30), Peter's sermon (Acts 2:14–40) also foreshadows much of the story to follow in his citation of Scripture (Joel 2 in Acts 2:16–21), now seen to be the basis of Jesus' prophecy and of the peculiar experience of the eschatological Spirit among the disciples: As the Spirit "is poured out" upon "all flesh," "men and women" will "prophesy,"

"visions" and "dreams" will be "seen," and "signs" will be performed upon the earth. This fulfillment of the Spirit of prophecy becomes both the keynote and the leitmotiv in the plot of Acts.

For all four visions/auditions (see below) Luke includes: *(a)* prophecy from the Scriptures now fulfilled; *(b)* a description of the eschatological coming of the Spirit; *(c)* the dual warrant of Scripture and Spirit for a particular mission "to all flesh"; and *(d)* subsequent visions/auditions that confirm and/or develop the mission and clarify the working of the prophetic Spirit. All the visions or auditions, therefore, are tied through the prophecy-fulfillment pattern to the Pentecost vision and its fulfillment:

VISION 1: The 120 Disciples Gathered
(2:1–4 [5–42])

a. Joel 3:1–5 (LXX); Pss. (LXX) 15:8–11; 109:1. It is the exalted Messiah who now "pours out" the eschatological Spirit to fulfill his own prophecy of the "promise of the Father" (Acts 2:29–36 → Luke 24:49). This prophecy is dovetailed with Jesus' own anointing by the Spirit as the prophet-Messiah of Isaiah 61 (Luke 3:21–22 → 4:18–30), which in turn is a fulfillment of John's prophecy (Luke 3:15–16). We have the resulting chain of prophecies: Joel and David → John the Baptist → Jesus → now fulfilled in the 120 disciples.

b. Acts 2:4–13.

c. Acts 2:14–40. Diaspora Jews resident in Jerusalem prefigure the mission to all the nations of the earth (2:5–12 → 2:39 → 10:43 → 11:15–18 → 15:14!).

d. Acts 5:17–21; 12:6–11(12–19). The apostles' mission as "witnesses" (1:8; Luke 24:48 → Acts 5:32) is confirmed precisely in the midst of suffering (4:1–31 → 5:17–42 → 12:1–5).

VISION 2: Stephen and the Seven
(7:55–56 [7:1–54, 57—8:3])

a. Deut. 18:15; Amos 5:25–27; Isa. 66:1; and "all the prophets." Israel's persistent history of resisting the prophetic Spirit which culminates in the murder of Jesus, the Righteous One, continues on in the death of Stephen (7:54–60): Moses → all the prophets → Jesus (Righteous One) → Stephen.[21]

b. Acts 7:55; cf. 6:3, 5, 8, 10, 15; 8:14–16.

c. Acts 6:3, 5, 8, 10, 15; 7:1–53. The persecution of the exalted Jesus, the Son of Man, through the stoning of Stephen leads to the extension of the journeying history of salvation to Samaria, Gaza (Judea), and eventually to non-Israelites (1:8 → 8:4–40 → 11:19–20).

d. Acts 8:26, 29. Fulfillment of the eschatological Spirit in Samaria (8:4–17) is followed by an anticipation of fulfillment to the nations (Ethiopia, 8:27–28) and linked with the suffering mission of Jesus as the fulfillment of Isa. 53:7–8 (8:29–35).

VISION 3: Peter and Cornelius
(10:3–8, 9–16 [17–48; 11:1–18; 15:6–21])

a. "All the prophets" (Acts 10:43); Jer. 12:13; Amos 9:11–12; Isa. 45:21 (Acts 15:16–18) point forward to the mission to non-Jews.

b. Acts 10:44–48.

c. Acts 10:34—11:18; 15:6–21. In reciting the events of God's good news "through Jesus the Christ" who had been "anointed with the Holy Spirit and with power" (10:36–38 → Luke 3:21–22; 4:18), Peter includes the apostles' charge to be Jesus' "witnesses" "to the people" (Acts 10:42 → 1:8) and "to all who believe in him," just as "all the prophets bear witness" (10:43). Later when justifying this mission to "the uncircumcised" (11:4–18), Peter recalls the "falling" of the Spirit upon Cornelius's household and interprets this event by citing Jesus' word to them about John's water baptism but of their baptism by "Holy Spirit" (11:16 → 1:5, 8 → Luke 24:49 → Luke 3:16). Still later, James mentions Peter's reference and then cites from "the words of the prophets" (Acts 15:14–18). Again we have the chain: "all the prophets" → John the Baptist → Jesus → fulfilled in Peter's mission.

d. Acts 12:6–11—ties in especially also with the more general vision of 2:1–4.

VISION 4: Paul and Ananias
(9:3–7 [8–9], 10–16 [17–19]; 22:6–10 [11–16],
17–21; 26:13–18 [9–12, 19–23])

a. Isa. 42:6, 7, 16; 49:6, 9.

b. Acts 9:17–18; cf. 13:9, 52; 19:6.

c. All three accounts of the "heavenly light" "send" Paul to Israel and to the nations as one who must suffer[22] (9:15–16; 22:15, 18, 21; 26:16–17) as he was persecuting the church and its Righteous One[23] (22:14; cf. 26:16; 9:4–5; 22:7–8; 26:14–15). Paul is thus welded into the chain of persecutions of Moses → "all the prophets" → Jesus → the apostles → Stephen. More particularly, Paul's inclusion into the company of "witnesses" (22:15; 26:16) with the mission of the suffering prophet of Isaiah as light to the nations, Isa. 42:6, 7; 49:6, 9 → Acts 13:47 → 26:22–23 (Moses and the prophets) links him directly to the promise-fulfillment schema of Acts 1:8 (Isa. 49:6) → 1:5 → Luke 24:49 → Luke 3:16, and also to the Simeon oracles (Luke 2:32) with its prophecy of suffering (2:34). The following chain of prophecies and prophets ensues: Moses → suffering servant of Isaiah → all the prophets → Simeon → John the Baptist → Jesus → apostles → Stephen ("your witness," 22:20)[24] → fulfilled in Paul and his mission.

d. Acts 13:1–3; 16:9–10; 18:9–10; 22:17–21; 23:11; 27:23. Each vision/ audition is anticipated by the promise/prophecy of the original Damascus vision (26:16b)[25] and reveals either the necessary suffering or the specific journey mission "to the end of the earth" or both (e.g., 23:11; 27:23).

2. *Sent to Proclaim the 'Word of the Lord.'*[26] By distilling the essence of the Spirit's utterance (2:4b), Peter's Pentecost address outlines the message or "word" (λόγος) of eschatological prophecy for the rest of Acts (2:33). "His [Peter's] word" (2:41) becomes "the word" (4:4)[27] which is taken to Israel and the nations as the fulfillment of "Moses" and "all the prophets" (3:18–26 → 10:43 → 13:26–33 → 26:22–23). This "word," however, is far from merely a cognitive capsule of what the earliest communities believed. Rather, it is an energizing *dynamis* that can "grow" (6:7; 12:24; 13:49; 19:20) in engendering and nurturing eschatological communities of salvation (e.g., 2:40–41; 13:26, 47–48). Moreover, it was an eschatological message *sent* by God through the *preaching* of Jesus Christ, concerning the "baptism which John *proclaimed*": the anointing of Jesus by God with Holy Spirit and power (10:36–38 → 1:5, 8 → Luke 4:18 → Luke 3:16). And this word continues to be proclaimed by the chosen witnesses (μάρτυρες, 1:8 → v. 22 → 2:32 → 3:15 → 5:32 → 10:39–41 → 13:31 → 22:15[20] → 26:16) who, more accurately, are bearers of the suffering but resurrected Messiah, the one in reality who is both the *proclaimer* and the *proclaimed* through the "word" (10:39–42 → 14:3 → 26:22–23).

Accordingly, verbs of proclamation are frequent and can be subsumed under the particular vision mandate:

διαμαρτύρομαι/μαρτυρέω[28]
VISION 1   2:40; (8:25); (10:42)
VISION 2   8:25
VISION 3   10:42; (15:8)[29]
VISION 4   18:5; 20:21, 24; 23:11; 26:22; 28:23

εὐαγγελίζομαι
VISION 1   5:42; (8:25)
VISION 2   8:4, 12, 25, 35, 40; 11:20
VISION 3   10:36[30]
VISION 4   13:32; 14:7, 15, 21; 15:35; 16:10; 17:18

κηρύσσω
VISION 2   8:5
VISION 3   10:37,[31] 42
VISION 4   9:20; 19:13; 20:25; 28:31

3. *'Mighty Works' That Demonstrate Prophetic Authority.* Again as with the mission of proclamation it is Peter's sermon that functions as a programmatic prophecy of the manifestations of the eschatological Spirit

in powerful works (δυνάμεις). Continuing the fulfillment of the Spirit upon Jesus (2:22; 10:38), the disciples will be granted power (1:8) and signs[32] (2:19) to perform. If Jesus healed a paralytic (Luke 5:17–26), so do the apostles (Acts 3:1–10), especially Peter (9:32–35) and Paul (14:8–18); if he raised people from the dead (Luke 7:11–17; 8:40–42, 49–56), so Peter does also in Judea (Acts 9:36–42) and Paul in the Diaspora and Gentile mission (20:7–12). In every instance these "signs and wonders" are to be apprehended as attending and issuing from powerful preaching and not vice versa. Hence, while they are not to be confused as proofs or as the essence of the fulfilled salvation (8:9–13, 18–24; 19:11–20), they serve nevertheless as conduits of the true prophetic power/authority[33] legitimated by the eschatological Spirit at the Pentecost fulfillment. Again we discover a line of prophetic authority reaching back to Moses:

σημεῖα (καὶ τέρατα): Moses (7:36) → Jesus (2:22) → apostles (2:43; 4:16, 22, 30; 5:12) → Stephen (6:8) → Philip → (8:6, 13) → Paul and Barnabas (14:3; 15:12).

δύναμις/δυνατός: Moses (7:22) → Jesus (2:22; 10:38; cf. Luke 24:19) → apostles (Luke 24:49 → Acts 1:8 → 3:12; 4:7, 33) → Stephen (6:8) → Philip (8:13) → Paul (19:11).

We shall see that for Luke it is not merely coincidence that "signs and wonders" is also a prominent LXX phrase in Deuteronomy to describe Moses' leading the people out of bondage from Egypt, at the Red Sea, and in the wilderness.

4. *Suprapsychic Perception.* If Jesus can read the hearts of people, so can the Spirit-filled disciples (e.g., Acts 5:1–11 and 8:18–24—Peter; 13:8–12; 16:16–18—Paul). As Acts 5:12 and 8:6, 13 make clear, the authority to pronounce judgment or exorcise evil stems from the fulfillment of the eschatological Spirit in Jesus (10:38) and at Pentecost (10:41–42 → 1:5, 8). Further, if prophets foretell and forthtell the mission of Messiah Jesus in Luke 1—3 and Jesus himself characterizes the outcome of his own movements (e.g., 4:24–27; 5:35),[34] so now in the Acts "prophets" predict future events (e.g., Agabus: 11:27–28; 21:11) and anticipate their own fate (Paul: 20:25, 29–30; 21:13; cf. 19:21). We shall see that Paul's perspicacity creates a special solidarity with Jesus as a suffering, rejected prophet.[35]

Conclusions: Prophecy and Fulfillment in Luke-Acts

1. It is Jesus as the *Christ* who brings a fulfillment of "Moses and all the prophets" as he is the bearer and then the giver of the eschatological Spirit. Joel 3 (LXX) functions as the pivot for an axis of prophecies and

(partial) fulfillments stretching through both volumes. In barest outline:
Luke 3:16(4:18)—Isaiah 61 → (Luke 24:49) Joel 3—Acts 2:17-21(1:5,
8) → 28:25-28—Isaiah 6
Throughout this entire history of salvation[36] it is the Spirit of prophecy
that is the principle of both continuity and newness.[37]

2. It is Jesus as the *Christ* who fulfills a long line of Spirit-inspired
prophets as he is the anointed eschatological prophet. In the church the
Spirit continues to "raise up" prophets for the purpose of extending the
messianic salvation to the end of the earth. While not all the believers are
depicted as prophets, all potentially *may* prophesy, that is, proclaim
boldly the "word of the Lord."[38]

3. It is Jesus as the *Christ* who constitutes the center of the fulfillment
of all the Scriptures—of "Moses and all the prophets"—as he is the
suffering eschatological prophet. What follows at every critical turn of
events in the Acts is the way of suffering for the disciples-prophets as the
appointed witnesses to the end of the earth. First the apostles, then
Stephen followed by the whole community of disciples in Jerusalem, and
then Paul all "suffer for the sake of the name" (see, e.g., 9:16; 14:22). It is
this suffering of Messiah and of his appointed witnesses, then, that sums
up the "appointed plan and prescience of God" (2:23) in the "divine
necessity" (δεῖ)[39] of salvation for both volumes.

The PROPHETIC CAREER *of* MOSES
ACCORDING *to* DEUTERONOMY

It should come as no surprise, then, if in the Central Section Luke
should present Jesus as a prophet. Indeed, given the overarching prophetic emphasis, we should expect it. But how does the prophetic figure
in the Central Section compare with the eschatological prophet-Messiah
of the two volumes, especially in the light of the form-content discrepancy that stalks Jesus throughout 9:51—19:44? Does a distinctive prophetic figure ever coalesce in this section? We shall argue on the basis of
9:1–50 that Jesus emerges from the Galilean ministry bound for Jerusalem as the anointed *Prophet like Moses of Deuteronomy*. In Part IV we
shall conclude this argument for the entire Central Section. In order to
bring this prophetic profile into focus, we will first paint in broad strokes
the picture of Moses' vocation in the story of Deuteronomy.

Through many "signs and wonders"[40] (see, e.g., Deut. 34:11–12) Moses
has led all Israel[41] out of Egypt to the borders of the Promised Land at
Beth-peor (3:29; cf. 34:6). There, shadowed by the funereal slopes of the
Nebo massif (32:49–50; 34:1; cf. 1:37; 3:27; 4:21–22), he takes the people

through a renewal of the covenant that had been established at Mt. Horeb. The whole book in fact purports to be the *words* of Moses (1:1-5) and can be classified according to Moses' (1) delivering the commandments;[42] (2) parenesis, including haggadic appeals to Israel's salvation history;[43] and (3) pronouncements of blessing and warning of judgment.[44] As a prelude to the recounting of the Law he leads the pilgrim tribes back in memory to their momentous experience at that mountain and their ensuing wilderness wanderings of forty years (Deuteronomy 1—11). And here (Deuteronomy 1—5, 9 esp.) it becomes clear just what prophetic role Moses was to play.[45]

When at the mountain out of the midst of the fiery cloud God began to speak to the gathered assembly of Israel (4:12-13, 33, 36; 5:4, 22, 24; 9:10; 10:4), the people were so terrified that they implored Moses to mediate the voice (φωνή) of Yahweh for them (5:4-5, 23-31). This then becomes Moses' great calling, to utter the voice of the Lord to the people[46] (e.g., 5:27-28, 30-31; cf. 30:2, 8, etc.) by teaching them all his commandments that they might live in the land which they were to possess as an inheritance (e.g., 4:5, 14).[47] But though they had promised fidelity to Moses' God-given word (5:27), even while Moses is still on the mountain speaking "face to face" with God (34:10), the people at the base rebel by worshiping an image, the molten calf (9:8-21; cf. 4:15-19). The Lord's anger is so overwhelming that only Moses' suffering submission in intercession[48] can appease his wrath sufficiently to save the people from total annihilation (9:18-20, 25-29; 10:10-11).

So the Lord continues his promise to them by *sending* Moses onward from Horeb at the head of the people to the land of promise (10:11; 1:7). But it would seem to no avail. Despite the searing discipline (4:36)[49] of seeing the very glory of God[50] on the mountain (5:24) and hearing his great voice from the cloud of fire (4:11),[51] the people are intractable in rebelling. At Kadesh-barnea, some eleven days' journey (see 1:2), all Israel and especially Israel's "men of war" (2:14, 16) spurn the voice of the Lord through Moses and spite Moses' leadership altogether as first they "murmur" against the call to battle and then go up against the Lord's command (1:19-46). With that, two epoch-making judgments fall upon Moses and his calloused coterie: (1) Only the children[52] (παιδίον, 1:39; cf. vv. 34-38) of the assembled people at Horeb will become the future possessors of the land; the entire older generation will be wiped out (1:35; 2:14-16).[53] (2) "On account of"[54] (1:37; 3:26) the people's intransigence, Moses must suffer the anger of the Lord, the anguish of being choked off from the land of promise, and thus ultimately die without the promised deliverance—all because of[55] the sin of his people (1:37; 3:26; 4:21-22; cf. 9:18-20, 25-29; 10:10-11; 31:2, 14; 32:49-52; 34:4).

These two themes become the double-beat leitmotiv which like a dirge undertones the entire story of Deuteronomy. The first is sounded as the relentless, interminable stubbornness[56] of *all* Israel to heed God's voice through Moses, even from the moment they left Egypt.[57] They have been rebellious[58] as long as Moses has known them (9:24). They are "wicked" or "presumptuous,"[59] "sinful,"[60] "proud,"[61] slow to believe and "hearken,"[62] refusing discipline and training[63] without "understanding."[64] They need new "eyes to see and ears to hear"[65] (29:4). Or as Moses himself sums up, they are en masse a "stiff-necked," "faithless," and "crooked generation" (32:5, 20; 1:35).[66]

It is only against this strain that the echo of Moses' suffering and death (item 2) can be heard as a clarion call to effect deliverance precisely through this means.[67] For it is not the case that the younger generation, the "children" on the mountain who take possession of the land, are blameless while their "fathers," the "men of war," receive the punishment.

Rather, it is curious how this generation at the "border" is lumped with its predecessors as one mass of a disobedient, perfidious people, such that their fate is linked to that of their "fathers," on the one side, but also to the necessity of Moses' tragic fate, on the other. First of all, the present generation's distinction as the innocent ones "without knowledge of good or evil" (1:39) is completely nullified by their eyewitness incorporation in "all the great work of the Lord" (11:7b), which had begun in Egypt and had continued through the wilderness period right up "until you came to this place" (11:5). Because they are one with their "fathers" in experiencing this *Heilsgeschichte* (11:1–7), they are also now without excuse in their responsibility to heed the commandments of the Lord once they have entered the land (11:8–9, 13–25). Second, their stubborn ways, which mimic those of their "fathers," are dovetailed directly into that "evil generation's" rebellion at Horeb and at Kadesh-barnea:[68]

> Hear, O Israel, you are to pass over the Jordan this day. . . . Do not forget how *you* incensed the Lord in the wilderness. . . . Even at Horeb *you* provoked the Lord to wrath. . . . And when the Lord sent *you* from Kadesh-barnea . . . then *you* rebelled against the commandment of the Lord. . . . Circumcise therefore the foreskin of your heart and do not be obstinate any longer. (9:1a, 7a, 8a, 23; 10:16)

Any distinction in culpability between them and their "fathers" is again obliterated. But, finally, there is one undeniable difference: this generation *does* enter the land of promise. Yet the story of this imminent fulfillment is at pains to make clear that this salvation is a gracious act of Yahweh that neither stems from any conceivable merit on the part of the people (e.g., 9:4–

6) nor is conceivable without dire consequences for their leader. At three crucial junctures in the story time[69] the necessity of Moses' death is woven into the progression and ultimate completion of the present generation's deliverance: (1) Moses' suffering mediation and intercession for the people at Horeb, which allays Yahweh's wrath sufficiently to continue the otherwise aborted Exodus redemption, is welded to Yahweh's sentence at Kadesh-barnea. Moses' cry for relief from the "burden and strife" of a contrary people *"at that time"* (1:9)[70] is granted—ironically, if not heartlessly—in the subsequent and explicit announcement of his death (1:9, 12 → vv. 34–40; cf. 9:7–21 → vv. 22–24). (2) As if to dispel any notion that Yahweh's anger was assuaged by the death of the older evil generation or that the Exodus continued to the borders of Canaan through the "uprightness" or innocence of Caleb or Joshua or the "children" of the mountain, the narrator has Moses repeat Yahweh's sentence to him *"at that time"* (3:23)[71] when the possession of the Transjordan area was completed. Moses' plea to enter into the land is met with "anger on your account" (3:26a). Because of the sin of the audience Moses is addressing, he must die (3:27). (3) The third announcement removes any vestige of the possibility that Moses' death is, after all, merely parallel to the main event of deliverance or that his denial outside the land is simply an example "of the tragic dimension of human experience."[72] After reviewing the affairs at Beth-peor from the time of the second declaration of his demise, Moses harks back to the revelation of Yahweh at Horeb to warn against apostatizing and uses that watershed event with its sequel at Kadesh-barnea to typify his audience's present state of affairs "this day" (4:20b). They stand freed from their bondage in Egypt, ready to pass over into the land, to be sure (4:20), but—again—Moses must die, precisely because "on account of you,"[73] Yahweh *"swore* that I should not cross the Jordan nor enter into the good land which the Lord your God is giving you as an inheritance. For *I*[74] must die in this land, *I* must not cross the Jordan, but rather *you* shall cross over, that you may take possession of that good land" (4:21–22). In short, without Moses' death they would not receive the gracious act of deliverance that Yahweh is now bringing to pass[75] (cf. 31:2, 14; 32:48–50;[76] 34:4). But they are also forewarned; if they continue their rebellious ways once they have entered the land, they will meet the same fate as their "fathers" (4:23–28). Thus it is at each of the three critical turns of events in the developing story that *Moses' death* moves the action of Yahweh's deliverance forward to its climax at the boundaries of the land and enables the people to cross over to their promised inheritance.[77]

The pen portrait is now distinct. Moses has emerged as a suffering mediator, sent from Horeb to lead the faithless and crooked generation of "children" to the promised salvation by dying outside the land. More precisely, we can distinguish a fourfold dynamic to his prophetic vocation.

(1) On the mountain Moses' calling to be the mediator of God's life-giving words (the Law) on the Exodus journey is revealed most formidably by the *voice* out of the fiery cloud to the gathered assembly of *all* Israel. (2) From the mountain the persistent *stubbornness* of the people to hearken to this voice is divulged through the twisting of this voice in the image of the molten calf; this defiance in turn illustrates the unwillingness of the people to "hear" this voice from the beginning. (3) Accordingly, while Moses is still on the mountain and as he descends and is *sent* on the Exodus his calling is disclosed to be a *suffering journey* to *death*. (4) As a result, his calling does not effect deliverance for all those who follow him to the Promised Land but only for the renewed people of the land, the *"children* of the mountain."

At the core of this dynamic is the double stroke of Israel's stiff-necked opposition to the voice of the Lord through Moses and the consequent tragic fate of this prophet. As later generations of the Deuteronomists were to color his career, Moses' death outside the land was a *necessary* punishment for the sin of all Israel—even of the "children" who like their fathers proved themselves to be a "stubborn" and "crooked generation."

The PROPHETIC PARALLELS *of* MOSES *in* DEUTERONOMY *to* JESUS *in* LUKE 9:1–50

It has often been noticed that Luke's account of Jesus' mountain transfiguration (9:28–36) introduces his subsequent "journey" (9:51—19:44).[78] But from the standpoint of the story the whole of 9:1–50 performs such a function through Luke's[79] carefully carved continuity in audience and scenery. In this way, before the journey is signally announced (9:51), Luke sets forth a fourfold exodus typology of the prophetic calling of Jesus which conforms closely to that of Moses in Deuteronomy as we have outlined it above. This typology in fact becomes *the organizing principle* for the form and content of the whole of the Central Section. As the scheme is set out, it is important to bear in mind that the correspondence in type is not a function of a mechanical, rote-like parallelism in the sequence of events or description of details. It is *not* suggested that a one-to-one analogy in the chronology of episodes in Deuteronomy exists in Luke 9:1–50 or that every event or subject in the one has a mirror image in the other. Rather, what we discover is a profound correspondence in the calling, execution, and fate of the calling of the one who is the Prophet like Moses (Deut. 18:15–19), effecting a New Exodus for a renewed people of God:

1. Only Luke of the three Synoptists speaks of Jesus' transfiguration taking place "while he was praying" (9:28b–29a); like Moses, Jesus is one who speaks directly with God (cf. Deut. 34:10). As his robes begin to

"flash like lightning" and the appearance (εἶδος)[80] of his face is altered, suddenly Moses and Elijah "appear" "in glory" (9:29b–31a) with him. Luke alone would have his readers behold three glowing personages who must have created a spectacle for these unwitting spectators. As with the Horeb theophany, the mountain was "burning with fire" (Deut. 5:23). Again it is only Luke who states that the three disciples saw Jesus' glory (τὴν δόξαν αὐτοῦ, v. 32b) "and the two men standing with him." They thus become witnesses to the divine glory, just as the Israelites are shown this glory on the mountain (τὴν δόξαν αὐτοῦ, Deut. 5:24). Peter, dumbfounded and stumbling over his words, suggests that they make three tents (9:33b) when, just "as he was speaking," a cloud[81] comes and "overshadows" them (9:34).[82] The disciples are "frightened" as the cloud engulfs them and a "voice (φωνή) from the cloud" declares, "This is my Son, my Chosen One, hearken to him" (αὐτοῦ ἀκούετε, v. 35). Now it is the heavenly voice (φωνή) of Horeb which, Moses reminds the people time and time again, is their life.[83] To hearken is to live, to disobey to die. And it is this voice to which they are to hearken in Moses and in the prophet like him who shall arise (ἀνίστημι) "among his brethren after him" (Deut. 18:15–18; esp. v. 15b, αὐτοῦ ἀκούσεσθε).[84] Here it is curious that of the three versions of this heavenly voice, only Luke in both vocabulary and word order matches the LXX of 18:15b. Thus, like all Israel, who on the mountain hundreds of years earlier witnessed the authoritative revelation of the divine voice through Moses, so now on the mountain the three disciples, representing the Twelve and hence the twelve tribes of all Israel, witness the definitive revelation of the divine voice through Jesus, God's Chosen Son. *Like Moses, Jesus is called to mediate the voice of God.*

2. It is only Luke of the Evangelists who dares mention that while Jesus is transfigured in glory with Moses and Elijah the disciples "were heavy with sleep!" (9:32a).[85] Only "when they were fully awake" (διαγρη-γορήσαντες, v. 32b) do they "see" Jesus' glory and the two men. What is more, Luke does not spare Peter and his companions further embarrassment when Peter, astir with "greatness in the air," thinks that the group needs a booth for each of the glorious figures—"not knowing what he was saying" (9:33b). It is then, "as he was speaking" (9:34a), that a cloud comes and the "voice out of the cloud" commands the terrified disciples to obey the voice of God in Jesus, his elect Son. Like the people of Israel on Horeb, who in their stubborn resistance to obey the voice of God through Moses had to be disciplined by the shock of the thundering voice from the fiery cloud (Deut. 4:36), so the disciples in their stuporous response to the voice of God through Jesus also have to be overwhelmed by the traumatic voice from out of the cloud. Luke continues (9:36) that "after the voice had spoken Jesus was found alone" and the disciples

"were mute," "telling no one in those days[86] anything of what they had seen" (ἐώρακεν). For it was true of them that they had "this day" "seen" (εἴδομεν) God speak with human beings and humankind still live!" (Deut. 5:24b).

It may be objected already that this second analogy hardly holds together when it is recalled that, in fear of their own lives, the Israelites eagerly accepted Moses' mediation of the divine voice on the mountain in contrast to the halting ambivalence of the disciples who do not even seem to comprehend the "life and death" matters in their midst at all. But what we are presenting is a typological correspondence far more fundamental than a specific sequence or episode within a momentous revelation. To penetrate these deeper dimensions it will be necessary to see how Luke's casting of the disciples on the *mountain* is, as in Deuteronomy, carefully engrafted into the behavior of the crowd below on the *plain* (Luke 9:1–27, 37–50).

In 9:1–6 Jesus sends out the Twelve with power and authority (v. 1) to continue the same activity in which he himself has been engaged, that is, healing and preaching the Kingdom of God (v. 2; cf. 9:11). Herod's stance to both Jesus' and his emissaries' amazing feats is then dovetailed into this sending out (9:7–9): Herod has "heard of all the things that were being done"; folk are buzzing with speculation that "John the Baptist had been raised" (ἠγέρθη) or that "Elijah had appeared" (ἐφάνη) or that "one of the prophets of bygone days had arisen"[87] (ἀνέστη, cf. Deut. 18:15, 18); as for Herod, he is at a loss just what to think—he must see (ἰδεῖν) this Jesus for himself! (9:9; cf. 23:6–12). The disciples' activity here is without doubt identified with Jesus' fame; to hear about their work is to force a decision about Jesus.[88] They appear to be one with their master in the *power* and *authority* granted them.

The Twelve return (9:10) and report, but no response by Jesus is given except that he takes them apart to Bethsaida.[89] "The crowds" (οἱ ὄχλοι, 9:11), however, who have thronged Jesus for some time now,[90] learn where he is going and follow him. While it is not explicitly stated that these crowds represent the same folk who are voicing their opinions about Jesus (9:7–8), yet it is interesting that right at this point, after Jesus has spoken about the Kingdom of God, healed,[91] and with his disciples fed these crowds in a desert place (ἐν ἐρήμῳ τόπῳ, 9:12b; cf. Deut. 8:2, 16—ἐν τῇ ἐρήμῳ), Jesus asks his disciples just what these crowds are thinking about him (9:18). And they report almost verbatim the same sentiments that are troubling Herod's ears (vv. 18–19). The popular feeling is that Jesus is a great prophet, comparable to the greatest of the OT figures. The reader is led to believe, then, that these opinions are emerging essentially from the same crowds. Peter, on the other hand, not content to be marked by such commonality, goes beyond this stance, acknowledging Jesus to be God's own "Anointed" (9:20). But unlike the other Synoptists, no praise or blessing by Jesus is accorded this insight; no period of private teaching is awarded the disciples' confession.[92] Instead, Jesus, charging and commanding them to silence and in the same breath (εἰπών)[93] telling them that "the Son of Man must suffer many things" (vv. 21–22), continues on by telling (ἔλεγεν,[94] v. 23) *all* that they too must suffer if they want to save their lives by following him (9:23–26). The sequence here is quite different from Mark and Matthew. For Luke presents one continuous scene in which the same crowds remain close by as a theatrical backdrop for the disciples' performance. Gone are both the intimate instruction as well as the rebuke to Peter which in Matthew and Mark draw attention to the special teaching to which the disciples were privy. This lack of interaction of Jesus with his disciples might appear to "level" them with the masses, to join them with the popular currents of the crowds. All must follow Jesus and all alike must suffer. Yet, different as this picture is, without Mark and Matthew as foils and stylistic variances notwithstanding, Luke's account is straightforward and intrinsically logical. The disciples are distinguished from the crowds *confessionally* and *spatially* by a relative privacy where Jesus is praying alone, in addition of course to their commissioning (9:1–6) and special assistance in feeding these multitudes (vv. 12–17).

As we pursue the advancing lines of the plot, however, this suspicion is borne out as the disciples' solidarity in power and authority with Jesus takes marked turns in the opposite direction. The divergences in audience and sequence with Mark and Matthew do indeed become signposts of a fundamentally different terrain which lies ahead. The great tableau of Jesus' following, which extends from 9:10–27, climaxes with Jesus prophesying to all that some among them will not taste death before they see (ἴδωσιν, v. 27) the Kingdom of God. "Now about eight days *after these sayings,*" Peter, James, and John—in spite of themselves—see (εἶδον, v. 32) Jesus' glory on the mountain. The next day when they have descended, Jesus is met by a great crowd (ὄχλος πολύς, 9:37b) only to learn from one of them (ἀπὸ τοῦ ὄχλου, v. 38a) that his disciples were unable to heal this man's "only son" (vv. 38b, 40). Jesus' response is: "You faithless and crooked generation!" (ὦ γενεὰ ἄπιστος καὶ διεστραμμένη, 9:41a). Here Jesus lumps his disciples together with one solid mass of a disbelieving, perverse people. Indeed, just as earlier the people's faithless twisting of God's commandment in the molten calf at the base revealed their stubborn perversity as Moses descends the mountain, so now as Jesus descends the mountain the disciples' faithless twisting of their divinely bestowed power and authority with the man's only son at the base reveals the stubborn perversity of the whole generation. Moreover, Moses' charge to the people that they are a "stubborn and crooked generation" (γενεὰ σκολιὰ καὶ διεστραμμένη, 32:5), and a "perverse generation, children in whom there is no faith" (οὐκ ἔστιν πίστις, 32:20), is matched here by Jesus: in both, the zealous anger of the Lord who confronts an obdurate generation "in the wilderness" comes to expression. And Moses' cry of desperation at Horeb, "How can I bear alone the weight and burden of you and your strife?" (1:12),[95] is echoed remarkably again by Jesus here at the base of the mountain: "How long am I to be with you and bear you!" (9:41). Jesus laments that he must endure this faithless mass any longer. Even the disciples, who hardly more than a week earlier had confessed his Messiahship, are identified with this crooked lot. They in fact are the very provokers of this outburst. Their impotence at the base of the mountain becomes a striking demonstration of their ambivalence at the top. The *whole generation*, disciples and all, are like their Horeb counterparts—one disobedient, rebellious mass.

That this portrayal is not happy coincidence is startlingly confirmed as the scene unfolds. Luke moves at a quick pace. While the crowds "marvel at the majesty (μεγαλειότης, 9:43) of God . . . and all that he was doing," Jesus tells his disciples again in sobering if not stern words, "Let these words sink into your ears (ὦτα)" (v. 44a). The disciples fare no better this time than with Jesus' first prediction of his Passion as Luke stresses in four different phrases their incapacity to grasp these words: They *(a)* do not understand *(b)* that which has been concealed from them, *(c)* "in order that they should not perceive"; and *(d)* "they were afraid to ask him about this saying" (v. 45). They are like their frightened wilderness predecessors who remain slow to believe and hearken (Deut. 9:23; 32:20), a people "without understanding" (32:28), even though they had witnessed the majestic (μεγαλεῖος) deliverance of God (11:2-7). Despite the mighty signs in their midst and the glory on the mountain, they reembody that people to whom Moses so well observed: "You have seen all the things the Lord did . . . the signs and those great wonders. Yet the Lord has not given you a heart (καρδία) to know or eyes to see or ears (ὦτα) to hear, even to this very day" (29:2b-4).

But as with the Israelites, the disciples' and the whole generation's crooked perfidy is not simply summed up by uncomprehending unbelief. For immediately Luke continues on at the same time and in the same "crowded" arena with the disciples arguing "which of them is the greatest" (Luke 9:46-48). That they could squabble about their own importance before these crowds right when they had failed miserably at casting out a demon (v. 42) from one of their children seems almost as if Luke here has resorted to burlesque. With the powerful perception of a prophet, Jesus penetrates to their hearts (καρδία, v. 47a) and places a child by his own side. The point: Unless a person can humble one's puffed-up "heart," and "in my name" associate with, that is, receive (δέχομαι) a person as small (μικρότερος) and insignificant as a child, that one will be *unable* to "receive" Jesus and thus also the One who has sent Jesus (v. 48). There is no point in being at Jesus' side unless one is humble enough to be at a "child's" side. The rebuke to the disciples could hardly be more scathing. They are failing to obey Jesus' voice through "proud and patronizing hearts."

That this is the pith of the problem in its Lukan context is illustrated by the next pericope, which again continues on uninterrupted in setting. John answers that they (i.e., the disciples) "saw someone casting out demons in your name"; they "forbade him, because he does not follow with us" (cf. 9:11, 23). Not only are the disciples blind and deaf to the true authority of Jesus' voice, but their presumptuousness also makes them numb to Jesus' discipline. What they "see" in this Jesus who performs mighty works is that which makes themselves mighty as well: they cannot recognize and fall in line with Jesus' authority but insist that true following (cf. 9:23–27) require a "falling in line" with them. The resonance of ἐν τῷ ὀνόματί σου (v. 49) with ἐπὶ τῷ ὀνόματί μου (v. 48) is loud and clear. Jesus' retort is also equally unequivocal. He forbids them to forbid (κωλύω) the person who is working "in Jesus' name,"[96] since such a one is obviously not against the disciples but is "for them" (v. 50). Jesus' pointing to the child in v. 48 as an object lesson in submission to his authority has been of no account whatever. The disciples are too caught up in their own prominence to stoop down to the side of the child. They are like their obstinate antetypes—refusing discipline and training (Deut. 9:6—10:5; cf. 4:36; 5:23–30; 8:2–5, 14–20; 11:2–7). Their glimpse of Jesus' divine glory on the mountain has revealed their own self-glory on the plain (Deut. 5:24; Luke 9:32).[97]

We are now in a position to see how the incidents at the base of the mountain interpret the behavior on the summit and in fact all that precedes the ascent (9:1–27). The contrast of the disciples with the unknown exorcist could not be starker. He has the power and authority to exorcise demons because he works in Jesus' name: he has submitted to the divine voice in Jesus. This incident (9:49–50), which at first seems to be attached arbitrarily by Luke, indeed renders Jesus' lament and charge in 9:42 fully comprehensible. The disciples are unable to exorcise the demon from the child because they have not submitted to this divine voice. They cannot, because their "hearts" are bloated beyond response to the "child" in their midst. They are at *base* no different from the rest of the twisted, unbelieving generation of the crowds. Thus what we have is the same fundamental distortion of the divine voice as at Horeb. In both, the command to hearken to the authority of the Lord through his mediator is completely contorted to the authority of their own *imag*ination. As the image of the molten calf divulges the refusal to obey the voice of God in Moses, so the image of self-importance of the disciples reveals their refusal to obey the voice of God in Jesus. The idol of the one is as real as the idol of the other. *Thus in both Deuteronomy and Luke 9 the reluctance and fear of listening to the voice of God on the mountain is truly a foreboding revelation of the twisted generation on the plain.*[98] And the incomprehension, strife, conceited hearts, imperviousness to discipline, and so forth, all become salient signs of "this generation's" crooked unbelief. We can schematize this basic dynamic of response in both Deuteronomy and Luke 9 as follows:

> Reluctance and Fear of Hearing the Voice on the Mountain → Stubborn Perversion of This Voice on the Plain → Incomprehension, Strife, Conceit, Rejection of Discipline, etc., by the Whole Generation.

What was true of the miraculous signs and feeding in the wilderness for the *laos* of God becomes true again for the *laos* of God in Luke: "You have been rebellious against the Lord from the day that I knew you" (Deut. 9:24; cf. 8:3, 15–20).

3. Of the Gospel writers it is only Luke who discloses that while the disciples slumber Moses and Elijah converse with Jesus about "his exodus (ἔξοδος) which he was to fulfill in Jerusalem" (9:31). We have already seen that Luke explicitly links Jesus' words (9:28; cf. v. 26) about bearing a cross and losing one's life (vv. 23–27) directly to the mountain glorification. These words are in turn an amplification of the Son of Man's suffering rejection and death at the hands of "elders, chief priests, and scribes" (v. 22), that is, by the Sanhedrin in Jerusalem. Moreover, in the context of 9:51 where "the days [pl.] of his taking up" in Jerusalem are "becoming completely full" (i.e., "had already arrived"),[99] it is certain that the exodus that Jesus fulfills *in* Jerusalem is also one that he fulfills on his way *to* Jerusalem, that is, through a journey to that city. Hence his exodus is both a "going out" to as well as a "departure" from Jerusalem. *Like Moses, then, Jesus' calling to journey to death is revealed to those on the mountain who would follow behind him to reach the "promised land" of salvation* (Deut. 10:11; 1:7; Luke 9:22–25 → v. 32 → v. 51).

As Jesus descends and is met by the crooked generation, his cry of desperation, like Moses' lament, reveals the palpable necessity of his suffering. "How long must I be with you and put up with you" voices the sentiment not of a normal mortal but of one who is clearly reckoning with a departure from "this generation"[100] in the imminent future. This necessity is suddenly voiced again, this time in the most ironic of settings. As the chorus of the crowds of "men" marvel approval, Jesus tries to shake his disciples from the monolithic snare of sin by warning them of these same "men" into whose hands he is "about to be delivered" (παραδίδωμι ... ἄνθρωποι,[101] v. 44b; cf. vv. 23–25, 18). It is not only the Sanhedrin who is going to kill Jesus but also this same twisted generation! The base of the mountain again confirms what has already been divulged at the top. But as at Horeb, this warning falls on deaf ears (cf. Deut. 1:43). As Jesus and his following continue from the mountain on the exodus it becomes all too transparent that the disciples can only think of calling down more of that glorious fire (9:29–34) to vindicate their own status as the mighty men of war for their Messiah-Deliverer (9:54; Deut. 1:41; 2:16). But for Jesus' stiff rebuke the disciples would "gird on his weapons of war and go up and fight" (Deut. 1:41). Even their most noble of Elijanic intentions is totally askew, "unfit" for the death journey which lies ahead (9:61–62; cf. v. 53; Deut. 1:41a; 1 Kings 19).

The grounding for the death of Jesus is thus the same as for Moses in Deuteronomy. *Because of* the intransigent sin of the people, a stiff-necked resistance so powerful that even gestures of redemption are spurned with contempt, Moses/Jesus *must* suffer and die. Though the first Passion prediction (Luke 9:22) occurs before the ascent, while Moses' necessity to suffer is disclosed upon the mountain, yet the overall portrait in both is intriguingly similar. For as later generations of Deuteronomists came to view Moses' whole calling as one of suffering and dying outside the land, so Luke and the traditionists before him became convinced that Jesus was born to die. Thus running through the narrative sections of Deuteronomy, both before and after the large teaching section on the commandments (Deuteronomy 12—26) are the notices of Moses' suffering and death (1:12–13, 37; 3:25–28; 4:21–22; 9:18–21, 25–29; 10:10; 31:2, 14, 23; 32:50–51;[102] 34:4). Even as early as 1:9, 12 and explicitly at 1:37 the reader is impressed with the passion of Moses as the signet for the whole. Similarly, in Luke's story the reader is informed of Jesus' tragic but redeeming destiny from the outset (2:34–35; 4:16–30!). But more significantly for the Central Section, the indicators of Jesus' Passion are concentrated both before and after a large teaching section (10:25—18:30) which is buttressed by the Deuteronomic "pillars" at 10:27 and 18:20 on the commandments (9:22, 23–25, 31, 41, 43b–45, 51; 18:31–34; 19:47; 20:9–18, 19, 20, 26; but cf. 12:49–50; 13:31–33; 17:25). It also becomes clear that Herod's beheading of John the Baptist with his desire to see Jesus (9:9) is an omen of ill on par with the crowds' (9:11–19) or the disciples' (9:20, 27, 28–36, 37–50) ability to "see" Jesus. Already then with Herod symbolizing the devious nation as a whole, the disciples' desire to dismiss rather than feed the *laos* in the wilderness (9:13) is,[103] like the Exodus antetype (Deut. 8:2–5, 14–17), a poignant demonstration of the whole stubborn generation's refusal to accept discipline and hence inability to heed the voice of the mountain revelation. *Consequently in Luke 9, as in Deuteronomy 1—3, the necessity of Jesus' suffering and death is first adumbrated and then announced in advance of the fuller manifestation on the mountain.*

4. It is only Luke of the Synoptists who links the figure of a child directly to the mountain revelation. Only the childlike can heed the voice of the mountain and receive this Jesus who has been sent by God from the mountain. Already in 9:23–25 Jesus had set forth the indispensable conditions of this receiving or of this following him on his exodus to Jerusalem. One must deny oneself, take up one's cross daily and follow him (v. 23); for the one who wishes to save one's life will in fact lose it (v. 24a). What we now find in 9:46–47 are the disciples trying desperately to save their lives, promoting instead of denying themselves. With the child at his side Jesus says in effect that such behavior can only lead to destruction of life as it stifles the life-giving liberation of the Son of Man's exodus to death and exaltation. That is precisely why the anonymous exorcist (vv. 49–50) is for (ὑπέρ) the disciples, since his childlike submission is a powerful promotion for the following, that Jesus demands.

As Jesus proceeds on his exodus he is quite adamant that only the childlike will inherit the blessings of the land (10:17–24; 12:32; 13:34; 15:3–7; 17:1–2, 33; 18:14, 15–17). The Seventy(-two),[104] Samaritans,[105] women,[106] the "poor,"[107] the sick and possessed,[108] tax collectors and "sinners"[109] all constitute the renewed "children" of the promise, the *laos* whom Jesus gathers and sifts from among the Horeb covenant *laos*.[110] Here it is curious that following relatively closely in Luke's story is Jesus' terming the Seventy(-two) "infants" (10:21) as those who, in following him to Jerusalem, work great exorcisms with power and authority *in Jesus' name* (10:17–20).[111] But this is only one of many instances where it becomes certain that only those who hearken to him, who hear the word of God in him and keep it, inherit the life of the New Exodus Land.[112]

But as with the first Exodus, so now even the "children" become representatives of the "faithless and perverse generation" responsible for Jesus' death. For just as the children of Horeb turn away and, like their "fathers," perpetrate the death of Moses in the end, so also the whole *laos* turn away and become, with their leaders, collaborators in Jesus' death at the fatal end.[113] And yet the story is not at an end. *For just as through Moses' death the children do enter the land of deliverance, so through Jesus' death the childlike who submit to the Prophet like Moses, whom God "raised" up from among his own folk* (Acts 3:22a), *do receive the blessing of the covenant promised to Abraham* (3:24–25). "You shall hearken (ἀκούω) to him in whatever he tells you. But it shall be that every person who does not hearken to that prophet shall be destroyed from the people" (Acts 3:22b–23 quoting Deut. 18:15b–16a, 19). Though the people, as did their forerunners hundreds of years earlier, acted in ignorance (Acts 3:17), yet the *laos* now have the unprecedented opportunity—through faith in the powerful presence of Jesus' *name* (3:6–7, 11–16)—to be released from their wickedness (πονηρός, Acts 3:26; Deut. 4:25; 9:18; 28:20; 31:29). "Those days" proclaimed by Moses and "all the prophets" (3:22–25) have been fulfilled. The *monolith* of stiff-necked disobedience is at last at an end (3:19); cf. the "rejected stone" and "the builders" in Acts 4:11 and Luke 20:17–18).

CONCLUSIONS

Luke then tells his readers in 9:1–50 that the story of the Prophet like Moses of Deuteronomy is about to unfold in a New Exodus journey to the promised salvation. We can illustrate this Moses-Deuteronomic typology by arranging our results into a literary-functional cross section of Luke 9:1–50. Through a tightly knit progression in audience and scenery Luke presents two tableaux, or, perhaps better, plateaus, divided by the mountain of revelation:

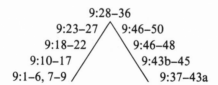

(1) Each incident on the one side has its mirror image on the other side of the mountain. What the one reveals about God's gathering, training, and disciplining a people through his prophetic voice, the other reveals about the ignorant, stubborn, and even perverted opposition of a people who make the suffering and death of this voice an absolute necessity. (2) The disciples are patent examples of this "stiff-necked generation." (3) Like Mt. Horeb, the mountain of Luke 9:28–36 forms the apex of God's selection of a special people through his chosen voice and this people's monolithic resistance to this selection. Upon this summit the fourfold career of the Moses of Deuteronomy for Jesus is divulged for the rest of Luke's Central Section. As in Deuteronomy, the mountain manifests most mightily the magisterial authority of the Lord's prophet-voice but also the tragic terrain of suffering and death ahead. (4) As Luke's travel

narrative progresses and the Jerusalem ministry culminates in the death-exaltation and Pentecost of the Acts, the mountain revelation is confirmed as the sending of the Prophet like Moses of Deuteronomy (18:15–19) to bring deliverance from wicked disobedience to the "children of the mountain" who submit to God's voice.

Hence the other side (base) of the mountain divulges the double-beat leitmotiv of Deuteronomy which the first side poses proleptically:

Luke 9:1–50
9:28–36
(4-fold Moses–Deut. Typology)

9:23–27	*9:46–50*
Suffering "Losing of Life" for *All* Following to Jerusalem Discipline & Submission to Authority of One Sent *Some* to "See" the Kingdom	Suffering Rejected-"Gaining Life" by Own "Kingdom" Numb-Discipline & Authority of One Sent to Jerusalem Submission of *One*-Model for *All*
9:18–22	*9:46–48*
Prophet's Preeminence Acknowledged/ S. of M. *Must* Suffer & Die in Jerusalem No Private Teaching but Taught Before Crowds	Disciples' Preeminence Acknowledged/ Suffering S. of M. Rejected for Rank of "Greatest"/Disciples Taught Through *Child* Before Crowds
9:10–17	*9:43b–45*
"Not by Bread Alone" Authority Revealed to 5,000 Disciples' Reluctance to Feed Marveling Crowds Through Ignorance & Disbelief	Discipline-Deaf Ears Disciples Miss Revelation c. 5,000 of Authority Reluctance-Ignorance & Fear Before Marveling Crowds—→ Necessity of Death by Crowds
9:1–6, 7–9	*9:37–43a*
Solidarity-Power & Authority c. Prophet Death of John —→ Herod's "Seeing" This Prophet of the Old Testament Era	Solidarity-Faithlessness & Perversity/Twisting Prophet's "Voice" to "Imaged" Powerless Authority Imminent Departure & Burden of Prophet

In short, as in Deuteronomy, the mountain of revelation forms the watershed for the plot to follow.[114]

Notes

1. See Exod. 19:3–6, 20–25; 20:21—24:2; 24:9—32:14; cf. Deut. 5:22–31; 9:9–20; 1 Kings 19:9–18.

2. Matthew: προφητεύω, four times; προφητεία, once; Luke: verb, twice; προφητεία, not at all.

3. See, e.g., G. Friedrich, "προφήτης," *TDNT* 6:828–48; L. Gaston, *No Stone on Another: Studies in the Significance of the Fall of Jerusalem in the Synoptic Gospels,* NovTSup 23 (Leiden: E. J. Brill, 1970), 276ff., esp. 276, 282; P. S. Minear, *To Heal and to Reveal: The Prophetic Vocation According to Luke* (New York: Seabury Press, 1976), esp. pt. 2; L. T. Johnson, *The Literary Function of Possessions in Luke-Acts,* SBLDS 39 (Missoula, Mont.: Scholars Press, 1977), 1–126; F. Gils, *Jésus prophète d'après les évangiles synoptiques,* Orientalia et Biblica Lovaniensia II (Louvain: Publications Universitaires, 1957), 9–47; and D. Hill, *New Testament Prophecy* (Atlanta: John Knox Press, 1979), 156–59.

4. Cf. L. Goppelt, *Typos: The Typological Interpretation of the Old Testament in the New* (1939; Grand Rapids: Wm. B. Eerdmans Publishing Co., 1982), 61–82; and D. L. Tiede, *Prophecy and History in Luke-Acts* (Philadelphia: Fortress Press, 1980), 19–63.

5. For a survey of "prophetic" features and the phenomenology of oracular speech in the Mediterranean basin, see D. E. Aune, *Prophecy in Early Christianity and the Ancient Mediterranean World* (Grand Rapids: Wm. B. Eerdmans Publishing Co., 1983); for prophecies of the risen Christ, see M. E. Boring, *Sayings of the Risen Jesus: Christian Prophecy in the Synoptic Tradition,* SNTSMS 46 (Cambridge: Cambridge Univ. Press, 1982).

6. See below, Part III, introduction, and B; cf. J. F. Ross, "The Prophet as Yahweh's Messenger," in *Israel's Prophetic Heritage,* ed. B. W. Anderson and W. Harrelson (New York: Harper & Brothers, 1962), 98–107 (repr. in *Prophecy in Israel,* ed. D. L. Petersen [Philadelphia: Fortress Press; London: SPCK, 1987], 112–21).

7. Cf. Minear, *Heal and Reveal,* 87.

8. See also Luke 9:48, 51; 10:16; 11:49; 13:32–34; 15:3–32; 16:24–31.

9. Cf. Exod. 24:9–14; Numbers 13; Deut. 1:22–33; 2 Kings 2:1–18; 9:1–13; etc.

10. See also Luke 6:12–17; 7:11–17; 9:1–6; 10:1–20; 19:29–34; 22:8–13.

11. In Luke 3:16 no further description is given of John's "I baptize you. . . ."

12. For prophets "anointed," see OT—1 Kings 19:16; Isa. 61:1; Qumran—CD 6:1; 2:12; 1QM 11:7; cf. 1QS 9:11; for the connection of the "Messiah's" anointing with the Holy Spirit, cf. *1 Enoch* 49:3; *Pss. Sol.* 17:42; 18:8; CD 2:12; *T. Levi* 18:2–14; and *T. Jud.* 24:2–3. In 11QMelch the Qumran sectaries connected the *měbassér* of Isa. 52:7 and 61:1 to a "messiah" "(māšîaḥ)/anointed one of the spirit" (1:18). Thus one of the functions of this anointed messiah-prophet for Qumran was the announcing of the reign of God's salvation. Cf. J. A. Sanders, "The Old Testament in 11 Q Melchizedek," *Journal of the Ancient Near Eastern Society of Columbia University* 9 (1973): 373–82; D. E. Aune, "A Note on Jesus'

Messianic Consciousness and 11Q Melchizedek," *EvQ* 45 (1973): 165; R. B. Sloan, Jr., *The Favorable Year of the Lord: A Study of Jubilary Theology in the Gospel of Luke* (Austin, Tex.: Schola Press, 1977), 48–54; S. H. Ringe, *Jesus, Liberation, and the Biblical Jubilee* (Philadelphia: Fortress Press, 1985), 50–80; and R. Meyer, "προφήτης," *TDNT* 6:812–28; for the Spirit and "anointed" prophecy in Luke-Acts, see G. Muhlack, *Die Parallelen von Lukas-Evangelium und Apostelgeschichte,* Theologie und Wirklichkeit 8 (Frankfurt: Verlag Peter Lang, 1979), esp. 117–40; see also below, Part III, "Josephus, the Qumran Covenanters, and the Deuteronomistic Perspective."

13. Luke 4:36; 5:17, 26; 9:1; 10:13–20; 24:19.

14. But on the role of "signs," see below, Part III.A.1 and 3.

15. Luke 6:8a is unique to Luke; cf. Mark 3:3; Matt. 12:13.

16. Luke 7:39–47 is unique to Luke; cf. Mark 9:36; Matt. 18:2.

17. Cf. Minear, *Heal and Reveal,* 83ff., 105–6; esp. 85: "I am convinced that this prophetic succession was more decisive for Luke than any 'apostolic succession.'"

18. See E. E. Ellis, "The Role of the Christian Prophet in Acts," in *Apostolic History and the Gospel: Essays in Honour of F. F. Bruce,* ed. W. Gasque and R. P. Martin (Grand Rapids: Wm. B. Eerdmans Publishing Co., 1970), 55–67, esp. 67.

19. See also Acts 15:35; 17:19; 18:11; 20:20!; 21:21, 28; 28:31.

20. In Acts 2:18b the verb is repeated (cf. v. 17) but cannot be supported by any extant Joel text; see below, n. 32.

21. For Stephen as a prophet in the mantle of the "prophet like Moses (Jesus)," whose suffering/death is crucial to the history of Israel's messianic fulfillment, see now D. P. Moessner, "'The Christ Must Suffer': New Light on the Jesus-Peter, Stephen, Paul Parallels in Luke-Acts," *NovT* 28 (1986): 220–56, esp. 227–34.

22. Ibid., esp. 247–55.

23. For a discussion of the title ὁ δίκαιος and its possible messianic overtones, cf. G. Schrenk, "δίκαιος," *TDNT* 2:182ff., esp. 186–87; Str-B 2:289–90; 4:213, 799ff.; Gaston, *Stone,* 293–94; and L. T. Johnson, *Possessions,* 70–76. Cf. also the messianic use of "the righteous one" in *Shemone Esre* 14 (Pal. rec.); *Pesiq. R.* 36.

24. See Acts 8:32–35 and Philip's extension of Stephen's "witness."

25. Cf. Acts 22:15; 26:16–18: Paul is a witness (μάρτυς) of the things he has "seen and heard" (22:15b).

26. Cf. "word of God" (Acts 6:2, 7; 8:14; 11:1; 12:24; 13:5, 7, 46; 18:11); "word": "of salvation" (13:26); "of his [Lord's/God's] grace" (14:3; 20:32); "of good news" (15:7).

27. Cf. Acts 4:4; 6:4; 8:4; 10:36!, 44; 11:19; 14:25; 16:6; 17:11; 18:5; for the function of "the word" in Acts, see, e.g., B. S. Childs, *The New Testament as Canon: An Introduction* (Philadelphia: Fortress Press, 1985), 22–25.

28. These verbs obviously include more than "proclaiming," whether by word or deed; the "witness" of suffering is critical (see esp. author's study, n. 21, above). The Scriptures continue to "testify" to the active "word of God" (Acts 10:43; 13:22).

29. God is the subject of the activity.

30. God is the "preacher."

31. John the Baptist is the preacher.

32. No known text of Joel includes "signs"; see above, n. 20.

33. ἐξουσία is not used directly for this line of authority, as in the Gospel, but cf. Acts 8:19; 26:18.

34. See also Luke 9:22-27, 44; 10:23-24; 12:49-50; 13:32-35; 14:27; 17:25; 18:31-33; 19:30-34; 22:10-13, 37, 53; 23:43.

35. See below, Part V, "The Literary Function of the Travel Narrative in Luke-Acts"; and Moessner, "'The Christ Must Suffer,'" esp. 247-55. Cf. M. D. Goulder, *Type and History in Acts* (London: SPCK, 1964), 35-36; and G. Bouwman, *Das dritte Evangelium: Einübung in die formgeschichtliche Methode* (Düsseldorf: Patmos Verlag, 1968), 70-75; Bouwman bases his conclusions primarily on the remarks of H. J. Cadbury (*The Making of Luke-Acts* [New York: Macmillan Co., 1927], 231-32): "It may be conjectured that the arrangement in Luke's Gospel of Jesus' prolonged progressions to Jerusalem and death has been affected by the geographical character of Paul's career, particularly by the latter's ominous approach to Jerusalem and his often anticipated arrival at Rome." Whether Jesus' journey was patterned after Paul's or vice versa remains a moot point.

36. σώζω in Joel 3:5 links up with the σωτήριον of Isa. 40:5 in Luke 3:6 and Acts 28:28 to span the beginning, middle, and ending of Luke's two volumes.

37. Cf., e.g., J. Jervell, "Sons of the Prophets: The Holy Spirit in the Acts of the Apostles," in Jervell, *The Unknown Paul: Essays on Luke-Acts and Early Christian History* (Minneapolis: Augsburg Publishing House, 1984), 96-121; e.g., p. 97: "The Spirit in Acts confirms and supports prophecy, that is, the prophecy in the Holy Scriptures, which contains the gospel verbatim."

38. See esp. Acts 4:31.

39. Luke 13:33; 17:25; 22:37; 24:7, 26, 44-46 — Acts 1:16; 9:16; 14:22; 17:13; 19:21; 23:11; 27:24; see esp. E. Fascher, "Theologische Beobachtungen zu δεῖ," in *Neutestamentliche Studien für Rudolf Bultmann,* ed. Walther Eltester, BZNW 21 (Berlin: A. Töpelmann, 1954), 228-54; and Tiede, *Prophecy and History,* 97-103.

40. σημεῖα καὶ τέρατα is a characteristic phrase in Deuteronomy to describe miraculous works performed through Moses in Egypt, at the Red Sea and in the wilderness: 4:34; 6:22; 7:19; 11:3; 13:1, 2; 26:8; (28:46); 29:3; 34:11; see K. H. Rengstorf, "σημεῖον," *TDNT* 7:208-43; and L. T. Johnson, *Possessions,* 45.

41. Deut. 1:1; 5:1; 11:6; 13:11; 18:6; 27:9, (14); 29:2, (10); 31:1, 7, 11(twice); 32:45; 34:12.

42. Deuteronomy 12—26; but see below, n. 43.

43. Deuteronomy 5—11, essentially. Cf. also Deuteronomy 29—30; 31:1-8. It is generally agreed that one of the distinctive features of Deuteronomy is its homiletical-rhetorical style, even in the "legal" section, Deuteronomy 12—26. E.g., G. von Rad (*Deuteronomy,* 19): "This trend towards exhortation is the real characteristic of the Deuteronomic presentation of the law . . . from specifically legal formulations towards pastoral exhortation and encouragement." For von Rad's ground-breaking form-critical studies on the parenetic character of Deuter-

onomy, see "Die formgeschichtliche Eigenart des Deuteronomiums und seiner sakralen Traditionen," in G. von Rad, *Deuteronomium-Studien,* FRLANT n.f. 40 (Göttingen: Vandenhoeck & Ruprecht, 1948), 7–16; M. Weinfeld calls attention also to the "rhetorical technique" of Deuteronomy in his *Deuteronomy and the Deuteronomic School* (Oxford: Clarendon Press, 1972), 171–78; in addition to a whole series of ad hominem expressions (e.g., "your eyes see"/"you have seen"— 11:7; 29:1 et al.; "this day"; "and now"), Weinfeld points out the appeal to large audiences: "This emphasis on vast audiences . . . and the detailed enumeration of the various leading classes participating in them is peculiar to the book of Deuteronomy and deuteronomic literature" (p. 173). Cf. R. Polzin, "Reporting Speech in the Book of Deuteronomy: Toward a Compositional Analysis of the Deuteronomic History," in *Traditions in Transformation: Turning Points in Biblical Faith,* ed. B. Halpern and J. D. Levenson (Winona Lake, Ind.: Eisenbrauns, 1981), 193–211; Polzin speaks of "the monologic word" of Deuteronomy with perhaps "a hidden dialogue between two 'Mosaic' voices" (p. 211) which overall exalts Moses' authority but also exalts the narrator "at the expense of Moses' uniqueness" (ibid.).

Deuteronomy 1:1—4:43, the "first discourse," with the core a historical retrospect (1:6—3:29), is "historical narrative" already "homiletical-parenetic." Deuteronomy 5—11, the "second discourse" with its Decalogue (5:1–21) and the hortatory Shema (6:4–5), contains in 6:10—9:6 a "block of sermons of a very special kind" (von Rad, *Deuteronomy,* 20) which are not linked to any specific legislation and which sum up repeatedly the heart of Israel's faith. We are interested especially in these two types of parenesis as they portray the character of Moses' calling vis-à-vis the saving events and Israel's corresponding rebellion. For further details, see esp. E. W. Nicholson, *Deuteronomy and Tradition* (Oxford: Basil Blackwell, 1967), chap. 2, "The Structure and Unity of Deuteronomy," 18–36, esp. 18–19, 26, 30; and G. W. Anderson, *A Critical Introduction to the Old Testament* (London: Gerald Duckworth, 1959), 21–22, who speaks of Deut. 1:1—4:40 and 4:44—11:32 as an appeal to past history as a witness of God's love; cf. p. 38 for rhetorical phrases. See below, Part IV, "The Relation of Form to Content in Deuteronomy and in the Central Section of Luke."

44. Deuteronomy 27:9—28:68; chap. 33. The rhetorical character of the book (see above, n. 43) along with the "blessings" and "curses" has suggested a "cultic" setting to many scholars. A considerable number, foremost von Rad, have linked the origin and form of Deuteronomy to the ancient covenant renewal ceremony as outlined for instance in Exodus 19—24; cf. Joshua 24. Deuteronomy follows this pattern: (a) recounting of the *Heilsgeschichte* (Deuteronomy 1—4) with parenesis for obedience (Deuteronomy 5—11); (b) promulgation of the law (12:1—26:5); (c) reenactment or renewal of the covenant with renewed pledges of obedience (26:16–19); and (d) blessings and curses (27:11—28:68). Deuteronomy 31:9–13 itself provides for such a covenant renewal at the Feast of Tabernacles. Although von Rad's theory that the Sinai traditions grew independently and were celebrated at Tabernacles while the Exodus-Conquest traditions were celebrated at the Feast of Weeks has not gained overall credence, the covenant renewal pattern as the *Sitz-im-Leben* for many of the Deuteronomic traditions

has wider support (cf. Nicholson, *Tradition*, 39ff., for a presentation of various opinions and discussion of the issues). The frequent phrase "this day" (e.g., 5:2–3; 8:18; 11:26, 32; 26:17–18) fits admirably with this theory. For contra, see Weinfeld, *Deuteronomy*, 173–78.

45. The first four chapters serve as an introduction to the Decalogue (5:1–21) and the Shema (6:4–5). Deuteronomy 4:1–43 is primarily hortatory and appears to bridge the historical retrospect (Deuteronomy 1—3) with the presentation at Horeb. M. Noth (*Überlieferungsgeschichtliche Studien I, Die sammelnden und bearbeitenden Geschichtswerke im Alten Testament* [Halle: Niemeyer, 1943]) argued that Deuteronomy 1—4 was the work of the Deuteronomistic historians as an introduction to their great work. If so, it is not the least strange that here particularly the calling, status, and role of Moses the prophet is telescopically reviewed, a fitting introduction to a theologumenon on Israel's prophetic history. See further, S. Mittmann, *Deuteronomium 1₁-6₃: literarisch und traditionsgeschichtlich untersucht*, BZAW 139 (Berlin and New York: Walter de Gruyter, 1975); N. Lohfink, "Darstellungskunst und Theologie in Dtn 1, 6—3, 29," *Bib* 41 (1960): 105–34, esp. 107–10; and below, Part III, introduction.

46. Cf., e.g., G. von Rad (*Old Testament Theology*, 2 vols. [New York: Harper & Row; London: SCM Press, 1975], 1:294): "The most impressive corroboration of this all-embracing mediating office of proclamation is of course the fact that the corpus of Deuteronomy is put into the form of words of Moses (and so not of Jahweh) spoken to Israel"; and W. Eichrodt (*Theology of the Old Testament*, 2 vols. [Philadelphia: Westminster Press, 1961], 1:290): "He is explicitly displayed as the supreme preacher of the divine will, . . . as *the mediator between God and his people* (5:24–28)."

47. Deut. 4:40; 5:31–33; 10:5; 32:46–47; etc.; cf. 30:1–20.

48. It is clear from the text (cf. esp. Deut. 9:6—10:11) that Moses himself would have been spared for lack of any wrongdoing; see below, nn. 53, 65.

49. LXX—παιδεῦσαί σε. For Hebrew (MT) and fuller details, see D. P. Moessner, "Luke 9:1–50: Luke's Preview of the Journey of the Prophet like Moses of Deuteronomy," *JBL* 102 (1983): 582–87.

50. Deut. 5:24 (LXX)—ἔδειξεν ἡμῖν κύριος ὁ Θεὸς ἡμῶν τὴν δόξαν αὐτοῦ.

51. Deut. 4:11b (LXX)—πυρὶ . . . σκότος, γνόφος, Θύελλα, φωνὴ μεγάλη; φωνη μεγ. >A. Cf. 5:22.

52. Deut. 1:39 (LXX)—παιδίον νέον; cf. 11:2, where Moses, speaking to the "children" of Horeb, tells them he is not speaking to their own "children" (παιδία) "who do not know and have not seen the discipline of the Lord" (ὅσοι οὐκ οἴδασιν ἴδοσαν τὴν παιδείαν κυρίου). Cf. also 31:13; in Deut. 4:9–10 the "children" of Horeb are to "teach" (διδάσκω) their children the law and their children's children; cf. 4:25, 40; 5:9, 29; 6:7; 11:19, 21; 12:25, 28; 14:1; 17:20; 29:22, 29; 30:2; 32:5, 20, 46.

53. Except for Caleb (and his family) and Joshua (Deut. 1:67–68).

54. Deut. 1:37 (LXX)—δι᾿ ὑμᾶς; 3:26 (LXX)—ἕνεκεν ὑμῶν.

55. Cf. T. W. Mann ("Theological Reflections on the Denial of Moses," *JBL* 98 [1979]: 486): "Nowhere in the deuteronomic explanations does Moses refer to his own responsibility; the blame falls squarely on the people."

56. One expression is (lit.) "stiff-necked," e.g., Deut. 9:6, 13, (LXX) σκληρο-τράχηλος; or "stiff-hearted," e.g., 10:16 (LXX) σκληροκαρδία; e.g., 31:27 (LXX) σκληρός; 9:27 (LXX) σκληρότης; cf. 29:19, "to walk in the error of (one's) heart" (LXX) ἐν τῇ ἀποπλανήσει τῆς καρδίας μου πορεύομαι.

57. E.g., Deut. 9:6, 7, 13, 27; 10:16; 12:8; 29:19; 31:27.

58. E.g., Deut. 1:26; 9:7, 23, 24; 21:18, 20; 28:65; 32:51 (LXX) ἀπειθ-εῖν/ής.

59. E.g., Deut. 9:4, 5, 27; 17:13; 18:20, 22; 19:16; 25:2 (LXX) ἀσέβ-εια/ειν/ημα.

60. E.g., Deut. 5:9; 9:18, 21; 15:9; 19:15; 21:22; 23:21, 22; 24:15, 16; 30:3 (LXX) ἁμαρτία.

61. E.g., Deut. 8:14; 17:20 (LXX) ὑψωθῆς τῇ καρδίᾳ.

62. E.g., Deut. 1:43; 9:23; 21:18 (LXX) εἰσακούειν.

63. E.g., Deut. 8:3, 5: "And he afflicted you . . . that he might teach you that humankind does not live by bread alone."

64. E.g., Deut. 32:28 (LXX) ἐπιστήμη.

65. LXX—ὀφθαλμοὺς βλέπειν καὶ ὦτα ἀκούειν.

66. E.g., Deut. 32:5 (LXX) γενεὰ σκολιὰ καὶ διεστραμμένη; cf. Luke 9:41 (Matt. 17:17); Acts 2:40.

67. See von Rad (*Old Testament Theology,* 1:295): "The death of Moses outside the land of promise . . . was vicarious for Israel. It is because of Israel that Jahweh's great wrath was directed upon Moses, with the result that Jahweh refused to allow him to set foot in the land of promise."

68. E.g., the younger generation was an eyewitness (Deut. 11:1–7). Moses bears the wrath of God for the younger generation which is about to enter the land (3:26; 4:21). The whole format of the Mosaic addresses assumes the participation of the hearers in the *Heilsgeschichte,* including their stubbornness—9:24.

69. See above, Introduction, "Method and Scope of This Work."

70. Deut. 1:6, 19 makes it clear that the Horeb episode is meant.

71. For the lapse of time to Moses' present address, see Deut. 3:29—4:1.

72. So Mann ("Denial," 486), referring to H. Barzel, "Moses: Tragedy and Sublimity," in *Literary Interpretations of Biblical Narratives,* ed. K. R. R. Gros, et al. (Nashville: Abingdon Press, 1974), 129.

73. See S. R. Driver, *Deuteronomy,* ICC; 3d ed. (Edinburgh: T. & T. Clark, 1902), 27, for the three parallel expressions (Deut. 1:37; 3:26; 4:21).

74. Notice that the emphatic "I" is twice contrasted with the emphatic "you."

75. Cf. Driver, *Deuteronomy,* 71.

76. Usually ascribed to the P account; see, e.g., von Rad, *Deuteronomy,* 201; cf. below, n. 102.

77. We are not suggesting that a developed, theoretical explanation of Moses' death as atoning or redemptive is offered in Deuteronomy. Rather, Moses' death vis-à-vis the older generation is vicarious in the sense of a shared participation in their punishment, and it is redemptive for the younger generation as it finally enables or allows their deliverance to be consummated. For "vicarious" in the sense of "substitutionary" and/or "representative," see, e.g., von Rad, *Old Testament Theology,* 1:294–95; idem, *Deuteronomy,* 45, 201; and G. E. Wright, "Exegesis of Deuteronomy," *IB* 2:339–40. For the explicit development in Mosaic

tradition (e.g., Isaiah 53), see von Rad, *Old Testament Theology*, 2:261–62; G. Vermès, "Die Gestalt des Moses an der Wende der beiden Testaments," in *Moses: In Schrift und Überlieferung* (Düsseldorf: Patmos Verlag, 1963), 78–86, esp. 79–80; and L. Ginzberg, *The Legends of the Jews*, 7 vols. (Philadelphia: Jewish Publication Society of America, 1910), 2:302.

78. So, e.g., Conzelmann (*Theology*, 59): "a means of strengthening . . . for the road that lies ahead." Cf. also J. H. Davies, "The Purpose of the Central Section of St. Luke's Gospel," *SE II* = TU 87 (1964), 164–65; D. Gill, "Observations on the Lukan Travel Narrative and Some Related Passages," *HTR* 63 (1970): 218–21; W. Grundmann, "Fragen der Komposition des lukanischen Reiseberichtes," *ZNW* 50 (1959); and idem, *Lukas*, 191–93; R. H. Lightfoot, *Locality and Doctrine in the Gospels* (London: Hodder & Stoughton, 1938), 136–37; C. C. McCown, "The Geography of Jesus' Last Journey to Jerusalem," *JBL* 51 (1932): 64–66; and P. von der Osten-Sacken, "Zur Christologie des lukanischen Reiseberichts," *EvT* 33 (1973): 482–84.

79. Or perhaps his sources'.

80. Cf. (LXX) Exod. 24:10, 17: only Luke has this verbal link with the Exodus account.

81. Cf. (LXX) Exod. 40:35; Pss. 90(91):4; 139(140):7; Prov. 18:11.

82. Whether the disciples, or Jesus and Moses and Elijah, are meant is not decisive for our thesis; cf. Marshall, *Luke*, 387.

83. Deut. 4:11–13, 33, 36; 5:22, 23, 24, 25, 26; 8:20; 18:16; cf. future days: 4:30; 13:4, 18; 15:5; 26:14, 17; 27:10; 28:1, 2, 9, 13, 15, 45, 62; 30:2, 8, 10, 20.

84. It must not be overlooked that the authority of the prophet like Moses is tied directly to Moses' authority revealed at Horeb (18:16–17).

85. For a discussion of linguistic issues, see Marshall, *Luke*, 385.

86. On "in those days," see Deut. 17:9, 12; 19:17; 26:3.

87. This phrase is unique to Luke.

88. On "apostles" (9:10!) and the *shaliach* concept, see C. K. Barrett, "*Shaliaḥ* and Apostle," in *Donum Gentilicium: New Testament Studies in Honour of David Daube*, ed. E. Bammel and W. D. Davies (Oxford: Clarendon Press, 1978), 88–102.

89. Contrast this "return" to that of the "Seventy(-two)" in Luke 10:17–20! For history of traditions issues, see F. Hahn, *Mission in the New Testament* (London: SCM Press, 1965), 40–48, 129–30.

90. E.g., Luke 6:17, 19; 7:9, 11, 12, 24; 8:4, 19, 40, 42, 45.

91. These first two activities match those of the Twelve (9:2).

92. Contrast Mark 8:31–32; Matt. 16:17–19, 21, 24–28; for the disciples as recipients of private teaching, see, e.g., R. P. Meye, *Jesus and the Twelve: Discipleship and Revelation in Mark's Gospel* (Grand Rapids: Wm. B. Eerdmans Publishing Co., 1968), 30–88, 118–36.

93. Cf., e.g., Grundmann, "Fragen," 255–56.

94. Cf. Marshall (*Luke*, 373): "He went on to say"; for this use of the imperfect, cf. BDF, §329. For Luke's unique "daily" (9:23) as a requirement for following in suffering to the cross at the level of Luke's story, cf. F. Schütz, *Der leidende*

Christus: Die angefochtene Gemeinde und das Christuskerygma der lukanischen Schriften, BWANT 89 (Stuttgart: Kohlhammer, 1969), 15–20.

95. The disciples are "at strife" in 9:46–48; see below.

96. There is no indication by Jesus that his authority is being abused by the "unknown" exorcist.

97. A comparison with the portrayal of the disciples in the corresponding Matthean and Markan passages discloses that only Luke reflects a developed complex of Exodus motifs that determines the whole tenor and structure of the story of Jesus: Mark 9:14–50—the disciples are bound to Jesus through their confessing, though naive and insufficient, faith and as such are set apart from the unbelieving and even hostile crowds; Matt. 17:14—18:35 — even more than Mark the disciples are distinguished from the unbelieving and perverted crowds (17:17a) by their faith and responsibilities as guardians of that faith. Cf. E. Lohmeyer, *Das Markus-Evangelium,* KKNT, 10th ed. (Göttingen: Vandenhoeck & Ruprecht, 1937), 184–97, esp. 190–91; idem, *Das Evangelium des Matthäus,* KKNT (Göttingen: Vandenhoeck & Ruprecht, 1956), 271; J. Schniewind, *Das Evangelium nach Markus,* NTD 1 (Göttingen: Vandenhoeck & Ruprecht, 1963), 91; and idem, *Das Evangelium nach Matthäus,* NTD 1 (1963), 195.

98. Does the desire to be *sheltered* by a "tent" or "booth" (σκηνή, οἶκος; cf. Luke 9:33; Deut. 5:30) perhaps reflect an early typological explanation of the disciples' reluctance to hearken to the divine voice in Jesus? In both Deut. 5:30 and Luke 9:33 the "witnesses" are eager to have this "voice" in their midst but only on their own terms (cf. also Deut. 1:27; 31:14–15; 1 Kings 19:9–15; Luke 16:9; Acts 7:43, 44 and the wordplay of σκηνή and σκήνωμα with οἶκος in Acts 7:46–50!). In Deuteronomy the "tent" (σκηνή, σκήνωμα, 16:13; 33:18) symbolizes the joy of God's saving presence when the nation is in an obedient relation to its covenant law and hence covenant God (cf. Acts 15:16); cf. also the "shame" of Luke 9:26–27 and the disciples' behavior in 9:40–50!

99. Cf. Acts 2:1 for best analogy; cf. also J. H. Davies ("Purpose," 165) for clear discussion of the linguistic relation of 9:51 to 9:31.

100. Luke 7:31; 11:29, 30, 31, 32, 50, 51; 17:25; cf. 16:8; 21:32; Acts 2:40; see M. Dibelius, *From Tradition to Gospel* (Cambridge: James Clarke & Co., 1971), 278.

101. Luke 9:23–25 along with probable paronomasia on ὁ υἱὸς τοῦ ἀνθρώπου with χεῖρας ἀνθρώπων (cf. J. Jeremias, *TDNT* 5 [1967]: 715) indicates a generic sense of "humanity," or the generation of Jesus' day. Luke 17:25 (cf. 9:41) indicates expressly that "this generation" rejects "the Son of humankind" and thus is responsible for Jesus' "suffering." In 23:13–25 Pilate delivers (παραδίδωμι, v. 25) Jesus over not only to the religious leaders but also to the *laos;* cf. below, Part III.C, esp. "The Journeying Guest Is Rejected in Jerusalem (Luke 19:45—23:49.)"

102. The tradition of Moses' death outside the land of promise in Deut. 32:48–52, that because of his own sin he is excluded from the land, is regarded as non-Deuteronomic material, perhaps from the Priestly Writings (P) (cf. the closely parallel Num. 27:12–14). That it does not harmonize with the distinctive Deuteronomic view is evident. Von Rad (*Deuteronomy,* 201) sums up much of critical

opinion when he avers: "In the tradition of Deuteronomy and that of the Deuteronomic history this fate was accounted for in quite a different way, namely that Moses had to die vicariously for the sake of Israel's sin (Deut. 4.21; 1.37)."

103. Only Luke places "Peter's confession" immediately following the "feeding" (9:10b–17).

104. Luke 10:17–24.

105. Luke 10:29–37; 17:11–19.

106. Luke 10:38–42; 13:10–17.

107. Luke 12:13–15, 16–21, 22–32, 33–34; 14:12–14, 15–24, 25–33; 15:11–32; 16:14–15; 19:31; 18:18–30.

108. Luke 10:1–12, 17–20; 11:14–23; 13:10–17, 31–33; 14:1–6, 15–24; 18:35–43.

109. Luke 14:15–24; 15:1–7, 8–10, 11–32; 18:9–14; 19:1–10.

110. Cf. P. S. Minear, "Jesus' Audiences According to Luke," *NovT* 16 (1974): 81–109, for Luke's use of *laos*.

111. Cf. ὄφις and σκορπίος (Luke 10:19) in Deut. 8:15!

112. ποιέω, ἀκούω, and φυλάσσω are the key verbs: Luke 10:25–28, 29–37, 39; 11:27–28, 42; 12:43, 47–48; 13:9, 22–30; 14:35; 15:1; 16:3, 4, 8, 9, 29, 31; 18:18–30; cf. 12:17–18, 38 [D]; 19:48; 21:38; 23:34.

113. Deut. 1:37; 3:26–28; 4:21; 9:24; 11:1–7; 31:14, 16–22, 26–29; 32:5, 20; 34:4–5; Luke 22:3–6, 24–27, 31–33, 35–38, 54–62; 23:13–16, 17–23, 35; Acts 3:12; cf. Luke 2:34; 13:34–35; 19:41–44. Cf., e.g., P. S. Minear, "A Note on Luke xxii 36," *NovT* 7 (1964–65): 128–34; and J. Kodell, "Luke's Use of *Laos*, 'People,' Especially in the Jerusalem Narrative (Luke 19,28—24,53)," *CBQ* 31 (1969): 327–43.

114. Our findings support in a general way the significance of "the mountain" as the place of revelation in Jesus' ministry as stated by Conzelmann, *Theology*, 57–59. But this mountain is not the general mythical mountain of religious manifestation but the particular mountain of the covenant God of the OT.

It is clear that Luke 9:1–50 combines various types of plot devices such as parallelism, repetition ("equivalence"), predictions, and anticipatory references. For instance, the transfiguration not only points the reader both backward and forward within Luke 9 but also repeats and predicts "actions" that come both before and after this point in the story time of the larger Gospel, e.g., "to enter into glory" (cf., e.g., 2:9, 32; 19:38; 24:26).

III

The Deuteronomistic View
of Israel's Prophetic History
and the Central Section of Luke

III

We have shown that the figure of the prophet is integral to much of Luke's story material. Moreover, we have demonstrated that this language and lineage of prophets become conceptual girders for a prophecy-fulfillment framework through which Luke structures his two-volume story. We are also maintaining that Luke 9:1–50 distinguishes itself by pointing ahead to the story in the Central Section as the unfolding drama of Jesus as the Prophet like Moses of Deuteronomy.

Before we marshal evidence from the Central Section itself to give substance to our claim that Luke has a specific plot development in mind, we here raise two questions concerning method: (1) How do we avoid superimposing a schema and plot that are alien to the author's intention? Since the name "Moses" appears only twice in the Central Section, and both times in the same pericope (16:29, 31), we must be careful in proposing grandiose typologies and parallels that Luke himself did not perceive and thus certainly did not intend. (2) Closely related is the functional significance of the characterization and plot of the Prophet like Moses of Deuteronomy for the Central Section. Suppose we succeed in showing that Luke has the Mosaic figure in mind. To what extent does this profile function to motivate and integrate the material within the Central Section itself as opposed to competing figures and plots? Further, how central to the larger story of Jesus and his witnesses in both volumes is the Mosaic prophet of Deuteronomy? In short, for both the shorter and the larger literary units of Luke, is the Mosaic prophet at the heart of Luke's overall portrait of Jesus, or is it only one of several equally or more significant figures?

In the first case, we should recall the crucial role that prophets play in Luke's view of the history of Israel's salvation and especially in their expectations of the end time salvation. The rationale for all the prophets' activity is their anticipation of this definitive act of salvation. Thus it is that Luke finds prophetic inspiration to be the center of Israel's Scriptures and favors the expression "[all] the prophets" to represent the whole of this scriptural revelation.[1]

We must, therefore, inquire further how Luke regards the calling of Jesus as prophet in the Central Section, particularly in relation to Jesus' fulfillment of the OT prophets' own role in pointing forward to the final salvation. To do this we must allow the peculiar figure defined by the dissonance of form from content to emerge while paying primary attention to Jesus' function vis-à-vis "all the prophets" in the actual "story stuff." In other words, any notion of the Prophet like Moses' role must inhere fully within Luke's larger presentation of prophetic fulfillment and must itself illumine and help to integrate this overarching story. To the extent that this integration is not possible, the greater is the danger that we are imposing false characterization and plot upon the story.[2]

In addressing the second question we will not present a comprehensive analysis of the Mosaic prophet within Luke's two volumes, although we will probe several trajectories through which this figure links Acts with the Gospel (Part V). We will also compare and contrast various statements about the prophets in the Central Section with views in writers contemporary to Luke. Often such extrinsic literary comparison has the merit of bringing a particular writer's formulations of plot and character into bolder relief. But more than that, if Lukan perspectives are found to match or closely resemble concurrent notions about prophets within Jewish or Christian writers, then the risk of fabricating alien interpretative grids for the Central Section is again reduced. Not only would certain prophetic traits become more poignant within Luke's presentation but also Luke would be seen as depicting Jesus in terms and with expectations that at least some audiences of his own day could comprehend.

In Luke 11:47–51 and 13:34, Luke has Jesus make the astounding claim that Israel has persecuted or killed a line of prophets that reaches all the way back to Abel's murder and extends up to the murder of Zechariah in the Temple and that therefore his generation will be held accountable for their blood. Where has Luke derived such logic and received such an uncompromising notion of Israel's guilt? And how does this view of Israel's history square with a messianic salvation that is a *fulfillment* of all the prophets? In particular, what possible lines of connection are there between this perspective and an anointed prophet like Moses who journeys to his death and exaltation in Jerusalem?

In his monumental study of intertestamental and NT sources regarding the role and fate of "the prophets" in Israel's history, O. H. Steck claims that for the Palestinian Judaism of about 200 B.C.E. to 100 C.E. one overriding framework of understanding permeated all of its extant literary activity, whether explicit or presupposed.[3] He delineates four tenets of what he calls a Deuteronomistic conception of the prophetic sayings within the Deuteronomistic comprehensive view of Israel's history:[4]

A. The history of Israel is one long, persistent story of a "stiff-necked," rebellious, and disobedient people.

B. God sent his messengers, the prophets, to mediate his will (i.e., the Law), to instruct and admonish (parenesis) them in this will, and to exhort them to repentance lest they bring upon themselves judgment and destruction.

C. Nevertheless, Israel en masse rejected all these prophets, even persecuting and killing them out of their stubborn "stiff-neckedness."

D. Therefore, Israel's God had "rained" destruction upon them in 722 and 587 B.C.E. and would destroy them in a similar way if they did not heed his word.

Such a conceptual canopy did not create one homogeneous Judaism, Steck explains, since within this view many modifications and novel solutions were proffered for emerging problems.[5] But what was viewed as constant was the monolith of disobedience and the acrimonious rebuttal of the prophets by their ancestors.

It is the thesis of Part III that this Deuteronomistic understanding provides the conceptual world in which the disparate traditions of the Central Section of Luke become coherent and present a cohesive picture of a prophet rejected by the unmitigating obduracy of Israel. Moreover, it is this rejection that serves as the basis for the fulfillment of all the prophets as the whole of Israel's history of salvation is seen to come to its intended goal in the death of the Deuteronomistic prophet Jesus, who, however, stands alone as the anointed Prophet like Moses. In Part III we shall present evidence for Jesus as a Deuteronomistic prophet. Then in Part IV we will demonstrate that the distinctive Mosaic traditions of Deuteronomy have been fully integrated with the Deuteronomistic view in Luke's journey to Jerusalem.

If we succeed in establishing our thesis, then we will have accomplished the following: (1) The Deuteronomistic profile will have been derived independently of the fourfold Moses typology of Deuteronomy. This procedure is in keeping with Steck's own conclusion that the fate of Moses in Deuteronomy did not serve as the model for the developing Deuteronomistic perspective of the violent fate of the long line of prophets, a line which nonetheless harks back expressly to his seminal career.[6] (2) If we can show that the Deuteronomistic landscape is not an alien canvas draped upon the text but, on the contrary, is endemic to it, then we will have provided one type of external safeguard for our hypothesis that a specific prophetic figure—as opposed to any other figure or type[7]—stands behind the plotting of the form and content of the Central Section. In other words, it will be a posteriori the more probable that *Jesus as prophet* serves as an integrating principle for Luke's story in 9:51—19:44. (3) Since Deuteronomy forms the keystone for the great Deuteronomistic history with its view of the tragic "end" of the prophets, and since Moses, though distinct, stands historically at the head of this line, we will at the least have elucidated traditiohistorical trajectories in which a comparison to Moses in Deuteronomy for Jesus would be a priori the more probable. Irrespective of Steck's observation of the independent status of Moses vis-à-vis the tragic end of *all the prophets* in his lineage, as decisive a figure as Jesus could well invite a typological correspondence to Moses conceived fully within the Deuteronomistic framework. Indeed, given the pervasive influence of the Deuteronomistic view, such a comparison is not at all inconceivable for a figure purported in the triple tradition to have appeared upon a mountain with Moses (Matt. 17:1–9; Mark 9:2–10; Luke 9:28–36).

We will now view briefly the Deuteronomistic conception of Israel's history in writings roughly contemporary with Luke in order to facilitate recognition of this perspective if it should appear in the Central Section.

JOSEPHUS, *the* QUMRAN COVENANTERS, *and the* DEUTERONOMISTIC PERSPECTIVE

For Josephus, the story of Israel's prophets is a tale of tragedy. In two passages especially he gives his readers a taste of the bitter fate that accrued almost unfailingly to the messengers of God. Describing in his *Antiquities* Hezekiah's reform and the invitation to the Passover (2 Chronicles 30), he instances the reaction of the northern Israelites to the king's messengers:

> When the envoys came and brought them this message from their king, the Israelites were not only not persuaded, but even laughed at his envoys as fools, and, when their *prophets* exhorted them in like manner and foretold what they would suffer if they did not alter their course to one of piety toward God, they poured scorn upon them and finally seized them and killed them. And not stopping even at these acts of lawlessness, they devised things still worse than those mentioned, and did not leave off until God punished them for their impiety by making them subject to their enemies. . . . However, many of the tribes of Manasseh, Zabulon and Issachar heeded the prophets' exhortations and were converted to piety. And all these flocked to Jerusalem to Hezekiah that they might worship God.   (*Ant.* 9.265–67)[8]

Here all four of Steck's categories are explicit, with a particular emphasis on elements B and C:[9] B: the prophets' task is primarily that of exhorting (παραινεῖν) the people to return to the "ancient custom" of "reverence" or "piety toward God";[10] C: they are opposed to the point of ridicule, death, and untold "acts of lawlessness."[11] Acts of violence and the death of *prophets* in the North are nonscriptural details that must derive from other traditions. 2 Chronicles only mentions "couriers" "sent" from Jerusalem who are "jeered" and "mocked" (2 Chron. 30:1–2, 6, 10). While 2 Kings 17:7–41 and Nehemiah 9 speak of the prophets' rejection[12] and death,[13] it is evident that Josephus's text is not simply reflecting the vocabulary or style of these passages but is voicing sentiments independent of the biblical texts and still current if not influential in Josephus's day.[14]

In *Ant.* 10.38–39, continuing with Hezekiah's son, Manasseh, Josephus declares:

> For, setting out with a contempt of God, he killed all the righteous men among the Hebrews, nor did he spare even the prophets, some of whom he slaughtered daily, so that Jerusalem ran with blood. Thereupon God, being wrathful at these things, sent prophets to the king and the people, and through these threatened them with the same calamities which had befallen their Israelite brothers when they outraged Him. They were not, however, persuaded by these words, from which they might so have profited as not to experience any misfortune, but had to learn from deeds the truth of what the prophets said.

Here again the lines of living Deuteronomistic tradition are distinctly visible. A comparison with 2 Kings 21:1–16, on the one side, and 2 Chron. 33:1–17, on the other, indicates the Deuteronomistic bias of Josephus's interpretation. Yet because, as in the first passage, he includes details such as the killing of the prophets and righteous men which are not present in 2 Kings 21,[15] it becomes all but certain that Josephus is depending upon a fundamental Deuteronomistic understanding of Israel's disobedient past which had continued to generate extrabiblical traditions on the fate of Israel's prophets.

We can conclude that the fourfold Deuteronomistic view of Israel's past was well known and shared by Josephus. It is quite possible that he was promoting a theological explanation of Israel's catastrophes in 722 and 587 widely circulated and upheld by a number of groups contemporaneous with his own experience with different "schools" of Judaism.[16] Be that as it may, it is interesting to note that at several points he evinces features of the Mosaic portrait in striking conformity to that of Deuteronomy: (1) Moses is the great mouthpiece of God. As Deut. 34:10 states, Moses was unequaled as "prophet," since "in all his utterances one seemed to hear the speech of God Himself" (*Ant.* 4.329). He was in fact the "interpreter" (ἑρμηνεύς)[17] of God. (2) Sent as God's spokesman, Moses is the untiring exhorter[18] of a stubborn people to heed God's commandments which form the very constitution of their subsistence. (3) But as the people persist in their stiff-necked disobedience, they harass and persecute Moses as the scapegoat of their predicament. Moses' response is to intercede and plead before God in their behalf.[19] That is to say, for Josephus as in Deuteronomy, Moses is the great suffering mediator for Israel.[20] "'God,' said he, 'and I, though vilified by you, will never cease our efforts on your behalf'" (*Ant.* 3.298).[21] Here it is significant that Josephus in four different passages[22] mentions the Israelites' intent to stone Moses, which in *Ant.* 3.21 is tantamount to "pronouncing sentence upon God."[23] These extrabiblical traditions once again make it all the more certain that Josephus is reliant upon Deuteronomistic conceptions of Moses[24] which in their basic structure adhere to the fourfold dynamic.[25] As the rejected mediator of God's will and intercessor for Israel, Moses is the greatest of the long line[26] of prophets who follow in his path of suffering.[27]

The covenanters of Qumran exhibit the same Deuteronomistic framework as Josephus, albeit from a point of vantage distant from his. The author(s) of "The Damascus Rule" (CD) declare(s):

> For when they were unfaithful and forsook Him, He hid His face from Israel and His Sanctuary and delivered them up to the sword. But remembering the Covenant of the forefathers, He left a remnant to Israel and did not deliver it up to be destroyed. And in the age of wrath, three hundred and ninety years after He had given them into the hand of King Nebuchadnezzar of Babylon, He visited them, and He caused a plant root to spring from Israel and Aaron to inherit His Land and to prosper on the good things of His earth. . . . And God observed their deeds, that they sought Him with a whole heart, and He raised for them a Teacher of Righteousness to guide them in the way of His heart. And he made known to the latter generations that which God had done to the latter generation, the congregation of traitors, to those who departed from the way. This was the time of which it is written, 'Like a stubborn heifer thus was Israel stubborn (Hos. iv, 16), when the Scoffer arose who shed over Israel the waters of lies. He caused them to wander in a pathless wilderness . . . that He might call down on them the curses of His Covenant and deliver them up to the avenging sword of the Covenant. . . . And the anger of God was kindled against their congregation so that He ravaged all their multitude, and their deeds were defilement before Him. (CD 1:3—2:4)[28]

The entire preexilic period is one block of faithless "abandonment" (1:3a). Tenet A is thus forcefully expressed. But now, instead of the usual dual form of the prophets' calling and fate (B, C), the judgment of 587 ensues (i.e., D, 1:3b–4a), followed by a remnant that is allowed to survive this destruction (1:4b–6).[29] From this remnant the covenanters are constituted by God to enjoy the blessings of the covenant salvation (1:7–8a, 10b–11a), while the great mass of stubborn Israel, the "congregation of traitors" of the "last generation," reap the fiery extinction of God's wrath (1:12–13a, 17; 2:1). Tenets B and C are telescoped into tenet D as the history of monolithic rebellion of preexilic days continues right up to the present and final generation. Only the covenanters themselves comprise the people of the covenant, the true Israel of the patriarchs (1:4b–5; cf. 1:16). How different this is from Josephus, who is intent to describe four "schools" of Judaism of the empirical Israel of his day.[30] Though Josephus allows for the repentance of smaller groups within a wayward Israel at certain stages of Israel's history,[31] he does not make a definitive distinction in eschatological terms between the one true covenant remnant and the great mass of the condemned.

Given this historical application of the Deuteronomistic orientation by the covenanters, it is passing strange that the Qumran scrolls never speak of the prophets being *sent* to a disobedient Israel to preach repentance or warn of judgment.[32] It is as though Israel's history is conceived as a mass apostasy and that such a sending would have proven sheer folly. As the covenanters are themselves the only true Israel, it is no longer conceivable to speak of God's saving actions directed to those outside their community in the present. Nevertheless, the classical twofold view (tenets B, C) of the prophetic calling emerges at several points in their estimation of Israel's past. The prophets are those who were sent to convey God's *law* to Israel (the first of the three functions of tenet B). But Israel did not hearken, rejecting these messengers of God. The comment on Hos. 2:10 in 4QpHos. 2:3b–6 avers: "But they forgot God who. . . . They cast His commandments behind them which He had sent [by the hand of] His servants the Prophets, and they listened to those who led them astray. They revered them, and in their blindness they feared them as though they were gods."[33] Though Neh. 9:26 and 2 Kings 17:13 are instructive parallels in the twofold Deuteronomistic pattern, it is again evident, as with Josephus, that this evaluation of Israel's prophetic ministry in the Deuteronomistic mold is cut from living traditions vital to the Qumran community. In addition, in 1QS 1:3 and 8:15–16 "Moses" and "the prophets" are mentioned as the mediators of God's law to which their community alone is obedient.[34] Moses and the prophets, then, are those who were sent to reveal God's law but were shunned from any true "hearing."[35]

It is when we look more closely at this rejection that the thinking of Qumran stands out in greatest relief from Josephus. For in the covenanters' view of things, not only did Moses and the prophets foretell their own rejection, they also believed that all the commandments that Moses and the prophets uttered and that were written down were intended to achieve full significance only at the time of the last generation, that is, only within their own covenant community. So, for instance, 1Qp 2:5-10 on Hab. 1:5 intones:

> This saying is to be interpreted [as concerning those who] will be unfaithful at the end of days. They, the men of violence and the breakers of the Covenant, will not believe when they hear all that [is to happen to] the final generation from the Priest [in whose heart] God set [understanding] that he might interpret all the words of His servants the Prophets, through whom He foretold all that would happen to His people and [His land].

Thus it is in the person of their founder and guiding light, the Teacher of Righteousness,[36] that the consummate meaning of the mysteries revealed to Moses and revealed anew in successive stages to each of the prophets had now been made fully clear. Indeed he is the one who received the interpretations of their *written* words from the very "mouth of God."[37] "The prophets," then, are conceived by these Essene covenanters always through the conceptual sieve of their Teacher who himself in so many outstanding features resembled the prophet Moses in Deuteronomy.[38] Like Moses, he is sent and commissioned by God to utter words from God's "mouth"; like Moses, "all the mysteries of the words of His servants the Prophets" (1QpHab 7:5) were divulged to him in his teaching and exhortations to the community. And like the great founder of the covenant community in the wilderness, so the Teacher himself founds a community of the "New Covenant"[39] in the wilderness. Although it is still disputed whether the Teacher was regarded as the eschatological "prophet like Moses" (Deut. 18:15-19), yet as W. A. Meeks observes, "It can hardly be doubted that the Teacher of Righteousness functioned as *a* prophet like Moses."[40] For like the figure in Deuteronomy 18 the words the Teacher utters carry with them the eschatological ultimacy of salvation or damnation. To decide against the Teacher is to decide against God himself.

As scholars have often noted, the conception as well as the inception of the Dead Sea community is based on the recapitulation of the Exodus-wilderness conditions of the Mosaic covenant.[41] Whether in their exodus-exile,[42] the organization around and renewal of the covenant,[43] or even the institutions of the holy war patterned after Moses' legislation in Deuteronomy and Numbers,[44] the whole phenomenon of the community of the Dead Sea Scrolls must be set within the hermeneutical framework of an Exodus–New Exodus typology. It is no wonder, then, that the

Testimonia parchment of Cave 4 speaks of the expected eschatological prophet of Deuteronomy 18 who is ranked in importance alongside the coming Messiahs of Aaron and Israel.[45] That the Qumran community at some stage of its history awaited the prophet like Moses of Deut. 18:15–19 cannot be doubted. That the Teacher of Righteousness himself, whose own coming either anticipated or actually fulfilled the expectation of this prophetic figure, carved a deep impression in a Mosaic vein is equally clear.[46] Consequently, the final redemption for the community, like its very constitution in the desert, was to have been a repetition or rather consummation of the original redeeming acts of God in the wilderness exile.

Summary. In the Qumran literature we find an active anticipation of a prophet like Moses (Deut. 18:15–19) who is sent to utter the words that God himself has placed into his mouth and commanded him to speak. On the one hand, this prophet matches the overarching description of Moses in Deuteronomy. On the other hand, this prophet exhibits astounding lines of affinity to the actual activity of the community's founder—the Teacher of Righteousness. By the same token, this expectation was framed by the Deuteronomists' historical perspective of the entire course of Israel's disobedience. Like Josephus, the covenanters believed that Israel was punished for its monolithic rebellion by the exile of 587 to Babylon. But unlike him, they held that this "Babylonian captivity" had never ceased. For except for the remnant out of which their own congregation grew, the rest of the nation remained one apostate mass. For this reason they themselves had to undergo a "counter exile," an exodus away from the congregation of the wicked to the desert, where they would recover and revitalize the covenant of Moses. It is this narrowing of the panorama to the typological landscape of the wilderness–New Exodus which accounts for the fewer instances of tenets B and C in the Dead Sea Scrolls over against Josephus. All attention now is focused on the mission of the last days, the climax of the work of the Teacher of Righteousness in interpreting the written words of Moses and the prophets, rather than on the living memory of their preaching and rejection. Yet in several glimpses of Israel's prophetic past and perhaps even more markedly in the fate of their own Teacher of Righteousness, the covenanters, like Josephus, testify to the proverbial "stiff-necked" rejection of Israel's prophets.[47]

Conclusions

We have discovered the fourfold Deuteronomistic framework to be a constant in such variables as Josephus and the Qumran covenanters. That this historical-theological understanding persisted in varying forms into intertestamental and NT times is an assured result. Moreover, we have seen that one function of the pluriformity of Judaism is the perceived exception to the rule of monolithic disobedience. The nation as a whole has been rebellious—without a doubt—but there have been groups from time to time who have repented and followed the will of Yahweh; or perhaps only one group has returned to the true religion of Mosaic revelation. In other words, tenets A and C as well as tenet D have built into them the prophets' "unless you repent." The idea of a faithful remnant is in no way contradictory to the Deuteronomistic "mass" mentality. What is more, we have encountered at least one active, contemporary expectation of a redemption that looks back to the Exodus-wilderness redemption of the Mosaic period. Even the eschatological "prophet like Moses" was to come to usher in this salvation. Therefore, any notion that the typological lines between Moses' career in Deuteronomy and Luke's Central Section *must* be accidental or purely stylistic devices can already be laid to rest.[48] Needless to say, these lines, drawn as they are within Luke's lineage and language of the prophets, must be given serious consideration (see Part IV). Finally and most significantly, the interpretative grids for both Josephus's and the covenanters' estimates of Moses—whether in the past or as an eschatological figure—are distinctively Deuteronomistic. And equally important, we have discovered Mosaic portraits in the intertestamental gallery that combine the unmistakable hues of Deuteronomy with the telltale shades of the Deuteronomistic historical perspective. The way ahead for us is thus clear. We must now demonstrate the conformity of the Central Section to the four-point Deuteronomistic perspective *independently* of the fourfold typological lines of Moses' calling in Deuteronomy.

The CENTRAL SECTION
and the DEUTERONOMISTIC HISTORICAL VIEW

In our analysis of the fourfold typology in Luke 9:1–50 we have already encountered the Deuteronomistic tenets A—C: As Jesus descends from the mountain and is sent on his exodus with the voice of God (9:31, 35, tenet B), he confronts the stiff-necked obduracy of the wilderness generation (9:41, tenet A).[49] Tenet C is intimated at 9:9 and 9:22–24 and is vividly illustrated by the disciples' repeated inattention to heed the voice of the prophet Jesus (9:37–50). Moreover, tenet D is alluded to at 9:5 and 9:26 but otherwise is not present. It is, however, the disciples' solidarity with the faithless mass of the people (tenet A), so poignantly accented by Luke's carefully carved continuity in the crowds and scenery changes, which imprints 9:1–50 with the Deuteronomistic outlook.

We shall now examine tenets A—D to see whether the Central Section exhibits their characteristic features. If not, our thesis disintegrates:

A. The Present Generation Is an Evil, Crooked One and as Such Demonstrates Its Solidarity with Their "Fathers"

From the day that your fathers came out of the land of Egypt to this day, I have persistently sent all my servants the prophets to them, day after day; yet they did not listen to me, or incline their ear, but stiffened their neck. They did worse than their fathers!   (Jer. 7:25–26)

1. **Luke 11:29–32 (with literary context, 11:14–54).** * This larger section, containing seven pericopes, begins in 11:14–23[50] with a controversy between Jesus and "some" and "others" of "the crowds" (οἱ ὄχλοι, v. 14b, 15a, 16a) and ends with Jesus at table in the home of a Pharisee (vv. 37–54).

No mention has been made of "the crowds" in 11:14 since 9:18 and 9:27–28, though, as we have seen, their presence is assumed by Luke up to 9:50. It is not entirely clear who is following along with Jesus "on the way" (9:57; cf. 10:2) to Jerusalem; in 9:52 some "messengers" are sent on ahead, while in 10:1ff. seventy(-two) "others" are likewise sent on ahead "into every town and place where he himself was going to come" (10:1b). We also learn that "on the way" certain individuals (9:57, 61) voice their readiness to follow Jesus and that Jesus himself even recruits another to follow him and to "proclaim the Kingdom of God" (9:59–60). It is certain that a group of disciples are with Jesus at certain points, since Jesus turns to them privately (10:23), partakes of a meal in one of their homes (10:38–42—Mary and Martha), and "in a certain place" (11:1) teaches and encourages them to pray (11:1–13). It is sometime subsequent to this last episode, while Jesus is casting out a demon, that the crowds are explicitly present, "marveling" (θαυμάζω) at a deaf-mute who can now talk (11:14). This feat is impugned by "some of them," however, as accomplished ultimately by "Beelzebul, the prince of the demons" (11:15), while "others" try to "test" (cf. 10:25; 4:2) his authority by "seeking a sign" (σημεῖον, 11:16). Again, with prophetic acuity, Jesus, "knowing their thoughts" (11:17), pits against these foes the authority of God himself ("finger of God") behind his own exorcism (11:20). Those who do not acknowledge this authority (i.e., who do not "gather" "with" him) are guilty[51] of "scattering" (i.e., are "against" him, 11:23).[52] We hear

---

* Please consult K. Aland, ed., *Synopsis Quattuor Evangeliorum* (Stuttgart: Württembergische Bibelanstalt, 1975), for the divisions of the tradition units (pericopes) utilized in this study, and the tables below, pp. 131 and 211.

echoed here the same basic for/against dichotomy of 9:50; this time, however, it is Jesus' rather than an unknown disciple's "casting out a demon" (11:14; cf. 9:49) that has ignited the flames of controversy.

After describing how a person cleansed of an unclean spirit can end up worse than ever (11:24–26) and how important it is to hear the word of God and to keep it (11:27–28),[53] Jesus makes his own accusation: "This generation is an evil ($\pi o \nu \eta \rho \acute{a}$) generation, it seeks a sign" (11:29).[54] Two points are striking here: *(a)* Jesus takes the offensive *"when the crowds were increasing."*[55] By the uninterrupted flow of pericopes it is clear that these crowds are the same as the ones out of which "some" and "others" accuse Jesus of dubious authority. *(b)* Still, Jesus addresses the crowds as one evil generation; though only "some" and "others" are designated as opponents, right when the masses in contrast marvel approvingly (11:14b–16), the whole generation seeks a sign. Here again, as in Luke 9, we find a part that is distinguished from the whole (here by "testy" unbelief, there by belief in his Messiahship) as the standard-bearer for the whole generation, including, of course, his disciples. If it seems that those who do not put Jesus in league with Satan, but rather are skeptical only of his authority, should receive fairer treatment from those who do, Jesus shatters such logic when he continues: "The Queen of the South will arise at the judgment with the men ($\mathring{a}\nu\delta\rho\epsilon\varsigma$) of *this generation* and bring charges against them" (11:31a); "the men of Nineveh will rise up at the judgment with *this generation* and bring charges against it [her]" (11:32a). A distinction between the "men" of this generation and "this generation" itself may be merely a stylistic (chiastic) contrast of gender between the "queen" (fem.) and the "men" (masc.), and the "men" (masc.) as opposed to this "generation" (fem.). In any case, there is no doubt that the entire lot of people, male and female, will stand condemned at the final judgment, because they did not hear the word of God in Jesus (cf. 11:27–28) and repent (11:31–32) accordingly. Verses 31–32 make it clear that "evil" in v. 29 is not an abstract generalization from the lips of a self-styled moralist. Rather, it is the unequivocal word of judgment from one who claims to be "charged" by the "finger of God," whose active presence invokes the very arrival of the Kingdom of God (11:20; cf. 11:19— $\kappa\rho\iota\tau\alpha\acute{\iota}$). In short, we here have the conception of a "stiff-necked," "perverted" people who, despite warning from God's commissioned prophets, remain stubborn. Not only is tenet A explicit but so also are tenets C and D, while tenet B is implicit.[56] As in 9:37–50, Jesus' response to an unbelieving group is one of a wholesale charge to the entire generation; not only those "others" but the whole generation seeks a sign. It is in its entirety no better than those who align Jesus with Satan; all will stand judged at the final day of reckoning. Thus, while the disciples' inability and lack of authority to cast out a demon provokes Jesus' charge in 9:37–50, the charge by "others" against Jesus' ability and authority to cast out demons bestirs the same retort. The effect is unmistakable: all are leveled to a position of radical disobedience before God.

Jesus proceeds,[57] using the metaphor of the eye as the "lamp of the body," to warn the same crowds against any partial reception of the light that is radiating in their midst (11:33–36;[58] cf. Jesus is in the midst of the crowds, he is "here," [ὧδε] 11:31–32). Any darkness at all, that is, any partial vision (v. 36a), any "unsoundness" or "sickly condition" (πονηρός, v. 34b) of the eye, results in complete darkness. "Therefore, beware, lest the light in you actually be darkness" (v. 35; i.e., any partial illumination is in reality total darkness!). This parable thus illuminates what has immediately transpired: As partial vision distorts and darkens the whole existence of an individual, so partial reception of Jesus' authority by some distorts and darkens the whole generation (hence the significance of v. 33 as a linking member is made clear; cf. 11:23).[59]

It is at this point—"when he had finished speaking" (aorist infinitive)—that a Pharisee invites Jesus to dine[60] with him. Jesus "enters" and "reclines at table" (11:37).[61] But when the Pharisee sees that Jesus does not "first wash before the meal"[62] he "marvels" (θαυμάζω, 11:38). Several observations catch our attention at once: *(a)* Jesus has just inveighed against a partial or "unsound" reception of the light, which as we have seen in that context refers to the illumination of revelation that emanates through his authoritative presence as God's agent for his Kingdom. Jesus is "here" (11:31–32) in their presence, bringing the presence of the Kingdom upon them (11:20). Now suddenly ("as he had finished speaking") we have a concrete example of a Pharisee receiving Jesus into his home. It is curious, however, that Luke does not use δέχομαι or its cognates to express this reception (as, e.g., in 9:53 [Samaritan village]; 9:48 [Jesus and the child; cf. 18:17]; 10:38 [Martha and Jesus]; cf. also 19:6 [Zacchaeus and Jesus]; 16:4, 9 [the dishonest steward]; and esp. 9:11 [the "five thousand" and Jesus before he feeds them]). Jesus is asked and simply "enters." What kind of reception he will be offered surfaces at the outset as a leading question.[63] *(b)* This Pharisee is one of those who make up the crowds of 11:14–36, because of the temporal connection in v. 37a.[64] *(c)* The Pharisee "marvels" (θαυμάζω) at Jesus' crude manner at table. Surely this teacher (cf. 11:45) must observe the proper laws of ritual purity as handed down by "their fathers"![65] (cf. 11:47–48). θαυμάζω is in itself a neutral term; it can express "wonder," "astonishment," and "amazement" both in a positive or a negative sense, depending upon the context of its referent.[66] Why does Luke employ negatively the same term here that he uses for the crowds in 11:14b in what must there be a positive sense?[67] What is more, this is the same expression he uses of the crowd (ὄχλος) in 9:43b of their response to Jesus' casting out a demon (9:42) just after Jesus calls disciples and crowds alike an "unbelieving and crooked generation."[68] This usage may be merely coincidence, although certainly other words were at hand had Luke or his source(s) wanted to have employed them.[69] What we are suggesting is not a "theology of response" to Jesus based on θαυμάζω, but rather that in Luke's particular juxtaposition of this term here and its reflection of amazingly similar circumstances and responses in 9:37–43 we have discovered one of the several clues to the unfolding dynamics of *Jesus as a prophet* and the ever-increasing monolith of rejection of him among the dramatis personae. What we see here already is a hint that the Pharisees' response to Jesus, though critical, is fundamentally the same kind as the crowds' admiring stance. We have already seen this solidarity to be true for the disciples and the crowds despite their varying responses.

Verses 39–52 follow, with Jesus again taking the offensive in a series of "woes," three directed against the Pharisees (vv. 42–44) and three against the lawyers (vv. 46–52).[70] In v. 39 Jesus accuses the Pharisees of "greed" and of "wickedness" or "evil" (πονηρός); in v. 42 they have neglected "justice and the love of God"; in v. 44, of defiling, like the graves of the dead, "unknowing," helpless humans (ἄνθρωποι). In v. 46 the lawyers "load" folk with "unbearable burdens" which they themselves do not even begin to "touch"; vv. 47–48—they "build the tombs of the prophets," thus betraying their participation, their "consent" in the murder of "all the prophets" (v. 50) by "your fathers";[71] v. 52—they have "removed the 'key of knowledge'" and in so doing have not "entered" themselves and have "hindered" "those who are entering." The consequence: "the blood of all the prophets from the foundation of the world" is "required" (ἐκζητέω)[72] "from this generation" (v. 50)! "Yes, I tell you, it shall be required from this generation" (v. 51). On what basis can such brutal attacks be justified? What kind of involvement have the Pharisees-lawyers had with Jesus thus far in Luke's presentation that could spark such a reaction, especially in the light of their hospitality toward him here (cf. 7:36–50)? How can they, in particular, be made responsible for the death of all the prophets whose blood now cries out for vengeance "from this generation"? These questions will be pursued throughout the rest of this study (see esp. Part III.D). Several revealing trails, however, can already be detected.

First, Jesus' castigation of the Pharisees-lawyers (11:39–52) is fourth in a row of climaxing denunciations: *(a)* In 11:19a Jesus defends himself against the Beelzebul charge by asserting that the accusers' sons would be their judges for scattering Jesus' flock (11:23). *(b)* In 11:28 Jesus rebukes a woman from "out of the *crowd*" for facile praise not inbred with an obedience to the "word of God"; such admiration cannot be "blessed." *(c)* In 11:29–32 Jesus incriminates all the crowds, "[the folk of] this generation," of judgment at God's final court. The movement is from an anonymous smaller group to a nameless individual to an immense but still faceless crowd to a very tangible, distinct smaller group, the Pharisees-lawyers. All of these actors emerge to make their debut from the midst of the ever-present crowds.[73]

Second, five different types of response to Jesus are leveled to one evil, guilty generation: *(a)* "marveling" (θαυμάζω) approval (11:14b); *(b)* direct opposition (11:15); *(c)* challenging skepticism (11:16); *(d)* naive admiration (11:27–28; cf. 11:44b—οὐκ οἴδασιν); and *(e)* critical, "offended amazement" (11:38—θαυμάζω). In his parables of the return of the evil spirit (11:24–26) and concerning light (11:33) and the sound eye (11:34–36), Jesus colors all such responses as "evil" (11:26) and full of "darkness" (11:34b, 35).

Third, the "men of this generation" or "this generation" is that group or "evil" antagonist held responsible ultimately for these various responses to Jesus. In 11:14–54 this phrase is used no fewer than six different times,[74] all in contexts of opposition to Jesus where he in turn launches assaults of his own. In 9:41 we have already heard his epithet for "the crowd": "You faithless and twisted generation."[75]

Fourth, the Pharisees-lawyers are brought into special connection with this "evil generation" of the crowds through the opprobrium *at table* in 11:39–52. They are guilty of both defiling folk (ἄνθρωποι, 11:44) (i.e., causing them to be corrupt or "evil") and taxing folk (ἄνθρωποι, 11:46) with "overburdening requirements" which "hinder" or "prevent" (11:52) them from "entering" the redemptive history willed by the Wisdom of God (11:49–51). It must be assumed from the context that these folk constitute the public, those who would make up at least part of the crowds, since the Pharisees'-lawyers' encounter with folk at "the synagogues" and in "the marketplaces" is singled out (11:43; cf. 11:41: giving alms). In their "love" for the "first seats" in the presence of these folk (11:43–44) they are at the same time derelict in their "love for God" (11:42). No wonder they themselves have not "entered" (11:52).

Last, the Pharisees-lawyers are uniquely related to this history of the "sending" (ἀποστέλλω) of prophets and apostles by their incriminating involvement in the murder of these ambassadors (11:47–48). Twice it is stated that they are actively participating in the deeds "of your fathers" (vv. 47, 48). In other words, they are the "sons"[76] of previous forebears or generations who likewise demonstrated their "crooked perversity" by murdering Wisdom's special agents. Thus the Pharisees-lawyers are peculiarly forged to this evil generation. Though it is not stated that they are exclusively culpable, yet they are distinguished, arraigned, and indicted for the blood required of "*this* generation." One question immediately arises: If they are the "sons" linked so intimately with the "men" of "this generation," who and whose are "the sons" who serve as judges (11:19)?

To sum up: That Deuteronomistic tenet A is a ruling idea in 11:14–54 has now become clear. "This generation"[77] and particularly the Pharisees-lawyers (with their ancestors before them) form a mass of active opposition to God's redemptive history. We pass on to another passage to probe deeper into the identity of the characters in the plot we have unraveled so far.

2. **Luke 17:20–37.**[78] Luke 17:25 speaks of the necessity (δεῖ) of the Son of Man's (cf. v. 24) "suffering many things" and "rejection" "by" or "from this generation." This suffering and rejection are linked to Jesus' fate at least indirectly in two ways:

a. In 17:22–37 Jesus is speaking to his disciples about a subsequent revelation of the "Son of Man" (17:30) who in "one of his days" (v. 22) will appear "as lightning flashes and lights up the sky" (v. 24). This day his disciples will not "see" (v. 22b), even though "people [they] will say, 'Look, there it is' or 'Look, here it is'" (ἰδοὺ ἐκεῖ ἤ ἰδοὺ ὧδε, v. 23). This explanation follows the Pharisees' question of when the Kingdom of God comes (17:20), to which Jesus replies that it is not coming with "observable signs" when "they" will say, "Look, here it is, or there it is" (ἰδοὺ ὧδε ἤ ἐκεῖ)! The fact is, Jesus avers, "the Kingdom of God is already in your midst" (v. 21).[79] It is sometime between this presence "in the midst" and the latter "day" that the Son of Man must "first" "suffer" (v. 25).

The similarities of this first "presence" (17:20–21) to that of 11:14–54, esp. 11:29–32, should already be clear. There as here Jesus declares that the Kingdom of God is already present "upon them" or "in their midst" (11:20–21). There as here there are no objectifiable signs that lead folk to say, "Look, here (ὧδε) is the Kingdom," despite the fact that something greater than Solomon or Jonah is ὧδε (11:31–32). The very opposite is true; folk like the Pharisees in 17:20 are asking for a "sign." Jesus' exorcism which brings the Kingdom "upon them" is anything but convincing. Jesus' response is to state as in 17:20–21 that no "sign" points to this coming—except, that is, the "sign of Jonah." Whatever the precise meaning of this sign, it is certain that it is not an "observable" one of the type to which Jesus makes reference in 17:21.[80] More important, unlike the "men of Nineveh," "this generation" rejects this "sign of Jonah."

b. The "sign of Jonah" is linked directly to the Son of Man in 11:30. And this figure is linked indirectly to Jesus' presence in the midst of the crowds through the "something greater"[81] which is "here" (vv. 31b, 32b). Moreover, we have seen that this "sign" is clearly related to the request for a sign in 11:16. There through several arguments Jesus points to his own exorcisms as evidence of the Kingdom's presence (11:17–20). At the very minimum, Luke has Jesus himself make an indirect connection between his own active presence and the Son of Man's presence as the "sign of Jonah" with "this generation."

We conclude, then, that 17:20–37* is an instructive parallel to 11:14–54. In the former the Pharisees receive the same core of teaching that the crowds (including Pharisees and disciples) hear in the latter, while the disciples in 17:22–37 are granted teaching geared especially for them. As we shall see (Part III.D), this contrast will place in even bolder relief the Pharisees' definitive relationship to "this generation." For now we can conclude that "this generation" in 17:25 is responsible for the Son of Man's suffering rejection, and in 11:37–54 the Pharisees-lawyers are held uniquely responsible for "this generation's" guilt in the deaths of "all the prophets." Finally, we can anticipate what will congeal in Part III.C: the suffering "rejection" of the Son of Man (17:25) already resonates with the Passion predictions in 9:22 and 9:43b where the "Son of Man must suffer many things and be rejected" (9:22) "and be delivered into the hands of men" (9:44b). This second prediction is especially intriguing, since it is spoken to the disciples while their counterparts, the "unbelieving and perverted" generation, are looking on approvingly, "marveling at all that he was doing." We shall have to trace this path of murder ($\dot{\alpha}\pi o\kappa\tau\epsilon\acute{\iota}\nu\omega$, 9:22) to those "deaths" in 11:37–54 ($\dot{\alpha}\pi o\kappa\tau\epsilon\acute{\iota}\nu\omega$, 11:47, 48, 49), below.

3. **Luke 7:18–50.** Outside the Central Section, Luke presents a series of Q narratives and sayings interspersed with "L" material (7:18–35) in which the overall technique, from a literary-source point of view, resembles Luke's compositional style in the first half of the Central Section.[82] Jesus has finished his "sermon on the Plain" "in the hearing of all the people" ($\lambda\alpha\acute{o}s$, 7:1; cf. 6:17), healed by fiat the centurion's "servant" in the presence of the "crowd" ($\ddot{o}\chi\lambda os$, 7:9), and "raised" (7:14; cf. 7:16, 22; 9:7, 22) the widow's "only" (cf. 9:38!) son from the dead (7:12), accompanied by his disciples and a "great crowd" (7:11) and met by a "large crowd" (7:12b) in Nain. "All" are overcome by fear and glorify God by exclaiming that "a great prophet has arisen among us" (7:16b) and that "God has visited his people" (7:16c). John's disciples then tell their master "about all these things" (7:18), which must include at least the raising of the widow's son if not the healing of the centurion's servant and much more besides.

It is at this point that John, through dispatching two of his disciples, questions these acts as appropriate demonstrations of Jesus' unique authority as the "coming one"[83] (7:19–20). Luke emphasizes John's wavering by repeating his question verbatim: "Are you the one who is coming or shall we look for another?" (7:20 — 7:19). Jesus' answer indicates that the OT prophecies of the final salvation in Isaiah are being fulfilled in the very acts John is beginning to doubt (7:22).[84] Again it is only Luke who places special stress on these deeds by having Jesus perform them right before the eyes and ears of John's messengers (v. 21), including the casting out of *evil spirits*. The upshot of this action? "Go and tell [i.e., again, 7:22 → 18] John that which you have seen and heard." The following list in Luke includes the curing of the "blind," the "lame," "lepers," the "deaf [or mute]" (κοφοί; cf. 11:14), the "dead being raised," and the "poor" having "good news preached" to them. When we understand that John's disciples had already told him about Jesus' mighty deeds (7:18), we perceive that Jesus' instruction to them is a direct "slap in the face" to their master's questioning.[85]

John, "This Generation," and Jesus (7:18–30)

We have in 7:18–30 a development arrestingly similar to 11:14–54:

a. Jesus' reaction to a stance that places his signs on a par with those of other miracle workers or which in any way denigrates his special authority from the One who sent him is to launch his own challenge to that person's ability to "see and hear" what is taking place in their midst: "By whom do your sons cast them out? Therefore they shall be your judges" (11:19b). "But if it is by the finger of God that I cast out demons, then the kingdom of God has come upon you" (v. 20). "Blessed rather are those who hear the word of God and keep it" (v. 28). "For they repented at the preaching of Jonah, and look, something greater than Jonah is here" (v. 32). "Be careful lest the light in you be darkness" (v. 35). "You have taken away the key of knowledge; you did not enter yourselves and you have hindered those who are entering" (v. 52b).

b. In so doing, Jesus points to his own activity as the corroboration of his authority (7:21–23 — 11:19, 20, 22, 30–32, 33, 36, cf. v. 49). In both passages Jesus refers the challenger not just to his miraculous works but also to his preaching[86] ("the poor have good news preached to them," 7:22c; "the sign of Jonah, . . . for they repented at the preaching of Jonah," 11:29b, 32b; cf. 9:11b; 4:18–19). That is, the faulty hearing as well as seeing is assailed by Jesus (7:22 — 11:14, 27–28, 31–32, 33–36; cf. 7:1, 3, 7). The blind see, the deaf hear (7:21–22), the deaf-mute speak (11:14), the centurion hears (7:3), the *laos* hear (7:1) and see (7:16) and glorify God (7:16); yet John wants more proof (7:19–20), others want a sign (11:16), this evil generation wants a sign (11:29).

c. Jesus' offensive even calls into question the doubter's own blessedness in the presence of these acts of the final salvation. He lances his rebuff to John with, "Blessed is the one who takes no offense at me" (7:23). While in the following narrative Luke indicates that John is not judged "out of" the Kingdom by Jesus, yet the full force of this warning cannot elude even this one who is the "greatest of humankind" (7:28a).[87] As in 11:14–54, each and every one who cannot be fully satisfied with Jesus' performance finds her- or himself teetering on the precipice of unbelief over the caldron of judgment (cf. 11:19b, 22, 26, 30–32, 34–35, 47–52). To be offended by Jesus is nothing less than rejection of him as is illustrated so graphically by the Pharisees-lawyers (11:38) who "do not enter themselves" (11:52). We see then already that Jesus' response in both contexts brooks no partial belief. In the time of eschatological decision, indecision is tantamount to "falling away."

When these messengers depart, Jesus begins to challenge the same "crowds" (7:24) who have just witnessed Jesus' healing, exorcising, and rebuke to John and his disciples (7:21–23).[88] "What did you go out into the wilderness to observe?" (7:24). "Just what did you go out to see?" (7:25a). Jesus answers his own question: "A prophet? Yes, I tell you, even more than a prophet" (v. 26). John indeed is the eschatological "messenger" of Mal. 3:1 and Exod. 23:20 (cf. Isa. 40:3–6; Mal. 3:23–24 = ET 4:5–6) who is "sent" "before *your* face to prepare *your* way" (v. 27). Though from a surface reading it is not certain who the "your" is referring to in these apparently "enriched" OT texts, yet there is absolutely no doubt that John is considered by Jesus to be the forerunner of the final days of salvation, while Jesus considers himself to be activating the very presence of this salvation through his own preaching and deeds (7:21–23). In fact, "among those born of a woman no one is *greater* than John" (7:28a). But there is an immediate qualification. "The one who is least (ὁ μικρότερος) in the Kingdom of God is *greater* than he" (v. 28b). Praise for a "great" man—greater than all the prophets, to be sure—but there are these insignificant ones, these "least" who, in the Kingdom of God, are greater than John!

It is amazing how many exegetes resort to linguistic gymnastics to cushion Jesus' trenchant reproach (7:28b) into merely a distinction of the aeons[89] or an accenting of the decisiveness of the present decision,[90] or of the importance of entering the Kingdom over against respect for John.[91] The context surely supports all of these, and they can be included in the meaning of this statement. But it is precisely as we look at this broader context, which Luke has joined through the crowds and Jesus' mighty acts, that we cannot sidestep the issue that intrudes at every point: Just who is Jesus? What does one go out to see in him? (7:18, 19–20, 21, 22–23). Blessed is the one who does not take offense at him! Here lies the pulse of the whole section as Jesus presses the crowds with this question (7:24–27) and builds to his climactic conclusion in v. 28b. John and his disciples are clearly marching to a different beat.

Luke continues with a comment (v. 29) that leads the reader into the upshot of Jesus' words: "When all the *laos heard* and the tax collectors" too, "they declared God to be right, since they had been baptized with the baptism of John." As we have seen, "John's baptism" is what John had preached (3:3) in fulfilling his role as the one who "prepares the way of the Lord" (cf. κύριος, 3:4⁹²—7:19). In 3:7–18 before the crowds of Israel (v. 7), in a way parallel to Jesus' confrontation of the crowds in 7:24–35, John upbraids the whole lot as a "brood of vipers" and warns them to flee the ax that is already in the hand of the "mightier one" who "is coming." To submit to the "baptism of John," then, is to realign oneself with the works of the true "children of Abraham" (vv. 8–14) in preparing to meet the one who wields the "winnowing fork" of the eschatological judgment (v. 17). Now from these crowds a repenting *laos* is formed in solidarity already with Jesus by means of the baptism of John (3:21). The "baptism of John" therefore is that event in the "plan of God" (7:30) which forges "the children of Abraham" to their Messiah, Jesus, "the anointed one" (3:15), the "Lord" (3:4b). The governing idea throughout, again: Who is Jesus? What does one go out to see in him?

The lights and shadows in this behavior portrait of John in 3:7–18 could not be in sharper contrast to the one in 7:18–28. In the latter he is the epitome of indecision, doubt, and unbelieving in-submission. The *laos* have just declared God to be right as they hear the voice of Jesus proclaim the fulfillment of the "greater" Kingdom of God in his own ministry (7:27–28), while John and his disciples wonder whether Jesus is the "one coming." They need a "sign," while the *laos* and the tax collectors (7:29; cf. 7:16), like the Gentile centurion (7:3), respond at once to the "greater one" in their midst.⁹³ John in fact mirrors the "questioning" that the *laos* had earlier concerning his own status (3:15), whereas Jesus' questioning the crowd (7:24–26) prompts immediate belief from the *laos*. Luke's observation in 7:29, then, is no chance remark that might also save face for John.⁹⁴ It is a reference back to the very ones, including tax collectors (3:12, 15, 18), who now in contrast to John embrace the good news and repent.

Luke provides another foil (7:30). Now antagonists appear, the same characters we have already met in 11:37–54—"the Pharisees and the lawyers." For these have openly rejected the "purpose" or "plan of God concerning themselves"⁹⁵ by refusing to submit to this baptism. Like the Pharisees and lawyers in 11:37–54, they do not fit in with the acts of salvation, willed by God, that entail those who are even now present directly before them (7:21–23). Luke has us see again that the crowds (7:24) are comprised of various groups, including the Pharisees whom we have already encountered in a similar setting (11:14–54; cf. 17:20–21, 22–37).

With this clash of opinion forming the springboard to the conclusion of Jesus' address (vv. 31–35), it is all the more striking that (just as in 11:14–54) Jesus reduces all the varied responses to one generation of scornful rejection. He has just spoken of all folk born of a woman (7:28) and now continues with these same "folk." "To what then shall I compare the folk of this generation or what are they like?" (v. 31). Jesus again answers his own question (cf. vv. 24–28): "They are like children (παιδίοι) sitting in the marketplace (ἀγορά) and calling to one another:

> 'We played the flute for you, and yet you did not dance;
> We sang a dirge, and yet you did not mourn' (v. 32).

Jesus immediately applies this parable (γαρ, v. 33) in vv. 33–35: "John the Baptist has come (ἐλήλυθεν)[96] not eating any bread nor drinking any wine and *you* say, 'he has a demon.' The Son of Man has come (ἐλήλυθεν) eating and drinking and *you* say, 'look, a glutton and a tippler, a friend of tax collectors and sinners.' Nevertheless, Wisdom is declared to be right by all her children." "This generation" is charged with linking John with evil and ranking Jesus with the shysters and riffraff of society. But what is the justification of such an accusation on Jesus' part, and who more precisely holds John and Jesus in such contempt? Furthermore, what is the point of the sharp contrast again with the "tax collectors" (v. 34; cf. v. 29) and the addition of "sinners" (v. 34) and "Wisdom's children" (v. 35)?

John, Jesus, and the "Children" of This Generation (7:18–35)

The parable of "the children in the marketplace" (7:31–32) is notoriously difficult to decipher.[97] Yet in its present context the main lines are clear enough:

a. The particle οὖν ("therefore") in v. 31 is crucial to the flow of the entire passage 7:18–35. Jesus' statement in vv. 31–35 purports to capsulize his word to the crowds (7:24–28). And, unless Luke's comments on the crowd response in vv. 29–30 are an awkward intrusion to his own unfolding story, we should expect vv. 31–35 to summarize or at least harmonize with them.

b. Jesus' application of the parable[98] links the "children" to "the folk of this generation" on the one side (v. 31) and to the "you say" on the other (vv. 33–34). But the "you say" can refer to no one other than the same crowds of vv. 24–28 and vv. 29–30. In other words, any cohesion in meaning will have to refer consistently to these crowds. It is they who are "the folk of this generation."

c. The odium of John's "having a demon" (v. 33a) is ironically the same stigma attached to Jesus in 11:15 by "some" from the crowd. Do we have any hints from Luke's story pointing to a group or groups behind the charge in 7:33? In a passage curiously parallel to 7:30, Luke speaks of "the scribes" who as part of the cast of challengers in 20:1–47 did not submit to the "baptism of John" since they did not "believe him" (20:1–6). Just before this incident, Luke has drawn a contrast between the leaders of the *laos,* including "the scribes," and the *laos* themselves who "hang on to every word" of Jesus (19:47–48, cf. 7:29–30). And in 20:6 the *laos* are liable "to stone" their leaders, since they were "convinced that John was a prophet" (cf. 20:19, 26, 45–47; 22:2). From 11:53 we know that Luke equates the "lawyers" with the "scribes"[99] (cf. 11:45, 52), so that along with their association with the Pharisees in 5:21, 30; 6:7; and 15:2, we can safely link the lawyers of 7:30 to the same category, "scribes," in 19:47—20:47. Thus in both 7:29–30 and 19:47—20:8 the lawyers-scribes are set opposite the *laos* who did submit to the "baptism of John" (cf. 3:21). Furthermore, when it is reemphasized that in both 7:18–28 and 11:14–54 Jesus' reaction even to benign uncertainty from some of the crowds is to align the whole generation squarely against the salvific plan of God (7:18–23, 28b; 11:14–26, 29–36), then it is tempting to take Luke's comment in 7:30 as divulging for the reader the primary antagonists of this "will of God." Nevertheless, direct evidence for the reproach of "having a demon" is lacking; it is only highly possible that such a connection is in mind.

d. In contrast, our evidence to pinpoint the "censors" of 7:34 could hardly be more direct. In 5:30 when the Pharisees and "their scribes" eye the disciples' table companions, they "murmur" (γογγύζω) to the disciples, "Why do you eat and drink with tax collectors and sinners?" More pertinently for the Central Section, in 15:1–2 the Pharisees and the scribes "murmur" (διαγογγύζω; cf. 19:7) when they see "the tax collectors" or "sinners" "drawing near to *hear*" (cf. 9:35!) Jesus as "this man receives" (cf. 9:11) "and eats with them" (15:2). Whoever else might be included in Jesus' statement in 7:34, within Luke's developing plot the main allusion is to the Pharisees-scribes (lawyers) of 7:30.

In sum, we have encountered what appears to be a most unusual shift in Jesus' stance toward John. From a stinging rebuke of his doubt and equivocation which culminates in 7:28b, Jesus then excoriates the crowd for refusing to accept John's sending (v. 33a; cf. 7:27a). What is more, it is most probable that Jesus is aligning John's mission with his own in vv. 33–34[100] as he points to the religious leaders who are not able to stomach Jesus' eating and drinking with tax collectors and sinners. How this apparent retreat from a rebuttal is to be interpreted is brought to light by v. 35.

e. In v. 35 Jesus singles out another group of "children" who declare "Wisdom to be right" (ἐδικαιώθη). There are at least three reasons to make the conclusion irresistible that the tax collectors and *laos* of v. 29 are designated here. First, Luke has just stated that it was they who "declared God to be right" (ἐδικαίωσαν, v. 29). We know from Jesus' parable in 18:9–14 that the tax collector was one of several types of "immoral" people (cf. 18:11) who, though considered to be sinners (18:13b) by the Pharisees in Luke's story, are those who repent. As we have seen, this larger group who repent at the preaching of John are called the *laos* by Luke in 3:15, 18, 21; (cf. 1:17, 77). Thus Jesus makes exception to his sweeping denunciation in vv. 33–34 by referring to those very ones of the *laos* in the crowds who are *not* now saying, "He has a demon . . . a glutton and drunkard." Second, Jesus' charge in v. 34 already includes within it a dichotomy between the crowds who are accused (the "you say") of opposing Jesus and John on the one side and the "tax collectors and sinners" with whom Jesus is aligned on the other (i.e., v. 34b). It is difficult to escape the impression that *Luke's* contrast in vv. 29–30 is meant to comment directly on *Jesus'* contrast in vv. 34–35. Third, since in vv. 29–30 the *laos* and the tax collectors are aligned with John's mission of 3:1–22, these "sinners" are the ones who do accept John's sending of no eating and drinking (v. 33; cf. 1:15b). Thus again the contrast of v. 35 points to a group within the crowds who exonerate God precisely for this sending of John which includes within it preparation for "the coming one," the Son of Man who *comes* eating and drinking with them as tax collectors and sinners (v. 34). To this can be added that in 11:47–51, as in 7:35, it is "Wisdom" representing God's sending of the prophets and the apostles (cf. 7:29–30) who is opposed by the scribes of the Pharisees. And there as here, these latter are linked to the guilt of "this generation" (11:50–51; cf. 7:31).

The "children of the marketplace" (vv. 31–32) thus reveal a generation that is monolithic in its rejection of John and Jesus and yet, at the same time, divided in its response. Jesus speaks to the crowds "about John" (vv. 24–28). The subject of his address never changes as he uses the wavering response of John to undertone the whole generation's response to himself. They are like children who cannot decide on the tune they want to play. "This generation" cannot march to the beat of the ascetic John and the reveling Jesus, even as now John and his own disciples are decidedly out of step. Jesus thus colors John's wilderness sending as concordant with his own mission (7:33) but declares in no uncertain terms that his doubt now is a sign of the whole generation's discordant response. His demand for a convincing "demonstration" is at base no different from the whole generation's perverted scorn of John's and Jesus' behavior. Yet paradoxically in the midst of these children are other "children" who are clearly "dancing" to the tune of the Son of Man.

Consequently in 7:18–35 we have a dynamic of the crowd's response closely parallel to 11:14–54. One group that is doubting is used by Jesus to label the whole mass as fundamentally wrong in its response. Just as a request for a sign is portrayed as essentially evil (11:16 → 11:29), so the expression of doubt is essentially offense (7:19–20 → 7:23). And just as the desire for a sign on the part of others (11:16) leads to the charge "This generation seeks a sign" (11:29), so one specimen of offense (7:23, 28b) shadows the whole lot with the charge of offense (7:33–34). It is not mere accident that Jesus uses the stinging illustrations of offense in 7:33–34 to parrot John's own offense in vv. 18–23, 28. For, as we have already observed, partial response is tantamount to an evil response, and an evil response on the part of some stains the response on the part of all.

It may be objected at this point that v. 35 appears to contradict tenet A in excepting a group of "children." How can the principle of solidarity in disobedient obduracy possibly be supported here? We recall that it was characteristic of especially Essene Judaism to regard their own communities as the exceptions to the rule of a mass rebellion to God.[101] Their own generation can be perverse, while they themselves stand alone as the upright folk of the true covenant religion. Moreover, we have already discovered (9:18–50) how the disciples confess Jesus' Messiahship, receive classified information on Jesus' death, experience special revelation on the mountain and yet are branded a "crooked and faithless" generation. So too, although "the crowds" in 11:14–54 marvel in approval over Jesus' mighty works, nevertheless Jesus lumps the whole generation together as evil. On the contrary, it is particularly characteristic of tenet A to assert mass rebellion and evil precisely at the point of a mixed or varied response among the masses.[102] Even with certain faithful responses, all share at base in the same rebellious state.

We have just such an assertion in 7:18–35. Despite "Wisdom's children" who declare God to be right, Jesus still declares all of them, the whole generation, to be wrong. Whereas in 9:37–50 it is Jesus' disciples who spark Jesus' condemnation, and in 11:14–54 the "others" who require a sign, in 7:18–35 it is John's disciples who spur such a judgment of the whole. Now, however, Luke's comment in 7:29–30 gives added weight to the truth that within this unbelieving generation of "children" there are the "children" who do submit and follow Jesus' authority—they justify God in the Jesus who is "here." In short, Luke's programmatic statement points to a pattern of acceptance as well as rejection that we shall notice throughout the Central Section (see esp. Part III.C and D). Yet, equally true, as Luke's story goes on to relate only too well, in the end all are numbered among the "lawless" (e.g., 22:37; 23:13).[103]

Before summarizing our results for 7:18–35, we need to probe deeper into Jesus' image of "children." It is curious that Jesus likens his generation to "children" ($\pi\alpha\iota\delta\iota o\iota$, v. 32) *after* referring to the "one who is the least" ($\dot{o}$ $\mu\iota\kappa\rho\acute{o}\tau\epsilon\rho o\varsigma$, v. 28), on the one hand, and *before* speaking of "Wisdom" and her "children" ($\tau\acute{e}\kappa\nu\alpha$, v. 35), on the other. Is Jesus' simile of v. 32 perhaps a catchword connection or can we detect an inner coherency in Luke's composition? The response of "the one who is least" is extolled as "better" or "greater" than that of John and his disciples. If it could be shown that John's response in 7:18–28a is contrasted to the image of children in v. 28b, then both a linkage with the parable and the special significance of "children" in the parable would not only be strengthened, but also John's response as definitive for all the "children" would assume a greater potency and consistency. In short, the cohesion of the passage as we have presented it would be substantiated all the more.

We have a close parallel context of the dynamics of response in 9:37–50. In 9:37–43 the inability of Jesus' disciples to perform a "mighty work" in the midst of the crowds is a bald contrast to the powerful healing by Jesus in v. 42. As we have seen, the disciples' response is to argue among themselves which of them is the "greatest" (v. 46).[104] If ever piping was not met with dancing, it is here with the disciples' bizarre behavior! Just as significant, Jesus' reply is to take a "child" ($\pi\alpha\iota\delta\iota\sigma\nu$; cf. 7:32), place him or her by his side (cf. 7:34), and tell his disciples that if they were responding fittingly to Jesus' authority (i.e., "in my name," v. 48), they would be aligning themselves with such "little ones." For, as Jesus continues, it is in reality these "little ones," these who are "the least" ($\dot{o}$ $\mu\iota\kappa\rho\dot{o}\tau\epsilon\rho\sigma s$!) "among you all,"[105] who are "great" (9:48b; cf. 7:28b).

If John and his disciples challenge Jesus' "greatness" by doubting his authority (7:18–28), so Jesus' disciples discredit Jesus' "greatness" by promoting themselves over against his authority (9:46–50; cf. 1:32).[106] If John and his disciples cannot accept the "mighty works" of Jesus which "glorify God" in their midst (7:16, 18, 21–22), so Jesus' disciples do not properly receive Jesus' divine display of magisterial power in their midst (9:43, 46–48). Jesus' procedure after John's messengers leave (7:24) is to instruct the crowds about his own authority, using the example of "children" (7:35, 31–32). Similarly, Jesus uses the child to teach his disciples what his authority is all about (9:47–48). Even more intriguing, as Jesus utilizes the response of John and John's disciples to color the response of the whole crowd ("this generation," 7:31–34), so he uses the response of his own disciples to do the same for "this generation" (crowds, 9:40–41). Finally, in both passages Jesus is the Son of Man who "has come" (7:34) or has been "sent" (9:44, 48).

It is not much of a leap to conclude that "the one who is the least" in 7:28b, like "the one who is the least" in 9:48b, is the figure of the child to denote those among the crowds (7:29, 35) or the disciples (9:48) who are humbly submitting to Jesus' authority. Direct proof is lacking. But we submit that all the parallels in this closely knit pattern of authority and response are not happenstance, that they in fact represent the same Deuteronomistic point of view of tenet A. Consequently, the *laos* and the tax collectors of 7:29 are concrete examples of the childlike, those who are "the least" but who are "greater" than John in the Kingdom of God (7:28b).

We have then the example of the "child" as a foil to John's response in 7:28 which Jesus takes up again in 7:32 in order to illustrate the malignant effect of both John's and the Pharisees' response upon the whole generation of confused and divided "children." Though the image of the "child" is not univocal in its connotation, its denotation is consistent throughout as "the folk of this generation" upon whom the authority of Jesus presses its claim. Thus, whether response to Jesus is skepticism or, as the dynamics of the passage make clear, repudiating scorn, the net effect of Jesus' speaking "about John" is to demonstrate the mass of resistance to Jesus. And yet if the Pharisees have their "children," so does the "Wisdom" of God (7:35; see 12:54—13:9 below, and Part III.D).

Our results thus far: In 7:34 the Son of Man's penchant for hobnobbing with "tax collectors and sinners" is elevated to a paragon of offense for this generation. What is now transparent also is that the "marvel" of shock of the Pharisee in 11:38 is one of a kind with the "scandal" in 7:34. And with the antitheses in 7:29–30 and 7:34–35 we can now assert what we did for 11:14–54: the Pharisees-lawyers (scribes) stand in a unique relationship to "this generation" as those most representative of its opposition to the salvation which is "sent" by the "Wisdom of God" (11:49–51). While in 7:18–35 they are not rebuked explicitly for their evil influence as in the latter passage (11:42–52), yet the notion of their leadership endangering the salvation of the whole generation is already here forcefully expressed. Jesus refers to himself as the Son of Man who is ridiculed to the ranks of the "swindlers" and "scum" of Israel's covenant society. Like the undesirables with whom he "carouses," Jesus' "eating and drinking" exposes in the one instance what his unwashed hands divulge in the other: he himself is a "defiled" "glutton and drunkard, a companion of tax collectors and sinners." As we shall see, it is this charge by the Pharisees-scribes which is pivotal in the Central Section's depiction of the whole loaf of this generation spoiled by the "leaven" of the Pharisees (12:1). Suffice it to say that already by 7:18–35 the response ascribed to these Pharisees-lawyers is imputed to "the folk of this generation."

We therefore have the following pattern of response in 7:18–35 and 11:14–54:

1. Jesus' works of healing and exorcism are met with incredulity and disenchantment on the part of some in the crowds (John and disciples, 7:18–23; "others," 11:16).
2. This dubiety is treated by Jesus as a blatant affront to his authority (7:23–30; 11:20–26).
3. This challenge on the part of some in turn is transferred by Jesus to the crowds as a challenge on the part of the whole generation (7:31–34; 11:29–36).
4. Out from this resistance emerge the Pharisees-lawyers as the vanguard or prime movers behind "this generation" to climax Jesus' offensive against the "offense" of "this generation's" twisted response (7:33–34; cf. v. 30; 11:37–54).

We may wonder whether there is not a line that leads from a sample of the evidence (skepticism on the part of some) to an arraignment of the accused (the whole "crooked" generation) to the root cause of the crime (the scornful influence of the Pharisees-lawyers). For now, we discern that in 7:18–35 the Pharisees-lawyers are not unmasked as the instigators but as the orchestrators of the children's refusal to "dance" or to "mourn" in the marketplace. We can schematize the dynamics:

equivocating *disenchantment* (some)	→ perverted *resistance* (whole generation)	→ scornful *influence* of leading antagonists (Pharisees-lawyers/scribes)

Jesus' reaction:

offensive vs. a direct challenge to his authority by disenchantment (some)	→ *charge* of an evil perverted generation (the crowds)	→ direct *reproach* to the offense of Jesus' "eating and drinking" (Pharisees-lawyers)

"This Generation" at Table (7:18–50)

It is noticeable at once that the diagram above does not allow for the discrepancy that in 7:24–35 Jesus is addressing the crowds when he assails the scornful attitude of the Pharisees-lawyers, while in 11:37–54 he is at table with the Pharisees-lawyers in one of their homes. But, in fact, a Pharisee does invite Jesus to his home for a meal (7:36–50) following Jesus' address to the crowds (7:24–35) as in 11:14–36 → vv. 37–54.[107] That this table scene[108] forms a parallel to 11:37–54 and thus a "one act" dramatization of the crowds' response will become evident as the scene unfolds.

As soon as Jesus has "reclined at table," "suddenly a woman in the city who was a sinner" is behind him, weeping at his feet (7:37, 34b). When the Pharisee sees this (v. 39a; cf. 11:38) he takes offense because Jesus allows a ritually defiled "sinner" to touch him.[109] If this man were a *prophet*, he would have the special perception to avoid contact with her (v. 39b; cf. 7:16). In other words, he is "a friend of tax collectors and sinners"; his "eating and drinking" is defiled (cf. 7:34; 11:38). And the woman? She is without doubt one of "Wisdom's children" (7:35). For she extends to Jesus the hospitality, the receiving due to the one before whom childlike repentance is the only proper response. Like the child of 9:47b, she is at Jesus' side, submitting to Jesus' prophetic authority, receiving him and the One who sent him. Luke goes on to tell us that this woman has her "sins forgiven" (vv. 47, 48). Unlike the crowds in 7:18–35 and 11:14–36 who do not repent before the prophet greater than Jonah (cf. 11:29–30, 32), this "sinner" is one with the "tax collectors" and the *laos* who "declare God to be right" because the "greater" or "mightier" one is "here" (3:16; 7:16, 21, 28, 29; 11:20, 21–22, 31–32). The disparity between her response and the negative criticism of Simon the Pharisee is so conspicuous by v. 40 that Luke hardly has to mention the "reception" that Simon had failed to give Jesus (vv. 41–46). But when he has Jesus chide him for not receiving him into his home with the proper acts of hospitality (vv. 38, 44–46), the foil of 7:29–30, 34–35 could not be more boldly paraded in front of our eyes.[110]

We can now extend our parallel between 7:18–35 and 11:14–54: Not only are the Pharisees-lawyers singled out in the crowds as the epitome of "this generation's" opposition to Jesus, their resistance is pinpointed to their offense at Jesus' disregard for ritual purity at table. Even more, this offense is displayed in the homes of Pharisees in the midst of their own *habūrah* table fellowship.[111] Whatever the particular history of tradition of these table scenes, it is clear that as narrator Luke could not have picked a more telling setting to impress his readers with the stark anti-thesis of response between the Pharisees-lawyers and "Wisdom's children." And though the intensity in this contrast has not begun to reach the proportions of 11:37–54, still we see the potential for "this generation's" twisted hostility toward the Son of Man writ large on this earlier stage of the drama. We can enhance our diagram of response:

equivocating *disenchantment* (some)	→	perverted *resistance* (whole generation)	→	scornful *influence* of leading antagonists (Pharisees-lawyers)	→	*offense* of this generation unmasked *at table* (Pharisees' *habūrah* meals)

Now is the time to present a tabloid summary of the parallels we have observed between 11:14–54 and 7:18–50:

Luke 7:18–50

1. Equivocating Disenchantment of *Some* (John the Baptist and his disciples) (7:18–23) in Crowds (7:24) → Erroneous, misguided Resistance of *whole* Generation (7:31–34) → Leading Antagonists in *Pharisees-lawyers'* Offense (Jesus' Eating and Drinking, 7:34, 39; cf. v. 30) Exemplified in Fellowship *Meal* in a *Pharisee's* House (7:36–50).

2. Jesus' *Offensive* to the Crowds (7:24–30) Against a Direct Challenge to His Authority by *Disenchantment* of Some (Baptist and disciples) → *Charge* of an *Evil, Perverted* Generation of the Crowds (7:31–34) → *Direct Reproach* to the Pharisees-lawyers' *Offense* Expressed by Pharisee *at Table* (7:39–47).

3. Healings and Exorcisms Sufficient Sign of *Authority* (7:21–23; cf. vv. 28–30, 1–17).

4. "Children," i.e., "the folk of this generation" (7:31–32) *Dominated* by Pharisees-lawyers (7:33–34).

5. *Wisdom's Children* (*Laos*, Tax collectors, "Sinners," 7:35, 30, 34) versus *Pharisees-lawyers* (7:30, 33, 34).

6. A Great *Prophet* Arisen (7:16)—*Laos* of Crowds Visited by God (7:16, 18–23; cf. vv. 26–28, 29) → Defiled Eater and Drinker (7:34, 39)—*Pharisees-lawyers of Crowds* (7:30, 36–50).

7. *The Son of Man* has come (7:34).

8. John the Baptist is *demon-possessed* (7:33).

9. Deaf-mutes hear (one of the *healing* signs, 7:22).

10. The Folk of This Generation in the *Marketplace* (7:31–32) *Influenced* by the *Pharisees-lawyers* (7:33–34; cf. 7:30).

Luke 11:14–54

Equivocating Disenchantment of *Some* ("Others") (11:16) in Crowds (11:14) → Erroneous, misguided Resistance of *whole* Generation (11:29–36) → Leading Antagonists in *Pharisees-lawyers'* Offense (Jesus' Eating and Drinking, 11:38) Exemplified in Fellowship *Meal* in a *Pharisee's House* (11:37–54).

Jesus' *Offensive* to the Crowds (11:29–36; cf. vv. 20–26, 27–28) Against a Direct Challenge to His Authority by *Disenchantment* of Some ("Some," 11:15; "Others," 11:16) → *Charge* of an *Evil, Perverted* Generation of the Crowds (11:29–32) → *Direct Reproach* to the Pharisees-lawyers' *Offense* Expressed by Pharisee *at Table* (11:37–54).

Exorcisms Sufficient Sign of *Authority* (11:14–23).

"Unknowing folk" (11:44) "of this generation" (11:50–51; cf. v. 29) *"Defiled"* (11:44) and *"Hindered"* (11:52) by Pharisees-lawyers.

Wisdom's Messengers (all the prophets) (11:47–51) versus *Pharisees-lawyers* (11:47–51).

The Crowds Marvel (11:14)—They have Kingdom of God "Come upon you" (11:20) by a *Prophet* greater than Jonah (11:32) → Defiled "Eater and Drinker"—*Pharisee* of the Crowds Marvels (11:38; cf. v. 37).

The Son of Man "is here" (11:30–32).

Jesus is *Beelzebul-possessed* (11:15).

A deaf-mute speaks (one of the *exorcism* signs, 11:14, 20).

The Folk of This Generation (11:31; cf. vv. 29–30, 32, 50, 51) in the *Marketplace* (11:43–44) *Influenced* by the *Pharisees-lawyers* (11:43, cf. vv. 44, 46, 50–52).

4. **Luke 12:54—13:9.** One further passage needs to be considered in the light of the Deuteronomistic tenet A. A quick perusal of its context will be helpful here.[112]

We left Jesus' dinner invitation in 11:37–54, with the scribes and the Pharisees "acting in a very hostile manner"[113] (11:53) to Jesus and "waiting to catch him at anything he might say" (v. 54). Luke then tells us immediately that "in the meantime" (12:1) "the crowds" who marvel in 11:14 and are "increasing" in 11:29 are now "gathering" by the "thousands" (i.e., "myriads"), even to the point of "trampling upon one another" (12:1). In the midst of this confusion Jesus concentrates "first" on his disciples, cautioning them to be on their guard against the "leaven of the Pharisees which is hypocrisy" (ὑπόκρισις, 12:1b!). What follows is an oscillating audience of *crowds* and *disciples* for Jesus' primary focus. That is to say, "the crowds" remain the backdrop throughout all of 12:1—13:9 in such a way that they never seem to be out of range of Jesus' speech even when he is concentrating upon the disciples (cf. esp. 12:41). Through this fluidity in audience Luke gives dynamic expression to both a solidarity as well as a distinction between these and other groups, an identification and yet a growing separation of the crowds and the disciples which we have already seen to be characteristic of the other passages we have reviewed.

In 12:54 "the crowds" capture Jesus' attention. He has just warned the disciples in the sternest of terms to be ready for the coming judgment of the Son of Man (12:40): "That servant who knew his master's will, but did not make ready or act according to his will, shall receive a severe beating" (v. 47). Now in even harsher words Jesus castigates the crowd for their dullness in discerning "the appearance" of "this present time" (τὸν καιρὸν . . . τοῦτον, v. 56). They "know" how to interpret such characteristic "signs" of the weather as cloud formations and prevailing winds. But they act completely dense to the "signs," the "prevailing winds" of their own day. They are, in fact, "hypocrites" (ὑποκριταί, 12:56)!

Several characteristic signs of Deuteronomistic tenet A are already observable:

a. "This present time," though certainly capable of various levels of time reference,[114] at the level of Luke's story of Jesus cannot but refer to the time, the period in which the audience, the crowds, are now faced with decision from the Jesus in their midst. Verse 57 makes it absolutely clear that they are "on their way" (ἐν τῇ ὁδῷ) to a judgment that brooks no turning back (cf. 9:62). Only one course is now expedient, namely, "coming to terms," "reconciliation" with their accuser (12:58). It is again made clear, in 13:1–5, that "unless you repent, you will all likewise perish" (vv. 3, 5). That is, they will be dragged to the "judge" and to the "bailiff" of

12:58, who will throw them into prison. The accuser is in their midst. The thought thus closely parallels 11:29–32, where "this evil generation" is "deaf-mute" (cf. 11:14) to the "sign" right in their midst ("here"). There as here, their perception is clouded by a darkness (11:33–36) that callouses them to the "preaching of repentance" (11:32 — 12:13–21, 35–48, 49–53, 54—13:9; cf. 3:3, 18; 7:29–30). "This present time" is hence a temporal equivalent for "this generation." What the first emphasizes as the point of decision the latter emphasizes as that group of people for whom this time of accountability has indeed arrived (cf. 11:50–51 — blood is "required of this generation"). Both are bound together by the presence of the "sign" (11:29ff. — 12:54–56), that is, the prophet "greater than Jonah" (11:32), the "accuser" who accompanies them to the judge (12:58; cf. 11:19b). His presence defines "this present time" for "this generation."

b. The *tertium comparationis* in v. 56 seems to be that just as they "know how to discriminate" the natural signs, they should know how to discriminate the activity in their midst. But yet "they do not know how to"! Therefore the question is, "Why do you not know how to discriminate the present time?" (v. 56b). These crowds are unable because of lack of knowledge. They fit perfectly the description of the "folk" who are defiled by the Pharisees because "they do not know" (11:44) and thus have the "key to the knowledge" (11:52) of entering the Kingdom removed from them (11:52). That there is an allusion in 12:54–56 to a group such as the Pharisees-lawyers is strengthened by Jesus' following question: "Why then do you not judge *for yourselves* what is right?" (v. 57).[115] The point is that they are ignorant (unknowing) and thus unable to judge the present time because someone else is exercising or has control of their own discriminating abilities. Someone is *hindering* them (11:52)! Verse 57 is thus both rebuke and plea. It is an admonishment to open their eyes (cf. v. 54; 11:33–36; 7:22, 25, 26) *to see* for themselves, to exercise their full discerning powers lest the light in them be darkness (11:35)! We may not have sufficient evidence at this point to tie the Pharisees-lawyers to this passage; yet influence by others must be intended here, since a tension is set up by "for yourselves" in conjunction with the crowds' own ability to judge natural signs *for themselves* (vv. 54–56).

c. Further weight is given to our suggestion that the Pharisees-lawyers are alluded to in 12:54–57 by the epithet in v. 56a, "hypocrites."

Now Jesus has just warned his disciples to beware of the "leaven of the Pharisees, which is hypocrisy" (12:1). The crowds are excoriated for the same behavior. Their "unknowing" inability to judge is adjudged no better than those who possess the "key to knowledge" (11:52) and yet "did not enter themselves." Their failure to discern for themselves is fundamentally no better than those who pride themselves in judging who and what is "clean" and "unclean" (7:39; 11:38, 39, 40) and yet defile others like "unseen graves" (11:44). And while they may be able to discern the more obvious signs in nature (cf. 17:20), their incapacity to discriminate the signs of the "present time" is at heart no better than those who bask in the praise of "folk" and yet "neglect justice and love for God" (11:42–43). They are as blind to the Prophet-Messiah Jesus in their midst as are the Pharisees. In essence, by 12:56 they have become what the Pharisees-lawyers are already. Their behavior betokens a response no different at base from the hypocritical demeanor of the Pharisees. They are in-*deed* "this evil generation" (11:29) from whom the blood of all the prophets will be required (11:50–51). The Pharisees who emerge from the crowds and the crowds themselves all stand together as one great lot (tenet A).

And now as if to press home this point even further Luke relates that "at that very time" (ἐν αὐτῷ τῷ καιρῷ!)[116] there were "*some* present" or who "had arrived" who told Jesus about the Galileans' "blood bath" at the hands of Pilate (13:1). Jesus' response is to wipe out any hierarchy of moral achievement; all who do not repent stand under the one judgment —"*all* perish" (13:3, 5). It was characteristic of the beliefs of at least certain Pharisees that a catastrophe was punishment for sin.[117] Jesus discounts any such notions at once; "all" are as sinful as their acknowledged "sinners" (cf. 7:29); repentance before the accuser "at that very time" is what is all-significant. The time for the fruit of repentance (13:3–9) is almost over; the crowds are already "on the way" to the courts (12:58–59). We are reminded of John the Baptist's preaching concerning the indispensable "fruit of repentance," that is, an immediate decision coupled with decisive action, which is a gaping omission on the part of the crowds (3:7–14). The gardener is still at work, fertilizing the tree, but the next year it will be cut down (13:8–9).

It is to be noted again that the point of view of a certain group (13:1) from within the crowds is an occasion for Jesus to equalize all the crowds into one mass of unrepentant folk. The "fig tree" (v. 6) undoubtedly symbolizes the entire nation or people of Israel (cf. Mark 11:13; Hos. 9:10; Joel 1:7).[118] Thus Jesus demonstrates by his parable in vv. 6–9 that the "all" in vv. 3, 5 is referring to the crowds before him and indeed the whole nation. A calamity experienced by some (vv. 1–2, 4) is a ready illustration of the calamity awaiting all[119]—unless of course they repent! We have here exactly the Deuteronomistic warning of the prophets—utter doom for the whole nation unless they turn back to Yahweh.[120] And though there may be a faithful remnant or various groups exhibiting a repentant spirit, nevertheless, unless the masses, the nation as a whole, repent, the whole nation faces judgment and destruction. All are implicated in its guilt.

Conclusions

We have discovered features of the Deuteronomistic tenet A in Luke 11:14–54 and 12:54—13:9 as well as in 9:1–50. We have also sighted its distinctive panorama in 17:20–37, though its individual features there are more veiled than boldly defined. The beginning, the center, and the end of the Central Section display its unmistakable contours. In addition, we have charted 7:18–50, where the landscape is identical and its lines exhibit maplike pointers to the territory ahead. Disciples (9:1–50), smaller groups from the crowds (11:14–55; 12:54—13:9), Pharisees (17:20–37), and John the Baptist and his disciples (7:18–50) all serve as graphic reliefs of the entire twisted terrain. Most especially, the bearing of the Pharisees-lawyers toward Jesus on the one hand, and toward the crowds on the other, has veered toward a constant reading on our compass as Jesus proceeds to Jerusalem: the response of "this generation." Finally, we have stopped twice at the dwellings of the Pharisees themselves, there to observe at table the most salient characteristics of this evil generation's blinders to the one critical signpost in their midst: the Jesus who is "here." It is now time for us to view the Central Region of Luke's Gospel from another vantage point, Deuteronomistic tenet B.

B. God Has Sent Jesus as a Prophet to Israel, like All the Prophets Before Him

> You shall say to them, "Thus says the Lord: If you will not hearken to me, to walk in my law which I have set before you, and to heed the words of my servants the prophets whom I send to you urgently . . ."
> (Jer. 33:4–5a [LXX])[121]

Although we are demonstrating that, independent of the fourfold Moses-Exodus typology of Deuteronomy, the profile of Jesus in the Central Section closely resembles that of "all the prophets" (see introduction to Part III), nevertheless it will become clear at the level of Luke's plot that any attempt to sever Jesus' prophetic sending from his sending on the mountain (9:28–36) is artificial.

Sent to Mediate the Divine Will

> The Lord, the God of their fathers, sent urgently to them by the hand of the prophets and by sending his messengers.   (2 Chron. 36:15a)[122]

1. **Luke 9:46–48.** We have already seen how the mountain revelation forms a focal point in the story of Jesus' sending to Jerusalem (see Part II). Yet when 9:46–48 is treated as a separate tradition apart from its present context, the self-consciousness of Jesus' ministry as a whole is crisply expressed: he has been sent (ἀποστέλλω, v. 48) to be received (δέχομαι, v. 48). Jesus is the object of God's sending; the authority to represent the divine will directly, as in "thus says the Lord," is unequivocally present here.

2. **Luke 10:16.** This verse, which articulates conversely the same awareness of Jesus' own sending to be received as in 9:46–48, will be treated again in the context of the sending out of the Seventy(-two), in 10:1–15, below. It is sufficient to point out here the direct connection back to the mountain sending of 9:28–36. "The one who hearkens to you hearkens to me, but the one who rejects you rejects me, and the one who rejects me rejects the One who has sent me." "Hearken to him!" (9:35).

3. **Luke 11:49–51.** This Q tradition encapsulates the whole historical dynamic of the Deuteronomistic view (tenets A—D). At table with the Pharisees, Jesus identifies himself with the entire line of those "prophets and apostles" sent (ἀποστέλλω) to Israel by the Wisdom of God.[123] The phrase προφῆται καὶ ἀπόστολοι is unique in the NT as well as in Jewish literature and may summarize all the messengers of God during the OT period (προφῆται) and their successors during the intertestamental period (ἀπόστολοι).[124] Whatever the particular history of this wisdom tradition, it is important to grasp the way that Luke has integrated its viewpoint into his overall picture of the activity of Jesus.[125] Followed by v. 52, this saying forms the climax of a growing resistance of "this generation" to Jesus' sending.[126] And when Luke adds in v. 53 that as Jesus "went out (ἐξέρχομαι) from there the scribes and Pharisees began to act in a very hostile manner . . .," he may be indicating that the journey of this rejected prophet continues on, under the closest surveillance, but undistracted to its destined denouement.

4 and 5. **Luke 13:31–35*** (→ **19:44**). By joining the *locus classicus* in the "L" source of Jesus' understanding of his own mission and fate (13:31–33)[127] with the ensuing judgment oracle of Q (vv. 34–35), Luke ties the Deuteronomistic conception of a prophet's sending directly to his thematic development of the journey. Though Jesus' tandem retorts (vv. 32–33) to certain Pharisees' advice (v. 31) present a host of exegetical puzzles, the present text can be interpreted logically without recourse to hypotheses about later interpolations/excisions.[128] In v. 32 Jesus shuns the temptation to follow a human scheme for the remainder of his journey sending. As in 4:40–44, Jesus *must* continue on "today and tomorrow" through "other cities also" (4:43), healing and casting out

demons (cf. 9:1, 42, 49; 11:14, 15, 18, 19, 20!). Not until "the third day" does he "consummate" this sending (cf. 4:18; 7:21–22). "Indeed"[129] (v. 33), precisely because of this sending he "must journey" (δεῖ . . . πορεύεσθαι) onward "today and tomorrow and on the next day, because it is not possible that a prophet should come to an end outside Jerusalem." Whether v. 33 is an independent saying, a part of vv. 31–32 originally, or Luke's own comment to fuse the latter to vv. 34–35,[130] it forges the Deuteronomistic conception of a prophet's tragic end to an unbreakable chain both backward to 9:51 with the mountain sending (9:31; cf. 9:52–53; 10:38; 13:22) and forward to Jesus' arrival in Jerusalem (14:25; 17:11; 19:28). As J. H. Davies, D. Gill, and others have demonstrated, πορεύομαι[131] (with compounds) functions as a technical term to describe the resolute determination of Jesus in 9:51 to reach his goal. Far from contradicting v. 32, the πορεύεσθαι of v. 33 graphically restates in *spatial* imagery the resolve expressed *temporally* in v. 32 as a crowning "on the third day." Jesus says in effect to the Pharisees, "Not I but you go away from here, for my course is already set by the One who has sent me."

Verses 34–35 articulate the Deuteronomistic viewpoint as poignantly as 11:49–51. But now, with the juxtaposition of προφήτης in v. 33 with προφῆται in v. 34, Jesus' sending as a prophet to Israel is made explicit (vv. 33b, 34a). As in 11:49–51 Jesus is aligned with the whole company of prophets whom "Jerusalem" has killed and with "those sent to her" (τοὺς ἀπεσταλμένους πρὸς αὐτήν)[132] whom she has stoned (v. 34, tenets A—C). What follows in v. 35a is the inevitable consequence of this dynamic of rejection: Jerusalem is left abandoned[133] (tenet D).

But while this devastation for the sin of the whole nation in rejecting Jesus is generally noticed, the role of the Pharisees in provoking the judgment pronouncements in 11:49–51; 13:34–35; and in 19:41–44 is often passed over. We can isolate the following parallels:

a. *The Pharisees.* In all three passages the Pharisees stand over against Jesus in a relation of hindering his sending. In 11:44 they are defiling folk and preventing/hindering them from entering the history of salvation in their midst (v. 52); despite their hospitality in inviting Jesus to a meal, he calls them killers of the prophets (and implicitly of himself) as they build their tombs (vv. 47–51). In 13:31–33 Jesus' rejoinder to the Pharisees' plan for his course is met now with an intensity incommensurate with a friendly concern on their part. It is in fact a riposte to their attempts to veer him off course and it leads immediately and logically to a judgment on the *whole* nation (or generation) precisely as we have it in 11:47–51. Now Jerusalem, or the whole nation, is the killer of the prophets (13:34). In 19:28–40, after Jesus goes on (ἐπορεύετο) before the throngs and sends (ἀποστέλλω) two of his disciples ahead to prepare for his descent into Jerusalem, as he draws near (v. 37) and the whole company of disciples ring out the messianic praise of Ps. 118:26 (117:26), "some of the Pharisees" tell Jesus to restrain his disciples (v. 39). Jesus' answer is again inconsistent with any attempt to protect him from possible recriminations.[134] When his disciples no longer extol him, then "the stones will cry out" (v. 40). Thus his retort to their resistance is again joined with a pronouncement of guilt over the *whole* nation (vv. 41–44). The doom is sealed. There is now no longer any promise of seeing Jesus in the future as in 13:35. In all three passages, then, we find the resulting schema: *Pharisees'* Hindering of Jesus' Sending → Judgment Oracle by Jesus Upon the *Whole* Nation.

    b. Jerusalem. In each of the three passages Jerusalem is pinpointed as the center of a disobedient, even hostile opposition to the gestures of repentance offered by God's ambassadors, the prophets. In 11:47–51 Jerusalem is alluded to in v. 51: whatever the exact identity of the prophet Zechariah, he lost his life between the altar and the sanctuary (ὁ οἶκος).[135] The Temple, with its sacrificial system, forms the omega point for the whole "bloody" history of the prophets (cf. 13:1).[136] In 13:35 Jerusalem is the killer and stoner of these ambassadors; its "house will be left abandoned." The phrasing here undoubtedly echoes the Deuteronomistic Jer. 7:10–11; 12:7; and 22:5 (e.g., "I have forsaken my house, I have abandoned my heritage," 12:7a; see LXX). In Jer. 22:5 (LXX), οἶκος represents successively the king's palace, the whole nation (descendants/ lineage), and the city of Jerusalem (cf. vv. 6–8).[137] That "house" can symbolize a people through a particular structure or dwelling (i.e., metonymy/synecdoche) is well known (cf., e.g., Acts 7:46–48).[138] In the present Lukan context the referent of "your house" would appear at one level to be the nation as a whole; Jesus has journeyed across it with a divine commission only to be rejected by it as were all the prophets before. Yet Jerusalem's Temple may well lie behind the imagery of its "house," especially if there are grounds for linking this verse not only back to 11:51 but also forward to 19:41–44. In 19:41–44 as Jesus weeps over the city (v. 41) he addresses it (v. 42) as one whose "children" (v. 44) will be ravished because "you" did not know the time of "your visitation" (ἐπισκοπῆς σου). This thought of a visitation comes most interestingly right at the point when Jesus with the host of disciples visits Jerusalem and he himself enters the Temple which should be "my house, a house of prayer" (19:46a) but instead is a "den of thieves" (v. 46b; Jer. 7:11!). Jerusalem (19:41–44), and even more precisely its Temple (vv. 45–46), is the focal point of this rejection of its royal visitor.

Is it possible to link Jesus' statement in 13:35b—"You [Jerusalem] will not see me until you say, 'Blessed is he who comes in the name of the Lord'"—to his "triumphal entry" when the disciples acclaim him as, "Blessed is the King who comes in the name of the Lord" (19:38)? Two major objections by commentators are lodged: (1) The quote in 19:38 does not reproduce 13:35b exactly: "The King" is inserted before 19:38 continues on in doxology. (2) The people of Jerusalem do not herald Jesus, but his disciples do. Therefore Luke cannot intend to link these two passages; 13:35b must be referring to the eschatological salvation of the coming Messiah or the return of the Son of Man.[139] Yet this kind of reasoning fails to take account of the Deuteronomistic thinking that binds these three passages. First, the quotation of Ps. 118:26 is close; the insertion of "the King" fits well with the probable *Sitz im Leben* of the psalm's earlier cultic background. This psalm was evidently used as a greeting to the king as he approached the Temple to worship God.[140] Second, the fact that Jesus, proclaimed as the King, does go immediately to the Temple to reclaim its true status as the house of prayer—a place of worship—can surely not be accidental. Last, exegetes overlook the symbolic value of the Pharisees as representative of the whole disobedient nation. As we have demonstrated (see tenet A), disciples, admiring crowds, table hosts, active opponents—all form the stiff-necked front of "this generation." In other words, the prophecy of 13:35b can be and is fulfilled when some of Jerusalem's children (the disciples) do hail him in the words of the psalm. That Jerusalem stands for the whole nation in 13:35 and 19:41–44 is beyond question. That 13:35b can be fulfilled only by the literal inhabitants of the city precincts must then be rejected as illogical. It should further be remembered that a multitude, including the *laos,* in the not too distant future will cry out for Jesus' crucifixion in 23:13–25.[141] Therefore Jerusalem in all three passages is the fulcrum of a stiff-necked rejection of the prophets; that its Temple is also singled out is probable, given the explicit mention of its precincts in 11:51 and 19:45–46 as well as the resonance of "house" in 11:51; 13:35a; and 19:46.

c. Judgment. In all three passages Jesus' sending to Jerusalem is bound up directly with the fate of judgment for the whole nation. Luke's mention of the Pharisees' determination to trip up Jesus in any possible way (11:53–54), coming immediately after Jesus' pronouncement upon "this generation," leads inescapably to the conclusion that his death at the hands of "this generation" (cf. 17:25) results in the final, definitive judgment upon the whole history of Israel's stubborn disobedience. In 13:34–35 this connection could not be made more explicit. Jesus' sending to Jerusalem (13:32–33) is at the same time the rejection of his attempts to gather Jerusalem's children (vv. 33b–34). The result: "Your house is left to you forsaken." And finally in 19:41–44 as Jesus' journey (v. 28) to

Jerusalem nears its end, the nation's blindness to his visit is the cause[142] of Jerusalem's devastation (vv. 42b, 44b). The parable of the returning nobleman (19:11–27) clears up any doubt about the significance of the royal visitation of 19:44: The citizens "hated him and sent a delegation after him saying, 'We do not want this man to reign as king (βασιλεῦσαι) over us'" (v. 14). The result: *Not one stone will* be left upon another (v. 44a; cf. 19:27).

The development within the three passages is now clear: The Pharisees' resolve to catch Jesus in 11:53–54 is demonstrated in 13:31–35. Jesus' warning of judgment upon "this generation" in 11:47–52 is now made into a categorical pronouncement of a *fait accompli* in 13:35a. Nevertheless, as is true with the Deuteronomistic warning by the prophets of the coming judgment, there is the built-in "unless you repent" (13:35b). Jesus continues on his journey, eating with Pharisees (14:1–24), gathering the lost of Israel (14:25—15:32), warning of judgment (16:19–31), teaching disciples (17:1–10), healing (17:11–17; 18:35–43), pleading for repentance (17:22—18:14), and so forth. But as he nears Jerusalem the force of the intractable opposition to his authoritative sending becomes at the same time all too apparent and overbearing—Jesus weeps. The frustrated yearnings of 13:35a can issue only in mourning.[143] As with Jeremiah (8:18ff.; 15:5ff.), Jesus' sorrow wells up from the springs of an inevitable disaster that *must* befall the prophet's own beloved but perfidious people. Though the time of repentance is not over (19:47—21:38), Israel's rejection of the prophet Jesus is already an assured outcome.

Our results yield the following schema: Guilt of All Israel Exhibited at Their Temple (11:47–51) → Judgment Begins at This Vortex of the Crime (13:35a)[144] → Judgment Spreads to the Whole City (Nation) (19:41–44).[145]

6. **Luke 13:22–30.** From 13:31–33, 34–35, it is clear that when Luke[146] says in v. 22 that Jesus "was passing through (διεπορεύετο) towns and villages, teaching and making journey toward Jerusalem," he is linking this teaching and journeying to the sending of the prophet in 13:32–33, on the one side, and to the sending from the mountain, on the other (9:31 → 9:51). As we shall see, the whole of the Central Section is characterized by this teaching function; and as this pericope unfolds, it becomes certain that when the inquirer addresses Jesus as "Sir"/"Lord" in v. 23, he is also addressing the "lord" (v. 25) of the banquet room of vv. 24–30. For it is this "lord" of the household who, like Jesus in v. 22, teaches in their streets (v. 26b). It is this teacher who controls the door into the banquet hall of salvation: "I tell you, I do not know where you come from; depart

from me, all you workers of iniquity" (v. 27). This teacher is the voice of the divine will; in his ministry of teaching (and eating and drinking!) in the streets is concentrated the life-giving voice of God—"Hearken to him."

To sum up: These six passages link the distinctive Deuteronomistic view of the prophets' sending to utter the voice (will) of God with Jesus' sending from the mountain on his journey to Jerusalem. The beginning, the middle, and the end of Jesus' journey portray him as sent as a prophet in the long line of all the prophets before him. We have the following chain:

9:31 → 9:46–48 → 9:51 → 10:16 → 11:47–51 → 13:22–30 → 13:31–35 → 19:41–44.

Sent to Instruct and Admonish the People in God's Will

Thus says the Lord: Go and say to the person of Judah and to those who dwell in Jerusalem, "Will you not receive instruction to hearken to my words?" (Jer. 42:13 [LXX])[147]

It has often been observed that in Luke 4:14—9:50 the *works* of Jesus are presented, whereas in 9:51—18:14 the *words* of Jesus in parables, instruction, table discourses, individual logia, and so forth, are given.[148] Although this is fundamentally correct, the fuller implications remain hidden until placed within the perspective of Jesus' commissioned sending and hence within Luke's pattern of authority.

First of all, it is true that Jesus is predominantly a speaker in this section: 81.1 percent of the verses in 9:51—18:14 contain utterances by him, mostly in longer and shorter addresses to crowds or larger groups. A high 88.6 percent of the core of the Central Section, 12:1—17:10, is composed of these sayings, a telling indicator of its peculiar pulse.[149]

Second, the concentration of stories of mighty works is significantly reduced. Whereas in Jesus' Galilean ministry (4:14—9:50) seventeen pericopes treat a "mighty work" of Jesus, in 9:51—19:44 only six pericopes do so (10:17–20; 11:14–23; 13:10–17; 14:1–6; 17:11–19; 18:35–43). Moreover, these accounts are scant, hardly more than an introduction to a longer address or a pronouncement in a controversy setting. For example, Luke merely states the bare facts in one quick verse of Jesus' casting out a demon from a deaf-mute (11:14). It is as though a longer story has been whittled down to the roughest and hence most general of outlines: type—result—crowd reaction. Immediately a protest is lodged (vv. 15–16) and Jesus launches into a mounting offensive in 11:17–36 which, as we have seen, climaxes in Jesus' tirades against the Pharisees at table (vv. 37–54). The mighty event is clearly in itself of secondary importance, serving rather to demarcate the lines for the ensuing battle over Jesus' authority.[150] This same function of the "mighty work" is found again in 13:10–17 and 14:1–6 which in the first instance provokes a heated skirmish over Jesus' healing on a Sabbath with an official of a synagogue (v. 14), while in the latter this same issue prods a multipronged challenge on Jesus' part against his censorious table hosts, the Pharisees-lawyers (see tenet C, below).[151] Who are the true leaders of Israel? Who possesses the authority to interpret Israel's law? These are the questions posed both to Jesus' audiences and to Luke's readers in his Central Section.

In this connection it is significant that the phrase "mighty works" (αἱ δυνάμεις) occurs not only at the beginning of the Central Section but also at its end (10:13; 19:37). As Jesus sends out the Seventy(-two) disciples, he pronounces judgment over three cities of Galilee for their failure to repent at the display of a mighty work by Jesus in their midst (10:13–15). These works are signs of Jesus' authority as they bring the powerful presence of God's reign upon those around him. But they are not expressions that in and of themselves are to be relished as the essence of Jesus' authoritative presence; they are not to be viewed as infallible proofs of Jesus' identity which in themselves epitomize his whole mission. This is clear from the episode following in 10:17–20 as the Seventy-(-two) "mighty workers" return. Their joy at the sight of such awesome power over the evil powers (v. 19) should not be savored for the raw authority that it obviously demonstrates. Neither in establishing their own authority nor in Jesus' are they to take delight. Rather, their elation should be based entirely on the objective purpose that these works are to effect: the saving presence of God's reign. Yet, they are palpable signs of the mission of bringing life which alone is to be the touchstone as well as the sine qua non of Jesus' identity and authority.

We have already noticed the way in which this understanding of mighty works is structured by Luke in 11:14–36. The request for the sign in v. 16 is completely rejected by Jesus as a proof of his authority and in fact is turned around in its purport by him to mean something entirely different. His prophetic word which demands repentance is the sign, the quintessential demonstration of his authority. It is that powerful display of the something greater than the preaching of Jonah and the wisdom of Solomon which makes Jesus' authority absolutely unparalleled (vv. 29–32). The thought here is precisely the same as in 10:13–15, 17–20, 21–24; the Galilean cities have missed or rejected this mighty word of Jesus (cf. 10:5, 9, 10–12 esp.); they have refused to repent even with the display of mighty works (10:13–15; cf. v. 9a). Many prophets (like Jonah) and kings (like Solomon) desired to see and to hear that which the Seventy(-two) have just "seen" and "heard" (10:24). Now, according to 10:20, 21–23, what this group has just seen and heard is the revelation of Jesus' identity as the Son of the Father—the Son who reveals the Father (10:22). Jesus exults (v. 21) that these emissaries in their powerful mission have seen and heard the true identity of Jesus.[152] He is the Son. "All things" have been given by the Father to him. And these things have been revealed to the Seventy(-two) (i.e., to infants, v. 21). The connection back to the revelation of the authoritative voice of God upon the mountain in the person of Jesus, his Son (9:35), is unmistakable. Both speak of a mighty revelation of the Father occurring through the Son; in both, this revelation is witnessed by Jesus' disciples. And in both, the image of the child presents the posture necessary to seeing and hearing this revelation.[153] It is this revelation that the cities of Galilee have not "seen and heard," and which the Twelve disciples have not received in 9:1–50. The relation of Jesus' mighty works to his sublime authority has not been grasped by these.[154] Therefore when the throng of disciples in 19:37 in the fervor of the royal messianic praise of Ps. 118:26 exult and bless God on account of or because of[155] all the "mighty works" which they had "seen," the reader should be wary of understanding these disciples as those "children" who have had the veil of his authority lifted.[156] In fact, we have already seen that such an understanding of "power" leads Jesus to the charge of a faithless and perverse generation (9:37–50) whose house is left forsaken (13:35a, b).

Third, the function of the mighty works in the Central Section thus confirms what their paucity has already divulged: Jesus is the authoritative voice of God, the teacher par excellence. This portrait can be highlighted further by a comparison with the pattern of Jesus' sending in the Galilean phase, 4:14—9:50. At the beginning of Luke's prelude to the journey (9:1–6), mighty works appear as Jesus gathers the Twelve and sends them out with power ($\delta\acute{u}\nu\alpha\mu\iota\varsigma$) and authority ($\acute{\epsilon}\xi o\nu\sigma\acute{\iota}\alpha$) "over all the demons" to proclaim the Kingdom of God and to heal the infirm (v. 2). This we know is exactly what Jesus himself does in 9:11.

But this bifocal thrust in 9:1–6 is clearly a continuation of what Jesus has been doing all along, from his first encounter with the demoniac in the Capernaum synagogue (4:31–37) to his "raising the dead" in 8:40–56. It is in fact around Capernaum where the crowds, astounded by the authoritative word of his teaching which also drives out the evil spirits (4:31–32, 36–37), in a "desert place" try to prevail upon Jesus not to leave (v. 42). But he counters that he "must preach the good news of the Kingdom of God to the other cities also, because for this reason I have been sent" (v. 43b). Luke adds (v. 44), "and he continued preaching in the synagogues of Judea." In 6:17–19 as Jesus prepares to deliver his manifesto of the Kingdom to his disciples and to the *laos* who have come "to listen to him" (6:17–18), "all the crowd were seeking to touch him because power (δύναμις) was coming forth from him and healing everyone" (v. 19). Later, Jesus takes the Twelve along with many women on a "preaching" (8:1) tour through "towns and villages, proclaiming the good news of the Kingdom of God." Again, demoniacs are healed (8:26–39), those with insufferable maladies are cured (vv. 42b–48), and with his powerful word even the waves and the wind are at his beck and call (vv. 22–25). Luke 8 provides a cross section of the whole Galilean period; teaching (vv. 4–21) is mixed in with his mighty deeds (vv. 22–25, 26–39, 40–42a, 49–56, 42b–48), all in the framework of the itinerant preacher (vv. 1–3) sent to the cities of his countryfolk. There is no doubt that Jesus is fulfilling the prophetic anointing of Isaiah 61 and 58 which he was sent to do (4:18–19).[157]

But now in Luke 9 the focus shifts perceptibly. After the mountaintop transfiguration we no longer hear of Jesus preaching the Kingdom of God.[158] This role is given essentially to the disciples whom Jesus sends out (9:59–60; 10:1–12, 13–15; cf. 9:52–53). They become the heralds of the Kingdom "in every town and place in which he was about to come" (10:1b). Jesus journeys instead as the teacher,[159] now preoccupied with defending his interpretation of the Law with lawyers, synagogue leaders, and Pharisees; instructing his disciples in this "law" and admonishing them to faithful adherence to this "law" in the midst of "temptations to sin"; teaching the people in their synagogues and in their streets along the way, warning the crowds to heed his voice lest they be shut out of the Kingdom of God. Thus for more than one-third of the Gospel, Luke presents a teaching journey of the great mouthpiece of God which culminates in the Temple as Jesus is ensconced there by the fervor of the *laos* as the *teacher*[160] of Israel (19:48; 20:1, 2, 6, 8, 9, 19, 26, 45; 21:38; 22:2). He has the authoritative word against which the chief priests, scribes, and elders (cf. 9:22) can only protest, "Through what authority do you do these things? Who gave you this authority?" (20:2). "He stirs up the people, teaching throughout all Judea, starting from Galilee up to this place!" (23:5). The voice of the mountain indeed thunders the answer to this challenge against the one whose "words" "will never pass away" (21:33): "Hearken to him."

Fourth, the parenetic emphasis in 9:51ff. illustrates from yet another angle the decisive turning point of the mountain of revelation in the picture of Jesus. It already can be observed that Jesus is the great pleader to Israel in two large tableaux, 12:1—13:9 and 14:25—17:10. In the first, Jesus has just excoriated the Pharisees-lawyers at table, when in the meantime myriads of the crowds are pressing for Jesus' attention. He turns to these multitudes, alternately admonishing disciples (12:1b–12,

35–48, 49–53) and crowds (vv. 13–20, 54–56, 57–59; 13:6–9) to heed his words and beware of the leaven of the Pharisees (cf., e.g., vv. 8–9, 41). In the second, Jesus again has just warned the Pharisees at table (14:1–24) when he repeats the same admonition to "many crowds" (14:25–35) and then, after a defense of his "company" (15:1–32),[161] focuses upon his disciples (16:1–13). Following yet another challenge by the Pharisees in 16:14 in which Jesus repeats the warning of 14:15–24 in even bolder terms (16:16–31), he again turns to his disciples to exhort them to faithful following lest they stumble helplessly over the great obstacles in their midst (17:1–10).[162] Thus in these two settings and elsewhere Jesus is sketched in the Deuteronomistic shades of the prophet who not only delivers and expounds upon the law of God but also exhorts Israel to faithful adherence. "For it is easier for heaven and earth to disappear than for one jot of the Law to become invalid" (16:17).

We have thus shown how the Central Section exhibits in the form of Jesus' words the unique pattern of Jesus' sending through the didactic and parenetic content of this section. We now turn to its overall form or structure. It has been pointed out that the Central Section is framed or buttressed by the Deuteronomic "pillars"[163] of the Shema, 10:26–27 (Deut. 6:4–5), and the Decalogue, 18:20 (Deut. 5:6–21); in both instances the leading question is: "What shall I do to inherit eternal life?" What is not always noticed is that in both instances one of the leaders of the *laos* (a lawyer, 10:25; a ruler, 18:18) addresses Jesus as "teacher" (διδάσκαλε). The issue is life and the question is whether Jesus has the words of life for the covenant people. How one receives the life of God is the pulse of the whole middle portion of Luke (10:25—18:30).

In 9:52–62; 10:1–24 Luke presents journey episodes that point to Jesus' distinctive authority. His mission to Jerusalem presses greater claims upon would-be participants than the ministry of the mighty Elijah (9:57–62, esp. vv. 61–62). In 10:1ff. he has the authority to send out his own ambassadors with an eschatological message that brooks no rival. Any resistance must realize that it will be more tolerable for Sodom on the day of judgment (10:12). Indeed anyone who rejects his childlike ambassadors (v. 21) rejects not only Jesus the Son but also God, the "Father," who sent him (10:16, 21–24 → 9:35!).

Now in v. 25, quite abruptly, a "great one" in the Law, one of the "wise and learned" (v. 21!) scribes stands before Jesus to test his credentials. If Jesus is a true teacher of Israel, he should be able to answer questions that concern the life of God. Jesus' response is to point him immediately to the Law (v. 26). The Law is life! But the crux of the matter is, "How do you read it?" (v. 26b). The right understanding makes all the difference. The lawyer returns by quoting Deut. 6:5 and adding Lev. 19:18. To this,

Jesus replies: "You have answered correctly. *Do* this and you will *live.*" It would seem that each has passed the other's orthodoxy test. But in fact the lawyer is not satisfied as he suddenly finds himself on the defensive. He has to demonstrate that his "reading" is correct as against that of Jesus, so he seizes the offensive once again. In what follows it becomes evident that the special bone of contention between them is, "Who can do the Law?" Who are the covenant people? For whom is life available in the Law?

As Jesus tells his parable of the uncompassionate priest and Levite, the lawyer cannot possibly escape the sobering conclusion: Israel's leaders are not doing the Law. They do not possess the love required by the Law not only for God but also for the neighbor. Not only this, Jesus' parable becomes a paradox. It is the nonelect foreigner, the hated Samaritan, who loves the neighbor as himself and thus does the Law. The lawyer's question is thus turned inside out. It is not a question of circumscribing the elect to define the locus of the life-giving Law but rather of defining who does the Law to circumscribe the locus of the life-receiving "elect."[164] But more than that, it has now also become obvious to the lawyer that Jesus is demonstrating his authority to give *halakah* that is pitted against Israel's most revered interpreters of the Law—himself and his colleagues. Jesus, not he or even the priests and the Levites, bears the authority to interpret and reinterpret the Law. "Go and *do* likewise" is the command of "Thus says the Lord." In short, 10:25–28, 29–37 pose the same issue as we found in the miracle-controversy stories in 11:14–54 and esp. 13:10–17 and 14:1–6 (Pharisees-lawyers): Who are the true leaders of Israel?

As the Central Section progresses, Jesus' journey is studded with this theme. Only those who hearken to him, who *hear* the *word* of God in him and *keep* it, inherit the *life* of the covenant promises in the Law: Mary "was *listening* to his word"; she "has *chosen* the better part" (10:39b, 42). "Blessed rather are those who *hear* the word of God and *keep* it!" (11:28). For you "pass by justice and the love of God; these you ought to have *done* without neglecting the others" (11:42) (the very pillars of Deuteronomy, esp. Deuteronomy 1—11). "Blessed is that servant whom his master finds so *doing* when he comes" (12:43). "And that servant who knew his master's will but did not *make ready* or *do* according to his will shall receive a severe beating. . . . Of whom much is given, will much be *required"* (12:47–48). "But he will say, 'I tell you, I do not know where you come from, depart from me all you *workers* of iniquity'" (13:27). "The one who has ears to *hear,* let that one *hear"* (14:35). "Now the tax collectors and sinners were all drawing near to *hear* him" (15:1). "I have decided what to *do*. . . . The master commended the dishonest steward because he had *acted* shrewdly" (16:4, 8). "They have Moses and the prophets, let them *hear* them." "He [Abraham] said to him, 'If they do not *hear* Moses and the prophets, neither will they be convinced if someone should *rise from the dead'"* (16:29, 31). What we have here is the voice of one who claims to utter the very word of God, a word that claims to interpret Moses and the prophets aright, that not only stands in line with them but also consummates them through the raising up of this voice from the dead. What Luke presents, then, is eschatological *halakoth* from the one who not only is conscious of being a prophet but who also fulfills their utterances by reinterpreting them over against Israel's leaders. Jesus' voice thus demands a doing of the Law in the most profound sense of doing the eschatological will of God; his voice presents a hermeneutic claiming nothing less than the authority of the author of the Law.

Consequently it is when the ruler[165] of 18:18—again following upon the example of children entering life (18:15–17)—asks the Teacher about inheriting the promise of life through the Law that Jesus not only directs him to its commandments but also challenges his understanding of Jesus' authority: "No one is good but God only!" (v. 19b). And as the episode unfolds, it again becomes clear that Jesus' interpretation of the Law holds the answer to life. For the "one thing" the ruler lacks is submission to the voice of God in Jesus which would place himself as the "poor" before God and follow Jesus to Jerusalem. Jesus declares the will of God directly: "What is impossible with humans is possible with God. . . . Truly, I say to you, no one has left . . . who will not receive manifold more in this period, and in the coming age eternal life" (vv. 27–30).

In 18:31—19:44, as in 9:51—10:24, the journey episodes appear again in rapid succession. Jesus' authority to heal and to reveal the eschatological will of God is again at stake (18:35—19:44): "Your faith has saved you" (18:42). "Today salvation has come to this house, since he also is a son of Abraham" (19:9). "I tell you, . . . from the one who has not, even what that one has will be taken away. But as for these enemies of mine, who did not want me to reign over them, bring them here and slay them before me" (19:26b–27). "I tell you, when these are silent, the very stones will cry out" (19:40). "And they will not leave one stone upon another in you, because you did not know the time of your visitation" (19:44b).

The overall structure of the Central Section, then, is made up of journey incidents at the beginning and at the end that stress the sending of Jesus to Jerusalem as the ultimate prophetic speaker for and consummator of God's will in the Law and the Prophets and of eschatological *halakah* that spans the Deuteronomic pillars of 10:25–28 and 18:18–23.

Therefore, the contour as well as the content of the Central Section displays the telling imprint of the Deuteronomistic view of the prophets who are sent to instruct and exhort the people to obedience to God's will. Again we discover a prophet who claims unique authority in this role as one sent from the mountain of revelation.

Sent to Call the People to Repentance Lest They be Destroyed by the Judgment of God

> Yet the Lord warned Israel and Judah by all his prophets and every seer, saying, "Turn from your evil ways and keep my commandments and my statutes in accordance with all the Law which I commanded your fathers and which I sent to you by my servants the prophets." But they did not hearken but hardened their neck stiffer than their fathers . . . until the Lord removed Israel out of his sight, as he had spoken by his servants the prophets.
> (4 Kgdms. 17:13–14, 23a)

This classic Deuteronomistic[166] compass of Israel's history and the warning of repentance through Yahweh's spokespersons, the prophets, sets the tone for much of Jesus' and his disciples' activity in the Central Section. We have established the theological as well as the literary contexts of this activity in the light of tenet A,[167] so that a rehearsal of this evidence will not be necessary here. We now present briefly Jesus' calls to repentance.

1. **Luke 9:37–43a**. Jesus' mournful outburst in v. 41 is at the same time a warning against an unbelieving and crooked generation that has not repented. The Twelve's "preaching the gospel and healing everywhere" (9:6b) had been met with enthusiastic reception (9:7–9, 10) but not with the true repentance that Jesus has demanded (10:13–16). It is a generation that will force Jesus' "exodus" from it in the immediate future (9:41b).

2. **Luke 10:1–16.*** Not only Jesus but the Seventy(-two) disciples are also portrayed as calling Israel to repentance. In 10:1 Jesus commissions them and sends them on ahead (cf. 9:52) into the towns and places where "he himself is about to come" (10:1). Luke thus directly links this sending to Jesus' own sending to Jerusalem. In this respect the Seventy(-two) are cast in the same mold as the "messengers" of 9:52–53 who are to "make ready" for Jesus' reception in a Samaritan village (cf. δέχομαι, 9:53; 10:8, 10; 9:48).

But Luke gives a far more detailed sketch of what these emissaries were to accomplish. In the form of an address (10:2–16), Jesus stresses that their mission is the eschatological gathering of the people of God. The towns that do not receive Jesus' representatives are to know that though the Kingdom of God has come "near" to them, yet it has not come "upon them" (v. 6b) for salvation from the coming judgment. "I tell you, it shall be more tolerable on that day for Sodom than for that town" (v. 12). The "greeting of peace" to the households (vv. 5–6) is therefore not simply the customary salutation upon entering a household or the greeting along the way (v. 4b) but the eschatological imparting of peace (cf. Luke 19:42; 2:14, 29; Acts 10:36). Not to receive the missionaries' word is to unleash a judgment so horrendous that the very shaking off the dust as the prophetic sign already generates the eschatological abandonment of the Kingdom from these houses (Luke 10:11; cf. 13:35a).

This interpretation is supported and illumined by Jesus' "woes" in 10:13–16. Looking back to his ministry in the three Galilean cities of Chorazin, Bethsaida, and Capernaum, Jesus mournfully pronounces the eschatological judgment upon these towns. "Alas for" Chorazin and Bethsaida is the deep cry of the anguish of divine judgment that has not been lifted, because these folk have not repented (μετανοέω, v. 13). Not even the "mighty works" that were performed and that the Seventy(-two) are to continue (v. 9; cf. vv. 17–20) were sufficient signs of the authority of the Prophet. The Gentile towns Tyre and Sidon, citadels of godless debauchery, will fare better "in the judgment" than this stubborn folk. "You shall be brought down to Hades!" (v. 15). We meet again the unmistakable contours of tenets A, B, and D. It is true that the message of Jesus and his prophetic band has been transmuted from the call back to the covenant oath into the dynamic presence of the Kingdom of God. But as we have seen above, this Kingdom is conceived as the fulfillment of Moses and all the prophets so that Jesus, along with his disciples, stands in continuity with a long line of the prophetic sending to Israel.[168] Jesus' exhortation in fact closes with this immediate consciousness: "The one who hearkens to you hearkens to me, but the one who rejects you rejects me, and the one who rejects me rejects the One who sent me" (v. 16). Not only is Jesus as the *Shaliach* of God boldly reasserted (cf. 9:35 → 9:48) but now also his Seventy(-two) disciples are incorporated with him in this sending as they, like he, are presented in the distinctive tones of the preachers of repentance to Israel.

3. **Luke 11:14–54**. In 11:29–32 Jesus rails at a generation that does not repent (v. 32). The mounting opposition to Jesus here sharpens the picture of 9:1–50 and places Jesus' "preaching the gospel" in the new perspective of the Central Section: When faced with the monolithic

opposition of a stubborn generation, the eschatological good news of the Kingdom in Jesus issues in the news of the coming destruction as signified by the presence of this same Jesus. The sign of Jonah is in their midst (vv. 20–32). The coming judgment is already at hand—it shall be required of this generation (11:47–51).[169]

4. **Luke 12:54—13:9.** In 12:40 Jesus has warned the disciples to "be ready" for the coming judgment in which the returning master ($\kappa\acute{\nu}\rho\iota o\varsigma$) will "cut in pieces" or "severely beat" the wicked servant and put him with the "unfaithful" (cf. 9:41a). In 13:3, 5 Jesus declares to the crowds that "unless you repent, all of you will likewise be destroyed." We thus have the same preaching of repentance placed now in even greater eschatological urgency: The accuser in their midst is already *on his way* to the judge to throw them into prison (12:57–59).[170] The ax is already laid to the root of the tree to cut it down and throw it into the fire (13:6–9; cf. 3:7–9, 17b).[171]

5. **Luke 13:22–30.** Now the "accuser on his way" is the Lord of the eschatological banquet, teaching and eating and drinking his way to Jerusalem. The warning is equally acute and even more precise. "Many will seek to enter" the feast of the Kingdom of God "but will not be able" (v. 24). This "Lord" will take those who have "eaten and drunk" in his presence and who heard his teaching and banish them as "evildoers" (v. 27). They will sob and grind their teeth when they see Abraham and Isaac and Jacob and all the prophets in the banquet hall, while they themselves are being thrown out (v. 28). "At that very hour" Jesus declares, "Look, your house is abandoned" (13:31a, 35a).

6. **Luke 14:15–24.** (See Part III.C, below.) Here it suffices to point out the image of the eschatological banquet again being used by one who is eating and drinking on his way to Jerusalem (cf. v. 25) to pronounce warning and judgment to those who are not accepting the call of this "voice" in their midst. "For I tell you, none of those folk invited shall taste my banquet!" (v. 24).

7. **Luke 15:1–32.*** The three parables of the 'lost' are Jesus' response to the charges that he "receives and eats with" "tax collectors and sinners" (v. 2b). In each parable a shepherd or a householder actively seeks to "find" and restore a "lost" or "perishing" entity under each's care. The implication is clear: Jesus is the one sent by "heaven" (vv. 7, 10, 18b, 21) to Israel to bring about a restoration characterized by repentance (vv. 7, 10, 17–19, 21; cf. vv. 28–30). For it is these "tax collectors and sinners" who are hearkening ($\mathring{\alpha}\kappa o\acute{\nu}\omega$, v. 1b) to the voice that demands total submission to heaven's call as it journeys to Jerusalem (14:25). Those who do not hearken will be "cast out" (14:34–35); therefore "let the one who has ears to hearken, hearken!" (v. 35b).

8. **Luke 17:22–37.** The Son of Man[172] will "suffer many things and be rejected" by a generation that, like Noah's and Lot's, "eats and drinks and marries and buys and sells and plants and builds" (vv. 26–30), unaffected by the prophet's warning; as with their "fathers," the "flood" and "fire and brimstone" will take them by complete surprise to destroy them *all* (v. 30). But this judgment effects the final separation of the faithful from the wicked (vv. 34–35).[173] It is the same eschatological trauma that breaks in unexpectedly like the thief into the house (12:39–40). Thus it is the same day and hour of the Son of Man which, Jesus says, demands a total state of readiness (cf. 12:40, 46). "Remember Lot's wife!" (17:32).

9. **Luke 19:1–27.*** Jesus as Son of Man "has come" "to seek and to save the lost" (v. 10). Zacchaeus, a "tax collector," "receives" Jesus joyfully (v. 6b; cf. 15:5–7, 9–10, 22–24, 32), "repents" (v. 8), and is restored as a "son of Abraham" (v. 9). Luke ties the response of the "grumbling all" (v. 7; cf. 15:2) to the parable of 19:12–27 via v. 11. The crowds accompanying Jesus (19:3–4, 7) are those who "do not want this man to reign over us" (v. 14b). The presence of the Kingdom in their midst is shunned for a great manifestation to come in Jerusalem (v. 11b). Consequently, "these enemies of mine, who did not want me to reign over them, . . . slay them before me" (v. 27). Though the distinctive Deuteronomistic language is lacking, nevertheless Jesus' sending as a messenger of repentance and portent of judgment à la Deuteronomistic conception is pregnantly profiled.

Conclusions

We have seen that the Deuteronomistic depiction of the prophet's calling to Israel is a distinctive portrait for the Jesus of Luke's Central Section. The words of Jesus in his teaching, exhortation, and warning calls to repentance attested by his "mighty works" all point to a prophet who is sent with the authoritative, living words of God from the mountain of revelation to the center of the covenant nation. Beginning, middle, and end, contour and content, parts and the whole—all alike testify to this telling tale of the prophet. The central role of Jerusalem in this story breaks through again and again. On the one hand, Deuteronomistic tradition speaks of its utter desolation as symbolic of the whole corrupt and calloused nation. On the other hand, it is the point of consummation for Moses and all the prophets. This peculiar dialectic is significant for the tension of the Central Section: Jesus travels as a prophet to meet a prophet's reward. But precisely because Jerusalem cannot be separated from the sending from the mountain, Jesus fulfills no ordinary prophet's task. He journeys, rather, as the authoritative prophet, uttering the voice of God's will which is the eschatological salvation of the covenant law. Journey episodes at beginning and end point to this unprecedented authority, while the large central teaching sections and parenetic tableaux present the life, the eschatological *halakah* of this salvation. The prophet Jesus—not the Pharisees or their doctors of the Law or the priests and the Levites—is the true leader and teacher of Israel. In short, we have discovered in the Central Section the Deuteronomistic hermeneutic of the prophet as the voice of God.

The Content of the Prophet Sent to Israel
9:51—19:44[174]

Sent to Mediate the Divine Will	To Instruct and Admonish in This Will	To Warn of Repentance
9:51	9:57–62	10:1–12, 13–
10:16	10:1–12, 16, 20, 23–24,	15, 16
11:49–51	25–28, 29–37, 38–42	11:14–23, 24–26,
13:22–30, 31–33,	11:1–4, 5–8, 9–13	27–28, 29–32,
34–35	12:1, 2–9, 10, 11–12	33, 34–36, 37–
19:41–44	13–15, 16–21, 22–32,	54
	33–34, 35–48, 49–53	12:54–56, 57–59
	13:10–17, 18–19, 20–21,	13:1–9, 22–30
	22–30	14:15–24
	14:1–6, 7–14, 15–24,	15:1–2, 3–7,
	25–33, 34–35	8–10, 11–32
	15:1–7, 8–10, 11–32	17:22–37
	16:1–9, 10–12, 13, 14–15,	19:1–10, 11–27
	16–17, 18, 19–31	
	17:1–3a, 3b–4, 5–6,	
	7–10, 20–21, 22–37	
	18:1–8, 9–14, 15–17,	
	18–23, 24–30	
	19:11–27	

C. Nevertheless, This Generation Rejected Jesus the Prophet, Even Killing Him out of Their Stiff-necked Resistance

Nevertheless they turned and rebelled against you and cast your law behind their back and killed your prophets who brought warning against them to turn them back to you, and they committed great provocations.

(2 Esd. 19:26 = Neh. 9:26)[175]

Retrospect

In tenet A it became clear that a variety of characters from Luke's dramatis personae—Jesus' disciples, John's messengers, individuals

from the crowds, the crowds of "this generation," the Pharisees-lawyers
—all become illustrations of a generation that is stubbornly hardened to
God's covenant relationship and to the redemptive pleading of his messengers. Moreover, we uncovered a distinctive dynamic: Doubt and
disenchantment and even facile enthusiasm on the part of smaller groups
and individuals from the crowds lead to the charge that the whole generation is crooked. We also detected a hindering influence which surfaced
as a scornful skepticism on the part of some of the Pharisees-lawyers.
This trail in turn led to the table fellowship of these Pharisees-lawyers
where offense at Jesus' "eating and drinking" is turned around by Jesus to
their offense of killing the prophets. Thus we noticed that from 7:18–35
(the programmatic introduction to this dynamic) to 11:14–54 a development in the intensity of resistance takes place. Jesus' reprimand of Simon
the Pharisee has become a trenchant rebuke and pronouncement of
judgment in the "Woe to the Pharisees and lawyers" of 11:37–54. By
12:54—13:9 Jesus has blanketed all the crowds with the indictment—
"hypocrites"—so that, like the Pharisees-lawyers, they await the same
fate. We concluded that not just isolated passages in the Central Section
but rather the whole contour divulges this Deuteronomistic outlook.
Thus to cite only those passages which betray the distinctive Deuteronomistic mentality, without charting their function within the developing
plot, would be not only to miss the characteristic dynamics of the
Deuteronomistic view but also to rupture Luke's presentation of his
"connected narrative" (1:3).

     In tenet B this conclusion was borne out. First, we treated only those
verses with the clear Deuteronomistic sending from God to utter the
divine will: these verses not only link the mountain sending to the arrival
in Jerusalem but also evince the same fundamental progression in plot as
in tenet A. What is more, this chain then revealed itself to be only the
skeleton of an entire body of the prophet's sending to teach and admonish and call the people back to the will of God. Nearly the entire Central
Section, infrastructure and building blocks, unfolds the dynamic story of
the Prophet as the Teacher of Israel, the voice of God to the nation.
Therefore, again, we cannot content ourselves only with explicit Deuteronomistic references to Jesus' rejection and death but must also follow
the developing lines of this dynamic in order to measure the pulse of the
rising opposition to the prophet Jesus.

Jesus the Journeying Guest Is Not Received (Luke 9:52—19:44)

     Under tenet A we discovered that the explicit lines of the Deuterono-
mistic dynamics, A—D, tended to converge at meal settings with the
Pharisees. Jesus is their guest and yet he is not "received" as he is by a

Mary and Martha or a Zacchaeus (10:38; 19:6—ὑποδέχομαι) at table. Indeed we have already seen how Luke avoids using the δέχομαι word group with those who do not submit to Jesus' prophetic voice.[176] Under tenet B we observed the way Luke forges the Deuteronomistic sending of the prophet to Jesus' journeying to Jerusalem. We propose, then, to concentrate on Jesus, the journeying guest, as a heuristic device in charting the rejection that comes to expression in tenet C.

1. **Luke 9:52-56.** Jesus sends out messengers "to prepare for him" at an unnamed Samaritan village. Whatever else the verb ἑτοιμάζω denotes, it includes preparations for the hospitable reception of the stranger customary in the ancient world as δέχομαι in v. 53a and 10:8, 10 indicates. But beyond this usual referent, Luke states immediately (v. 53) that Jesus is refused hospitality because he ("his face") was "journeying to Jerusalem." This may be an indication that ἑτοιμάζω in 9:52 signifies more than the preparations for the usual hospitality[177] (see especially the eschatological sense in 12:40, 47; 14:17; 17:8 and preparations for the Passover meal in 22:8, 9, 12, 13). Jesus is on his "exodus" (9:31) from the mountain to his "receiving up" (9:51) as the prophetic voice of God. It is this sending which Luke now signals to be the decisive factor in the Samaritans' refusal of hospitality and which continues to unfold in the following pericope.

2. **Luke 9:57-62.** Verse 57 describes the continuation of the journey from v. 56. What follows is three encounters with individuals who either desire to follow Jesus on this journey or are so requested by Jesus (v. 59). In v. 57 a certain individual wants Jesus to know that regardless of how Jesus is treated by unobliging folk (cf. v. 53) he will follow wherever Jesus goes. Jesus' response is a sobering confirmation of this commitment while at the same time a challenge to count the cost of such a decision: he has "no place to lay his head."[178] In the present context, v. 58 could mean that Jesus is referring to his rejection by the Samaritan village that same day so that he continues on without a place to spend that night. Or it could represent a gnomic synopsis of the journey as a whole—it will be characterized by rejection. Or the saying could include both these senses. From the stringency of Jesus' sayings that follow in vv. 59–62, in addition to the gnomic character of v. 58 itself, it would appear that Jesus is using the Samaritan village rejection as a dramatic demonstration of what this enthusiastic aspirant can expect "down the road." In essence, then, Jesus announces here already that all along his way to Jerusalem his unique sending will be met with inhospitable resistance.

In vv. 59–60 the nature of this "unwelcome" journey is widened from another angle. Upon Jesus' challenge, "Follow me," another individual evidences every willingness to do so but for an a priori duty to fulfill a most uncompromising requirement of the Law—to bury one's dead. As W. Grundmann summarizes: "This duty releases one from the study of Torah and from all other obligations which the Torah requires."[179] Yet Jesus' command bears the force of one whose authority is clearly above the Law as it is perceived and enforced. "Leave the dead to bury their own dead." Thus we meet the same authoritative voice of tenet B whose mandate is extended back to the seminal revelation of 9:28–36.[180] "But as for you, you go and declare the Kingdom of God" (v. 60b). The Kingdom as it is actualized in the authoritative presence of Jesus takes absolute priority over any current interpretation and practice of the Law. The implication seems unavoidable that the dead who are to bury their own are those who are missing the life of the fulfillment of the life-giving Law—the presence of the Kingdom of God.[181] Not to follow this journey and to proclaim the presence of life is to negate the life-giving Law (10:25–37) into death. Note also that following Jesus includes the sending out from his entourage to proclaim the Kingdom of God. It may well be that one of the activities of the sending out of the messengers in 9:52 is being reflected here. But the juxtaposition here of this command to proclaim ($\sigma\grave{\upsilon}$ $\delta\grave{\epsilon}$) with that in v. 60a adds currency to this notion of the "dead." Proclamation of the Kingdom of God brings life.

This interpretation is supported by the third encounter which again pits familial commitments precedented by the Law (cf. 1 Kings 19:20–21) against an immediate and unequivocal "hearkening" to the voice of Jesus. To "say farewell" to one's home ($\acute{o}$ $o\mathring{\iota}\kappa\acute{o}s$ $\mu o\upsilon$) is certainly a reasonable if not charitable thing to do (cf. 10:25–27). Yet Jesus' rejoinder is more radical; not even Elisha's calling by Elijah compares in significance with the Kingdom's calling by Jesus. To return to one's own and share a meal together as Elisha did (1 Kings 19:21) is to render one unfit for the Kingdom of God. This allusion to Elisha's practice may not be gratuitous in its present context.[182] In any case, Jesus' command is absolute.

In sum, although the "killing of the prophets" of Deuteronomistic tradition is not articulated in these traditions, the general rejection of God's messengers sent to Israel (tenet C) is already surfacing through the plot. *(a)* Jesus' journey mission from the mountain (9:31, 51) carries the life-giving words of God as conceived in tenet B. *(b)* Jesus' sending (tenet B) is implicit as he sends out others on missions with this authoritative voice. In both cases, whether through Jesus or his messengers, the Kingdom of God now epitomizes the eschatological will of God vis-à-vis the Law, and any opposition to this journey sending is direct opposition to the presence of God's eschatological rule in this journeying guest. Luke continues to spin out this story in an ever-tightening web.

3. **Luke 10:1–24.*** The first twenty-four verses of Luke 10 form a unit

based on the mission of the "Seventy(-two)."[183] Analysis of smaller units will, however, provide a firmer grasp of the whole:

10:1. It is evident that Luke intends the following narrative to be a continuation of the journeying-guest story:

(i) Through the use of κύριος, ἀποστέλλω, πρὸ προσώπον αὐτοῦ, and ἔρχομαι, an immediate resonance with vv. 52, 53, 54, 56, 57, and 59–60 is produced. (ii) Jesus repeats the procedure of 9:52; those from his entourage are sent out ahead of him along the very route Jesus himself will follow. Whatever may differentiate the Seventy(-two) from the messengers/envoys of 9:52, their basic assignment as forerunners is the same. (iii) Luke explicitly calls the Seventy(-two) "others" (ἕτεροι). Because in Koine idiom ἕτερος could take on virtually the sense of ἄλλος, it is not certain from this word alone whether the sense here is *(a)* continuous in a comparative manner or *(b)* discontinuous in a contrasting sense: *(a)* "He sent seventy(-two) more" (i.e., messengers of 9:52). *(b)* "He sent seventy(-two) different ones" (i.e., different types of ambassadors from those of 9:52). Most likely *(b)* can be ruled out on the basis of (ii) above; Luke is straightforward in his description of their preceding the "Lord's" own journey. Though there is an obvious analogy with the sending out of the Twelve (9:1–6), yet the contrasting colors into which their mission is cast as well as the different literary context which begins in 9:51 militate against the primary referent of ἕτεροι being the Twelve;[184] (iv) Μετὰ δὲ ταῦτα (v. 1a) is an explicit, albeit general, time connective to the preceding developments.

10:2–3. Jesus' address (vv. 2–16) to commission the Seventy(-two) begins. The metaphor of gathering a harvest (v. 2) mirrors Jesus' self-proclaimed goal of gathering in 11:23 as well as John's picture of Jesus' ministry in 3:17 (cf. 13:6–9; 15:1–32). What needs to be underscored here is the urgency of this task. As workers in this harvest, they are to pray that more be added to the "few"; because this harvest is "great," not even Seventy(-two) are nearly enough. Apparently this is no seasonal gathering of people. In fact, they are to pray to the "Lord of the harvest" to have more "sent out" into their harvest; Jesus can only mean that God is the one who is harvesting. As these disciples are about their master's/Lord's work (ὁ κύριος, v. 1), they are at the same time about the business of God himself. A passage such as Isa. 27:12 (LXX) comes to mind: "On that day the Lord will thresh . . . and you will gather the sons and daughters of Israel one by one." The "you" refers to the people of Israel who, after gathering their own people from their exile in Assyria and Egypt, will come to the holy mountain in Jerusalem to worship the Lord. In the light of Jesus' (the "Lord's") journey to Jerusalem which climaxes in his "purifying" the Temple,[185] this OT allusion may be in the background here. In any case, we have already demonstrated the eschatological character of the Seventy(-two)'s preaching of repentance.[186] Now it is certain that this harvest is the eschatological gathering of God's people (cf. Joel 3:13 [LXX] on the eschatological gathering of the nations).

In v. 3 the sending is emphasized again (cf. 9:52; 9:1–6). In this mission they will be *like lambs amidst wolves!*[187] Here the rejection of 9:52–56 and 57–58 returns. Some commentators find an inconcinnity here with an abundant harvest in v. 2.[188] But it should be noted that a great ($\pi o \lambda \acute{v} s$) harvest can designate the large number of fields that need to be harvested without indicating the size or the productivity of what is actually reaped. The Seventy(-two) have an immense task ahead of them; the potential is great but so are the dangers.[189] They are indeed to experience the resistance that their "Lord" (v. 1) knows firsthand and continues to experience (cf. also 9:23–26). But they also go with the authority of the "Lord of the harvest" (cf. v. 16).

10:4–6. Their provisions for the journey (v. 4a) leave them radically "provisionless" (cf. 22:35). In this, Jesus' strictures match the Essenes (cf. Josephus, *War* 2.124–27). But unless the Seventy(-two) were always to meet up with friends or sympathizers, their plight would be more precarious than the desert nomads who could find hospitality with members of their own group or allied conventicles. Verses 5, 6, and 10 make it certain that this was not to be the case. In other words, the cost of following Jesus to Jerusalem is as uncompromisingly depicted here as in vv. 57–62. No money, no nourishment, no extra clothing—in short, these emissaries have to be totally dependent upon their *being received as guests* by the towns and homes along the way. They are not even to greet anyone along their path (v. 4b). Like Elisha's messenger, Gehazi (2 Kings 4:29), they are dealing with "life and death" matters such that formal, drawn-out acts of hospitality on the roadside must be dispensed with.[190] Thus they could not even fall back upon these wayside encounters which often provided relief for the more desperate traveler.

In vv. 5–6 the rationale for such austere measures comes to light. The household ($o \tilde{i} \kappa o s$, $o \grave{i} \kappa \acute{i} a$), not the road, is to be the center of their activity. For they are to utter the powerful word of peace immediately upon entering. No time is to be wasted along the road for the urgent message of peace to be conferred upon these homes. That this peace is not the customary salutation upon entering a house is disclosed by vv. 10–12.[191] It is, rather, the *eschatological peace,* the "peace of heaven" heralded by the great company of disciples as Jesus enters Jerusalem (19:42) and construed by Peter in Cornelius's household as the essence of Jesus' public proclamation (Acts 10:36–37). If the householder is a "son of peace"[192] (v. 6), then the peace of the messenger will "find rest upon him."

The ancient idea of the powerful, performative word (cf. Isa. 55:10–11) which is sent out and can return is present here. This word of peace indeed returns upon the messenger when a "son of peace" is not there (v. 6b).

Now from vv. 10–12 the full significance of this greeting is divulged as nothing less than the effective presence of the eschatological salvation of the Kingdom of God. To refuse this greeting is to reject this salvation and make effective the final abandonment of this presence from that household. Consequently the household is both the starting point and the ultimate destination of the messengers' special mission. If the household does not *receive* the message of peace, then the whole town is left desolate of this salvation. "The Kingdom of God has drawn near," to be sure (v. 11b), but not "upon them" (v. 9b; cf. v. 6a).

10:7–9. Once the householder has received their "peace," the ambassadors are to remain *in that particular house,*[193] eating and drinking what the host provides (v. 7a). "For the worker is worthy of his wages" (v. 7b). The image of "the worker" hired for the harvest in v. 2 is picked up again here and is pivotal for understanding the actual activity in mind. What is not being said (contra most commentators) is simply that preachers of the gospel are to be rewarded for their spiritual giving by material gifts.[194] Rather, the Seventy(-two) are "workers" in the eschatological harvest of gathering a people for the Kingdom of God, and their "wages" are the fruit of this gathering—the meal fellowship of this Kingdom. Or to use the phrasing of v. 8, they are employed *to be received* ($\delta\acute{\epsilon}\chi o\mu\alpha\iota$) into the homes to *eat.*

That this is the crux of the matter in v. 7a and v. 7b is substantiated by the following points:

(i) Verses 7–9 form the climax of vv. 1–6. Once the eschatological peace is received, the guests are to set about the following work. Thus vv. 2–6 relate the necessary conditions and precautions without which the "abiding" in the homes remains ineffective. (ii) Since the effect of the greeting in the household and *not* "on the way" (vv. 5–6) is ultimate, the "eating and drinking" which receives this greeting is ipso facto no ordinary eating and drinking! At the very least, it represents a fellowship of those in the saving presence of the Kingdom of God. (iii) The injunction (v. 7b) not to transfer from house to house casts suspicion on a purely utilitarian interpretation of the eating and drinking in v. 7a. For if the main goal were the evangelizing of as many houses as possible, then the messengers should not tarry too long at one household. In this rapid transition they would need to rely upon their hosts primarily for provisions and could justify this service as their rightfully "earned" wages of preaching.[195] But it is clear that this kind of movement is not envisioned. Rather, the activities within or through this house constitute a primary end in themselves. (iv) This understanding of this goal is borne out by vv. 8–9 which, through a paratactic string of imperatives, link the ambassadors' *receiving* by a particular town (v. 8a) to the *eating* of whatever is set before them followed by the *healing* of people in this town as well as by *proclaiming* the presence of the Kingdom of God upon them. The syntax of the Greek text betrays the goal as well as the result of the "receiving" of these messengers. (v) The repetition of the imperative to "eat" in v. 8b places a special emphasis upon this function of the Kingdom's presence: *(a)* Unless παρατίθημι is nonsensically pleonastic, it can only mean "whatever is set before you." The strict dietary laws for the Jew are not to be in effect.[196] *(b)* This strongly suggests that at least part of their journeying will take them through marginal Jewish regions like Decapolis, Perea, Gaulanitis, if not also Samaria.[197] This in turn points to the mission of the Seventy(-two) as the adumbration, if not actual initiation, of the Samaritan-Gentile mission which is carried out later by the church in Acts 8ff. (cf. Peter's vision of "unclean" food in Acts 10). The eschatological gathering of vv. 2–3 may well be, then, the eschatological gathering of the nations. But *(a)* and *(b)* must also be viewed in the light of vv. 4, 7c–8a above. The messengers could have taken their own undefiled provisions along or bought them selectively along the way (cf. John 4:8) or even have relied upon Jewish friends. But the fact that they are not to take such provisions (v. 4a) nor carry money (v. 4a) or rely upon sympathizers (vv. 4b, 6, 10–12) indicates the importance of sharing even "unclean" food with their hosts. We meet again the eschatological ultimacy of Jesus' command which inheres with the authority to (re-) interpret the Law. And like Peter's vision in Acts 10, "unclean" food not only symbolizes the breaking down of ethnic and legal barriers in the Kingdom of God; eating and drinking of it becomes a palpably powerful demonstration of the unifying of Jew and Greek as in Cornelius's own house.[198] (vi) Verses 10–12 leave no doubt about the primacy of *receiving* these journeying guests; when a town does "not receive you," then "say. . . ." Like Jesus in 9:46–48, they themselves are the object of the sending (cf. vv. 1–3). When they are not received, the presence of the Kingdom departs with them (v. 11b). This amazing relationship finds its grounding in v. 16: to reject these ambassadors is simultaneously the rejection of Jesus who commissioned them (v. 1) and of God who sent Jesus. The *shaliach* concept is succinctly articulated here.[199] The presence of the Kingdom of God with these messengers therefore is the presence of Jesus, "the Lord" (v. 1), as well as the presence of God, the "Lord of the Harvest" (v. 2). Consequently the "eating and drinking" of vv. 7 and 8 is the *table fellowship of the presence of God in God's eschatological Kingdom* (cf. vv. 12–15).[200] (vii) Finally, notice the eschatological "woes" of vv. 13–15. Integral to receiving is repenting. To be a "son of peace" (v. 5), therefore, is to place oneself in a posture of repentance before the saving presence of the Kingdom. The "eating and drinking" of vv. 7–8 is thus a meal fellowship of repentant sinners who acknowledge their need for the saving efficacy of this Kingdom. Consequently Jesus' emissaries are sent on ahead to prepare repentant households who not only receive Jesus in the visitation of these guests but who are also ready literally to receive him into their homes when he comes through their towns (10:1).

For all these reasons the "eating and drinking" of v. 7 does not refer merely to the perquisites due these "hired laborers of the harvest." Rather, Jesus, the Lord, is already *on his way* to meet a gathered, prepared people. Urgency is required because time is pressing ineluctably to its climax in Jerusalem (9:51, 59–60, 61–62). The task of the Seventy-(-two) is therefore not to evangelize in as wide an area as possible but to ensure rather that Jesus (and his entourage) find households along his way to *receive* him. This is exactly what is depicted in 9:52–56. *To prepare for Jesus is to prepare a repentant people,* which in this instance ends in rejection. But when the Seventy(-two) are told to remain in the same house before moving ahead to another town, the reasoning is now clear. They are to establish a "banquet fellowship" where the presence of the coming King[201] is celebrated and anticipated as the "eating and drinking" of salvation. This fellowship becomes the center of healing and the heralding of this presence for the whole town. The order, then, of vv. 4–9 is not simply an arbitrary collation by Luke or Q but reflects a definite mission strategy of which we have glimpses of Jesus' alleged practice elsewhere (e.g., 10:38–42; 11:37–54; 14:1–24; 15:1–2; 19:1–10; cf. 5:29–39—a gathering of Levi's friends in his house; cf. 5:17–26— healing and proclamation occur in a house). "Receiving" in v. 8 (cf. v. 10) is thus a summary term for this whole procedure in which the very presence of Jesus is brought right to the tables of these repentant households.[202]

10:10–16. These verses all anticipate *rejection* of these journeying guests. Verses 10–11 may mirror what in essence took place in the Samaritan village of vv. 52–56. When no "sons of peace" are to be found, then they are to move on with the prophet's sign of authority. Verses 13–15 intimate that what Jesus has experienced as stiff-necked opposition will be the lot of these messengers as well. Verse 16 brings Jesus' address to a crisp conclusion by stating the raison d'être for the whole mission: *the dynamic presence of God in Jesus* is to be received in these missionaries. The identity of their presence with Jesus and God is inseparable; therefore their identity with them in rejection is inseparable as well. These messengers will learn the meaning of bearing a cross daily as they follow the One to Jerusalem who has no place to lay his head (9:57–58; cf. 9:23–26).

10:17–24. In vv. 17–20 the story of the sending continues in the *return* of the Seventy(-two). Apart from the logistical problems of such a rendezvous, the language of this unparalleled material changes considerably from vv. 2–16, so that problems of origin cast doubt upon the credibility of such a conclusion within the earlier strata of tradition.[203] The focus now seems to be entirely upon the "spiritual" power received and experienced by the emissaries rather than their being welcomed or received as heralds of their coming Lord-King. This complex history of tradition notwithstanding, careful analysis reveals a basic consistency on Luke's part in the developing plot:

> The Seventy(-two) "return"[204] not to the point from which they were sent out but to their Sender who has continued on his journey. A final point for regrouping all the messengers before reaching Jerusalem is not so difficult to imagine. Accordingly, v. 17 can be conceived along the lines of 9:52–56 and may suggest that vv. 17–20 stem from this same "L" source.
>
> Even more significant is the thrust of their report: *(a)* Verse 17a: "Even the demons are subject"—points directly to a "successful" healing activity and hence indirectly to the messengers being welcomed and thus received by various households. *(b)* Verse 17b: "in your name"—links up directly with the authority structure of vv. 1, 16. "By the authority of *your sending* us, the demons . . . *(c)* Verse 19: "Look, I have given you authority . . . over all the power of the enemy." The authority and consequent power of their sending from the Lord and Lord of the harvest of vv. 1–3 is articulated similarly to the sending of the Twelve in 9:1–6 (cf. 9:1).[205] This same power is expressed, albeit in a perverted fashion, by James and John in 9:54. More directly, the performative power of Jesus' word bestowed to these messengers in vv. 5–6 and especially vv. 9–12 is acknowledged once again in terms of its eschatological ultimacy. Now even Satan (v. 18) is being overcome with all the power that he wields (v. 19). They indeed have been in the midst of wolves (v. 3). But they have been victorious with that unequaled power which can declare, "It shall be more tolerable on *that day* for Sodom" (v. 12; cf. vv. 9, 11, 14–15). *(d)* Verses 17a, 20b: "With joy. . . . Rejoice, because your names are written in the heavens." Joy is to be the keynote of their mission but not the kind that glows over power. Interestingly enough in Luke-Acts, "joy" is an eschatological phenomenon joined peculiarly to the meal:[206] "And coming home he calls together his friends and neighbors, saying to them, *'Rejoice* with me.' . . . Even so I tell you, there will be more *joy* in heaven" (15:6–7). "And when she has found it, . . . there is *joy* before the angels of God" (vv. 9–10). "Bring the fatted calf and kill it, and let us eat and *make merry*. . . . It was necessary that we should make merry and *rejoice*" (vv. 23, 32). Zacchaeus celebrates his repentance in a home-meal fellowship (19:5–6). After the resurrection, the disciples "were still disbelieving for *joy* and marveling when he said to them, 'Do you have anything here to eat?'" (24:41). "And day by day . . . breaking bread together in their homes they partook of food with *joyful* and generous hearts" (Acts 2:46; cf. 16:34). It is the same joy these emissaries were to have experienced in the "eating and drinking" with their repentant hosts who had received them and thus the eschatological

salvation;[207] and it is the joy they were now to experience again with Jesus as he exults in the Holy Spirit over their salvation.

The upshot of these observations is not only that the journeying guest is implicit in vv. 17–20 but also that this theme is integrally developed from 10:1–16. The Seventy(-two) were indeed sent out and were received into households as guests along the way. The power that was manifested as salvation in these houses attested to the presence of the kingly reign of God in Jesus through these ambassadors. This salvation and not the thrilling display of mighty works is to be the object of their joy. In this way we find the same understanding of the mighty work as we traced above under tenet B.[208] They are signs of the more significant receiving of salvation upon "hearkening" to Jesus' voice. It is just this experience that the Seventy(-two) have had (cf. 10:16). Here again in vv. 17–20 we find the journeying guest to be an extension of Jesus' mountain sending (9:28–36). By the same token, although these emissaries met opposition by the demons, the preponderant emphasis is upon their overpowering "success." The rejection theme of v. 16b is not picked up again (cf. 9:42–50). Instead, caution against misdirected joy is sounded.

In vv. 21–24 this most curious of Q traditions[209] follows chronologically in Luke's scheme ("in that very hour," v. 21). And the theme of eschatological joy continues uninterrupted as well (v. 21a); there is no doubt that Luke intends the narrative in 10:1–20 to culminate in these verses. The object of Jesus' "exulting" is the revelation of "these things" to "infants" ($\nu\dot{\eta}\pi\iota\sigma\iota$) which at the same time are "hidden" from the "wise" and "learned." Though "these things" appears to lack a precise antecedent or precise antecedents, both the chronological link and the thematic link of v. 21 to vv. 17–20 strongly suggest that it represents the experiences of the Seventy(-two) affirmed and qualified by Jesus in vv. 17–20.[210] This revelation has taken place according to the gracious will (v. 21) of the Father (the "Lord of heaven and earth"), and "all things" have "been delivered over" to Jesus, the Son "by my Father" (v. 22). Therefore, v. 22 divulges the ultimate basis of the Seventy(-two)'s experience of salvation and reception of revelation in vv. 17–20. Jesus as *the Son* has *revealed* it to them.

This connection can be substantiated by the following: *(a)* Jesus addresses God as "Father" in v. 21 and then calls him "my Father" in v. 22. *(b)* In v. 21 revelation has been received by infants on account of God's gracious will or favor; in v. 22 revelation is given on account of the Son's own "will" or "choosing." *(c)* It is inescapable that the speaker of "my father" (i.e., Jesus) of v. 21 is "the Son" of v. 22, since Jesus declares that "all things" have been given over by this Father "to me" (v. 22a). *(d)* Therefore, with the theme of "mutual knowledge" and the bestowal of "all things" to the Son of v. 22, the reception of "these things"[211] of v. 21 must not only be encompassed by the "all things" of v. 22 but must also be dependent upon the revelatory structure or ordering for the "all things." *(e)* "All things" refers not only to "knowledge" but also to "authority," since authority over all creation is predicated of the Father by Jesus in v. 21 in addition to the Father's authority to choose those upon whom he bestows his revelation.[212] *(f)* The mutuality and yet explicit subordination of the Son to the Father through the bestowal of the "all things" appears to be a direct reflection of the *shaliach* concept of 10:16; there rejection of Jesus is tantamount to rejection of God, yet Jesus is the one sent by God.[213] As we have seen, this sending issues from a bestowed authority upon Jesus by God in 9:35. *(g)* The acceptance or rejection of the Seventy(-two) (and of Jesus and of God) is dependent upon the message of peace or announcement of the *presence of the reign of God* (cf. 10:5–6, 9, 11). We can conclude, therefore, that the structure of authority and revelation in the present form of 10:1–24 makes the connection of the revelation of the Father by the Son in v. 22 to the revelation to the emissaries and to their hosts in the "these things" of vv. 17–20, 21 not only probable but also logically necessary.[214] An inner coherence is disclosed in what Luke presents outwardly as one continuous story. The literary climax (vv. 21–24) is matched by the substantive culmination of the eschatological mission: in the deeds and words of the Seventy(-two) the "disciples" experience the fulfillment of the age of salvation longed for by people of the Old Covenant but never realized. The era of eschatological joy and peace has only now arrived (10:5–9).[215]

But this means, then, that the mission of the Seventy(-two) is stamped by the revelation of the Son to those who hearken (10:16) to them as journeying guests. But that is yet another way of linking the mountain revelation of the Son and his exodus-sending-journey to Jerusalem with the Jesus who journeys as guest to Jerusalem in 10:1–24 (as well as in 9:52–56, 57–62). The whole of 9:51—10:24 exhibits this direct link back to the mountain sending of 9:28–36. *To journey with Jesus means to participate in the self-unveiling of his authority as the Son as he advances to Jerusalem!* And this revelation is the effecting of salvation for those who receive him and his ambassadors which is most sublimely mirrored in the eschatological joy of the home-meal fellowship. As the "disciples" journey to Jerusalem, they "see" and "hear" the events hoped for but not experienced by prophets and kings. Not even John had "seen" or "heard" this fulfillment (7:18–35)!

Summary. In 9:52—10:24 Jesus journeys to Jerusalem as guest to be received, revealing his authority as the Son in his own deeds and words and through his ambassador-guests. In 9:52, 60, and 10:1 Jesus sends out these messengers to prepare repentant households that will eat and drink with their guests in the presence of the eschatological salvation and receive Jesus as he passes through that town. A Samaritan village refuses this hospitality (9:53). This rejection is used by Jesus to typify the whole of his journey (9:58). And yet the Seventy(-two) in probably nominal or peripheral Jewish regions experience decisive victories over Satan and enjoy an obvious reception among the townspeople as they eat and drink, heal, and proclaim the dynamic presence of the reign of God. The rejection of 9:52–56 and 9:58 (cf. 10:3) is not characteristic of their mission; consequently in 10:2–23 they are portrayed in contrasting colors to their lord.

Behind the imagery of the journeying guest is the unmistakable prophet-messenger of Deuteronomistic tradition sent to Israel with words of repentance (tenet B). But now with Jesus as "the Son," who himself reveals directly the words of "the Father" and sends out his own messengers, Jesus and his ambassador-guests carry with them the words of the final message of repentance. The time of eschatological decision has arrived. Those who reject this pleading call down upon themselves the final judgment of the reign of God. Moreover, the "journeying guest" graphically expresses developing Deuteronomistic tradition (e.g., Jer. 26:15 [LXX 33:15]; 2 Chron. 36:14ff.) in which the prophets themselves, rather than simply their message, are to be received.[216] Tenet C consequently is formulated as the rejection of these messengers. Such is the portrait Luke provides of the Samaritan rebuff, of the expectations for would-be followers (9:58), and of the Seventy(-two) (10:3, 10–15). The Seventy(-two)'s apparent reception of revelation as "infants" and reception in the homes in marginal Jewish areas certainly sets them in relief and raises anew the question of the kind of reception Jesus will encounter as he continues his journey as guest to the heart of Israel.

4. **Luke 10:25–37.**[*217] The lack of temporal and spatial connections to the preceding material indicates a break in the flow. Yet in pointing the lawyer to the Law for life, Jesus relates a story of a Samaritan, who as he journeys (ὁδεύων, v. 33) shows compassion to a stranger by taking him to an inn (v. 34; cf. 15:1–2). This act of hospitality becomes a paragon of *receiving* as well as of *giving* life: By receiving the "unclean" neighbor, the Samaritan aligns himself with the love for God and the neighbor required by the Law (10:27–29); by doing the Law he receives its life. He thus proves himself a "child" who submits to the authority of God as structured in this Law, in blatant contrast to the "wise and learned" (cf. v. 21) priest and Levite who, as guardians of the official covenant religion, "pass by" its own demands.[218] At the same time, as the one who reaches out to the outcast and receives such a one *as he journeys,* the Samaritan brings life to Israel and as such becomes a "type" of Jesus' own sending (tenet B).

Both the "childlike" response to Jesus and the life-giving journey of Jesus are mirrored by this foreigner. The positioning of this parable immediately after the Seventy(-two)'s reception as guests by undoubtedly nominal Jewish or even Samaritan hosts is not gratuitous to Luke's "connected narrative" (1:3). What is evident now also is that opposition to Jesus' sending (tenet C) is coming from leaders of the people who are "testing" Jesus (v. 25; cf. 11:45, 46, 52!). Hence the rejection by the Samaritan village seems to fade in its signal effect as a Samaritan is pushed into the limelight of childlike response to God and the neighbor.

5. **Luke 10:38–42.**[219] The theme of journeying guest is picked up in v. 38 from 10:1–24 and then illustrated in vv. 39–42 through both a broadening and a qualifying of the childlike posture of 10:29–37. In v. 38 the movement of the journey is resumed with reference to both Jesus and the disciples of 10:23; in v. 38b only Jesus is described as entering a "certain village," with no hint of his disciples joining him later in Mary and Martha's house.[220] Apparently there was no need for disciples to precede him immediately, as in 9:52–56, perhaps because this preparation had already been accomplished by members of the Seventy(-two).[221] In any case, the contrasting parallelism of this verse with 9:52–53 appears to be deliberate: *(a)* An unnamed village is entered. *(b)* But a woman "receives" Jesus in contrast to the Samaritan village that "did not receive" (9:53) him. *(c)* Already the mistress of the house is named as Martha; thus the specific household of the mission strategy of 10:5–9 is identified over against the general refusal by the whole Samaritan town (cf. 10:10).

Though textual difficulties abound,[222] in vv. 39–42 Jesus places a priority on "listening to him" vis-à-vis the act of hospitality per se. Martha's "service" ($\delta\iota\alpha\kappa o\nu\acute{\iota}\alpha$, v. 40a) is not placing her in a position of submitting to Jesus' authority; to the extent that preparations for a meal stifle the life-giving words of Jesus, to the same degree the meal itself can no longer manifest the saving revelation of this life-giving presence. Whether Jesus' words (v. 42) are simply a rebuke to Martha for distracting Mary or whether they also intend to halt Martha's activity, the acts of hospitality achieve their full significance only when they "serve" Jesus' authority. To make excessive preparations for a meal is to deny its intended purpose, to block the self-revelation of the Lord's (vv. 39, 41) word (v. 39b) and thus the revelation of the Father by the Son (10:21–22, 9–11).

In the light of this understanding of *receiving,* it is Mary who exhibits the childlike response required by Jesus (cf. 9:46–48) by "hearkening ($\mathring{\eta}\kappa o\upsilon\epsilon\nu$) to his word." In 10:29–37 a Samaritan, in 10:1–20 seventy(-two) "others," and now here a woman are the "infants" receiving revelation for which Jesus gives praise to the Father (10:21–22). Clearly ethnic and sexual distinctions are transcended in the life-giving journey of this guest;

yet in 9:52–56 and 10:38–42 Samaritans and a woman respectively either reject or detract from this authoritative sending; opposition to Jesus likewise transcends ethnic and sexual barriers (cf. lawyer in 10:25–29). At this stage of the narrative it is too early to tell how this opposition will grow and coalesce eventually to kill Jesus the Prophet. But refusal of hospitality (9:52–56), testing of Jesus' authority (10:25–37), and distraction from his word (vv. 38–42) all constitute the "looking back" which is not "fit" for the Kingdom of God (9:62). Significantly, in the last two instances this opposition is contrasted to the right reception of Jesus by the "child" through the explicit development of the journeying-guest motif.

6. **Luke 11:1–13.**[*223] In 11:1 no indication of progress to Jerusalem is given, as in 10:25 there appears to be a break in a "travel narrative." Nevertheless, as in 10:1–24; 10:25–37, and 38–42, two important themes are extended further in 11:1–13 without a sense of interruption: The journeying-guest motif is interwoven with a childlike response to Jesus' authority. Similar to 10:23–24, "disciples" are present in semiprivate surroundings in which a childlike posture to Jesus' authority prevails. The "certain place" of 11:1 fits well the description of "every place" of 10:1b where Jesus himself was to pass through on his way to Jerusalem.

In the midst of his own praying (11:1a), Jesus tells the disciples to address God as "Father" (v. 2), the very name he uses in praying to God (10:21);[224] moreover, they are to look to God each day for their "bread" (v. 3). This petition reflects a journey setting like that of the Seventy(-two) in which they are thrown back upon their hosts for their daily meals.[225]

The disciples' own journey setting then is mirrored straightway by a parable of a friend on a journey in need of hospitality (vv. 5–8). The meal is again the palpable sign of receiving the guest and sharing the sustenance of life with him. But more than this, this hospitality-household imagery depicts the caring nature of God in contrast to the unwilling householder. The disciples can be assured that when they are in need, they can ask, seek, and even knock (vv. 9–10) like the friend at midnight (vv. 5–8) and find a caring Father more than willing to meet any need. Their own experience of knocking on doors to receive their livelihood becomes an apt figure for receiving instruction on total dependence on God through prayer by the One who speaks directly to God as "Father" (11:1a → 10:21 → 9:29, 35).[226] Tenet C is not expressed here.

7. **Luke 11:14–54.** Opposition to Jesus returns and crescendos to a first climax in the house of a Pharisee. Jesus draws sharp lines within the "house" of each individual who hears his preaching; only total submission to Jesus' authority produces a people who "gather with" him (11:17–23; cf. 10:2!). This gathering (10:1–24) constitutes the eschato-

logical defeat of "Satan's house" (11:17–18, 21–22)[227] and provokes in Jesus the classic denunciation (à la tenet C) of Israel's resistance in the house-meal setting of their leaders, the Pharisees-lawyers: "This generation" is held accountable for the murder of the prophets from the very foundations of history (vv. 47b–48, 49b, 50b–51a). It is transparent now that the meal can also be the setting for the obfuscation and rejection of the revelation of the journeying guest, the "lord" (v. 39) of the banquet who is here (cf. vv. 31b, 32b).

8. **Luke 12:1–12.*** Luke 12 begins a large "teaching" section which, as we have seen, is considered by many to be a static compilation of disparate traditions that all but destroys the rhythm of progress to Jerusalem. Not only does Jesus "stand still" but so does Luke's ability to fashion a believable travel narrative.[228] But against this conclusion we have two explicit themes in v. 1 which, protruding like tips of an iceberg, signal the necessity of further exploration. First, there are the "increasing crowds." Second, there is the "leaven of the Pharisees which is hypocrisy." This hypocrisy in the context of the Pharisees' meal fellowship, on the one side (11:37–54), and of teaching directed "first" to the disciples, on the other, not only invites but requires greater illumination. What does the teaching of vv. 2ff. have to do with *hypocrisy*?

Verse 2 speaks of that which is "covered up" or "hidden" coming into a full and recognizable form (i.e., it "will be revealed"). In the light of the revelation of Jesus as the prophetic voice and Son of the reigning presence of God, which is both manifested and celebrated (10:1–24; cf. vv. 38–42) or stifled and denied in a meal setting (11:37–54; cf. 10:38–42), the referent of this revelation must be carefully delineated. Verse 3 gives the clue. "Because[229] whatever *you* have said in the dark will be heard in the light, what you have spoken in the inner rooms will be proclaimed upon the housetops." *"You"* can refer only to the disciples whom Jesus is addressing. But where in Luke's narrative have the disciples spoken privately within the confines of a home? Only in the mission of the Seventy(-two) where the "house" is the center of proclamation![230] That is, the disciples' message of peace accepted and celebrated by the hosts will be "hearkened to" (ἀκουσθήσεται) like a public announcement from the rooftops. Their mission will not be squelched by the resistance of hypocrisy, the leaven that conceals the allegiance of one's heart.[231] Now it is precisely the Pharisees of 11:37–54 who, on the one hand, have attempted within the public perusal to maintain a cordial, even engaging, friendship with Jesus by listening to his teaching and inviting him to their meals. On the other hand, they refuse to acknowledge his authoritative word and to receive him like children as the journeying Prophet, the Son of the Father (11:39–52). Therefore vv. 2–3 are a direct rebuttal of the

Pharisees' rejection of Jesus' authority—a denial that "defiles folk," "removes the key of knowledge," "kills Israel's prophets," and thus hinders or prevents people from entering the presence of the reign of God mediated through the Son. This hypocritical behavior will be fully exposed (v. 2)!

This link of vv. 2–3 with 12:1 and 11:37–54 not only demonstrates a logical progression in Luke's presentation but is further substantiated by the continuing sequence.[232] Verse 4: "I tell you, my friends, do not fear those who kill the body." This admonition seems totally out of context; who is committing murder that anyone should fear? But Jesus has just accused the lawyers of consenting to the deeds of their "fathers" who killed the prophets (11:47–51). These same Pharisees-lawyers are now acting in a hostile manner to Jesus (11:54). The connection back to them continues from vv. 1–3; the disciples are not to fear those who cannot destroy anything more than the body. Rather, there is only one person to fear—God, who possesses the authority to "cast into Gehenna" (v. 5). It is this fear of God which removes all fear of people,[233] because God protects and upholds folk, whose hairs are numbered and who are of much greater value than the sparrows which even he does not neglect (vv. 6–7). The fatherly provision and concern of God of 11:1–13 is here again declared by Jesus, whose own authority is given in the following verses. Everyone who declares allegiance to Jesus before other human beings, that one the Son of Humankind will also acknowledge before the angels of God (v. 8). Irrespective of Jesus' relation to the Son of Man in this verse, how "men" relate to Jesus in the present determines their ultimate fate before God. Thus Jesus possesses the authority to declare to these same "men" what God is like and how humankind must relate to him; the content and authoritative resonance of his statements here echo not only his teaching in 11:1–13 but also statements in 10:17–20, 21–24. "But the one who has repudiated or disowned allegiance to me before fellow human beings, that one will be repudiated before the angels of God" (v. 9). Fearlessness of other people through fear of God is therefore equated to submission to this authority in Jesus.

But who are those who have denied Jesus' authority before other people (v. 9)? Jesus states that the Pharisees-lawyers of 11:37–54 have removed ($\mathring{\eta}\rho\alpha\tau\epsilon$) the key that opens folk to knowledge of the Kingdom in their midst and have prevented ($\grave{\epsilon}\kappa\omega\lambda\acute{\upsilon}\sigma\alpha\tau\epsilon$) them from entering (11:52). Consequently, those like the Pharisees-lawyers who have hindered others stand in the danger of being denied by God at the judgment; certainly there is no reason for the disciples, Jesus' friends,[234] to fear. For it is only the one who blasphemes against the Holy Spirit (v. 10b) who will not be forgiven; there is still hope for those who speak against the Son of Man (v. 10a). Presumably Luke intends this Son of Man to be Jesus' self-designation.[235] Then the thrust is this: Those like Simon the Pharisee, or like Peter, who will oppose Jesus out of failure to recognize or accept his authority, can still be forgiven; but those who have resolutely determined (aorist) to deny Jesus' revelation of the Father (10:21–22) and granting of the Holy Spirit to others (11:13) cannot be forgiven. Not only do they deny life for themselves but in so doing destroy life for others. Such opposition is blasphemous, because in essence it takes the presence of God and confines it to the presence of evil folk (cf. 11:15–16). But that is the same as covering up that which is being revealed, or hiding that which is being known (v. 2) in Jesus' and his disciples' journeying ministry—a maneuver Jesus terms "hypocrisy." It is thus that "leaven" which prevents this generation from repenting and from receiving Jesus' authority.[236] Here again vv. 9–10 are alluding back to the opposition of the Pharisees-lawyers of 11:37–54.

Verses 11–12 confirm this connection. The thought is on the continuing mission of the disciples, whether in the immediate journey or the future. Reference to folk bringing them to synagogues and civil rulers makes no sense here at all unless the resistance of vv. 9–10 and especially of v. 4 with its connection to 11:37–54; 12:1–3 is taken into account. Jesus has already warned the Seventy(-two) that they will encounter wolves (10:3, 10–12) and has told all who would follow him that cross bearing (9:23) with loss of life (9:24) and no place of hospitality (9:57–58) is the daily agenda. And now in the light of Jesus' accusation of the Pharisees-lawyers' murder of the prophets (11:47–51), their determination to corner him (11:53–54), Jesus' warning against their influence (12:1b–2), and mention of the disciples' counter mission in households (12:3) with fear of fierce opposition (12:4), the defense of their allegiance before synagogue officials and other authorities makes complete sense. But, says Jesus, they are not to worry (cf. 10:41) about denying their bonds to himself (12:9) or about blaspheming the Holy Spirit (12:10b), for this same Spirit will instruct them in their defense at that hour of testing. Here again is the promise of the Holy Spirit (11:13) to those who have aligned themselves with the authority of Jesus as the spokesman for God (11:2–13 — 12:4–11). The intimate relation of Jesus with God and the Spirit is in evidence again as in 10:17–20, 21–24; 11:1–4, 9–13, especially in the coordinate function of Jesus teaching the disciples what to say in 11:1–4 as the Spirit will do in Jesus' absence (12:11–12).

In sum, the threat of the Pharisees-lawyers of 11:53–54 is taken up at once by Jesus with his disciples by direct reference to their mission as journeying guests (12:3). Though this reference is easy to miss in the light of the seemingly arbitrary and disconnected order of sayings in 12:4–12, yet it is precisely this motif which brings cohesion to the whole of 12:1–

12 and integrates it to the preceding story of Jesus as guest with the Pharisees. That the corresponding tradition in Matthew is placed in the mission charge of Luke 10 should come as no surprise. Now in Luke a signal warning is sounded against the leaven of these Pharisees; Jesus declares that this invisible influence can lead to no less than the denial of this generation before God. Their resistance is a matter of eternal life and death. The journeying-guest motif again links up with Deuteronomistic tenet C as the murder of all the prophets is brought to bear upon the disciples. Not only Jesus but they as well are meeting the opposition which issues in the monolithic murder of the prophets. Thus through the "journeying guest" we discover again (see tenet A) that 11:14–54 forms the watershed for the rejection of Jesus that propels the drama throughout the Central Section to its climax in Jerusalem. It is the opposition from Israel's recognized religious authorities as pictured in the lawyer of 10:25–37, and not from the Samaritans (9:52–56) or of the distraction of *diakonia* (10:38–42), that gives form and substance to the distinctive Deuteronomistic view and hence to the shape of the Central Section.

9. **Luke 12:22–34.** * After an interjection by one from the pressing crowds (cf. 12:1) in 12:13–21, Jesus focuses again upon his disciples in 12:22–32, 33–34,[237] now referring explicitly to God as the disciples' Father (v. 30; cf. 11:2; 10:21–22). The concern is with seeking material wealth which all the nations of the world (v. 30) pursue and which has been so graphically illustrated by the "rich fool" (vv. 16–21).[238]

But one may wonder why the disciples' concern for material things is mentioned at all here. Merely because someone in the crowd is anxious for one's own inheritance (21:13–15) does not mean that the disciples themselves are preoccupied with accruing wealth.[239] Again it is only the journeying-guest motif which adequately illuminates the positioning of this teaching on anxiety and possessions. For these concerns mirror the situation of mission (cf. 11:1–13 and 12:1–12). In contrast to the nations (v. 30),[240] Jesus' disciples, called to follow him to Jerusalem (9:23–27, 57–62), are to set their sights constantly on this goal and not upon provisions which the Father will grant. It is already clear that certain individuals had difficulty with the cost of this kind of commitment (9:59–62); that some of the disciples would worry about daily provisions is most likely. What is more, the "hard sayings" of v. 33 take on a rationale not otherwise possible in the present context. The disciples are to sell their possessions and give alms, not only because these will encumber them as they journey but also because their maintenance (growing old, thieves plundering, moth destroying) will distract them from their real treasure which is the Kingdom (v. 32), the presence of the One "in the heavens" (v. 33) that does not fail! Like the Seventy(-two), they are not to carry a purse (v. 33b),[241] for where their treasure is, there will be the heart of their commitment.

10. **Luke 12:35–48.** Continuing on without change of audience, Jesus exhorts the disciples to be "ready" (v. 40), like servants waiting to receive (προσδέχομαι;[242] cf. 15:2) their master when he returns from a great feast[243] (vv. 35–38;[244] cf. 14:8). There is thus an immediate tie-in with the rich man of 12:16–21 who is caught off guard by God in the midst of his foolish dissipation in "eating, drinking, and merry making" (vv. 19–20). But whereas in 12:13–21, 22–32 the accent is on the disciples' need to be rich toward God, now attention shifts to the disciples' need to be awake in exercising the eschatological stewardship entrusted to them (12:41–48). We can untangle three interwoven strands of the journeying-guest motif:

a. The Coming of the Lord. The journey theme is expressed by ἔρχομαι in vv. 36, 37, 38, 39, 40, 43, 45 and by ἥκω in v. 46. Like the Lord of 10:1 (ὁ κύριος) who is "about to come," the lord of vv. 36–38 is about to come from a banquet, while the lord of a household in vv. 42–48 is expected to come from a journey. Yet he comes at an unexpected day and unknown hour (v. 46) to servants unprepared to meet him (vv. 45–48). In v. 41 Peter addresses Jesus as lord, while the narrative uses this same appellative in v. 42. Thus another line of continuity from previous journeying-guest material is maintained (cf. Luke 9; 10; 11). Jesus, "the Lord" of 11:39, "comes out" (ἐξέρχομαι) from a banquet (11:37–52) to the crowds and disciples in 11:53–54, while the Son of Man "comes" in 12:40. It would appear to be more than coincidental that in 7:34; 9:58; 11:30; 17:25; 18:8;[245] and 19:10 *Jesus is the Son of Man who has come or is coming to Jerusalem as the journeying guest.*[246]

b. The Coming of the Lord of the Household. The "house" imagery of Luke 9—12 is developed in 12:35–48. The "house" (chapters 9—12) and particularly the knocking and opening of a door to receive a neighbor as journeying guest (11:5–8) are now transformed into the journeying lord of the household who himself returns from a banquet (12:35–38).

Not only is the excuse that the door is already shut and the household asleep not valid but also the closed door becomes symbolic of servants unfit for their lord (v. 36b). The demand for "watchful" servants is pointed in vv. 39–40. Here even the "master of the household" is taken by surprise by the coming (ἔρχομαι) thief. Like the goods susceptible to the thief in 12:33, the house in v. 39 is plundered. *A minore ad maius,* do the *servants* have to be on their guard!

As Jesus makes inescapably clear, the Son of Man comes as lord of the house when *you* (the disciples) do not think he will come. As in 9:57–62;

10:1–20; and 12:2–12, no other pursuits can be allowed to distract the disciples *at the present time!*[247]

That the stakes are no less than in 9:57–62; 10:1–24; 12:2–12 becomes manifest in the third parable of vv. 42–48, where everything revolves around the performance of the "house steward" (v. 42).

> If he faithfully exercises his duties with *a sense of the urgency of the situation,* then he will be rewarded when the master comes (vv. 43–44). But if not, then the master will come at a totally unexpected time[248] and punish this servant by "cutting him off" from the lot of the blessed.

The language of ultimate fate in the judgment is prominent here (cf. vv. 47–48).[249] Consequently the common trait of all three parables is the coming of the Lord with either blessing for those faithfully prepared to meet/receive him or judgment for the unfaithful who are caught unprepared.

c. The Serving of a Meal by the Coming Lord of the Household. In addition to the journeying-house-householder stock vocabulary the meal-food imagery is equally evident: *(i)* The servants of vv. 35–38 are waiting for their master to return from a banquet (v. 36). *(ii)* Upon finding alert, girded servants, this master girds himself and serves them a meal (v. 3). *(iii)* The faithful, alert servant is the one who distributes food[250] to the rest of the servants of the household at the proper time (v. 42b). *(iv)* The unfaithful, dissipated servant is symbolized by an eating and drinking to drunkenness (v. 45) and hence unpreparedness (v. 46).

"Food" and a "meal" are metaphors for the proper relation of the disciples to Jesus. Jesus is saying that there is a master-servant relation with eschatological significance in their midst. How the disciples relate to the Master by conducting his stewardship *in the present* is all-important. It should not be surprising within the context of a mission journey of both Jesus and his disciples that Jesus would select the meal imagery as paradigmatic of the disciples' relation of submission and total dependence upon their Lord. For not only were the disciples dependent upon their identification with Jesus to receive hospitality from their hosts but also the home meal itself became the fullest expression of the relationship of blessing and salvation to the presence of the Lord in their midst. But now this image is developed distinctly in the direction of *service.* To be rightly aligned with the authority of this Master is to enjoy his presence at the table at which he serves: *Jesus is the host.* But we have already seen Jesus host the feeding of the five thousand when he receives the crowds. And as guest, Jesus seems to assume the role of host at table (cf. esp. 13:26; 15:2; 19:5). Moreover, we have seen that, for Luke, Jesus' disciples play an important role in distributing the food as Jesus serves the five thousand.[251] Now this role becomes parabolic of faithful servanthood or stewardship in 12:42 as they follow their Master's example as they in turn follow him to Jerusalem.

But there is also a different kind of serving—the eating and drinking of the food that was supposed to be distributed to the household (vv. 42–43, 45). This eating and drinking becomes a token of the unfaithful servant who, in spite of *knowledge* of the master's will, still does not make ready[252] nor act[253] accordingly (v. 47). Because he has been given much responsibility, much will be required ($\zeta\eta\tau\eta\theta\acute{\eta}\sigma\epsilon\tau\alpha\iota$) from him (v. 48).

We have just witnessed an eating and drinking by the Pharisees with Jesus in 11:37–54 that ends with the solemn declaration that they will be held accountable ($\grave{\epsilon}\kappa\zeta\eta\tau\eta\theta\acute{\eta}\sigma\epsilon\tau\alpha\iota$)[254] in the judgment for a whole history of rejection. They have not "entered" despite holding "the key of knowledge" of salvation. We will have to suspend judgment at this point as to whether the Pharisees are distinctly mirrored in vv. 45–47.

It is clear that Jesus' warning to his disciples of an eating and drinking that is not prepared to receive the Master when he comes is as pressing as the warning against the "leaven" of the Pharisees in 12:1ff. Opposition is definitely in the air and it is already infecting the disciples (v. 40b). Peter wonders whether Jesus should not actually be addressing the crowds instead of them (v. 41). After all, the disciples are the ones who have left their goods behind and are following Jesus; surely they are prepared for any inbreaking of the Kingdom in the coming Son of Man. But Peter's protest prompts an even sterner warning. Only that servant who is faithfully serving the stewardship *at the proper time* will meet with blessing. Moreover, that same servant (v. 45) may be tempted to "eat and drink" to destruction (v. 46). The situation is now worse than in 12:1–12; the threat is laced now with no consolation (cf. 12:2–8, 10a, 11–12). Even the one who does not know the Master's will will be punished (v. 48a).[255] In conclusion, the "journeying-guest" motif has revealed an increase in opposition to Jesus, the Lord (cf. vv. 41–42); tenet C, however, is only indirectly expressed.

11. **Luke 12:49–53.** Jesus continues uninterrupted. "I have come" (v. 49). Now it would appear that the dramatic buildup of opposition pictured in the parables is stated in the open and applied directly by Jesus to himself. The use of $\H{\epsilon}\rho\chi o\mu\alpha\iota$ here, following its occurrence seven times in 12:35–48 (four times in the aorist tense, referring to people's preparedness once the "lord" has come; vv. 36–38, 43), should at least signal a possible connection in thought. It is precisely a response to one who has *arrived* in the crowd's midst which vv. 49–53 bring to focus. Jesus

announces that he has already come to kindle division within the *house* (v. 52). Now instead of being the center of the unity of the presence of the Kingdom (e.g., 10:1–24), the household is the heart of disunity (v. 51). The greater intensity of opposition to Jesus in 12:35–48 is thus manifest. But in addition, Jesus' coming is not over: *(a)* the fire of division has not been kindled yet (v. 49); *(b)* Jesus' "baptism" has not yet been finally accomplished (v. 50); and *(c)* "from this point on" the dissension will take place in the house (vv. 52–53).[256] *Jesus is thus the one who has come and who is coming.*

The temporal relation of the thief who has already come to the Son of Man who is coming in 12:39–40 is an exact parabolic counterpart,[257] while the house and the disturbance of its peace is the univocal link of warning in both passages. Moreover, the temporal relation of Jesus' activity as a source of strife and division in 11:14–54 to that of the Son of Man's appearance as a sign in 11:29–32 is strikingly close: the one greater than Solomon and Jonah who is already here and who destroys the peace (v. 21; cf. 12:51) in the palace (11:21–23) and brings disturbance to the "rest" of the house in 11:24–26 is the *sign of Jonah* which *is* and *shall be*[258] the *sign of the Son of Man* to this evil generation!

Therefore we can conclude that the decided weight of the evidence points to *the three parables of 12:35–48 as a self-description of Jesus' arrival as the Lord of the household and of his imminent coming or journeying in the present and immediate future.*[259] From now on, Jesus declares, his journeying will pit members of the household dead set against each other. We thus see already that Jesus' prophecy in 12:2–3 of an open, publicly declared mission that leads to persecution and even murder (12:4–12) is already on the point of fulfillment. And in 12:54–56, 57–59, Luke goes on to declare that the "crowds" likewise are hypocrites, that in fact they are also journeying but to the judge with their accuser, the "caster of fire," in their midst. The note of *opposition* and *rejection* which leads to the persecution and *murder* of the prophets à la tenet C in 11:47–51 is thus extended throughout the whole of Luke 12. How this opposition can congeal so quickly from a comforting of the disciples in 12:2–12 to the sternest of warnings to this same group—from that servant who is blessed to the same one "cut in pieces" in 12:35–48, 49–53—will be the ongoing thrust of our investigation.

12. **Luke 13:22–30.**[260] At 13:10 the tableau of 12:1—13:9 shifts to Jesus' teaching in a synagogue where "all his adversaries," "you hypocrites" (v. 15; cf. 12:1, 56), are "put to shame" (13:17). Following his teaching there (13:18–19, 20–21), the travel notice of 13:22 only articu-

lates expressly what the reader has been witnessing all along through the mission of 9:52ff. and the growing resistance in Luke 11 and 12: "Now he continued to pass through [imperfect tense] towns and villages, teaching and making progress toward Jerusalem." When an anonymous person asks about those "being saved," Jesus answers with the home-meal imagery of the journeying-guest motif—not at all unlike his response to Peter's question in 12:41.

    a. The figure of the householder shutting the door (v. 25) is reminiscent of 11:7 and the knocking (13:25) on the door of 11:9c, 10c; in both passages the Kingdom of God is depicted, but the contrast in tone is as great as possible. Now instead of picturing God's gracious care of Jesus' disciples, the householder is the uncompromising judge who does not "give" when asked or "open" when people knock (11:9–10); hence the imagery of the journeying-guest mission is used to warn and even pronounce judgment, in keeping with Jesus' instructions in 10:6b, 10–12.

    b. The "eating and drinking" of v. 26 effects the same result as that "eating and drinking" of 12:45—exclusion from the household: those who ate "in the presence of" Jesus did not recognize him as the host. Consequently they are not known by Jesus the journeying Lord of the house (13:23, 25).[261] So far in the Central Section those who have eaten and drunk with Jesus and failed to recognize and submit to his authority are Martha of 10:38–42 and the Pharisees of 11:37–54 (cf. 5:29–39; 7:36–50).

    c. The banquet of the Kingdom of God in v. 29 as hosted by "the Lord of the house" closely parallels the meal served by the Lord of the house in 12:35–38 (cf. "sitting at table," 12:37 and 13:29).

    d. The interrogator (13:23) represents a larger group whom Jesus both exhorts to enter (v. 24a) and yet immediately describes their exclusion (vv. 25–28). Is Luke's portrayal credible here? The present/future relation of the "Lord" (i.e., Jesus) of v. 23 to the "lord" of v. 25 is analogous to that of Jesus to the Son of Man in 11:14ff. and of the three parables of 12:35–48, with the difference that the future referent here describes the journeying ministry of the "Lord" from a point of view when it is already completed and being consummated in the final banquet of the Kingdom of God (vv. 28–29). This relation is thus quite close to 12:8–10, where the Son of Man acknowledges before God those who have acknowledged Jesus on his journey (cf. 11:53—12:3). What we have in 13:22–30, then, is a group who are headed for the judgment (like those of 12:54–56, 57–59) but still have the possibility of altering this course. However, the situation has deteriorated to an even greater extent. Now the threat of judgment of 12:57–59 has become a pronouncement of judgment (v. 27); their future exclusion is painted in all too vivid terms.

    e. The tension of *d.* coupled with the frustrated striving of v. 24b which yields only impotence suggests the ignorance and inability of judging the "present time" by the crowds in 12:57–59.[262] Self-discernment appears to be incapacitated. Again we find evidence of a *hindering* influence that leads to prevention; the thought of 11:52 is not far away. In return, Jesus vows that there are those who are "the first" (v. 30; cf. 11:43; 14:8; 19:47)[263] who will become the last, and "the last," like the Gentiles (v. 29), who become the first.

We can conclude that the home-meal imagery of the journeying-guest motif has disclosed once again an opposition to Jesus' authority which is augmenting steadily as he approaches Jerusalem. Though tenet C is not explicit, yet it is clear that the Lord of the Banquet who consummates all the prophets (v. 28) by eating and drinking and teaching in the streets of Israel (v. 26) is not received.

13. **Luke 13:31–33,**[264] **34–35.**[265] Jesus, sent to an Israel (tenet B, v. 34a) that has always stoned and killed God's messengers (tenet A, v. 34a), must continue his journey of rejection through its towns and byways in order to reap the prophet's "reward" (tenet C, vv. 31b, 33, 34b). Indeed he must continue to "exorcise demons" and "effect cures" in the villages and homes of Israel as he journeys as guest (vv. 32b–33a, 34b, 35b; cf. esp. 10:9, 17; 11:14–15, 18–20). But because of Israel's calloused reception of the one who again and again has attempted to gather her children (v. 34b; cf. esp. 10:2; 11:23, 29–32; 12:32), the judgment of God must fall upon this nation (tenet D, v. 35a).

In this pithy summary Luke has fully integrated the journeying-guest imagery with the Deuteronomistic conception of the prophets' reception. According to Luke, Jesus' entire journey mission is comprehensible only under the Deuteronomistic rubric; our use then of the journeying-guest motif to measure this contour is substantiated.

In the light of the threefold lines of connection of 13:34–35 with 11:47–52 and 19:41–44 (see tenet B),[266] the question arises whether "your house" of v. 35a must not also be construed within the journeying-guest motif.

We have already shown the high probability of "house" standing simultaneously for "the whole nation" and the "Temple." Further, we have just seen not only that "house" can represent the Kingdom of the Lord of the journey (12:35–48; 13:22–30) but that a hindering presence in 13:22–30 also results in "many" not being able to enter the "house" in which "all the prophets" gather. The convergence of the house imagery with the theme of judgment on the one side, and with the hindering of the journeying prophet on the other, both already combined in 13:22–30, argues strongly against a fortuitous clustering of these conceptions in 13:31–35. Rather, Jerusalem's "house" symbolizes all that is dead set against Jesus' "house." The strife within the "house" of 12:49–53 seems already to be won by this "house" of opposition to Jesus, since its children "would not" (plural verb; v. 34b).

In conclusion, then, 13:31–33, 34–35 brings the journeying-guest motif to a new climax: Jesus as journeying guest–prophet is denied the receiving commensurate with his authority. Though the journey is only half completed,[267] tenets A—D are already distinctly developed and have determined the shape of this half.

14. **Luke 14:1–24.***[268] In 14:1 Jesus, "the coming one" (13:35b), "comes" as guest to the house of "one of the rulers of the Pharisees."[269] In 14:25 "many crowds journey with" him and are told to "come after" him with their crosses. The journey to death of 13:33–34 through villages and houses continues (cf. 10:1ff.; 9:51ff.).

Opposition to this sending is the keynote of his visit; already in v. 1b "the lawyers and Pharisees" (v. 3) are "watching"[270] Jesus to catch him in a violation of the Law. The plan of 11:53–54, and example of that in 13:31–33, appears to be unfolding here.

> That the objection of the "ruler of the synagogue" in 13:14 should also be included in this scheming seems probable, given the same Sabbath controversy[271] of healing, the use of "adversary" to describe this objection (13:17), the epithet "hypocrites" joined with an instance of a hypocritical violation of the objectors' own interpretation of the Law (13:15—14:5), and the inability of the opposition to withstand Jesus' counter-offensives (13:17a—14:6; cf. 11:37–38, 39–52).

To be sure, a certain friendliness must be assumed, since again Jesus is included in the sacral meal fellowship.[272] Further, the reader is led to believe that Jesus is in an entirely different locality in 14:1–24 from that in 11:37–54, so that a conspiracy between the two groups would appear unlikely. And in marked contrast to 11:39–52, Jesus' teaching in 14:7–11, 12–14 is not studded with venomous barbs. The tone seems to be that of a concerned friend who wishes to assure his fellow guests of reward in the resurrection of the just (v. 14). Jesus uses the language of the home-meal fellowship of his present situation to teach the meaning of "humility" (v. 11). He has noticed how the guests were striving for the "first seats" of honor and chides them by using the setting of a banquet akin to 12:35–38 and 13:22–30. The host is one who, when he comes (vv. 9, 10), rewards or punishes those at table like a householder taking charge over his servants (12:36–38) or the lord of the household controlling his banquet room (13:25–27). To the Pharisee who invited him, Jesus cautions against an inclusion of only his friends, relatives, and rich neighbors which yields no heavenly reward (vv. 13–14); rather, the "poor," the "crippled," the "lame," and the "blind" should be invited.[273] It would seem that vv. 7–14 follow vv. 1–6 rather oddly, since the table dynamics appear to have improved drastically.[274] Yet with Luke picturing Jesus as the Lord[275] of the house of the Kingdom of God and host of the banquet of salvation, the imagery in 14:7–14 should alert us that far more is at stake than friendly words of correction about rewards. By the time Jesus finishes comparing the banquet in the house (v. 23b) of vv. 16–24 with the banquet that is before him, it has become certain that it is the "house" of the Pharisees of 13:35a which is to be "vacated" of salvation:

> *(a)* The "poor," "crippled," and others of v. 13 are those receiving the blessings of the "coming one" in 7:19 for whom Jesus is sent (7:19–20; 4:18– 19) and who form a foil to the Pharisees and the lawyers in 7:18–35. To invite this group to a banquet would be to imitate Jesus' practice as well as to symbolize the banquet of the Kingdom of God (cf. 7:34–35, 36–50; 10:8– 9).[276] *(b)* In v. 15 one of the table guests apparently attempts to qualify Jesus' restriction in vv. 13–14 by referring "blessedness" to all who participate in the heavenly banquet. It would seem that Jesus' admonitions in vv. 7–11, 12–14 have fallen on deaf ears. *(c)* This speculation is borne out by the overriding point of Jesus' parable in rejoinder: the many who are originally invited end up being excluded from the banquet by excluding themselves (vv. 18–20, 24). Not all those who think they will dine in the great feast will be permitted to come.[277] Like the servants of 12:45–48 who were not ready (v. 47) to receive the Master, so those invited (vv. 17–20) are not ready (cf. 14:17) to receive the invitation through the servant of the Master when he comes. *(d)* The warning of exclusion is given specific application by the mention of "the poor and crippled and blind and lame" in v. 21, the very group that the Pharisee host should be inviting, and by allusion to those "outside" the boundaries of God's people (v. 23); by not too subtle inference the friends, relatives, and rich neighbors of the host (i.e., *the guests around the table*) are the ones who shall not "taste my banquet" (v. 24).

What has occurred, then? By the end of the meal scene, the level of conflict has reached and even surpassed the opening confrontation over the Law.[278] None of the "many" invited will receive the "blessedness" of the Kingdom of God (cf. 13:25–28; 13:35a). Now the Pharisees are told not only that they bear the responsibility for the "many" in the coming judgment but that they themselves are entering the phase when they will no longer be invited![279] They not only "have not entered themselves" (11:52) but can no longer expect an "invitation." Behind the figures sent to the "many" by the master in vv. 16–24 are the indelible imprints of tenets B and C. From the vantage point of Jesus' mission, therefore, the parenetic thrust of vv. 7–14 must be understood as an ultimate warning.[280] The Pharisees' own meal practice and especially their own *eating and drinking* with Jesus are not allowing them to recognize the Lord of the Banquet in their midst (cf. vv. 21–23). They are too puffed up with self-esteem in interpreting and guarding the Law that they are numb to the invitation by the Lord of the household (v. 21) at their own table. Guest and host have fully converged in 14:1–24. As journeying guest, Jesus uses the home-meal imagery of the Kingdom and its banquet to announce that he is the host. Only those who receive him as guest in their home can receive him as Lord and host of the Banquet of the Kingdom of God.

15. **Luke 14:25–33.**[281] Apart from the verb παρατηρέω in 14:1, in 14:1–24 Luke does not broach the idea of a violent rejection of Israel's messengers. Though the "servant" (v. 17) of the Master is not accorded the proper response, there is no hint of his maltreatment. But through the frame of v. 25 followed by the demand of "bearing a cross" (vv. 26–27), the "watching" in 14:1–6, the "hypocrisy" of the Pharisees-lawyers (vv. 7–14), and Jesus' judgment of their exclusion (vv. 15–24) are all darkened by the shadow of Jesus' violent fate in Jerusalem. In 14:1–24 Luke consequently recapitulates the growing hostility to Jesus of 9:52—13:35 by portraying in microcosm the increasing rejection of the journeying guest–prophet–Lord of the Kingdom (i.e., from table fellowship, 14:1, to the shattering of this fellowship, vv. 15–24). The judgment of 13:35a is palpably presented. It is not coincidence that from this point on Jesus is never again at table in the "house" of the Pharisees.[282]

16. **Luke 15:1–32.**[283] After pronouncing judgment on certain Pharisees-lawyers in 14:15–24, "the Pharisees and the scribes" return the compliment in 15:2. The murmuring (διαγογγύζω) against Jesus' table fellowship echoes the same complaint of 5:30 and 7:34 (cf. 7:30). But now the "tables" are fully turned! Jesus is the host and he decides who is fit and "clean." He "welcomes" or "receives" the ones who are hearkening to him as his "guests" at table! The "great reversal" of 14:15–24 is already coming true as the outcasts invited in 14:21–22 are the ones coming to the "banquet" with Jesus in 15:1–2.[284] Though this ministry of Jesus is not new, what now becomes lucid in the light of the journeying-guest motif is that Jesus journeys to Jerusalem, inviting folk in the present as Lord of the household of the Kingdom to his banquet. And it is the Pharisees-lawyers (scribes) who are the arch antagonists to this journeying.

Three parables illustrate this sharp demarcation, using the "journey-ing-guest" home-meal language. In 15:4–7 after the shepherd journeys to find the lost sheep, he rejoices with his friends and neighbors in his "home" over a meal. Likewise a woman (15:8–10) searches diligently for a lost coin until she finds it and then invites her friends and neighbors to her home for a meal celebration. In both instances Jesus does not allow the point to escape his Pharisees-scribes audience: He is like the shepherd and the woman by seeking out the lost and separated folk from society and bringing them to the table fellowship of repentant sinners (15:7, 10). With the authority to voice how God ("heaven"/"angels," vv. 7, 10) views "sinners," Jesus etches an impression of his own sending to invite and receive sinners who repent. We thus have the same mission portrayed as that of the messengers and the Seventy(-two) in 9:52–56 and 10:1–24, with the difference that Jesus as host summons his guests not to his own but to his Father's "house" of the Kingdom of God.

In 15:11–32 the division in the households of this mission (12:49–53) is graphically painted, with the antagonists highlighted in the elder son. The profligate, "unclean" sinner son (vv. 13–14), who eats the food of the uncleanest animals (v. 16), and "devours" the father's living with the uncleanest of humans (v. 30) but repents of his sin[285] and comes (vv. 18, 20, 30) to the father (vv. 17–21), becomes an object of repugnance to his older brother, who refuses to enter the house to have table fellowship with him (vv. 25–32; cf. imperfect verb, v. 28b; 11:52b). The parallel to 15:1–2 is obvious. Just as the Pharisees-scribes criticize Jesus for receiv-ing such unclean folk and eating with them, thereby forcing Jesus to defend his practice (vv. 3–10), so the older son criticizes the father for doing the same, forcing him to give an account of his eating and drinking (vv. 30, 32). And just as Jesus entreats the Pharisees to enter the banquet house of the Kingdom (14:1–24), so the father entreats the son to enter his house for the feast (v. 28b).[286] But in both cases the entreaty appears to be of no avail (cf. 14:15; 15:28). The home-meal fellowship is split asunder.

In sum, 15:1–32 mirrors the dynamic of affairs in 14:1–24. Though talk of Jesus' denouement is not expressed, yet opposition is sounded by the Pharisees right from the beginning. In both scenes Jesus' association with "unclean" at table casts the gravest aspersion upon his "house."

17. **Luke 16:1–15.*** The parable of the unjust steward is extremely difficult to decipher.[287] The journeying-guest motif may provide some clues:

a. There is an audience change to the disciples in v. 1, though the Pharisees are still within earshot (v. 14).

b. There are several parallels of comparison/contrast to previous parables: (i) Like the prodigal son, the steward realizes that a decisive action is necessary to retain at least some of the well-being that he enjoyed in the master's (vv. 3, 5, 8) house (16:3–7; cf. 15:14–20a). And as with the prodigal, this action follows a "squandering" (16:1; cf. 15:13) of the master's/father's goods. The goal of their action consequently is "to be received" into the house or the houses (16:4; cf. 15:25). (ii) Like the Pharisee host of 14:12–14, the steward uses material wealth to place others in his debt. Through the management/manipulation of this wealth, others become dependent upon them for favor and/or have the obligation to pay them back (cf. 14:14). (iii) Like the householder/lord of 13:22–30, the lord of the house in 16:1–9 casts out or dismisses people from his house. (iv) Unlike the "wise steward" (12:42; cf. 16:8) of 12:42–47 who mismanages the master's house and eats and drinks what he should be distributing and hence is punished, the steward of 16:1–9 is commended for his dishonest handling of the food distribution/accounts (16:8), though on the basis of his action only after he had been formally dismissed. (v) Unlike Jesus' exhortations to the disciples in 12:22–32, the steward worries about what he will eat and wear and "all the rest" (16:3–4). (vi) As with the rich man of 12:16–21 and of 16:19–31, the steward's actions are controlled by mammon; there seems to be no escape from its snare. (vii) Like the Seventy(-two) in 10:1–20, the steward is dependent upon being received into homes for his sustenance; but in complete contrast to them, he uses material wealth to control in advance the outcome of this receiving (cf. 9:52–56—messengers). (viii) Similar to the "creditor" of 7:41–43, the steward builds up favor/love by remitting the debts of the dependents. Thus the steward receives the love/favor which is ultimately due the master.[288]

The closest parallel to the steward's behavior is undoubtedly that of the Pharisee in 14:12–14. The steward/Pharisee knows how to use material goods to the utmost for one's own advantage (cf. the attitude of wanting the "first seat" in 14:7–11). The rich master commends the steward because he has shown great shrewdness and adroitness in the business world, where material advantage determines the vitality of life. That is to say, the steward is exalted among the folk of his *own generation*[289] (v. 8b) as a man deft in the spirit of his age[290] (v. 8b). The point for the disciples, then, is that they are to treat material things in a way that is equally adroit but in a just way that does not enslave them to master mammon (v. 9). Like the steward, they are to make friends by their use of material goods but only in a way that at the same time prepares them to be "received" into the eternal dwellings[291] (v. 9b). Like the faithful and shrewd steward of 12:42–45, they are to exercise proper management of material things which ultimately are not their own but pass away (v. 9b). That the Pharisees are primarily in mind as Jesus describes the "dishonest steward" can already at this point be supported by the following:

(1) The steward's behavior closely parallels the Pharisee of 14:12–14; moreover, the great social pride and vanity of the steward's remark (v. 3b) is akin to the pride of the first seats in both 14:7–11 and 11:43.

(2) Jesus tells the Pharisees point blank that they (you) are the "ones who justify yourselves in the sight of others" (16:15a); this comes directly after the narrative comment that they are "money lovers." Such a combination leads to an exalted position in society but is an "abomination in the sight of God" (16:15b). Thus like the steward who is exalted among folk and who uses mammon to justify his own status vis-à-vis his generation, so the Pharisees are driven by mammon. God knows their hearts (v. 15a), just as Jesus claims to know the inner condition of the Pharisees of 11:37–54 as greed and covetousness (11:39). Jesus' direction to them there is to give alms (11:41); such may be in mind in 16:9a[292] as in 12:32, as an antidote for the disciples (cf. 16:10–12).

(3) While the steward's shrewdness to act decisively with his "possessions" at the point of crisis is held up as exemplary by Jesus, his attempt to serve both mammon and his master at the same time is pictured as a fiasco (16:1–2). This is the climax of the application of 16:10–13 in 16:13: God and mammon cannot be served as joint masters. To this the Pharisees react with scoffing. Since they are "lovers of money," the implication is that they regard Jesus' illustration (16:1–9) and application (16:10–12) as an absurd insinuation. The harshness of Jesus' retort in turn is indication enough that the Pharisees' personal ire has been raised (cf. 11:45).

(4) The stark either/or of an undivided loyalty in 16:13, 14–15 relates back to the exclusive choices of 14:15–24, 25–33, 34–35; 15:11–32: one must either accept the invitation or serve self and possessions (14:15–24); loyalty to Jesus' journeying ministry must be absolute even to the degree of renouncing all of one's possessions (vv. 25–33); salt is either good or useless, there is no in-between (vv. 34–35); either the house is united over table or it is divided (15:11–32).

(5) In 16:8 the steward's shrewdness in dealing with his generation is compared with the "sons of light"; whoever are denoted by the latter, the idea is clear that they do not exercise nearly the control or influence upon their generation as the former;[293] the steward's manipulation of the relation between the debtors and their "lord" is the paradigm for the "sons of this world." We have already detected a definite hindering/manipulating influence by the Pharisees-scribes vis-à-vis the crowds in accepting Jesus' authority: In 11:52 they are hindering/preventing others from entering the Kingdom; their hypocrisy will be fully exposed (12:1–4) as the disciples carry out

their mission amidst persecution (12:4–12); a ruler of the synagogue, one of certain hypocritical adversaries, counters Jesus before the gathered worshipers in 13:10–17; people must continue to strive to enter the banquet of the Kingdom, since many, though seeking, will not be strong enough to enter; at that very hour some Pharisees attempt to veer Jesus from his journey mission (13:22–30, 31–33) and Jesus declares that Jerusalem's children have resisted his gathering (13:34–35); in 14:1–6 the Pharisees-lawyers oppose Jesus' healing, while the parable of the banquet speaks of "many" who have been excluded through inattention to the importance of the invitation in their midst; in 14:25–33 many multitudes are warned of heedless following, while the Pharisees-scribes murmur against Jesus' association with sinners (15:1–2). We shall again observe that it is more than likely that the Pharisees' leaven of influence over the crowds is alluded to in 16:8.[294]

In sum, the parable of 16:1–9 in its present Lukan context poses the choice between two stewardships (16:10–13): the disciples can choose to be stewards either of the household of God or over the house of mammon of the "sons" of this age. It is precisely the Pharisees who have sold out to the house of mammon, resulting in favor and influence among their generation. The disciples therefore are to be aware of and beware of this influence lest what is exalted among human beings be an abomination before God. The home-meal imagery of the journeying-guest motif has thus again revealed two "houses" of the one divided house. The opposition has become all too clear: not only is the Pharisee's "house" evacuated of salvation (13:34–35), it is also an "abomination before God." Though violent resistance to the prophets is not articulated, opposition to Jesus pulsates with a fever pitch. Jesus is identified with the stewardship of God (v. 13) through the authority to pronounce God's view of the Pharisees' hearts (v. 15). Journeying per se is not explicit, but the imagery of being received into homes reflects the journeying-guest mission of Jesus and the disciples (tenet B). Such language would be a poignant reminder of where their loyalty is cast and upon whom their life depends.

18. **Luke 16:19–31.** In yet another "L" pericope, most of the themes within the journeying-guest motif come together in a distinctive blend. The Pharisees are the primary audience (cf. 16:14–18): *(a)* Another rich man is described as feasting or making merry in sumptuous fashion (v. 19). *(b)* A poor man lies outside the rich man's gate, desiring to be fed from the crumbs of his table (v. 21). *(c)* The poor man (Lazarus) dies and is taken by angels to the bosom of Abraham (vv. 22–23) which most probably refers to reclining at table in the heavenly banquet[295] (cf. 13:28–29). *(d)* In torment the rich man asks Abraham to send Lazarus to come and serve him[296] (v. 24). *(e)* He also requests Abraham to send him to his

father's house (v. 27). As with the house of 12:49–53, there are five inhabitants, and a journey mission to this house is conceived (cf. v. 30). And as with the mission of the Seventy(-two), the house is to be called to repentance (v. 30). *(f)* Abraham's reference to "Moses and the prophets" recalls "Abraham, Isaac, and Jacob and all the prophets" at table in 13:28–29; yet the delineation of the "law and the prophets" (cf. 2:22; 20:28, 37; 34:27, 44) in 16:16 suggests here the OT Scriptures read in the synagogue. Nonetheless, in conjunction with a sending (vv. 24, 27) and with a "hearkening" (vv. 29, 31) the themes of Deuteronomistic tenet B in general[297] and of the mountain sending with Moses and Elijah in particular (9:28–36) are brought into focus again. *(g)* Resurrection of the dead harks back to the stir over Jesus among Herod and the crowds in Luke 9. There we noticed that Jesus' unique authority as a prophet like Moses was adumbrated in the rumblings of the people (9:8b), predicated in Jesus' own prediction of his being raised (9:22), and revealed in splendor upon the mountain (9:35, 31, 51).[298] In his journeying to Jerusalem, it is precisely when Jesus speaks of the divided house that he reminds his disciples of the journey to death that he has to accomplish (12:49–53); and it is when he has announced that this division becomes irreversible, that access from one side to the other is cut off (13:25–27; 16:26), that Jesus declares again that he must complete his journey to death (13:22–30, 31–33, 34–35). The idea therefore of a raising "from the dead" in connection with a journey mission links up inevitably with the ongoing drama of Jesus' own sending. What Abraham is stating, then, (see *f*), is that if Moses and the prophets are not read correctly, then the authority of one raised from the dead will not be recognized as well. The continuity of this authority from the OT is thus underscored as in 16:16. But that is exactly what we discovered about Jesus' prophetic status (see Part II) and of his sending (Part III.B, above). *(h)* Tenet C is brought out directly through the refusal to hear the message of those sent to Israel (vv. 30–31) and indirectly through the reference to a death.

We have already demonstrated the great probability that the Pharisees are depicted by the unjust steward of 16:1–9. Now with a rich man (cf. 16:14–15) contrasted to a poor man of the very group the Pharisee of 14:1–24 has not invited to his feast (14:12–14) and the type they deride in 15:1–2, the lesson of 16:19–31 is clear enough. The house of the Pharisees is like the rich man's, where repentance has become impossible through enslavement to "master mammon" (cf. 16:14–15). Whereas the "elder brother" epitomizes the proud Pharisee who begrudges Jesus' "bad company" (15:1–2), the rich man is the symbol of those Pharisees who are exalted among "men" through their manipulation of wealth (16:1–9, 14–

15). Jesus' house or stewardship is thus aligned with the "poor," just as in 14:1–24 and 15:1–32.

In sum, the journeying-guest motif brings the themes of 14:1—16:15 to a head and thus advances the drama to a stage beyond the semiclimax in 13:22–30, 31–33, 34–35. In 15:3–32 Jesus defends his "eating and drinking" by evoking the very joy of God over the table fellowship of sinners. To the sneers of Pharisees over Jesus' warning to beware of the deadening influence of their riches (16:1–9, 10–13), Jesus launches his own offensive in 16:15 by casting them as the rich man of 16:19–31. Repentance is a dead option (tenet C). They are eating and drinking themselves to Hades (16:19–23). Thus again two houses with two kinds of eating and drinking are pitted against each other.

19. **Luke 17:7–10.**[299] Jesus turns to his disciples in 17:1–4 to alert them against those who would tempt others to fall away or be scandalized (vv. 1–3), and to forgive and promote repentance and forgiveness among their cohorts (vv. 3b–4). But to the apostles Jesus appears to give a rebuke (vv. 5–6). If their faith were even as great as a grain of mustard seed, they could command miraculous power and authority. Then in 17:7–10 Jesus continues this rebuke by pointing to the standard of servanthood that they should be following. As little as they would expect a slave of theirs to be waited on for a meal after a day's duty, so little should they expect to be served by compliments or praise for doing their duty before God. Thus Jesus is warning the apostles against an attitude of hypocritical authority which expects recognition for a position of privilege that they do not possess.

There are some clear lines of contrast between the servant of 17:7–9 and the "unjust steward" of 16:1–9: *(a)* Unlike the servant (17:7), the steward of 16:1–9 does not perform that which he ought to have done (cf. 17:10). Not only is he dishonest (16:1–2), but instead of giving an account of his stewardship, as he is commanded (16:2b), he distorts the bookkeeping even more (16:4–7). *(b)* The dishonest steward is complimented by his master for his decisive but devious action; the servant of 17:7–9 receives no gratitude from his master for faithful performance. *(c)* The steward speaks and acts for the master without duly guarding respect for the master's authority.[300] He thus justifies his own dishonest, wasteful ways "before folk"[301] by currying their favor. In exactly the opposite vein the servant is treated by his master as one who is there to obey, and so the servant behaves. He does not expect special favor, nor does he receive any. The relation between master and servant is kept distinct and thus intact. *In sum, what the apostles are warned against becoming (17:10) is the figure of 16:1–9.*

It is significant that the *apostles* are signaled out for the parable in a context (17:1–6) in which there will be unavoidable barriers of stumbling (17:1–3a), dissensions among the disciples (17:3b–4), and faith of the apostles that is smaller than even the "tiniest amount of faith":[302]

> *(a)* In 9:46–48, 49 John represents the authority of the twelve apostles as Jesus corrects their misuse of authority. *(b)* Again, in 9:54–55, it is John with James who wants to execute their authority in an ill-conceived manner; Jesus strongly rebukes them. *(c)* In 12:41 Peter acts surprised that the disciples would be told to be prepared for an unsuspecting coming of the Son of Man. Jesus should preach rather to the crowds. Jesus' response is to speak of a steward who, though placed over other servants, does not endure in faithful service precisely because he does not know when his master is coming. Instead, he begins to usurp authority for himself by maltreating the servants and with profligate eating and drinking (12:42–46). *(d)* In 17:2 "little ones" (μικροί) are in danger of "stumbling," while in 18:15–17 the disciples are rebuked for hindering (κωλύω) children coming to Jesus—of entering the Kingdom of God (vv. 16b–17). Perhaps the apostles' stewardship has itself produced a hindering influence. *(e)* In 18:28 Peter proudly asserts that they have left their homes and followed Jesus. Jesus answers that *anyone* who has left homes and family for the sake of the Kingdom of God will receive the blessings of life. *(f)* In 18:31–34 it becomes apparent that the Twelve do not recognize the *coming* of the Son of Man as alerted to them by Jesus in 12:39–40. This is demonstrated by the fact that Jesus' reference in 16:30–31 to the coming of one in line with Moses and the prophets raised from the dead has not been understood by the Twelve as an allusion to their Master. For when Jesus says the Son of Man will be killed but on the third day rise to fulfill everything written by the prophets, they do not even begin to make the connection with Jesus, let alone understand what fate lies ahead for the Son of Man (v. 34).

In sum, the Twelve—at the center of Jesus' coming (tenet B)—are not receiving him properly. The context divulges, in fact, a growing *hindering* among the disciples; apparently the apostles' attitudes of privilege are at least partially to blame for this predicament. Opposition to Jesus (tenet C) has not curtailed in the slightest; in fact, Jesus' own select group of apostles seems to be infatuated with a stance strikingly close to the Pharisees in 16:1–31. The Pharisees' leaven appears to be "working" infectiously close to "home."

20. **Luke 17:11–19,**[303] **20–37**. Though journeying is absent in 17:7–10, we have already discovered Jesus' sending in 15:1–32 and 16:19–31 in illustrations and allusions to his journeying to the lost of Israel. Now again, as in 14:1–24, we discover that Jesus' teaching in 17:1–10 is framed by references to this journeying. Luke 17:11 thus does not protrude as an alien idea out of the thick of static teaching. What follows this

reference to journeying along the border of Galilee and Samaria[304] is a Samaritan who serves as a foil not only to the apostles but to the whole stubborn nation of Israel as well (tenets A and C): *(a)* He submits to Jesus' authority (vv. 15–16a) by giving Jesus thanks (v. 16a; cf. 17:10); and *(b)* his *faith* (cf. 17:5–6) is the instrument not just of miraculous healing but also of the presence of eschatological salvation among Samaritans over against the mass of a recalcitrant Israel.[305]

In 17:20–21[306] we meet "this generation's" leaders again who are apparently in Jesus' entourage or at least encounter him at this point, as in other instances (cf. 13:31–33; 16:14–15). To their question concerning when the Kingdom will come, Jesus asserts that it is not a temporal question of when, as heralded by observable events, but a spatial one of the where of the Kingdom in their midst.[307] But that is to assert quite clearly again that Jesus *comes* bearing the Kingdom of God as he journeys to Jerusalem (17:11). We have here the same idea of his coming as in the mission of the journeying guest (cf. 10:1) where his authoritative presence brings the Kingdom of God to the space of the towns and villages (10:9, 11b). And like those Pharisees in 11:37–54; 13:31–33; 14:1–24; 15:1–2; 16:14–15, they do not recognize this journey and thus do not receive him and the Kingdom of God.

We have already analyzed 17:22–37 in the light of tenet A and discovered tenet C in the monolith of opposition by "this generation" (vv. 25–30). They are a lot dissipated with the frenzy of gaining life (cf. v. 33)—marrying, buying, selling, planting, building—and *eating and drinking* their way to destruction. Not only do they persecute the Son of Man (v. 25), rejecting him out of hand, but they are so weighted down with their own pursuits that they are oblivious to "his day" when he is revealed (vv. 24b, 30). It is the same hypocritical generation that is unable to discern the present time (12:56) of Jesus' repentance preaching to Israel (cf. 16:27–31) as they head for their judgment (Luke 12 and 17). Now the disciples must glimpse the time when the house (v. 31) will no longer be the center of mission but of judgment (vv. 31–35). In conclusion, the "eating and drinking" of "this generation" is like that of the rich man (16:19–31), the "elder brother" (15:28), the Pharisees (14:1–24; 11:37–54), the inquisitors (13:26), the steward (12:45), and the rich fool (12:19): it does not recognize the Lord of the Banquet when he comes.

21. **Luke 18:1–8,**[308] **9–30.**[*309] Apart from the opening two parables, the pace of the journey quickens in a series of encounters in the continuing progress to Jerusalem. Luke 18:1–8 poses the same issue raised in Luke 16 and 17: as Jesus the Son of Man journeys to Jerusalem will he find faith (tenet C)? Whether the disciples' weakness and vulnerability to miss Jesus' authority or the Pharisees' hindering influence is uppermost, the point remains the *growing* hostility on the one side, and the increasing

imperviousness on the other to Jesus' prophetic authority (cf. Luke 12). As in 12:39–40; 17:20–21, 24–30 the Son of Man's coming inheres with the *bifocal coming* to Jerusalem.[310] In 18:9–14 a Pharisee and a tax collector are juxtaposed to warn those in Jesus' audience who thought they were "right" (δίκαιος) before God while snubbing[311] others. Only the tax collector, who placards the posture of Wisdom's children (cf. 7:34–35), goes down to his "home" accepted by God. Now Luke mentions that some people were beginning to bring[312] children to Jesus, that he might bless them. When the disciples attempt to *hinder* them, Jesus leaves no doubt that the children's coming to him is analogous to entering or receiving the Kingdom of God. Here only traces of the distinctive themes of the journeying-guest motif are present: coming, house, receiving. That these traces stem from such a mission *Sitz im Leben* is highly questionable. Nevertheless, in Luke's present ordering, such ideas take on a greater significance: they sustain the dynamic of a journey and develop the subthemes inherent to the journeying-guest theme.

As in 10:25–28, one of Israel's leaders[313] addresses Jesus as "teacher," wanting to know how "to inherit eternal life" (18:18). After pointing him to the commandments, Jesus puts his finger on the one thing he still lacks: *the one thing needful* (cf. 10:42)—*to submit to his authority.*[314] As with the rich man (16:19–31) and as Jesus commands the disciples (12:22–34), to become like the "poor" is indispensable in following Jesus to Jerusalem (18:22b; cf. 9:23, 49, 57, 59, 61; 18:31). Obedience to the Law is in fundamental continuity with this following of Jesus.[315] It is placed alongside this demand of discipleship without hint of opposition. It is the same conceptualization as in 16:19–31: Moses and the prophets are joined by one whose sending speaks of the same "bosom of Abraham." And as we have seen, this sending is conceived by Jesus as a following to Jerusalem which brooks no rival in any human pursuit or attachment (9:57–62). Thus when Peter exclaims that they had left their homes to follow Jesus, he is asserting that they have met the requirements of the journeying-guest mission as so strongly laid out by Jesus, the Son of Man, in 9:57–62. Though this bold claim of Peter does not portray the disciples, and especially not the apostles, in a good light,[316] yet it still marks them as distinct from the "ruler."[317] For this ruler mimics the excuses of the invited guests of 14:15–24; he cannot leave his home (18:28; 14:20) because of his many possessions (18:23–25; 14:18–19). That is to say, he epitomizes the rich Pharisee (14:1–24), who invites only rich guests and like-minded neighbors, and the Pharisees (16:14–15) whose love for money excludes them from entering the Kingdom in their midst.[318] Here in 18:18–30 Luke presents a real-life fulfillment of what Jesus has already depicted and predicted (cf., e.g., 16:19–31). Consequently when Jesus speaks of the impossibility of the rich entering (present tense; v. 24) the

Kingdom of God, he is drawing upon the full cluster of ideas generic to the journeying guest. Like the Pharisees of 11:52, the ruler does not enter the Kingdom by refusing to acknowledge Jesus' unique authority. It is only the "children" coming to Jesus who are entering (18:17) the Kingdom in their midst. In conclusion, in the parable of 18:9–14 and in 18:15–17 the humble, unpresumptuous entering of the Kingdom is contrasted to the wavering, even presumptuous faith of the disciples and to the deadening influence of riches.

22. **Luke 18:31–34**.[319] Several distinctive features of this pericope should be noted:

a. By his going up to Jerusalem, Jesus' journey sending "will be consummated"; the idea of a culmination links up not only with the express notices of Jesus' goal (9:51, 53; 13:22, 31–33, 34–35; 17:11; cf. 9:22, 31, 44) but also with passages of the divine necessity of Jesus' or the Son of Man's coming (9:57–58, 61–62; 10:1; 11:29–32; 12:35–38, 39–40, 41–48, 49–53, 57–59; 15:1ff.; 16:30–31). *Jesus' mandate is about to be fulfilled.*

b. This divine mandate has been written by the prophets (v. 31) about the Son of Man. Here again a central motif interwoven with the journeying guest comes to a near-climax. The convergence in 16:27–31 of the written testimony of the prophets with a sending that culminates in resurrection from death is strikingly close to the thought in 18:31–33.

c. Only Luke speaks of Jesus' "shameful treatment" (v. 32) which may echo the suffering of the "righteous" in the OT.[320]

d. Peculiar to Luke is also the incomprehension of the Twelve. As in the hindering by the disciples (18:15–17), by the Pharisees (16:14–31), and by the "stewardship" of the Twelve themselves (17:5–10), the presence of this detail here should come as no surprise. It has become typical of Jesus' journeying that he is not received.

In sum, the singular character of this "Passion prediction" is due to the journeying-guest motif and tenets B and C. Though Jesus is delivered over to the Gentiles, his violent death and resurrection are the ineluctable fate of a prophet sent to journey to the center of the nation of Israel. It is because he receives the "prophet's welcome," as written by the prophets themselves, that Jesus is "delivered over" to death.[321] Thus despite any prima facie impression to the contrary, 18:31–34 both continues the ongoing drama of the journeying prophet and expresses this fate within the characteristic Deuteronomistic mold.

23. **Luke 19:1–10.** In the story of Zacchaeus the journeying guest reaches a penultimate climax. In these verses the definitive themes of this motif are integrated into a live, one-act portrayal of Jesus' entire journey:

a. After a blind man, whose faith has saved him (18:42b; cf. 17:19), follows Jesus on his journey (18:43), Jesus enters and passes through Jericho, still coming through towns on his journey to Jerusalem (10:1; 9:51–52).

b. Zacchaeus is a chief tax collector. He thus is at the zenith of that despised profession which was so attracted to Jesus (15:1; 18:10–13).

c. Zacchaeus is rich (v. 2b) and is thus classed with those for whom it is humanly impossible to enter the Kingdom (18:18–27) or banquet of salvation (14:15–24; 16:14–15, 19–31).

d. Like the many prophets and kings who desired to see Jesus' journeying-guest ministry of salvation (10:24), Zacchaeus too desires to see Jesus as Jesus travels on his way to Jerusalem (v. 3a; cf. 7:22; 9:9, 27, 32; 12:54; 13:35; 17:22; 19:37).

e. Zacchaeus is a "little" man (μικρός, v. 3b); it may not be a trivial detail that "smallness" is linked to his being a tax collector (cf. μικρός in 7:28; 9:48; 17:2).[322] Jesus has just warned of those who cause these "little ones" to stumble (17:2), and we have just seen the disciples hinder the little children from coming to Jesus (18:15–17).

f. Jesus is depicted as coming to the place (v. 5) where Zacchaeus was (cf. 10:1–16). Jesus is the coming one whose presence demands response (cf. 12:35–48; 13:35; 19:38).

g. Jesus must stay at Zacchaeus's *house* (v. 5b). Moreover, Jesus assumes the role of *host* by inviting himself and determining the time of his *visitation* (σήμερον, 19:9; cf. 4:21; 13:32–33; 14:16–17; 15:1–2; 19:44).

h. This staying is a divine must (δεῖ); as in 13:31–33, Jesus' course is plotted by God; it is a divine sending.

i. At once Zacchaeus receives (ὑποδέχομαι, v. 6) Jesus in his home as journeying guest. Like the servants of 12:35–38, Zacchaeus is ready to open to Jesus, the Lord (v. 8; cf. 12:36–38), when he comes (v. 15).

j. Zacchaeus receives him with rejoicing (v. 6b), like the joy of the celebration feasts of 15:3–7, 11–32 which mirror the heavenly banquet.

k. All who see this "murmur" (v. 7) at the disgusting sight of someone about to be defiled in the home of a sinner.[323] Thus we have the same reaction as in 15:1–2 by the Pharisees and the scribes but now encompassing the crowds—all are aghast at Jesus' eating and drinking!

l. With Zacchaeus branded as a "sinner" (v. 7b) by the onlookers, Luke presents a real-life counterpart to the tax collector–sinner of 18:9–14, with the grumbling of 19:7a corresponding to the disdainful pride of the Pharisee in that pictorial lesson.

m. Jesus enters "to find lodging"[324] (cf. 9:4; 10:5, 8, 10). Here again we find a literal representation of the heavenly banquet into which folk must enter as guest of the Lord of the house.

n. Zacchaeus addresses Jesus as "sir"/"lord" (v. 8); his subsequent confession demonstrates that Jesus is received as Lord of the house.

o. The verb σταθείς (v. 8a), perhaps indicating the standing up from table,[325] denotes a decisive response[326] to the revelation of Jesus in the home-meal fellowship.[327] Thus in word and deed (v. 8b) Zacchaeus hearkens to the voice of the Son as a "son of peace" (cf. 9:35; 10:5).

p. By giving "half of all" his possessions to the "poor" (v. 8),[328] Zacchaeus now identifies with that group which enters the heavenly banquet (14:13, 21; 16:20, 22). But that is another way of saying that he does just the opposite of the rich ruler who "cannot" enter the Kingdom of God (18:22–23). Like the faithful and wise steward (12:42–44), Zacchaeus distributes the goods of his Master's "household" and does so when he comes. And like the servant (17:7–10), he shows his abiding gratitude for the privilege of serving the Lord by continuing to serve others. In short, he has humbled himself (14:11; 18:14).[329]

q. By paying back fourfold whomever he has defrauded (v. 8b), Zacchaeus, by this decisive action, imitates the unjust steward (16:1–9). But Zacchaeus also repents, shows that he will serve only the one master (16:13), the Lord of the house, and is thus faithful to receive the true riches of salvation (v. 9; cf. 16:10–12). As he repents he fulfills the Law, and as he does the Law he goes beyond its strict adherence to demonstrate his love for God and his neighbor (10:27); hence he experiences the life of the Law (10:28). He thus stands in contrast to the lawyer (10:25), to the synagogue official (13:10–17), to the rich ruler (18:18–30), and particularly to the Pharisees (11:37–54; 14:1–24; 16:14–15).[330] This means that Zacchaeus is likened to the "child" who can receive Jesus as the Lord and thus enter the Kingdom of God (9:46–48; 10:21–24; 18:15–17).

r. "Today salvation has come to this house"; the Kingdom of God's rule in Jesus the journeying guest has rested upon Zacchaeus (cf. 10:6–9; 13:23).[331] Thus Zacchaeus joins that company of those who are "saved" and "being saved" (13:23; 17:19; 18:42), as a "son of Abraham" (cf. 13:16; 3:8, 12–13). Again the Lord of the house is designated the Son of Man who has come (v. 10) and is coming (v. 1; cf. 12:40; 18:8).

s. He "has come to seek and to save the lost." The verbs ζητέω and ἀπόλλυμι (v. 10b) resonate the activity of the shepherd and of the woman[332] in 15:3–10. Thus, like the unclean and despised prodigal of 15:11–32, Zacchaeus "comes home" to the banquet of his Father's house in the midst of *all* the "elder brothers" who stand and shake their finger.

In sum, Zacchaeus represents that person for whom Jesus the Lord is sent on his journey and who receives this Lord as guest and Lord of the household when he comes. As such, he crowns the journeying-guest mission which is revealed upon the mountain (9:28–36) and heralded upon entering Samaria (9:52–56). All of the main subthemes of this journey converge in this story of Jesus the Son of Man who eats and drinks with tax collectors and sinners when he comes (7:34)! And the parallel rise of opposition and rejection of this journeying prophet now reaches a peak in 19:7. The *hindering* of the Pharisees-lawyers (scribes) has encroached upon the large number of crowds in Jesus' company. "All" stand outside the house, building themselves a "house of scorn." All but the explicit consequences of tenet C are summed up by their menacing "murmur."

24. **Luke 19:11–27.**[333] Luke states (19:11) that the crowd of 19:3 (cf. 19:7b) heard Zacchaeus's confession and Jesus' affirmation (19:8–10). How ironic that the crowds still do not recognize the Kingdom in their midst. They suppose it is still to come, and because Jerusalem is within sight, its coming will be immediate as it appears in Jerusalem. Thus the crowd holds the identical view of the Kingdom as the Pharisees in 17:20–21: it is something that will appear in a convincing form; it is certainly not effective in Jesus' journeying in the present.

The thrust of Jesus' parable confirms this interpretation of the comment in 19:11. The nobleman journeys to a distant land to receive a kingdom though he already has citizens (v. 14) over whom his influence is not insignificant: they already hate him (v. 14), even to the extreme of dispatching a delegation to hinder any further development in his authority over them (v. 14).[334] In addition, the servants that are entrusted with the master's wealth are held accountable for their stewardship during the period *even before their master receives the kingdom!* They are to give an account when he *comes* (v. 13b). The point is unmistakable. Jesus already journeys (cf. v. 12) with the authority to declare the fate of those he encounters vis-à-vis the Kingdom of God. He already journeys with a mass of people who hinder his authority and resist his "ruling" over them. And the goal of his journey is Jerusalem, where he will be taken up (9:31, 51) as the resurrected, rejected prophet to receive the power of the Son of Man "at the right hand of God," and shall return and appear "like lightning" in judgment (22:69; 17:24–35). Moreover, how his servants, the disciples, manage the wealth of his dominion *as he journeys in the present to receive* the Kingdom determines their well-being when he returns (9:57–62; 12:22–34, 35–38, 39–40, 42–48; 16:1–9; 18:24–30). Therefore Jesus once more warns the crowds that their response to the Kingdom in their midst determines their fate in the Kingdom that he is on his way to receive in power. The imagery of a nobleman and servants does not appear to stem from the journeying-guest mission. Yet these figures, within the journeying context of one in authority, fit admirably into the dramatic buildup of Jesus' own journey as guest. As with the citizens who hated the "nobleman-lord," so it becomes clear as Jesus approaches Jerusalem that his "citizens" "do not want this man to reign over us."[335]

25. **Luke 19:28–40,**[336] **41–44**. The "Lord" (vv. 31, 34) continues on his journey (v. 28). At the descent of the Mount of Olives the whole company of disciples—not the crowds or Jerusalem's residents—hail Jesus as the King, the one who comes in the authority of the Lord. Jesus' prophecy of 13:35b is thus fulfilled, while his self-description as the nobleman to be received with kingly authority is paraded in front of the crowds' eyes. But Jesus' entry is not so triumphant. After an attempt by some Pharisees to dampen Jesus' acclaim, he weeps over a city that does not recognize his visit (ἐπισκοπή). The irony of 19:11–27 is again pregnantly present: Jesus laments over his rejection even as he is hailed as king. The division of the two "houses" is drastic and yet ultimately insignificant. Jerusalem's "children" (v. 44) are depicted as the "wise and learned" of 10:21. Jesus' coming is *hidden* (19:42b — 10:21) from them. Their *eyes* (19:42b — 10:23) are sealed. The disciples, however, recognize Jesus as king. They "see" what many prophets and kings longed to see but did not. And like the Seventy(-two), they *rejoice* in the mighty demonstrations of *power* they had seen (cf. 10:19, 20). Yet coming as it does at this point in the journey, there is a hollow ring to their praise. Compared to Zacchaeus's contrite confession as sinner and his acts of repentance, their enthusiasm over the acts of power sound quite a different note. Indeed Jesus' own rejoicing over Zacchaeus (19:9–10) and others like him (e.g., 15:1–32) poses a stark contrast; it is not by accident that Jesus' example to the Seventy(-two) of exulting over their salvation rather than the display of power is the same note of triumph that Jesus warns should prevail throughout the journey (10:20; 11:28; 12:32; 13:16, 28–29; 14:5, 10–11; 15:3–32; 16:22; 18:9–14, 16, 29–30, 41–42).

Thus, though ironic, it is not at all surprising that as Jesus contemplates his entrance into Jerusalem (cf. 13:34–35), he knows that her children, the nation as a whole, will reject him in the end. The word Jesus uses for his own ministry which goes unrecognized is a most fitting synopsis of the whole journey sending. It is a *visitation* by God for the salvation of the nation as typified by their *Exodus* (Gen. 50:24–25; Exod. 3:16): Jesus has journeyed on an *exodus* (9:31) with the authority and presence of God. He does indeed come to visit in the name of the Lord. But as in the OT, when the "word of the Lord" is not heeded and people cry "Peace, peace" "when there is no peace" (Jer. 6:14; 8:11), then the Lord visits his people for destruction (Jer. 6:15; 10:15; cf. Isa. 29:6).[337] So also here tenet D follows irrevocably upon the refusal to receive God's messengers (19:43–44). Thus as in 12:56 the crowds with Jesus do not recognize the time of their journeying guest: *Jesus has not been received.*

Conclusions

We can now summarize our findings under two headings:

The Journeying Guest as an Integrating Motif

An astonishing fifty-two of the seventy-three pericopes in the Central Section divulge the distinctive marks of the journeying-guest motif. Jesus is cast as *the bearer of the dynamic presence of God* as he journeys to be received.

1. In Luke 9:52—10:24, episodes from Jesus' and his disciples' journey as guests in a home-meal mission on their way to Jerusalem are presented, while in 11:1–13; 12:1–34 images from this mission are used to teach the disciples about their absolute dependency upon God as their Father as Jesus, the Son and Son of Man, speaks for him. In 12:35ff. the emphasis shifts to Jesus' dynamic role as Lord of the house and host of the banquet of the Kingdom of God:

a. The disciples are pictured as stewards and servants. There is the gravest danger that their stewardship as servants will be found wanting when the Lord, the Son of Man, comes.

b. This danger is depicted as a counterstewardship symbolized by a dissipated "eating and drinking." Consequently two types of "eating and drinking" are arrayed against each other.

c. The significance of this cipher lies in the revealing presence of God's rule through the Son at the meal fellowship in the houses where Jesus and his messengers are received as guests.

d. Therefore to be ready to receive the Son of Man when he comes is to submit to this guest as host to share in the heavenly banquet. Not to receive him is to miss this coming and to "eat and drink" to exclusion from the banquet hall.

e. As the Lord of the household of the Kingdom of God comes, he splits the household of the Kingdom of Israel into strife; Jerusalem's "house" is thus pitted against the house of the Lord of the Banquet. From 16:1ff. especially, dissipated "eating and drinking" or profligate stewardship is portrayed as service or servanthood to mammon. Such service is at base a justification of self to one's society, a breeding of a self-"rightness" incapable of repentance.

f. Israel's divided house discloses a monolithic fortress of rejection facing Jesus the journeying prophet. Only the "sinners," those already excluded from the feasts of the rich and pious leaders of the people, show themselves "children" of the house of the Lord of the Banquet.

2. It is because Jesus is the dynamic bearer of God's rule that *each of the actual meal settings in the Central Section is linked to a travel notice* (10:38–42—v. 38; 11:37–54—v. 53;[338] 14:1–24—v. 25 and 13:31–33,

34–35; 19:1–10—18:43 and 19:11): *At table* Jesus reveals himself as the Lord-Host of the Heavenly Banquet which is now dynamically being fulfilled in his *journeying* to Jerusalem.

In all the parables, episodes, and illustrations of the journeying guest there is a remarkable consistency in the use of the images. Though not univocal, the "house" nevertheless constitutes simultaneously the means as well as the goal of the mission. As the goal, its fellowship around the meal is at once the fulfillment of the presence of God's rule (salvation) in the Son and an anticipation of the consummation of that presence in the banquet of the "house" of the Kingdom of God. This pervasive language throughout the whole of the Central Section produces a dynamic coherency which either has not been recognized or has not been properly appreciated by critical scholarship. Jesus is either journeying or teaching about his coming and the reception he will receive. Consequently he hardly "stands still." What we find in the way Luke has told his story and thus arranged the various traditions in his text is an integrated, consistent picture of Jesus the journeying guest on the way to Jerusalem, who is host and thus Lord of the Banquet of the Kingdom of God.

The Journeying Guest and Tenet C

The Deuteronomistic conception of a prophet's sending and rejection provides the conceptual framework for the journey mission:

1. It is the prophet himself and not only his message that is refused. Therefore it is not fortuitous that *the explicit utterances of Jesus' violent fate come exclusively in journeying or in meal settings* (11:47–51, 53–54; 12:49–53; 13:31–33, 34–35; 17:25;[339] 18:31–34; cf. 14:27; 16:30–31; 19:41–42, 44b). Jesus is rejected as he is sent (journeying) or is not received hospitably (home meal) as an authoritative messenger (voice) from God. We have also seen that tenet B becomes thoroughly entwined with the journeying-guest motif. Luke 9:51—10:24 especially links the mountain sending to Jesus' journeying and his reception, while this link is direct in several other instances, particularly in the travel notices. Therefore it is clear again that the journeying guest both is given its ultimate signification by tenets B and C and itself, serving as the narrative currency, the "story stuff," illuminates the Deuteronomistic conceptualization of Jesus in the Central Section.

2. The journeying-guest motif divulges the various sources of opposition through the divergent development of its subthemes:

    a. The journeying Samaritan (10:29–37) negates the significance of a Samaritan village rejecting Jesus. Thus Samaria as a whole is not singled out as the point of resistance to Jesus; rather, the "Good

Samaritan" figure is aligned against the leaders of the people represented by the lawyer of 10:25–29.

b. The first three meals (10:38–42; 11:37–54; 14:1–24) indicate the authority of the "Lord" which is received (Mary—10:39, 42) but mostly unrecognized, challenged, and even disdained. By sounding tenet C in 11:37–54 (12:1–12), Luke discloses that it is the Pharisees and the lawyers who are the "Lord's" primary opponents. Thus as we have discovered, 11:37–54 forms the watershed for the massive resistance Jesus is beginning to face. Hence 10:25–37 serves as a frontispiece to this opposition which will intensify throughout the journey. Luke 14:1–24 links up with these previous pericopes along with 13:31–33, 34–35 and its tenet C to disclose the intensifying dynamic of the Pharisees-lawyers' opposition to Jesus' journeying as Lord of the Banquet. Finally, the fourth meal (19:1–10) sums up the journeying-guest motif by combining the various subthemes of the parables and food imagery with the actual meal setting. Only the "little" folk like the tax collectors and sinners receive Jesus as Guest and "Lord," while the Pharisee-inspired "grumbling" has now become characteristic of the crowd.

c. The imagery of householder and servants is directed primarily to the disciples as a warning against the leavenlike influence of the Pharisees-lawyers. A sloven, unfaithful, and greedy stewardship is depicted as that which is being rejected in the present by Jesus the Lord of the house.

d. This counteropposition discloses a "house" controlled by the Pharisees-lawyers that is pitted against the house of Jesus the Lord who has come and is coming. It would appear that the discredited stewardship represents the Pharisees-lawyers as leaders of the people.

e. Commensurate with the increase in the "hindering" influence of the Pharisees is Jesus' emphasis on the disciples as servants. Servanthood means no claim whatever upon the Master, on the one hand, and no basis for self-justification before others, on the other hand. The ultimate grounding for this service is the example of Jesus himself, who, as host, assumes the role of the house servant.

In sum, that Jesus as journeying guest, Lord, and host of the Kingdom of God is not received is displayed in the Deuteronomistic pageantry of 9:52–56. As such, this opening scene is a most appropriate introduction for the whole journey of rejection.

We can now sketch several critical points of a developing opposition according to tenet C:

9:52–56, 57–58
Announcement of *Rejection*
for Whole Journey
in Tones of *Tenet C*

10:25–28, 29–37
Rejection Posed by *Lawyer*
as Introduction to
the Primary Opposition
Tenet C in nuce

11:37–54
Pharisee Meal as
Watershed of *Tenet C*
for the Rest of
the Journey

12:35–48, 49–53
Division of House of Israel
Into House of the Lord
of the Banquet and House
of the Pharisees-Scribes:
Goal of the Journey =
Tenet C

13:22–30, 31–35
Climax of Journey
Anticipated Through
Tenet C;
Judgment on Jerusalem's
House; *Tenet D*

14:1–24, 27
Guest and Host Fully Converge
but Pharisees and the "Many"
Exclude Themselves as *Meal
Fellowship Broken* by Refusal
to Repent: *Tenet C*

16:19–31
House of Pharisees-
Lawyers = House of Mammon;
Repentance *Impossible* Through
False Eating and Drinking:
Tenet C implicit

19:1–10
Crowning of Journeying
Guest in Receiving of
the "Least"; Monolith of
Crowds=House of Scorn:
Tenet C explicit

19:38–40, 41–44
Jerusalem's Blindness Complete;
Judgment on the Whole Nation
according to *Tenets C* and *D*

The Journeying Guest Is Rejected in Jerusalem (Luke 19:45—23:49)

A number of the themes of the journeying guest are introduced in the Galilean Section which are taken up again, developed, and sustained in the journey to the descent from the Mount of Olives into the Temple precincts. Does this motif end with the Temple? Let us sketch the resolution of the journeying guest in Luke's own resolution of "all that Jesus began to do and teach until he was taken up" (ἀνελήμφθη, Acts 1:1–2; cf. Luke 9:51).

The Passion Meal of the Journeying Guest (Luke 22:7–38)[340]

In 19:45 Jesus takes control of the Temple by driving out those "taken up" with mammon (cf. 17:28). In citing the OT,[341] Jesus claims Jerusalem's "house" (cf. 13:35a) as his own as he is ensconced there by the people (ὁ λαός) who will come day after day to hear his teaching (19:47–

48; cf. 21:37–38). Immediately the opposition sets to work. Representatives of each of the three groups of the Sanhedrin are already plotting (v. 47) to kill Jesus. With the mention of "the scribes" we meet again the lawyers-scribes of the Pharisees, the arch antagonists of the journey. It would seem that tenet C is moving without a hitch to its denouement. Yet again with the strongest of irony, Luke states that this ploy was itself *hindered* by "the people."[342] They "hung on every word" of Jesus (v. 47). In 19:28–40 only the disciples hailed Jesus' entry; now it is Jerusalem's children who are receiving him as Jesus receives them into his house, or so it would seem.

In 20:1–8 the plotters' direct attempt to discredit Jesus' authority before the people goes awry. In fact, once again Jesus turns the tables! By telling the people the parable of the wicked tenants in the shocking tones of the Deuteronomistic view of Israel's mistreatment of the prophets (20:9–18),[343] Jesus makes a powerful and embarrassing countersurge against "the scribes and the chief priests . . . who perceived that he had told this parable against them" (20:19).

In 20:45–57 after another frustrated foray by the same tandem, Jesus thrusts a warning to his disciples who are now singled out within the "hearing of all the people." They are to watch out for "the scribes," "who love greetings of respect in the marketplaces and the most important seats in the synagogues and the prime seats at feasts. They devour widows' houses (v. 47) and for appearance's sake they pray at a distance of others (20:46–47)."[344] We have already met these same charges against the Pharisees-lawyers (scribes), the first three at the table scenes of 11:37–54; 14:1–24, while the last is illustrated by the Pharisee of 18:9–14. And as in that parable, the lowly (cf. widows) are contrasted to the pretense of the Pharisees' public image. For this reason, as in 11:47–51, the scribes will be held more accountable at the judgment (v. 47b). Moreover, following this remark Jesus contrasts the rich with a poor widow (21:1–4). It is precisely again the Pharisees-lawyers who have been earmarked by their riches in both table scenes and in the latter half of the journey: the dynamics of opposition to Jesus and the hindering of the people along the journey continue on in Jerusalem as well. Yet despite this organic unfolding, one significant difference must not be obscured: Jesus is no longer the journeying-guest who is received into homes. Instead, as only Luke sums up the whole period of the Jerusalem teaching, Jesus would take his lodgings upon the Mount of Olives (21:37–38), while it was all the people who would get up early to come and hear him in the Temple. Jesus has reached his destination, the city that murders the prophets and does not recognize his visitation. What will be her "children's" next move?

Just when we hear of the same plotters, the chief priests and the scribes, persisting in their scheme to kill Jesus as Passover is at hand, we encounter the irony of ironies: one of the *Twelve* makes the decisive move against his master (παραδίδωμι, 22:4, 6).[345] What Jesus forecasts to the disciples before the crowds in 9:44 and discloses privately to the Twelve in 18:32 is now set in final motion by one from this innermost band of followers. Instead of Jesus the accuser handing the crowds over to the judge (12:57–59),[346] one of his own disciples hands him over to the judges of the Sanhedrin! "This generation of Jerusalem's children" (13:34; 17:25) becomes concrete in Judas, "one of the number of the Twelve" (v. 3b)!

Thus it is all the more striking that precisely at this point the journeying-guest motif returns. Jesus sends Peter and John to find hospitality (cf. v. 11; 19:7) in Jerusalem. According to Luke, Jesus is determined to continue his "journey" by entering the city proper[347] (v. 10; cf. 10:1). So, as in 9:52–56, Jesus sends two of his disciples ahead (v. 8) to make preparations (vv. 8, 9, 12, 13). They are to enter into a house (v. 10) to tell the householder that the teacher is going to eat (v. 11; cf. v. 8) a meal (the Passover) with his disciples (v. 11b). Thus, as with Zacchaeus, Jesus again as Lord of the Banquet takes the initiative to be received as guest.

The peculiar features of Luke's account of the Passover meal are patent. But what is not sufficiently taken into account are the lines that extend from the journey meals and converge in this Passion meal. To be sure, commentators have noticed "eucharistic touches" in some of the meals, especially in the feeding of the five thousand and the Emmaus episode.[348] But what is considerably more constitutive to Luke's unique "Lord's Supper" is the way this final meal before Jesus' Passion is the crowning point of the journeying-guest motif.

To continue these features from Luke 22:7–13 we can mention the following in 22:14–38:

1. Verse 14: As he had sat previously with the Pharisees in their fellowship meals, Jesus sits down at table (11:37; cf. 14:10; 17:7) and immediately assumes the demeanor of the host.[349] Now, however, Jesus has been careful to arrange a private room to eat the Passover only with his apostles.

2. Verse 15: Luke's use of a Septuagintism to stress Jesus' *longing* to eat this particular meal with his apostles anticipates the climactic nature of this event.

3. Verse 15b: The verb "to suffer" links explicitly with the first Passion prediction in 9:22 and with 17:25 of the journey. How one eats and drinks with Jesus has a direct bearing on Jesus' suffering fate. Hence it is no accident whatever that this Passover meal becomes the quintessential Pas-

sion meal for Jesus. It is the culmination of the monolithic rejection of a hardened generation (tenet A) which has not recognized the Lord of the Banquet at their own table but rather hangs him upon a cross.

4. Verse 16: This Passion meal is to be *fulfilled* in the Kingdom of God. Thus again this meal becomes the crowning point for all the meals of the journey of the Lord of the Banquet as *the* anticipation of a future fulfilled meal in the Kingdom.

5. Verses 17–20: Jesus as the host serves his apostles at table. He thus resembles closely the example of the "lord of the house" in 12:35–38 who after a journey from a feast serves his servants at table (cf. 17:7–10).

6. Verse 18: Jesus vows that "from now on" he will not drink wine until the Kingdom of God comes. On the journey, Jesus as Son of Man comes bearing the Kingdom of God. Here a further coming is envisioned.

7. Verse 20: If the longer reading is accepted,[350] then Jesus declares that in this Passion-Passover meal a "new covenant" is established through his blood, a reference to the sacrificial blood required to make a covenant and therefore a reference to his impending death.[351] In connection with a Passover meal the theme of the covenant brings to mind the Exodus in general and a passage like Exod. 24:8 in particular.[352] Thus Jesus' vicarious death "on your behalf" (vv. 19–20) is linked not only to the Exodus tradition but also specifically to the Exodus traditions of the Book of Deuteronomy. Like Moses and the Horeb covenant, this covenant must be followed by the vicarious death of the one who has led the people on the exodus journey to the promised land. In addition, a vicarious sacrifice calls to mind the work of the Servant of Deutero-Isaiah. As we shall see shortly, Jesus' death is the necessary consequence of the sin of the whole generation. Consequently, tenet C is dovetailed into the prophetic fate of Moses in Deuteronomy with the distinctive dress of the "suffering Servant."[353]

8. Verses 21–22: The one who instigates the fulfillment of tenet C is the Jesus at table; again the irony is profound but consistent with the peculiar link of Jesus' "murderers" as fellow guests *at table.* Not by accident Jesus' "woe" to Judas (v. 22b) resounds Jesus' woes to the Pharisees-lawyers (esp. 11:47–51; cf. "blood of prophets," 11:50–51, and "my blood," 22:20).

9. Verse 22: The Son of Man still has a way to go; the "journey" is not completely over (cf. v. 18b). This journey is "determined" as part of the entire journey to Jerusalem (cf. esp. 13:31–33; 18:31–34).

10. Verses 23–26: As the apostles begin to discuss with one another who the betrayer could be, they argue over which of them is the greatest (cf. 9:46). The resonance with 9:46–48, 49–50 is indeed impressive: *(a)* Both arguments follow Jesus' direct statement to the disciples/apostles that he will be *delivered over* (παραδίδωμι) to the violent judgment of "men." *(b)* The *Son of Man* is the one so betrayed in both instances. *(c)* With v. 24 juxtaposed to v. 23 Luke makes it clear that their questioning about the betrayer betrayed *no* real understanding of the impact of Jesus' words. Thus as in 9:45, it becomes clear, even at this late date, that the inner band, the apostles, do not begin to

grasp the incredible ordeal awaiting their master. *(d)* Jesus again uses the example of the "least significant," the "child/youngest," to illustrate proper response to his sending (cf. πορεύομαι, v. 22; ἀποστέλλω, 9:48). Here again as Jesus speaks of a journey that is about to take place (cf. 9:51) the "child" moves into the foreground. *(e)* As in 9:49–50, members of the apostolic Twelve were at the center of the disciples' strife over rank. In sum, not only is their behavior fundamentally not any different from what it was at the start of the journey but their posture at table here unites them with the striving for rank of the Pharisees-lawyers (14:7–11).

11. Verse 27: Jesus repeats in private essentially the same point he had made to the disciples in the midst of the crowds (12:35–38). Their *servant* status in the Lord's house/Kingdom during the journey (cf. esp. 17:7–10) has been given its final justification: As one who is facing imminent death (v. 15b), Jesus as Lord and host still has taken on the role of the house servant, who waits upon others at table (vv. 17–20).

12. Verses 28–30: What appears to be only a marginally related topic is explained by the journeying-guest motif. Hand in hand with true servant-hood (vv. 26–27) goes faithful stewardship (cf. esp. 12:35–38 → vv. 42–48; 16:1–9 → vv. 10–13)—the apostles will sit on thrones "judging" (i.e., ruling and judging; cf. Dan. 7:10; 9:12) the twelve tribes of Israel. Jesus' promise to the apostles of a kingdom is virtually the same as to all the disciples in 12:32. There, in the journey, their receiving the Kingdom in the present is linked, on the one hand, to the heavenly treasure where their future will be (12:33–34) and, on the other hand, to faithful servanthood and stewardship (12:35–48).[354] However, the special role of the apostles is, as we have seen, totally foreign to the journey section where they are, for the most part, placed in an unfavorable light. There appears to be a development of the tradition in 22:24–30 from the distinct standpoint of the *journeying-guest* motif.

13. Verses 31–34: The postulate of item 12 is supported by the focus on Peter (v. 34; "Simon," v. 31) which is remarkably similar to the controversy surrounding him in 12:41ff.: *(a)* In both passages Peter is singled out as one whose grasp of the significance of Jesus' presence in their midst is far from firm. In 12:41 he insinuates that Jesus' warning to be *ready* is not pertinent to the disciples; here he claims he is *ready* for whatever lies ahead in Jesus' path. Jesus has just indicated that his path, his coming, is not over, 22:22; in 12:40 his coming takes place at an unexpected hour. *(b)* Peter is the representative for all the disciples/apostles in both passages (ὑμᾶς, 22:31 — 12:41). *(c)* Luke 22:14 indicates that *the hour* has arrived (cf. 12:40: the "unexpected *hour*"). *(d)* In both contexts Jesus has referred to himself as the Son of Man who journeys (22:22; 12:40). *(e)* In both, the apostles'/disciples' eating and drinking in the Kingdom is followed by a challenge of their ability to be faithful stewards when the Lord *comes* (22:33; 12:43). It is Peter's objection which elicits this challenge.[355] *(f)* In 22:33–34 Peter's objection is followed by the prediction of his *renouncing* his Lord (cf. 12:9); in 12:41ff. Peter's objection is followed by a scenario where that steward, not recog-

nizing the significance of the lord's coming nor knowing the hour, *renounces* his allegiance to his lord.

While all the parallels may not be exact, still this cluster of ideas strongly suggests that the shaping of the traditions in 22:21–34 is inseparably linked to the traditions in 12:32–48. But that is to argue that the journeying-guest motif is the constitutive link. Accordingly, with this background it is all the more interesting that it is precisely Peter and the apostles (cf. John and James—9:54–56) who are now not only shaded in a bad light but are presented as those who desert their master at the crucial end (cf. 10:21–24). But this falling away is a demonstration of tenet C; even though they have persevered with Jesus in his trials and opposition, they become at the decisive "hour" part of this monolith (cf. v. 32b). Hence 22:31–34 divulges once again the depth of the Passion as definitive of this meal. Jesus establishes a new covenant with those who betray and deny him; his blood is shed on their behalf (cf. v. 33b). As such, he is like Moses, dying on behalf of those he has led on an exodus but who reject and betray his authority. This paradox of the "gospel" explains the promise of the apostles' rule in the midst of their rejection (vv. 28–30).

14. Verses 35–38: A reference back to the "Sending Out of the Seventy-(-two)" in v. 35[356] all but gives proof to our suggestion that the journeying-guest motif is culminated in the table talk of this Passion meal. It appears as though the traditions involving the Twelve exclusively at the Last Supper have been refocused through the lens of this motif. Now Jesus, the Lord (v. 38), announces that the period of being received as guest is over for him and for the disciples. They can no longer count on hospitable reception at least by a few friends or tax collectors–sinners. For this journey's end is determined ($\delta\epsilon\hat{\iota}$) by Scripture. Again this thematic pulse of the whole of Luke-Acts possesses a special bearing to the journey (cf. 13:31–33; 18:31–34). For it is only as Jesus completes this course that "what is written about me achieves its goal" ($\tau\epsilon\lambda\circ\varsigma$ $\epsilon\chi\epsilon\iota$, v. 37b).[357] All else that will follow in the Acts is the spreading effect of this journey. For at the end of this path Jesus is "reckoned with the lawless" (Isa. 53:12—v. 37a).[358] Like Moses, who must be numbered with those who persistently broke the Law and deserved its punishment,[359] so Jesus as the Servant must be counted among those most reprehensible in his society. And again with utmost irony, as the disciples mistakenly carry their swords to link up with the "swords and clubs" of the arresting "crowd" led by "one of the Twelve," they unwittingly join this generation in numbering Jesus "with the lawless" (22:47–53).[360]

In sum, Jesus' journey does not end in the Temple. By sending out messengers to enter the city proper, Jesus signals the resumption of the journey in a fashion imitating the beginning in 9:52–56. Though the disciples find hospitality, Jesus is the host of a Passover-Passion meal that climaxes all of his eating and drinking during the journey. Jesus has not been received at table, and his receiving tax collectors and sinners at table has only exacerbated an opposition that has already surfaced in a plot by Jerusalem's children to kill him. Now at this last fellowship supper, cast in the distinctive lines of the journeying guest, the apostles also join this plot. Tenet C becomes actual from within Jesus' closest following. As such, they prove their membership in that growing opposition which has been so palpable at table throughout the journey. But as the suffering, rejected one, Jesus hosts the anticipatory meal of the consummate Kingdom of God. For by his suffering, Jesus is the Mosaic Servant whose vicarious death establishes the new covenant in which the apostles will eat and drink and judge the tribes of Israel. Even as they turn against him, Jesus reveals to them what true servanthood is like by serving them at table as one who is "the least." Jesus' exodus to Jerusalem, then, as it is already set out by Scripture, has culminated in a new redemption through the prophet like Moses of Deuteronomy whose vicarious death allows the people to enter the promised feast of the Kingdom of God. As they get up from table, this exodus reaches its *telos* "as the Son of Man goes as it has been determined" (v. 22). Like the unfaithful steward, the apostles do not know the hour when their Master comes!

The Journeying Guest Is Received (Luke 24:13–53)

From the guest room of 22:7–38 the action proceeds quickly. Jesus returns to his place of lodging on the Mount of Olives (cf. 22:40). As he prays, the disciples *sleep,* calling to mind the sleeping of the three on the Mount of Transfiguration in 9:28–36. Thus as he rises and *comes* (ἔρχομαι) to them they are not *ready* to meet him when *the hour* is at hand (22:45–56, 53b). For at that very moment one of the *Twelve* leading a crowd (ὄχλος) of officials approaches Jesus to *deliver over* (παραδίδωμι) the Son of Man (v. 48). In claiming the Temple as "*my* house," Jesus had split the nation at its very center (cf. 12:49–53). Now in retaliation, the *leaders* of the nation of Jerusalem's "house" were striking back (vv. 52–53). Only Peter follows—at a distance—as Jesus is seized and taken into the *house* (οἰκία) of the high priest. He renounces anything to do with his "Lord" (v. 61). Meanwhile the official representatives of the people (λαός), the Sanhedrin, including that old nemesis, the scribes, were gathering. The next morning they question Jesus, the Son of Man (vv. 67–69), and condemn him for claiming to be the *Son of God* (cf. 9:35; 10:21–22). They proceed to take him to Pilate, where they insist before a gathered crowd (ὄχλος) that Jesus has been misleading and stirring up the people (λαός) through his *teaching,* even from Galilee up to Jerusalem (23:1–5). Thus Jesus' whole journey to Jerusalem and his presence in the Temple is defined as a false teaching, a prophet uttering a false word.[361] Pilate sends

Jesus to the nation's "king" who eventually, after "seeing" Jesus (cf. 9:9), joins his soldiers in mocking Jesus, while the chief priests and the scribes vehemently accuse him (23:10–11). Sent back to Pilate, Jesus stands one final time before the crowd, now called "the people," who in turn stand with their leaders and the chief priests (23:13–25). The whole nation is assembled! The *laos*, their leaders, their priests, their king, their Gentile governor of the kings of the nations (22:25)—all condemn Jesus to death. One by one in a mounting suspense of murder and treachery "the hands of men" of "this generation" join together to take Jesus to the cross as a false teacher and prophet, a king without a people or throne. The whole nation of Israel and its "benefactors" (22:25) have struck back. Tenet C has now become fact. Three times Pilate tries to persuade release of Jesus; but each time it falls on deaf ears of a nation that is stiff-necked and unrelenting. At last Pilate *delivers* him *over* to their will (23:25; cf. 9:44; 18:32). Jesus must die.

Jesus begins the final leg of his long exodus journey (23:27–32). The *laos* follow behind, while "daughters of Jerusalem" carry out the official rites of mourning for the condemned (cf. *b. Sanh.* 43a).[362] Luke's irony shines through again: the nation that goes out to witness its condemned also provides its own lament. The relief is now set for Jesus' final turning to those who at stages have followed along in the arduous journey. He pronounces judgment over the whole nation (tenet D): If such a sin-riddled nation condemns an innocent man to a violent fate, how much greater will God's retribution upon them be when their guilt is fully ripe! Thus before tenet C reaches its conclusion Jesus once again pronounces tenet D.

Jesus *comes* (23:33) to "the Skull." There as he hangs on the cross rejected by the people, mocked by their leaders as the chosen one (v. 35; cf. 9:35) sent from God, one of the "lawless" criminals hanging alongside him submits and receives Jesus' authority. Jesus declares that this man will be with him *today* when he "*comes* into [his] kingdom" (v. 42). With that the curtain of "his house" is torn in two (v. 45; cf. 12:49–53), while a Roman Gentile "praises God" and declares Jesus to be innocent (δίκαιος) of any wrong. With darkness over the land, the crowds sense that a gross injustice has taken place, as they return "beating their breasts" (v. 48). All the while, Jesus' acquaintances and the women who had followed him all the way from Galilee stand by passively, observing all that was happening. Jesus breathes his last. The journey is over.

The Journeying Guest Is Lord of the Banquet (Luke 24:13–53)

On the third day, after all these things had occurred, two men journey (πορεύομαι) toward Emmaus,[363] heads hanging, voices somber, disillusioned by yet another false messiah and "redeemer of Israel" (24:13–14,

17b, 19–21). As they converse, another joins their party and journeys with them (v. 15b). The stranger asks them what they are talking about. They are astonished[364] that this journeying stranger (παροικέω, v. 18; cf. Acts 7:6) to Jerusalem does not know about that Jesus of Nazareth who was a "prophet powerful in deed and word before God and all the people" (v. 19) whom the chief priests and the leaders had condemned to death. And now it has been reported by some women that they had seen angels who said this man was alive. But as it has turned out, no one has "seen" him. The stranger replies by chiding their dullness in failing to believe "all that the prophets had spoken." After all, "it was necessary (δεῖ) that the Christ should suffer these things before entering into his glory." He then begins to interpret for them the Scriptures *"beginning from Moses and all the prophets"* (vv. 25–27).[365] The two approach their village of destination, while the stranger appears to be going on. But they strongly urge him (v. 29)[366] to *stay with them.* So the *journeying guest* "enters to stay with them" (v. 29b). As he is received at table and reclines with them, this guest behaves most unusually: he takes over as host. Taking bread, he blesses it and begins to give it to the two men. At once "their eyes were opened." The journeying guest is known to them at table (cf. v. 35).[367] This is the "Lord of the Banquet."

In what is one of his most exquisite literary achievements, Luke brings his Gospel to a dramatic close. It is again the "journeying guest" which is fundamental by providing the constitutive link between Jesus the journeying prophet–Lord of the Banquet and the one testified by Scripture who is killed by sinful folk but rises on the third day (24:7 → 18:31–34; 9:44, 22). The individual themes of the "journeying guest" are plain enough that they do not warrant a relisting here. What is primary[368] to the Emmaus episode and may be regarded as the interpretative key for all the meal scenes in Luke is the recognition of the journeying guest who is revealed at table as the Lord (v. 35) and as Lord, the host of the banquet in the Kingdom of God (cf. the passive verbs in vv. 16, 17, 31, 35).[369] Through the structure as well as the movement of this "reverse-journey narrative," then, there is a momentous revelation of Jesus the journeying prophet as the same Lord who promised that his disciples would eat and drink in his Kingdom and who had received and forgiven repentant tax collectors and sinners at table.[370] Consequently, we may regard this unique story as generic to all the meal scenes we have discussed and an organic development and logical outcome of the meal fellowship with the Lord of the house of the Kingdom of God. Like the Seventy(-two) whose eyes had seen what had been hidden from the wise, so these two see the Lord in their midst.[371] "He was known to them in the breaking of the bread" (24:35).

As the two return to Jerusalem to join the gathered disciples, Jesus himself appears[372] (24:36–49) and pronounces the "peace" upon them in a way similar to that by the Seventy(-two) in the homes of the journeying-guest mission. While they are taken aback and "marvel" (θαυμάζω) in disbelief, Jesus eats before them (v. 43). Again this eating is linked to revelation of his identity: "he opened their minds to understand the Scriptures." The whole of Scripture points forward to the suffering death and resurrection of the Messiah which Jesus had already declared to them (v. 44). Now a new direction is given which continues to fulfill the divine necessity of the prophetic function of Scripture: a mission to the Gentiles must be undertaken so that repentance and forgiveness of sins may be extended to them (vv. 47–49). But before this mission of proclamation (v. 47; cf. 3:3; 4:18–19, 44; 8:1; 9:2; 12:3) "in his name!" begins, they are to receive power from on high. Thus a new journey is announced (cf. 9:51), starting from Jerusalem (v. 47b), a journey that curiously resembles the journeying-guest mission of the Seventy(-two):

(a) "Power" (cf. 10:19, 13) from God goes with them. (b) They go in Jesus' "name" (cf. 10:17; 9:48–49). (c) Repentance is the aim of their proclamation (cf. 10:13; 3:3, 8; 5:32; 15:7, 10; 16:30; 17:3–4). (d) Non-Jewish or Gentile areas are to be their goal (cf. 10:2–3, 8, 17–20). (e) The mission is tied to revelation of Jesus' identity at a meal (cf. 10:5–11). (f) And this mission reveals the one whom the OT period prophesied and anticipated (cf. 10:23–24). (g) The authority behind this commission is one that has been rejected by Israel and has thus resulted in a suffering death (tenet C) but also resurrection (cf. 9:51, 53, 57–58; 10:1, 18–19). (h) The mission is attended by "joy" (10:17).

Though the journeying-guest themes are not as concentrated as in the Emmaus story, still there are those distinct links to that mission in 9:52—10:24, in particular, and to the more comprehensive conception of Jesus' mission in the Central Section in general.

As Jesus leads his followers out to Bethany before he is taken up into heaven (vv. 50–51), the new journey begins even as the journey to Jerusalem reaches its fulfillment (cf. 9:51 — Acts 1:10–11). It is the journey of the church called to proclaim the one who was not received by his own and "killed by the hands of lawless folk" (Acts 2:23; cf. Luke 22:37), the one "sent to Israel with the good news of peace" "beginning from Galilee," whose presence brought the dynamic reign of God for healing and the forgiveness of sins (Acts 10:36–38, 43b; cf. Luke 10:1–24). When the disciples return to Jerusalem they bless God continually in the Temple, eating and drinking together with great joy,[373] knowing that the journeying Jesus continues to reveal his presence among them as the "Lord of the Banquet" (Acts 2:42, 46–47; 9:19; 10:48b; 16:15, 34; 20:7–12; 27:33–38).

D. Therefore God Will "Rain" Destruction Upon Israel as in 722 and 587 B.C.E. Because They Did Not Hearken to Him

Thus I will cast them out among all the nations which they have not known, and the land behind them will be made utterly destitute of any traversing or returning there: indeed, they have made the chosen land a desolation.

(Zech. 7:14 [LXX])[374]

Consolidation of Tenets A—C → D

Tenets A—C lead inevitably to God's destruction of a stiff-necked people (tenet D). Although tenet D in earlier Deuteronomistic tradition consists of the historical fact of this judgment upon Israel in 722 and 587 B.C.E., later tradition ascribes to the prophets' own message the announcement of the judgment that the Lord will bring again in similar fashion upon an unrepentant people.[375] As we have seen, this later function corresponds precisely to Jesus' pronouncements of judgment upon Jerusalem and "her children" in the Central Section.[376]

In tracing tenets A, B, and C we have been led to see tenet D in 11:31–32, 50–51; 12:57–59; 13:24–30, 35a; 14:24; (16:27–31);[377] 17:26–30; 19:27, 41–44.[378] This pronouncement either erupts in the midst of the *crowds'* and of the *Pharisees'* active resistance to Jesus' authority or it comes as a warning to the *crowds* and *disciples* whose capacities to discern the "sign" in their midst are becoming increasingly vitiated. In 13:35a Jesus' oracle of judgment on Jerusalem's house brings the journey to a semiclimax as the "triumphal tragedy" of the end is already adumbrated. What has transpired from the Pharisee meal (11:37–54) to this midpoint is the growing influence of the Pharisees-scribes upon the crowds and Jesus' disciples to such a degree that Jesus must launch a vigorous counterwarning to divide Jerusalem's "house" (12:1—13:9). And though it is clear that Abraham's children constitute the one side of the divided household (13:16), the question thrust before the reader in 13:17, 22–30 is which side the burgeoning (12:1, 13, 54) and approving (13:17) crowds will occupy. Are those children of Abraham who are being saved many or few (13:22)? Can it be that even those who have eaten and drunk in the "Lord's presence" (13:26) will not be included in the banquet of Abraham's children (13:27–28)? Luke 13:31–33, 34–35 leave absolutely no doubt concerning the fate of the nation's "children" in this Deuteronomistic capsule of Jesus' career. Because of this prophet's tragic rejection and violent death, Jerusalem's house will be forsaken!

Now it would seem that the second half of the journey could only be anticlimactic. But such is hardly the case. We have witnessed Jesus' renewed attacks on the Pharisees' greed and service to mammon in response to the growing sentiment that Jesus' eating and drinking with tax collectors and "sinners" completely disqualified him from any authentic word of prophecy. By the time we reach the prediction of Jesus' Passion in 18:31–34—with the Twelve's ability to receive Jesus' teaching and warnings not increased in the slightest—the overwhelming crush of the monolithic opposition hits the reader with the most sordid of conclusions: even Jesus' closest followers will play into the brutal "human hands" (9:44) of "this generation" (17:25) to deliver Jesus over to the authorities (9:22; 18:32) for death. Despite the voice of the Son and "all of his glorious deeds," Jerusalem's children will be *one unified house of rejection.* Therefore, not one stone will be left upon another (19:41–44).

Thus we have now demonstrated the way Deuteronomistic tenets A, B, C, and D determine both the overall shape of the Central Section and its basic dynamics. Now it is time to see how Luke's dramatis personae "act" in a continuous, unfolding plot to bring about the journeying prophet's death and, ultimately, the destruction of an immovable people.

The Leaven of the Pharisees-Scribes

1. The Pharisees in Luke-Acts

In order to appraise the distinctive role this group plays in the story of Luke's Central Section one needs to observe Luke's treatment of them throughout his two-volume work, Luke-Acts.

The Acts

Acts 5:34. The explicit mention of "Pharisees" first occurs in the "apostles'" arrest and defense before the Sanhedrin (5:27). It is the Sadducee "party," driven by the jealousy of the chief priests, which has determined to stop the young, brash movement that teaches the resurrection from the dead "in Jesus" and stirs up the *laos* (4:1ff.; 5:12ff.). In fact, during the early days of this movement in Jerusalem the only group directly opposing the "disciples" is the Sadducees, who become so enraged that only the death of the community's leaders[379] would seem to provide appeasement (cf. 5:33). In the midst of this furor it is ironically a Pharisee, Gamaliel I, a noted scribe in the Sanhedrin,[380] who argues effectively for restraint in opposing what may be a movement "from God" (5:33–39).

Acts 15:5. Though Luke's detail of "some believers from the party of the Pharisees" is tantalizingly scant, at least the reader is informed that certain numbers of Pharisees were included in the early Christian community. The dispute that follows, though serious and not without far-reaching consequence, is still portrayed by Luke as a "family fight"; the Pharisees here are not opponents but working members of the Jerusalem community.

Acts 23:6–9. Paul, lynched by the mobs of the *laos* in Jerusalem and arrested by the Roman tribune (21:30–36), is hauled before the Sanhedrin (22:30—23:1). In a stunning "courtroom coup" Paul suddenly declares, "I am a Pharisee, a son of Pharisees," thus throwing the whole chamber into bedlam (23:7–10). Then "some of the scribes of the party of the Pharisees" stand up to defend Paul. His view of the "resurrection of the dead" (23:6b) appears to match theirs. They can "find nothing wrong in this man." Consequently, by a brilliant identification with this aspect of a shared hope—which in Acts characterizes both the continuity and the distinctiveness of the Christian movement vis-à-vis Israel—Paul manages to escape adjudication from the Sanhedrin by throwing its Sadducee members into a bitter feud against the minority Pharisee faction. What is evident and important for our purposes is that we hardly find the suspicious hostility of the Pharisees against Jesus that we encountered in the Central Section of the Gospel. On the contrary, in both Acts 5 and 23 "the Pharisees" constitute the apostles' greatest "official" support.

Acts 26:5. In another trial scene Paul contends before Agrippa and Festus that with respect to the Jews he has lived according to the strictest party of "*our* religion" (i.e., as a Pharisee). He asserts again that his appearance in such a setting is a travesty, since he believes only what was promised as hope to "our fathers" to which "our twelve tribes" hope to attain—resurrection from the dead.

In short, in Acts we have a picture of the Pharisees that is in striking contrast to that of the Gospel's Central Section. Pharisees not only make up part of the Jerusalem community of disciples, but as outstanding a disciple as Paul, an apostle,[381] even declares that he is one with them in hope and in the life he has lived. Far from opposing the movement of Jesus "the Nazorean" they stand up for it before their rival faction the Sadducees. Moreover, and just as noteworthy, the Pharisee scribes who form the brunt of Jesus' most stinging rebuke in the Central Section[382] are now seen to produce some of the disciples' most articulate defenders.[383]

Luke 1—8

Luke 5:17–26. Only Luke of the three Synoptists records the presence of the Pharisees in the healing of the paralytic let through the roof (5:17, 21); they are linked in both verses with the scribes. Luke so structures his account that these Pharisees and scribes are introduced at the beginning as if they were an "inspection team" who, coming from every village of Galilee and Judea, as well as from Jerusalem, become official representatives of all Israel in evaluating Jesus' teaching (v. 17). As in Matthew and Mark, they inwardly accuse Jesus of blaspheming when he declares the paralytic's sins forgiven. Thus their opinion at this early stage of the Gospel is censorious; only God can forgive sins (v. 21b).

Luke 5:27–39. Like Matthew and Mark, Luke presents the Pharisees' ("and their scribes"—Luke; "scribes of the Pharisees"—Mark) objections to the eating (and drinking—Luke) with tax collectors and sinners at Levi's banquet (vv. 27–32).[384] But only Luke continues the story with characters and setting unchanged as the Pharisees once again look a-skance at the disciples' "eating and drinking" (vv. 33–39) in contrast to John's and their own disciples' fasting. Coming directly after the Pharisees'-scribes' negative review of Jesus in 5:17–26, the distinct impression is that this murmuring by the Pharisees-scribes reveals now a significant scandal which might well develop into a dominant note of opposition in Luke's plot of the Jesus movement (cf. 4:16–30).[385]

Luke 6:1–5. Luke's story moves on to a Sabbath controversy (cf. 4:16–37). The antagonists: "some of the Pharisees," who again protest the indecorous eating of Jesus' disciples. Jesus again intervenes to defend his disciples' practice. Far from transgressing the Law of the Sabbath, they are only doing what the OT already depicts in David's eating of the showbread and his distribution of it to those with him. The points of this analogy are not difficult to grasp: *(a)* Jesus is comparable to David in that he was responsible for the eating of those in his company. What the disciples are doing, then, is indeed authorized by Jesus himself. *(b)* As David's authority equalled that of the priests by eating that which only they were authorized to eat, so Jesus reinterprets the Law of the Sabbath with the authority equal to the scribes of the Pharisees who interpret the Law through the traditions of their fathers.[386] But Jesus' authority does not end there. For "the Son of Man is Lord of the Sabbath" (v. 5). We meet the same assertion of authority as in 5:17–26 of the Son of Man, who claims to speak for God. By using the term "Lord," Luke presents a Jesus whose authority in interpreting the Law is tantamount to God's. Thus we encounter here in the first third of the Gospel the primary focus of the Prophet and Son of Man in the Central Section who utters the voice of God. What is more, as in the Central Section, Jesus' eating and drinking is singled out here as the trademark most decidedly canceling any credence to that claim. For Jesus links his disciples' practice unmistakably with his own mandate from God. To oppose his disciples is to oppose the one who has come, eating and drinking to call sinners to repentance (5:32) and to proclaim the will of God in the Law (6:5). The connecting thread of all four pericopes is the Pharisees'-(scribes') resistance to this mandate from God. And in the last three pericopes the disciples' eating and drinking is the critical center. We have, consequently, some of the rudiments of the "journeying guest," without, however, the final goal of the journey stated or the means of being received into the homes clearly exemplified.[387] The effect, then, of 6:1–5 is to extend the Pharisees' building opposition to Jesus as one unfit to teach and heal and observe the Law.

Luke 6:6–11. Continuing on "on another Sabbath," Luke relates yet again "the scribes' and the Pharisees'" deprecatory stance to Jesus' behavior. As in 5:17–26, Jesus is teaching and heals a paralytic; but now the Pharisees'-scribes' questioning and murmuring of 5:17—6:5 reaches a new stage in the developing hostility: they begin to "watch closely" or "scrutinize" (cf. 14:1; 20:20) Jesus' movements *"in order that they find grounds to bring charges against him in legal proceedings."*[388] Jesus' counterstrategy of healing the man meets only a greater determination to throttle him: "They were filled with fury and were discussing with each other what they might do to Jesus" (v. 11). Now in the context of accusations of blasphemy (5:17–26), violations of purity, dietary, and Sabbath regulations, and a plotting to take Jesus to court, Luke's comment of furious wrath and renewed opposition (v. 11) can only with the greatest of difficulty be construed as having nothing to do at all with a desire to take his life.

> It is true that this goal is not expressly stated; but planning to bring charges against Jesus under suspicion of blasphemy can lead logically to the conclusion that such a thought had at least been entertained. The programmatic character of 5:17–26 should warn the reader that representatives from all Israel are already alarmed over blasphemous assertions from Jesus' lips. For Jesus himself claims to possess the authority on earth to forgive sins and not just to utter a prophetic word concerning the mind or decision of God to forgive. Hence, "blasphemy" must be interpreted as a "violation of the power and majesty of God" which was to be punished by death.[389] Therefore to conclude, as some have, that, vis-à-vis Matthew and Mark, Luke has "softened" the Pharisees' stance or relates traditions less ominous in import[390] is to disregard the story plot that Luke is developing within his Gospel.

Yet, for all this, it must be admitted that Luke betrays no clear-cut conspiracy to destroy Jesus; the options remain open and indeed are being discussed. To be sure, the Pharisees-scribes are not any less hostile or more favorably disposed to Jesus when compared to Matthew or Mark. Rather, Luke's story thus far presents a stage in which the explicit plan to kill Jesus has not yet been formulated. As I. H. Marshall comments, "The impression given is that they are at their wits' end and do not know what to do."[391] But by joining five units in sequence in which the Pharisees-scribes are the antagonists and which end in an enraged effort to stop his blasphemous actions, Luke leaves no doubt that their opposition is deadly serious and building momentum.

Luke 7:18–50. The next appearance of the Pharisees-scribes is not until after Jesus' lengthy address to his disciples in the hearing of the *laos* (6:12–49) and following two mighty deeds (7:1–17). The effect: the momentum of opposition by the Pharisees-lawyers is all but lost. When they do appear again in 7:30 there is no direct linkup with their scheming to halt Jesus' movement in 5:17—6:11. Instead, they reject the purpose of God for themselves by failing to be baptized by John and taking heart at Jesus' preaching. It is not until the parable of the children playing in the street and its application (7:31–35) that the Pharisees'-scribes' role in opposing John and Jesus begins to bear any relation to their opposition in the earlier phase of the Gospel. And even here, the dynamics of this opposition are of a fundamentally different kind. Instead of contrasting the censorious connivings of the Pharisees-scribes with the near ecstatic awe of the crowds (5:15, 26), their scornful stance is now related to the primal disobedience and rejection of Jesus' movement by the same ecstatic crowds. The Pharisees' influence upon the rest of the nation is now the subject of attention as they are singled out as the orchestrators of a movement that will grow to include the whole of the folk of this generation in murmuring against the Son of Man. Moreover, as this new picture is introduced, the Pharisees ironically are no longer treated as a block of resistance. Rather, we glimpse an individual Pharisee, Simon by name, who even extends a home-meal invitation to Jesus. That is, some of the Pharisees are portrayed as friends or at least sympathetic or open to the prophetic signs accomplished by Jesus (cf., e.g., 7:16, 18–23). Whereas Luke 5:17, 21, 30, 33; 6:7 and 7:30 speak of *the* Pharisees and scribes as a generic group and 5:17, 21 portray them as representing all of Israel so that "some of the Pharisees" in 6:2 is only a stylistic variation, 7:36 introduces a new factor into the plot: the Pharisees engage Jesus in his sending as the journeying-guest prophet. It is precisely these meals with Pharisees which serve as a barometer of "this generation's" response to Jesus. Consequently, even as the meal fellowship is broken off with *some* of the Pharisees (11:37–54; 14:1–24), so all the crowds are joined to the ranks of the now consolidated opposition of *the* Pharisees-scribes. Thus in this way, 7:18–50 is a frontispiece to the Central Section, while at the same time it is a bridge to the earlier opposition of the Pharisees-scribes (5:17—6:11). Notice that the home-meal motif of the "journeying guest" carries 7:18–50 forward to the journey (9:51ff. and 11:37–54). But this "eating and drinking" (7:34) also binds this section to the main charge against Jesus in 5:17—6:11.

In short, the Pharisees-scribes are important antagonists in the first third of the Gospel. Though there is no explicit plotting of Jesus' death, they are nonetheless opposed to him and his disciples and scheme among themselves to put an end to his blasphemous claims. The intensity of their hostility is thus linked qualitatively with that in the Central Section. In an important bridge passage (7:18–35) Luke summarizes the rejection of Jesus by the Pharisees-scribes to that point (7:30) and then introduces a more complex dynamic of acceptance and rejection (7:31–50) which is developed in and becomes characteristic of the Central Section. The momentum of resistance in Luke 5 and 6, however, is not sustained in Luke 7 and 8.

Luke 19:45—21:38

Curiously the "Pharisees" are not mentioned by name at all in this or the final section of the Gospel. They last appear so identified in 19:39–40. The question immediately arises whether Luke wishes to exonerate them of any official complicity in Jesus' death or whether their resistance in the earlier parts of the Gospel is now carried on by the scribes, who appear frequently in the attempts to arrest Jesus.

Luke 19:47. For the first time in the Gospel, Luke mentions a specific scheming to kill Jesus, undertaken by representatives of each group of the Sanhedrin. Thus for Luke, a plan to stop Jesus' activity by the death penalty is an official plot to be carried out by the chief court of the nation. Consequently the listing of the *functionaries*—rather than the religious parties or preferences within the Sanhedrin—is to be expected.[392] The question is still completely moot as to which religious groups were primarily involved, especially in any unofficial, behind-the-scenes maneuvering. Yet already by using the expressions εὕρισκον . . . ποιήσωσιν and ὁ λαός, Luke creates connections back to the Pharisees'-scribes' scheming in 6:7, 11 (climax of 5:17ff.) and 7:29 (contrast to the *laos*). It is quite possible that the Pharisees-scribes of this earlier "chapter" of the story are now, from an official legal basis, fulfilling their desire to "find grounds to bring charges against him in legal proceedings" (6:7b).

Luke 20:1, 19. On another occasion the Sanhedrin representatives try again to execute their plans by challenging Jesus' authority. Again fear of the *laos* prevents them from carrying out their ploy (20:6, 19). The stark contrast with 7:29–30 is again evident.

Luke 20:20–26. Though the word "scribe" does not occur in this section, the strategy of 20:1ff. continues with the same actors, "the scribes and the chief priests" (20:19a), now contriving to hand Jesus over to the

Roman governor (20:20b) for trial.[393] That Luke understands these scribes to carry on the determinations of the *scribes of the Pharisees* from the pre-Jerusalem phase can be argued by the following:

a. Like the scribes and the Pharisees of 6:7 and 14:1, the scribes of 20:22ff. are "watching closely" (παρατηρέω) for the right opportunity[394] to bring charges against Jesus.

b. The spies sent who pretend to be "righteous" (δίκαιος) match the description of the Pharisee of 18:9–14 and those to whom the parable is addressed (δίκαιοι) as well as the lawyer of 10:25–37 and the Pharisees of 16:14–15 who attempt to justify (δικαιόω) their righteousness before others. Moreover, the Pharisees-scribes are told that the "righteous" are not the raison d'être for Jesus' eating and drinking (5:32 and 15:7). By implication the Pharisees-scribes stand over against the "sinners" as those "righteous" who do not suppose they have a need for a "physician." Furthermore, this *hapax legomenon* here, ὑποκρίνομαι, resonates Jesus' charge in 12:1 to beware of the hypocrisy (ὑπόκρισις) of the Pharisees.

c. Like the scribe of 10:25–37 and the scribes and Pharisees of 11:37–54, the "spies" here attempt to catch Jesus at something he might say which could lead to his arrest.

d. "Teacher" (v. 21) is the characteristic appellation for Jesus among the non-"disciples"; of the eleven occurrences in the vocative, seven are from Pharisees/scribes or a "ruler,"[395] while the Sadducees address him as such in 20:28. Thus "teacher" is the common title for Jesus used by the Pharisees-scribes.

e. It is unlikely that Sadducees would tell Jesus that he "spoke and taught accurately" and "truly taught the way of God" when they differed with him (as with the Pharisees) in such a basic tenet as the resurrection[396] (cf. 20:27–40; 14:14). When the Sadducees do appear as a religious group, Luke considers it appropriate to give them a special introduction, since they represent such a contrast to the previous questioners in their way of thinking (v. 27b).

f. Both in vv. 20b and 26a these spies are identified as potentially capable of catching Jesus in error or at odds with the "righteousness" of the Law[397] (cf. v. 21—"the way of God";[398] v. 22—"Is it lawful?").

g. Again Luke mentions the *laos* as "holding the lid" upon any attempt to arrest Jesus. The foil of 7:29–30 is again conjured up. The Pharisees as the religious leaders of the people were precisely those who would find themselves in a delicate situation in trying to maintain this leadership in the face of a powerful rival.

h. Therefore, as in 14:6, Luke adds that they were "unable" to trap Jesus. That is to say, again the sharpest scribal minds cannot outwit Jesus, as had been tried previously (cf. 5:30–39; 6:1–5, 6–11; 7:40–50; 11:37–41, 53–54; 13:31–33; 14:1–6; 15:1–2).

We conclude, then, that the weight of the evidence points to the scribes and their "spies" in 20:20–26 to be Pharisees.[399] They are thus continuing the plan and desire of the Pharisees-scribes of the pre-Jerusalem period to bring charges against Jesus.

Luke 20:27–40. After Jesus' convincing two-pronged refutation of the Sadducees' trick or "mocking question,"[400] *some* of the scribes chime in unison that Jesus (i.e., "teacher") has answered "well."[401] The impression is that Jesus' audience in 20:20–26 has continued on with the same "spies"-scribes witnessing Jesus' masterful confutation of the Sadducees and now venting glee that their archrivals have been made to look impotent. That Luke is not suggesting that these "some" (of the scribes) are now favorably disposed to Jesus, and thus backing down from their scheme to arrest Jesus, is evident from two facts: *(a)* Verse 40 states that they backed down from challenging Jesus *because* they did not *dare* put themselves into another embarrassing and humiliating situation. Thus their "compliment" in v. 39 is more an expression of release from their chagrin, and a gloating over their rivals' discomfiture, than a sincere attempt to win Jesus' favor. *(b)* This interpretation is supported all the more by Jesus' immediate response in 20:41–47 in which he first challenges the scribes' messianology and then adds insult to injury by criticizing their way of life. Hence the "scribes" of v. 39 are Pharisees.

Luke 20:45–47. Note that in vv. 45–57 Jesus repeats the same fundamental charges that he has directed against the Pharisees-scribes of 11:37–54 and 14:1–24[402] (20:46b is a doublet of 11:43; cf. 14:7). Like the Pharisees-scribes of 11:46–52, the scribes of v. 46 "will receive the greater condemnation."[403]

In short, the "scribes" of the Jerusalem ministry are the scribes of the *Pharisee* party. Luke informs his readers that now within the official council of the Sanhedrin, they, along with others, are laying plans to fulfill the scheming of their counterparts in the pre-Jerusalem period by seeking to arrest Jesus and deliver him over to death. Nowhere does Luke give the impression that these scribes are unrelated to the scribes of the Pharisees in the earlier parts of the Gospel.

Luke 22:1—24:53

Luke 22:1–2. As the Passover approaches, the chief priests and scribes "were plotting" how to "kill" or "do away with" Jesus. The plan of 19:47 is nearing fulfillment but again is hindered by the potential reaction of the people. Every indication is that the scribes here are the same representatives of the Sanhedrin as in the Jerusalem period. Thus there are no grounds for contending that the Pharisees disappear altogether in the Passion narrative. What Luke does go on to say is that Judas is interested in delivering Jesus over to the chief priests and the Temple police.[404] This is perfectly logical, given the authority and responsibility of the priest-controlled Temple police to make arrests as well as to ensure order in the Temple precincts. The scribes' role in the plot is not in the least diminished (cf. 22:52–53, 66).

Luke 22:66. At dawn, according to Luke, the Sanhedrin convenes; at the center of its investigation and decision to deliver Jesus over to Pilate for death are the scribes. There is no slackening of the Pharisees'-scribes' role in the plotting and execution of Jesus' death. Luke 22:1–2 is now consummated as the fulfillment of 19:47ff.

Luke 23:10. Before Herod the same duo of "chief priests and scribes" accuse Jesus (cf. 23:2). By using the verb κατηγορέω ("to accuse"), Luke brings to a head the "scribes' and the Pharisees'" "watching" of Jesus throughout the Gospel to bring him to court, which is stated expressly in 6:7 (cf. 14:1; 20:20). At 23:13 Pilate assembles chief priests and other Jewish leaders along with the *laos,* who then together with *one* voice cry out for Jesus' death. That is to say, the dynamics of acceptance and rejection have changed remarkably to that of the Central Section.[405] No longer do the *laos* and the crowds stand in sharp relief to their leaders, the chief priests and the scribes (see Luke 1—8; 19:45—21:38), but join in "murmuring" against Jesus.

In short, the scribes continue their active role from within the Sanhedrin to bring about the arrest and conviction of Jesus to death. In the Passion narrative the scheming of Luke 5—6 and the intensifying opposition in the Central Section of the Pharisees-scribes come to fulfillment. For Luke, their role is consistent throughout, both as instigators of Jesus' arrest and death and as leaders of the people, however the dynamics of the latter may vary from section to section. Here it is notable that primarily in the Passion narrative, the dynamics of the Deuteronomistic view of the prophets' fate dominate as the *laos,* disciples, and all of "this generation" combine with their leaders to "murder" the prophet Jesus.

We can therefore draw the following conclusions:

a. In contradistinction to the Gospel in general and the Central Section in particular, the nonbelieving Pharisees and their scribes are given a sympathetic treatment by Luke in Acts. The Pharisees form the closest link to the young community's growing awareness of both its continuity with but also growing differentiation from the Temple and synagogue worship of their "brethren." There is none of the hostility of the Gospel posed *directly* by the Pharisees in Acts. This stark contrast must be taken into full consideration in analyzing the portrait of the Pharisees within the Gospel as well as vis-à-vis Matthew and Mark.

b. In each major section of the Gospel it is the Pharisees and especially their scribes who are Jesus' leading opponents. Consistent throughout is their challenge of his credentials to understand "the way of God" in the

Law and hence to teach and heal with any prophetic authority. In Luke 5—6 Jesus' forgiving of sins leads to accusations of blasphemy, and the eating and drinking of his disciples and violation of Sabbath laws provoke them to look for every opportunity to press charges against him. In the Central Section this same disgust at Jesus' defiling eating and drinking and gross perversion of Sabbath laws propels them onward in their plan to trip him up. It is not, however, until the Jerusalem ministry that Luke expressly equates this plan with an intention to seek his death. And because during this phase the word "Pharisee" does not occur, it is tempting to distance them from the scheme for his life, if not extricate them altogether. Our literary analysis, however, has rejected this view precisely because Luke links the scribes of the Sanhedrin to the scribes of the Pharisees in the pre-Jerusalem ministry. These lines of connection are both substantive and strategic. The most that can be maintained is that without the ring of the word "Pharisee" in the last part of the Gospel, especially as Jesus is crucified, the contrast to the tolerance of the Pharisee Gamaliel in Acts 5:34 and the other occurrences in Acts is not as stark as it might have been.[406] Be that as it may, for Luke, it is the scribes of the Pharisees who through the whole of the Gospel push for the doom of Jesus' ministry.

    c. In the first third of the Gospel, the Pharisees and their scribes are pitted against the enthusiastic acclaim of Jesus' words and deeds by the crowds and against the eating and drinking of the disciples. The one exception is Simon the Pharisee of 7:36–50, who, with Luke's treatment in 7:18–35, ushers in the Deuteronomistic dynamics of acceptance and rejection of Jesus the prophet. These dynamics are constitutive of the Central Section but are mitigated at the beginning of the Jerusalem ministry (19:45ff.) where the pattern of opposition resembles that of Luke 5—6. The crowds, now termed the *laos,* form the positive but unwitting screen of resistance to the Pharisees'-scribes' and chief priests' maneuverings to entrap Jesus. Yet it is clear that these dynamics are not to last for long. Already in the Deuteronomistic shades of Luke 20:9–19 Jesus describes the leaders' rejection of God's messengers, the prophets, and the giving of the "vineyard" to new tenants. In 20:45–47 the disciples, as in the Central Section, are again singled out from the crowds and warned about the deleterious presence of some of those leaders—the scribes. Suddenly the "childlike" widow appears (21:1–4); and the disciples are warned against dissipation and drunkenness before the coming destruction of Jerusalem (tenet D) (21:5–36).[407] Thus the ground has been prepared for the reemergence of the journeying-guest motif in the Passion narrative (22:1ff.) and with it the full flowering of the Deuteronomistic dynamics of the Central Section. As the leaders, *laos,* and disciples join in the plot to crucify Jesus, it becomes clear that the leaven of the Pharisees-scribes has carried the day. The whole nation is a land of the "lawless." Consequently 19:45—23:56, in microcosm, recapitulates the overall pattern of acceptance and rejection in the Gospel. And most revealingly, it is the "journeying guest" which transforms the *laos* from hanging on to every word of Jesus to a ruthless mob who hang this prophet on a Roman cross.

2. The Leaven of Hypocrisy of the Pharisees-Scribes

We can now outline the developing plot of the "rising leaven" of the Pharisees-scribes in Luke's Central Section.

Luke 10:25–37. The lawyer stereotypes the scribal superiority in matters of the Law among the Pharisees in their attempt to secure a position superior to Jesus' "movement." Thus within the Central Section, 10:25–37 serves as a frontispiece to this *hindering*.

Luke 11:37–54. The climax to this watershed of rejection in the Central Section proper sets in motion a renewal of the scheme to thwart the prophet's sending, now foreshadowed in the death knell of tenet C (vv. 47–51, 53–54): by removing the key of (and to) the knowledge of God, the Pharisees-lawyers stand[408] as an immovable obstacle to entering the salvation in their midst.

Luke 12:1–12. Jesus announces a countermission that will fully expose the "leaven" of the Pharisees which prevents the crowds from repenting and submitting to Jesus' authority. The "hypocrisy" of the Pharisees is thus their engaging Jesus as a son and teacher of the covenant (e.g., at their sacral meals), while not hearkening to his authoritative voice vis-à-vis this covenant.[409] The direct result is not only the denial of folk before God but also the persecution of Jesus and his followers (tenet C: 12:4–5, 8–10).

Luke 12:13–34.* The hindering influence of the Pharisees upon the crowds can already be detected in the story immediately following the warning of 12:1–12. It is the greed (v. 15) for mammon which characterizes these multitudes and endangers the disciples' seeking and embracing the Kingdom in their midst (vv. 30–31). The disciples, addressed as "little of faith" (v. 28c), must stop "worrying" (v. 26b) about their material well-being. What the Pharisees are guilty of "within" (greed, 11:39b), the crowds and disciples must beware of "without" (e.g., 12:16–21, 22–30, 33–34), lest where their "treasure" is, there their heart be also (v. 34).

Luke 12:35–48. To the warning of covetousness Jesus adds the dimension of preparedness to a faithful stewardship of the Lord's household. There is the gravest threat posed to the disciples of an "eating and drinking" oblivious to the master's coming and in defiance of the urgency of

the present time. This unfaithful stewardship is embodied by the Pharisees-scribes who are caught unprepared by the coming of Jesus the Lord
and Son of Man on his journey to Jerusalem. And because as leaders of
the people they have received much responsibility with God's gracious
provisions, the Pharisees-scribes shall receive the greater punishment for
their dereliction in meting out this "food" at the proper time. The disciples and not just the crowds must take the strictest of precautions not to
succumb to this tempting but ultimately destructive stewardship.

Luke 12:49–53. The effect of this dissipated stewardship is to split
Israel's house right down the middle (vv. 52–53). Jesus' countermission
to the Pharisees' leaven of hypocrisy will "cast this fire" of division upon
the "household" and ensue in his death "baptism"[410] in Jerusalem (tenet
C—vv. 49–51). The persecution and murder of 11:47–51 and 12:4–12
are on the brink of becoming reality.

Luke 12:54—13:9. The profligate eating and drinking of the Pharisees
which does not exercise faithful stewardship in the present time (12:42)
of the Lord's coming now becomes characteristic of all the crowds'
inability to discern this present time (12:56). The leaven of hypocrisy has
overtaken them; they all are hypocrites because they continue to
entertain Jesus in their midst through enthusiastic approval of his mighty
works without submitting to his call for repentance (13:1–9). And unless
they discern for themselves and make reconciliation with the accuser in
their midst, they also will receive the same condemnation (13:3, 5, 6–9).
As Jesus' exhortation comes to an end (12:1—13:9), the Pharisees'
hindering influence has become pervasive over the whole nation (13:6–
9); "all will likewise perish" (tenets A and D: 13:3b, 5b). The dynamics
consequently parallel 11:37–52, where the Pharisees' hindering leads to
the judgment of the whole nation (cf. 13:31–35; 19:37–44).

Luke 13:10–21.* In this Sabbath healing Luke describes a ruler of the
synagogue, most likely a Pharisee,[411] directly *hindering* the crowd's
response to Jesus' mighty deed. The result is a mirroring of the division
of Israel's house in 12:49–53 and the continued blindness of the crowds
to repent (12:54—13:9): those who actively oppose Jesus (v. 17) are
called hypocrites (v. 15) because they pose a narrow understanding of the
Law in the way of one who has the authority to declare the will of God in
the Law directly (v. 16; cf. 10:25–37; 11:37–52). The crowd thus continues its facile praise of Jesus' mighty works without the praise of God
that comes from a repentant heart (v. 13).[412] But, Jesus declares, though
this opposition is great, it will eventually be surpassed by the counter-
"leaven" of the Kingdom (vv. 20–21). Though small like a mustard seed
and invisible like yeast, this leaven nevertheless will work and grow to a
kingdom of the greatest proportions (vv. 18–21).

Luke 13:22–30. With Luke's notice of the progressing journey comes the corresponding increase in the *hindering*.[413] The Pharisees' eating and drinking with Jesus of 11:37–54 has now become emblematic of the crowds' presence with Jesus in their towns (v. 26). The judgment of 12:57–59 is graphically described as it is pronounced (vv. 25–30).

Luke 13:31–35. "At that very hour" Pharisees try to veer Jesus off his journey course. Luke's temporal detail is no happenstance. It is the emergence of the Pharisees from the crowds of this generation as in 11:14–37 and 7:18–30, with a link back to 11:53–54 and the Pharisees' eating and drinking (11:37–52). By this center-point, then, the Pharisees' hindering is anticipated as completely successful; the nation as a whole is not and will not receive the journeying-guest prophet. Yet as Luke has Jesus prophesy, even this blanket rejection is a divine must, "for it is not possible that a prophet should come to his end away from Jerusalem" (v. 33b).[414]

Luke 14:1–24. Now the Pharisees' eating and drinking with Jesus comes to a head. Their hypocrisy of guarding the Law while refusing to submit to the one who utters the voice of God directly is shattered by their own inconsistent keeping of the Law (v. 5). That which is hidden is becoming fully known (12:2)! Consequently their "watching"/engaging Jesus (14:1–6) ends in their exclusion from the Banquet of the Kingdom. They and "the many" they control will "not taste my banquet."

Luke 14:25–35.* The crowds are warned by Jesus that unless they extricate themselves completely from the deceiving, deadening influence of the Pharisees-scribes, they cannot be his disciples. The cleft must be absolute; to follow Jesus means to renounce material and societal status (vv. 26, 32) and to follow him to the cross. The fire of division of 12:49–53 is already falling; "salt" that is no longer pure is thrown away (vv. 34–35). For that which has been covered up is now being fully exposed (12:2)!

Luke 15:1–32. The Pharisees-scribes, taking advantage of the "undesirables" that congregate about Jesus, try to retaliate against Jesus' stinging condemnation of their sacral meals (14:7–24) by attacking Jesus' own meal practice! Jesus responds in kind by showing that it is the Pharisee "elder brother" and those like him who are the "lost" who will not be found in the Banquet of the Kingdom (cf. the "ninety-nine" and "nine" in 15:3–7, 8–10). The two types of eating and drinking are mutually exclusive. The house is completely divided (13:52–53; 15:25–32).

Luke 16:1–13.* The dishonest steward epitomizes the Pharisees'-scribes' mismanagement of the stewardship of the household of God. The disciples no less than the crowds in 14:25–33, 34–35 and the Pharisees themselves in 15:11–32 are presented with the stark alternative between two "houses." They can serve only one or the other (v. 13). To be sure, if they "swallow" the Pharisees' leaven and serve the house of mammon, they will have great influence and status as "sons of this age" vis-à-vis the folk of this generation. But this house stands condemned; it is an abomination in the sight of God (v. 15b).

Luke 16:14–15. The Pharisees' hindering-opposition continues to be open and direct (cf. 15:1–2) but now takes on an unparalleled vituperous tone: they "sneer" at Jesus directly to his face. Jesus' riposte seems equally charged. He compares their love of money and resulting influence among society with an "abomination" (cf., e.g., Isa. 1:13) which provokes God's greatest judgment (cf., e.g., Isa. 2:11–19; 5:14–16). It may be that the thought of the abomination in the Temple (cf. Dan. 9:27; 11:31; 12:11 of Antiochus Epiphanes; also cf. 1 Macc. 1:54; 6:7; Matt. 24:15; Mark 13:14) is in mind. In turn it may resonate with the evacuation of the presence of God from the Pharisees' "house" as symbolized by Jerusalem's Temple in Luke 13:35a. At any rate, there is now no turning back in the bitter strife raging between the house of the Kingdom of God and the house of mammon of the Pharisees.

Luke 16:16–18.* Verse 16 with its Matthean parallel is one of the most difficult of the dominical sayings in the NT. But in the context of the Pharisees' *hindering* the crowds and disciples from entering the Kingdom there is a promising solution for this enigmatic saying. Now that the Kingdom of God is being proclaimed, Jesus states that *everyone who wishes to enter it must force one's way into it.*[415]

That βιάζομαι in the middle voice can take on the sense of "force a way for oneself," "try hard," and, with εἰς τι, "enter with force into something" has been amply evidenced.[416] The sense of "must force . . ." is reinforced by the larger context: In 11:52 Jesus castigates the Pharisees-scribes for hindering ("stopping"—NEB) those who are entering the Kingdom; in 12:4–5, 11–12 the prospect of persecution and violence is raised to the disciples in connection with the leaven of the Pharisees; in 13:10–17 an effort is made to prevent people from receiving the healing power of the Kingdom; in 13:24–30, though people are and will strive zealously to enter the Kingdom, they will be incapacitated; in 14:23 the "outsiders" are compelled to come into the Kingdom, while in 15:11–32 the younger brother enters the feast only at the strong protest of the elder brother. Moreover, in 16:1–9, 10–13 it is the steward's (Pharisees') dishonest management of the "household riches" which is coupled with the warning to use these "riches" ultimately for entering the "eternal habitation": the Pharisees are exploiting the material benefits of their status in a way that does not lead the people into the eternal "riches" of the Kingdom of God. Because of this unfaithfulness in mammon, the Pharisees can no longer be entrusted with the true riches (16:11). Their interpretation of the Law to their own favor and prestige (cf. 11:39–44), which justifies their way of life to the masses (16:15a), leads to an incapacitating dullness among the people to discern the signs of the Kingdom in Jesus (cf. 12:54–59). Though the invitation to *enter* the Kingdom has and is being extended by proclamation from the time of John[417] (v. 16), those who desire to enter must force their way in over the resistance of their leaders, the Pharisees-scribes.[418]

Further, vv. 17 and 18 make excellent sense within this context. For, Jesus says, however "dishonestly" the Pharisees are manipulating the Law, both to their own advantage and to the obscuring of the Kingdom of God in the people's midst, it would still be easier for heaven and earth to pass away than for anything within the Law to lose its force (v. 17). Despite their erroneous stewardship, it is still true that, for instance, every man who divorces his wife and marries another commits adultery. Here Jesus gives an example of OT Law (cf. Deut. 24:1–4) and now sharpens it to bring out its true and eternally abiding validity.[419] Regardless of the injustice to the Law, on the one side, and the forced pressure of entering the Kingdom, on the other, the revealed will of God in the Law receives its *full due within the era of the preaching of the good news of the Kingdom of God* (v. 16).

Luke 16:19–31. The hindering of the rich Pharisees is graphically "enacted" by the rich man who excludes the "poor" man from the riches of the banquet table. Because this rich man is unfaithful with the "unrighteous mammon" (16:11), he is denied the true riches of the heavenly banquet in the eternal habitation (16:9, 11b). What is more, his prevention of the "poor" man out of greed for mammon has created a permanent prevention of repentance *within his own house* (vv. 27–31). The *eating and drinking* of the Pharisees has led to an unbridgeable chasm within Abraham's house (v. 26). By being unfaithful with the things of another, they cannot even receive that which is their own (16:12).[420]

Luke 17:1–10.[*421] As the attention shifts to the disciples, so does the growing influence of the hindering leaven among them. There is a grave danger that "these[422] little ones" will be led astray into sin or apostasy. "Woe" to such a one who causes this stumbling (v. 1b; cf. 11:39–47— "woes"). It would be better for that person to be dead than face the consequences of such action in the judgment. The heat of Jesus' condemnation equals his fire of rebuke to the Pharisees in 16:15. And this is no theoretical or abstract possibility to worry about in the future. On the contrary, the threat is concretely real now among the disciples themselves! Therefore, "take heed to yourselves!" (v. 3a).

The identity of these "little ones" is widely debated.[423] Are literal children signified here?[424] Or does Jesus mean weaker and more vulnerable disciples?

Or are perhaps the "poor" in the sense of 14:13, 21; 15:1–2; 16:20, 22, i.e., the sick and "sinner" outcasts of society, in mind? We have already demonstrated Luke's symbolic value of μικρός for a "childlike" response to Jesus' authoritative presence in 7:18–35 and 9:46–48. It is significant that in the former passage the "poor," including the "blind," "lame," "deaf,"[425] and so forth, are posed as examples of those who receive salvation by Jesus in the presence of the crowds just before Jesus refers to one who is "least" being greater in the Kingdom than John. Moreover, this same passage refers to "taking offense" or "stumbling" (7:23) with respect to Jesus' bringing salvation as he eats and drinks with tax collectors and sinners (7:34). Further, the Pharisees'-scribes' reaction is contrasted to that of the *laos* and Wisdom's children (7:29–30, 35). With all of these themes and actors present immediately before 17:1–10 in 14:15—16:31, and, as we have seen, active in positive response to Jesus in the midst of growing rejection, the reference to the "children" or "little ones" here as the "poor" and outcast is forcefully corroborated.[426] For Jesus is warning the disciples in the severest terms against their hindering these weak and powerless from following him in faithful submission. Events leading to a "falling away" are "impossible not to come" (i.e., the events of a violent death ahead in Jerusalem). Therefore the disciples must "take heed for themselves" lest their own demeanor "play the fool" in these events.

The disciples must be zealous to root out these temptations to sin among one another by rebuking and seeking repentance from the offenders. It is only as they stay united and free from strife and jealousy among themselves that they will withstand the temptations within their own circle (17:3–4). The "apostles," conscious of their leading role among the disciples, ask for greater faith in which to combat such influence (v. 5). Jesus rebukes their request by likening their attitudes in leading to the Pharisees' own self-importance with the masses of the people (17:6, 7–10). The apostles are imitating the specious stewardship of the Pharisees-scribes by their air of superiority among the rest. They are exhibiting a hypocrisy commensurate to theirs by assuming privileges in authority that they do not possess. The leaven of the Pharisees has "risen" effectively within the very core of Jesus' following.

Luke 17:11–19. The massive resistance to Jesus' unique authority fermented by the Pharisees' leaven is rehearsed by the nine Jewish lepers over against the one Samaritan. Only the "foreigner" returns to praise God at Jesus' feet (cf. 10:25–37). His *faith* has uprooted a mighty tree (17:6)!

Luke 17:20–37. The Pharisees, oblivious to the Kingdom of God in their midst through such acts of power (cf. 11:20), expect to see observable signs of its coming sometime in the future (17:10–21). Anxious to suppress their increasing grip on the minds and attitudes of the disciples, Jesus launches into a refutation of the Pharisees' ideas about the visible coming of the Kingdom (vv. 22–37). It does not come as "they" claim: "Look here or look there" (v. 23; cf. v. 21). They therefore must not follow those who do!

Luke 18:1–14.* In the light of the temptations to sin and "to lose heart" (v. 1) before the Kingdom comes in triumphant power (17:30, 37), Jesus encourages his disciples to pray. Though persistent prayer until this final Kingdom comes constitutes the thrust, yet Jesus has a more immediate danger in mind (πλήν,[427] v. 8b). Will the disciples be able to endure in the present crisis? As Jesus the Son of Man *comes* to Jerusalem, will he indeed find faith (v. 8b; cf. 17:11–19)? Will in fact the Pharisees' hindering leaven prevail?

That in 18:8b Jesus is concerned about the immediate threat of the Pharisees' leaven is brought out by the following parable that he points at certain ones of his disciples who entertained notions of their own right standing before God,[428] while disdaining others! The negative example to shun is none other than the Pharisee of 18:10–14 who disdains the tax collector and thanks God for his special status of acceptance with the masses.[429] Thus it is the Pharisees-scribes in Jesus' present journey to Jerusalem whose negative influence upon the crowds and now especially the disciples continues to work with increasing effectiveness.

Luke 18:15–30.* The alarming effect on the disciples is suddenly manifested. As "little children" (v. 15; cf. v. 16) come to Jesus, the disciples hinder them. The disciples are perilously close to fulfilling Jesus' direst warning against leading "little ones" astray (17:2)! And they are now guilty of the charge leveled against the Pharisees-scribes at table in 11:52: they have become like the Pharisees! For in their rebuke of the parents in v. 15, they imitate the Pharisee of 18:9–14, who exalts himself, and copy those among them who "treat others with snubbing" (18:9).

As the rich ruler comes upon the scene, we observe another contrast to the "children" (18:15–17). As we have seen,[430] "unrighteous" mammon ties him to the behavior of the Pharisees. But what is most interesting is that Luke indicates the solidarity of sympathy with the ruler from *all* those who have heard the conversation, both disciples and crowds alike (v. 26). If this rich person cannot enter the Kingdom, who can? Jesus' answer refers back to the children in 18:15–17 and the tax collector of 18:9–14 (i.e., those who can bring no merit of performance to the Kingdom). Only such people who submit humbly to God's "impossible" act of accepting them are those who enter the Kingdom (v. 27). Peter, however, thinks he has grasped the import of Jesus' word and claims for him and his friends the obedience that would fulfill Jesus' demand to the ruler (v. 28). Jesus does not deny the sacrifice that his disciples have made but stresses at the same time that this sacrifice is meant for all and thus is valid for all. Though the disciples' obedience is affirmed on the one hand, their special status is denied on the other. All will receive the blessings of new relationships[431] in the Kingdom now as well as the coming eternal life. The leaven of self-importance appears to transcend even the attachment to mammon.

Luke 18:31–34. The Twelve's selection as leaders is shown to be completely gratuitous on Jesus' part as the real goal of his journey remains elusive (v. 34).[432] Thus Peter's claim (18:28) is shown to be vacuous of the self-sacrifice that is ultimately demanded and significant for eternal life: *the way of the cross.* Jesus' earlier question becomes all the more pertinent: "When the Son of Man is delivered over to death [i.e., comes], will he find faith?"

Luke 18:35–43. Jesus finds faith in the blind man of Jericho (v. 42b; cf 17:19) along the "path" (v. 35; cf. 9:57) of eschatological salvation. But this beggar must persist against the hindering of "those who were leading the way" ("rebuke," v. 39; cf. 18:15b). Who are meant by this designation—the Twelve, some of the disciples, or perhaps even some Pharisees (cf. "rebuke," 19:39)? Luke does not specifically identify this group. But the presence of this hindering here should come as no surprise. We have just seen the disciples hinder children after being warned against an attitude of superiority and privilege (18:9–17). Jesus must now stop and "command" the blind man to be brought to him (v. 40).

Luke 19:1–10. Within the widening path of blindness to Jesus' authority, Zacchaeus's *small* stature (v. 3) joined to the crowds' hindering him from "seeing" (v. 3a) Jesus is not without distinct irony. Zacchaeus embodies the "inferior" of Israel who form the brunt of "those who trust in themselves that they are upright while treating others with contempt" (18:9). With 19:7 Luke has reached a new plateau in the dramatic journey to Jerusalem. The solidarity of "this murmuring generation" which kills the Son of Man (17:25) is now in place. The leaven of the Pharisees has leavened the whole lump. Jesus indeed journeys as a glutton and winebibber, a friend of tax collectors and sinners.

Luke 19:11–27. As Jesus had begun his journey to his exodus-exaltation (ἔξοδος—ἀνάλημψις) to receive a kingdom, he charged his disciples with certain responsibilities.[433] But while he is en route, it is clear that the masses of citizens who follow behind him resist and hinder his "reigning over them" (v. 14). When he returns, Jesus pointedly warns, will he find that all the stewards have been faithful (vv. 15–26)? The disciples and the crowds as a whole thus reflect the thinking of the Pharisees in 17:20–21 who miss the Kingdom of God in their midst while awaiting the glorious triumph of this Kingdom in Jerusalem.[434] As a result, declares Jesus, when he returns, all those who resist his rule will be slain "before me" (v. 17, tenet D).

Luke 19:28–44.* Although the mass of resistance has formed, it would be erroneous to think that a consensus has developed on the exact identity and authority of Jesus. It is clear especially from the parable (cf. 19:11) that a considerable number accompanying Jesus linked the manifest coming of the Kingdom with Jesus' own arrival there. While they remain blind to his unique authority, they certainly esteem him as one who journeys with a special God-given mission. In 19:35–40 this expectation is illuminated when the disciples spontaneously vent their hope that Jesus is the Messiah according to Zech. 9:9, the one who is to come in the authority of the Lord (cf. 1 Kings 1:33; 2 Kings 9:13; Luke 13:35b; 7:19–21). It is therefore ironic that as he is bestowed royal honor, Jesus prophesies and laments his rejection by these same "children" (19:44; cf. 9:18–20, 54–55).

Yet while the disciples erupt with effusive (but naive) praise, Luke lets the reader know that others certainly did not go along with this estimate of Jesus' approach to the city. "Some of the Pharisees from the crowd" attempt to silence the disciples. For them, Jesus is a "teacher"[435] who should not tolerate such misguided ardor. Thus again, in this final episode of the journey, the now familiar antagonists are at work in their hindrance of Jesus. As the "secret" of Jesus' Messiahship (9:22; 12:2) overflows publicly, the Pharisees try quickly "to contain" it. Their leaven is active up to the end. Jesus' response is not that his Messiahship must come out into the open or that such royal heraldry must attend his entrance into the city. Such praise, though sincere, is not commensurate with the "following" and "hearkening" that Jesus the Son of Man demands (cf., e.g., 11:27–28!). Rather, as in 12:35 and 19:11–27, Jesus combines the misunderstanding of his Messiahship with the prophecy of the destruction of the nation (tenet D): "When these [the disciples] become silent, the stones will cry out!" Jesus thus prophesies of the time when Jerusalem's children will en masse reject him, with the toppling stones of ruin crying out like Hab. 2:11 against the perpetrated evil. The reference is thus to his imminent rejection and death in Jerusalem with the irrevocable consequence of the destruction of the nation (tenet D). It is the shrieking stones of v. 40 which testify to their fate in v. 44.[436] The distinctive tones of the Deuteronomistic conception resonate! Even as "the whole multitude of disciples" sing his praise, the prophet declares the entire lot to be an "evil generation" which demands a sign (19:34) and from whom the blood of all the prophets will be required (cf. 11:27–29 → 47–51).

Thus far our results: We have discovered and traced an indelible imprint of the Pharisees-scribes throughout the Central Section. It is their "leaven of hypocrisy" which is the counterpoint to the "journeying guest." With this theme of opposition Luke creates an ever-mounting drama of Jesus' journey to Jerusalem with a dynamic tension all its own. The entire section is a story of two opposing forces vying for the allegiance of the crowds of Israel. It is a drama fought to the death. We can delineate five major stages:[437]

1. *Luke 11:14–52.* Partial resistance represents in actuality a monolith of opposition. At table the Pharisees are revealed to be the prime movers behind this opposition which will lead to the judgment of God.

2. *Luke 11:53—13:21.* The crowds' imperviousness to the "signs" of Jesus' presence at "the present time" have increased to the point of resembling the hypocritical leadership of the Pharisees. Riches and especially an unfaithful stewardship of the divine riches by the Pharisees-scribes are the prime forces of this hindering resistance. Judgment upon the whole nation is threatened.

3. *Luke 13:22–35.* The powerful influence of the Pharisees-scribes is demonstrated by the assimilation of their eating and drinking by the crowds! The journeying guest is entertained in their streets and dined in their households without their hearkening to his authoritative voice. The Pharisees attempt to hinder Jesus' actual movement in the journey. Judgment is pronounced.

4. *Luke 14:1–35.* Jesus directly attacks the Pharisees' eating and drinking. Salvation for the throngs can come only through total extrication from this "eating and drinking" which makes repentance impossible and exclusion from the heavenly banquet an assured outcome. Judgment is again pronounced on the Pharisees-scribes and their "many."

5. *Luke 15:1—19:44.* The last part of the journey constitutes a rigorous effort on Jesus' part to prevent the disciples from succumbing fully to the leaven of hypocrisy. From 15:3 Jesus in succession teaches and exhorts against the hindering influences that have been exerted thus far in the journey: *(a)* 15:3–32: the resistance to his association with "sinners"; *(b)* 16:1–13: the stewardship of the Pharisees which disqualifies them to lead the people in the true riches; *(c)* 16:16–18: the Pharisees' interpretation of and obedience to the Law; *(d)* 16:19—17:10; 18:9–30: the Pharisees' greed and manipulation of riches which produces "super-

iority" and contempt for others; and *(e)* 17:20—18:8: the Pharisees' view of the coming Kingdom. By the end of the journey, Jesus' efforts have already proved unsuccessful, as his final parable illustrates (19:11–27).

In short, the hypocrisy of the Pharisees is their leadership over Israel which, though continuing the traditions of the Law and the prophets, covers up from the people and themselves the true fulfillment of this whole history of Israel in Jesus the Prophet. Its result is the opposite of repentance which turns enthusiastic praise and eating and drinking into the specter of the cross. Accordingly, each new stage of the plot sounds the doom of Deuteronomistic tenet D!

CONCLUSION: *The* STORY *of the* DEUTERONOMISTIC JOURNEYING-GUEST PROPHET

It is now time at last for us in highlights to *tell the story* of the Deuteronomistic journeying-guest Prophet.

Jesus has announced to the captivated crowds in the vicinity of Bethsaida that he must embark on a journey to death in Jerusalem. Whoever will follow with their own cross will gain life (9:23–27). Now convinced that Jesus is the Messiah, the disciples, bristling with expectation of great things ahead, begin to vie for rank and honor. The authority of the Son on the mountain has translated into privilege and "power" on the plain (9:46–50). Meanwhile, talk about an "exodus" to a cross is strange and threatening, better to repress with exhilarating thoughts of the journey ahead than to probe more deeply (9:43b–45).

The journey begins. Jesus launches into Samaria by sending messengers ahead of him to herald the coming of the King with his salvation in the Kingdom of God. But these ambassadors are refused hospitality, for no one whose sights are fixed on Jerusalem can bring the promised deliverance. Jesus the "king" is flatly rejected. Those who wish to follow any farther are forewarned: they will have no place to lay their heads. Proclamation of the Kingdom of God will require the sacrifice of ties with home and cherished notions of the Law. No one who keeps looking back to the status quo of Israel's covenant faith will be fit to journey ahead to its fulfillment in the Kingdom of God. Such is the cost of "following" this Lord-King.

Later, as the journey continues, Jesus dispatches seventy(-two) "other" messengers to proclaim the arrival of the Kingdom in the journeying-guest Prophet who has not been received. The results of their mission are astounding. As they go in pairs through the towns and regions that Jesus himself was to traverse not too long afterward, they are received by "sons and daughters of peace." In these homes they establish a banquet fellowship where the presence of salvation is manifest through their eating and drinking with their hosts as they announce the coming of the Lord of salvation and heal the sick. Subsequently, when they rendezvous together, they are ecstatic with the powerful manifestations of the Kingdom's presence. Jesus confirms their joyful childlike reception of the revelation on their journey. He himself is the Son of the Father who reveals the Father to the "children" who receive Jesus and his emissaries with grateful repentance. As with the five thousand near Bethsaida, so again it becomes clear that Jesus is the Lord of the Banquet of the Kingdom of God. But Jesus cautions that now one may not luxuriate in the power that is at hand in the Kingdom but rather in the Kingdom salvation which is being secured through this power. Jesus underscores this message by instructing a larger group of disciples in private: the eschatological fulfillment of the history of salvation of Israel's "prophets and kings" is only now unfolding in their very midst!

Jesus' caution is immediately accentuated by active resistance to his authority. A leading authority in the Law, a scribe from the Pharisees, questions his ability to interpret life as the goal of the Law. Consequently, as the journey proceeds, Jesus begins to stress to his disciples at table and in certain locations along the way that the life promised by the Law is now found only in the one thing needful—hearkening to his voice (10:25—11:13). Only as the disciples submit to him do they receive the life of the Father in the Holy Spirit that Jesus manifests.

As Jesus continues to reveal the Kingdom in the powerful exorcism of demons, the resistance of the scribe proves to be anything but an isolated occurrence. Some of the crowds who are also coming out to see these marvels are restive (11:15–16); Jesus must prove his authority. Even the masses, fascinated and thrilled by Jesus' exhibitions of power, and whose ranks are now beginning to swell (11:29), demonstrate what Jesus had declared already before the beginning of the journey: they are a stubborn and faithless lot, unrepentant before the one wiser than King Solomon and more authoritative than the prophet Jonah. The reason for this obstinate evil soon emerges. "This generation" of Israel is under the control of the hypocritical leadership of the Pharisees-scribes that continues to murder the prophets as did their ancestors before them. The Pharisees' entertaining of Jesus at their meals does not manifest but rather stifles the Kingdom of God in their midst. These leaders thus produce a "leaven" among the crowds which does not receive the journeying-guest Prophet, Lord of the Banquet.

After this decisive meal with certain Pharisees, Luke tells his readers, tens of thousands of the crowds of "this generation" of Israel come out to "see" Jesus. The Pharisees-scribes have now begun to treat Jesus with great hostility, so that Jesus must launch an ambitious counteroffensive. Those who are willing to endure this animosity and openly confess their allegiance to the Son of Man must declare "from the housetops" the presence of the Kingdom in this journeying guest. The battle for the nation of Israel is for its very soul. It is a battle between life and death. But even as Jesus sounds this clarion call to his disciples, a voice from the crowds reveals what Jesus has already sensed—the pervasive influence of the Pharisees'-scribes' leaven even upon the disciples. The battle cry of the Kingdom is already being drowned out by the greed for riches and security in the present. Jesus turns alternatively to disciples and crowds, teaching, exhorting, and warning in such a way that "all Israel" is the audience of this great Prophet. The disciples' tenuous situation is reflected by this audience oscillation as they are at once both distinct from, but yet at one with, the crowds of this generation. Two stewardships, two visions of "the coming Kingdom," in short, two "eatings and drinkings" are at loggerheads. The whole generation is a band of hypocrites and will all perish. Yet "from now on," Jesus cries, this house will be split apart as the Son of Man comes to Jerusalem to die (12:1—13:9).

As Jesus moves on, the divided house meets him at every turn. But it is now "the many" who build the growing monolith as, like their leaders, they eat and drink with Jesus without entering the Banquet in their midst. Only the "least" or Wisdom's children, those sick and possessed and destitute, and so forth, are those "being saved." By the time Luke has completed half of this journey, then, the rejection of the journeying guest by the Samaritan village has become emblematic of the whole. The whole house of Jerusalem's children headed by the Pharisees will be forsaken, even though some of them will still herald him as "coming in the name of the Lord" (13:10–35).

On one of the Sabbaths, Jesus is again present at one of the homes of the Pharisees-scribes. The table talk sums up the course of the journey thus far and sets the tone for the remainder by juxtaposing the Pharisees' idea of the banquet of the Kingdom with that of the Lord of the Banquet. The two are now mutually exclusive. The "prophets" of the streets and alleyways and hedges and highways continue to stream into the banquet, while "the many" remain oblivious to the presence of its Lord. Again as Jesus leaves the Pharisees' home the crowds are swollen, now surging to many as Jesus turns one final time to "all Israel" who are now "accompanying" but not "following" him. Only the latter course, Jesus warns, leads to life. Only as they renounce all of the cares and duties that their leaders have placed in the way of the Kingdom in their midst can they follow as true disciples *to the cross* (14:1–35).

The leaders appear again, and again they place stumbling blocks in Jesus' path. They are now incensed over Jesus' rebuff of their eating and drinking and launch into a public attack on Jesus' "culinary company." Jesus' defense is to paint three miniatures depicting the altercation ahead. The sinners and tax collectors represent the way of the despised and rejected, while the Pharisee elder brother forms the path of antipathy marked by the cross at its end. The disciples are then presented an ultimatum: either they serve the god of mammon of their leaders or they serve God. At this point, as the Pharisees overhear Jesus' assault on them, Jesus alternates in turning to them and to his disciples. The precarious plight of the disciples who stand so close to the leaders of this generation is heightened even more. Now it is alarmingly evident that some of the disciples have joined in belittling "little" "sinners" in their company (15:1—17:10).

As the audience tableau comes to an end, a growing parade of "Wisdom's children" demonstrates how wide the gap between them and "this generation" has become. The disciples even try to prevent some from receiving Jesus and the salvation "today" of the Kingdom that he brings. As the journey draws to a close, Jesus looks back to color the caravan of all Israel that now approaches the "city of the murdered prophets." Though many eagerly anticipate the glorious appearance of the Kingdom, Jesus the journeying guest portrays them as citizens who have not and will not receive their king. To be sure, there are his servants, the disciples, some like Wisdom's children who are faithful as he journeys. But then there are the not so faithful, those who have even identified with the citizens by refusing to submit to his authority. The crowds and the disciples then are mixed, with various degrees of understanding, ambitions, and expectations. Yet they represent as a whole one nation that stubbornly persists in their failure to repent. While Jesus the journeying Prophet and Son brings salvation to the homes and hearths of all Israel, the citizens shake their heads as they look forward to the greater things to come in Jerusalem. Even as the band of disciples ring out with praise for all the mighty acts this Prophet-Messiah has performed—thus to fulfill his own prophecy—Jesus knows where this praise will lead. The way of peace has been concealed from them even as the visitation of the voice of the Son has gone unheeded. Jesus knows all too well the fate that awaits those who are sent to the nation's heart. And as he looks over the city below, he weeps, for he also knows the destiny that awaits a stiff-necked and disobedient people.

**Table of Contents of the Central Section
and its Deuteronomistic Prophet**

Tenets

A.	*B.*	*C.*	*D.*
"This Generation" —"Stiff-necked" like Their "Fathers"	Jesus Sent as Voice —Mediate Will/ Instruct, Admonish/ Warn Repentance	"This Generation" Rejects Jesus-Prophet and Kills Him	Therefore God Will Rain Destruction on the Whole Crooked Nation
11:29–32, 49–52	9:51, 52–56, 57–62	9:51, 52–56, 57–58	(10:12, 14–15)
12:54–56, 57–59	10:1–12, 13–15, 16, 17–20, 21–24, 25–28, 29–37, 38–42	10:3, 10–11, 13, 16, 25	11:31–32, 50–51
13:1–9, 22–30, 34	11:1–4, 5–8, 9–13, 14–23, 24–26, 27–28, 29–32, 33, 34–36, 37–54	11:14–23, 24–26, 29–32, 47–54	12:57–59
16:27–31	12:1, 2–9, 10, 11–12, 13–15, 16–21, 22–32, 33–34, 35–48, 49–53, 54–56, 57–59	12:49–50, 54–56	13:24–30, 35
17:25–30	13:1–9, 10–17, 18–19, 20–21, 22–30, 31–33, 34–35	13:1–9, 14–17, 25–30, 31–33, 34	14:24
18:8	14:1–6, 7–14, 15–24, 25–33, 34–35	14:1, 24	(16:27–31)
19:41–42, 44b	15:1–7, 8–10, 11–32	15:1–2	17:26–30
	16:1–9, 10–12, 13, 14–15, 16–17, 18, 19–31	16:14–15, 16, 27–31	19:27, 41–44
	17:1–3a, 3b–4, 5–6, 7–10, 11–19, 20–21, 22–37	17:25–30	
	18:1–8, 9–14, 15–17, 18–23, 24–30, 31–34, 35–43	18:8, 31–34	
	19:1–10, 11–27, 28–40, 41–44	19:7, 14, 39–40	

EXCURSUS 1
Audience Criticism of the Central Section

Analysis of Jesus' audiences[438] in the Central Section reinforces the dramatic plot and sharpens the contours of the Pharisees' hindering of Jesus' sending. There are three recurring audiences—crowds, disciples, and Pharisees—for the words of Jesus, with the following changes of address:

Crowds (9:57–62)	In 9:57ff. Jesus addresses potential followers to Jerusalem who meet him along the way; there is no mention of a "crowd" per se.
Disciples (10:1–24)	The seventy(-two) disciples are given instructions for their mission and debriefed at a rendezvous point.[439]
Pharisee (10:25–37)	A lawyer (undoubtedly of the Pharisees), from an unspecified audience, poses a challenge which Jesus addresses.
Disciples (10:38—11:13)	Jesus addresses Martha in the midst of teaching Mary; the disciples are taught after "one" of them requests instruction.
Crowds (11:14–36)	Challenges from smaller groups in the crowds evoke teaching/parenesis by Jesus (vv. 14–26); a woman from the crowd is addressed (vv. 27–28); and as the crowds increase, Jesus teaches/exhorts them as "this generation" (vv. 29–36).
Pharisees (11:37–54)	At the astonishment of Jesus' lax ritual cleanliness at the Pharisees' meal fellowship, Jesus attacks their defiling "leaven."
Disciples (12:1–12)	With the crowds now in "myriads" in the background, Jesus warns and teaches his disciples about the leaven of the Pharisees.
Crowds (12:13–21)	A request from "one of the crowd" sparks a warning call of repentance to *all.*
Disciples (12:22–53)	With the crowds within earshot, Jesus teaches and exhorts his disciples to live in accordance with the Kingdom their Father is already giving them.
Crowds (12:54—13:9)	Jesus warns them against a hypocritical behavior in the present leading them straight to judgment; a concern from a group within the crowds provokes warning of destruction upon *all.*
Crowds-Pharisees (13:10–21)	A woman in the synagogue crowd sets the scene for warning and teaching to both the crowd and Jesus' hypocritical opponents,

	most likely the Pharisees and their sympathizers.
Crowds (13:22–30)	Again an individual from the *many* that Jesus meets on his way evokes a warning and teaching fitting to all.
Pharisees (13:31—14:24)	The Pharisees who emerge from the crowds to hinder Jesus' journey provoke judgment on all of "Jerusalem's children." A meal with the Pharisees again leads to judgment of the *many* (cf. 11:47–51).
Crowds (14:25–35)	As *many* crowds now accompany Jesus, he again warns/instructs them of the dangers of not following as true disciples.
Pharisees (15:1–32)	The Pharisees' murmuring provokes teaching/warning in three parables.
Disciples (16:1–13)	In the hearing of the same Pharisees, Jesus characterizes their misguided stewardship of Israel.
Pharisees (16:14–31)	The Pharisees now listen to Jesus expound the eternal validity of the Law even as he portrays their disobedience to and separation from the "house" of the patriarchs, Moses, and the prophets.
Disciples (17:1–10)	Temptations to apostasy and pride are singled out for special warning by Jesus. The apostles are the object of address in vv. 6–10.
Crowds-Disciples (17:11–19)	Though the audience in vv. 17–18 is difficult to specify, it is probable that all those accompanying Jesus are addressed, with perhaps a special message to the apostles on the issue of faith (cf. 17:5–6).
Pharisees (17:20–21)	The powerful healing of 17:11–19 may spark the Pharisees' question about the coming of the Kingdom in manifest signs.[440]
Disciples (17:22—18:17)	Jesus concentrates on a false view of the coming Kingdom, apostasy, and "puffed-up" self-esteem in teaching/exhortation. Hindering of children leads to rebuke and warning of exclusion.
Crowds (18:18–30)	A rich ruler, possibly a Pharisee, spawns interaction of Jesus with both the crowds and the disciples who are addressed as one unified group.
Disciples (18:31–34)	For the first and only time in the journey the Twelve are singled out for private teaching.[441]

Crowds (18:35—19:27)	Individuals who are set apart from the crowds "see" and "hear" Jesus (18:35—19:10); the solid front of crowds and disciples receive a final warning from Jesus.
Disciples (19:28–36)	As at the beginning of the journey, Jesus gives disciples instructions and sends them on ahead to make necessary preparations.
Pharisees (19:37–40)	With the backdrop of the chorus of the disciples, the Pharisees emerge from the crowds again to hinder Jesus' journeying. In a final rebuke, Jesus prophesies the destruction of the nation.
Crowds (19:41–44)	Jesus' address to Jerusalem is a lament over all of her children. The crowds in the background will soon be within Jerusalem's walls, visiting children awaiting the visiting destruction of God.

Observations

1. The "crowds" are addressed most frequently by Jesus, that is, some ten (eleven) times.[442] The "disciples" are addressed nine (ten) times,[443] whereas the "Pharisees" or individual representatives are singled out eight times by Jesus. The relatively equal instances of address to each group are already an indication of the potential interaction among them.

2. Audience Changes

Analysis i: *Crowds ⇄ Disciples*

9 times   (9:62—10:1; 11:13–14; 12:12–13; 12:21–22; 12:53–54; 18:17–18; 18:30–31; 18:34–35; 19:27–28)

a. Out of the nine changes, five occur before the midpoint and pronouncement of judgment according to tenet D (13:35).

b. Whereas in the first five changes the accent is upon the stark contrast between the crowds' expectations and the demands of discipleship, three of the last four[444] stress the similarity of the disciples' thoughts and actions with the crowds'. Now the "childlike" serve as a counterfoil.

c. Three of the first five changes occur within one major audience arena of crowds and disciples (12:1—13:9). The changes thus take on an oscillating effect, with each group not far removed from the other.

d. The second large teaching tableau (14:25—17:10) is void of this exchange, as is the smaller teaching section, 17:20—18:14.

e. The last four changes occur only after the final journey incidents are taken up (17:11ff.).

Luke is thus interested in the crowds'-disciples' interaction particularly within the first half of the journey and the last few journey incidents before the arrival at Jerusalem.

Analysis ii: *Disciples* ⇄ *Pharisees*
>9(8) times   (10:24–25;   10:37–38;   11:54—12:1;
>15:32—16:1;   16:13–14;   16:31—17:1;
>[17:19–20]; 17:21–22; 19:35–36)

a. Out of the nine (eight) changes, only three occur before 13:35; that is to say, there is double the interaction in the last half.

b. The large teaching section (15:3—17:10) and the smaller unit (17:20—18:14, 15–17) are devoted entirely to this exchange (five [four]) times.[445]

c. Seven of the nine exchanges occur after the Pharisees' resolution to trap Jesus (11:53–54).

The marked presence of the Pharisees with the disciples in the second half and the lopsided exchange between the two groups is in keeping with our sketch above of the stages of the drama. There, particularly from 15:1ff., it was seen that Jesus launches a rigorous attempt to prevent his disciples from succumbing fully to the Pharisees' leaven. Moreover, it again appears that the concentrated exchanges may bear some relationship to the Pharisees' meals and their determination to halt Jesus' public influence (11:53–54).

Analysis iii: *Crowds* ⇄ *Pharisees*
>7(6) times   (11:36–37; 13:9–10; 13:21–22; 13:30–
>31; 14:24–25; [17:19–20]; 19:40–41)

a. Four of the six (or seven) occur before the midpoint, 13:35.

b. All but one (or two) occur before the large teaching tableau (14:25—17:10).

c. The first four occur between the two Pharisee meal scenes, while the fifth is a transition from the second meal to the large teaching tableau (14:25—17:10).

d. Whereas the first audience change in the Central Section is between eager, prospective disciples in the crowds and the disciples, the last change is between hindering Pharisees and the crowds, prompting Jesus' condemnation over the whole nation (tenet D—19:41–44).

e. In at least two and probably three instances, it appears that Luke describes the Pharisees interacting with Jesus by emerging directly from the crowds (11:36–37; 13:30–31; and probably 17:19–20).[446]

The main interaction occurs between the end of the first large crowd scene (11:14–36) and the second large teaching tableau (14:25—17:10), that is to say, precisely where the Pharisees'-disciples' exchange is scarce. It again appears that the Pharisee meals serve as important markers in the developing drama and that the crowds from 14:25 on are dominated or represented by Pharisees.

Analysis of the audience changes cannot in itself determine the profile of the plot. But these changes do reinforce, supplement, and/or modify the results of our literary-thematic investigation. Data from the three individual audience changes dovetail to form one coherent picture for Luke's portrayal of Jesus' turning to Israel. Throughout the entire journey Jesus' aim is to call out and gather disciples from the crowds. As an audience, these crowds are generally distinguished from the disciples as those who have not repented and submitted to Jesus' unique authority—those who are not "receiving" the Kingdom. But as the journey proceeds, the situation becomes considerably more complex:

(1) The Crowds ⇄ Disciples (analysis i) corresponds to Jesus' aim insofar as it reveals an active interchange with these two groups, especially in the first half of the journey and in the last journey episodes.

(2) The Crowds ⇄ Pharisees (analysis iii) begins to qualify this picture. In fundamental agreement with the thematic analysis of the Pharisees' hindering, it betrays an active interchange of Jesus with the Pharisees and the crowds especially in the first half of the journey where the former are a distinct audience but yet fluidly present in the crowds. Hence the presence of a powerful contender for these same crowds is illuminated by this active exchange, especially in the area of overlap with the Crowds ⇄ Disciples interchange (i.e., between the two Pharisee meals). Clearly two conflicting forces are determined to lead the crowds!

(3) Lastly, the Disciples ⇄ Pharisees (analysis ii) illumines yet another angle of this profile. The concentrated interchange of Jesus between the Pharisees and his disciples reflects the growing effect of the leaven upon those disciples. Whereas in the first half Jesus contends with the Pharisees for the adherence of the crowds, in the second half he contends with these Pharisees for his disciples. Instead of concentrating upon the crowds to win disciples, Jesus is now forced to concentrate on the disciples to prevent them from blending back into those same crowds! The watershed character of 11:37–54 is thus illustrated again. From that meal scene to the next the Pharisees launch a vigorous campaign among the crowds à la 11:53–54, which is resonated by Jesus' pleading, cajoling, and warning them to shake off their hypocritical stance to him. By the time the audience shifts to the disciples, Jesus has declared the crowds to be an evil generation that has already succumbed to the Pharisees' leadership. Their house will be abandoned! (13:35a—tenet D). The question is now clear: When the Son of Man comes to Jerusalem will he find any faith at all?

EXCURSUS 2
A Gallery of the Characters of "This Generation"

Here is Luke's profile of characters as they appear in the two major audiences of the Central Section:

The Crowds

Given the dynamic nature of the crowds' responses, a static portrait is hardly adequate. Yet Luke portrays the crowds as representing the *laos,* the people of Israel who come out to "see" Jesus and his mighty works, to be healed, and to hear his teaching. From this group Jesus recruits his disciples, and to this group he directs his strongest pleas for repentance. In the introduction to the journey (9:1–50), at times the crowds can follow Jesus (e.g., 9:11) and persist with his disciples in meeting him upon his return from a private excursion (9:37). But it is not certain in the first half of the journey (9:51—13:35) whether some of these crowds continue to follow Jesus from Galilee as he sets his sights on Jerusalem. Luke 9:57–62 may indicate a following by those outside the band of disciples from whom individuals express their desire to continue as members of that band. One fact, however, is certain: as Jesus proceeds toward Jerusalem, the crowds continue to increase—from "increasing crowds" (11:29) to "myriads of the crowd" (12:1) to "many crowds" (14:25). Jesus' parable in 12:57–59 divulges that the myriads of the crowd are on their way with Jesus to Jerusalem. In 14:25 it is expressly stated that the many crowds are accompanying Jesus, so that toward the end of the journey, when Luke depicts "the crowd" as passing through Jericho and so swollen as to prevent Zacchaeus from seeing Jesus, one gains the impression that *all Israel* is following Jesus into Jerusalem. The "many crowds" representing the *laos* covenant people, from Galilee all the way to Jerusalem, are indeed the "citizens" (19:14) of Israel who "do not want this man to reign over us!" (19:14b). As the journey progresses in the second half, the crowds per se are addressed only once (14:25–35), though certainly the whole caravan is addressed in 19:11–27, 41–44.[447] This shift in audience is due to Jesus' concerted efforts to prevent "the disciples" from being swallowed up into the crowds from where they have originated. It is ultimately Jesus' failure to prevent this consolidation which leads to the cry for his death by the *laos*-crowds of 23:1–25.

We can profile the crowds in a more dynamic sense by identifying the specific audiences that emerge from them:

Unidentified individuals and groups (9:57–62; 11:15–28; 12:13–21; 13:1–9, 23–30; 17:12–14).[448] As the crowds represent the whole *laos* of Israel, so these anonymous individuals and groups "present" these faceless throngs. The growing leaven of the Pharisees upon the crowds is mirrored in the growing severity of Jesus' retort to the questions, desires, and attitudes of these individuals and groups. As they emerge to submerge again into "the crowds," it is clear that the way in which Jesus characterizes them is characteristic of this whole generation. Attachment to the Law, the need for manifest signs of the Kingdom's presence, fascination but failure to repent, riches—all epitomized by a false "eating and drinking"—are all evidence of a hypocrisy which we have traced directly back to the influence of the Pharisees-scribes. It is not by accident that all but one of these "crowd-presenters" occur in the first half, where by 12:54–56 Jesus has already castigated these crowds as hypocrites!

Pharisees, scribes (lawyers), rulers (10:25–37; 11:37–54; 13:14–21, 31–35; 14:1–24; 15:1–32; 16:14–31; 17:20–21; 18:18–25; 19:36–40). The Pharisees-scribes are the leaders, the rulers of these crowds of "this generation"; they appear regularly throughout the Central Section.[449] In the first part of the journey they emerge from the crowds as individuals or smaller groups, whereas in the latter part, except for the final journey episodes, they appear en masse as "the Pharisees" alongside the disciples. In this way Luke demonstrates what the crowds and their individuals have already shown: the intensifying solidification of their grip over "this generation." The two meal scenes (11:37–54; 14:1–24) form the crucial junctures along this development. In 11:37–54 an invitation by an individual Pharisee from the crowd is transmuted into a scathing condemnation on all the Pharisees and scribes present. Luke 11:53–54, however, broadens this to a categorical intent of *the* Pharisees and *the* scribes. The rest of the journey unfolds this group's determination "to provoke him to speak about many things" (11:53). In fact, 12:1ff. begins a teaching section in which Jesus does speak of "many things" that constitute the leaven of the Pharisees (12:1). And after an attempt by "some of the Pharisees" to steer him off course (13:31–35), one of the houses of the Pharisees reveals again the undying resolve of the whole lot to trip him up (14:1–6). Jesus' admonition to individuals (14:12–14) and to a larger number (vv. 16–24) involves the fate of the whole group of scribes and Pharisees (v. 24), which, from this point until 18:18, he treats as an undifferentiated whole. Now we have the distinct impression that within this traveling caravan there are a considerable number of Pharisees! Their coordinate presence with the disciples is a vivid visual device by which Luke divulges not only the domination of the crowds by the Pharisees but also their encroachment upon the disciples. Even when Jesus speaks to the disciples it seems he is not out of the Pharisees' range (cf., e.g., 16:14). The solitary figure of the rich ruler would seem to be an exception to the solidified movement of the Pharisees to squelch Jesus' mission: "he became sad" (18:23b). Luke may be indicating that as the boundary between crowds and disciples becomes less defined, not all the Pharisees were "acting in a very hostile manner toward him" (11:53a; cf. 17:20–21)! Some may still have debated whether he was a legitimate "teacher" (cf. 17:20–21; 11:45; 10:25; 7:39). Yet the ruler's unwillingness to repent places him in the front of Pharisees, disciples, and swelling crowds—they all cannot receive Jesus and the Kingdom like a child. Finally, when Luke says that "some of the Pharisees from the crowd" (19:39), trying to hinder the disciples, address Jesus as "teacher," the fundamental distinction between the crowds and the disciples, and the Pharisees' control of the former, is not to be forgotten. For in spite of the fluidity of the boundaries, the crowds still do not perceive Jesus as their King-Messiah. Though like the disciples they are aglow with Jesus' glorious works—"a prophet mighty in deed and word before God and all the people"[450]—yet his messianic identity, covered over by the leaven of hypocrisy, has not been penetrated. Jesus remains the "teacher" (cf., e.g., 19:47—21:38).

The Disciples

The disciples are those who respond to Jesus' call to leave behind their daily commitments and "to follow" him to Jerusalem. It is evident already in 9:1–50 that the disciples link Jesus with the Messiah and the coming of the Kingdom of God (9:2, 18–22). This conviction is emphasized at the beginning of the journey where new recruits are sent out "to proclaim the Kingdom of God" (9:60b). It is also true of the disciples that God "their Father" is giving them this Kingdom (12:32–34). But the great question as the journey progresses is whether the disciples will be true to this Kingdom in their midst, whether they will be faithful stewards and confess the Son of Man before others (9:57–62; 10:38–42; 12:1–12, 22–53). The distinctive status of the disciples is illustrated, on the one hand, through the concentrated teaching they receive on the journey of rejection and suffering that must stamp their following of the Son of Man (12:1–12, 49–53; 17:22–25; 18:31–34; cf. 9:22, 43b–45). But, on the other hand, the crowds and even the Pharisees hear about this journey to death (13:31–33; 14:25–33; cf. 9:23–27). Jesus' teaching is characterized by a public openness among all who come out to hear and follow. The impression is that Jesus' words to the disciples are never fully out of range of the crowds (9:57–62; 10:17–22; 12:1ff.; 15:1ff.; 18:31–34; cf. 9:18–27, 43–50). This impression is enhanced when we notice that Luke mentions only one explicit teaching in private (10:23–24).[451] Hence the boundary between crowds and disciples is open and fluid, depending upon the state of alertness and commitment to heed the voice of the Son of Man as he comes to Jerusalem. This dynamic potential is, as with the crowds, best illustrated by the various audiences that emerge from "the disciples."

The Twelve, apostles, and individuals (9:54–55; 12:41; 17:5–10; 18:28, 31–34). The "Twelve" and especially Peter are presented in the introduction (9:1–50) as the leaders and spokesmen for the larger group of disciples (cf. 9:1–6, 10–17, 18–22, 28–36, 49–50). This role is evidenced in the Central Section proper but not at all emphasized (e.g., 9:54; 12:41; 17:5–6; 18:28, 31–34). The "Twelve" occur only at 18:31; "apostles" at 17:5 (cf. 11:49).[452] Peter's utterances evince a grave and growing misunderstanding of the Kingdom's presence, representative of "the disciples" in general. Even though before the journey Peter had led the disciples in confessing Jesus' Messiahship, now toward the end of the journey the apostles are chided by Jesus for their minuscule faith which is polluted by a vainglorious view of their own leadership over the others. The Twelve thus become leaders of the disciples' triumphalist view of their journey to the Kingdom which, hand in hand with the Pharisees' leaven, produces a growing hypocrisy unable to submit as a child to the King-Messiah in their midst.

The Seventy(-two) (10:1–20). On the journey, seventy(-two) "others" and not the Twelve are sent out with the special power and authority to preach, eat and drink, and heal. To them as journeying guests and to their hosts has been revealed the presence of the Son—the voice of the mountain—and hence the fulfillment of the eschatological salvation in Jesus the journeying-guest prophet. This revelation is linked to their childlike posture, and it is celebrated as salvation realized in their midst. Upon their return, their joy is, however, linked to a triumphalist notion of power which is noticeably void of the cross (cf. 9:57–58). Closely aligned with this notion is the powerful presence of the Holy Spirit (10:20–21) with "the disciples" in the next two audience arenas (11:1–13; 12:1–12). Though the Seventy(-two) are not mentioned again, one wonders whether "the disciples" here are not particularly aligned with their mission, perhaps as recruits from the homes along the streets and country roads (cf. 14:21–23).[453] In any case, a critical turning point in the plot is disclosed. From 12:22ff. the disciples display a growing vulnerability to the hindering leaven of the Pharisees. Now submission to the Lord of the Banquet whose presence reveals the crisis of eschatological salvation in their midst is being transformed subtly to seeking after material security and privilege in the coming triumph of the Kingdom of God. Instead of seeking the Kingdom in the Jesus (12:31) who has no place to lay his head, they seek it in the mighty works which already herald the coming blessings of the Kingdom.

Unnamed groups ("all who hear," etc.; 18:9–14, 26–30, 39–40; 19:7–10, 11–27, 41–44). It is not entirely clear whether the crowds or disciples are principally signified, though no change of audience (e.g., 18:8–9), an apostle's question (18:28), and "those leading the way" (18:39) point toward the latter. But this confusion points precisely to the situation that has obtained as the journey climaxes. Self-assured status and privilege (18:9–14), riches (18:26–30), disdain for social outcasts (18:9–12, 39–40; 19:7–10), and hope in the glorious Kingdom about to appear (19:11–27) are traits of the whole caravan oriented against a childlike entering of the Kingdom. As 19:41–44 makes manifest, the pilgrims represent "all Israel" which for its disobedience will be destroyed.

Wisdom's children (10:1–24, 38–42; 13:10–13, 28–30; 14:4, 21–23; 15:1–2; 16:19–31; 17:1–2, 15–19, 33b; 18:13–14, 15–17, 40–43; 19:5–10). Though described under different names—"children of Abraham," the *"laos,"* the "little ones"—these disciples constitute the "poor" of Israel (i.e., the sick, destitute, women, "sinners," and tax collectors) and are joined by Samaritans and Gentiles. Their chief characteristic is their unassuming submission to Jesus' authoritative presence. This childlike coming to Jesus is expressed sometimes as "faith" and ensues in glory to God for salvation received today. The presence of these "children" among the disciples is not only to be assumed by their welcome response but is also explicitly stated in 17:1–3a, a passage reflecting 9:46–48 in the introduction. In the former passage the disciples are a "divided house," with the "little ones" the focus of "temptations to sin" (17:1). The path of those being saved (13:32–33) is thus a source of strife not only among the crowds of the *laos* of Israel but also among the disciples. A glance at the appearances of Wisdom's children discloses that as the journey progresses, the number of these childlike responses increases: at the same time that the leaven of the Pharisees steadily intensifies, so does the stream of "the least" to Jesus. It is indeed this tension of two simultaneous and opposing movements which gives the Central Section its unique dramatic tension, climaxing ultimately in the death-exaltation of Jesus. It is of course the company of the childlike sinners and tax collectors that provoke Pharisees and crowds alike to reject the authoritative voice of the Son; and it is their presence among the disciples which, hand in hand with the Pharisees' influence, leads to grandiose ideas of status, making childlike submission for some impossible. With this path of Wisdom's children, then, Luke points to the other side of the house, those responding to the invitation to the eschatological feast (14:21–23). As Jesus arrives at Jerusalem, the *laos* are divided into the unrepenting crowds and into the *laos* who repent (12:49–53; cf. 7:29–30; 18:43b), with perhaps many of "the disciples" wavering between both sides.[454] As 12:49–53 and 13:31–33 make clear, it is this path of division and growing hostility which leads directly to the death of the Prophet. Whether Luke believes that Wisdom's children pierced the messianic veil of the death of Jesus, the Son of Man, remains uncertain and perhaps doubtful in the light of the events before Pilate, 23:1–25 (cf. 23:49). Yet it is certain that these "poor," in their own following and eating and drinking with Jesus, do embody the fate of the despised and rejected one (e.g., 15:1–2; 18:43; 19:1–10). Though they are not fully exonerated from the *laos'* collaboration in Jesus' crucifixion, yet by their childlike submission they "justify" Wisdom and the salvation of the Rejected One she has sent.

In sum, the story of the Central Section is a dynamic of two opposing forces that fulminate in the tragic death but glorious exaltation of the journeying-guest Prophet who "comes" to Jerusalem. Through the cast of Jerusalem's and Wisdom's children, Luke paradoxically shows how the one house of Israel—divided and yet a monolith of solid resistance—becomes the house in which not one stone is left upon another.

EXCURSUS 3

The Literary Design of "Eating and Drinking"

To illustrate how the drama of the calling and fate of the Deuteronomistic journeying-guest Prophet is enhanced by the literary design of the "eating and drinking" of the main actors, we can sum up the following pattern of the meal scenes:

Luke 10:38–42. This first setting at table in the Central Section depicts the journeying-guest, home-meal mission of the messengers-disciples and the Seventy(-two) (9:52–56; 10:1–20). At the same time, it illustrates the opposition that has begun to set in against the authority of the Lord of the Banquet's voice (cf. 10:25–37). Already Jesus must take care that his disciples not become a divided house as they continue their journey (cf. 11:1–13; 12:1ff.). Consequently this meal reviews the journey up to that point and previews the development to come (cf. 12:22ff.).

Luke 11:37–54. This first Pharisee meal serves as the watershed for the dramatic tension of the remainder of the journey. The main elements of the opposing leaven of the Pharisees-scribes are articulated that will be developed throughout the rest of the plot: (i) "greed" for mammon (v. 39); (ii) differing interpretation and application of the Law of life (vv. 38, 42);

(iii) self-righteous pride and "superiority" over others (v. 43); (iv) a leadership-stewardship, in general, detrimental to the people for the attaining of life (vv. 44–45). The entire opposition is summed up as a killing of the prophets sent to Israel by the Wisdom of God, that is, tenets A—D (vv. 47–51). Jesus' role as the fulfiller of this sending by bringing the Kingdom of God is encapsulated in vv. 50–52.

Luke 14:1–24. The second Pharisee meal presents the heightened opposition to Jesus by summing up the effect of the leaven among the dramatis personae: *(a)* the Pharisees-scribes, the rich, and their friends (vv. 1–6, 7–11, 15); *(b)* the "many" of the people of Israel (vv. 16–20, 24); *(c)* the "poor" and outcast of Abraham's/Wisdom's children (vv. 1–6, 13–14, 21–22); *(d)* the aliens (Samaritans) and Gentiles of Wisdom's children (v. 23). Again the main themes of the virulent leaven are delineated which set the tone and agenda for the rest of the journey: (i) "greed" for mammon (vv. 12, 18–19); (ii) differing interpretation and application of the Law of life (vv. 1–6, 12–15); (iii) self-righteous pride and "superiority" over others (vv. 7–12); (iv) a leadership-stewardship, in general, detrimental for the attaining of life (vv. 5, 12–14, 15–24). Verse 15 witnesses to the misleading view of the coming of the Kingdom as dealt with in 17:20–27 and the rest of the journey as a whole (cf. 11:52).

Meal-Food Parables. As the opposition to and the rejection of Jesus magnify, so do the number of "eating and drinking" parables between the actual table scenes. In this way Luke provides a graphic commentary on the rejection of the journeying guest epitomized in these meals. These meal-food parables are directed to the crowds and Pharisees, as well as to the disciples, and exhort against the hypocritical leaven of the Pharisees-scribes. Interestingly enough, only the disciples are the primary focus for the parables of stewardship and/or serving at table (12:35–38, 42–48; 16:1–9; 17:7–10). They, and not the Pharisees-scribes, are assuming the stewardship of the people of Israel in the Kingdom of God (cf. 22:14–29).

10:38–42 —— 2—→	11:37–54 —— 4 —→	14:1–24 —— 6 ——→ 19:1–10
Parables	Parables	Parables
(11:5–8, 9–13)	(12:16–21, 35–38,	(15:3–7, 8–10, 11–32;
	42–48; 13:22–30)	16:1–9, 19–31; 17:7–10)

Luke 19:1–10. This meal scene with a tax collector–sinner is the crowning portrayal of the rejection of the journeying guest by Jerusalem's children. This generation of unrepentance stands by as Wisdom's child repents. Only these "poor," sick, outcast children receive the revelation of Jesus the Lord of the Banquet.

Notes

1. Luke 1:70; 13:28; 18:31; 24:25; Acts 3:18, 21, 24, 25; 7:42; 10:43; 13:27, 40; 15:15; 26:27; see above, Part II, "Luke's Language and Lineage of the Prophets."

2. Especially in the light of L. Goppelt's conclusions in his *Typos: The Typological Interpretation of the Old Testament in the New* (1939; Grand Rapids: Wm. B. Eerdmans Publishing Co., 1982), esp. 198–205.

3. Steck, *Israel.* We shall not concern ourselves with the extent of the Deuteronomistic view in Jewish literature of Palestinian provenance; that Steck has proved his thesis for a vast amount of this literature is beyond question (see, e.g., J. H. Elliott, *JBL* 87 [1968]: 226–27). I want to illustrate briefly the uniformity of this understanding within the plurality of the appropriations of this perspective by citing such diverging witnesses as Josephus and the Qumran covenanters.

4. I follow Steck's enumeration of this schema with A, B, C, D. For a clear explanation of the four tenets, see Steck, *Israel,* 60–64.

5. Ibid., 81–109 and throughout.

6. Cf. ibid., 201–2 n. 4; for Mosaic lineage, cf. 96–97 n. 4, 199–200 for Hos. 12:13–14 et al.

7. Not that a prophetic figure does not overlap with our figures but that prophetic functions dominate the "story stuff" of the character.

8. Josephus, *Antiquities,* LCL (Cambridge: Harvard University Press, 1961). Citations and translations of Josephus throughout this section are based on this edition, unless otherwise indicated; italics mine.

9. On the characteristic twofold thrust of the Deuteronomistic prophetic "savings" traditions, see Steck, *Israel,* 62–63, 68, 71.

10. σέβειν τὸν θεόν, Josephus, *Ant.* 9.264; εὐσέβειαν τοῦ θεοῦ, 9.265; cf. 9.267, "the exhortations of the prophets" (οἷς οἱ προφῆται παρήνεσαν).

11. Josephus, *Ant.* 9.265–66.

12. 2 Kings 17:13–15; Neh. 9:30; cf. 2 Chron. 36:16.

13. Neh. 9:26.

14. Steck, *Israel,* 84; see above, n. 11.

15. To be sure, the basis for such a development is 2 Kings 21:16; 24:4. G. Vermès ("Die Gestalt des Moses an der Wende der beiden Testaments," in *Moses: In Schrift und Überlieferung* [Düsseldorf: Patmos Verlag, 1963], 87–88, 92) contends that from the Exile haggadic traditions began to grow and coalesce into an organic unity that is reflected primarily in the catechetical traditions of the Targumim and Midrashim. Despite the wide variety of traditions on a given theme, this tradition determined, for instance, an underlying unified view of Moses in both Hellenistic Diaspora and Palestinian Judaism. See Vermès on Josephus's exegesis of the Moses stories (p. 88); see below, n. 27.

16. See Josephus, *Life* 10–12; cf. *War* 2.119ff.; *Ant.* 13:171–73; 18.11.

17. Josephus, *Ant.* 3.87; cited also by W. A. Meeks, *The Prophet-King: Moses Traditions and the Johannine Christology,* NovTSup 14 (Leiden: E. J. Brill, 1967), 138.

18. Josephus, *Ant.* 3.13–21; 4.24–34, 177–93; e.g., παρόντων—*Ant.* 3.14; παραινῶ—*Ant.* 4.192.

19. E.g., Josephus, *Ant.* 3.22—Moses, confronted by an angry mob bent on stoning him, after "smooth" words of persuasion, deems it necessary, "ἐφ ἱκετείαν τοῦ θεοῦ καὶ παράκλησιν ἐλθειν"; cf. *Ant.* 3.310—πεσόντες ἐπὶ τὴν γῆν τὸν θεὸν ἱκέτευον . . . [Moses and Aaron]; *Ant.* 4.194—Moses the "intercessor" (παρακαλῶν)

dies outside the land of promise (cited by Meeks, *Prophet-King,* 137); cf. *Ant.* 3.315—παρακαλέω.

20. E.g., Josephus, *Ant.* 2.327–29, 334; 3.11–12, 295–99; 4.22, 40–50, 177–79.

21. See Meeks, *Prophet-King,* 137–38.

22. Josephus, *Ant.* 2.327; 3.12–22, 307; 4.22; in the OT only at Exod. 17:4; Meeks, *Prophet-King,* 140.

23. τοῦ θεοῦ κατακρίνειν; cf. Luke 13:34 for the startling parallel in thought, i.e., the "stoning" of those sent to Jerusalem perceived as a direct refutation of God and hence demanding God's retribution or "sentence upon" Jerusalem. Cf. Meeks (*Prophet-King,* 140), who attributes this motif in Josephus only partially to the "divine man" (Θεῖος ἀνήρ) while linking it primarily to "older traditions"; we are contending (Steck, *Israel,* 85 n. 10) that these "older traditions" are essentially Deuteronomistic.

24. In addition, the title στρατηγός (e.g., Josephus, *Ant.* 3.2, 67, 102; 4.165, 194, 329; idem, *Against Apion* 2.158) connotes both "military leader" and "ruler." As Meeks (*Prophet-King,* 134) argues, the former "fits one aspect of the biblical picture of Moses, particularly of Deuteronomy, which idealizes him as the leader of Israel's holy war." For fuller details, see Meeks, *Prophet-King,* 132–36; στρατηγός is linked with προφήτης for Moses in *Ant.* 4.329; for Joshua, as Moses' successor, in *Ant.* 4.165.

25. Points (1) and (2) = B; (3) = a microcosm of the entire history of preexilic Israel, i.e. = A and C; points (1) — (3) cohere to the basic twofold dynamic of the prophetic sayings traditions which Steck defines as central to the Deuteronomistic view (*Israel,* 62–63, esp. 62 n. 4; 68; 73 n. 1); D = punishment of the people for their disbelief in Moses and their rejection of him, occurs frequently, e.g., *Ant.* 4.51ff.; 3.299; the crowd's attempt to stone Moses at the borders of Canaan and their rebellion at the reports of the spies are punished by the "exile" of forty years of wandering (*Ant.* 3.300–314).

26. For a Mosaic succession of the prophets in Josephus, the Apocrypha, and the Pseudepigrapha, cf. Meeks, *Prophet-King,* 142–45, 154–56; and Steck, *Israel,* 200 n. 4.

27. That many traditions concerning Moses' great prophetic status were alive and influential in Josephus's day is of course almost a tautology, given the centripetal force of the "Law of Moses" for the many faces of Judaism. Josephus, *Ant.* 3.317: "The admiration in which that hero was held for his virtues and his marvellous power of inspiring faith in all his utterances were not confined to his lifetime; they are alive today." Cf. above, n. 15.

28. G. Vermès, *The Dead Sea Scrolls in English,* 2d ed. (Harmondsworth, Eng.: Penguin Books, 1975). Citations are from this edition (unless otherwise indicated), although the verse numeration is based on E. Lohse, ed., *Die Texte aus Qumran: Hebräisch und Deutsch,* 2d ed. (Munich: Kösel-Verlag, 1971).

29. See also Steck, *Israel,* 166.

30. Josephus, *Ant.* 4.11; cf. above, n. 16.

31. See, e.g., Josephus, *Ant.* 9.267: "many" from the larger mass of the northern

tribes respond favorably to the preaching of repentance by the "prophets" and go to Jerusalem to worship God at Hezekiah's invitation. See further, e.g., *Ant.* 3.315: the Israelites repent of their rebellion to Moses at the borders of Canaan, though they have opposed Moses repeatedly en masse. See shortly thereafter (*Ant.* 4.1): "They [the Hebrews] refused to remain inactive in obedience to the words of Moses. . . . They proceeded to accuse and suspect him of scheming to keep them without resources."

32. See Steck, *Israel,* 168.

33. See Steck (*Israel,* 167), who points to Neh. 9:26 and 2 Kings 17:13 as earlier Deuteronomistic tradition forming the pattern of 4QpHos 2:3ff.

34. See also CD 2:12 and 5:21—6:1: "God's "anointed" are the *prophets* who like Moses mediate the inspiration of God's "holy Spirit" by revealing God's law.

35. Cf. also 1QpHab 2:6–10.

36. E.g., 1QpHab 2:2, i.e., the "Priest" of 2:18.

37. 1QpHab 2:2-3.

38. Cf. Meeks, *Prophet-King,* 173–75; e.g., 175: "The sect's principal midrashic teacher and lawgiver functioned as a new Moses." See Vermès ("Gestalt des Moses," 79–86), who considers Deut. 18:15–18 as the point of departure for later Mosaic messianic expectations and concludes that the teacher was identified as the "prophet like Moses," the "new Moses," the "forerunner" of the messiahs of Aaron and Israel.

39. The expression occurs in CD 6:19.

40. Meeks, *Prophet-King,* 170; cf. above, n. 38.

41. E.g., G. Vermès, *Scripture and Tradition: Haggadic Studies,* SPB 4 (Leiden: E. J. Brill, 1961), 43–49; and Meeks, *Prophet-King,* 171–73.

42. E.g., CD 6:5.

43. I.e., the "new covenant"; see above, n. 39.

44. Among others, see, e.g., 1QM 2:7 (Num. 16:2); 2:6 (Deut. 15:1–8); 3:13ff. (Numbers 1—2); 7:5–7 (Deut. 23:2–15); 10:6 (Num. 10:9).

45. Cf., e.g., Meeks, *Prophet-King,* 169; and Vermès, "Gestalt des Moses," 80–84.

46. See above, n. 38. Although the Teacher is never called a "prophet," nor is "sent," nor is placed alongside the "prophets" with respect to his violent fate, yet his whole career so closely parallels that of Moses in the wilderness as the revealer and mediator of the law of God that this typology is unavoidable. See further, Steck, *Israel,* 168–69; and Vermès, "Gestalt des Moses," 79–84; cf. below, n. 47.

47. For the persecution of the Teacher of Righteousness, cf., e.g., 1QpHab 11:4ff.; 4QpPs 37:14–15; 1QH 2:9ff., 32ff.; 4:8ff.; 5:5ff.; 9:1ff.

48. By "stylistic devices" we mean a language of "exodus" to evoke a general mood of an exodus deliverance without conscious typological ties to Moses and the specific events of that exodus journey.

For the "New Exodus" as a central if not the most decisive conception and typology for the coming final salvation, see, e.g., Vermès ("Gestalt des Moses," 79), who instances the false messiahs who led the masses into the desert and similar episodes (Josephus, *Ant.* 18.85ff.; 20.97–98; 20.169ff.; *War* 2.258ff.; 7.437ff.).

49. See above, Part II, "The Prophetic Parallels of Moses in Deuteronomy to Jesus in Luke 9:1–50," item 2.

50. Many scholars view 11:14–23 (24–26)—the "Beelzebul Controversy" in Luke—as stemming essentially from Q, while Matthew (9:32–34; 12:22–30) combines Mark and Q. This of course is disputed. See esp. F. Katz, "Lk 9.52—11.36: Beobachtungen zur Logienquelle und ihrer hellenistisch-judenchristlichen Redaktion" (diss., Mainz, 1973), 166–213, esp. 168–79, for different views. Katz holds that a Hellenistic Jewish-Christian community composed 11:14–26 by adding sayings close in content to a kernel of tradition already ordered in sequence to form a speech of Jesus similar to 10:1ff. (pp. 212–13). For a consensus point of view, see, e.g., Grundmann, *Lukas,* 237.

51. Cf. 11:19, those who link Jesus' exorcisms with Beelzebul will have their own "sons" as "judges."

52. On the theme of "gathering"/"scattering," see further, Part III.C.1—4, below.

53. Debate over this "pronouncement story" (Bultmann) centers on whether it comes from Q (so, e.g., H. Schürmann, *Traditionsgeschichtliche Untersuchungen zu den synoptischen Evangelien,* KBANT [Düsseldorf: Patmos Verlag, 1968], 231) or from "L" (so, e.g., Grundmann, *Lukas,* 241). It is also possible (whether from Q or "L" or another source) that it is a doublet of Mark 3:31–35; cf. Matt. 12:46–50. Luke has already given this form in 8:19–21 (cf., e.g., Klostermann, *Lukas,* 127–28; Bultmann, *Syn. Trad.,* 30 [see Part I, n. 12]. Cf. also *GTh* 79. That it coheres with Luke's present text at the level of his story is argued below.

54. On the history of the tradition in the "Sign of Jonah" (11:29–32), see esp. Marshall, *Luke,* 482–83, for a helpful synopsis of various views. Chief among several issues is whether the original "sign" in the sayings of Jesus is "no sign at all" (Mark 8:11–12 par. Matt. 16:1–4), the "sign of Jonah" as in Luke 11, or the "sign of Jonah" with the "resurrection" as explanation (Matt. 12:40). Another alternative is that two original sayings of Jesus have been preserved in varying forms, one that spoke of *no* "sign" at all, while the other designated "Jonah," in some fashion, as a "sign." General opinion, however, favors one original saying of Jesus with two basic versions, Q and Mark. Marshall concludes: "The sign will be the attestation of the preaching of Jesus by the resurrection or the parousia, seen as a divine vindication of his message" (p. 483). We shall argue that for Luke's story of Jesus, the sign of Jonah is the preaching of repentance which reflects the Deuteronomistic view of one of the major prophetic roles. See Part III.B, "Sent to Call the People to Repentance Lest They Be Destroyed by the Judgment of God."

55. For "audience criticism," see Part III.D, "Conclusion," Excursus 1.

56. See below, Part III.B, "Sent to Mediate the Divine Will," item 1.

57. Cf. Plummer (*Luke,* 308): "There is no break in the discourse, and this should hardly be printed as a separate section: the connexion with what goes before is close. Christ is still continuing His reply to those who had demanded a sign."

58. Cf. the doublet to Luke 11:33 in 8:16 par. Mark 4:21. The two sayings, 11:33 (par. Matt. 5:15) and 11:34–36 (par. Matt. 6:22–23), are generally held to be from Q. See the commentaries on these passages.

59. Luke 11:36b repeats and rounds off the linking idea of v. 33b: the "lamp" (vv. 36b, 33a, 34a) must not in any fashion be obscured! Commentators often miss this connection. These two parabolic sayings thus illustrate the main point of the preceding story, a procedure typical of Luke's literary style elsewhere: e.g., 10:25–28 followed by 29–37; 11:14–23 by 24–26, 27–28; 12:13–15 by 16–21; 15:1–2 by 3–7, 8–10, 11–32; etc.

60. ἀριστάω—"eat breakfast" or, generally, "eat a meal, dine" (s.v., BAGD). Probably the ἄριστον, i.e., the midmorning or noon meal, is meant, the ἀκράτισμα being the earliest meal or snack before the day's work, and the δεῖπνον the main meal of the day in late afternoon. More well-to-do Jews followed the Roman custom of having two main meals, ἄριστον and δεῖπνον; cf. *prandium* and *cena* (see Marshall, *Luke,* 493; and Plummer, *Luke,* 309). Possibly the noon meal (ἄριστον) after the synagogue service on the Sabbath is the occasion here (cf. 14:1ff.; see below, Part III.C, n. 272).

61. A majority of exegetes believe that Q forms the backbone of 11:37–54, though what exactly Q encompasses in comparison with the Matthean parallels (23:1ff.) is divergently perceived. Bultmann (*Syn. Trad.,* 118–19, seven "woes"), Grundmann (*Lukas,* 246), Marshall (*Luke,* 491–93), and others, hold to a Q basis, though not excluding the influence of other sources. But Ellis (*Luke,* 170), Schlatter (*Lukas,* 303–8), Rengstorf (*Lukas,* 150, a "Proto-Luke"), and others, designate Luke's special source "L" as the primary tradition into which bits from Q are inserted (essentially the "woes" of vv. 42–44, 46–52). Most consider Luke to have added his own touches here and there, probably creating bridge verses such as 45, 53–54. This opinion is shared especially regarding the table setting (11:37–38). Generally, however, those holding to an "L" source think that the meal scene is inherent to it. Marshall (p. 491), however, suggests that Luke has retained the original Q setting at table which Matthew did not need, since he has placed the dispute in a Markan setting. Mark 7:1–5, though similar in the controversy, contains different details and lacks the characteristic "woes."

62. βαπτίζειν most likely refers to "hand washing," not to ritual baths. See Grundmann, *Lukas,* 247. J. Neusner ("First Cleanse the Inside," *NTS* 22 [1975–76]: 486–95) provides evidence that with respect to Jesus' retort in 11:38–41 the Shammaite ruling on the cleanliness of the outside/inside of utensils held sway before 70 C.E. Accordingly, the cleanliness and the uncleanliness of the inside or outside are separate questions, the one portion not governing the other, so that Jesus' criticism is quite pertinent. In effect, by using the cup and plate as metaphors for the moral cleanliness of a person, Jesus chides their petty distinctions as missing the point of the Law altogether, "that the inner traits of man are what matter" (p. 494). Jesus' own thought in 11:40–41 is close to the Hillelite thinking that the "inner part" controls the state of the "outer" (see esp. pp. 492–93). The Pharisee's disapproving "astonishment" at Jesus' "unwashed hands" (11:38) thus reflects the Shammaite worry that unclean hands, when touching, for instance,

the liquid on the outside of a cup, render all the liquid and hence the inside of the cup unclean. Jesus would thus be defiled.

63. For the significance of δέχομαι, s.v. W. Grundmann, *TDNT* 2:50–59: Luke uses it "for the hospitality which was everywhere honoured and regarded as sacred in the ancient world" (p. 51). See further below, Part III.C.

64. In the ten instances in Luke-Acts where Luke uses ἐν τῷ + aorist infinitive, the sense is almost always that of a previous action conceived punctiliarly as coming to an end while a new action or event follows on immediately or is simultaneous to the point of the conclusion: Luke 2:27; 3:21; 8:40; 9:34, 36; 11:37; 14:1; 19:15; 24:30; Acts 11:15. Only 19:15 may be translated more imprecisely as "after that," i.e., "sometime after his return," though here the point is surely that the "king" first returns before he calls his servants to account. The urgency of the situation (cf. 19:23) points, rather, to an immediate action on the part of the returning nobleman. Thus BAGD (ἐν, II.3) and Robertson (§1073), *pace* BDF (§404), are correct at least for Luke's usage. For our purposes it is clear that Luke links the Pharisees' meal invitation *directly* to the preceding action. He has a definite dynamic or progression in mind.

65. For the Pharisees' claim of a direct lineage to Ezra and the men of the "Great Synagogue" back to Moses, Joshua, the elders, and the prophets, see *m. 'Abot.* 1:1.

66. BAGD, s.v. "Θαυμάζω." H. Flender (*Heil und Geschichte in der Theologie des Lukas,* BEvT 41 [Munich: Chr. Kaiser Verlag, 1965], 138–39 is closer to the Lukan usages when he speaks of an "undecided stance" (p. 139). He avoids for the most part G. Bertram's ("Θαυμάζειν," *TDNT* 3:27–42) tendency to "theologize" the word by building into almost every usage the "astonishment and awe let loose" at the "mystery of the divine" (p. 38).

67. Positive, i.e., from the point of view of "the crowds." δέ in 11:15a already introduces an adversative "mood."

68. Cf. also Luke 8:25 (of the disciples): 20:26 (of those "who were acting as though they themselves were righteous"; 20:20); and 4:22 (of the Nazareth townspeople!).

69. E.g., ἐκπλήσσομαι. Cf. 9:43a; ἐξίστημι; cf. 2:47; Acts 2:7, 12.

70. Whether Luke's division or Matthew's order of seven "woes" is closer to the tradition (e.g., Bultmann) is widely disputed. It is possible that both versions represent variances due already to the oral stage so that Matthew and Luke are *not* dependent upon a common written source. See further, J. Jeremias, *Jerusalem in the Time of Jesus: An Investigation Into Economic and Social Conditions During the New Testament Period* (Philadelphia: Fortress Press; London: SCM Press, 1969), 246–67. Jeremias argues that Luke's division correctly differentiates the largely lay movement of Pharisees from their leaders, i.e., predominantly the ordained scribes or doctors (lawyers) of the Torah. Whereas the woes to the "lawyers" (vv. 46–52) pertain to their control of other folk in religious affairs and to their own privileges in social life, those to the "Pharisees" are a refutation of their generally hypocritical religiosity based on an inner impurity. Cf. Schlatter, *Lukas,* 305: the "L" tradition does not inveigh against the hypocrisy

of incongruent outward appearance/action with inner corruption but against a serious pursuit of the Law grounded upon a false understanding of it; see below, Part III.C, n. 231.

71. On Luke 11:47–51, see J. D. M. Derrett ("'You Build the Tombs of the Prophets' (Lk 11, 47–51, Mt 23, 29–32)," *SE IV* [= TU 102], 187–93), where he argues that behind οἰκοδομεῖν (v. 47) stands the Heb. *boniyn (boniym)*, "builders," which can equally be read as "understanders" ("scholars") and "sons" (cf. Isa. 54:13). Jesus is thus making a wordplay on the Pharisees' conception of themselves as "builders" (i.e., authoritative interpreters, scholars) of Torah by charging that what they are really "building" (i.e., understanding/perceiving) is the tombs of the prophets! By misunderstanding God's will, which the prophets conveyed, and perhaps also by literally building monuments as adornments to their tombs (cf. Matt. 23:29) they participate both in word and action in the "murdering" of the prophets' living word. Regarding the wisdom oracle, 11:49–51, Steck (*Israel,* 51–53) thinks that this quotation is a prophetic messenger formula and derives from pre-Christian wisdom circles who considered themselves to carry on the line of the prophets. Either Jesus or more likely the church (i.e., Hellenistic Jewish Christian) used this Jewish wisdom saying to pit Jesus' authority against Pharisaic opponents of their own day. Whether Steck's derivation is correct or not, what we are arguing is that in Luke's presentation Jesus is identifying himself with Wisdom's *emissaries* (not with "Wisdom" per se) as expressed in the *Deuteronomistic* idiom of the violent fate of the prophets and messengers (cf. 13:33–35). That ἀπόστολος could be used to denote a "prophet" or "messenger" *sent* with God's authority in the OT period is clear from 3 Kgdms. 14:6 (of Ahijah) (cf. O. J. F. Seitz, "The Commission of Prophets and 'Apostles': A Re-examination of Matthew 23,34 with Luke 11,49," *SE IV,* 236–40). See further, Fitzmyer, *Luke,* 1:949–52.

72. See 2 Sam. 4:11; Ps. 9:12; Ezek. 33:6, 8 for the seeking of *required* vengeance for blood.

73. While Luke does not specifically state that the Pharisee who invited Jesus to "lunch" was in the crowds, Luke's temporal connection of 11:37a (along with other evidence) makes it certain that the Pharisee's behavior is representative of the crowd's.

74. Luke 11:29, 30, 31, 32, 50, 51.

75. Cf. Marshall (*Luke,* 391): "The wording echoes Dt 32:20. . . . The phraseology thus reflects that of God when confronted by the faithless and disobedient generation in the wilderness."

76. See Derrett ("You Build," 189) on "sons": "The word only means membership of the same clan, company, or ethnic group."

77. Cf. also in the Central Section the parable of the unjust steward (16:1–9), which speaks of "the sons of this age" vis-à-vis "their own generation" (see below, Part III.C.17).

78. The bulk of this material is generally assigned to an "apocalypse" in Q. There are no certain parallels in Matthew to Luke 17:22, 25, 28–29, 32, 34, 37a. And it is debated whether Luke derives some of his material from Mark 13 (the

"little apocalypse"), e.g., 17:23 par. Mark 13:21; or 17:25 from the Markan Passion predictions. Many hold vv. 20–21 to have been composed by Luke (e.g., Bultmann, *Syn. Trad.,* 24, a Greek *chreia;* cf. *Ps. Arist.* 10), though Marshall (*Luke,* 652) thinks it possible that the setting with Pharisees stems from tradition. For our purposes, at the level of Luke's "orderly account, the link between the "sign of Jonah" (11:29), Jesus' person, and the Son of Man is unmistakable.

79. Cf. Mark 13:21. The sense of ἐντός as "among" or possibly "in your domain" is to be preferred here simply because (as, e.g., Marshall, *Luke,* 655, points out) nowhere else in Luke is the Kingdom regarded as something internal, nor does it ever "enter" a person but rather vice versa. If our arguments are correct, then this translation is confirmed and the presence of the Kingdom in the presence of those Pharisees is the primary thrust of the saying as opposed to the sudden emergence of it in the future.

80. BAGD, s.v. "παρατήρησις": "'The Kingdom of God is not coming with observation' i.e., in such a way that its rise can be observed." Cf. also Marshall, *Luke,* 654, for various nuances.

81. Marshall, *Luke,* 486–87.

82. "L" = 7:20, 29–30; because the three pericopes (7:18–23, 24–28, 29–35) are paralleled closely in vocabulary and sequence in Matt. 11:2–19, many scholars hold this section to be taken from Q. Whether Luke's unique material is his own additions to Q through editorial comments or from a special source, or whether Matthew has omitted verses from Q, is a moot point. For our purposes, what is significant is that vv. 29–30 in their present context cannot represent words of Jesus but are a commentary by the narrator.

83. See J. Schneider, "ἔρχομαι," *TDNT* 2:666–84; and Marshall, *Luke,* 290. The term recalls John's designation of Jesus as the one who is "coming" (3:16, i.e., "who is mightier than I"), and bears a messianic thrust (cf. 3:15). Cf. Ps. 118:26 (117:26); Hab. 2:3; Mal. 3:1; Dan. 7:13. Schneider (p. 670) refers to the two forms of the Messiah's coming that the rabbis held, i.e., in glory or in humility. See also Str-B 4:872ff. The rabbis also link the figure of Ps. 118:25–26 (117:25–26) to David (*b. Pesaḥ.* 119a) or to the final redemption (*Midr.* Psalm 118, §22, 244a). There is apparently no evidence of the use of this phrase as a *title* for the Messiah (see Schürmann, *Lukas,* 408–9, who, however, points to Hab. 2:3 as the basis of the language). For a different opinion, see Bultmann (*Syn. Trad.,* [Ger. ed.] 168 n. 2): "already in Judaism a secretive messianic title." The passages in which Jesus speaks of his own "coming," e.g., Luke 12:49, 51 (cf. 13:35), should also be taken into account for Jesus' messianic self-consciousness *according to Luke;* see below, Part III.C.10.

84. See Schürmann, *Lukas,* 411.

85. Luke is much stronger here than Matt. 11:4–6. Luke has Jesus refer directly to the miracles he has just performed before their eyes and ears (v. 21)—in essence a repeat of 7:18. Notice the stark contrast here with the centurion's "faith" based simply on "hearing" about Jesus (Luke 7:3, 7, 9).

86. Schürmann (*Lukas,* 411) notes that the "preaching of good news to the poor" comes at the end of the list of Jesus' activities in 7:22 and considers this to

be significant: "Apparently salvation, strictly speaking, first comes in Jesus' proclamation."

87. Cf. Schürmann, *Lukas*, 412.

88. See the commentaries; e.g., Marshall (*Luke*, 292, on 7:24–28): "It is directly linked to the preceding conversation."

89. E.g., Plummer (*Luke*, 205): "John belonged to the old dispensation; he was its last and highest product"; Ellis (*Luke*, 119): "John is the 'messenger' (27) of the new age, 'the Elijah' promised by God. . . . Yet his place in redemptive history belongs to the time of the promise, the pre-messianic era."

90. Marshall (*Luke*, 293, on v. 28b): "Its point is rather to stress to Jesus' hearers the significant decision that faces them." He correctly pinpoints the thrust of "decision" for Jesus but in so doing mistakenly softens the brunt of Jesus' retort.

91. See, e.g., Conzelmann, *Theology*, 22–27. For the unlikely view that "the least" (7:28) refers to Jesus, see Leaney, *Luke*, 58; Marshall, *Luke*, 297; and Fitzmyer, *Luke* 1:675.

92. For the significance of Isa. 40:3–5, see W. Wink, *John the Baptist in the Gospel Tradition*, SNTSMS 7 (Cambridge: Cambridge University Press, 1968), 66, 69–70.

93. It is not suggested in 7:21 that Jesus performs cures and exorcisms in order to help convince the "people" or "crowds" of his status. Nor does Luke state that Jesus faces John's doubting as a challenge which has to be met with a "sign" to verify his authority. Rather, Luke simply states that "at that hour" (7:21a) John's emissaries witnessed Jesus doing precisely what he was "sent" to do (7:22; cf. 4:18–19). In other words, Jesus responds to John's questioning by *being* the "anointed one" (cf. 3:15) and giving John one more opportunity to accept Jesus' real calling. That these works should therefore at the same time bear the force of a "sign" is clear from the inherent objective convincing power that they should carry for John (7:22a). See F. Mussner, "Der nicht erkannte Kairos (Mt 11, 16–19 = Lk 7, 31–35)," *Bib* 40 (1959): 599–612, esp. 604 n. 1.

94. Luke's remark serves to draw out the two extreme positions to Jesus and obfuscate John's wavering stance. The stern reproach (7:28b) is still allowed to stand but now in the wider perspective of the ultimate "plan" of God (v. 30).

95. Plummer (*Luke*, 206): The expression "the plan/will of God" is unique to Luke in the NT (Acts 13:36; 20:27); cf. Wis. 6:4.

96. For a discussion of the "authenticity" of the "has come" (ἦλθον) statements, see, e.g., Bultmann, *Syn. Trad.*, 166–68 (later church formulations); and Grundmann, *Lukas*, 269 (1QH and the Teacher of Righteousness' self-professed recognition of his own status "necessitated" a similar profession by Jesus in his earthly mission).

97. There are two main issues: (1) The dynamics within the parable: Are the two groups of children represented as *(a)* exchanging reproaches (ἀλλήλοις), or *(b)* does only one group reproach the other first for not dancing and then for not mourning?

(2) The symbolic value: If *(b)* is preferred in (1), do the reproaching children, *(c)*

represent Jesus' audience, i.e., the Jews, against John and Jesus, or *(d)* do they symbolize John and Jesus and their following as scolding their unresponsive contemporaries? For (2), *(c),* see J. Jeremias (*The Parables of Jesus* [London: SCM Press, 1972], 160–62), who thinks ἀλλήλοις does refer in earlier tradition to *two* "scolding" groups but that Luke has gotten it wrong; Matthew's form is correct. Schürmann (*Lukas,* 424) counters that the sense of ἀλλήλοις need be only that of the typical bantering back and forth between children without representing the reproaches of two different groups. He interprets (pp. 423–24) the complaining children to be God's messengers (e.g., John and Jesus) who find no response to any of their message, i.e., (2) *(d).* Mussner ("Der nicht erkannte Kairos," 599–601, 605–6) tries to avoid an allegorical application of two groups by following Jülicher's (*Die Gleichnisreden Jesu,* 2 vols. [Tübingen: J. C. B. Mohr (Paul Siebeck), 1910], 2:25–26) application that just as children at play become ill-tempered, fickle, and "pig-headed," so "this generation" is toward John and Jesus (vv. 33–35). For full discussions, cf. further, Plummer, *Luke,* 207; Lagrange, *Luc,* 223–25; and Fitzmyer, *Luke,* 1:677–78.

98. Mussner ("Der nicht erkannte Kairos," 605–6) argues that the application goes back to Jesus himself, since the judgment of the parable needed to be applied to someone to make any sense originally.

99. Cf., e.g., Bultmann (*Syn. Trad.,* 113): "the same meaning."

100. See Mussner, "Der nicht erkannte Kairos," 610 n. 2.

101. See above, Part III, "Josephus, the Qumran Covenanters, and the Deuteronomistic Perspective."

102. See above, Part II, "Prophetic Career of Moses According to Deuteronomy."

103. See below, esp. Part III.C.

104. See above, Part II, "The Prophetic Parallels of Moses in Deuteronomy to Jesus in Luke 9:1–50."

105. ἐν πᾶσιν ὑμῖν (9:48b) could refer to the "crowds" (9:37, 38) (cf. πάντες, 9:43a, 43b), but more likely to the μαθηταί (9:43b); cf. ἐν αὐτοῖς (9:46). In any case, it is clear from Luke's story that among these crowds are the *laos* (9:13; cf. 7:29) and "tax collectors" (cf. 7:29) and "sinners" (7:34; cf. 6:17; 7:1), some of whom in part constitute the "disciples" (e.g., Levi in 5:27–35). See below, Part III.D.

106. In a curious way the disciples' behavior in 9:46–50 mirrors the "children of the marketplace" (7:32); they quarrel among one another (vv. 46–48) and take sides (v. 49) against other disciples who do not "play their tune," i.e., do "not follow with us!" Leaney (*Luke,* 57–59) tries to forge a link between 7:28 and 9:46–48 by making Jesus the symbol of the child in both passages. This is possible only by not taking into account the dynamics of acceptance and rejection of Jesus in both contexts.

107. While Luke does not connect this meal setting by a temporal phrase to the audience scene (as in 11:37), nonetheless the story itself exhibits direct lines of development from 7:18–35.

108. The history of tradition in 7:36–50 is as Bultmann admits, "difficult and uncertain" (*Syn. Trad.,* 20–21). The majority opinion accepts the bulk of the

story from "L" with probably some cross-influence from Mark 14:1–9, perhaps already at the oral stage. See the commentaries on Luke 7:36–50. There is little doubt that the *point* of the whole is to contrast the "sinner's" humble submission of faith (and love) (vv. 47–50) with the skeptical offense of the Pharisee (vv. 39–40, 44–46). The woman's faith is a response to the prior forgiveness, just as the love of the debtor responds to the prior forgiveness of the creditor. That is to say, the parable is one of *response,* whether "love" or "faith" is the medium. Therefore G. Braumann's arguments ("Die Schuldner und die Sünderin, Luk. VII. 36–50," *NTS* 10 [1963–64]: 487–93, esp. 488–89) are amiss, since the parable illustrates the contrasting response of the one who recognizes his great "debt" over against one who does not. This response is the "all or nothing" which Braumann otherwise correctly designates as the import of the *story:* "doubting Jesus' authority" (p. 492). Hence we are contending that the Pharisee's doubt—in the Deuteronomistic understanding—is leveled to "nothing," i.e., rejection of Jesus. Cf. also U. Wilckens, "Vergebung für die Sünderin (Lk 7, 36–50)," *Orientierung an Jesus, Zur Theologie der Synoptiker,* für Josef Schmid (Freiburg: Herder & Herder, 1973), 394–424; he argues that the parable (7:41–42) must have had a setting at an early stage in the tradition for it to have any significance at all. Most likely the two were together from the beginning (*pace* Bultmann, *Syn. Trad.,* 20–21).

109. For the possible *halakic* ramifications of anointing by an "unclean sinner" and Jesus' response, see J. D. M. Derrett ("The Anointing at Bethany," *SE II,* 174–82). Derrett, however, interprets Luke 7:36–38 in the light of Mark 14:3–9 and parallels and thus imputes motives from the latter into the former (e.g., p. 180). For a more lucid explanation of the purity laws, including the possible significance of being touched by a "defiled" person, see Neusner, "Cleanse the Inside."

110. Jesus' reproach is of course milder than his offensive in 11:37–54. For this development in opposition to Jesus, see below, Part III.C and D.

οὗ χάριν, "for this reason" (BAGD) (i.e., *receiving* Jesus properly in his authority), signifies the basis of her forgiveness. See Jeremias (*Parables,* 127), who argues that the woman's love (v. 47) expresses the deepest gratitude and probably translates the Hebrew (Aramaic) *berekh,* "to bless." "The story therefore implies that Jesus in his sermon had offered forgiveness." Cf. below, n. 111.

111. Cf. Jeremias, *Parables,* 126. The meal in 7:36–50 was a Sabbath banquet (cf. "recline," v. 36) in Jesus' honor as a prophet after he had preached the synagogue sermon.

112. Three pericopes, Luke 12:54–56, 57–59; 13:1–9, are in question. Luke 12:54–56, 57–59 are Q. For arguments over whose "Q" is the more original, see the commentaries.

Luke 13:1–9 is "L," though as usual its origins are greatly disputed. Bultmann (*Syn. Trad.,* 23) considers vv. 1–5 to be a church creation to introduce the parable in vv. 6–9. Contra Bultmann: J. Blinzler ("Die Niedermetzelung von Galiläern durch Pilatus," *NovT* 2 [1955–58]: 24–49) offers evidence for a historical basis to vv. 1–5 in the setting of Jesus' ministry (Galilee).

These three texts, as well as 12:49–53, are linked by the common theme of the "imminent crisis" which is already impinging upon Jesus' audiences through his words and deeds (i.e., "presence").

113. δεινῶς ἐνέχειν (BAGD).

114. See G. Klein, "Die Prüfung der Zeit (Lukas 12, 54–56)," *ZTK* 61 [1964]: 373–90. Klein refers the import in its present Lukan context to the time of persecution and crisis in the church.

115. Plummer *(Luke)* on 3:9: "The δὲ καὶ . . . is Lk's favorite method of giving emphasis."

116. Probably paronomasia on *kairos* (12:56).

117. See Marshall, *Luke,* 553; and Str-B 2:193–97.

118. Cf. also Jer. 8:13; 24:1–8; Mic. 7:1. Marshall *(Luke,* 555) thinks that the fig tree is "hardly . . . a standing symbol for Israel" but that its fruit "is symbolical of the Jewish people." See also Fitzmyer, *Luke,* 2:1008.

Are the "three years" here possibly an allusion to Luke 4:25, i.e., about the length of the famine announced by Elijah, who subsequently goes to Gentile territory because Israel would not repent?

119. Pilate's "bloodbath" (13:1) is an ominous example of being turned over to the ἄρχοντα of 12:58!

120. E.g., Deuteronomy 29—30; 1 Kings 18; 2 Kings 17; Jeremiah 7; 25. See esp. Part III.B, below.

121. MT = Jer. 26:4–5. See Steck, *Israel,* 72–74, for Deuteronomistic background.

122. Steck, *Israel,* 74–80. 2 Chron. 36:14–20 represents the stage in which the prophets themselves are regarded as sent and rejected, and as personal ambassadors are mocked. Cf. Luke 9:46–48; 10:16; 13:31–35.

123. See above, Part III.A.1.

124. Steck, *Israel,* 222–27. Cf. above, Part III.A, n. 71. Steck argues that the wisdom circles that produced this judgment oracle (Luke 11:49–50) had merged with traditionists of the Deuteronomistic point of view during the Hasidic period.

125. The analysis and use of the Deuteronomistic viewpoint in Luke as evidence for our thesis does not depend upon Steck's particular view of the history of these traditions during the intertestamental period. Naturally we are indebted to his identification of certain of these individual traditions in Luke-Acts. Cf. below, n. 169.

126. See above, Part III.A and chart, p. 110.

127. See, e.g., Conzelmann, *Theology,* 63–65, 68, and above, Part I, n. 12.

128. For a discussion of various views, see Marshall, *Luke,* 568–73. Blinzler's suggested emendation ("Die literarische Eigenart des sogennanten Reiseberichts im Lukasevangelium," in *Synoptische Studien,* Studies for A. Wikenhauser, ed. J. Schmid and A. Vögtle [Munich: K. Zink, 1953], 42–46) has generally not been accepted because it is *unnecessary.* Instead of 13:33 standing in "offenkundigem Widerspruch" (pp. 42–43) to 13:32, it is much more reasonable to explain this relation from paratactic style. In v. 32 the sending of 4:18–19 (cf. 4:40–44) is expressed, whereas in v. 33 the sending from the mountain (9:31–35) is articu-

lated. In Semitic style, these two statements are set alongside each other, with the reader expected to understand their relation from the context. πλήν is an attempt to make this explicit; here it is only mildly adversative and has more the sense, "Indeed, for all of that" I must go. See Plummer *(Luke)* on 6:24; he cites Curtius and J. B. Lightfoot and then concludes, "It sometimes restricts, sometimes expands, what precedes" (p. 182). Here it expands v. 32. For πλήν as "indeed," "moreover," cf. Marshall *(Luke,* 572), who cites M. E. Thrall, *Greek Particles in the New Testament,* NTTS 3 (Leiden: E. J. Brill, 1962), 20–21.

129. Ibid.

130. So Steck, *Israel,* 44.

131. See above, Part I, "Characterizations of the Dissonance of the Central Section."

132. For the Semitic use of the third person αὐτή in direct address, cf. Grundmann, *Lukas,* 289–90.

133. "Abandonment" is a typical Deuteronomistic expression for Jerusalem's "destruction"; when God leaves the "city," it falls prey to its enemies; cf., e.g., Ezek. 9:1—10:22; 11:22–25; *1 Enoch* 89:56, 66–67; *Pss. Sol.* 7:1ff.; *2 Apoc. Bar.* 8:1–2; cf. Steck, *Israel,* 228 n. 4, 229 n. 1, and esp. 79 n. 1.

As Steck observes *(Israel,* 227–28), the singling out of Jerusalem as the great killer of the prophets is unique to Deuteronomistic tradition. Yet there are close parallels: In Lam. 1:7–8 "Jerusalem" is a punished sinner (cf. 1:14, 18); in Tob. 13:9–10; Bar. 4:12 (a widow left desolate by sinful children; cf. "your children," Luke 13:34b); *Pss. Sol.* 2:3 (Jerusalem's offspring are sinners); or in *2 Apoc. Bar.* 3:1ff.; 10:16; 4 Ezra 9:38ff.; Lamentations 1; Bar. 4:8ff., 31–33 (Jerusalem is a mother herself worthy of destruction; cf. mother "hen" in Luke 13:34b). The closest parallels, however, are in the Qumran literature where Jerusalem is attacked directly as *place* guilty of the sin of the whole apostate nation: QpHab 12:6b–9, commenting on Hab. 2:17, "as for that which he said, 'Because of the murders committed in the city and the violence done to the land,' the explanation of this is (that) *the city* is Jerusalem, where the Wicked Priest committed abominable deeds and defiled the sanctuary of God" (A. Dupont-Sommer, *The Essene Writings from Qumran,* 2d rev. ed. [Oxford: Basil Blackwell, 1961], 267). 4QpIsa.b II, on Isa. 5:8–10, 11–14, 24–25: "Interpreted this saying concerns the last days, the devastation of the land by sword and famine. At the time of the Visitation of the land there shall be 'Woe . . .' (Is 5:11–14). These are the scoffers in *Jerusalem* who have 'despised the Law of the Lord and scorned the word of the Holy One of Israel' (5:24f.). This is the congregation of Scoffers in *Jerusalem*" (cf. 4QpIsa.c 10–11). In these and especially the Qumran quotes it is clear that Jerusalem by metonymy stands for the whole nation of Judah or the people of Israel as a whole. And the context of Luke 13:34–35 bears this sense out as well. Jesus must traverse through the land before he arrives in Jerusalem, the symbolic center of the climax of the whole course of his ministry (13:32–33).

134. E.g., reprisals from authorities for a disruptive messianic demonstration. For this and other suggestions, see the commentaries.

135. I.e., "the temple building" (BAGD); cf. Matt. 23:35—ναός.

136. With the cluster of ideas of the Temple and the blood *required* for the murder it would seem fairly certain that the murder of Zechariah, son of Jehoiada (2 Chron. 24:20–22), is referred to here. This Zechariah was stoned in the court of the Temple ("house," v. 21b), probably the court of the priests where the altar of burnt offering was located and prayers of penance were offered (cf. Steck, *Israel,* 35–36 n. 3). Since Chronicles stood last in the Jewish canon of that time, the murders of Abel and Zechariah are the first and the last of the OT. And in both cases vengeance for the murder is demanded (Gen. 4:10; 2 Chron. 24:22)! Moreover, 2 Chron. 24:19 expresses the telling Deuteronomistic fate of the prophets. For the view that in Matt. 23:35 Zechariah, son of Barachias, refers to the son of Bareis, who was slain by zealots in the Temple at the outbreak of the Jewish War in 67 C.E. (Josephus, *War* 4.334–44), cf. Steck, *Israel,* 37–40. On this view, Matthew continues the long history of the prophets' murders up to the fall of Jerusalem, namely, another 587 B.C.E.

137. Cf., e.g., A. Weiser, *Das Buch des Propheten Jeremia,* ATD 20 (Göttingen: Vandenhoeck & Ruprecht, 1952), 189–93; for the vocabulary of the LXX and the Deuteronomistic view in the judgment oracles of both Luke and Acts, see D. P. Moessner, "Paul in Acts: Preacher of Eschatological Repentance to Israel," *NTS* 34 (1988): 96–104.

138. For "the house" as the Temple, cf. the many instances in the OT: e.g., 1 Kings 5:19b; 6:2ff.; 2 Kings 12:6, 7, 8; 22:6; 2 Chron. 2:4; 3:4ff.; 23:10; Ezra 3:12; 5:11; for intertestamental: e.g., *Jub.* 49:19; *2 Apoc. Bar.* 8:2.

139. For the messianic interpretation of Psalm 118, cf. Str-B 1:849–50, 876; cf. Zech. 9:9–10. Steck (*Israel,* 236–37) concludes somewhat dubiously on the basis of one text that the Messiah cannot be referred to here because in *Psalms of Solomon* he returns to a repentant Israel which 13:35a contradicts. He opts therefore for the "Son of Man." But there is no evidence for Ps. 118:26 being used with this figure; nor can "the coming one" be tied with any certainty to Dan. 7:13 (Steck) where the Son of Man is ascending, not coming to humankind or to Jerusalem. For "the coming one" as "messianic," see above, Part III.A, n. 83.

140. Cf. Marshall (*Luke,* 715), who cites G. W. Anderson, in *Peake's Commentary,* 439.

141. See further below, Part III.C, "The Journeying Guest Is Rejected in Jerusalem (Luke 19:45—23:49)."

142. Literally (ἀνθ᾽ ὧν) "in return for which" (BAGD); for the 587 B.C.E. cause, cf. above, n. 133.

143. Both Luke 13:34–35 and 19:41–44 present a prophetic judgment oracle within the lament. Cf. Steck, *Israel,* 56, 58–59, 227; T. W. Manson (*The Sayings of Jesus* [London: SCM Press, 1957], 126, 319–22), who on 13:34–35a (p. 126) cites C. F. Burney (*The Poetry of Our Lord: An Examination of the Formal Elements of Hebrew Poetry in the Discourses of Jesus Christ* [Oxford: Clarendon Press, 1925], 146) for the *kinah* poetical form, i.e., the rhythm of the old Hebrew elegy or dirge. Luke 19:43–44 also exhibits poetic form.

For the conception of God's presence (or the *Shekinah*) dwelling in the Temple, see Str-B 2:311, 314–15; in *1 Enoch* 89:56 and *2 Apoc. Bar.* 8:2; 64:6 and in Josephus (*War* 6.5.3) God leaves the city by departing or leaving the Temple! See already this idea in Ezekiel 9—11, and cf. above, n. 133. For the imagery and theological conceptualization of the three judgment oracles (Luke 11:47–51; 13:34–35a; 19:43–44) closely mirroring prophetic conceptions of 587 B.C.E., esp. in Jeremiah, Isaiah, and Ezekiel, see C. H. Dodd, "The Fall of Jerusalem and the 'Abomination of Desolation,'" *JRS* 37 (1947): 47–54; for Paul's judgment oracles in Acts reflecting this Deuteronomistic perspective, see Moessner, "Paul in Acts," 101–3.

144. The present passive ἀφίεται has a future sense; cf. BDF §323; and Steck, *Israel,* 228 n. 4. But like the prophetic perfect in Hebrew (cf. Gesenius-Kautzsch §106), the present tense here signifies a present and definite reality, which though not completed has already been set in motion and thus is as good as accomplished.

Cf. 4QFlor 1:5, where šmm = ἀφίημι (cf. LXX Jer. 12:7; Luke 13:35a) denotes a "laying waste" or a defiling/desolating of the Temple in the context of their expectation of a new Temple made by God which cannot be corrupted. This parallel again adds evidence to ὁ οἶκος in 13:35a referring to the Temple as an image for the whole nation (cf. LXX Jer. 22:5).

145. Cf. Luke 21:6ff. In Acts the Temple remains the center of the whole nation; e.g., 3:1ff.; 5:12, 20–21, 25, 28 (center for preaching repentance); 21:17ff. (center of worship for the Christian community!). See esp. Part V, "The Literary Function of the Travel Narrative in Luke-Acts," below; and D. P. Moessner, "'The Christ Must Suffer': New Light on the Jesus-Peter, Stephen, Paul Parallels in Luke-Acts," *NovT* 28 (1986): 243–56.

For "visitation" as both the redemption and the judgment of God, cf., e.g., H. W. Beyer, "ἐπισκοπή," *TDNT* 2:603–8.

146. Or his source.

147. MT Jer. 35:13. For the prophets as the teachers of Israel, see Jer. 35:13, 15 and Steck, *Israel,* 73 n. 6. This role matches that of Moses in Deuteronomy and of Jesus in Luke 9:51ff.!

148. E.g., McCown, "The Geography of Luke's Central Section," *JBL* 57 (1938): 51, 56–58, 65 (see Intro., n. 26); Blinzler, "Eigenart," 27–28 (see Part I., n. 5); J. Schneider, "Zur Analyse des lukanischen Reiseberichtes," in Schmid and Vögtle, *Synoptische Studien,* 219ff. (see Part I., n. 3); B. Reicke, "Instruction and Discussion in the Travel Narrative," papers presented to the International Congress on "The Four Gospels in 1957" at Christ Church, Oxford, *SE I* = TU 73 (Berlin: Akademie-Verlag, 1959), 209ff. (see Part I, n. 7); W. Grundmann, "Fragen der Komposition des lukanischen Reiseberichtes," *ZNW* 50 (1959): 259ff. (see Part I, n. 13); G. W. Trompf, "La section médiane de l'évangile de Luc: l'organisation des documents," *RHPR* 53 (1973): 141–54; and L. T. Johnson, *The Literary Function of Possessions in Luke-Acts,* SBLDS 39 (Missoula, Mont.: Scholars Press, 1977), 105–7 (see Part I, n. 77).

149. When it is noted that many of the "non-words" verses in this core serve mainly as framework (introduction/conclusion) for Jesus' words, then the didactic character is even more pregnantly perceived.

150. This emphasis along with the dearth of so-called miracle stories is in fundamental agreement with the Deuteronomistic prophetic sayings which never speak of the prophets' role as one of "mighty works" or "signs and wonders." The latter is used normally for God, but cf. Deut. 34:11; cf. also Steck, *Israel,* 147 n. 4, 240 n. 1, 248; and above, Part II, n. 40; below, Part IV, "The Relation of Form to Content in Deuteronomy and in the Central Section of Luke."

151. Luke 17:11-19 provides more details which serve, however, to set in relief Israel's mass rejection of Jesus with the believing, submitting Samaritan. See below, Part III.C.20.

152. I.e., the identity and at the same time calling that was confirmed to Jesus at his baptism, Luke 3:21-22.

153. See above, Part II, "The Prophetic Parallels of Moses in Deuteronomy to Jesus in Luke 9:1-50"; see also the theophanic language of "lightning" in Luke 10:18 and 9:29; cf., e.g., Deut. 32:41; Exod. 19:16; Ezek. 1:4, 7.

154. Cf. the same understanding of "mighty works" as in Luke 7:18-35 (above, Part III.A, esp. nn. 85, 86, 93). In 7:29 the *laos* and tax collectors "justify God" upon the hearing of Jesus' word, not upon seeing the mighty works in 7:21!

155. περί—cf. BAGD, 1.b.

156. Cf. above, n. 154.

157. See above, Part II, "Luke's Language and Lineage of the Prophets."

158. The only occurrence of εὐαγγελίζομαι at Luke 16:16 indicates the whole period of Jesus' activity. At the same time we are not suggesting that Jesus' teaching is not a "preaching of the gospel" (cf. 20:1). As 16:16 indicates, the whole period of Jesus' ministry is typified by "good news." Rather, in the Central Section the focus is on (1) the actual context or the teaching itself; and (2) teaching directed to specific groups in a context of growing opposition so that the "good news" has become primarily parenesis and "warning," which, to be sure, are part of the "gathering" function of the "good news" (see below, Part III.C and D).

159. Cf. esp. J. Schneider and Grundmann, in Part I, "Characterizations of the Dissonance of the Central Section"; and see the chart at the end of Part III.B.

160. διδάσκαλος: Luke 9:38; 10:25; 11:45; 12:13; 18:18; 19:39; 20:21, 28, 39; 21:7; 22:11; διδάσκω: 11:1; 12:12; 13:10, 22.

161. For the connection of 14:25-35 to 15:1ff., see Plummer (*Luke,* 367) on v. 1; cf. below, Part III.C.15 and 16.

162. See below, Part III.C.19 and 20.

163. To my knowledge, M. D. Goulder ("The Chiastic Structure of the Lucan Journey," *SE II,* 196) is the first to use the term "pillars" in commenting upon C. F. Evans's observations ("The Central Section of St. Luke's Gospel," in *Studies in the Gospels: Essays in Memory of R. H. Lightfoot,* ed. D. E. Nineham [Oxford: Basil Blackwell, 1955]) on Luke's handling of the Markan outline.

164. Cf. the similar kind of reasoning in Rom. 2:6-29, esp. vv. 13ff.!

165. Cf. Luke 13:14: ἀρχισυνάγωγος.

166. Cf., e.g., Steck, *Israel,* 66-72, 77-80, 200-201.

167. See esp. Part III.A.1 and 4, above.

168. See below, n. 169.

169. See above, Part III.A.1. Steck (*Israel*, 288) concludes that Q represents a collection of sayings from the Jewish Christian (Palestinian) community primarily to instruct their preachers of repentance to Israel. This community stands in a very close relationship, although not in an unbroken line, to the "late Jewish" sapientially and eschatologically oriented Deuteronomistic traditionists which carried on the Hasidic movement into the period of the NT (cf. esp. *1 Enoch*).

170. See above, Part III.A.4.

171. See above, Part III.A.3.

172. See above, Part III.A.2.

173. The final advent, however, is conceived as a coming that the present generation of disciples should be prepared to meet. "Folk" will say to them, 'Look here or there' (17:23).

174. As would be expected, extensive overlap occurs. The line, for instance, between admonition and warning is sometimes impossible to draw, e.g., Luke 17:22–37. See chart at the end of Part III.D, below.

175. According to Steck (*Israel*, 60–66), the oldest formulation of the *violent* fate of the prophets à la the Deuteronomistic historical view.

176. See above, Part III.A.1.

177. Links to Jesus' movement: τὸ πρόσωπον; πορεύομαι; εἰς Ἰερουσαλήμ. Cf. D. Gill, "Observations on the Lukan Travel Narrative and Some Related Passages," *HTR* 63 (1970): 203, for pilgrimage routes; see Josephus, *Ant.* 20.118; *War* 2.232; *Life* 269.

178. For the possibility of a Wisdom saying as the background, see Grundmann, *Lukas*, 204; and Marshall, *Luke*, 410; cf. *1 Enoch* 42:1–2.

179. Grundmann, *Lukas*, 205; Grundmann points to *m. Ber.* 3:1; *b. Ber.* 18a; cf. also Gen. 50:5; Lev. 21:1–3; Tob. 4:3.

180. See above, Part III.B, pp. 114–20.

181. Cf. Grundmann, *Lukas*, 205: "What people call life is for Jesus death."

182. Jesus is calling men and women to the eschatological banquet which is the crowning of all the sacral familial, covenant meals of the OT. Cf. Luke 10:1–24, below.

183. Cf. F. Schleiermacher's (*Schriften*, 167 [see Part I, n. 52]) judgment: "Up to 10:24 we surely have a narrative that was connected together from the beginning." Contrast Bultmann (*Syn. Trad.*, 145–46), who considers 10:2–12 to stem from the community of the resurrected Lord but preserved in Q as mission instructions for the church in the form of instruction to the disciples during the ministry of Jesus. See further, e.g., F. W. Beare, "The Mission of the Disciples and the Mission Charge: Matthew 10 and Parallels," *JBL* 89 (1970): 9–10.

184. See esp. Part II, "The Prophetic Parallels of Moses in Deuteronomy to Jesus in Luke 9:1–50," item 2, above. No exulting in the work of the Twelve is given in Luke. Cf. Mark 6:30–31, where the Twelve, fresh from their campaign, seem, like their master, to be in demand from the "many who were coming and going." Jesus takes them away to a "desert" or deserted place to "rest."

185. Above, Part III.B, pp. 115–19; see also the "messenger" of Mal. 3:1–2 who

is sent before the "Lord's" own coming to the Temple, to purify the sons of Levi. In Luke 10:1 messengers are sent ahead toward Jerusalem anticipating the "Lord's" own coming to purify the Temple. In Mal. 3:22 (LXX, MT = 3:23; ET = 4:5) this messenger is identified as Elijah who brings about repentance to Israel. In Luke 10:1–20 the Seventy(-two), like the messenger-disciples of 9:59–62, are sent on a repentance mission greater than that of Elijah's first mission. They, and no longer John, fulfill the eschatological mission of Elijah (Luke 7:27).

For the idea of "apostleship" in the early church rooted in OT ideas of prophets' sending, see Steck, *Israel,* 229–30 n. 5: repentance-preachers in the Hasidic period and later regarded themselves as sent out by Wisdom, just as earlier the prophets had been (cf. Luke 11:49; 13:34; see above, Part III.B, n. 169.

186. See above, Part III.B, pp. 127–28.

187. Cf. Marshall (*Luke, 417*), who cites J. Jeremias's (*TDNT* 1:340) quotation of *Tanchuma toledot* 32b: "Hadrian said to R. Jehoshua (c. 90 A.D.): There is something great about the sheep (Israel) that can persist among 70 wolves (the nations). He replied: Great is the Shepherd who delivers it and watches over it and destroys them (the wolves) before them (Israel)." Cf. also examples of lambs defenseless before wolves: Isa. 11:6; 65:25; Sir. 13:17; Homer, *Iliad* 22.263.

188. E.g., Leaney, *Luke,* 176–77; Katz, "Lk 9.52—11.36: Beobachtungen zur Logienquelle," 65–66 (see Part III.A, n. 50).

189. In any case, to use the imagery of sheep, it takes only a relatively small pack of wolves to wreak havoc on a large flock of sheep!

190. See above, n. 185.

191. See above, Part III.B, pp. 127–28.

192. I.e., a person "worthy of" or "destined for" peace; cf. Marshall, *Luke,* 420.

193. Either αὐτός is used as a demonstrative, "that" house, or it translates the Aramaic proleptic pronoun, "in it, namely the house" (so Marshall, *Luke,* 420).

194. Though this meaning is not necessarily excluded; for commentators who interpret as essentially material reward for the preacher, see, e.g., Marshall, *Luke,* 420; Grundmann, *Lukas,* 210; Ellis, *Luke,* 156; and Danker, *Luke,* 214.

195. Contrast this tarrying to the injunction in *Didache* 11.5 concerning the journeying "apostle" or "prophet" not to remain more than two days (when necessary) at one house: "If he remains three days, then he is a false prophet." In *Didache* 12.1ff.: "Anyone who comes in the name of the Lord" can stay "when necessary" "two or three days" (12.2).

196. M. Hengel ("Die Ursprünge der christlichen Mission," *NTS* 18 [1971–72]: 15–38) traces this attitude to Jesus himself (p. 36). Because for Hengel the mission charges of the Gospels do not betray specific christological content, these reports must go back to Jesus' (the "original missionary's") own practice (p. 36).

197. Cf. Schlatter, *Lukas,* 274–75, 277.

198. Acts 10:48b. See J. Navonne, "The Lucan Banquet Community," *The Bible Today* 51 (1970): 161.

199. See above, Part II, n. 88.

200. Cf. P. J. Bernadicou ("Biblical Joy and the Lucan Eucharist," *The Bible Today* 51 [1970]: 162–71), speaking of Jesus' meals in Luke: "Jesus put men

before the actual reality of God and mediated an experience of friendship with this God through his own friendship with men" (p. 169).

201. I.e., the royal presence of God in his Kingdom through Jesus his ambassador ("apostle"—10:16); cf. Luke 19:11–27, 38; 1:32–33; 23:42.

202. Cf. A. Schlatter (*Der Evangelist Matthäus: Seine Sprache, sein Ziel, seine Selbständigkeit* [Stuttgart: Calwer Verlag, 1929], 304): What baptism was for the Baptist—i.e., a bath removing uncleanness—was for Jesus the fellowship meal.

203. There are three main positions for vv. 17–20: (1) *From Q:* e.g., Schürmann (*Untersuchungen,* 146 n. 37)—Matt. 7:21–23 reflects the Q of Luke 10:17–20. (2) *From "L":* e.g., Manson (*Sayings,* 74)—Luke 22:35 is from "L" and corresponds exactly to 10:4 which is different from Mark 6:8–9, par. Luke 9:3; "L" encompasses 10:1, 4–7, 17–20, while Q vv. 2, 3, 8–12, 13–16. (3) *From Luke's editorial activity:* e.g., P. Hoffmann (*Studien zur Theologie der Logienquelle,* NTAbh n.s. 8 [Münster: Aschendorff, 1972], 248–54)—10:1 and 17 as Lukan framework to recast isolated sayings, in part grouped and reworked by Luke (e.g., 10:18–20) to express his theology of mission at a time when missionaries no longer demonstrated charismatic power.

204. "Return" is an unfortunate translation; the sense, in the context of the cycle of their sending out, is "to turn back" (s.v., BAGD; s.v., LSJ).

205. Hoffmann *(Logienquelle)* points out the Lukan theme of "power" over Satan and the demonic powers in Acts (e.g., Acts 8:7; 10:38; 13:8–12; 16:16–18; 19:13–14; 28:3–6).

206. Cf. esp. E. Lohmeyer, *Lord of the Temple: A Study of the Relation Between Cult and Gospel* (London: Oliver & Boyd, 1961), 79–81; Bernadicou, "Joy," 169–71; and B. Reicke, *Diakonie, Festfreude und Zelos: In Verbindung mit der altchristlichen Agapenfeier,* UUA 1951:5 (Uppsala: Lundequistska, 1951), 167–79, 201–22.

207. In Acts 8:8 χάρα is linked with the σημεῖα (8:6, 13) and exorcisms of unclean spirits (πνεύματα) by *Philip,* one of the Seven, in Samaria—the same linkage as in Luke 10:17, 20. Moreover, 10:1ff. is tied thematically to the mission activity in Samaria of 9:52–56. See below, Part V, "Reflections on the Theological Implications of the New Exodus Travel Narrative for Interpreting Luke-Acts."

208. See above, Part III.B, pp. 120–27.

209. For a discussion of the history of the traditions, see Marshall (*Luke,* 431–32), who points to the parallels in Jewish wisdom circles and the present unity of the section as a whole, esp. between v. 21 and v. 22, even though vv. 23–24 probably at an earlier stage were separate.

210. Cf. below, Part III, "Conclusion," Excursus 2. The form of Jesus' prayer in v. 21 is that of the *Hodayoth,* or thanksgiving hymn: e.g., 1QH 7:26: "I thank Thee, O Lord, for Thou hast enlightened me through Thy truth. In Thy marvelous mysteries . . . Thou hast granted me knowledge" (trans. G. Vermès). For the concept of "knowledge" in Qumran, see W. D. Davies, "'Knowledge' in the Dead Sea Scrolls and Matthew 11:25–30," *HTR* 46 (1953): 113–39. Davies shows how the coordination of knowledge of the eschaton with an intimate knowledge by the

mediator of God's mysteries with God closely matches Luke 10:21 and Matt. 11:25–30 and their literary contexts. He agrees with B. Reicke's assessment (cf. "Traces of Gnosticism in the Dead Sea Scrolls?" *NTS* 1 [1954–55]: 137–41). The significance of these and other parallels to Jewish Palestinian thought for our study is that the *Sitz im Leben* in the story of Jesus that Luke presents for the revelation to the Seventy(-two) *on the journey* to Jerusalem is conceivable with a Palestinian provenance for the tradition.

For the "wise" and "learned" as those unfit to receive God's revelation because of their arrogance/sin, cf. 1QS 11:6–7; 1QpHab 12:4; 1QH 2:8–10; Sir. 3:19–20; Wis. 10:21—11:1; Bar. 3:9–37.

211. Davies ("'Knowledge,'" 137) takes *tauta* in 10:21 "to refer not only to the fall of Satan and the writing of the names in heaven, but also to the woes on the cities, as well as to all those things which 'prophets and kings have desired to see and have not.'"

212. See B. Reicke, "πᾶς, ἅπας," *TDNT* 5:895, on Luke 10:22.

213. Cf. this same structure of authority in Luke 10:2.

214. Indeed, Luke 10:22 states that only those willed by the Son receive revelation. For the Semitic parallelism of v. 22, cf. J. Jeremias, *New Testament Theology: The Proclamation of Jesus* (London: SCM Press, 1971), 56–59. For text-critical matters, as well as poetic structure, cf. P. Winter, "Matthew XI 27 and Luke X 22," *NovT* 1 (1956): 112–48.

215. Cf. Luke 2:14; 7:22–23; 12:49–53; 19:41. Cf. Isa. 52:15; 60:3, where kings will see the final era of salvation! It may well be that in the sending out of the Seventy(-two) Luke is reflecting a midrash on Isaiah 52—53 in which Jesus as the voice (φωνή, Isa. 40:3, 6, 9; 42:2; 50:10; cf. 48:20; 51:3) is the *měbassér* or ὁ εὐαγγελιζόμενος (40:9; 52:7) who sends out preachers of good news, i.e., "voices" à la Isa. 52:8. In the LXX these "voices" return from their journey mission and report to the ὁ εὐαγγελιζόμενος and à la 52:8 rejoice together! In the LXX the "voice," the "preacher of good tidings," and the "servant" are identified as one figure. Moreover, this servant-voice-preacher of good news leads "the new exodus" of the final salvation in which his presence brings the very kingly presence of the Lord himself to Jerusalem (52:6–7)! Thus Jesus is the κύριος (Luke 10:1, 17) who reveals and bears the presence of the "Lord of heaven and earth" (10:21b) and fulfills that which all the prophets and kings longed to see (Isa. 52:15; 60:3). In thus fulfilling Isaiah, he sends out ambassadors of good news to anticipate his own coming.

216. See above, Part III.B, n. 2.

217. For a synopsis of the complex history of the traditions—Markan, "L," and Q?—see Marshall, *Luke,* 440–41, 444–46; and Fitzmyer, *Luke* 2:877–79, 882.

218. That this reference to a Samaritan alongside Jerusalem officials stems from Jerusalem circles in the church is rigorously defended by Conzelmann, *Theology,* 71–72.

219. See Grundmann, *Lukas,* 225. Cf. Bultmann, *Syn. Trad.,* 33, for a discussion of an "ideal scene" of a biographical apothegm.

220. Cf. Luke 10:1: "every city and place where he himself was about to come."

221. There is no indication that Jesus already knew Mary and Martha before entering their home. The "Mary" of 8:2 is not identified by Luke with the "Mariam" of 10:39, 42.

222. See Marshall, *Luke,* 453–54.

223. For the argument that 11:5-8 ("L") actually comes from Q, see Schürmann, *Untersuchungen,* 119.

224. The disciples, however, are never presented as calling God "*my* Father."

225. Cf. J. B. Mathews, "Hospitality and the New Testament Church: An Historical and Exegetical Study" (Th.D. diss., Princeton Theological Seminary, 1965), 28–60, 70–139, 198–234, 271–84.

226. Marshall (*Luke,* 462–63) is correct in refusing to choose between the two alternatives of God's contrasting goodness *or* persistent prayer: If even a human responds to the pressing needs of a friend, how much more will God provide for his children in all that they need (cf. v. 8b). Therefore take heart and keep on praying, whatever the exigencies. The "wisdom" character of this parable is evident along with its connection to 18:1–8, the unjust judge; cf. also 16:1–9.

227. See above, Part III.A.1. Cf. the "house" imagery of 11:24–26, 33–36 which mirrors the need for a full acceptance of Jesus' authority, i.e., of the "Son of Man who is here" (11:29–32). The "journeying guest" *Sitz im Leben* may be responsible for the imagery of 11:24–26, 33–36; for this setting in the church, see below, Part V, "Reflections on the Theological Implications of the New Exodus Travel Narrative for Interpreting Luke-Acts."

228. See, e.g., Part I, "The Dissonance of Form from Content," above.

229. Plummer, *Luke,* 318.

230. "The disciples" in 12:1 refers to a larger group than the Twelve. Therefore while the mission of the Twelve (9:1–6) is not excluded, the primary referent is the larger mission of the Seventy(-two) and of "others" (e.g., 9:60) who have journeyed with Jesus.

231. See U. Wilckens ("ὑποκρίνομαι κτλ.," *TDNT* 8:559–71), who points out the semantic shift in Diaspora Judaism from classical usage. Moreover, in "primitive Christianity as in the LXX the word group is always used in *sensu malo*" (p. 566). He sees a general synoptic sense: "failure to do God's will is concealed behind the pious appearance of outward conduct" (pp. 567–68). This contradiction between "inner" and "outer" reality became the essence of the meaning of "hypocrisy" for all of later antiquity as influenced by Christianity (pp. 567–68 n. 46). Note that purposive or conscious dissembling is not necessarily included in the sense. One can be sincerely motivated and yet "hypocritical" vis-à-vis another's point of view; cf. above, Part III.A, n. 70.

232. Contra, e.g., Marshall (*Luke,* 510): "The connection of thought is somewhat artificial, with several motifs intertwined." For the reconstruction of composite sources, see pp. 509–11.

233. Cf. Grundmann, *Lukas,* 253–54.

234. The only time in the Synoptics that "friends" is used for Jesus' disciples; cf. John 15:14–15; 3 John 15; James 2:23.

235. Cf. above, Part III.A.2.

236. Cf. Caird (*Luke,* 160): "The opposite of hypocrisy is repentance."

237. The differences in wording and one inversion with Matthew's Q (6:25–34, 19–21) lead Marshall to appeal to more than one Q-rescension (*Luke,* 525).

238. Cf. above, Part III.B, pp. 120–24, on parenesis.

239. Cf. below, on Luke 16:1–31, pp. 159–64.

240. Does reference to "the nations" indicate peripheral Jewish areas like the Decapolis or Samaria through which the Seventy(-two) have journeyed? Jesus would then be using graphic illustrations from that mission as the journey continues.

241. The only other occurrences of this word in the entire NT are in Luke 10:4; 22:35–36, which refer to the mission of the Seventy(-two)! See below, "The Journeying Guest Is Rejected in Jerusalem (Luke 19:45—23:49)," pp. 180–81. "Purses that do not grow old" is the equivalent of being "rich toward God," 12:21b.

242. In the sense of anticipation to receive or experience something, as in Luke 2:25 and 23:51. But cf. the meal setting here and in 15:2.

243. Here γάμος is in the plural, "great feast," without necessarily a reference to a wedding feast (singular) (so BAGD, s.v.).

244. For the view that this parable stood in Q, cf., e.g., Manson, *Sayings,* 115–16; Schürmann, *Untersuchungen,* 124–25 (=Mt 24:42); and Marshall, *Luke,* 553 (cautiously); from "L," e.g., Fitzmyer, *Luke,* 2:984.

245. No distant coming is necessarily implied vis-à-vis Jesus' own presence. The future of εὑρίσκω is subsequent to a coming of the Son of Man of which the precise time framework is not given.

246. Cf. Luke 11:3–32: the Queen of the South (explicitly) and Jonah (implicitly) both journey.

247. Cf. Luke 9:58 and 11:30 and "the Son of Man."

248. The element of "delay" (12:45) is nowhere tied to a previous coming of the master. It is a pure eisegesis to speak of a "return" of the master in the sense of another *coming.* The story within the parable speaks of a master who is away and who will reward a faithful steward *when he comes.* Therefore it is wrong, as, e.g., A. Weiser (*Die Knechtsgleichnisse der synoptischen Evangelien,* SANT 29 [Munich: no pub., 1971], 175–77, 204–14), to speak of a shift of audience where a "delay" *must* now refer to the situation of the church waiting for the Lord's *return coming.* Further, ἀναλύω in the first parable, v. 36, should be translated "depart" or "leave." Totally apart from whether Jesus reckoned with and thus prepared his disciples for a period after his departure, the parable as a literary/rhetorical device to image an analogous situation must be read as a story coherent within itself before the question of its application is posed (cf. below, n. 289). (For a use of ἀναλύω as "depart" from a feast, cf. Josephus, *Ant.* 11.34.)

249. See O. Betz, "The Dichotomized Servant and the End of Judas Iscariot," *RevQ* 5 (1964): 43–58. Betz shows that διχοτομέω in 12:46 probably reflects the idea of being "cut off" from the faithful as in, e.g., 1QS 2:16, where *nikrat* "cuts off" the wicked from "all the sons of light." This Essene background fits in well also with the reference to "knowledge" (γινώσκω) which in the same verse refers

to the steward's ignorance of the "hour" of the master's coming; for eschatological "knowledge" of the final events which Yahweh will bring about, cf. 1QpHab 7; cf., e.g., W. D. Davies, "'Knowledge,'" 122–25. We are arguing for an eschatological interpretation for Jesus' journey to Jerusalem in the story of Luke. See esp. below on 12:44–53.

250. *Hapax legomenon* in Greek Bible.

251. See above, Part II, "The Prophetic Parallels of Moses in Deuteronomy to Jesus in Luke 9:1–50."

252. Cf. the eschatological references above, on 9:52–56, p. 133.

253. See above, Part III.B, pp. 123–26, on "doing the Law."

254. BAGD: a synonym of $\zeta\eta\tau\acute{\epsilon}\omega$, "to require," "to demand."

255. Cf. the Pharisees who "reject" the $\beta ov\lambda\acute{\eta}$ of God in 7:30.

256. Cf. the future verbs in vv. 52–53.

257. This analogy, however, does not rule out a bifocal image, i.e., a reference to a coming subsequent to this first coming.

258. Note the future tense: $\delta o\theta\acute{\eta}\sigma\epsilon\tau a\iota$—11:29; $\check{\epsilon}\sigma\tau a\iota$—11:30; cf. $\mathring{\eta}\lambda\theta\epsilon v$, 11:31, to describe the journey of the "Queen of the South," though Solomon and Jonah, and not she, are a "type" of the "sign" of the Son of Man.

259. In 12:35–38 an arrival is followed by serving at table; this is precisely the way Jesus' journey is depicted as he continues to "come" and arrive at places along the way, e.g., 13:25; 15:1–2; 22:14–38; cf. 24:13–35. In 12:42–44 an arrival is followed by an allotment of stewardship over food distribution; in 9:10–17 the Twelve are set over the distribution (literally) of food after Jesus arrives at Bethsaida. In 10:1ff. the Seventy(-two) are set over the food as they effect meal fellowships in the homes after they arrive. Neither parable of course excludes the final eschatological messianic meal which the meals on Jesus' journey initiate and thus anticipate. See O. Hofius, *Jesu Tischgemeinschaft mit den Sündern*, Calwer Hefte 86 (Stuttgart: Calwer Verlag, 1967), 19.

260. For the history of the various traditions, see Marshall, *Luke*, 563–64 (sayings from Q that were available to Matthew in a variant form); and Fitzmyer, *Luke*, 2:1021 (less certain).

261. Cf. above, Part III.B, pp. 119–20.

262. See above, Part III.A.4.

263. In Luke 11:43; 14:8 the Pharisees "love" the "first seats," as the "scribes" do in 20:46; the "first of the people" in 19:47 probably refers to the "elders."

264. On the history of tradition and literary difficulties of 13:32–33, see above, Part I, n. 12; Part III.B, nn. 128, 130.

265. For Jerusalem as the "murderer" of the prophets, see above, Part III.B, n. 133. There are three basic positions on the origin of the logion, vv. 34–35, as a "wisdom" saying: (1) Wisdom herself is being quoted (e.g., Steck, *Israel*, 230–31; and Bultmann, *Syn. Trad.*, 114–15). (2) The Q community has drawn upon Jewish wisdom sayings to formulate an utterance of Wisdom (for bibliog., cf. Marshall, *Luke*, 574). (3) A dominical saying has been preserved in which Jesus himself drew upon wisdom conceptions (e.g., Hoffmann, *Logienquelle*, 173–74). Cf. above, Part III.B, n. 143; Part III.A, n. 71.

266. See above, Part III.B, pp. 114–20.

267. I.e., about one half of the text.

268. For questions of tradition and redaction of the parable and its relation to the similar Matthean parable (Matt. 22:1–14), see Jeremias, *Parables,* 61–63, 65–67, 175–77 (see above, Part III.A, n. 97); Marshall, *Luke,* 584–87; and Fitzmyer, *Luke,* 2:1049–50. Although there is considerable agreement that the two forms go back to one earlier version or form, there is widespread disagreement concerning the stage at which this precursor can be reconstructed: oral, Q, or other pre-Evangelist redactor? A third variant is found in *GTh* 64.

269. This phrase has three possible referents, according to J. Ernst, "Gastmahlgespräche: Lk 14, 1–24," in *Die Kirche des Anfangs,* FS H. Schürmann, Erfurter Theologische Studien 38 (Leipzig: Sankt-Benno Verlag, 1978), 64: (1) a local synagogue president (cf. Luke 8:41; 13:14); (2) one of the leaders of the Pharisee movement; and (3) a Pharisee member of the Sanhedrin.

270. On 14:1, BAGD (παρατηρέω): "watch (maliciously)," "lie in wait for."

271. Cf. Luke 6:1–5, 6–11; 13:10–17.

272. Cf. above, Part III.A, nn. 60, 70, 111. Cf. *m. Šabb.* 16:2; *b. Šabb.* 117b, 118a, 118b; and Josephus, *Life* 279, for descriptions of the three prescribed meals on the Sabbath, the main meal around noon, called "the meal" *(s'wdh),* following the synagogue service when guests were often included (*b. Šabb.* 119a). On weekdays the Jewish people normally ate only two meals: "breakfast" *(ptšhryt, ἀκράτισμα, jentaculum)* sometime before or at noon, and the main meal of the day *(s'wdh, δεῖπνον, cena)* in the late afternoon. The breakfast was usually very light, salt and bread (e.g., *b. B. Meṣ.* 107b; cf. Str-B 2:204–5).

The scribes or "lawyers" usually did not make the effort to eat the first main meal or breakfast until noon, which then took on the larger proportions of the ἄριστον or *prandium* of the Romans; but as Billerbeck points out, "We hear in fact also about a snack which one would take early in the morning before attending the house of study" (p. 205). The ἄριστον of Luke 11:38 is probably the noon meal; if a Sabbath meal is meant, then it would be the major meal of the day comparable to the δεῖπνον or *cena.* Billerbeck also points out that it was only in the circles of the Rabbis and "well-to-do" Jews that the "breakfast" took on the proportions of the larger noon meal or *prandium* (cf., e.g., *Pesiq. R.* 16[81b]) as in Luke 11:37–54.

273. The wisdom character of Luke 14:7–11, 12–14 is marked. Cf. on the ordering of seating, e.g., Prov. 25:6: "Do not promote yourself in the king's presence; for it is better to be told, 'Come up here,' than to be put lower in the presence of the prince." Luke 14:8a reproduces a wisdom formula: e.g., Sir. 31:12: "When you sit at a great man's table . . ."; or Prov. 23:1. On Luke 14:22, cf. Sir. 3:17: "My son, in all your activity, be humble. . . . The greater you are, the humbler you should be; then you will find favor with God." Cf. also *Ep. Arist.* 263; James 4:6; 1 Peter 5:5; *1 Clem.* 30:2; Ign. *Eph.* 5:3; for further warnings against seeking rank, cf. Str-B 1:774, 914–15. On Luke 14:12–14, cf. *1 Enoch* 108, e.g., v. 10, commenting on the "poor" *('nwym)* of the psalms: "And he hath assigned them their recompense, because . . . though they were trodden underfoot of wicked men . . . yet they blessed me." Cf. *m. 'Abot.* 1:5: Jose ben Johanan of

Jerusalem (ca. 140 B.C.E.) said: "Let thy house be opened wide, and let the poor be thy household" (R. T. Herford). For commentary, cf. *'Abot R. Nat.* 7 (Str-B 2:206). For Greek views of the "poor" and "sick" included in a meal, cf., e.g., Plato, *Kriton* 53a; and Xenophon, *Symposion* I,15.

For the motif of the poor invited to meals in the OT, cf. esp. Deut. 14:29; 16:11, 14; 26:11 (cf. Reicke, *Diakonie,* 350–64; see esp. Part IV, "The Journeying Guest, Lord of the Banquet as the Prophet like Moses of Deuteronomy," below. L. C. Crockett ("The Old Testament in the Gospel of Luke: With Emphasis on the Interpretation of Isaiah 61.1–2" [diss., Brown University, 1966], 280ff.) demonstrates a highly developed Isaianic "banquet midrash" in which the "poor, the maimed, the lame, the blind" (e.g., Luke 14:13, 21) represent those of Isa. 61:1–6 (cf. Luke 4:18–19) and similar texts such as Isa. 58:6–8; 25:2–9; 56:4–7; 65:13–14, and 5:27—the "exiled" of Israel—who along with the Gentiles constitute the redeemed of the eschatological banquet. It is indeed this eschatological character and claim which distinguishes Jesus' sayings and Luke's entire scene from Jewish and secular parallels.

274. It has become common to speak about the "Lukan symposium" of 14:1–24 in order to explain the grouping of alleged disparate teaching material in the setting of a meal combined with a healing (e.g., Grundmann, *Lukas,* 290; and F. Hauck, *Das Evangelium nach Lukas,* THKNT 3 [Leipzig: Deichert, 1934], 187). Ernst ("Gastmahlgespräche," 57–63, 74–76) shows that the topics at table here— choice of guests, seating precedence, punishments for refusing an invitation, inviting the poor and infirm—are all common to the ancient symposium. See also E. S. Steele, "Luke 11:37–54—A Modified Hellenistic Symposium?" *JBL* 103 (1984): 379–94. Moreover, the parallels to Wisdom demonstrate the widespread interest in these themes in the ancient world. Given these facts, then, it does not necessarily follow, as Ernst, Grundmann, and others argue, that *Luke must* be credited with the structuring of 14:1–24 into such a "symposium." In any case, it is clear—whether from Luke or his sources—that there are many parallels between the structuring and course of Jewish meals and their subsequent *mischtītā* and the Greco-Roman symposium (cf. G. Dalman, *Jesus—Jeshua: Studies in the Gospels* [1929; reprint, New York: Ktav, 1971], 134 [cited by Ernst, 61]).

The topics at the table (14:7ff.) proceed directly from the larger story of Luke: Jesus has already warned both his disciples and the Pharisees against seeking precedence and religious pride—e.g., 9:46–50; 11:43—and he will warn the people again by using the scribes as example in 20:45–47. In 14:7–11, 12–14 in the same vein Jesus, using wisdom ideas, is criticizing a conception reflected in Qumran (e.g., table seating: 1QS 6:4–5; 1QSa 2:17–22; the "lame": 1QS 2:4ff.; 1QSa 2:4–10; CD 13:4–7; cf. 2 Sam. 5:8) in which the eschatological people of God exclude the "unclean." Jesus is therefore attacking the Pharisees' conception of their own fellowship, their meals, and their relationship to the eschatological messianic meal of the Kingdom of God (cf. the "excuses" of 14:18–19 reflecting Deut. 20:5–7 which "enriches" the Isaianic midrash; so Crockett, "Old Testament," 295–98). It should also be remembered that precisely in an eating and drinking context (7:33–50) Jesus aligns himself with the Wisdom of God.

275. Notice that κύριος is *not* used to describe the Pharisee host, either in Luke 11:37-54 or in 14:1-24.

276. Cf., e.g., Ernst, "Gastmahlgespräche," 70; Jeremias, *Parables,* 191-92; and Crockett, "Old Testament," 301-2.

277. For the history of interpretation of the "Great Banquet," see F. W. Beare, "The Parable of the Guests at the Banquet: A Sketch of the History of Its Interpretation," in *The Joy of Study,* FS F. C. Grant, ed. S. E. Johnson (New York: Macmillan Co., 1951), 1-14.

278. Cf. Ernst, "Gastmahlgespräche," 65.

279. πολλοί in 14:16, 24 points to the hindering influence of the Pharisees as enunciated by Jesus in 11:52; see esp. Part III.D, "The Leaven of the Pharisees-Scribes," below. Cf. Marshall (*Luke,* 586): "Jesus' comment on the 'pious' in Israel who neither entered the kingdom themselves nor allowed others to enter (11:52)."

280. See also Ernst, "Gastmahlgespräche," 68.

281. For parallels to the two peculiar Lukan parables (14:28-29, 31-32), cf. *GTh* 98.

282. See esp. Part III, "Conclusion," Excursus 3, below.

283. For the literary structure as a *chreia* similar to 13:1-9, cf. W. R. Farmer, "Notes on a Literary and Form-Critical Analysis of Some of the Synoptic Material Peculiar to Luke," *NTS* 8 (1961-62): 301-16.

284. Cf. the periphrastic and imperfect forms in 15:1-2. For possible interpretations of the time sequences within Luke's presentation, see Plummer, *Luke,* 367-68. Cf. above, n. 259.

285. "Against heaven and before you" (v. 21) summarizes the twofold thrust of the Law, esp. à la Deuteronomy; cf. Luke 10:27; 18:20.

286. Cf. Lydia's "entreating" Paul and Silas to come and stay with her in Acts 16:15; cf. 27:33.

287. For a synopsis of varying approaches, cf. Marshall, *Luke,* 614-15; and Fitzmyer, *Luke,* 2:1095-99.

288. Whether or not the steward technically had the authority to change the debtors' accounts is beside the point. It is clear that only after his dismissal does the steward instruct the promissory notes (τὰ γράμματα) to be altered, and only for the purpose of his own welfare (vv. 2-4). His commendation (v. 8) is hardly elicited because he put the master in a favorable light; cf. v. 8b: "shrewdness" is extolled, not generosity! Cf. J. D. M. Derrett, "Fresh Light on St Luke XVI,I: The Parable of the Unjust Steward," *NTS* 7 (1960-61): 198-219, esp. 216-17. Derrett musters considerable evidence that the steward of the large farm or *latifundium* (cf. Grundmann, *Lukas,* 317) had the authority to reduce the absentee landlord's bills, in this case the interest charged and due the landlord. The steward may have brought favor to the landlord, but this is hardly a point in the story of the parable.

289. Marshall (*Luke,* 621) refers to 1QS 3:14, where *drt* signifies character rather than a chronological succession. Cf. above, n. 274, for Jesus' teaching reflecting an anti-Qumran mentality.

290. A Semitic idiom; see Str-B 2:219.

291. Cf. 4 Ezra 2:11; and *1 Enoch* 39:4.

292. Cf., e.g., F. E. Williams, "Is Almsgiving the Point of the Unjust Steward?" *JBL* 83 (1964): 293–97.

293. Probably Essene communities are denoted by "sons of light." Outside the NT (John 12:36; 1 Thess. 5:5; cf. Eph. 5:8) the main occurrences are in Essene literature: *1 Enoch* 108:11; 1QS 1:9; 2:16; 3:13, 24–25; 1QM 1:3, 9, 11, 13.

294. See below, Part III.D, "The Leaven of the Pharisees-Scribes."

295. See Str-B 1:226 for citations which are relatively few, e.g., *Pesiq. R.* 43 (180b): the phrase can mean either a fellowship characterized by love (as of a child in a mother's bosom) and/or the fellowship of joy and blessedness (as of a meal in which the reclining participants' heads are near or upon the breast of the neighbor, e.g., John 13:23). See the tradition that Abraham was the first operator of an inn/restaurant (e.g., *Tg. Yer. I* Gen. 21:33).

296. Marshall, *Luke,* 637. For the suggestion that Lazarus represents a Gentile, based on Genesis 15 and the conjunction of "Abraham" with "Eliezer" (Lazarus), cf. C. H. Cave, "Lazarus and the Lukan Deuteronomy," *NTS* 15 (1968–69): 319–25. Cave rejects the basis of Deut. 24:6ff. and hence the parallel ordering suggested by Evans ("Central") and the lectionary parallel of A. Guilding (*The Fourth Gospel and Jewish Worship* [Oxford: Clarendon Press, 1960]) and suggests the theme of the "Gentiles putting Israel to shame" for the lack of the latter's repentance, as based on a lectionary reading for *Shabuoth* of Genesis 15 and Isaiah 1. On this reading, according to our plot, "Lazarus" the "poor man" would tie in with both the "poor" of Israel and the Gentiles of the "highways and hedges" of the "Great Banquet" of 14:15–24 (i.e., those who are in Abraham's bosom at the messianic feast while the "leaders" of Israel exclude themselves).

297. Steck, *Israel,* 101–2 n. 5; but see below, n. 343.

298. See above, Part II, "The Prophetic Parallels of Moses in Deuteronomy to Jesus in Luke 9:1–50."

299. Cf. Weiser, *Knechtsgleichnisse,* 105–12, for this "L" parable as stemming from Q.

300. See above, n. 288.

301. Cf. Luke 16:15a: ἐνώπιον τῶν ἀνθρώπων in context of the Pharisees' greed.

302. Marshall, *Luke,* 643.

303. Some regard this "L" pericope to be a Hellenized version of Mark (Mark 1:40–45 par. Luke 5:12–14) created by the church (cf., e.g., Bultmann, *Syn. Trad.,* 33; and Klostermann, *Lukas,* 173).

304. See above, Part I, n. 7.

305. Like Naaman the leper (2 Kings 5:10–14), the Samaritan along with the "nine" is healed from a distance with a delay to test his/their confidence in Jesus' authority.

306. On the history of tradition, see above, Part III.A, n. 78.

307. See C. H. Roberts, "The Kingdom of Heaven (Lk xvii. 21)," *HTR* 41 (1948): 1–8. Roberts draws attention to three papyri in which ἐντός has the sense "in the hands of," "within the power of," so that with ὑμῶν the import would be "within your reach or grasp" (cf. No. 1 of P. Ross, Georg. III, ca. 270 C.E.: "Send me the woolen jacket so that I may have it with me [ἐντός μου], p. 5 of Roberts). Subsequently in an interesting twist for our "journeying guest, Lord of the house"

story stuff, H. Riesenfeld ("'Εμβολεύειν—'Εντός") and A. Wikgren ("'ΕΝΤΟΣ," in *Nuntius* 4 [1950]: 27–28) established the sense of "in the house of" or "in the domain of" for the same papyri of Roberts to give the meaning "among you." Cf. above, Part III.A, n. 79.

308. Many exegetes view 18:8b if not 18:6–8 of this "L" parable as an addition by Luke (see, e.g., Marshall, *Luke*, 670). Whatever the history of the present text, all eight verses fit integrally into Luke's ongoing story.

309. Grundmann (*Lukas*, 355 n. 3) supposes that Luke 18:18–30 derives from an earlier form than Mark. Contra: e.g., Marshall, *Luke*, 686; Klostermann, *Lukas*, 181; Leaney, *Luke*, 237; and W. Manson, *Luke*, 204–6.

310. See above, pp. 150–53.

311. ἐξουθενέω: "despise, disdain" (s.v., BAGD); cf. Luke 23:11.

312. The inceptive imperfect emphasizes the disciples' hindering; see C. F. D. Moule, *An Idiom-Book of New Testament Greek*, 2d ed. (Cambridge University Press, 1971), 9.

313. "A member of the Sanhedrin or . . . the president of a synagogue" (Grundmann, *Lukas*, 354); cf. Schmid, *Lukas*, 284.

314. Jesus' challenge in 18:22 matches his challenge in 18:19. See above, Part III.B, pp. 120–27.

315. Cf. Luke 10:25–37!

316. Contra, e.g., Ellis (*Luke*, 217): "Peter represents the true disciple."

317. They have followed the requirement of Jesus in 9:59–62.

318. Cf. Marshall (*Luke*, 685) on the "ruler's" claim (v. 21): "The statement is not untypical of Pharisaic claims"; in addition to Luke 1:6; 18:11 and Phil. 3:6, he refers to Str-B 1:814–15.

319. Commentators generally hold to a Lukan revision of Mark 10:32–34 (e.g., Grundmann, *Lukas*, 355–56, though the shortened 18:31 along with Matt. 20:17 may reflect a more primitive stage; Marshall, *Luke*, 689–90; Danker, *Luke*, 302; and Fitzmyer, *Luke*, 2:1207–8: "inspired by "Mk," . . . considerably redacted by the Lukan pen"). Whatever the provenance of Luke's distinctive features, they certainly are organic to the developing plot.

320. Cf. Marshall, *Luke*, 690.

321. Cf. γάρ: v. 32.

322. See above, esp. Part III.A.3 (pp. 103–7); for fuller discussion, see below, Part III, "Conclusion," Excursus 2.

323. Cf., e.g., *Mek.* Exod 18:1 (65a) (Str-B 2:208). For a definition of "sinner," cf. *m. Sanh.* 3:3 (including a "usurer"—cf. Luke 19:8) and commentary, *b. Sanh.* 25b (including the tax collector!). On eating with "sinners," cf. *m. Dem.* 2:3 (Danby, 22): "He that undertakes to be an Associate . . . may not be the guest of an *Am-haaretz* nor may he receive him as a guest in his own raiment." Cf. *b. Ber.* 43b (Str-B 1:498): "Six things redound to the shame of the students of the scribes . . . he must not lie at table with people ignorant in the Law."

324. Cf. (LXX) Gen. 19:2: Lot and "angel" guests at Sodom; 24:23, 25: Abraham's servant, guest at Rebekah's father's home.

325. See the commentaries: e.g., Marshall, *Luke*, 697; Ellis, *Luke*, 221; and contra, Fitzmyer, *Luke*, 2:1224–25.

326. Cf., e.g., Plummer, *Luke,* 434–35; and Fitzmyer, *Luke,* 2:1225.

327. See above, Introduction, n. 11.

328. On Jewish regulation, cf. Str-B 4:546–47. Zacchaeus goes beyond that required by the Law (cf. Lev. 5:16; Num. 5:7) and in fact follows the restitution of sheep "rustlers," Exod. 22:1.

329. In all of his actions Zacchaeus is diametrically the opposite of the "unjust steward" of 16:1–9. Cf. Danker (*Luke,* 306): "In Luke's recital he is a living definition of the word 'repentance.'"

330. The contrast is also sharp with the "fool" rich man of 12:13–21 who revels in his wealth.

331. On the "house" as a center of a meal fellowship, see Acts 2:46; 9:9; 10:2; 12:12; 16:15, 31, 34; 21:10; cf. 5:42; 18:7; 20:7–12, 20. See below, Part V, "Reflections on the Theological Implications of the New Exodus Travel Narrative for Interpreting Luke-Acts."

332. See the commentaries: e.g., Marshall, *Luke,* 698; and Fitzmyer, *Luke,* 2:1226.

333. For a synopsis of the complex tradition history of this apparent "Q" parable, see, e.g., Marshall, *Luke,* 701–2; and Weiser, *Knechtsgleichnisse,* 255–58.

334. For the analogy to the experience of Archelaus, cf. Josephus, *War* 2.80–100; *Ant.* 17.299–320.

335. See esp. Part III.D, "The Leaven of the Pharisees-Scribes," pp. 197–207, below.

336. For the view that Luke's account is not entirely built upon Mark, cf. Manson, *Sayings,* 317; Schlatter, *Lukas,* 116–17, 408–12; Marshall, *Luke,* 709–11; Grundmann, *Lukas,* 366; and V. Taylor, *Behind the Third Gospel: A Study of the Proto-Luke Hypothesis* (Oxford: Clarendon Press, 1926), 94–95; contra, e.g., Fitzmyer, *Luke,* 2:1242–44.

337. Cf. 1QS 3:14, 18; 4:6, 11, 19, 26.

338. In the light of the journeying-guest context, Luke 11:53 should be included in the list of travel notices or journey indicators; cf. above, Part I, nn. 1, 2.

339. Note the rejection in the midst of profligate "eating and drinking" (17:27–28).

340. For a thorough and comprehensive style-critical analysis of Lukan sources in the Last Supper, see H. Schürmann, *Der Paschamahlbericht. Lk 22, (7–14.) 15–18;* idem, *Der Einsetzungsbericht. Lk 22, 18–20;* and idem, *Jesu Abschiedsrede. Lk 22,21–38: Einer quellenkritischen Untersuchung des lukanischen Abendmahls-berichtes. Lk 22, 7–38* (Münster: Aschendorff, 1953, 1955, 1957). The results of this exhaustive study: two pre-Lukan sources (Types 1 and 2) = 22:15–18, 19–20, 24–27, 28–30, 31–32, 35–38; Mark = vv. 7–14, 21–23, 33–34. Luke then made his own modifications in combining these sources.

341. Isa. 56:7; Jer. 7:11.

342. For a summary of Luke's use of *laos* in the Gospel, see below, Part III.Conclusion, Excursus 2.

343. See Steck, *Israel,* 279 n. 2. Because he has discerned neither the Deuteronomistic framework nor the plot of the Central Section, Steck thinks that Luke

is not familiar with the Deuteronomistic motif of the violent end of the prophets as "his redaction of the allegory of the wicked tenants in the vineyard, 20:9ff., demonstrates."

344. Cf. BAGD, s.v., on the use of the neuter μακρά.

345. To be sure, Satan and "mammon" join forces!

346. Note the ironic fulfillment of παραδίδωμι (12:58).

347. Conzelmann, *Theology,* 75–76.

348. In addition to commentaries, see esp. J. Wanke, *Beobachtungen zum Eucharistieverständnis des Lukas auf Grund der lukanischen Mahlberichte,* Erfurter Theologische Schriften 8 (Leipzig: Sankt-Benno Verlag, 1973), 31–59; and W. Bösen, "Das Mahlmotiv bei Lukas: Studien zum lukanischen Mahlverständnis unter besonderer Berücksichtigung von Lk 22,14–20" (diss., Saarland, 1976), 279–89, 373–92.

349. ἀναπίπτω; cf. also Mark 6:40; John 13:12.

350. So, e.g., J. Jeremias, *The Eucharistic Words of Jesus* (London: SCM Press, 1966), 133–53. Schürmann (*Einsetzungsbericht,* esp. 82–135) comes to the completely opposite conclusion (cf. Jeremias, 181–89) regarding the primitiveness of the longer reading (p. 133). Our thesis is independent of the longer or shorter reading.

351. See esp. M. Barth, *Das Abendmahl: Passamahl, Bundesmahl und Messiasmahl,* Theologische Studien 18 (Zollikon-Zurich: Evangelischer Verlag 1945), 25–39.

352. Cf., e.g., Marshall, *Luke,* 807; Ellis, *Luke,* 251; and P. E. Leonard ("Luke's Account of the Lord's Supper Against the Background of Meals in the Ancient Semitic World and More Particularly Meals in the Gospel of Luke" [diss., University of Manchester, 1976], p. 245): "To eat with God in Exodus is to participate in the covenant—to be admitted into the presence of God and to 'behold him' (Exod. 24:11)."

353. On the themes of the "Servant" of Isaiah and Luke 22:20, cf. Schürmann, *Einsetzungsbericht,* 99–100; Jeremias, *Eucharistic Words,* 216–23; and Leonard, "Luke's Account," 229–32.

354. On the apocalyptic sense of "trials" within the context of "testamentary disposition," see Marshall, *Luke,* 814–15.

355. In Luke 22:32 Peter is told to "strengthen" his "brothers." In 12:42–43 Peter's objection is redirected by Jesus to one who "feeds" the others.

356. See the commentaries: e.g., Marshall (*Luke,* 824): "He [Luke] is drawing here on the source which included the charge in ch. 10"; and Manson, *Sayings,* 341.

357. Alternatively τέλος ἔχειν can mean "to come to an end" (cf. BAGD, s.v. "τέλος," 1.a). The overall force of the verse in the context of death is the same; as Jesus' life ends, the Scripture is fulfilled.

358. Manson (*Sayings,* 342): "There can be only one end to His ministry; and that is the end foreshadowed in the fifty-third chapter of Isaiah."

359. P. S. Minear, *To Heal and to Reveal: The Prophetic Vocation According to Luke* (New York: Seabury Press, 1976), 129: "It is not impossible that Luke's

arrangement of the extensive table talk in the Upper Room was influenced by his idea of Jesus as a second Moses engaged in the deliverance of Israel from bondage" (cf. esp. pp. 102–21, where Minear draws together Mosaic parallels to Jesus). For the Mosaic character of the Servant, see von Rad, *Old Testament Theology*, 2:261–62; for the intertestamental period, see Vermès ("Gestalt des Moses," 74–86), who summarizes the Palestinian pseudepigraphical literature (p. 80): "The one who Deutero-Isaiah describes as the main figure of the New Exodus, the Servant of Yahweh—who suffers and dies for the sins of his people—can be none other than the 'new Moses,' who in detail most closely parallels Moses of the Scriptures."

360. Apart from the enigmatic nature of the "sword" sayings in 22:36, 38, the thrust of the "table talk" is to show not only the disciples' misunderstanding and captive thinking but also their unwitting but complete involvement in the treachery against Jesus. As P. S. Minear ("A Note on Luke xxii 36," *NovT* 7 [1964–65]: 130–31) points out, Jesus' prophecies at table are all fulfilled through the disciples in the immediately following scenes. So in vv. 35–38 when Jesus predicts that Isa. 53:12 will be fulfilled and uses the present tense ("is finding its fulfillment/end"), one should not be surprised to find the disciples immediately fulfilling this prophecy too. It is clear that when the *disciples* (pl.) produce a *sword* (vv. 49–50), they match Jesus' description of Judas and the arresting party (v. 52: *"swords"; cf.* "no more of this," v. 51a).

The "but now" of v. 36 therefore is denoting the changed situation of the disciples to Jesus in which they are no longer *one* with him "in my trials" (v. 28), but in fact are fulfilling Isa. 53:12 in Jesus' fate. Like Moses, Jesus does not escape the perfidy of his own people.

361. Cf. *b. Sanh.* 43b, and comment of C. H. Dodd, *Historical Tradition in the Fourth Gospel* (Cambridge: Cambridge University Press, 1963), 117 n. 1.

362. Cf. Jeremias, *Jerusalem,* 110.

363. For a thorough treatment of the literary-redactional questions of Luke 24:13–35, see J. Wanke, *Die Emmauserzählung: Eine redaktionsgeschichtliche Untersuchung zu Lk 24, 13–35,* Erfurter Theologische Studien 31 (Leipzig: Sankt-Benno Verlag, 1973). For parallels to the other Lukan meals, see Bösen, *Mahlmotiv,* 373–83; and Wanke, *Beobachtungen,* 31–44. For the unlikely suggestion that the Emmaus story was originally part of a longer ending to Mark, see N. Huffmann, "Emmaus Among the Resurrection Narratives," *JBL* 64 (1945): 205–26.

364. Literally, "they stood still" (v. 17b).

365. See esp. P. Schubert, "The Structure and Significance of Luke 24," in *Neutestamentliche Studien für Rudolf Bultmann,* BZNW 21 (Berlin: A. Töpelmann, 1954).

366. Cf. Acts 16:15: Lydia strongly urges Paul and Silas to "stay" in her "house."

367. Scholars generally agree that the "recognition" element forms the core of the tradition. See, e.g., J. Wanke, "'. . . wie sie ihn beim Brotbrechen erkannten': Zur Auslegung der Emmauserzählung Lk 24, 13–35," *BZ* 18 (1974): 180–92;

Wanke points out that "Emmaus" accents neither the (1) continuity of the crucified Jesus with the Resurrected One who disappears suddenly nor (2) a missionary commission, i.e., neither of the two themes deemed by form criticism as
constitutive of the resurrection appearance narratives (p. 180); cf. J. Dupont,
"The Meal at Emmaus," in *The Eucharist in the New Testament: A Symposium,*
by J. Delorme and others (Baltimore: Helicon Press, 1964), 105–21. On liturgical
influence, see R. Orlett, "An Influence of the Early Liturgy Upon the Emmaus
Account," *CBQ* 21 (1959): 212–19.

368. I.e., both the plot motivation and the framing of the story.

369. On revelation tied to the passives, see A. Ehrhardt, "The Disciples of
Emmaus," *NTS* 10 (1963–64): 183–85. Ehrhardt rejects the genre of the "dis-
guised wandering of [a] god" in preferring an "*epiphaneia* to wanderers," like the
Greek myth of Romulus (pp. 193–95). Cf. Dupont ("The Meal at Emmaus," 111):
"the edifying or moving story"; he compares the genre to John 20:11–17.

370. For the stress on this continuity in the view that Jesus' oath in Luke 22:16,
18 is fulfilled in the postresurrection meals, see Barth, *Abendmahl,* 39–51.

371. Note the accent on "power" (δύναμις, δυνατός) in Luke 24:19 and 10:13,
19, both within the conceptual canopy of Jesus the prophet who reveals himself!

372. This "appearance" exhibits both rudiments of the "typical" resurrection
episode: (1) continuity of Jesus as resurrected Lord (24:36–43); and (2) mission
charge (24:44–53). See Marshall, *Luke,* 900–901, 903–4.

373. Cf. Barth (*Abendmahl,* 40): "The messianic meal is to be a meal of
jubilation." See esp. Part IV, "The Journeying Guest, Lord of the Banquet as the
Prophet like Moses of Deuteronomy," below.

374. Cf. Steck, *Israel,* 143–44.

375. E.g., Bar. 2:20, 24; 4QDib Ham 3:12ff.; cf. Steck, *Israel,* 122 n. 1, 140 n. 5,
222; cf. 193–95.

376. Cf. esp. Part III.B, pp. 115–19, 128–29, above.

377. Tenet C (16:30–31) implies tenet D.

378. Tenet D is also foreshadowed in 10:12, 13–15.

379. The disciples' leaders are called "apostles" in 5:18, 29.

380. See, e.g., Str-B 2:527, 636–39, for rabbinic references: e.g., *m. Sota* 9:15:
"When Rabban Gamaliel the Elder died, the glory of the Law ceased and purity
and abstinence died" (Danby); Jeremias, *Jerusalem,* 241–43, 254–56; B. Reicke,
The New Testament Era (Philadelphia: Fortress Press, 1968), 150–52, 159, 162–
63, 189. On νομοδιδάσκαλος (Luke 5:17; 1 Tim. 1:7), see K. H. Rengstorf (*TDNT*
2:159): the term is "designed to mark off Jewish from Christian teachers."

381. Acts 14:14.

382. Luke 11:45–52.

383. In Acts 19:35 γραμματεύς is used for the town "clerk" of Ephesus.

384. Only in Luke (5:30) do the Pharisees-scribes criticize the disciples'
behavior; cf. Mark 2:16; Matt. 9:11.

385. On the prohibition of the Pharisees'-scribes' students (disciples) from
eating and drinking with "the people of the land," cf. *b. Ber.* 43b.

386. Cf. *Mek.* Exod. 31:14(109b): "The Sabbath is given over to you [Israel]
and not you to the Sabbath" (quoted by Marshall, *Luke,* 232).

387. Though stated in principle in Luke 5:31–32, 34–35.

388. See BAGD on κατηγορέω.

389. Cf. Marshall, *Luke,* 214, referring to H. W. Beyer, *TDNT* 1:621–25.

390. See, e.g., J. A. Ziesler, "Luke and the Pharisees," *NTS* 25 (1978–79): 146–57; cf. Grundmann, *Lukas,* 135.

391. Marshall, *Luke,* 236.

392. Ziesler, "Pharisees," 148–49.

393. Cf. Marshall, *Luke,* 733; and Fitzmyer, *Luke,* 2:1294.

394. See BAGD, s.v. "παρατηρέω," on Luke 20:20.

395. Luke 18:18, most likely a Pharisee. See above, Part III.C, nn. 313, 318. It is very unlikely that a Sadducee would sincerely inquire into inheriting eternal life.

396. "Who say that there is no resurrection" is in the triple tradition (Mark 12:18; Matt. 22:23).

397. Cf. δίκαιος, v. 20.

398. For ὁδός as God's requirement for human beings, see Acts 18:26; cf., e.g., Deut. 8:6; 10:12–13; Ps. 27:11; CD 20:18; 1QS 3:10, "to walk perfectly in all the ways of God which he commanded concerning the times appointed for him."

399. Cf., e.g., Marshall (*Luke,* 738): "Pharisaic types of discussion"; J. B. Tyson, *The Death of Jesus in Luke-Acts* (Columbia, S.C.: University of South Carolina Press, 1986), 64–72.

400. For this technique and conjunction of the other questions put to Jesus in the Jerusalem ministry, see D. Daube, *The New Testament and Rabbinic Judaism* (London: Athlone Press, 1956), 158–69.

401. They use the same tack of complimenting Jesus' teaching as the "spies" do in 20:21.

402. And cf. the Pharisee of 18:9–14, Part III.C.21, above.

403. Note also the similar contrast of the "rich" to the "poor" in 21:1–4 as in 16:14–15, 19–31.

404. See Reicke, *New Testament Era,* 146–52.

405. See above, Part III.C, "The Journeying Guest Is Received (Luke 24:13–53)."

406. Only in this way can it be said that Luke "softens" the role of the Pharisees in opposing Jesus (*pace* Ziesler, "Pharisees," e.g., 154–55).

407. Esp. Luke 21:20–24; on these and tenet D, see now Moessner, "Paul in Acts" (see Part III.B, n. 137).

408. See the three aorist verbs of 11:52—ἤρατε, εἰσήλθατε, ἐκωλύσατε. Luke is describing a definitive influence which at this stage in the plot is portrayed as irrevocable; cf. Plummer (*Luke,* 315): "The aorists indicate what was done once for all and absolutely" (cf. M. Black, *An Aramaic Approach to the Gospels and Acts,* 3d ed. [Oxford: Clarendon Press, 1967], 129, 260—the Aramaic perfect).

409. Cf. esp. Part III.C.7 and 8, above.

410. For the substantive connections of this "baptism" to the baptism of Jesus in Luke 3 and in Acts, see M. Barth, *Die Taufe—Ein Sakrament?: Ein exegetischer Beitrag zum Gespräch über die kirchliche Taufe* (Zollikon-Zurich: Evangelischer, 1951), 37–101, 133–85, esp. 37–41.

411. Danker (*Luke,* 260): "It is apparent that Pharisaic casuistry is a primary issue."

412. See esp. Part III, "Conclusion," Excursus 2, below.

413. See above, Part III.C.12.

414. Cf. above, n. 410.

415. That is, "everyone tries to force" = "everyone is forced to force"; cf. J. H. Moulton and G. Milligan, *The Vocabulary of the Greek Testament* (London: Hodder & Stoughton, 1930), 110.

416. S.v., BAGD; Moulton and Milligan, 110.

417. Cf. Luke 3:18; Acts 1:22.

418. Cf. Lagrange, *Luc,* 440.

419. Cf. Marshall, *Luke,* 631.

420. I.e., by being unfaithful with God's riches (both material and spiritual) they forfeit their inheritance in the Kingdom of (Abraham) God.

421. For a history of the traditions, see Marshall, *Luke,* 640–44; and Fitzmyer, *Luke,* 2:1136–47.

422. Marshall (*Luke,* 641): "The curious feature is the uniform use of οὗτος in the phrase presumably referring to people present."

423. For discussion, see W. G. Kümmel, *Promise and Fulfilment: The Eschatological Message of Jesus* (London: SCM Press, 1957), 93–95.

424. E.g., Manson, *Sayings,* 138 (see Part III.B, n. 143).

425. The list in Luke 7:22 partially overlaps that in 14:13, 21.

426. Cf. Kümmel (*Promise and Fulfilment,* 94): "Jesus by this altogether unusual expression meant none other than 'the poor' of the first beatitude . . . the same meaning as μικρότερος in Luke 9:48."

427. Marshall (*Luke,* 676): "A somewhat abrupt shift."

428. Cf. Josephus (*War* 1.110) on the Pharisees: δοκοῦν εὐσεβέστερον εἶναι τῶν ἄλλων.

429. *y. Ber.* 4.7d, 31; οἱ λοιποί = primarily the *'am ha'aretz* (see the commentaries).

430. See above, Part III.C.21.

431. Marshall (*Luke,* 688): "The idea of material loss and reward is not present in Lk."

432. Yet their selection is ultimately God's doing, as the passive of κρύπτω in 18:34 suggests, a verse unique to Luke (cf. commentaries). J. Jervell (*Luke and the People of God: A New Look at Luke-Acts* [Minneapolis: Augsburg Publishing House, 1972], 86–89) argues that Luke must demonstrate the validity of both Jesus' messiahship and his resurrection; therefore, independently of Jesus' calling and fate, witnesses are needed to testify. "Consequently, it must be shown that their authority goes back further than Jesus, namely, to God himself" (p. 89). Cf. also the passives in the "Emmaus" story, 24:16.

433. E.g., the mission tours of 9:1–6 and 10:1–20; the "feeding" of the five thousand (9:10–17).

434. The kingdom will "appear" (ἀναφαίνω, 19:11b) shortly.

435. See above, p. 193.

436. For this link with Hab. 2:11, see Schlatter, *Lukas,* 409–10.

437. Notice how a meal setting/parable is central to each stage; see esp. Part III, "Conclusion," Excursus 3, below.

438. For a general treatment of this technique, see J. A. Baird, *Audience Criticism and the Historical Jesus* (Philadelphia: Westminster Press, 1969); and A. W. Mosley, "Jesus' Audiences in the Gospels of St Mark and St Luke," *NTS* 10 (1963–64): 139–49.

439. Luke 10:23 may indicate that Jesus' prayer and exultation in vv. 21–22 were near or in the midst of crowds.

440. See P. S. Minear, "Jesus' Audiences According to Luke," *NovT* 16 (1974): 101.

441. Cf. παραλαμβάνω—18:31 (cf. BAGD, s.v.: "Private instruction"); the "disciples" receive private teaching in 10:23–24.

442. Depending on the audience of 17:11–19.

443. See the chart of the dramatis personae, Part I, "The Dissonance of Form from Content," above.

444. In 19:27–28 two disciples are set apart for a specific function.

445. If the audience is interpreted as the disciples in 17:11–19, then 15:1—18:17 is engaged entirely in this exchange.

446. We know from 19:35–36 that at that point the Pharisees are part of the great procession of the crowds.

447. Cf. Luke 18:18–30; 19:1–10—the crowds as "backdrop" audience.

448. The nine lepers who do not "repent" remain "faceless," thus representing the anonymous mass of the crowds who likewise do not repent, even though like the lepers they consider Jesus a "great teacher" (cf. ἐπιστάτα, 17:13b).

449. They appear in every chapter except chap. 9.

450. Luke 24:19b.

451. Cf. Jervell, *Luke,* 97–98; esp. p. 78: "Everything happens in public, while all Israel watches."

452. Jervell (*Luke,* 78): "In general, the apostles play a notably passive role during Jesus' earthly life." Jervell's comparison with Matthew and Mark (p. 78), however, on the role of the Twelve is specious; only in Acts do the Twelve play an important part as apostles.

453. Cf. the larger group of "disciples" that are gathered as the Seventy(-two) report back, 10:23–24.

454. Cf. the wavering or lapsing of 17:3b–4.

IV

*Jesus the Deuteronomistic
Rejected Prophet as the Prophet
like Moses of Deuteronomy*

IV

Our investigation in Part III yielded the coherent drama of the Deuter-onomistic journeying-guest Prophet who is not received by the people of all Israel. Contemporary critical theories that maintain an unmitigating dissonance of form from content for the story of Jesus' journeying (Part I) must now in the light of our analysis be judged as inadequate estimations of this unique and decisive portion of the Lukan corpus. We now intend to show how the fourfold Moses-Exodus-Deuteronomy typology (Part II) is constitutive of the overall literary-theological framework for this spe-cial story. It shall become even clearer how the vast teaching sections of the Central Section do not represent static heaps of disconnected tradi-tion but, on the contrary, form integral movements of the dynamic. In Part III we noticed that in both Josephus and Qumran distinctive traits from the portrait of Moses in Deuteronomy have been interpreted through the conceptual sieve of the Deuteronomistic perspective of Israel's history. We now contend that in the Central Section of Luke, *tradition portraits of the Moses of Deuteronomy have converged with the Deuteronomistic view.* What sets the Central Section apart from its coun-terparts is the development of a consistent typology based on the Moses of Deuteronomy *to form a coherent drama of a New Exodus for the Prophet Jesus who is the prophet like Moses* (Deut. 18:15–19; Acts 3:22–23; 7:37).

The FOURFOLD MOSES-EXODUS-DEUTERONOMY TYPOLOGY *as the* LITERARY-THEOLOGICAL FRAMEWORK *for the* CENTRAL SECTION

Though methodologically we have derived the Deuteronomistic por-trait of the prophet in Luke 9:51—19:44 independently of the fourfold Moses-Deuteronomy typology evident in 9:1–50, our exegesis of the former has shown how intricately interwoven this mountain calling is to the subsequent journey.

A. In this first of four tenets it became clear that the crowds that come out to see Jesus and eventually follow him to Jerusalem constitute a stubborn, disobedient nation that, like their forebears, does not hearken to the voice of God in his mediator. The beginning, the middle, and the end of the Central Section disclose the same faithless and twisted generation that *Jesus confronts as he descends the mountain in 9:37ff.* Consequently the first of the double-stroke leitmotiv of Deuteronomy is constitutive for 9:51—19:44 as well.

B. Jesus is the teacher par excellence, the voice of God that fulfills "Moses and all the prophets." Depending upon how one hearkens to this "Voice," the Son, who speaks with the authority of the author of the Law, determines whether one receives the life of the covenant law. The full content and infrastructure of the Central Section evinces this life-giving function of Jesus' voice: Beginning and ending with journey episodes that stress the authority of Jesus' sending to Jerusalem as the ultimate voice of God's will, the Central Section is dominated by the words of Jesus framed by the Deuteronomic pillars 10:25 and 18:20. Jesus delivers eschatological *halakah* as he exhorts the people to obedience and warns them to repent. Throughout this prophetic activity we encounter an unmistakable and unbreakable chain of *sending* and *hearkening* which links the voice of the mountain all the way to Jerusalem, where this voice is ensconced as the teacher of Israel. Like the voice of God through Moses, Jesus utters the very salvation or life of the covenant law *as he journeys from the mountain.* Once again one of the moments of the fourfold career of Moses in Deuteronomy is constitutive of Luke 9:1—19:44: "Hearken to him."

C. Jesus' journey not only leads to his death but is itself a journey of rejection. As the journeying Prophet, Jesus, in his sending to utter the voice of God, is rejected, and as the journeying-guest Prophet, Jesus is not received as he progresses from Galilee all the way to the nation's heart. It is because of "this generation's" refusal to be gathered as a repentant, obedient people that the journeying-guest Prophet must die in Jerusalem. It is a telling indicator that every one of the references to the *end* that awaits Jesus is in a journeying or "eating and drinking" context. His journey is itself an exodus of death. Like Moses, then, the generation "of human hands" (Luke 9:44) that *awaits Jesus as he descends the mountain* is the stubborn generation that makes his death an absolute (divine) necessity, the second of the double-stroke leitmotiv of Deuteronomy.

D. Alongside the growing rejection, there is a stream of "children" who hearken to Jesus' voice, and like the "today" of Deuteronomy,[1] "today" receive the exodus-journey salvation. These "least" exhibit the same posture that Jesus declares is characteristic of the "least" *among the disciples at the mountain.* Like the children of Horeb, then, these child-like ones receive the salvation of the exodus-journey while the "evil" generation brings upon itself the wrath of God. As Jesus proceeds from the mountain and like Moses leads all Israel to the promised fulfillment, he gathers a repentant *laos* from the Horeb covenant *laos* who inherit the promises of Abraham, Isaac, and Jacob (Luke 13:22).[2] But as the journey reaches its goal in Jerusalem, the whole faithless and twisted *laos* of the covenant mountain deliver Jesus to death. Just as Moses, so Jesus must die for the sake of "all"—stiff-necked and childlike alike. But again as Luke continues his story it becomes manifest that as in Deuteronomy *Jesus' death like Moses' brings the promised salvation only to the "children" of the mountain.* Only those who hearken to Jesus the prophet like Moses "inherit" the life of the exodus salvation, while the rest are cut off from the people (Acts 3:22–23). As it was true of the wilderness people at the border of the Promised Land, so it is true again that "whoever does not receive the Kingdom of God like a child shall not enter it" (Luke 18:17; cf. Deut. 1:39).

We therefore conclude that the calling and fate of the Moses of Deuteronomy is constitutive for the Deuteronomistic rejected journeying-guest Prophet. The career of Moses has indeed converged with the career of Jesus, who fulfills "all the prophets" "beginning with Moses" (Luke 24:27). As he is sent on a New Exodus, Jesus brings the promises of the covenant life to fulfillment precisely as he is rejected by an unrepenting people. The double-stroke leitmotiv of Deuteronomy is thus the driving force of Luke's plotting of the anointed prophet sent to Israel in the Central Section (tenets A—D). And the fourfold typology serves as the linchpin or overall frame within which this dynamic story is enacted. The rationale for all of this is not hard to discover, since Deuteronomy itself at 18:15–19 prophesies through Moses of one who, *like* himself and *according to Moses' own calling from the mountain,* will mediate the words of the Lord to the people: *(a)* Jesus is "like me" (18:15a)[3] in the calling and fate of the prophet who himself is *(b)* one "of the brethren" of Israel (18:15a).[4] *(c)* Like the trauma on the mountain, when the people feared for their lives as they heard the voice of the Lord and saw the great fire, so the people are now again to hearken to Jesus ("to him") "so that they shall not die" (18:15b–16).[5] *(d)* "Like you" (Moses), Jesus shall have "my [i.e., God's] words in his mouth" (v. 18b).[6] *(e)* Jesus "shall speak" to the people as God "commands him" (v. 18c).[7] *(f)* Finally, as it was true of Moses that "whoever shall not hearken to whatever words that prophet shall speak in my name I will take vengeance on that one" (v. 19), so it is true of Jesus whose speaking "in my name" leads to the recompense of God (tenet D).[8]

Luke then presents the journeying Jesus of the Central Section as *the Prophet like Moses of Deut. 18:15–19*. But at the same time that Jesus fulfills this prophecy—"written" by the prophet Moses—he is greater than Moses. Already before Jesus ascends the mountain it is clear that he is not one of "the prophets of bygone days" who "has arisen" (Luke 9:19). And as "all Israel" with Moses and Elijah testifies to Jesus' calling on the mountain, it becomes clear that Jesus is neither of these two prophets redivivus. His exodus surely cannot be simply a recapitulation of that first Exodus deliverance. For the disciples see Jesus' glory (9:32) as he stands with Moses and Elijah, who themselves have appeared in glory (9:31). Rather, Jesus' exodus is a journey from the glory of the mountain to the glory "of the Father and of the holy angels" in the Kingdom of God (9:26 → 9:51 → 24:26).[9]

Even as his transfiguration anticipates his resurrection-exaltation and parousia,[10] so does Jesus' *journey*. His coming to Jerusalem already precipitates the eschatological judgment upon those whom he meets. Not to be prepared to submit to his voice is to bring the judgment greater than Sodom and Gomorrah. For Jesus utters the eschatological fulfillment of the words of Moses in the Horeb covenant law (cf. 10:25; 18:20), and his eating and drinking already manifests the eating and drinking "before the Lord" in the fulfilled salvation of the New Exodus (see below). Jesus journeys, then, as the one like but greater than Moses. As he dies on account of the whole people, he brings them life. But he does not bring this life by dying and passing on his journey deliverance to a human successor like Joshua. Rather, he is "raised up" from the dead from "among his brethren" to send them the power from on high, the Spirit of the last days (24:46, 49; Acts 1:2, 4–5). This Spirit had already been present with Jesus and experienced by the disciples who submitted to Jesus as he journeyed as guest. Now as Jesus' baptism of death is completed (12:50)[11] in his journey-resurrection-ascension-exaltation, so also the disciples are baptized by this Spirit to begin a new but nevertheless continuing journey of the journeying-guest Prophet (Acts 1:5, 8; 3:20, 26).[12]

Jesus' exodus journey thus bursts the fourfold analogies with Moses' Exodus. But Israel's Exodus has now been fulfilled (9:31). For that reason "this crooked generation" (Acts 2:48) find themselves in the unparalleled situation of having a second chance to hearken to the voice of the Son in his Spirit-filled apostles.[13] Though they "killed the author of life," they "acted in ignorance" and thereby actually fulfilled what "all the prophets" had declared (Acts 3:15, 17–18).[14] As "offspring therefore of the prophets" and "of the covenant" of Abraham and the patriarchs, they must now repent (Acts 3:19, 25). For the first time they stand at that moment in Israel's history of which Moses and all the prophets who came afterward proclaimed—the coming of the Prophet like Moses (Acts 3:17–24). Jesus' journey then is a recapitulation but also a consummation. Jesus fulfills the type of Moses, but yet he stands unique. But all of that is to say that as the Prophet like Moses, Jesus is the Christ of God, the one from the mountain (Luke 9:20b) who must journey to suffer in order that he might enter into his glory (Luke 9:20b → 22:67 → 24:26, 44–46; Acts 2:31; 3:17, 20, 22–24).

The JOURNEYING GUEST, LORD *of the* BANQUET
as the PROPHET *like* MOSES *of* DEUTERONOMY

We have shown that the Deuteronomistic view of a prophet in Israel's history forms the conceptual girders for the journeying guest, and that as building blocks of the story the latter motif refracts the telltale shades and shadows of "all the prophets." But what connection does a meal on a journey have with a rejected prophet? What does "eating and drinking" in the presence of the Lord (Luke 13:25) have to do with the sending and tragic fate of all the prophets? The Prophet like Moses of Deuteronomy provides the missing link.

In Deuteronomy the goal of all of Moses' journeying with the people to the Promised Land is to inherit the blessings of the covenant to Abraham, Isaac, and Jacob as summed up by "eating" and "rejoicing" before the Lord. This goal is discernible from three main vantage points.

The Description of the Land

1. The first act upon entering the salvation of the land is to write the Law upon stones erected on Mt. Ebal, and there with a peace offering "eat and be filled and rejoice before the Lord" (Deut. 27:7). That is to say, the land is viewed as the fulfilling of all the blessings or inheritance of life promised to Israel's ancestors. For before entering the land, the people had not received the "rest" (12:9), that dwelling with the Lord in peace and harmony with his Law, safe from all their enemies (11:12).[15]

2. The land itself is repeatedly envisioned as "flowing with milk and honey" (6:3; 8:8; 11:9; 26:9–10, 15; 27:3; 31:20; 32:13–14).

3. Set apart and reserved for the people of Israel, the land is specifically contrasted to Egypt as a land of plenty where every need and particularly food will be fulfilled: "You will not eat your bread with want, and you will not lack anything. . . . For you shall eat and be filled and bless the Lord

your God upon this good land which he has given to you" (8:9–10; cf. vv. 7–8). "For the land into which you are entering to inherit is not like the land of Egypt . . . but the land shall drink water of the rain of heaven" (11:10–11).

4. Wine or "strong drink" is particularly symbolic for all of the blessing of the land. Along with eating the sacrifices of oxen and sheep, it represents that which most satisfies the "desire of the soul" (14:25–26) as one rejoices ($εὐφραίνω$, 14:26) before the Lord. It epitomizes what is most sublime in the land vis-à-vis all foreign lands.[16] For instance, during the wilderness wanderings, "You did not *eat* bread, you did not *drink* wine or strong drink" (29:6a). All of Israel's enemies in fact are characterized by their foul and bitter wine: "Their grape is a grape of gall, their cluster is one of bitterness. Their wine is the rage of serpents and the incurable rage of asps" (32:32–33). And as Moses looks ahead and prophesies Israel's punishment in exile, he distills the blessings of the land by describing "Jacob" as one who "had drunk wine, the blood of the grape" (32:14b).

In sum, to drink wine is to honor or fear the Lord by rejoicing in all of the gracious covenant blessings of the land (e.g., 14:23b).

The Central Section of Deuteronomy

The large "legal" section, Deuteronomy 12—26, evidences this same goal of *eating* and *drinking* and *rejoicing* before the Lord as the fulfillment of salvation in the land.

1. Indicative of the primacy of "eating" and "rejoicing" is the frequency with which both terms are commanded of the people in order to regulate and provide meaning for their life in the land.

$φάγω$—12:7, 15, 18, 20–21, 27; 14:23, 26, 29; 15:20, 22; 16:3, 7–8; 18:1, 8; 26:12. Of these seventeen occurrences in the imperative,[17] eleven enjoin this eating to take place at the central place or "the place which the Lord shall choose" (e.g., 12:5), that is, Jerusalem.[18] $εὐφραίνω$—12:7, 12, 18; 14:26; 16:11, 14, 15; 26:11, 12.[19] Of those nine instances, eight refer to "the place" in which this "rejoicing" is the sum and substance of "eating."

2. This injunction dominates the beginning of the middle section. Immediately following the commandment to destroy all foreign gods once they enter the land (12:2–4) is the positive counterpart (v. 5a): they are to seek out the Lord at the place where his "name" is present by journeying there ($ἔρχομαι$) to eat their sacrifices and offerings and to rejoice in all the things with which the Lord has blessed them (12:7). The whole of Deuteronomy 12 asserts the importance of this true worship of

the Lord in contrast to "following" (v. 30) the gods of the nations. Hand in hand, then, with the great Deuteronomic plea for the single and solitary devotion to Yahweh and his commandments is the effective consummation of this devotion by eating and rejoicing at the one place which the Lord shall choose. The seminal location of this injunction is fully in line with the explicit rationale for this form of worship: the central place is symbolic of the fulfilled covenant promises when the whole of the Law of the Lord is heeded. "Only in the place which the Lord your God shall choose in one of your tribes, there you shall offer your whole burnt offerings and there you shall *do* (ποιέω) *all the things that I command you today"* (σήμερον) (v. 14). Again at the end of this chapter the rationale for eating at the central place is given: "You shall do all the things that I command you in order that it may be well with you and with your children forever" (v. 28).

3. The act of eating and rejoicing as an expression of covenant loyalty and worship of Yahweh at the "place" is carried out "before the Lord" (ἐναντίον κυρίου;[20] ἐνώπιον).[21] It is this presence of the Lord that is described as "his name" which is to be called upon there.[22] Thus the consummate worship of the Lord in eating and rejoicing before the Lord takes place where his presence is accessible and manifest.[23]

4. Although the injunction to eat and drink wine and rejoice is presented by Moses to "all Israel," the basic unit for fulfilling this command is the "household."

a. Once Israel has crossed over into the land, their life is pictured frequently as distinct households especially within the cities of the former inhabitants.[24] Typical of the role and goal of the household with respect to obedience to the Law and hence life in the land is 19:1: "And when the Lord your God shall have destroyed the nations, that is, when he gives you the land and you inherit it and you dwell in their cities (πόλεις) and in their houses (οἶκοι), you must . . ."[25]

b. Each household unit is responsible for teaching the Law to its children (6:7, 9; 11:19–20). Commensurate with this, much of the legislation treats relations within and between households or society in general (e.g., 12:7; 14:26; 15:16, 20). Moreover, the household is responsible for ensuring that future generations know the true significance of heeding the Law: because Israel was brought forth from "the house of slavery" to the land of promise to live, they must now inherit this promise by heeding the commandments which alone is life (see esp. 6:1–25; cf. 5:6, 15; 7:8; 8:14; etc.).

c. It is precisely as the household revels together that the injunction to eat and rejoice in the land is fulfilled: (i) The whole household, including sons, daughters, male and female servants, are to enjoy the blessings of the covenant life by eating "meat" and "fruit" according to "all their desire" "in every city" (12:15–16, 20; 14:28–29; 15:22; 26:12). As a way of demonstrating this blessing over against their former slavery they are to share their firstlings and first fruits with the poor—the stranger, the widow, and the orphan—as well as with the Levite in their city (14:28–29; 26:12). The raison d'être for this eating is clear: to experience the joy in the salvation that is fulfilled in the land! All of Israel, both the household and those poor deprived of a household, are to frolic in the covenant blessings ("and they shall eat in your cities and be merry!"—26:12b). (ii) But it is preeminently at the "place" "before the Lord" that this eating and rejoicing is fulfilled by the household. Here again joy is the keynote as the household along with its poor and its Levite is to *journey* there with their sacrifices and offerings (see 12:5–18; 14:23–27; 15:19–21; 16:1–15; 26:1–11).

The supreme importance of this eating and rejoicing finds expression in the presentation of first fruits and firstlings in 14:22–27. If "the place" is too far for the household, then they should sell their produce and use the money at "the place" to buy whatever meat and wine or strong drink their heart[26] desires, "and you shall eat there before the Lord your God, and you and your household shall rejoice!" (14:26b).

5. The essence of the "eating and rejoicing" is distilled most clearly in the injunctions for the three great feasts of Israel. Three times a year all Israel as represented by their males is to appear before the Lord at the place to celebrate (Deut. 16:16). The Passover, linked with the festival of Unleavened Bread,[27] stresses the commemoration of the affliction left behind by their "quick" exodus from Egypt (16:1–8). Tabernacles or "tents" is a special time of revelry in the final harvest and in the vintage. The household in particular is enjoined to "rejoice in the feast," "in all your fruit," and "in the work of your hands" (6:13–15; cf. 31:10–13). But it is the Feast of Weeks (16:9–12) in which the joy of release from slavery, hearkening to the commandments of the Lord, and exulting in the blessings of the land *as a household* with its poor and its Levite are most closely intertwined. This revelry in the "first fruits" *as a sign of the fulfilled covenant promises* is in keeping with the special accent upon first fruits and firstlings throughout Deuteronomy.[28] The literal first fruits of the land are proof from the returning messenger-scouts that the promises of the inheritance to the patriarchs are about to come true (1:22–25; cf. v. 25b: "The land is good which the Lord our God is giving us"). Moreover, these fruits and firstlings epitomize the blessings of the land that fulfills the "desire of the soul" (14:22–27). It is for this reason that the poor as well as the Levite are to share in the eating and merriment of these fruits and firstlings (14:27–29; 18:4; 26:12–15); for, as distinct households, all Israel is united as the one people of the inheritance, as they eat and rejoice at the one "place" or cult before the Lord who is one (cf., e.g., 6:1–

5). Finally, the unique history of the people of Israel, their longing for the land of their forebears, and its fulfillment in their special destiny of inheriting the "land of milk and honey," is crowned by the offering of the first of their fruits once they have settled the land (26:1–11). It is no accident that the consummating point of Israel's peculiar Exodus salvation is the eating of the first fruits by the household and their rejoicing before the Lord in the place which the Lord will choose (26:1–4, 10–11).

Moses and the Journey of Eating and Rejoicing

The course of the journey of Moses and the people best sums up all that we have observed about the goal of eating and rejoicing:

As the people leave the slavery of Egypt, a land of want where nourishment was equated with backbreaking labor (Deut. 8:7–10; 11:8–12), Moses leads them toward the land of milk and honey (6:3), full of "wheat and barley, vines, figs, pomegranates," and "olive oil," "where there are torrents of waters and fountains" (8:7–9). Yet the way there through the "great and terrible wilderness, where there is the biting serpent and scorpion, and drought and no water" (8:15), proves to be a crucible of Israel's hearts (8:2). Though the Lord feeds them the bread of manna from heaven and water from the rock (8:3, 15–16), his care is meant to discipline them like a father with his child (8:5), that they might obey him. Manna and water become the very symbols of the people's humiliation in hunger and thirst and yet, at the same time, of the Lord's provision to prepare them for life in the land. For "you did not eat bread, nor did you drink wine, that you may know that I am the Lord your God" (29:6). All of his great signs and wonders in Egypt, at the Red Sea, and in the wilderness, his giving them food and clothing,[29] were meant to teach them to obey his voice, "that he might make you know that humankind does not live by bread alone, but . . . lives by everything that proceeds out of the mouth of God" (8:3).[30]

But the people rebel and persist in their stubborn ways. At Horeb when they refuse to hearken to the voice of the Lord, Moses intercedes in their behalf by fasting forty days and nights. Again bread and water become symbolic of the humiliating affliction that God pours upon his people, as it is now concentrated upon their representative Moses. "I neither ate bread nor drank water, on account of all your sins which you committed in doing evil before the Lord to provoke him to anger" (9:18; cf. v. 9). As they proceed from Horeb and Moses sends out twelve messengers to scout out the Promised Land, at Kadesh-barnea once again they prove themselves an incorrigible lot. When the messengers return with the first fruits of the land, the people refuse to accept these as tokens that the promise of the land through Moses is about to be fulfilled. Their refusal to hearken to the voice of God in Moses once again sets up a benchmark of twisted evil for the whole generation (1:34–37): Moses must die outside this land of milk and honey, this "good land which the Lord our God is giving us" (1:25b).

But the Lord did not give them the land so quickly. From Kadesh-barnea to the crossing of the brook Zered the people must wander thirty-eight years[31] in the wilderness (2:1). Now they are forced to entreat the nations for bread and water in order that they may eat and drink (2:6, 29). As they cross over the valley of the Arnon, they are refused hospitality. The messengers Moses sends on ahead to ensure safe passage and to request bread and water are flatly denied. Consequently, through a bloody "holy war" the Lord must deliver Sihon, king of Heshbon, and his land over to them (2:24–37).[32]

It is not until Bashan is similarly conquered that Moses can direct the people to the land of milk and honey by envisioning the central place as the goal of all their many long years of humiliation and frustrated wandering. As Moses renews the covenant of Horeb with the people, the fullness of all the covenant promises is to be crowned in the eating and drinking and rejoicing before the Lord:

> And it shall be that when you have entered into the land which the Lord your God is giving you as an inheritance and you have inherited it and dwell upon it, then you shall take from the first of the fruits of your land which the Lord your God is giving you, and put them into a basket and go ($\pi o \rho \epsilon \acute{v} \sigma \eta$) to the place which the Lord your God shall choose to have his name called upon there. And you shall come to the priest who is on duty in those days and shall say to him, "I declare today to the Lord my God, that I have come to the land which the Lord swore to our fathers to give to us." Then the priest shall take the basket from your hands and shall place it before the altar of the Lord your God. And you shall respond by saying: "My father abandoned Syria and went down to Egypt and sojourned there, few in number, but there became a great and populous nation. But the Egyptians afflicted us and humbled us and imposed harsh labor upon us. And we cried out to the Lord the God of our fathers, and the Lord hearkened to our voice and saw our humiliation and our toil and our affliction. And the Lord himself brought us forth out of Egypt with great strength and his mighty hand and his exalted arm, and with great visions and with signs and wonders. And he brought us to this place, and gave us this land flowing with milk and honey. And now, see, I have brought the first of the fruits of the land which you have given me, O Lord, a land flowing with milk and honey." Then you shall leave it before the Lord your God and worship there before the Lord your God and you shall rejoice in all the good things which the Lord your God has given you— you and your household and the Levite and sojourner with you.
>
> Deut. 26:1–11 [LXX]

But even as the consummation is announced, Moses foresees the shattering of these promises through the willful defiance of the Lord's voice, once they have entered and settled the land (28:15, 45, 62). A turning to the gods of the nations—that great abomination against which the Lord through Moses has repeatedly calumniated—will be at the center of a smug security in Yahweh's covenant. "Let good come my way, though I will walk in the error of my heart" (29:18–19). It is that adultery of the heart which will turn away from the Lord to play the harlot with the idols of the nations (31:16). It is indeed the same rebelliousness and stubbornness that characterizes the people throughout the Exodus journey (e.g., 31:27). Now fittingly this twisting of God's voice is symbolized by perverted eating and rejoicing:[33] "For I will bring them into the good land which I swore to their fathers to give to them, a land flowing with milk and honey. But when they shall eat and be filled and be satiated, then they will turn aside to other gods and serve them and provoke me and break my covenant" (31:20). "Take heed to yourself lest you forget the Lord your God, . . . lest when you have eaten and are full, and you have built fine houses and live in them, . . . you become exalted in heart and forget the Lord your God, who brought you out of the land of Egypt, from the house of bondage" (8:11–12, 14; cf. 6:10–12; 8:7–10, 15–20; 11:13–17). Thus this "eating and rejoicing" effects the very negation of the covenant fulfillment; it is its precise opposite, aligned directly against the culmination of the promises. As the Song of Moses concludes, "So Jacob ate and was full, and the beloved one kicked; he grew fat and thick and wide, and forsook the God who made him, and departed from God his savior" (32:15).

The consequence of such eating and rejoicing is unequivocal: the whole generation will be destroyed (cf. tenet D). In a list of the covenant curses, some four times longer than the blessings (28:15–68), the horrendous details are painfully described. Not by coincidence, considerable stress is laid upon the eating and rejoicing which will turn into starving and mourning: *(a)* A conquering nation will eat their fruit and their sheep and cattle (28:31, 33, 51), while they themselves hunger and thirst in abject slavery (28:48). *(b)* Their vineyards will bear fruit, but the worm will prevent them from drinking the vine (28:30, 39). *(c)* Their dead bodies will become the food for birds and beasts alike (28:26). *(d)* And in mock reference to the sacrificial practice of the pagan nations whose gods Israel will follow, a desperate Israel will eat their own sons and daughters and infants (28:53–57). Thus, the "eating and rejoicing" that perverts and hence destroys the life of the covenant fulfillment leads to the perversion and destruction of their own life. It is as this language of "eating and rejoicing" is understood as emblematic of the reversal of the whole climax of salvation that the references to an exile[34] and even return to bondage in Egypt make sense. Because Israel will forsake the covenant that the Lord made with them after he brought them out from Egypt (29:25), there they shall return—"a journey which I promised that you should never see again;[35] and there you shall be offered in the market to your enemies as male and female slaves even though no one will buy you!" (28:68). Moreover, this covenant breaking is conceived as a willful neglect in rejoicing properly in the good things that will come to fruition: "Because you did not serve the Lord with rejoicing and a glad heart for all the abundance of things, therefore you shall serve your enemies . . . in hunger and in thirst . . . and you shall wear a yoke of iron upon your neck until he has destroyed you" (28:47–48). The whole saving history appears then to be negated by this intransigent disobedience to the voice of God (cf. 28:15, 45, 62; 27:10).[36] The "way" of deliverance has come to an end.

And yet the way of salvation does not end here. Moses' prophetic vision of the way of the Lord continues on in a restored or new Exodus, a new path of deliverance even greater than the past (30:1–10). For when Israel finds itself scattered among the nations and remembers the covenant, then the Lord will gather them from their dispersion and once again bring them into the land of inheritance. The keynote of this New Exodus will be identical to that of the first—hearkening to the voice of the Lord (εἰσακούω τῆς φωνῆς κυρίου, 30:2, 8, 10). But as they "return" to the Lord (30:2, 8, 10), their restoration will be even greater than before: *(a)* The Lord will "heal their sins" (30:3). *(b)* Their descendants will be more numerous than their ancestors (30:5). *(c)* Their hearts as well as those of their offspring will be "purged and purified" by the Lord (30:6). *(d)* As a result (of *a—c*), the people will actually hearken to the Lord by *doing* his commandments (30:8). This New Exodus will thus be a restoration or recapitulation of the promises fulfilled in the first entrance of the land. This is expressed foremostly, and now as we would expect, as the return of a period of *rejoicing* in the great bounty of the land (30:9). But this New Exodus will also be a consummation of the Horeb covenant and the first entrance. For the people's stiff-necked rebellion and disobedience will at last come to an end through the Lord's own inner renewal of his people: the Lord will create the necessary conditions among his people for a perfect adherence to his voice. This notion is thus strikingly close to the "new covenant" of Jer. 31:31–34ff. and 32:39–41 (cf. Ezek. 36:24–38) in which the Law is written upon their hearts.[37] All that the Lord has spoken through Moses, through the perfect obedience of a cleansed heart, will finally be fulfilled (30:1, 8).

As Moses climbs Mt. Nebo to view the land that the Lord promised to Abraham, Isaac, Jacob, and their descendants, he ends his Exodus journey by dying outside the fulfilled promises. The people—even the children of the mountain—intractable to the end, will continue to disobey his voice once they have entered and begun to experience the "eating and rejoicing" before the Lord. But though Moses has been denied this culmination, he knows that the day is coming when this eating and rejoicing will find its perfect fulfillment. Not only will a prophet like him arise to speak the word from God that he has spoken but the people themselves will turn to the Lord to love him with *all* their heart and *all* their strength (30:2, 6, 10) in order that they may *live* (30:6b). Even as Moses dies on behalf of the people he looks ahead to a greater restoration, indeed a consummation where the land flowing with milk and honey is freed from the bondage of a stubborn, rebellious heart. "For this means life to you" (30:20b).

In the Central Section of Luke's Gospel this restoration takes place. As the Prophet like but also greater than Moses, Jesus leads the New Exodus to its consummation in the "New Covenant" of the Kingdom of God.

In the introduction to this New Exodus journey Luke presents Jesus as laying claim to and then demonstrating his identity as the Mosaic Christ of God. Like his predecessor, Jesus sends out a representative of each tribe of Israel to secure the "first fruits" of the land. But now this fruit is already enjoyed by the various households (Luke 9:4) of Israel that receive these representatives: the good news of the Kingdom of God is already preached and the power of the fulfillment is already experienced in the healing of the sick (9:1–6). Moreover, as in Deuteronomy, these "first tastes" of the consummated covenant divulge the attitudes or heart of the people.[38] They will indeed follow Jesus as John the Baptist or Elijah or even one of the old prophets raised such as Moses (9:7–9); but, as Luke foreshadows in the feeding in the wilderness and the disciples' confession, they are and will not hearken to him as the "Christ" of God. For Jesus reveals himself as the Prophet like but greater than Moses when he feeds the crowds of the *laos* of God in the "desert place" (vv. 12–13). Not manna from heaven but bread and meat from God through Jesus represents the life from God now being consummated. But as the descent from the mountain of revelation exposes the rejection of the whole generation of the wilderness, it has become clear that this people along with the disciples have not received the revelation in the bounty of the bread from their Messiah, nor grasped the discipline of the Lord in hearing the words of life that issue from the mouth of God (9:10–17, 28–36). They are a faithless and perverse generation. Therefore this Moses-Messiah must die to make the covenant of the New Exodus effective for the people (9:22–27, 31, 43b–45).

In Luke 9:51ff. the *gathering* of all Israel continues as Jesus is sent from the mountain of his messianic revelation. Now instead of feeding those who follow along, Jesus, like Moses, sends out messengers to secure food and hospitality for them. As if on cue, they are flatly rejected. But Jesus' strong rebuke prevents his disciples from waging "holy war" on the dissident Samaritans. Clearly then the deliverance of this New Exodus is different from the first Exodus. This difference is witnessed once again in the first fruits of the eating and rejoicing before the Lord which are already present. The Seventy(-two),[39] who are sent out to peripheral and non-Israelite homes (i.e., to the sojourner or stranger) to gather repentant households, eat and drink and rejoice in the eschatological banquet of the blessings of the land.[40] As they go in the power and authority of the Prophet-King who sends them, they go in the name of the one who himself is sent by God. Thus in the midst of the eschatological joy of the feast of the New Exodus these households eat and drink in the presence of the very *name* of the Lord. This presence of the Lord Yahweh in the Lord of the Banquet is experienced as the cleansing of the heart or the forgiveness (healing) of sins as these ambassadors are received. These are the households that are turning and hearkening to the voice of the Lord in the announcement of the arrival of the eschatological "rest" of the land (Deut. 13:9). Or in other words, the promise in Deuteronomy of households that eat and drink and rejoice in the peace that comes only from hearkening to God's commands had finally come true. Freedom from a twisted and rebellious heart has at last arrived; the household now manifests the life of freedom from the slavery of sin. At the same time, it is also disclosed that this eating and drinking and rejoicing is a foretaste of the feast in the banquet hall of the Kingdom of God which will be hosted by the Lord himself when he comes through their towns and villages. Thus, as in Deuteronomy, the fulfillment of the promises of blessing in the land within the individual households also points forward to the eating and drinking and rejoicing in the *place* that the Lord himself will choose. For as the Lord of the Banquet journeys on his exodus he meets and gathers households that follow him to the central place of all Israel—Jerusalem. Consequently the New Exodus culminates the original Exodus; but it does so by reversing the movement of that deliverance. Now instead of leading a gathered Israel to the Promised Land, where they will disburse into individual households, the anointed Prophet greater than Moses gathers the disbursed households and leads them to the central place where "all Israel" will worship and eat and rejoice before the Lord (Deut. 16:16). But that is precisely the way in which Moses envisions the restoration and the consummation of the promises to their forebears to take place. All Israel as households will eat and drink and rejoice before the Lord with a cleansed and fully devoted heart at the place that the Lord will choose. In Luke 9:51ff. this New Exodus consummation is underway!

But as the anointed Prophet continues on the way as the Lord of the Banquet, he meets an eating and drinking and rejoicing that is directly contrary to the consummation of the covenant. He in fact meets that eating and reveling which matches Moses' description of a hardened people who forget the graciousness of the Lord by neglecting the weightier matters of his commandments, such as the love of God for the poor and justice for the foreigner. It is in the meals with the Pharisees-scribes that this slavery to an unrepentant heart is the most pervasive. At table Jesus confronts a smug security in the blessings of wealth and prestige that the Pharisees-scribes enjoy as the leaders of "this generation" in the land. "How happy is the one who shall eat bread in the Kingdom of God" (14:15; cf. 18:9–14)! "But when you give a feast, invite the poor, the maimed, the lame, the blind, then you will be happy" (14:13–14a). Here is the same concern for the poor in sharing the blessings of the Exodus salvation as stressed in Deuteronomy. The Lord of the Banquet declares that these Pharisee meals are not the foretaste of the consummated covenant in the Kingdom of God. The Pharisees are excluding themselves from eating and rejoicing "before the Lord." Their exercise of prestige through their wealth has become an abomination, a false god before the Lord (16:14–15): "You shall eat and be full, but take heed lest your heart be deceived and you turn aside and serve other gods and worship them" (Deut. 11:16). "But you shall remember the Lord your God, that he gives you the strength to get wealth so that he may establish the covenant which the Lord swore to your fathers" (Deut. 8:18). It becomes obvious as the New Exodus journey progresses that the lawyer's question of how to inherit life reveals a stiff-necked opposition to the crowning of this life in Yahweh's voice, and hence a denial of the love for the Lord and the neighbor which the pillars of covenant life in Deuteronomy require (Luke 10:25–28; cf. 18:20).

As the rejected journeying-guest Prophet approaches Jerusalem, the joyful households of the fulfilled feasting form a decisive partition within the house of all Israel. The poor and outcast, women and tax collectors, in short the children of the covenant, are increasingly streaming to the Lord of the Banquet to eat and drink and rejoice in his presence, while the rest of all Israel persisting in their stubborn resistance shut themselves out. Though they have eaten and drunk "in the presence of the Lord" (13:26), they have not hearkened and repented to receive the renewed heart of the promises "to Abraham, Isaac, and Jacob and all the prophets in the Kingdom of God" (13:28–29). Even the disciples, who already in the feeding in the desert were called to serve this household of rejoicing, squander this stewardship of feeding the people. They join in, rather, in obstructing this presence in their midst.

Yet the anointed Mosaic Prophet is faithful in leading all Israel to the borders of the "Promised Land." As the Central Section leads into the Jerusalem ministry the journeying-guest Lord of the feast *chooses the place in Jerusalem* where he will celebrate the Passover with the household of the twelve disciples. True to the picture of Passover and Unleavened Bread at the place in Deuteronomy, this feast is a solemn remembrance of the flight from the house of affliction in Egypt. Constituting one of the many households that have accompanied Jesus to Jerusalem, the Twelve, representing the twelve tribes of all Israel, eat and drink the Passover before the Lord. But true to the New Exodus, this Passover is also the anticipation of the blood shed in the consummated Horeb covenant, even the "new covenant" of the land (Luke 22:19; cf. Jer. 31:31–34; Exodus 24; Deut. 30:6, 8–10). Combining the meaning of the sacrifices of the covenant meal, the Passover, and the death of Moses outside the land, this meal is the foretaste of the fulfilled banquet of the new covenant of the Kingdom of God wrought by the death of the Prophet like but greater than Moses. Even as bread and wine embodied the blessings of the land (Deut. 29:6), so now bread and wine are emblematic of the eschatological blessings of the new covenant salvation brought by the breaking and sharing of the body and blood of the Lord of the Banquet.

But as the feast of Passover points ahead to the frolicking in the bounty of the land in the Feast of Weeks (Pentecost), so Jesus' death celebrated with the "bread and wine of the land" points ahead to the eschatological joy in the feasts of the Kingdom of God. From the Passover meal, as Lord of the Banquet, the Prophet like Moses journeys to the cross, is "raised up from among his brethren," and is taken up to the Lord God *from the mountain* (Acts 1:12). It is only then as the journey of the New Exodus is "completed in Jerusalem" (Luke 9:31) that the promise to the "fathers" of eating and rejoicing before the Lord in the land is consummated for the crooked generation of the people of Israel (Acts 2:40b). For when the Feast of First Fruits arrives, the "power from on high" (Luke 24:49) produces the first fruits of the new covenant:

1. The stubborn hearts of the disciples and of the people of the Horeb covenant are "baptized" as they turn and repent (Acts 1:5; 2:1–4, 37–41; 3:19). The purified heart of Deut. 30:6a has been fulfilled.

2. Those who repent hearken to the voice of the Prophet like Moses (Acts 3:21–24) to bring about the obedience to God that Moses foresees in Deut. 30:2, 8.[41] Thus all the commandments uttered through Moses reach their consummation in Jesus.

3. The sins of the Jerusalem community are "released" (Acts 2:38) or "removed" (3:19) in the sense that their ill effects are "cured" or "counteracted"[42] according to the prediction of Deut. 30:3a.

4. The singleness or oneness of "heart and soul" (Acts 4:32) that characterizes the restored covenant community fulfills Moses' prophecy of the *oneness* or *wholeness of heart* devoted to the Lord in Deut. 30:2, 6, 10. Thus the consummated covenant community exhibits that singleness of devotion (love) to Yahweh which is the central plea not only in Deuteronomy but in the great Deuteronomistic history as well.[43]

5. As in Deuteronomy, the sharing of possessions or fruits of the land with the poor of the restored community demonstrates the heart that is wholly grateful to the Lord for the blessings of the land (Acts 2:42, 44–45; "as any had need"; 4:32, 34–36; cf., e.g., Deut. 14:28–29; 26:12–15). It is Ananias's and Sapphira's behavior that closely parallels the "exalted heart" of Deut. 8:12–20 that withholds gratitude to the Lord for his Exodus salvation and "goes after other gods." In both cases the unity of heart of the community is destroyed.

6. The ingathering of the dispersed people of Israel from all the corners of the earth as envisioned by Moses in Deut. 30:1b, 3b–5[44] is beginning to be fulfilled at the Feast of First Fruits in Jerusalem (Acts 2:5–12). It is from this group primarily that the first believers are drawn (cf. Acts 2:44), who "turn" to the Lord and hearken to the Prophet like Moses and hence love the Lord their God with all their heart and soul" (Deut. 30:2, 6, 10; Acts 2:37–47; 3:25–26).

All of these points of fulfillment in the restoration and consummation of the covenant are now crowned by the eating and rejoicing before the Lord by the young community: "Day by day, attending the Temple together and breaking bread in their households they partook of food, full of joy and with a singleness of heart,[45] praising God and finding favor with the whole people" (Acts 2:46–47a).[46] Here at last the goal of the first Exodus in Deuteronomy is reached (Deut. 30:9b: rejoicing restored). As *households* they constitute all Israel[47] that has gathered or rather has been gathered by the Lord at the central *place* (shrine) of the nation. Here the joy and revelry of the Feast of Weeks flows over into the eschatological jubilation effected by the New Exodus of the Prophet like but greater than Moses as the Lord of the Banquet. They eat and rejoice[48] and worship (2:47a) before the Lord as he is present in his name. Quoting Joel 2:32, Peter declares that the Lord is present as salvation in his *name* which can be *called upon* (Acts 2:21; cf., e.g., Deut. 12:5, 11, 21, 26, etc.). As Jews representative of the Diaspora are baptized in the name of Jesus the Christ they receive the Holy Spirit.[49] By the presence and power of this name a lame man is healed (3:6), and Peter subsequently declares that "this name, by faith in this name, has made this man strong" (3:16; cf. 4:12). The conception here matches exactly the presence and power in the name of the Lord in the sending out of the Seventy(-two) (Luke 10:17). Moreover, the joyous meal celebrations of that mission as well as those with tax collectors and sinners on the New Exodus journey are now fulfilled by all Israel at the place, where, according to Deuteronomy, the Lord will choose to place his name.[50]

The New Exodus of Deuteronomy 30 has been accomplished! The Prophet like Moses, even the Christ of God, has come. The joy of the feast has now been fulfilled. The covenant to Israel's forebears, their Exodus, and their inheritance in the land—the goal of the entire saving journey history expressed in eating and rejoicing in the first fruits of the land (Deut. 26:1–11)—after the long journey of Jesus to Jerusalem has now at last been consummated.

The RELATION *of* FORM *to* CONTENT *in* DEUTERONOMY *and in the* CENTRAL SECTION *of* LUKE

We have shown that (1) the rejected Deuteronomistic Prophet recapitulates and consummates the calling and fate of Moses as the Prophet like but greater than Moses of Deuteronomy and that (2) this Prophet executes the fulfillment of the first covenant and Exodus of Deuteronomy through the New Covenant of the New Exodus which climaxes in the eating and drinking and rejoicing before the Lord. In both these ways, therefore, the Moses of Deuteronomy has functioned constitutively as a literary-theological model for the Jesus of the Central Section of Luke. The following correspondences bear added testimony to this conclusion.

Form-Critical Considerations

The overall shape of the words of Moses in a journey framework closely resembles the words of Jesus in a journey framework. Form-critically, Moses' words can be divided into[51] (1) parenesis; (2) delivery and exposition of the Law or will of God; and (3) pronouncements of curses (judgment) and blessings:[52]

1. Though homiletical-rhetorical language characterizes the whole of the Deuteronomic style, including the legal material, Deuteronomy 1—4, 5—11, and 29—30 are the distinctively parenetic sections. Deuteronomy 1:6—4:40(43) constitutes the first discourse or parenetic tableau in which the release from Egypt, Horeb, and subsequent journey episodes form the core of a historical recalling (1:6—3:29). The haggadic appeals are used in the service of the appeal for obedience to the voice of the

Lord.[53] Deuteronomy 5—11 comprises the second discourse or tableau with the Decalogue (5:1–21), the Shema (6:4–5), and further parenetic material[54] such as the historical reminiscence of the molten calf (9:7b—10:11). Finally, 29:1—30:20 forms the "third discourse" or address, with its highly rhetorical style appealing both to the past journey as well as to a future restoration.

2. The second large parenetic tableau continues on as an address of Moses but now in the delivery of the specific ordinances of the voice of God (Deuteronomy 12—26). Yet here the peculiar rhetorical accent of the previous section is continued in periodic flourishes, with the result that one central tableau of teaching and exhortation is formed (5:1—26:19).

3. Deuteronomy 27:9[55]—28:68 is Moses' instructions for and the blessings and curses of the covenant which is being renewed. The content as well as style is most probably dependent upon the specific form and the regulations for the covenant renewal ceremony.[56]

In sum, the characteristic feature throughout Deuteronomy is the interweaving of historical recalling of the journey from Egypt with legal material to fashion a web of teaching, exhortation, and curses and blessings following from the Law of God. The Exodus journey forms the raison d'être of the covenant law (and hence of adherence to the *voice* of God as well as the hope of the coming consummation.[57]

We have already traced the contour of Jesus' words in the midst of a journey (Part III.B). Although the *forms* of the OT Deuteronomistic summaries of the threefold character of the prophets' words do not match the forms of Moses' words in Deuteronomy[58] or in Luke, nevertheless the content—mediation and teaching of the voice of God; exhortation to obedience (parenesis); call to repentance; warning of judgment—does correspond closely to the threefold content of Moses' words. This parallel is even more pronounced when it is recalled that the Deuteronomistic view of the prophetic sayings developed out of the watershed experiences of the fall of Israel and Judah in 722 and 587 B.C.E. (i.e., tenet D). These judgments from God were interpreted as the direct outworking of the curses (and blessings) of Moses in Deut. 27:9–10; 28:1–68.[59] Already in the thinking of the Deuteronomistic history writers, the prophets' utterances of warning of judgment or of blessing in their repentance preaching are based directly on Moses' utterance in Deuteronomy.[60] When in later Deuteronomistic tradition the prophets and/or their successors themselves took on the function of announcing the coming judgment of God, they did so in the shadow of Moses' prophetic words in the *covenant curse formulation. Tenet D was nothing but the arrival of the Mosaic curse.*[61] Therefore the sayings of Jesus in Luke that we have included under tenet

D conform likewise to the words of Moses. The result is an overall picture of the ministry of Jesus finely focused with that of his "type." The two large parenetic tableaux, Luke 12:1—13:9 and 14:15—17:10, correspond to the large parenetic tableaux in Deuteronomy, while the smaller parenetic passages in the Lukan Central Section reflect numerous such instances in Deuteronomy's "legal" section, Deuteronomy 12—26. In both cases, mediation of the will (voice) of God is interlaced with exhortations to obedience, calls for repentance, and warnings of judgment. What is more, in the light of Moses' directions for eating and rejoicing in the land, along with the Deuteronomistic expansion of this future as exile and restoration (Deut. 30:1–10), Jesus' words about eating and drinking in the banquet hall of the Kingdom of God and the coming Kingdom of salvation correspond to Moses' predictions and pronouncements of blessing. But not only do they match in content, they also effect for the first time the consummation of these Mosaic words. It is precisely then in this sense that Jesus utters the eschatological *halakah* of all the words of Moses. Not until the coming of the antitype does the "voice" on the mountain of Horeb find its final fulfillment. In short, in Luke's Central Section Jesus is the prophet "like me" who "will speak to them all that I command him" (Deut. 18:15a, 18b).

The Relation of the Sayings of Moses/Jesus to a Journey

When we recall that both Moses and his counterpart utter their words in the Exodus-New Exodus *journey* setting, the career of Moses in Deuteronomy as a model for the form-content relation in the Central Section becomes all the more apparent.

1. Whereas in Deuteronomy the Exodus to the border of the Promised Land has already taken place, while in Luke 9:51 the journey is only beginning, nevertheless in both texts travel notices point ahead to the final destination—the "land"/"Jerusalem." Typical of the travel notices in Deuteronomy is 6:18: "You shall do that which is pleasing and good before the Lord your God . . . that you may go in (εἰσέρχομαι) and inherit the good land, which the Lord swore to your fathers." Or again, Deut. 6:1: "These are the commandments and the ordinances, and the judgments, as many as the Lord our God commanded to teach you to do accordingly, in the land into which you are going to enter (εἰσπορεύομαι) in order to inherit it." That is, the notice of their imminent entering into the land is bound up with their entering life in the land as the goal of the whole journey. Similarly the travel notices in the Central Section are bound up with entering life in the Kingdom of God, again the goal of the whole journey.[62] For instance, Luke 13:22ff.: "He was going on his way (διαπο-

ρεύομαι), teaching and journeying toward Jerusalem, when someone said to him, 'Lord, are those being saved few?' And he said to them, 'Strive to enter (εἰσέρχομαι) through the narrow door, for many, I tell you, will seek to enter but will not be able.'" Or Luke 14:25ff.: "Now many crowds were *journeying* with him when he turned and said to them, 'If anyone *comes* to me but does not hate . . . . Whoever does not bear his own cross and *come* after me cannot be my disciple.'" Or again, Luke 18:31: "And taking the Twelve, he said to them, 'Look, we are *going up*[63] to Jerusalem, and everything that is written of the Son of Man by the prophets shall be consummated.'" In Deuteronomy these notices are tied intrinsically to the previous course of the journey, and especially to that part of the journey from Horeb, the mountain of God.[64] Thus a dynamic, bifocal tension is sustained, moving the story time from Moses' ascent of Horeb to his ascent of Mt. Nebo. The journey forward is always the resolution as well as the culmination of the previous journey. We have charted the same bifocal tension in the chain of travel notices which reach back to Jesus' ascent of the mountain in Luke 9 and sending to Jerusalem, where, again, he ascends a mountain to climax the journey (Luke 24—Acts 1). Jesus' forward progress always anticipates this resolution as well as culmination of the mountain revelation of his glory and of the stubborn disobedience of the people (see esp. 13:32–33). Therefore, we can conclude that the literary function of the travel notices in the Central Section is a striking reflection of their role in Deuteronomy.

When it is noticed that the ratio of the frequency of these travel notices to the rest of the so-called static material in both Deuteronomy and the Central Section of Luke's Gospel is virtually the same, the similarity of the relation of form to content is astonishing indeed.

> *a.* In both, journey notices are interspersed in the midst of pareneticdidactic sections.[65] When allowance is made for the greater length of Deuteronomy (calculated in total verses,[66] Deuteronomy is about 2.6 times longer than Luke 9:51—19:44), the ratio of the number of journey notices (total verses) to the rest of the material (total verses) in each is nearly the same: Deuteronomy—43/42—Luke 9:51—19:44.
>
> *b.* In both, these notices are concentrated before and after the large, predominantly parenetic-didactic sections, Deuteronomy 12—26 and Luke 10:25—18:30.
>
> *c.* Significant for the riddle of the Central Section of Luke, the ratio of its journey indicators to the "static"[67] material in the more concentrated parenetic-didactic section (12:1—17:10) is roughly the same as that ratio for Deuteronomy within its concentrated parenetic-didactic (legal) section, Deuteronomy 12—26: Deuteronomy 12—26—7/6—Luke 12:1—17:10 (Deut. 12:1—26:19 = about 1.9 times the length of Luke 12:1—17:10). In

other words, the most "static" section of the Central Section is hardly any more so than its counterpart.

2. The "legal" section of Deuteronomy 12—26 is far from a dry and stodgy rehearsal of static legislation.[68] The following points illustrate this:

a. The individual ordinances are laced with the parenetic potency of sermons to elicit obedience from the heart. As an example: "There shall not be a poor person in your midst, for the Lord your God will surely bless you in the land which the Lord your God is giving you by inheritance. . . . And if you will indeed hearken to the voice of the Lord your God, to keep and to do all these commandments, as many as I command you today, . . . then you shall lend to many nations . . ." (15:4–6). The section is replete with rhetorical expressions like, "Take heed" (12:19, 23; 15:9); "remember" (15:15; 16:12); "therefore I charge you" (12:28; 15:11; 19:7, 9); "if you will hearken to do" (e.g., 19:9); "beware and hearken" (e.g., 12:28).

b. Much of the parenetic power derives from a recalling of the delivery from slavery in Egypt and functions therefore as a reminder of the journey that has liberated them. For instance: "You shall remember that you were a slave in the land of Egypt but that the Lord your God redeemed you from there. Therefore I charge you to do this thing" (15:15). "The Ammonite and Moabite shall not enter into the assembly of the Lord, . . . because they did not meet you with bread and water on the way when you were journeying out of Egypt" (23:3–4; cf. vv. 5–7). Thus both the journey as a whole and specific episodes are appealed to: for example, 13:5; 24:9. Consequently journeying and obedience to the "voice" in Moses are inextricably linked.

c. Travel notices pointing forward to the goal of entering the land link obedience in the land to Israel's obedience to the Lord, who has already brought them thus far in the Exodus journey of salvation. For example: "For up to now you have not come to the rest nor the inheritance which the Lord our God is giving you. You shall therefore go over the Jordan and dwell in the land which the Lord our God takes as an inheritance for you. . . . And there shall be a place. . . . There you shall bring all the things that I command you today" (12:9–11). This goal of entering life is epitomized in the credal response which, with its bifocal journeying center, reaches back all the way to the patriarchs'[69] wandering to Egypt as well as to the people's own goal of entering the land. "And when you have entered into the land . . . and you shall go to the place . . . I have come into the land. . . . My father departed Syria and went down to Egypt . . . but the Egyptians afflicted and humbled us . . . but the Lord himself brought us out from Egypt . . . and he brought us into this place. . . . And now, look, I have brought the first of the fruits of the land" (26:1–11). Here the entire process of entering the life promised to Israel's forebears is perceived as a *journey*. Salvation from Egypt is a dynamic restoration and consummation of the whole of the elective promises of journeying into a "land of milk and honey" (cf. 17:14–17).

d. In addition, once the people are settled in the land, they are commanded to journey to eat and rejoice before the Lord at the central place. In other words, the goal of eating and rejoicing is linked to a variant form of travel notice: 12:5–7, 11–12, 26–27; 14:23–26; 18:6–8; 26:1–11. In 16:1–5 the Passover is linked to the past journey, while in 12:9–10; 18:9; and 26:1–11, the travel notices of entering the land link up directly with journeying to eat and rejoice after the people have settled in. But that is to demonstrate again that eating and rejoicing before the Lord as the goal of the journey is inseparably bound up with the life in the land that continues to be celebrated and reenacted by journeying to eat and drink and rejoice.

Corresponding to the above points are these in the Central Section of Luke:

a. Instead of the one large audience tableau of all Israel in Deuteronomy 12—26,[70] there are two in Luke (12:1—13:9 and 14:25—17:10), with the crowds increasing to the thousands upon thousands of all Israel. But these sections are replete with rhetorical phrases that both explain and stress the importance of hearkening to the voice of God in Jesus. For instance: "Therefore I tell you, do not be anxious about your life, what you shall eat. . . . How much more will he clothe you, O folk of little faith" (Luke 12:22, 28). "Temptations to fall away are sure to come, but woe to the one by whom they come" (17:1). "Take heed to yourselves. . . . So you also . . . say, 'We are unworthy servants; we have done only what we ought to do'" (17:13, 10).

b. As in Deuteronomy 12—26, several specific journey episodes are recounted (Luke 13:10–21, 22–30, 31–35; 14:1–24; 15:1–2) as well as references to the journey as a whole: "I have come to cast fire upon the earth. . . . As you go with your accuser before the magistrate, make an effort to reconcile with him on the way" (Luke 12:49, 58). "Look, I cast out demons . . . and the third day I consummate my course. . . . How often would I have gathered your children . . . but you would not" (Luke 13:32, 34). "Then I beg you, father, send him to my father's house. . . . If they do not hearken to Moses and the prophets, neither will they be convinced if someone should rise from the dead" (16:27, 31). Again, journeying and obedience to the "voice" in Jesus are inseparably linked.

c. Travel notices pointing to the culmination of entering Jerusalem (the "land" of the Kingdom of God) link obedience in the life of the

Kingdom of God to the Lord who has brought them thus far on the New Exodus. For example: "He continued to travel through cities and towns, teaching and making journey toward Jerusalem. . . . 'When once the householder has risen up and shut the door, you will begin to stand outside and to knock at the door, saying, "Lord, open to us." He will answer you, "I do not know where you come from." Then you will begin to say, "We ate and drank before you and you taught in our streets." But he will say, "I tell you, I do not know where you come from—depart from me all you workers of wrongdoing"'" (13:22, 25-27). "Now many crowds were journeying with him. . . . 'Whoever does not bear his or her own cross and follow behind me cannot be my disciples'" (14:25, 27). The peculiar link of the travel notices with eating and drinking even within 12:1—17:10 is striking. Luke 13:22, 32-35; and 14:25 connect the journeying Lord to the Lord of the Banquet who not only eats and drinks on his way to the consummated banquet in the Kingdom of God but who also reveals that there is another kind of eating and drinking that does not participate in the feast of the Kingdom of God.

d. As in Deuteronomy 12—26, there are journey notices linked to a feast that embodies the consummated salvation reached as the goal of that journey:

> (1) In Luke 12:35-38 the "Lord" departs from a banquet[71] to gird up and serve a *household* of servants who recline at table. The Lord is said to *come* (vv. 36, 37, 38) to reward the faithful servants with the feast that brings the joy of a consummated salvation.
>
> (2) In Luke 13:22-30 the link of the journey of the teaching Lord in vv. 22-23 to the feast in the banquet hall in vv. 25-30 is forged by the use of "Lord" in v. 25 and by "teaching" in v. 26. Again the feast of eschatological[72] rejoicing is described as the goal of a journey (vv. 28, 29).
>
> (3) The "eating of bread in the Kingdom of God" (14:15) is portrayed as a feast in a household that awaits those who journey to it after receiving an invitation from one who himself journeys to them (vv. 17, 20, 21, 23). The journey of the servant is described as a "leading in" (vv. 21, 23), while refusal of the banquet is a "reverse journey" (vv. 18, 19).
>
> (4) In all three parables of Luke 15 a feast follows a journey or a seeking that culminates in the joy of the "lost" being found (vv. 6, 9, 23-32).
>
> (5) Revelry in feasting (16:19) of a rich man[73] is contrasted to the bliss of the feast in the bosom of Abraham (16:19-31). The chasm between the two is impassable (v. 16), and the petition to send (vv. 24, 27) someone on a journey (v. 30) to households is now viewed as futile.

All these references in the context of the journeying-guest Prophet mirror the climax of Jesus' journey mission in a feast of joy. This feast crowns the meals of the Lord of the Banquet on his journey[74] and continues to be celebrated in the great pilgrimage feasts of Israel in Jerusalem (Luke 22:14–38; Acts 2:42, 46). That is, through the journey of the New Exodus the Prophet like but greater than Moses reenacts the entire *Heilsgeschichte* of Deut. 26:1–11. In so doing, he consummates the "eating and rejoicing" before the Lord that Moses proclaimed as the goal of Israel's salvation. What has now "come" are the first tastes, the first fruits, of the eternal feast of the Kingdom.

3. In both Deuteronomy and the Central Section of Luke's Gospel, journey episodes proceeding from the mountain of revelation are concentrated before the explanations and exhortation of the divine voice begins: Deut. 1:6—3:29 and Luke 9:52—10:24. In Deut. 4:1 and Luke 10:28 the rationale for heeding this voice is given: "Do this and you shall live."

4. More significantly, the density of journey episodes within the opening sections before the concentrated didactic-parenetic sections (Deuteronomy 12—26 and Luke 12:1—17:10) is astoundingly close. In Deut. 1:1—11:32, 49 percent of the verses recount the Exodus journey, while in Luke 9:51—11:54, 46 percent of the verses treat the events of the New Exodus.[75] In both of these sections these incidents are laced with teaching-parenesis regarding opponents, loyalty to the voice of the journey, pronouncements of judgment and blessings, and exultation over the salvation history.

5. Finally, both Deuteronomy and Luke's Central Section present Moses/Jesus as the voice of God from the mountain whose miraculous feats are only rarely described and, even then, usually summed up as a whole: Deuteronomy—"signs and wonders" (4:34; 6:22; 7:19; 11:3; 26:8; 29:3; 34:11);[76] Luke—"mighty deeds" (10:13; 19:37); "glorious things" (13:17); "performing cures" (13:32). In both, these mighty acts are subsumed to the journey as expressions of the saving power of God.

CONCLUSIONS

As the Deuteronomistic rejected Prophet, Jesus not only recapitulates the fourfold calling of Moses in Deuteronomy but as the anointed Prophet like Moses he also consummates Moses and all the prophets by journeying on the New Exodus from the glory of the mountain of revelation to his exaltation in the glory of God in the Kingdom of God. As such, he is the "Christ of God."

Jesus' meals with the "poor" and the Seventy(-two)'s meals with repentant households in the journey of the New Exodus are climaxed by the Passover meal of the New Covenant and the meals of First Fruits (Weeks) in Jerusalem, the place which the Lord has chosen. The goal of the journeying *Heilsgeschichte* as expressed by the Moses of Deuteronomy is thus consummated by the Prophet like but greater than Moses as the "eating and rejoicing" of stubborn, unrepentant hearts is replaced by the "eating and rejoicing" of cleansed, forgiven hearts before the Lord, in the name of the Lord of the Banquet of the eschatological Kingdom of God.

Both for the words of Jesus (i.e., content) and for his journeying (i.e., form), the Moses of the Book of Deuteronomy serves as a literary-theological model.

Therefore in his calling and fate, his prophecy of the future, and in the setting of a journey for his words, the portrait of Moses in Deuteronomy becomes the portrait of Jesus in the Central Section of Luke. It is here that the organizing principle for Luke's terrain is to be found.

Notes

1. See a concordance for the frequent occurrence of σήμερον in Deuteronomy.

2. "Inheriting" or receiving the promise "sworn" to Abraham, Isaac, and Jacob is a central motif in Deuteronomy (e.g., Deut. 1:8; 6:10; 9:5, 27; 29:13; 30:20; 34:4).

3. See Luke 9:10–17, 28–36; Acts 3:22–23; 7:37.

4. See Luke 1 and 2.

5. See Luke 10:25–27; 18:18–20.

6. See Luke 9:26; 10:21–22, 25–28; 11:27–28; 16:31; et al.

7. Se Luke 9:35; 10:21–22.

8. See Luke 9:48–49; 10:17; 13:35; 19:38; 24:47; cf. 21:8, 12, 17.

9. Cf. Luke 17:18; 19:38; 21:27; 22:69; 24:4, 51; Acts 1:9–12; 2:33–34; 7:2, 55. This journey of and to glory thus parallels the more developed theme in John (cf. esp. G. B. Caird, "The Glory of God in the Fourth Gospel: An Exercise in Biblical Semantics," *NTS* 15 [1968–69]: 265–77).

10. Cf. Luke 17:18; 21:27; see, e.g., J. G. Davies, "The Prefigurement of the Ascension in the Third Gospel," *JTS* 6 (1955): 229–33.

11. In addition to the linguistic evidence of Luke 9:31, Luke 12:50 argues strongly against Jesus' exodus journey only beginning upon his arrival in Jerusalem, i.e., from his death to his resurrection-exaltation (so J. Mánek, "The New Exodus in the Books of Luke," *NovT* 2 [1958]: 8–23; Mánek does, however, rightly point out [p. 13] that, according to Luke, Jesus regarded his own mission as an Exodus, "beginning with Moses," Luke 24:27).

12. Jesus is the "Christ" like Moses, now sent to Israel in the mission of the apostles; see J. Jervell, *Luke and the People of God: A New Look at Luke-Acts* (Minneapolis: Augsburg Publishing House, 1972), 98–102.

13. This second chance parallels the two sendings of Moses to "his brothers and sisters" as structured in Stephen's speech, Acts 7:17–29 and 30–43. See below, Part V, "The Literary Function of the Travel Narrative in Luke-Acts"; and D. P.

Moessner, "'The Christ Must Suffer': New Light on the Jesus-Peter, Stephen, Paul Parallels in Luke-Acts," *NovT* 28 (1986): 227–34.

14. See above, Part II, "Luke's Language and Lineage of the Prophets."

15. See O. Bauernfeind, "κατάπαυσις," *TDNT* 3:628. G. von Rad (*Deuteronomy*, 93) on 12:9: "Israel will belong altogether to its God and be wholly in his safe keeping."

16. See, e.g., "wine" with "grain" and "oil" as well as with sheep and oxen (e.g., Deut. 7:13; 11:14; 12:17; 14:23; 18:4).

17. These seventeen occurrences do not include dietary regulations or negative injunctions.

18. The central place is in Jerusalem, at least for the Deuteronomists. See, e.g., G. von Rad, *Deuteronomium-Studien*, FRLANT n.F. 40 (Göttingen: Vandenhoeck & Ruprecht, 1948), 25; and F. M. Cross, *Canaanite Myth and Hebrew Epic: Essays in the History of the Religion of Israel* (Cambridge: Harvard University Press, 1973), 278–85. See, e.g., 1 Kings 11:12, 13, 32, 34, 36; 15:4; 2 Kings 8:19; 19:34; 20:6.

19. Deut. 26:12 is the one exception in which the rejoicing is to take place in the individual town, but still "before the Lord" (26:13). For discussion of this puzzling "sacral formulation" which assumes a sanctuary, see von Rad, *Deuteronomy*, 159–61.

20. Deut. 12:7, 12, 18 [2x]; 14:26; 15:20; 16:11, 16; 18:5, 7; 26:5, 10; ἔναντι in 15:20.

21. Deut. 16:16; 31:11; cf. 4:10—Horeb.

22. Deut. 12:5, 11, 21, 26; 14:23–24; 16:2, 6, 11; 26:2; cf. MT: His name "dwells" there.

23. Cf., e.g., von Rad, *Studien*, 25–30; and idem, *Deuteronomy*, 90: "The name, which is present at the shrine in almost material form, is regarded almost as a person, and acts as a mediator between Yahweh and his people."

24. For the frequent instances of οἶκος/οἰκία, κατοικέω, and πόλις, consult a concordance.

25. Cf. Deut. 5:21: one of the ordinances of the Decalogue regards the "household" as a sacrosanct unit for fulfilling the covenant promises.

26. LXX: ψυχή.

27. See, e.g., J. C. Rylaarsdam, "Passover and Feast of Unleavened Bread," s.v., *IDB*.

28. E.g., Deut. 13:6–7, 11–12, 17–18; 14:22–27, 28–29; 18:4–5; 26:1–11, 12–15; see esp. J. C. Rylaarsdam, "Weeks, Feast of," s.v., *IDB*.

29. Deut. 8:4; 10:18; 29:5.

30. Cf., e.g., Deut. 4:32–40.

31. Deut. 2:14.

32. For the "holy war" idea in Deuteronomy, see von Rad's classic study, *Studien*, 30–41.

33. E.g., ἐμπίπλημι: Deut. 6:11; 8:12; 11:16; 31:20; 32:15.

34. See Deut. 4:27–31; 28:36–37, 41, 47–48, 64–68; 29:20–28; cf. 30:1–10. For this Deuteronomistic redaction and theology, see Cross, *Canaanite*, 285–89; and Steck, *Israel*, 139–43.

35. Cf. Deut. 17:16.

36. Von Rad (*Deuteronomy,* 176): Israel's future disobedience leads to "something like a liquidation of the whole history of salvation brought about by Yahweh"; but see P. D. Miller, "'Moses My Servant,'" *Int* 41 (1987): 251–54.

37. Cf. von Rad (*Deuteronomy,* 183–84) in designating 30:1–10 as the culmination of the entire Deuteronomistic historians' message: "Altogether the whole picture of the future of God's people healed and blessed by God himself resembles completely that in Jer. 32"; H. W. Wolff, "The Kerygma of the Deuteronomic Historical Work," in *The Vitality of Old Testament Traditions,* ed. W. Brueggemann and H. W. Wolff (Atlanta: John Knox Press, 1975), 93–96.

38. The *literary function* in both accounts (Deut. 1:19ff. and Luke 9:1–9) is the same: the "hearts of many are revealed" (Luke 2:35b).

39. Deut. 1:9–18 is an apparent combination of Num. 11:14–25 (seventy elders) and Exod. 18:13–27 (judges) (cf., e.g., von Rad, *Deuteronomy,* 39).

40. Cf. esp. Part III.C.3, above.

41. Deut. 30:8, 10: ποιέω, φυλάσσω; cf. above, Part III.B, pp. 114–20, 127–30.

42. ἰάομαι: "cure the effects of," "counteract" (LSJ). See esp. Acts 28:27; and D. P. Moessner, "Paul in Acts: Preacher of Eschatological Repentance to Israel," *NTS* 34 (1988): 101–4.

43. See above, n. 37.

44. Deut. 30:4: "from the end of heaven to the end of heaven."

45. See B. Reicke, *Diakonie, Festfreude und Zelos: In Verbindung mit der altchristlichen Agapenfeier,* UUA 1951:5 (Uppsala: Lundequistska, 1951), 203–4: ἀφελότης = "upright," i.e., "with a complete giving of the heart," "without any competing interests."

46. Joel (e.g., 2:26) is also drawn upon for eschatological joy and feasting; cf., e.g., Reicke, *Diakonie,* 193–94, 203.

47. In the representative sense that "all" Galilee, Perea, Judea, and the Diaspora are gathered, as well as the favor the young community finds "with the whole people" (Acts 2:47), "all Israel" is present at the central place!

48. Cf. Joel 2:22–27 on "food and feasting" in the restored land.

49. See this same connection in Joel 2:28–29, 32: "name of the Lord" and the "spirit." On the gathering of the Diaspora, see B. Reicke, *Glaube und Leben der Urgemeinde,* ATANT 32 (Zurich: Zwingli Verlag, 1957), 32–37.

50. Deut. 12:5, 11, 21 [26]; 14:23, 24; 16:2, 6, 11 [15]; [17:8, 10, 12]; 18:7; 26:2. But once the presence of the "name" is fulfilled at the central place, it is no longer confined to it; rather, "the name" continues a dynamic fulfillment of salvation in the spreading apostolic "witness": Acts 2:21, 38; 3:6, 16; 4:7, 10, 12, 17, 18, 30; 5:28, 40, 41; 8:12, 16; 9:14, 15, 16, 21, 27, 28; 10:43, 48; 15:14, 17, 26; 16:18; 19:5, 13, 17; 21:13; 22:16; 26:9. Cf. above, Part II, "Luke's Language and Lineage of the Prophets," pp. 50–56.

51. Cf. E. W. Nicholson, *Deuteronomy and Tradition* (Oxford: Basil Blackwell, 1967), 18–36; and von Rad, *Studien,* 7–16; cf. above, Part II, nn. 43, 44.

52. See von Rad, *Studien,* 9.

53. Cf. von Rad's "historical narrative" (see above, Part II, n. 43).

54. "Sermons of a very special kind" (von Rad; see above, Part II, n. 43).

55. Taking 27:9ff. as concluding 26:17–19 (see von Rad, *Deuteronomy*, 165–66).

56. E.g., Josh. 8:30–35; cf. above, nn. 51, 52.

57. Cf., e.g., Deut. 6:20–25; 26:1–11: the exodus journey enacts the promises to "the fathers."

58. For the Deuteronomistic historians' summaries, see Steck, *Israel*, 69–70 n. 2, 70 n. 1, 122 n. 1.

59. See esp. G. von Rad, *Old Testament Theology*, 2 vols. (New York: Harper & Row; London: SCM Press, 1975), 1:82; and Steck, *Israel*, 67 n. 7, 114 n. 1, 140–41.

60. Steck, *Israel*, 60.

61. Ibid., 67 n. 7; cf. 140 n. 5: "The understanding of tenet D as the arrival of the covenant curse corresponded already to the Deuteronomistic [historians'] view of Israel's history."

62. See above, Part III.B, pp. 114–20, and the link of the travel notices back to the mountain.

63. Note ἀναβαίνω: e.g., Deut. 1:21, 22, 26, 28, 41, 42, 43; 9:23.

64. Deut. 1:7–8; 1:21, 37–39; 2:29; 3:18, 25; 4:14; 6:1; 8:1; 9:23; et al.

65. The following list from Deuteronomy is based on LXX, and does not include notices to the central place, once Israel has settled the land: Deut. 1:7–8, 21(22–23), 37–39; 2:29; 3:18(19–22); 3:25(26–29); 4:1(2–4), 5, 14, 21–22, 26, 38; 6:1, 10, 18–19, 23; 7:1; 8:1(2–10); 9:1(2–5), 23, 28; 10:11; 11:8(9–12), 23–25, 29(30–32); 12:9–10, 29; 16:20; 17:14; 18:9; 23:20; 26:1–11; 27:2–4, 12; 28:21, 63; 30:16–18; 31:1–8, 13, 20–21, 23; 32:47, 52; 34:4—Luke 9:51, 52–53(54–56), 57; 10:1, 38; 13:22, 31–33(34–35); 14:25; 17:11; 18:31, 35, 43; 19:1, 11, 28, 41.

66. Verse totals are determined by the format of the *Biblia Sacra Iuxta Vulgatam Versionem* (Stuttgart: Württembergische Bibelanstalt, 1969). There are sixteen travel indicators in Luke 9:51—19:44; about forty-three travel indicators in Deuteronomy (see above, n. 65).

67. So called static; see above, Part III.C, on the plotted journey.

68. Cf., e.g., Part II, n. 43, above.

69. Actually Jacob, according to von Rad (*Deuteronomy*, 158).

70. From an audience-critical point of view, Deut. 5:1—26:19 is one long discourse—the "second discourse" (Deuteronomy 5—11) plus the legislation (Deuteronomy 12—26).

71. See above, Part III.C.10.

72. Notice how blessing and judgment are interwoven: e.g., Luke 13:28, as in the more parenetic sections of Deuteronomy.

73. εὐφραίνω is the goal of the "rich fool" in Luke 12:16–21.

74. Cf. also Luke 11:5–8; 10:33–35; and see above, Introduction, "The Problem and Purpose of the Investigation."

75. Narrative episodes on the journey: Deut. 1:6—3:29; 4:9–14, 41–43; 5:4–5, 22–31; 9:7–29; 10:1–5, 6–7, 8–9, 10–11; 11:2–9; Luke 9:51, 52–56, 57–62; 10:1–24, 25–29, 37, 38–42; 11:1 (53–54).

76. See von Rad, *Old Testament Theology*, 1:292–95.

V

Conclusions

*The Significance of the Travel
Narrative in Luke-Acts*

V

Our journey in Parts II—IV through the central portion of Luke's account "of the events that have been brought to completion among us" (Luke 1:1b) has brought us to the conclusion that Luke 9:51—19:44 with introduction (9:1–50) is indeed a travel narrative. Luke's Central Section is the story of the journeying salvation of the New Exodus prophesied by Moses to the people of the Horeb covenant as the fulfillment of the promises to Abraham and his descendants. As Jesus reaches the Temple and later enters the city of Jerusalem to die on behalf of this people, the people of the "new covenant" is established at the place which the Lord had chosen out of all Israel. The credo of Deut. 26:1–11 has achieved its goal. But before we can sketch the significance of this journey for the larger story of Luke-Acts, we must conclude our discussion with the exegetes in Part I[1] to establish more precisely what we mean by a travel narrative.

The NATURE of the TRAVEL NARRATIVE

The nearly unanimous opinion of contemporary critical exegesis is that the travel narrative is a makeshift arrangement of Luke to frame a large amount of disconnected traditions (see Part I). The resulting dissonance of form from content hardly lends itself to any credible journey account. But in the light of our demonstration that this dissonance is an erroneous perception of inadequate literary-critical categories, what kind of travel narrative does Luke actually present?

1. The Journey Indicators[2]

Their Incoherency. Our study has naturally not overturned the incontrovertible observation that Luke does not present a travel itinerary or travelogue with a sequence of day-to-day events or outline of specific routes of the travelers. But it has revealed no support whatever for the critical consensus that these travel indicators are contradictory or hopelessly confusing. This latter conclusion stems from an inappropriate supposition that Luke 9:51—18:14 must inevitably fit into the Markan sequence of 10:1–12. But Luke nowhere intimates that Jesus proceeded directly out of Galilee on a "straight line" or a direct route to Jerusalem. On the contrary, Luke 13:31–33 indicates that the journey itself consumes a definite time period of continued ministry analogous to the pattern of 4:14—9:50. Even if the time sequence in 13:32–33 is interpreted as a literal "three days" before arrival in Jerusalem, this timetable should not be confused with the average length required by Galilean pilgrims to reach the feasts in Jerusalem. For Luke has already presented a considerable amount of Jesus' activity up to this point with not the slightest hint that 9:52—13:30 should be compressed into a short two- or three-day period. The impression is quite the opposite with a journey into Samaria, a special mission of seventy(-two) messengers requiring them to remain in homes for indefinite periods, meals in homes, long teaching sessions, synagogue worship, discussions on the journey, and so forth. Our exegesis of Luke 10:1–24 has divulged the likelihood that Jesus' journey entailed extended forays into marginal or nominal Jewish regions such as Samaria, Decapolis, Gaulanitis, and even Galilee.[3] All of this journeying—whether moving geographically closer to Jerusalem or not—is conceived as an exodus through which the salvation "today" of the eschatological journeying *Heilsgeschichte* consummated in Jerusalem is brought ever closer.

Their Infrequency. This objection is robbed of any force when Luke's Central Section is viewed as a theological presentation of a historical period of Jesus' ministry. Jesus' overall movement from his origin of ministry in Galilee to his exaltation in the Kingdom of God at the place the Lord has chosen is conceived as the fulfilled Exodus journey. Not only does Deuteronomy, with its teaching sections interspersed with travel notices, provide a precedent but also the numerous indications of a journey or sending within the didactic material do portray Jesus on a dynamic mission that continually presses for and toward its resolution in Jerusalem. The static "wastelands" simply do not exist.

Their Indefiniteness. One of the extraordinary features of the Central Section, as confirmed by our investigation, is the vagueness of topographical information. Here, however, it is most curious that Jericho and its environs are painted in vivid detail, in bold contrasts to the grayness of "in a certain place," "through towns and villages," and the like. The concluding episodes of the journey from Jericho to the entrance into the

Temple precincts, in fact, continue this same interest in the specific movement of the pilgrim caravan.[4] Notice once again that although Samaria is singled out for special interest, topographical detail, like the bulk of the journey, is still nondescript. One must conclude either that Luke was not concerned to learn the specifics of the journey (cf. 1:3) or, more likely, in view of the Jericho depiction, that most of the material he received was already void of such information.[5]

2. The Traditions and the Journey Motif[6]

Our attention to the Deuteronomistic conception of "all Israel's" response to the messenger of God within the unfolding story of the New Exodus presents a plot sequence that fully explains the lack of strict temporal and spatial connections. It is the mounting tension of the swelling crowds of all Israel who come out to hear the prophet and follow him to the place of the prophets' tragic end, and not the precise details of a journey itinerary, which gives the Central Section its distinctive shape. Far from a random collection of disjointed material, sewn together only by virtue of common themes or catchwords, the Central Section discloses a very specific, fourfold plot based on the Prophet like Moses of Deuteronomy who leads the people from the towns and villages of all Israel to the redemption of the consummated Exodus deliverance. Time and space are not suspended in a convenient "journey scaffolding" but press ineluctably toward a culmination in the "house" of the journeying Lord of the Banquet.

3. Provenance and the Setting of the Journey Motif[7]

Once the twofold a priori of strict adherence to geographical and to Markan literary outlines is stripped away (see Part I), the objection to the presence of Pharisees along Jesus' journey is removed completely. In Luke's thinking, Jesus is not necessarily in Samaria or Perea when he dines at their houses. Moreover, it is clear toward the end of the journey that Pharisees are in the caravan of pilgrims with Jesus. Even Matthew and Mark depict Pharisees interacting with Jesus in Perea, which may reflect the more developed picture of Jesus' dealings with the Pharisees in the Central Section. The fact that the dramatis personae here are the same as in the Galilean phase is exactly what we should suspect, since it is Luke's intent to show Jesus gathering disciples from "all Israel," including Galilee, to follow him on his exodus to death and exaltation in Jerusalem. Many of the episodes appear to be doublets of the Galilean phase (see below).[8]

Once we have answered the objections and qualified the sense in which Luke's account is a travel narrative, we are still faced with the resulting problem: Is such a journey account credible? Can a theological presentation of a phase of Jesus' ministry be joined in any believable way to history? Although we have dispensed with such historical questions as an a priori, nevertheless we are led to face the inevitable dilemma. Within our literary-critical framework, however, we have concluded that what Luke presents does indeed match his intention to relate a story of the "events that have come to completion among us" in an "orderly" or "connected narrative" fashion. Luke purports to write history. He does in fact portray Jesus on a final journey, beginning in Galilee and climaxing in Jerusalem. And what is most significant, the travel notices do present a believable, historical route, so long as it is remembered that this route is not conceived as a direct or constant geographical progression from Galilee to Jerusalem. Despite the zigzags and forays into various areas of all Israel, including the mission of the Seventy(-two), Luke in 17:11 does take Jesus and his entourage from the border area between Samaria and Galilee—the Great Plain or the Valley of Jezreel (Esdraelon and Jezreel) —into Perea and back across the Jordan into Jericho at 18:35. That this general route is indicated is made clear by the almost inadvertent detail of 19:1 (i.e., that Jesus and the caravan were passing through Jericho after having already "drawn near" to it in 18:35–43). Luke 19:11 also corroborates this route, since Jesus is now "near" to Jerusalem, a very improbable phrase if Jesus were on the east or northeast side of Jericho.[9] This Perean route then accords with Mark's and Matthew's presentations (Mark 10:1—11:10; Matt. 19:1—21:9). But two caveats must be lodged here. First, it would be a mistake to call the travel narrative "the Perean Section." Nowhere does Luke mention Perea or "beyond Jordan" or refer any specific episode to this territory. The teaching of Luke 17:20—18:14 and the three episodes of 18:15–34 are not given a specific location, and 18:35–43 takes place already in the Jericho region. It is only "likely" from Luke's comment in 17:11 that this material is to be connected in the reader's mind with the vast expanse somewhere between the Valley of Jezreel and Jericho, perhaps along the well-known pilgrimage route on the Perean side of the Jordan.[10] Otherwise, there is no evidence, direct or indirect, that the large section 9:52—17:10 is to be linked to Perea. Second, it would equally be misleading to deny the possibility that a considerable number of the traditions of the entire travel narrative may have had a historical link with Perea, or the Decapolis, or even Samaria in their history of transmission. Investigation of such possibilities is beyond the scope of this study, except insofar as what we shall have to say shortly about the various internal clues to certain of the traditionists. It is clear that Luke does not provide much detail concerning the location of Jesus' words and deeds, even from 17:11 to 19:44.

We conclude, then, that Luke has presented a realistic picture of a journeying Jesus in what may be appropriately called a travel narrative. Luke narrates both a dynamic plot and a general journeying frame (Galilee—Valley of Jezreel—Jericho from Transjordan—Jerusalem) for a critical phase of Jesus' ministry. Indeed our analysis in Parts II—IV has demonstrated a narration characterized by an inner coherency between the journey framework and the words and events that are included within it. Jesus is the Prophet like and greater than Moses of Deuteronomy whose words bring life even as he takes all Israel to his death in the New Exodus deliverance of God.

We will now bring this travel narrative into focus within the larger story of Luke-Acts.

The LITERARY FUNCTION *of the* TRAVEL NARRATIVE *in* LUKE-ACTS

The Gospel of Luke

Like the story of the people of God in the OT, Luke continues the journeying of this people[11] and their prophets "beginning from Galilee . . . in the country of the Jews and in Jerusalem" (Acts 10:37b, 39a). Already in the opening stories of the families of John and Jesus, Mary travels from Galilee to Judah to visit her kinswoman Elizabeth around the time of the birth of John (Luke 1:39–56); Joseph and Mary journey from Nazareth to Bethlehem of Judea, where Mary gives birth to Jesus (2:1–7); and, almost in passing, Luke mentions that John, growing "strong in spirit," was dwelling "in the desert" until the time of his manifestation to Israel (1:80). Thus "journeying" and "sojourning" mark the beginning of the Gospel story.

Very quickly Luke relates three more journeys of the people of God, one again to Bethlehem by shepherds sojourning in the hills of Judea and two to Jerusalem by Joseph and Mary for the rite of purification in the Temple (2:22–39) and for the Passover (2:41–51). This second Jerusalem journey is especially interesting in the way that it foreshadows the large travel narrative of Jesus' journey to Jerusalem:[12] from the midst of Passover pilgrims Jesus goes to the Temple to amaze the teachers of Israel and "all those who hear him" with his words of teaching. Here already Jesus is prefigured as the teacher of all Israel.

Luke 3 sounds the beginning of the journey callings of both John and Jesus. John "comes" (3:3) into "all the region of the Jordan" to preach his baptism of repentance for the forgiveness of sins, which points directly forward to the journey sending of Jesus.[13] In the imagery of the New Exodus of Deutero-Isaiah (40:3–5), John fulfills "the voice of one crying in the wilderness: Prepare *the way of the Lord,* make straight his pathways. . . . And all flesh shall see the salvation of God" (3:4, 6). With John as his forerunner, Jesus also "comes" (3:16) into the wilderness with "all the people" (3:21, 15) to be baptized by John. After sojourning in the wilderness—again treading in the footsteps of John (1:80; 4:1–8), Jesus' journey mission suddenly takes an abrupt turn from his predecessor even as John's imprisonment casts an ominous shadow on the path ahead (3:19–20). Jesus is found once again in Jerusalem (4:9–13). But now instead of being in the Temple, demonstrating his authority to the nation, Jesus is upon its pinnacle, tempted by the devil to abuse this authority before this same people. Unlike the Jerusalem priest's son, John, Jesus cannot avoid his fate at the Temple. Thus before Jesus' public journey sending in Galilee commences, Jesus has already been led three times by others *to Jerusalem.* Consequently this nation's center already takes on the contrary tones that will color the whole of the central travel narrative. For Jerusalem is the place where Jesus must consummate the Law of the people of God—as adumbrated by the rite of purification at the Temple and the glory now redounding to the people of Israel (2:22–39). And yet Jerusalem represents the solidarity of rejection that will demand Jesus' death—as prophesied by Simeon (2:34–35) and intimated by the uncomprehending rebuke of Jesus' own family in his Father's house (2:46–50). This tension is thrust in Jesus' face already in the wilderness by the power of darkness in this initial climax at the Temple—that central place of all Israel (4:9–13; 22:53). Jerusalem and Temple occupy center stage from the very beginning of Luke's Gospel. It is there, Luke will tell his readers, that Israel's destiny will be made even as there Jesus must come to terms with his own fate. Galilee and the desert are clearly only preparatory stages for the momentous finale that must in Jerusalem be played for Jesus, "the coming one."

As Jesus returns "in the power of the Spirit" to Galilee in 4:14ff., it is even more manifest that he will not simply follow John's shadow. Far from preaching the good tidings of the Kingdom in the wilderness, Jesus "must" journey from city to city to preach in the synagogues and heal the infirm (4:42–44; 8:1–3; cf. 8:22–39—the Decapolis). The disciples of John must learn that the path that their master prepared does not lead from Judea to the desert but in the very opposite direction (7:18–30). It is thus when Luke sounds the solemn tones of 9:51 that he is announcing the beginning of the completion of those events which have already been put into motion from the story's inception. And here it is significant that before this decisive journey begins, Jesus is again found alone in the desert (9:12, 18). It is evident once more that Israel's destiny of the "glory of her people" leads from the desert to the very center of her history in Jerusalem (cf. 9:26). But this time Jesus must himself decide to go to Jerusalem; he cannot simply be led there by others. Therefore in a flourish of biblical metaphor Luke stresses Jesus' own (αὐτός) unbending resolve at this point to keep his journey directed toward Jerusalem. The point of no return has been reached. As Jesus departs from the desert, he knows that the fate of Israel and his own are now one.

We have noted that the journeying of Jesus the Prophet like Moses leads to the place of "the Skull." The Gospel, however, closes with a journey in a different direction. As two of the disciples head toward Emmaus and as other disciples gather in Jerusalem, the resurrected Prophet comes to direct them outward toward the "kingdoms of the earth" (cf. the temptation of 4:5–8). This then becomes the story of Luke's second volume, the journey missions of the one who is "raised up among his brothers and sisters" to be exalted in heaven (24:50–52).

The Acts of the Apostles

The plot of Luke's continuing story (Acts 1:1–5) is stated crisply in Jesus' command to his disciples to "be my witnesses in Jerusalem and in all Judea and Samaria and to the ends of the earth" (1:8; cf. Luke 24:48). Thus the "Acts of the Apostles" are actually the stories of the journeying of the people of God whose leaders imitate their Prophet Messiah in proclaiming the glad tidings of the Kingdom of God (1:3; 8:12; 14:22; 19:8; 20:25; 28:23, 31). We can divide the Acts story according to the journeying scheme:[14]

Acts 1:16—5:42. The Pentecost pilgrims to Jerusalem and the beginnings there of the messianic community.
Acts 6:1—9:31. The calling of the "seven," the witness and murder of Stephen, the journeys of the Stephen-Philip group into Samaria and Gaza, the persecution of Saul and his call-conversion at Damascus.
Acts 9:32—12:25. Peter's journeys along the Palestinian coastal plain, including the conversion of Cornelius at Caesarea; the journeying of the Stephen-Philip group to Phoenicia, Cyprus, and Antioch; Peter's imprisonment and departure from Jerusalem; Paul and Barnabas's journey to Jerusalem from Antioch.
Acts 13:1—15:35. The journeying of Paul and Barnabas from Antioch to Cyprus and south-central Asia Minor and journey to Jerusalem from Antioch for the Apostolic Council with return to Antioch.
Acts 15:36—19:20. Paul's journeying from Antioch through Asia Minor,

Macedonia, Achaia, and return via Jerusalem[15] to Antioch, followed by a return to Asia Minor and stay in Ephesus.

Acts 19:21—28:31. Paul's decision "in the Spirit" to journey to Jerusalem before the necessity of seeing Rome and the "end" of this journeying in a two-year period of house arrest in the capital of the Empire.

Each of these sections Luke concludes with a summary description of the effects or results of the preceding (journey) missions[16] (5:42; 9:31; 12:24–25; 15:35; 19:20; 28:30–31). Each unit is thus a thematic whole, following the movement of the church along the path announced in Acts 1:8.

We can gain a deeper insight into the import Luke attaches to this movement by concentrating on the last and largest journey section of Acts (19:21—28:31).[17] It is only this final one that speaks of a determined resolve (19:21) "in the Spirit" of the "main actor" to reach a destination. Certain parallels to the large travel narrative of the Gospel would thus seem to suggest themselves: (1) Like Luke 9:51—19:44, this final portion of Acts comprises one continuous journey story, though not one geographically straightforwardly moving account. From Ephesus, Paul heads in the opposite direction, northwestward to Macedonia and down to Achaia, before looping back to Troas and proceeding forward toward Jerusalem. (2) Both introductory verses speak of a "firm resolve" of the principal actor *to journey to Jerusalem.* For Paul it is a resolution "in the Spirit," whereas with Jesus it is the language of the prophet's calling in the OT.[18] But in both these ways the divine "must" comes to expression: Luke 9:51 continues the linkage of 9:31 with the δεῖ of 9:22; while in Acts 19:21, this δεῖ is explicit and links up directly with the divine direction (δεῖ) for Paul's journey in 23:11 and 27:24, with the Spirit's sending out messengers on divine missions (8:29; 10:19–20; 11:12; 13:2, 4),[19] and specifically with Paul's journeying to Jerusalem (20:22–23; 21:4, 11). (3) This divinely directed journey in both instances follows a period that itself brings a fulfillment of time: in Luke 9:51 as the days of an itinerant ministry within Galilee come to a close the days of his "taking up" are already being "filled to completion"; in Acts 19:21 as Paul's mission in the eastern Mediterranean has become "fulfilled" he must press forward to Jerusalem and Rome. Thus in sonorous tones both verses signal the beginning of the *climax* of the story. (4) Both journey sections occupy approximately one-third of the story text: Luke 9:51—19:44 = 36.8 percent; Acts 19:21—28:31 = 31.3 percent.[20] (5) Both sections contain longer and shorter speeches of Jesus/Paul within a journey framework (cf. Acts 20:18–35; 22:1–21; 24:10–21; 26:2–29; 28:25–28).[21] (6) Like Jesus at the beginning of the journey, so Paul sends some from his entourage ahead to where he himself will later come (Acts 19:22; cf. 20:1). (7) Both journeys begin with a rejection scene that leads Jesus/Paul to depart for another locality (cf. Acts 19:23–41) without returning (cf. Acts 20:16).[22] (8) Only a few miracles are reported (Acts 20:9–12; 28:3–6, 8–9).[23] (9) And both recount the hospitality and meals experienced as journeying guests (e.g., Acts 20:7–12; 21:4, 7, 8, 16, 17; 27:33–38; 28:7, 14, 23, 30).[24]

In spite of these parallels, a number of major differences must not go unnoticed. First, one has only to look at the vivid description of Acts 19:22–41 or the colorful unfolding of the voyage in 27:1—28:16 to see at once to what extent this detailed journey account, with its specific characters and localities, chronological connections, and even particular journey routes, varies with the Gospel travel narrative. Already Acts 19:21 mentions a specific route in contrast to the silence of Luke 9:51. It is also obvious at the outset that Paul reaches Jerusalem at 21:16, so that 21:17—28:31 should then be analogous to the Jerusalem period of Jesus' ministry and the Passion narrative and not to the Central Section of Luke's Gospel. Clearly at this level of the plot it would be misleading to speak of parallel journey narratives. Moreover, the percentage of Paul's words does not even begin to equal the density of Jesus' words in a comparable text length. Far more of the journeying and actions of Paul and his companions is recounted. When these facts are combined with the observation that some of the parallels above are only outwardly rather than substantially analogous, then the whole comparison of the two journeys is called into question.

Yet as we concentrate on the plot dynamics of the calling and fate of Paul in this final journey, a number of distinctive parallels become telling signs of a much profounder comparison:

1. As with Jesus' calling at the mountain, so Paul is called to suffer (Acts 9:16; 22:17–18; 26:16–17).[25] This fate is enhanced by Paul's reminiscences that he was called precisely at the moment when he was persecuting Jesus himself (22:6–9; 26:9–15).

2. As in the mountain theophany, Paul's calling takes place in a "great light from heaven" (Acts 22:6, 11—δόξα!; 26:13) and from the midst of this light comes a voice (φωνή, 22:7, 14; 26:14).

3. And as with the mountain sending, so Paul is sent on a journey mission (Acts 22:10, 21; 26:17–20), which will eventually reach its culmination in Jerusalem (19:21; 20:16, 22; 21:4, 11–13, 15, 17, 31; 23:11; 24:11).

4. As along Jesus' journey to Jerusalem, so it is also true of Paul's that predictions of suffering and death awaiting him there are made (20:22–25; 21:10–14; cf. 20:38; 23:11, 27; 25:3, 24; 26:23; 27:10).

5. Resistance to this journey arises from among the entourage (21:12, 14).

6. But it is Jesus'/Paul's appearance in the Temple where the opposition consolidates, leading to an arrest and eventual appearance before the Sanhedrin (Acts 21:26–36; 24:6, 11–12, 18; 26:21). As with the long journey of Jesus, the Temple once again forms the fulcrum of the hostility against the messenger of God.[26]

7. As in Jesus' arrest and trial, so both the Jewish leaders of the people and the *laos* combine to demand Paul's death (Acts 21:30–32, 36, 39–40; 22:30; 23:1–5, 12–22; 24:1–9; 25:1–12).[27] Moreover, as in Jesus' journey, already along the journey to Jerusalem plots against Paul emerge that are consummated after he reaches the Temple (Acts 19:23—20:1; 20:3, 22–30, 38; 21:4, 11).[28]

8. As in Jesus' arrest and incarceration, so in Paul's, the people and their leaders, the Roman governor and his authorities, and Herod, "King" of the Jews, collaborate (Acts 25:13—26:32).[29]

9. But it is the charges against Paul leveled by the people and their leaders which, upon closer scrutiny, reveal the most binding parallel to Jesus' calling and fate. Paul is accused of *(a)* teaching Jews of the Diaspora against "Moses" and circumcision and the "customs" (Acts 21:21), which is summarized as (against) the "Law" in 21:24; *(b)* teaching against "the people," the Law, and "this place" (i.e., the Temple) and of defiling the Temple with Greeks (21:28; 24:6); *(c)* creating agitation among all the Jews in the world and of being a leader of the "sect of the Nazoreans" (24:5; cf. Paul and the "Nazorean," 22:8; 26:9); *(d)* "offending against" "the Law of the Jews, the Temple, and Caesar" (25:8); and *(e)* "actions against the people and customs of our fathers" (28:17). These charges can be grouped together as against the Law (Moses), the people, the Temple, and Caesar, as a member of the "Nazoreans." Now in Jesus' arrest and trial he also is charged with "agitating" the people (Luke 23:5), "perverting" them with false teaching (23:2, 5, 14), and resisting allegiance to Caesar (23:2). We have already seen that this false "teaching" is tantamount to a teaching against the Law as defended by the chief priests, scribes, and elders of 19:47ff.[30] "Law," "people," "Caesar" again sum up the charges against Jesus, especially as they reach a fever pitch in Jesus' teaching in the Temple.

It is therefore evident that Luke presents Paul as following in the footsteps of his master in his journey-calling to witness to the Kingdom of God in suffering and affliction as he is rejected by an intractable people: like Jesus, he is to suffer the prophet's fate. This casting of Paul into the prophetic mold à la Jesus the Deuteronomistic Prophet like Moses can be focused with greater precision when we look once again at the story of Stephen,[31] who in Luke's understanding forms a crucial link in the interlocking careers of Jesus and Paul.

Stephen first enters the story in the second journey section of Acts through a conflict that arises between "Hellenists" and "Hebraists" in the young messianic community.[32] Because of the neglect of the Hellenist widows in the daily serving/distribution of food *(diakonia)*, presumably at or intended for the common meals,[33] seven men, including Stephen, are chosen to resolve this at least potentially dangerous rift in the unity of the community. But no sooner is this threat apparently relieved (esp. 6:7) when the reader is thrust into the tragic end of Stephen's ministry. In order to elucidate the intersecting lines between Jesus and Paul, the following outline summary will be helpful:

1. Garbed in the cloak of the prophet with his powerful signs and wonders,[34] Stephen ignites the fury of Diaspora Jews resident in Jerusalem, including the synagogue of the Cyrenians and those *from Asia.* Luke will tell his readers shortly that it was Christian converts from Cyrene, scattered from Jerusalem by Stephen's persecution, who along with men from Cyprus first preached the "Lord Jesus" to the Greeks (Gentiles) at Antioch (11:19–20; cf. 13:1). And then somewhat later Paul himself will be sent out from Antioch on a mission to the Greeks (Gentiles) in which Jews *from Asia* will emerge as his chief opponents (13:1–3ff.; 14:27–28; 19:23—20:1, 16; 21:27; 24:18).

2. As Stephen ends his defense before the Sanhedrin, the lynching mob incited by the Diaspora Jews suddenly rushes upon Stephen to drag him out of Jerusalem, there to stone him. As Stephen dies, Luke notes: "And Saul was *consenting* to his death" (8:1). It is revealing that, apart from the linking verse of 11:19, the only other mention of Stephen in the rest of Acts is in 22:20, where Paul in Jerusalem, just after he himself had nearly been lynched by a throng fomented by Jews from Asia, makes his defense before this mob. "And when the blood of Stephen your [i.e., Jesus'/the Lord's] witness was shed, I also was standing by and *consenting* and keeping the garments of those who killed him" (22:20). Equally as significant, the only other occurrence of this sympathetic witnessing (consenting)[35] in Luke-Acts is precisely in the *locus classicus* of the Deuteronomistic violent fate of the prophets in Luke 11:47–51 where Jesus aligns himself with this tragic fate: "So you are witnesses and you [are] *consent[ing]* [are sympathizers with] to the deeds of your fathers, for they killed them [the prophets] and you build their tombs" (v. 48). That this threefold linkage (Luke 11:47–51 → Acts 8:1 → 22:20) is not gratuitous is bolstered by four other interconnected parallels:

a. In all three instances, the idea of μάρτυς as an "active witness" in either opposing or promoting God's salvation through his messengers is present (Luke 11:48 in 11:47–52; Acts 7:58 in 7:54—8:3; 22:20 in 22:6–24).

b. In each passage the refusal of the people (or of "this generation") to accept God's messenger is brought to a climax in their livid hostility (Deuteronomistic tenets A and C are explicit). And with this response the mission to the Gentiles is proleptically announced or commanded (Luke 11:29–32 in context of tenet D in 11:50–51; Acts 7:23—8:3 → 11:19–20; 22:4–24).

c. In each divine sending the Temple plays a decisive role in epitomizing Israel's antipathy for the messenger-prophets (Luke 11:51 → 13:34–35; Acts 7:47–51; 22:17–21; 21:23–26).

d. And while Jesus aligns himself with the whole noble line of persecuted prophets in Luke 11:47–52, Stephen and Paul do the same by appealing (praying) directly to the persecuted Jesus (Acts 7:51–53, 55–60; 22:6–11, 17–21).

3. But as with Paul and Jesus, the most striking parallels are the charges leveled against Stephen: *(a)* "blasphemous words against Moses and God" (6:11); and *(b)* "words against this holy place and the Law," which is explained as promoting "Jesus, the Nazorean's" threat to destroy "this place" and "change the customs which Moses delivered to us" (6:13). Now instead of "the people" and "Caesar," blasphemy against God is focal,[36] while the "Law" and association with "the Nazorean" remain critical. Though nothing about destroying the Temple is lodged against Jesus at his arrest and trial, now interestingly Stephen is accused of propagating an anti-Temple stance of the Nazorean.[37] When we recall the astonishing analogies between Stephen's death ("stoning," 7:57–60) and Jesus' first rejection (Luke 4:16–30; cf. 13:34), Stephen's dying words and Jesus' words on the cross (Acts 7:60 — Luke 23:34; cf. Acts 7:59 — Luke 23:46), the common blasphemy charge (Acts 6:11 — Luke 22:70–71), and the link of the "Son of Man at the right hand of God" (Acts 7:56 — Luke 22:69), it becomes manifest that Stephen is a definitive "type" or "antitype" of the Deuteronomistic rejected Prophet like Jesus and the critical link between Jesus and Paul in this ongoing line.

But two questions are immediately relevant. First, in the context of the journey motif of Luke-Acts, how is Stephen a "type" of Jesus, the Deuteronomistic Prophet like Moses of the New Exodus whose journeying to Jerusalem is paralleled by the prophet Paul? Luke nowhere speaks of a journey ministry by Stephen. Second, does Moses play a specific role in the prophetic model in Acts, or does he simply stand behind the figure of the Jesus of the travel narrative who is proclaimed by the early community as the Prophet like Moses (Acts 3:22)?

It is when we look at the longest speech in Acts, Stephen's defense before the Sanhedrin (7:2–53), that the figure of Moses again looms paramount as in the Central Section of the Gospel. Moses and the Exodus occupy about 60 percent[38] of Stephen's recounting of the *Heilsgeschichte* in which the early community of disciples' own relation to the God of "our fathers" is justified.[39] A closer look at this story divulges the following *journey* stages of the people of God:

a. Upon a revelation (Acts 7:2) of God in Mesopotamia, Abraham moves to Haran after being commanded to "go out" and "come" to the "land" which God will show him (v. 3). But Haran is not the promised "land," since God "leads him to migrate" to "the land" "in which you are now living" (v. 4). From the outset, then, movement to the "land" of revealed promise is the dynamic pivot of the plot. It appears by the end of v. 4 that Stephen already anticipates the climax by pointing out to his hearers in Jerusalem that they are standing in the very land of the fulfilled promise.[40]

b. But the fulfillment did not come so quickly in their journeying history, simply because Abraham himself received no "inheritance" in the land. Instead, God "promised" "possession" (7:5) only after "his descendants" were to become enslaved as strangers in a foreign land. Only then, after some four hundred years, would they "journey out" and come "to worship *in this place*" (v. 7b). That is to say, first another journey is necessary—and indeed a journey to *the place* in the promised land—before the promised inheritance could be realized.

c. But even before this journey Stephen recounts the journey into slavery. First, out of scorn from his brothers, Joseph is sold into bondage in Egypt.[41] But delivered from his afflictions, raised up within the house of Pharaoh, and elevated above all the people of Egypt by God, Joseph becomes an anticipation of the Exodus deliverer by feeding the "twelve patriarchs," Jacob and his relatives, who are "sent" or later "journey down" to escape a devastating famine. Though unrecognized by his brothers on their first visit, this Joseph who was *cast aside* by his own becomes exalted among them as their "deliverer."

d. But as "the time of promise was drawing near" (7:17), this glorious period was not to last for long. Moses, himself one of the brethren of Israel (v. 20) but raised in the house of Pharaoh (v. 21),[42] also goes unrecognized by his own when he visits and "delivers" (v. 25) one of them from the brutal oppression of the Egyptians. On his return to reconcile a feud among his own folk he is spurned and *cast aside*. Thus he must flee to the land of Midian, an alien in his own "house," as well as a sojourner in a foreign land. It is only then that Moses, in the *desert* of Mt. Sinai, receives a calling from the *voice* of the Lord in the midst of burning fire to be *sent* on a journey to his people to deliver them from Egypt. So it is as the days of the long-awaited promise to Abraham and the patriarchs are beginning to be completely full that the Exodus journey begins (vv. 35–41). But although already repudiated by his people, Moses becomes their ruler and deliverer (v. 35b) to lead them out with "wonders and signs in Egypt, the Red Sea, and in the desert for forty years,"[43] and prophesied of one whom "God will raise up from your kinsfolk *like me*" (Acts 7:37 — Deut. 18:15), and received "living words" "in the desert" "upon the mountain." Yet despite all of this, Moses is scorned and *cast aside* a second time by his folk,[44] "our fathers," who "turned in their hearts back to Egypt" (v. 39). This epoch-making rejection is epitomized by the *calf*[45] to which they sacrificed and "were rejoicing in the works of their *hands*" (v. 41). Thus a perverted *rejoicing*[46] in the wilderness at the mountain forms the quintessence of an intractable people whom God gave over not only to idolatrous *worship* (v. 42) but also to the foreign land of Babylon (i.e., tenet D), "just as *it is written* in the book of the *prophets*" (vv. 42–43). Consequently, before the promise is fully realized, the pronouncement of judgment (tenet D) falls over the Exodus journey "to the place" in the land.

e. The journey, however, continues, led by "the tent of witness" which was with "our fathers in the desert" as it was built by Moses (7:44). This tabernacle formed the focal point for "our fathers" when God thrust out the nations during the time of Joshua and up to the days of David, who "found favor before God." Though David wanted to "find" a dwelling place for the God of the house of Jacob, it was his son Solomon who built him a "house" (vv. 45–47). But there is no doubt that this building of the Temple did *not fulfill* the promise to Abraham that his posterity (i.e., "house") would "journey" to "this place" to "worship" God (v. 7 → v. 17). For Stephen immediately qualifies the importance of the Temple by reminding his hearers that God does not *dwell* in such *hand*-made constructions "just as the prophet (Isa. 66:1) declares: 'Heaven is my throne. . . . What is the place of my dwelling? Did not my *hand* make all these things?'" (vv. 49–50 → v. 41!)[47]

f. The journey history for the "house of Jacob" was not over; the *coming* of the Just One[48] was still to be announced beforehand by *the prophets!* But instead of the events of this period being related, they are summed up as a whole by Stephen in an absolutely "scandalous" accusation: Just as "*your* fathers" "persecuted" and "killed" the prophets, so you have "betrayed and murdered" "the Just One" (tenet C, 7:52). The whole lot of them is a "stiff-necked" people, a brood of murderers who, "uncircumcised in heart and *ears*," have not *hearkened* to the Law (v. 53), even as they have "always resisted the Holy Spirit" (tenet A, v. 51). Therefore, Stephen concludes his rehearsal of the entire history of Israel by voicing *the same Deuteronomistic view*[49] that Jesus pronounces during the New Exodus journey in Luke 11:47–51 and 13:34–35. The whole nation is a "wicked generation."

It is true also, then, with Stephen that the story of Moses and the Exodus–journeying history of Israel reaches a high point. For even the stoning of this messenger in Jerusalem (cf. Luke 13:34) cannot halt the ongoing journeying history carried out by Philip to Samaria and Gaza, by others associated with the Stephen-Philip group to Phoenicia, Cyprus, and Antioch (Acts 11:19), and by Paul from Antioch through the eastern Mediterranean eventually to Rome (13:1—28:31). It is precisely the figure and fate of Stephen which, linking the fulfillment of the New Exodus journey of Jesus in the Jerusalem community of Acts 1:6—5:42 to the journey to the center of the Roman Empire, give birth to the exodus of the Jerusalem church on a "worldwide" mission. We can thus establish the following picture of the plot movement in Luke-Acts.

In the opening chapters of the story, the journeys between Galilee and the Temple at Jerusalem anticipate the fulfillment of the *Heilsgeschichte* through the New Exodus of Jesus the Prophet like Moses to the place of all Israel. This culmination is marked by the worship of the First Fruits (Pentecost) community in the eating and drinking, and rejoicing and worshiping of Yahweh at this central place in Jerusalem. In Acts 6, as the unity of this consummated community is threatened, Stephen sums up the journeying salvation history of Israel, which includes the recapitulation and consummation of this history through the coming of the Prophet like Moses (of the Gospel) to the central place, and sparks the next journeying phase through his prophetic warning of judgment. The nation of Israel as a whole remains a stiff-necked persecutor of God's saving agents. The result is that the fulfilled promises to Abraham go out as "a light of revelation for the Gentiles" that "all flesh may see the salvation of God" (Luke 2:32; 3:6).

It is not in the least accidental that in Stephen's recounting of this dynamic history the movement to fulfillment closely follows that of the credo in Deut. 26:1–11:

"My father" journeys from Syria to Egypt, only few in number → Multiplying to a great nation and being enslaved by the Egyptians, "we" are led out by Moses through "signs and wonders" and brought to this *place* which the Lord promised to "our fathers" as an inheritance → "I" have come to this place to eat and rejoice and worship the Lord our God.[50]

Stephen's speech thus draws together the story of Luke-Acts to that point and moves it on to its conclusion. Consequently, Acts 6:1—9:31, along with Luke 9:1–50, functions as a second watershed in the plot. Just as

Jesus' "reception" at the base of the mountain and his cry of desperation (tenet A) augurs the rejection once again of God's messenger by the whole nation at Jerusalem, so Stephen's "reception" upon recounting this long history of rejection with its accusation (tenet A) portends the rejection of God's messenger Paul by the whole nation at Jerusalem. We can schematize this movement with the pivotal points Luke 9:1–50 and Acts 6:1—9:31 like two foci of an ellipse:

The thrust of the story from Acts 9:32—28:31 centers upon the beginnings of the extension of the fulfillment to the Gentiles and culminates in Paul's rejection at Jerusalem with his concluding judgment at Rome against the whole nation of Israel in the distinct tones of tenet A:

> The Holy Spirit was right in saying to *your fathers* through Isaiah *the prophet,* "Go to this people and declare: You shall indeed hear but never understand . . . for the heart of this people has grown fat, they have become hard of hearing . . . lest they should hearken (ἀκούω) with their ears and understand with their heart and turn for me to heal them."

Paul, the great prophetic preacher of repentance to Israel, in nearly every city of his sending must turn to the Gentiles, for "they will hearken" (v. 28).[51] The journeying history of promise and fulfillment enacted through the Deuteronomistic dynamics of the tragic fate of God's messengers continues. But even as the irresistible movement to tenet D lurks ominously in the background, the promises of the Kingdom of God move forward uninhibited in the center of the world (28:30–31). For just as the twisted repudiation of Moses and all the prophets led to the New Exodus salvation of Israel in the Prophet like (and greater than) Moses, so this same stubborn rejection is now leading to the "new" Exodus of this salvation to the ends of the earth.

We can group our conclusions for the significance of the travel narrative (Luke 9:51—19:44) by summarizing the plot of the Prophet like Moses that moves through the pages of Luke-Acts (i.e., in "plotted" time):[52]

1. The calling to a journey sending is revealed by the voice of the Lord in great light:

Jesus ⟶	*Moses* (Stephen) ⟶	*Paul*
(Luke 9:29–35)	(Acts 7:30–32, 38)	(9:3–19; 22:6–11; 26:12–18)

Stephen's calling is likewise confirmed by the "Lord" in great light (Acts 7:55).

2. This calling is one to a suffering unrecognition and rejection by the whole people of Israel:

Jesus ⟶	*Moses* (Stephen) ⟶	*Paul*
(Luke 9:18–50)	(Acts 7:23–29)	(9:16–30; 22:18; 26:17)

Stephen's calling is likewise one of suffering rejection (Acts 6:9–15; 7:54—8:3). All three prophets in the context of Israel's journeying history pronounce the indictment of tenet A: Luke 11:47–51 → Acts 7:51–53 → Acts 28:25b–28

3. The suffering journey is a mission of deliverance (salvation) to the central place of all Israel—in Jerusalem:

Jesus ⟶	*Moses* (Stephen) ⟶	*Paul*
(Luke 9:51—19:44)	(Acts 7:7, 17, 35–46)	(19:21—28:31)

Stephen's suffering likewise leads to a mission of deliverance (salvation) which culminates in the central place—in Jerusalem (Acts 9:15–16 → 11:19–26 → 19:21—21:26; 21:27—28:31).

4. This suffering journey mission ends in the monolithic rejection of the "deliverer" by a stiff-necked nation. But through this tragic end, the salvation of the living words of the mountain is effected for the children of Abraham, even to the widow and stranger,[53] that is, to the outcast and to the nations of the earth, as foretold (written) by the prophets (cf. Luke 3:8):[54]

Jesus ⟶	*Moses* (Stephen) ⟶	*Paul*
(Luke 24:44–49; Acts 1:8)	(Acts 7:42–50)	(21:27—28:31)

Stephen's mission of suffering also leads to his tragic end, but thereby not only is salvation consolidated for "the Hellenists" (Acts 6:1–6) but is extended to "the Gentiles" as well (11:19–20; 9:15; 22:15; 26:19–23).

We find therefore the same fourfold pattern of Jesus the Prophet like Moses of Deuteronomy of the travel narrative (Luke 9:51—19:44)[55] extended throughout Luke's two-volume story. It is in fact this pattern which drives the action of the plot not only through the Central Section of the Gospel but also throughout the entire ongoing story of the fulfillment of that journey in Acts. And in this continuation as it is outlined in Acts 1:8, it has become clear that the Stephen-Philip group occupies a pivotal position. Without the journeys of persecution to Samaria and Antioch, the dynamics of the story would break down altogether. Luke then tells the story of the *glory of God* as revealed at the beginning and at three critical stages in the fulfillment of the history of salvation: Luke 2:9, 32 (Prophet-Messiah's birth) → 9:31–32; cf. 9:26[56] (the Mountain) → Acts 7:55; cf. 7:2[57] (Stephen's death) → Acts 9:3ff.; 22:11ff. (Paul to the Gentiles). It is to this glory which the disciples-prophets have seen and heard that they go forth as witnesses from Galilee (Acts 10:39; 13:31) to Jerusalem (Acts 1:8) and via Stephen (Acts 22:20) through Paul (Acts 22:15; 23:11; 26:11–18) to the ends of the earth on the journey of the Kingdom of God. We can schematize this story time of the history of the way (ὁδός) of salvation, from the promise to Abraham to the ends of the earth,[58] through the prophets like Moses, as disclosed in Stephen's "witness" and violent death: *Abraham* → (Joseph) *Moses* → *Jesus* (Messiah) → (Stephen) *Paul* → *Nations* of the Earth

REFLECTIONS *on the* THEOLOGICAL IMPLICATIONS *of the* NEW EXODUS TRAVEL NARRATIVE *for* INTERPRETING LUKE-ACTS

Our discovery that Jesus' long journey to Jerusalem presents the fulfillment of the promised New Exodus salvation of the Prophet like Moses carries with it conclusions that must be taken into consideration in penetrating the unity and purpose of the author of Luke-Acts. We shall look briefly at two dimensions of his story that call for a thorough rethinking in contemporary estimates of the Lukan point of view.

Eschatology and Luke's *Sitz im Leben*

Our analysis has been restricted primarily to treating Luke's text as a mirror.[59] Before substantial gains can be made in perceiving Luke's own aims and situation of his writing, thorough studies correlating the text as both mirror and window will have to be carried out. Our extrinsic literary comparisons, however, have uncovered a conceptual framework, a particular orientation to the world "of events that have been completed among us," through and from which our author writes his account. Our analysis both of the Central Section and of the larger journey motif within the story of Luke-Acts has revealed a lineage and language of the prophets conceived within the Deuteronomistic conception of Israel's history. The story of the Jesus who journeys to Jerusalem and the story of the journeys of the Stephen-Philip group and of Paul in the Acts are a continuing story of prophets sent to Israel to receive a prophet's "reward," beginning long ago in the promise of inheritance given to Abraham.[60] Whatever else Luke intends with his two volumes, he is clearly, if not foremostly, continuing the biblical story of the history of God's dealings with God's people Israel.

Luke writes, then, a history from a specific theological vantage point, or what we call a theological history. Our treatment of the calling and fate of the prophets like Moses reveals how impossible it is to separate history from theology or theology from history in Luke's thinking. Israel's history is primarily a succession of messengers, divinely sent in real time, to carry out specific events resulting in specific consequences. Luke is aware both of this historic succession and of the inner forces or dynamics of history that fundamentally link these stages and their results. But for Luke, both these successions and outcomes are subsumed to the more comprehensive divine δεῖ of the rule of God in the Kingdom of God. Unless Luke is a "crank," deceiving his readers by presenting an "orderly account of the events" that he himself does not believe (cf. Luke 1:1–4), it becomes certain that the fundamental parallels in the careers of Stephen and Paul with Jesus are not purely poetic devices to motivate and bring cohesion to the plot. Movement and cohesion, rather, are due ultimately to the divine δεῖ enacted through the Spirit of the God who from beginning to end dominates the story as the ultimate motivator and consummator of the plot. It is this comprehensive interpretation governing the Deuteronomistic dynamics of Israel's history which must be kept in the forefront of any discussion of Luke's eschatology and vantage point of his own writing.

Israel in the History of Salvation and the Imminent Expectation

It should strike the reader who is aware of the Deuteronomistic historians' succession of prophecy and fulfillment and the prophetic succession within that history that at the opening of the story (Luke 1:1—4:13) Luke indicates that this prophetic line is again being activated. It should also strike one as significant that at the very end of Acts, Paul, in the mantle of a prophet, speaks of this chain of prophecy and fulfillment as still actively in force. Where does Luke at the time of his writing stand in relation to this dynamic of history?

1. Paul's arrival and open preaching in Rome of "the Kingdom of God" is a distinct parallel to the opening of the story in Luke where John the Baptist is preaching good news (Acts 28:31 — Luke 3:3, 18). That is to say, even as Luke begins on a kerygmatic note, so he ends with this same kerygmatic emphasis. This is made all the more clear by the added description that Paul "was teaching about the things concerning the Lord

Jesus Christ." We have already seen that John points directly ahead to the coming one who is the "Lord" (3:4) and the "Christ" (3:15), and Jesus' journey to Jerusalem as well as the content of the preaching concerning him in the Jerusalem community centers upon his Lordship as the Prophet-Christ (e.g., Acts 2:36; 3:19, 22; 4:33). Moreover, the parallel fate of Stephen and Paul as explicitly cast in the same mold as this Lord-Prophet-Christ demonstrates the fundamental continuity of this kerygmatic line. In short, there is no indication whatever that Luke is "historicizing" the ministry of Jesus as a separate or distinct period or epoch followed by a secularized or "dekerygmatized" period of the church, as some from the "new look" had argued.[61] Far from pushing Jesus' ministry back to a time that is past and self-contained, the dynamic of the journeying Jesus, Lord and Prophet-Messiah like Moses, continues to the very end of Luke's story.[62] Paul is even cast as a journeying guest[63] who, after arriving at Rome, welcomes or receives[64] guests into his own place of residence (28:30; cf. 28:16).

2. The closing of Acts in the ominous tones of Deuteronomistic tenet A leaves the reader with the unmistakable impression that the story is building to an eruption of tenet D. It is certain from the end of Luke's plotted time that Jerusalem and the Temple are as vital as ever as the focal point of the nation. It has been only a little over two years since Paul came face-to-face with the "zealous" lynching mob at the Temple.

3. It is also the case that though the mission(ary) center shifts from Jerusalem to Antioch to Rome via the Stephen-Philip group and then Paul, it is not true that the "journeying center" in the history of salvation shifts away from Jerusalem to Rome.[65] On the contrary, we have seen not only that Paul's journey to Jerusalem at the end of Acts is purposely portrayed in the lights and shadows of Jesus' journey there but also that Paul still views the Temple as the historic center of the salvation that has come from Israel and out to Israel as this salvation is extended to the nations.[66] In his defense speeches in Jerusalem and Caesarea, Luke has Paul emphasize that as a model Israelite (à la Deut. 26:1–11, and like Jesus in Luke 2:41–50 and 9:51—22:38) he has come up to Jerusalem bearing his "first fruits" "to worship" the "God of our fathers" at the place (Acts 20:16; 24:11, 17–18; 26:21). He declares further before Festus and Herod Agrippa that he is on "trial" for "hope in the promise given by God to our fathers to which our *twelve* tribes wish to attain" (26:6–7). There is neither a shift away from the centrality of Jerusalem in the history of God's dealings with God's people nor the conception that the *laos* of God is now being replaced by the Gentiles.[67] Paul's "hope of the twelve tribes" articulates the same hope as the journeying Jesus, "Jerusalem, Jerusalem . . . How often would I have gathered your children together as

a hen gathers her brood under her wing but you would not" (Luke 13:34).

Though we will not launch into a fuller investigation of *laos*,[68] "Israel," and the "Temple"[69] in Luke-Acts, we have already noticed that within the Deuteronomistic framework the wholesale rejection of God's salvation by Israel leads to their judgment, destruction, and exile rather than a transfer of God's covenant promises to another people. This confusion has led to the erroneous assertions on the part of some contemporary interpreters that the end of Acts signals a "new people of God" or a "disengagement of Christianity from Judaism"[70] or the transition of Christianity to "a religion distinct from Judaism."[71] Nowhere does Luke state or intimate that Israel's rejection of Paul's message leads to a transfer of God's people qua people to the Gentiles. Rather, the same conception that dominates the travel narrative, namely, that from the Horeb *laos* a renewed *laos*—including the "outcast" and the Gentile—is being fashioned, also controls the Acts.

By the same token, Paul's sending to the Gentiles proceeds from the core of his original calling (e.g., Acts 26:19–20) and is *not* based upon the Jews en masse *first* rejecting the message. It may be true that when Paul is called on the Damascus road his own zealous persecution of the church is a prefigurement of the growing consolidation that eventually hands him over for legal proceedings. Yet it is equally true that at the height of this persecution in Stephen's death, Stephen's defense presents a "God of glory" whose dynamic presence and saving revelation are anything but confined to "the land" of the promise.[72] Thus hand in hand with Israel's growing rejection there remains a constant stream of a smaller number of Israel that do repent along with an increasing "turning of" the Gentiles to God (e.g., 13:42–48; 14:1ff.; 17:1ff.; 18:1–17; 19:1–10). At the practical or logistical level, this "turning of" the Gentiles is a result of increased "turning to" the Gentiles as Israel as a whole in various localities rejects Paul's preaching (e.g., "the Jews," 13:45; 14:4; 17:5; 18:5–6; 20:19). But at a deeper theological level, Israel's rejection is precisely the God-ordained means by which, through a smaller remnant, the "glory of Israel" is shed as salvation upon the nations (13:46–48; 26:22–23). Already at the beginning of the story in the Temple, Simeon sounds this theme of (Deutero-) Isaiah: "thy salvation which thou hast prepared in the presence of all the peoples, a light for revelation to the nations and for the glory of your people Israel . . . and for a sign that will be spoken against" (Luke 2:30–32, 34b).

Israel, then, is at the center for the sake of the nations. Luke's use of Deutero-Isaiah ought to be pursued further.[73] But we can observe here that just as all along his Mediterranean journeys Paul first goes to the synagogues and preaches there to all, including Gentile God-fearers, who will listen, so in Rome Paul first receives the local leaders of the Jews into his house before he pronounces Isaiah's judgment: "Some were convinced by what he was saying, but others did not believe" (28:24).[74] The Deuteronomistic conception of the remnant thus continues to the very end of Acts, with the parallel fomenting rejection of the Prophet's messengers. Yet in spite of this hostility, Paul does not make a decisive turn away from the Jews any more than before, for he "was welcoming[75] *all* who entered to [see] him" (28:30b). Israel and Jerusalem remain pivotal.

4. At the same time, with Israel's centrality a sine qua non, Paul's warning to that people in Acts 28:25b–28 makes it clear that God's patience does not bide an indefinite period of refusal of salvation. A thorough investigation of the relation of the story in Acts to the Deuteronomistic dynamics of history is needed.[76] But our analysis of this dynamic in the Gospel travel narrative and the subsequent Jerusalem ministry already sheds light on Paul's closing words. While teaching in the Temple, Jesus had already prophesied that not one of its stones would be left upon another (cf. Luke 19:40) by the merciless devastators of Jerusalem (tenet D). "But *before* all these things" "folk ['they'] will lay their hands upon you and persecute you" (Luke 21:12a). It is certain that this indefinite "they" refers to the disciples' fellow Jews by what follows in vv. 12b–13—"delivering you over to the synagogues and prisons, before kings and governors for the sake of my name. This will be a time for you to bear witness." This period and path of persecution portrays precisely Paul's predicament in his journey to Jerusalem and Rome: in his earlier journeying he had met persecution from fellow Jews (Acts 13:44–51; 14:5–7, 19; 17:5–9, 13; 18:6, 12–17; 20:3, 19) in the synagogues or from the Jewish leaders (13:4–45; 14:5;[77] 18:4–6); and now as he arrives in Jerusalem he is delivered over by the Jews to King Agrippa (26:2, 7, 13, 19, 26, 27, 30) and to the Roman governors Felix and Festus (23:24, 26, 33; 24:1, 10) and must bear witness to his association with the name "Jesus Nazorean" (24:5; cf. 22:8; 26:9). In other words, according to the story time, Luke closes his two volumes with a description of the period before the destruction of Jerusalem, an event that must still take place as a punishment for Israel's stubborn resistance.

"Jerusalem" is thus not deeschatologized by Luke. The dynamics of the New Exodus journey to Jerusalem are moving to an inexorable climax. Paul's parallel journey signals that God by no means has given up his people Israel in their history of election. The very fact that the history of Israel's disobedience from the Exodus occupation of the land to the destruction of Jerusalem and the Babylonian exile is now being recapitulated is a powerful demonstration that Yahweh is faithful to the covenant. Jerusalem's impending destruction is a divine certainty based on the history-creating word of the Lord spoken through his Prophet.[78] Consequently Luke does not give up on the idea of an "imminent expectation" of the Parousia.[79] It is the case, rather, that Jesus' prophecy of the end is moving exactly according to the path that he had described. Though hated, Paul has not lost his life (Luke 21:18–19 → Acts 28:30–31); the period of "witness" is still in force. But after this, Gentile armies will "surround" Jerusalem to desolate and "take into exile" her people "in the days of punishment" (Luke 21:20–24) *"to fulfill all that has been written!"* (v. 22). It is only then after this fulfillment that the "times of the Gentiles" will be completed and folk will see the "Son of Man *coming* in a cloud with power and great glory" (v. 27). As we have seen, all through Jesus' journey in the travel narrative and in the earliest Jerusalem community, Luke lays the stress on the eschatological *fulfillment* of the promises to Abraham as brought to completion in the Prophet like Moses. The story of the Acts is the ongoing saga of this *completion* in the hardening heart of Israel with the accompanying mission to the Gentiles which will ensue ultimately in its destruction as a nation but also in the repentance of some of Israel to form the center of the renewed, consummated people of God. Only in this sense can we speak of the relative unimportance of the imminent end which will come "suddenly like a snare" (Luke 21:34b).

It would be specious methodologically to go from the *Sitz im Leben* of the end of the plotted time directly to Luke's own *Sitz im Leben* at the time of his writing. "Narrative world" cannot be translated directly into "author's world." We have seen, for example, that themes significant to the story do not necessarily link up with "needs" of supposed communities. Nor can we read biographical facts into the author's situation from the biographical details he assigns to his leading characters.[80] Yet with this caveat in mind, our analysis of the story does produce several clues to the *possible* time of writing:

a. Our references to the journeying-guest theme in Acts need to be supplemented by two observations: (i) Most of Paul's final journey to Jerusalem and Rome is accompanied by the famous "we" passages (so, explicitly, 20:5—21:18; 27:1—28:16; cf. 16:10–17).[81] The vivid detail of the Jerusalem proceedings suggests that the "we" was never far away from the action. A narrator thus purports to have been an eyewitness to this journey which is modeled after Jesus' journeying-guest mission to Jerusalem. (ii) Apart from the earliest Jerusalem community in Acts 2:42, 46, the only descriptive accounts of a *meal* are in those "we" journeying sections, namely, the "breaking of bread" at Troas (20:7–12)[82] and the "blessing and breaking of the bread" on the ship off the coast of Malta (27:33–38).[83] It would appear, then, that the "we" narrator had a special interest in or attached a particular significance to the "breaking of bread" among the mission communities.[84] *If,* as is certainly possible, the "we" is meant to include the actual "I" of the Prologues in Luke 1:1–4 and Acts 1:1–5,[85] then this portrayal of meals links directly with the interest in the journeying-guest meal fellowship of the New Exodus travel narrative (Luke 9:51—19:44) and the Passion, Emmaus, and upper room meals of the Jerusalem period. The author of the two volumes would then be the companion of Paul on Paul's last journey to Jerusalem and Rome, who leaves the reader with Paul after two years in the capital of the Empire.

b. We discovered that the Deuteronomistic dynamics of the rejection of Jesus, God's messenger, were introduced at table with a Pharisee (Simon, Luke 7:36–50) in which a discussion between Jesus and Simon and his Pharisee friends is presented.[86] We also noticed that Jesus' warning judgment at table at a later stage in the journey leads to caustic exchanges between Jesus and the Pharisees and the absence of further table fellowship with them, on the one side, and an intensifying stream of outcasts to Jesus as "guests," on the other.[87] This development was then contrasted with the favorable portrayal of the Pharisees in the Acts.[88] Yet however careful Luke is to present the Pharisees as supporters of the new "way," he also subtly allows references to strife and dissension reflecting Pharisee sentiments to pierce through. The "some" of Acts 15:1 is connected in 15:5 to the "Pharisee believers'" insistence that all non-Jewish converts be circumcised in order to adhere to the law of Moses. This dispute is in turn linked to the "apostolic decree"[89] (cf. esp. 15:1 → v. 24) in which table fellowship is the central concern (15:20, 29). Moreover, Peter's visionary "conversion" to a fellowship with "unclean" Gentiles comes by way of meal-food imagery which Luke carefully links to the "circumcision party's" criticism of Peter's eating with Gentiles (10:9–16 → v. 28 → v. 48b → 11:3–10 → 15:1). When these facts are joined with yet a third series of developments—the table-service controversy between the "Hellenists" and the "Hebraists" in 6:1–6—a fuller picture indeed begins to emerge. In the "murmuring" (6:1) tones recalling the Pharisees' censoring of Jesus' meal practice, Luke quickly passes over the squabble by introducing the "Seven" and the stories of Stephen and Philip. This latter group is then tied uniquely to Antioch and the spread of the preaching to Gentiles[90] right at the juncture of Peter's defense of his eating with Gentiles to the circumcision party in 11:2–17 → v. 18 → v. 19. What Peter has just learned at Caesarea is already being promulgated in Antioch!

The composite picture that emerges, then, is that the table fellowship controversies so pregnantly depicted in the travel narrative find a distinctive echo in the stories of the Acts. The period of composition of the

Gospel represents *perhaps* a time in which table fellowship was a burning issue in the Jerusalem church and in the subsequent Jewish-Gentile mission churches.[91] Much in its resolution would turn upon how Jesus was remembered to have related to the "unclean" and those "ignorant" in the Law. It is possible that in the discussions of Jesus and his disciples at table with Pharisees in the journey narrative, we hear the notes of discord between "Hellenists" and "Hebraists" in Jerusalem and between Pharisees of the circumcision party and those of the Stephen-Philip Gentile mission group, the latter reflecting possibly the views of ritual and cultic law similar to Stephen's speech. It is clear that the conciliatory tone of Acts represents Luke's own viewpoint and that he can in no way be dubbed anti-Pharisee or even anti-Semitic. But his Acts *may* reflect a period when Zealots put extreme pressure on Jewish converts to separate from Gentile contacts in all matter of social intercourse and particularly from the common meal.[92] Historians have placed the table fellowship strife at Antioch, known to us from Galatians 2, around the early or middle 50s C.E.[93] The Acts could then depict this period and carry the story farther to the late 50s C.E. and the beginning of the 60s C.E. when the situation had grown increasingly worse, so much so that Luke has James warn Paul at his fateful and final arrival in Jerusalem (ca. 58 C.E.) that "myriads" of Jewish believers were "zealous" for the Law, and then surprisingly repeats the apostolic decree as if Paul has never heard it before (21:20, 25; cf. 15:22–35).[94] If again the "we" so interested in meals on this final journey is Luke, the author of Luke-Acts, then *perhaps* again we have an important clue to the time and situation of his own writing.

    c. The threefold scheme of the "new look" which replaced the twofold Markan eschatological framework for Luke has been rejected generally[95]—and rightly so. Nonetheless, the correlative assertion—Luke as a "third generation" Christian looks back at a "foregone" era from the 80s C.E. (at the earliest) or more likely from about 90–110 C.E.[96]—lingers almost impeachably as a foregone conclusion.[97] This dating may be right. But a third and possibly the most telling observation that tends against this later dating is the fact that the Deuteronomistic dynamics of Israel's history are not drawn out to their (inner) logical conclusion, namely, the death of Paul following in the footsteps of Jesus and Stephen and, even more important, the destruction of Jerusalem in 70 C.E. as the fulfillment of tenet D. To be sure, Luke could be writing to people who were familiar with Paul's death and the fate of Jerusalem and he knew very well that they could draw the obvious connections and conclusions. Nevertheless, there is still a considerable inherent thrust within the plotted time that begs for resolution if in fact Paul's fate as a prophet like Jesus (Moses) had already been sealed and had been matched by Jerusalem's destruction. The atmosphere, rather, of the Acts is one of an irenic appeal to various groups within Judaism and the church to unite within the one "hope of Israel"⁹⁸ at a time when clearly the break between synagogue and church was anything but complete. Paul goes to the Temple for a vow, the Jews in Rome receive Paul's word eagerly (Acts 28:22). This period of "engaged disengagement" just prior to 70 C.E. could well reflect the time of Luke's writing to "you, your Excellency, Theophilus" (Luke 1:3).

In sum, on the basis of our limited internal analysis of plot and plot motivation in Luke-Acts, a pre-70 C.E. date for the completion of the two volumes should be given new and serious contemplation. This evidence, however, is, again, restricted and needs to be supplemented by extrinsic literary and sociohistorical data. Unless, on other grounds, it could be demonstrated that the "we" within the "plotted time" of the last half of Acts is the real author of the two-volume story, our intrinsic evidence does not penetrate directly into the "author's world."

Clues to Certain Tradents of the New Exodus Travel Narrative

Further, traditiohistorical analysis would have to be carried out on the travel narrative traditions to gain a fuller picture of the identity of the "eyewitnesses and servants of the word" to whose accounts Luke claims to have access as he begins his story (Luke 1:1–3). Our study, however, has divulged distinctive lines of connection between the Seventy(-two) ("others") of the journeying-guest mission and the Stephen-Philip group of the Acts. A listing of these lines will suffice here:

1. *Emphasis on the dynamic or "enthusiastic" power of the Holy Spirit over evil spirits (demons) and through "signs" or demonstrations of power.* Though this "prophetic model" runs throughout Luke and particularly in Acts,⁹⁹ it is Stephen, followed by Philip, who most strikingly embodies this characteristic. Luke 10:17–24; cf. 11:13, 57; 12:1–12 → Acts 6:3, 5, 8, 10; 7:22, 25, 36, 51, 55; 8:6–13, 26–40.

2. *The Messiah as essentially a prophetic figure and indeed like Moses of the Exodus deliverance.*¹⁰⁰ Luke 9:51—10:24; cf. 9:1–50; 19:28–40 → Acts 7:9–45, 52, esp. v. 37; cf. 8:26–40. The emphasis on Jerusalem as the place of all Israel already accented in Luke 9:51—10:24 and carried out throughout the journey narrative is unusually prominent in Stephen's speech (Acts 7:7, 17, 45–46).

3. *The dynamic journeying history of the revelation of God not bound to land or shrine.* The whole of the travel narrative as poignantly displayed in Lk 9:51—10:24 (esp. 10:21–24) exhibits the dynamic presence of God for

salvation as revealed in the Jesus who journeys to the place in Jerusalem. This dynamic notion is featured in Stephen's rehearsal of the journeying *Heilsgeschichte* which culminates with the bringing of the tabernacle to the place (Acts 7:44–46) and is continued in the dynamic presence of the Spirit in the journey missions of the Stephen-Philip group (8:4ff.). The travel narrative is thus a journey of the "tabernacled glory" of God in Jesus. Luke 9:31 → 9:51 → 19:38 → 24:26 → Acts 7:(2) 55 → 22:11.

4. *The extension of this dynamic presence as salvation for Israel to the Gentiles.* The universalistic thrust receives its decisive impulse in the journeying-guest mission of Jesus and the Seventy(-two) and is carried out by the Stephen-Philip group and on through Paul.

5. *The journeying-guest mission of the New Exodus and its special interest in Samaria.*[101] Luke 9:52–56; 10:25–37; 17:11–19. Similarly, Stephen's speech bears distinct affinities with Samaritan ideas and traditions,[102] including emphasis on Joseph and the Messiah like Moses (cf. the Samaritan *Taheb*);[103] and as a result of the persecution of Stephen, it is Samaria which becomes the first object of the mission preaching and healing of the Stephen-Philip group: Acts 8:4–25.[104]

6. *Meals as a focal point for this dynamic presence of God as salvation.* The meals of the journey mission of the Seventy(-two) sound the keynote for the rest of the journey which climaxes in the eating and drinking and rejoicing before the Lord in the Jerusalem meals of the First Fruits community. It is Stephen and the "Six" who are appointed to administer this table service (Acts 6:1–6). The following themes draw together all five of the major connecting points above:

a. *Revelation of the dynamic presence* of the Lord of the Banquet in the mission of the Seventy(-two) climaxes at Emmaus where the "Prophet mighty in deed and word" is recognized as Jesus the journeying guest. The themes of this revelation scene are linked extraordinarily closely to the Stephen-Philip group: (i) Revelation is a dynamic presence not bound to Jerusalem or the Temple. (ii) Jesus, a prophet before God and the whole people, "redeems" Israel ($\lambda\upsilon\tau\rho\delta o\mu\alpha\iota$,[105] Luke 24:21 → $\lambda\upsilon\tau\rho\omega\tau\eta s$,[106] Acts 7:35—of Moses) by being rejected and killed (Luke 24:20, 26 → Acts 7:23–29, 35–36, 39–40, 52). This rejection is due to both a lack of recognition and a stolidity of heart (Luke 24:25 → Acts 7:51). (iii) This rejected Prophet-Messiah was prophesied by "Moses and all the prophets" (Luke 24:25, 27 → Acts 7:37, 52), whose spoken words are dynamic living words straining toward fulfillment (Luke 24:25 → Acts 7:37–38, 52). (iv) Jesus is termed "the Nazorean" (Luke 24:19 → Acts 6:14 → 22:8; 24:5; 26:9).

b. *The antipurity, antiritualistic stance* of the journey mission of the Seventy(-two) is echoed in the charges against Stephen (6:11, 13–14—against the Law and "the customs"), in his "living oracles" from Sinai (7:38), and in the table fellowship controversy in Acts which is sparked by the Gentile mission of the Stephen-Philip group.

c. *The anti-Pharisee outlook* concentrated at table in the travel narrative appears to emerge again around the table fellowship controversy between the Pharisee-circumcision party and the mission stemming from the dispersion of the Stephen-Philip group. This connection with the latter circle may well explain the exceptional anti-Pharisee posture—within an otherwise sympathetic portrayal by Luke—as an intra-Jewish rivalry.[107]

d. The Temple, symbolic of a stiff-necked nation and surfacing peculiarly "at table" with the Pharisees in the travel narrative (11:47–51), is mirrored in the anti-Temple charge against Stephen (Acts 6:13–14). In both instances the nation's stubborn rejection of the prophets sent to her is aligned with her "house" (Luke 11:47–51; 13:34–35; 19:39–47 → Acts 7:39–53).

e. The portrayal of *Jesus as the servant at table* in the New Exodus journey which climaxes at the Passion meal is emulated again by the Seven who are chosen to serve at table (Acts 6:1–3). The tension between serving at table and the hearing of the word in Luke 10:38–42 and the danger of lax and unscrupulous service at table in 12:35–48 and 17:7–10 may well represent such tensions as the Hellenist-Hebraist controversy in Acts 6:1–6. It is noteworthy that Peter as spokesman for the Twelve is pitched in an unfavorable strain in the Gospel; but after a change of posture toward "table fellowship" he becomes in the Acts a mediating figure in the conflict between the circumcision party of Pharisees and the Antioch mission community of the Stephen-Philip group (Acts 11:1–20; 15:1–11, 14).[108]

f. The monolithic rejection of Jesus, the prophet, which is vividly depicted at the beginning of the mission of the Seventy(-two) and is concentrated at table with the Pharisees in the New Exodus journey (Luke 11:37–54; 14:1–24), is linked to Stephen's speech and fate primarily through the Emmaus and upper room meals where Jesus is the rejected, suffering one (24:20, 25–27, 46). Moreover, this suffering rejection at table is joined with humble service at the Passion meal (22:21–27). Thus Jesus is cast as a "suffering servant" at table and is imitated later by Stephen, the suffering servant of tables.

g. The mission to the nations intimated in the journeying-guest meals of the Seventy(-two) is anticipated again at table with the Pharisees in the invitation by the Lord of the Banquet to the "poor and unclean" at the outskirts of Israel (14:12–24), embraced by this journeying Lord's eating and drinking with "sinners," and commissioned by this Lord at table to his disciples (including the two Emmaus disciples; cf. 24:35–36) who are to be his witnesses in the power of the Holy Spirit (24:46–49; cf. Acts 1:4–5). The Stephen-Philip group, table servants to widows, is the critical link in the fulfillment of this mission.

h. Jesus, the journeying-guest Lord of the Banquet, is related to the Wisdom of God, particularly at meals (e.g., Luke 7:31–35; 11:37–54). It is precisely the Stephen-Philip group of Seven who must be full of wisdom in order to qualify for table service (e.g., Acts 6:3; cf. 6:10; 7:10, 22).

These themes and emphases therefore characterize and cluster about specific actors in Luke's two-part drama. We have already seen that the Stephen-Philip group is pivotal to this flow and is constitutive to the plot of the Prophet like Moses of the New Exodus. We can now add that if the "we" actor in Acts represents the author of Luke-Acts, then the latter provides a description of his own contact with this group in Acts 20:5—21:14. From Troas through Assos, Mitylene, Samos, Miletus, Cos, Rhodes, Patara, Tyre, and Ptolemais, Paul and companions arrive in Caesarea to be received into "the house" of Philip, who, the "we" says explicitly, "was one of the Seven" (21:8). There "we stayed" (v. 8b) "for several days" (v. 10a), hearing Philip's four daughters "prophesy" as well as "the prophet" Agabus, who is reported to utter a "Passion prediction" for Paul which clearly resounds Luke 18:32a. Again at Acts 27:1–2 the "we" speaks as though he had been in Caesarea at least sometime prior to Paul's departure from there to Rome.

In general, the Stephen-Philip group (with the Seventy[-two]) exhibits traits that converge with ideas and outlooks of the old Northern Kingdom of Israel which survived in part in Samaria and perhaps in various Essene communities down to the days of Jesus:[109] (i) Rejection of the Davidic dynasty, though the Davidic era per se is not disavowed. (ii) The charismatic principle of the prophets' calling as exhibited in Elijah and Elisha, continued by Hosea, and reflected in Jeremiah. The Seven are clearly chosen on this basis and not by the "southern" dynastic principle, which is perhaps in part behind James's leadership. (iii) Moses as the preeminent "type" of Messiah rather than David. (iv) The ark and tabernacle as a dynamic witness of Yahweh's revelatory presence. With Jerusalem as the central place for this dynamic revelation, we must rule out a Samaritan group for whom Shechem and Mt. Gerizim would be central. It may be that circles in which the predominantly northern traditions of Deuteronomy were first collected and placed into a covenant renewal framework survived in the North[110] in outlying territories like Gaulanitis and Ulatha (i.e., the tetrarchy of Philip, OT Bashan), parts of the Decapolis such as the OT Gilead, Perea (Gilead, including the tribe of Gad), and areas as far away as the province of Syria, Ituraea, Trachonitis, and Abilene. Luke's chronological and geopolitical compass in Luke 3:1–2 (cf. 6:17) may then betray certain circles of his traditionists (cf. 1:1–4) if not certain readers of his as well. For the Stephen-Philip group, Jerusalem is the focal point for the unity of the tribes of Israel *and* Judah as well as the epitome of all that is wrong with the existing official Judaism of the South. The journeying Jesus' desire to gather "her children" (Luke 13:34) may reflect not only the New Exodus theme of Deuteronomy 30 and Deutero-Isaiah but also this same hope in Jeremiah 30—31 where Yahweh the good Shepherd (cf. Luke 15:3–7) gathers in the scattered flock as they stream to Jerusalem to receive Yahweh's *"new covenant with the house of Israel and the house of Judah"* (Jer. 31:31; cf. 31:7–25). It has been pointed out that Philip's mission to Samaria in Acts 8 may represent this group's belief that the Mosaic deliverer Jesus had come to reunite North and South, and consequently they saw their mission to Samaria as part of this eschatological fulfillment.[111] This view harmonizes well with the stress on the eschatological fulfillment that we found in the travel narrative.

In line also with this Samaritan connection, it is possible that the New Exodus travel narrative is a collection of traditions—stemming in part from the Seventy(-two) "eyewitnesses" (cf. Luke 1:2)—used as mission preaching and teaching by the Stephen-Philip group in Samaria. The dearth of topographical detail could then be explained through the kerygmatic and didactic superfluity of such detail as well as the unfamiliarity of Samaritans with Galilean towns and countryside. Such obscure villages as Capernaum and Gennesaret[112] would neither aid the Samaritans in receiving the good news of the New Exodus of their Mosaic Messiah *(Taheb)* nor present them with palpable sights and smells that would animate their picture of Jesus. In fact, such geographical illustrations might have offended some of them.[113] Luke 9:52–56 would then also be explicable as a demonstration of Jesus' love for the Samaritan people despite rejection by one of their villages. And the comment of 9:53 would make sense not only on the level of Jesus' journeying but also for the later journeying of the Stephen-Philip "messengers" who constantly confronted the "offense" of Jerusalem in their mission preaching.[114] Here it might also prove illuminating to compare the mission of the seventy(-two) *"others"* who are sent out to *eat* and *drink* where "the *harvest* is plentiful" to the Samaritan jaunt in John 4 where Jesus says to his disciples that they have entered (perfect tense) into the labor of *"others"* who have already "sown in fields" that are now "white for *harvest*" (John 4:35–38).[115] Here, interestingly, the disciples have just returned from buying food and admonish Jesus to *eat,* to which he replies: "My food is to do the will of him who sent me" (4:34a; cf. Luke 10:16)!

We have etched a profile, then, of possible eyewitness traditionists, with distinct northern affinities, standing behind certain of the traditions of Luke's Central Section. Here it would be interesting to speculate on a more precise provenance, though we must bear in mind the desiderata of further traditiohistorical comparisons. It is in the region of Bethsaida, Luke says, that the crowds followed Jesus and that he revealed himself as the Messiah to this *laos* as he received them, blessed and broke bread to feed them, and healed and spoke to them of the Kingdom of God (9:10–17; cf. esp. vv. 18–20). Here the main themes of the journeying guest, Lord of the Banquet first cluster about the *laos* that begin to follow Jesus just prior to the mountain revelation and confirmation of his calling from

Moses and Elijah.[116] It is here, then, that the New Exodus journey begins. It may well be that traditionists from this area of Gaulanitus (Bashan) and perhaps from the Decapolis (Gilead, e.g., Pella) and Perea assembled certain traditions—some of them overlapping with Jesus' activity in Galilee[117]—in the form of the Exodus journey of the Prophet like Moses who leads a reunited people to the salvation of the Mosaic wilderness period.

This hypothesis would accord well with the traditions of Deuteronomy, on the one hand, and with those of the *Assumption of Moses,*[118] on the other. This latter work, quoted only by church writers and closely connected to the *Testament of Moses,* purports to be an addition to the former book and relates Moses' "taking up" ($\dot{\alpha}\nu\dot{\alpha}\lambda\eta\mu\psi\iota\varsigma$) after his lengthy discourse to Joshua in Ammon (i.e., beyond Jordan in the tribe of Gad), the same area in which Moses makes his lengthy speeches in Deuteronomy. As we have seen, Deuteronomy displays a special interest in entering the land from Beth-peor in Gilead after the settling of the tribes of Reuben, Gad, and Manasseh from the valley of the Arnon in the south in Moab to Mt. Hermon north of Bashan (3:8),[119] and in Moses' dying upon the Pisgah-Nebo massif overlooking the Jordan Valley in Gilead opposite Jericho and Gilgal. It was also in this area that Elijah journeyed from Gilgal through Jericho across the Jordan to be taken up ($\dot{\alpha}\nu\epsilon\lambda\dot{\eta}\phi\theta\eta$) into heaven (4 Kgdms. 2:1–11). When all this is joined with our observation that in the travel narrative it is precisely in the area of *Jericho* that topographical details suddenly become quite precise and vivid, it may well be that our traditionists saw in Jesus' crossing of the Jordan *to be taken up* into heaven a recapitulation and consummation of his forerunners who had spoken "about his exodus that he was to fulfill in Jerusalem" (Luke 9:31). This suggestion could also explain why the term "beyond Jordan" never appears in the Central Section—indeed, not in Luke at all: certain traditions of the Central Section reflect the viewpoint of those who lived on the east side of the Jordan, for whom "beyond Jordan" would have signified something entirely different.

In any case, the resulting story would be about a community of the *laos* of Israel who are led out into the desert to be fed by their Prophet-Messiah like Moses and to be gathered with increasing numbers of Israel as they eat and drink and journey to their deliverance in Jerusalem in the Kingdom of God. At Jesus' death this community disintegrates. But as their redeemer rises from the dead to be exalted in heaven and bring the promise to their ancestors to fulfillment at the central place, so the banquet community is raised to new life in the eating and drinking before the Lord in the breaking of the bread of the early church (Acts 2:42, 46; cf. 1:4). And as eating and drinking with Jesus had become a kind of prerequisite or token of following him in the Exodus journey, so the daily breaking of bread in the Acts community becomes a watershed qualification or signification of the unity that will spread out to form new "banquet communities" on the journeyings to the end of the earth (e.g., Acts 1:4; 2:42, 46; 6:1-6). It is this story which is crowned with Paul in Rome "receiving" guests into his "house" (28:23) and "proclaiming the Kingdom of God" (Luke 9:11 → Acts 28:30-31).

The following traditiohistorical trajectories need to be pursued to establish the importance of the Stephen-Philip-Seventy(-two) connection for Luke-Acts:

1. The relation of Acts 7 to the Deuteronomistic view of Israel's history (tenets A—D), with special attention to concurrent expressions of this view such as the poignant form in the *Testament/Assumption of Moses,* on the one side, and to the Book of Deuteronomy on the other.[120]

2. The relation of the meals in the travel narrative (and Jerusalem-Emmaus meals) to Essene meal practice.[121] Especially relevant here is the messianic meal of Qumran of 1QSa 2:11-22,[122] where the Messiahs of Aaron and Israel are manifested to Israel.[123] In addition, the meals of the Therapeutae[124] as well as the conception of "eating and drinking" in certain of the *Testaments of the Twelve Patriarchs* are most promising. See, for example, *T. Sim.* 6:7: "Then I will arise with rejoicing and praise the Most High for his marvelous works. For God, by taking a body and *eating with* [cf. Luke 15:2] human beings, saved (cf. Luke 19:10) humankind."[125] Or *T. Ash.* 7:3: "The Most High shall visit [cf. Luke 19:44; 1:68; 7:16] the earth, and when he himself has come,[126] he shall eat and drink [cf., e.g., Luke 5:30; 7:34; 12:37; 13:26; Acts 10:41] with human beings, and shall without danger break the head of the dragon in the water. This one shall save Israel and all the nations, God speaking to humankind."[127]

3. The relation of the Stephen-Philip-Seventy(-two) connection to John the Baptist and his disciples. It might be significant that John or his disciples is mentioned just before the New Exodus journey begins and after the return of the Seventy(-two) to Jesus (Luke 9:7-9, 19; 11:1ff.). Moreover, not only is he linked with Jesus in the scandal of eating and drinking (7:33-35) but also his baptism is continuous with and yet decisively differentiated from Jesus'! Whereas John baptizes with water, Jesus *and* his disciples will baptize or be baptized with Holy Spirit (e.g., Luke 3:16; Acts 1:5; 8:9-24; 13:24-25; 18:25; 19:1-7). It is intriguing that Philip, that prophet with signs and power who preaches both the good news of the Kingdom of God and the name of Jesus Christ (8:12-13; cf. "in the name of" Jesus—Luke 10:17—the Seventy[-two]), is filled with the Spirit (Acts 6:3) and is "caught up" by the Spirit after baptizing the Ethiopian eunuch (8:39). Yet he does not himself baptize with the Holy Spirit but rather "only in the name of the Lord Jesus" (8:16)—a baptism that seems closely parallel to the baptism of John (cf. esp. Acts 18:25; 19:1-7).[128] It may be that the Stephen-Philip group represents a

baptist sect of either the Samaria or Transjordan area[129] who at some point were associated with the movement of John the Baptist, who was preaching in *"all the region round about the Jordan"* (Luke 3:3a).

4. Relation to the Fourth Gospel. Emphases on the Baptist, meals, and the feasts of Israel in Johannine trajectories suggest continued fruitful correlation with Luke-Acts.[130]

5. The relation of the "Prophet like Moses" Christology[131] to the "Suffering Servant" of Deutero-Isaiah,[132] on the one hand, and to the "persecution and exaltation of the Righteous Man" of wisdom circles,[133] on the other. It might be significant, for instance, that after the Seven are described as "full of wisdom" (Acts 6:3, 10) and Stephen imbues Joseph and Moses with "wisdom" qualities (7:9–13, 22–29), Philip takes on scribal characteristics by expounding the meaning of the Suffering Servant passage (Isa. 53:7–8). The extent to which the speeches in Acts (esp. 3:12–26 and 10:34–43) reflect Wisdom and Suffering Servant ideas would also have to be taken into account.[134] Furthermore, the relation of the Isaianic Suffering Servant Christology to the Isaianic "Banquet midrash"[135] would also need to be pursued, particularly with regard to the "poor" and "righteous" of the Qumran and pseudepigraphal traditions.[136]

6. The relation of the "Son of Man" of the travel narrative and the Passion stories to Daniel 7. We have seen that the Son of Man comes on a New Exodus journey to his exaltation in heaven: as in Daniel 7, the movement is that of ascent and not the alleged descent of the "divine redeemer myth."[137] It may be decisive that the only use of "the Son of Man" in Acts occurs at the end of Stephen's speech when this persecuted and dying "righteous" man, "full of the Holy Spirit," sees Jesus "the Son of Man standing at the right hand of God" (7:55–56).[138] A reference to the exalted Moses, interceding before God for his people Israel, may in fact be indicated here.[139]

In sum, it is only as these and other studies are carried out that the relation of Luke the author to the Stephen–Philip–Seventy(-two) group(s) can be more precisely determined. We have discovered already, however, that in his overall presentation of the journeying Jesus and the journeyings of the first Christian missionaries, this Luke exhibits a peculiarly close relationship to them.

Luke's Theology of the Cross

It has become axiomatic in Lukan studies that Luke imparts no atoning significance to Jesus' death. At most, one can claim that Jesus' crucifixion "corresponds to the will of God."[140] Conzelmann's conclusion still remains in force, that there is no "direct soteriological significance drawn from Jesus' suffering or death. There is no suggestion of a connection with the forgiveness of sins."[141]

Our analysis of the Central Section has led to the opposite conclusion.

As the Prophet like Moses of Deuteronomy, Jesus must journey to die in Jerusalem, not simply because God so willed it but because God so willed that the Exodus redemption led by Moses be consummated in the Exodus of the Prophet who, like him, must die to effect new deliverance for the people. And similar to Deuteronomy, this death stems at the same time from the stubborn disobedience of the people to hearken to Jesus' good news of the saving Kingdom of God which brings with it the demand for repentance. Thus Luke weaves together into one strand the so-called "misunderstanding on the part of the Jews"[142] and the "divine necessity" of God's will to present an atoning death on behalf of an intractably sinful nation. But now, unlike the first Exodus and death of Moses, the raising up of Jesus from the dead to his "place at the right hand" of God leads to the sending of the Holy Spirit with the power in the Christ's name to preach repentance and the forgiveness of sins to all nations (Luke 24:44, 53; Acts 1:1–11). Luke thus sees the journey Exodus, the suffering rejection and death of Jesus, and his resurrection and exaltation as one continuous journeying–saving event—Jesus' ἀνάλημψις (cf. Luke 9:51 → Acts 1:11). And the journeys to the ends of the earth in Acts are an extension of this event for the sake of all peoples.

We have brought to light the atoning significance of Jesus' death from the fourfold Deuteronomic-Exodus typology of the travel narrative itself (Luke 9:51—19:44). When, however, the Passion narrative is added, especially the Passion meal, we have seen how consistently the conception of Jesus' atoning death is developed. Whether the longer or the shorter readings of the "words of institution" are followed, Jesus must still "suffer" (22:15), his body must be broken (v. 19a), and he must be reckoned with the "lawless" (v. 37b). When the longer reading is preferred, then Jesus' death is explicitly described as a representative, and in that sense, a substitutionary vicarious death "for the sake of" or "on behalf of"[143] his twelve apostles who represent Israel. Here it would appear that sacrificial language, especially that of a covenant sacrifice, is uppermost, though not necessarily so. The language of the Servant's vicarious death also plays an important role. Both of these matters would have to be pursued. But in any case, it is certain that Jesus' death is an absolutely indispensable event which makes possible the new power of the life of the Kingdom of God *for the forgiveness of sins*. In short, for Luke, without Jesus' death there is no forgiveness (ἄφεσις) of sins.

It may still be objected that Luke's real theology of the cross is divulged only in the Acts with his preponderate reference to the resurrection. On this reading, the cross is pushed into the background—at the most, a heinous deed by the "ignorant" Jews—serving as a necessary *prelude* to resurrection and exaltation.[144] Jesus' resurrection has double prominence for Luke: it is an event in history, attested by witnesses, and therefore an anticipation of the future resurrection of all which will likewise take place *in* history (e.g., Acts 17:31; 23:6–9; 24:15, 21; 26:23). And yet Jesus' resurrection is also an eschatological event transcending history which leads to the fulfilled life "at the right hand of God" already available to the believer in history through the sending of the Christ (3:20, 26) in the mediating power of the Holy Spirit (e.g., 2:32–39; 5:31–32).

Nonetheless, even with this emphasis we have already seen how central the call and fate of suffering is for the apostles and the whole company of disciples in Acts.[145] And both Stephen's and Paul's careers are patterned after the suffering journey of their master, with Paul especially fulfilling Jesus' demands on the New Exodus to follow in the way of the cross (Luke 9:23–26; 14:25–27; cf. 12:49–50; 13:33; 17:25). How, then, is this notion of the cross to be squared with the dominant resurrection theme? From our analysis of the travel narrative the answer appears to lie in the converging picture of the Moses of Deuteronomy and the Deuteronomistic view of the "rejected prophet." Even as Jesus is rejected and brutally killed by his own people, he is one with them in their plight as sinners. Though he is righteous/innocent (δίκαιος) and perfectly fulfills and consummates the Law, yet he suffers and dies on their behalf (i.e., vicariously) to remove their stiff-necked disobedience. As Luke first underscores in Jesus' baptism and then highlights in his eating and drinking with tax collectors and sinners, there is a fundamental solidarity of Jesus with the sinful *laos* of God. Luke's emphasis on the resurrection, then, is a logical acclamation that this crucified one has been vindicated by God precisely as a means of bringing the eschatological fulfillment of new life to Israel and through Israel to the nations—despite Israel's ignorance and rebellion! The consequent coupling of this message with the appeal to repentance (and faith) for the forgiveness of sins confirms this relation of new life through resurrection and exaltation *as an extension of the forgiveness wrought by Jesus' death.* For a call to repentance means inherently an admission of one's own participation in Israel's stubbornness and an identification or solidarity with Jesus' death on Israel's (and the nations') behalf. This sense of identification with Jesus' suffering and death indeed lies behind such a statement as Acts 14:22b, "that through many tribulations we must (δεῖ) enter into the Kingdom of God." To be sure, this line of thought needs to be pursued in further study.[146] But it is apparent already that "resurrection" in Acts does not nullify or even push to the periphery Luke's theology of the atoning significance of the cross. It only elucidates and develops it.

CONCLUSION

The consummated Exodus journey of the Prophet like but greater than Moses (Luke 9:51—19:44) forms the dynamic center of Luke's unfolding drama of the journeying history of Israel's salvation. It is far from a secondary insertion of hodgepodge traditions into a traditional chronological framework. In it the journeying Jesus brings to fulfillment the longed-for promises to Israel's forebears, as proclaimed by all the prophets, and sets the pattern for the extension of this salvation to the end of the earth. Luke's story is both history and theology. In the bold contours of the Deuteronomistic view of Israel's history Luke shows how the people of Israel persisted in their stiff-necked rejection and killing of the prophets sent to them but how the Lord God of Israel was faithful to the promises, nonetheless. Yet this unrelenting obduracy brings with it no less the fulfillment of God's warning through the prophets. That Luke-Acts ends with this fulfillment unfilled as Paul is nearly killed at the Temple may suggest that from within these Deuteronomistic dynamics we have discovered a possible bridge from the narrative world of the text to the real world of Luke. In any case, whenever and wherever Luke is writing, he views the "events that have been completed among us" as the ongoing history of God's salvation to God's chosen but obstinate people. It may be that he considered his own two-volume work to be continuing the story of Deuteronomy (Genesis)—2 Kings.[147] As that great work of the Deuteronomist historians consists of the deliverance wrought for Israel in the Exodus story of Moses (Deuteronomy) and is completed by the unfolding history of that salvation (Joshua—2 Kings), even as Moses foresaw and prophesied, so Luke's first volume presents the consummation of the first Exodus in the New Exodus story of Jesus and is completed in the unfolding history of that salvation, even as Jesus foresaw and prophesied. This grand vision of Israel's salvation would then explain why it is that only Luke's description of Jesus' prophecy of the destruction of Jerusalem is a poignant echo of the prophetic predictions of the fall of Jerusalem in 587 B.C.E.[148] Luke thus may be the one author of the New Testament who brings the story of those words "spoken by the prophets" up to date as this journeying history reaches the ends of the earth.

Notes

1. See esp. Part I, "Dissonance of Form from Content," above.
2. See above, Part I, "Dissonance of Form from Content," pp. 14–16, 33 nn. 1, 2.

3. See above, Part III.C.3, pp. 137–39.

4. See below, "Reflections on the Theological Implications of the New Exodus Travel Narrative for Interpreting Luke-Acts," pp. 315–222.

5. See below, "Reflections on Theological Implications," pp. 318–20.

6. See above, Part I, "Dissonance of Form from Content," pp. 17–18.

7. See above, Part I, "Dissonance of Form from Content," pp. 18–20.

8. See below, pp. 318–20.

9. See, e.g., Marshall, *Luke,* 692; and Plummer (*Luke,* 439): "About six hours' march . . . or about 18 miles."

10. For the three main pilgrimage routes, see C. C. McCown, "The Geography of Jesus' Last Journey to Jerusalem," *JBL* 51 (1932): 122–29. If "Galilee" in 17:11 denotes Perea (see Marshall, *Luke,* 650), a general reference to the route east of the Jordan may already be indicated.

11. See F. V. Filson, "The Journey Motif in Luke-Acts," in *Apostolic History and the Gospel: Essays in Honour of F. F. Bruce,* ed. W. Gasque and R. P. Martin (Grand Rapids: Wm. B. Eerdmans Publishing Co., 1970), 68–77; R. Maddox, *The Purpose of Luke-Acts,* FRLANT 126 (Göttingen: Vandenhoeck & Ruprecht, 1982), 10–12, 168–70; cf. D. Daube (*The Exodus Pattern in the Bible,* All Souls Studies II [London: Faber & Faber, 1963], 12) on patterns of "deliverance" in the Bible: "I soon discovered that there was none remotely comparable to the exodus."

12. This journey of the twelve-year-old Jesus to teach in the Temple (2:42) prefigures the journeying of Jesus to the Temple to gather the Twelve tribes of all Israel in Jerusalem (9:51—19:44, 45—21:38; cf. Acts 26:6–8).

13. See above, Part III.A.3, pp. 102–5. For the "New Exodus" in Deutero-Isaiah (cf. Luke 3:4–6), see B. W. Anderson, "Exodus Typology in Second Isaiah," in *Israel's Prophetic Heritage,* ed. B. W. Anderson and W. Harrelson (New York: Harper & Brothers, 1962), 177–95.

14. See Filson's ("Journey Motif," 72–73) outline which has roughly the same journey divisions.

15. For "the church" as Jerusalem (Acts 18:22), cf. F. F. Bruce, *The Book of the Acts,* NICNT (Grand Rapids: Wm. B. Eerdmans Publishing Co., 1954), 379; F. J. Foakes-Jackson, *The Acts of the Apostles,* MNTC (London: Hodder & Stoughton, 1931), 171; and E. Haenchen, *The Acts of the Apostles: A Commentary* (Philadelphia: Westminster Press, 1971), 544.

16. Filson, "Journey Motif," 72.

17. Cf. Filson, "Journey Motif," 72–73, and Bruce, *Acts,* 393–94, for convincing demonstrations of the integrity of this schema as opposed to the "traditional" three missionary and Rome journey framework.

18. See above, Part I, n. 6.

19. See above, Part II, "Luke's Language and Lineage of the Prophets," pp. 48–56.

20. Text lengths are based on percentage of total verses.

21. See esp. Part III.B, pp. 123–27, above.

22. Both involve rejections of a sending in conjunction with temple worship: Acts 19:23–41—Temple of Artemis; Luke 9:52–56—the "Temple" cultic worship at Mt. Gerizim. In both instances, Paul/Jesus journeys to the Temple at Jerusalem.

23. See above, Part III.B, pp. 120–23. For the role of "miracle" in ancient sea voyages, see G. B. Miles and G. Trompf, "Luke and Antiphon: The Theology of Acts 27—28 in the Light of Pagan Beliefs About Divine Retribution, Pollution, and Shipwreck," *HTR* 69 (1976): 259–67.

24. See above, Part III.C.

25. Cf. BAGD, s.v. "ἐξαιρέω" on Acts 26:17: "deliver," "set free," "rescue"; for Paul's own theology of suffering, see especially J. C. Beker, *Paul the Apostle: The Triumph of God in Life and Thought* (Philadelphia: Fortress Press, 1980), esp. 198–212.

26. See esp. Part III.B, pp. 115–20, above.

27. Cf., e.g., Luke 23:9.

28. See esp. Part III.D, "The Leaven of the Pharisees-Scribes," above. Unlike the Central Section, "Jews" from Asia are the instigators (e.g., Acts 19:23ff.; 21:27); cf. D. P. Moessner, "'The Christ Must Suffer': New Light on the Jesus-Peter, Stephen, Paul Parallels in Luke-Acts," *NovT* 28 (1986): 250–53.

29. See esp. Part III.C, "The Journeying Guest Is Rejected in Jerusalem (Luke 19:45—23:49)," above.

30. See esp. Part III.D, "The Leaven of the Pharisees-Scribes," above.

31. See above, Part II, "Luke's Language and Lineage of the Prophets," pp. 52–56.

32. For discussions of the identity of these two groups, see e.g.: H. J. Cadbury, "The Hellenists," in *The Beginnings of Christianity,* ed. F. J. Foakes-Jackson and K. Lake (London: Macmillan Co., 1933), 5:59–74; O. Cullmann, *The Johannine Circle* (Philadelphia: Westminster Press, 1976), 39–49; idem, "L'opposition contre le temple de Jérusalem, motif commun de la théologie johannique et du monde ambiant," *NTS* 5 (1958–59): 157–73; idem, "Von Jesus zum Stephanuskreis und zum Johannesevangelium," in *Jesus und Paulus,* FS W. G. Kümmel, ed. E. E. Ellis and E. Grässer (Göttingen: Vandenhoeck & Ruprecht, 1975), 44–56; E. Dinkler, "Philippus und der ANHP AIΘIOΨ (Apg 8,26–40): Historische und geographische Bemerkungen zum Missionsablauf nach Lukas," in Ellis and Grässer, *Jesus und Paulus,* 85–95; E. Ferguson, "The Hellenists of Acts," *Restoration Quarterly* 12 (1969): 159–80; P. Geoltrain, "Esséniens et Hellénistes," *TZ* 15 (1959): 241–54; M. Hengel, "Zwischen Jesus und Paulus: Die 'Hellenisten,' die 'Sieben' und Stephanus (Apg 6,1–15; 7,54—8,3)," *ZTK* 72 (1975): 151–206; C. S. Mann, "'Hellenists' and 'Hebrews' in Acts VI 1," in *The Acts of the Apostles,* ed. W. F. Albright and C. S. Mann, Anchor Bible (Garden City, N.Y.: Doubleday & Co., 1967), Appendix 6, pp. 301–4; C. F. D. Moule, "Once More, Who Were the Hellenists?" *ExpTim* 70 (1959): 100–103; R. Scroggs, "The Earliest Hellenistic Christianity," in *Religions in Antiquity,* FS E. R. Goodenough, ed. Jacob Neusner, *Numen* Supplements 14 (Leiden: E. J. Brill, 1968), 176–206; M. Simon, *St. Stephen and the Hellenists in the Primitive Church* (London: Longmans, Green

& Co., 1958), esp. 167–83; E. Trocmé, *Le "Livre des Actes" et l'histoire,* Etudes d'histoire et de philosophie religieuses 45 (Paris: Presses Universitaires de France, 1957), esp. 190–91.

33. See J. B. Tyson, "The Problem of Food in Acts: A Study of Literary Patterns with Particular Reference to Acts 6:1–7," in *SBL Seminar Papers,* 1979, ed. P. J. Achtemeier (Missoula, Mont.: Scholars Press, 1979), 69–85, esp. 77–82. Tyson delineates what he calls a recurring "threat" pattern which moves the action in Acts, of which 6:1–7 is one such instance.

34. See above, Part II, "Luke's Language and Lineage of the Prophets," pp. 48–56.

35. See BAGD, s.v. "συνευδοκέω."

36. "Against God" probably reflects Stephen's polemic against the Temple (so Bruce, *Acts,* 134).

37. Note that Ναζωραῖος (18:37) or Ναζαρηνός (4:34; 24:19) occurs only once in the Galilean section of the Gospel. The term appears to cluster about Jesus' crucifixion in Jerusalem in the Gospel and about his death or persecution in the Acts (e.g., Acts 2:22; 4:10; 6:14; 22:8; 26:9; exceptions—3:6 and 24:5). But in all instances the Temple is never far removed as symbolic of the monolithic resistance first to Jesus and then to his disciples-prophets. In Luke 4:34 the synagogue at Capernaum is the setting. For historical and linguistic issues, see, e.g., W. F. Albright, "The Names 'Nazareth' and 'Nazoraean,'" *JBL* 65 (1946): 397–401; B. Gärtner, *Die rätselhaften Termini Nazoräer und Iskariot,* Horae Soederblomianae 4 (Uppsala: Appelberg, 1957); E. Nestle, "'He Shall Be Called a Nazarene,'" *ExpTim* 19 (1907–8): 523–24; idem, "Nazareth," *Protestantische Monatshefte* 14 (1910): 349–50; W. O. E. Oesterley, "Nazarene and Nazareth," *ExpTim* 52 (1940–41): 410–12; J. A. Sanders, "ΝΑΖΩΡΑΙΟΣ in Matt 2:23," *JBL* 84 (1965): 169–72; H. H. Schaeder, "Ναζαρηνός, Ναζωραῖος," *TDNT* 4:874–79; E. Schweizer, "'Er wird Nazoräer heissen' (zu Mc 1:24 Matt 2:23)," in *Judentum, Urchristentum, Kirche,* FS J. Jeremias, BZNW 26 (Berlin: A. Töpelmann, 1960), 90–93; P. Schwen, "Nazareth und due Nazoräer," *ZWT* 54 (1912): 31–55; idem, "Nazoräer und Nasaräer bei Epiphanius," *Protestantische Monatshefte* 14 (1910): 208–13; H. Zimmern, "Nazoräer (Nazarener)," *ZDMG* 74 (1920): 429–38; E. Zolli, "Nazarenus Vocabitur," *ZNW* 49 (1958): 135–36; and E. Zuckschwerdt, "Nazōraῖos in Matt. 2,23," *TZ* 31 (1975): 65–77.

38. The Exodus account covers (in percentage of verses) 59.2 percent, i.e., vv. 17–45 of Acts 7:2–50.

39. In addition to the commentaries on Acts 7, see, e.g.: B. W. Bacon, "Stephen's Speech: Its Argument and Doctrinal Relationship," in *Biblical and Semitic Studies: Critical and Historical Essays by the Members of the Semitic and Biblical Faculty of Yale University* (New York: Charles Scribner's Sons, 1902), 213–76; L. W. Barnard, "Saint Stephen and Early Alexandrian Christianity," *NTS* 7 (1960–61): 31–45; Cullmann, "L'opposition"; F. J. Foakes-Jackson, "Stephen's Speech in Acts," *JBL* 49 (1930): 283–86; W. Foerster, "Stephanus und die Urgemeinde," in *Dienst unter dem Wort,* FS H. Schreiner (Gütersloh: Bertelsmann Verlag, 1953), 9–30; J. Bihler, *Die Stephanusgeschichte im Zusammenhang*

der Apostelgeschichte, Münchener Theologische Studien 1/16 (Munich: Hueber Verlag, 1963); B. S. Childs, "Moses' Slaying in the Theology of the Two Testaments," in his *Biblical Theology in Crisis* (Philadelphia: Westminster Press, 1970), 164–83; idem, *The Book of Exodus, A Critical, Theological Commentary,* OTL (Philadelphia: Westminster Press, 1974), 573–81; N. Dahl, "The Story of Abraham in Luke-Acts," in Keck and Martyn, *SLA,* esp. 142–48; O. Glombitza, "Zur Charakterisierung des Stephanus in Act. 6 und 7," *ZNW* 53 (1962): 238–44; A. F. J. Klijn, "Stephen's Speech—Acts VII. 2–53," *NTS* 4 (1957–58): 25–31; B. Reicke, *Glaube und Leben der Urgemeinde,* ATANT 32 (Zurich: Zwingli Verlag, 1957), 115ff.; J. H. Ropes, "Bemerkungen zu der Rede des Stephanus und der Vision des Petrus," *TSK* (1930): 307–15; M. H. Scharlemann, *Stephen: A Singular Saint,* AnBib 34 (Rome: Pontifical Biblical Institute, 1968); Scroggs, "Hellenistic Christianity"; Simon, *Stephen and Hellenists;* idem, "Saint Stephen and the Jerusalem Temple," *JEH* 2 (1951): 127–42; and A. Spiro, "Stephen's Samaritan Background," in *The Acts of the Apostles,* by J. Munck, rev. by W. F. Albright and C. S. Mann, Anchor Bible, Appendix 5, 285–300.

40. But 7:51–53 makes it clear that they are not participating in this fulfillment.

41. Like Moses, Jesus, and Stephen, Joseph is σοφία; like Jesus and Stephen, he has χάρις before God and the people.

42. Cf. above, n. 41, and 7:22b: "δυνατός in word and deed."

43. For this triad, cf., e.g., Deut. 11:3–5.

44. See L. T. Johnson's (*The Literary Function of Possessions in Luke-Acts,* SBLDS 39 [Missoula, Mont.: Scholars Press, 1977], 71–76) observation on the speech revealing "the structure of Luke's thinking about Jesus and his place in God's plan." For sources and redaction, see, e.g., E. Richard, *Acts 6:1—8:4: The Author's Method of Composition,* SBLDS 41 (Missoula, Mont.: Scholars Press, 1978), esp. 13–31, 243–311.

45. Cf., e.g., Deut. 9:12.

46. On this theme in the New Exodus travel narrative, see above, Part III.C and D, and in Deuteronomy, see above, Part IV, "The Journeying Guest, Lord of the Banquet as the Prophet like Moses of Deuteronomy."

47. Dahl ("Abraham," 142–48) comes to a similar interpretation of the Temple polemic within the speech.

48. See above, Part II, n. 23.

49. Steck (*Israel,* 265–69) concludes that Acts 7 represents a Hellenistic-Jewish Christian type of repentance preaching to Israel based on the Deuteronomistic view of Israel's history and on such repentance preaching by Deuteronomistic traditionists during the intertestamental period who themselves were nurtured primarily in "wisdom" circles. Steck aligns the "Hellenists" of Acts 6—8 with the traditionists of Stephen's speech. We have left this latter question open, preferring instead to speak of "the Stephen-Philip group," which may or may not have belonged to the Hellenists. The disputed variant reading in Acts 11:20 makes this question, at the level of the story, virtually impossible to answer.

50. See below, "Reflections on the Theological Implications of the New Exodus Travel Narrative," pp. 312–22, for Paul as a model Israelite à la Deut. 26:1–11.

51. See above, Part IV, n. 42.

52. See the definition of "plot" in the Introduction, "Method and Scope of This Work."

53. Cf., e.g., Deut. 26:11 and see above, Part IV, "The Journeying Guest, Lord of the Banquet as the Prophet like Moses of Deuteronomy," pp. 266–67, 273.

54. Implicit in this prophetic model is the rejected prophet's vindication or exaltation: Moses is vindicated by Joshua and the Prophet like Moses; Jesus is raised up from the dead and "taken up" to the "right hand of God"; Stephen is granted the vision of the glory of Jesus the Son of Man "standing at the right hand of God"; Paul, in Rome, preaches openly as the message of the Kingdom of God goes out to the "end of the earth." In each case, vindication is the initiation of the extension of salvation beyond previous bounds.

55. See above, Part II.

56. The "mountain" is the proleptic fulfillment of "the Christ" "entering into his glory" (Luke 24:26); see above, Part II, "The Prophetic Parallels of Moses in Deuteronomy to Jesus in Luke 9:1–50," item 1; and D. P. Moessner, "'The Christ Must Suffer,'" 235–38.

57. The beginning of the promise of "the God of glory" to Abraham.

58. Cf. n. 52 above for story time; for the "way" of salvation, see Luke 1:76, 79; 2:44; 3:4–5; 7:27; 9:3, 57; 10:4, 31; 11:6; 12:58; 14:23; 18:35; 19:36; 24:32, 35; Acts 1:12; 8:26, 36, 39; 9:2, 17, 27; 13:10; 18:26; 19:9, 23; 22:4; 24:14, 22; 25:3; 26:13.

59. See above, Introduction, n. 25.

60. In Luke 11:47–51 this story goes back to creation (the "foundation of the world") with the "sending" of Abel.

61. E.g., Conzelmann, *Theology,* 95–136; Haenchen, *Acts,* 97–98; U. Wilckens, *Die Missionsreden der Apostelgeschichte: Form und traditions-geschichtliche Untersuchungen,* WMANT 5 (Neukirchen-Vluyn: Neukirchener Verlag, 1961), 202; S. Schulz, *Die Stunde der Botschaft: Einführung in die Theologie der vier Evangelisten* (Hamburg: Furche, 1967), 238, 284; and E. Dinkler, *Signum Crucis: Aufsätze zum Neuen Testament und zur christlichen Archäologie* (Tübingen: J. C. B. Mohr [Paul Siebeck], 1967), 334. For a summary of this position and response in contemporary debate, see W. G. Kümmel, "Lukas in der Anklage der heutigen Theologie," *ZNW* 63 (1972): 149–65.

62. Cf., e.g., B. Reicke, "The Risen Lord and His Church: The Theology of Acts," *Int* 13 (1959): 157–69, esp. 157–58, 161–65.

63. Cf. also, e.g., οἶκος—Acts 20:20; 21:8.

64. Cf. also Acts 21:17.

65. Contra Filson, "Journey Motif," 74–76.

66. Notice how Paul always goes first to the synagogues and preaches to the Jews "as was his custom" (Acts 17:2; cf. 17:10, 17; 18:4–5, 12).

67. So Jervell (*Luke and the People of God: A New Look at Luke-Acts* [Minneapolis: Augsburg Publishing House, 1972], 41–74) argues; but see Moessner, "Paul in Acts," for a different notion of eschatological Israel; cf. D. Juel, *Luke-Acts: The Promise of History* (Atlanta: John Knox Press, 1983), 101–12.

68. On the role of the *laos* as well as that of the leaders in the death of Jesus, see D. P. Moessner, "The 'Leaven of the Pharisees' and 'This Generation': Israel's Rejection of Jesus According to Luke," *JSNT* 34 (1988): 21–46.

69. E.g., K. Baltzer, "The Meaning of the Temple in the Lukan Writings," *HTR* 58 (1965): 263–77.

70. The phrase is found in Petersen, *Literary Criticism*, 87.

71. Haenchen (*Acts*, 539) as quoted by Petersen *(Literary Criticism)*.

72. As Reicke (*Glaube*, 129–57) observed.

73. But cf. below, Part III.C, n. 215, for the "messenger midrash." It is possible that Luke 2:30–32 was formulated in the light of those messenger texts through the "catchwords" λαός and ἑτοιμάζω. Cf. also Isa. 49:6 in Acts 13:47; 26:23. For the Servant theology in Luke-Acts, see D. P. Moessner, "The Ironic Fulfillment of Israel's Glory," in *Luke-Acts and the Jewish People*, ed. J. B. Tyson (Minneapolis/ Philadelphia: Augsburg Publishing House/Fortress Press, 1988), 35–50; and the articles by R. C. Tannehill (83–101) and D. L. Tiede (21–34) in the same volume.

74. E.g., Acts 13:43; 14:1, 4, 21; 17:4, 11–12; 18:4, 8, 10b, 27; 29:1–7.

75. The imperfect tense is used; Acts ends with Paul still actively at work, but note the aorist tense in v. 30; for a revitalization of the view that Paul's Gentile mission is an apologetic for the complete Jewishness of Paul, see R. L. Brawley, "Paul in Acts: Lucan Apology and Conciliation," in *Luke-Acts: New Perspectives from the Society of Biblical Literature Seminar*, ed. C. H. Talbert (New York: Crossroad, 1984), 129–47.

76. For a beginning, see Moessner, "'The Christ Must Suffer.'"

77. ἄρχων refers to Jewish leaders (so also Bruce, *Acts,* 287; and Haenchen, *Acts,* 421).

78. See G. von Rad, *Deuteronomium-Studien*, FRLANT n.F. 40 (Göttingen: Vandenhoeck & Ruprecht, 1948), 52–64.

79. E.g., Conzelmann, *Theology,* 98–100; Haenchen, *Acts,* 96; and E. Grässer, *Das Problem der Parusieverzögerung in den synoptischen Evangelien und in der Apostelgeschichte,* BZNW 22, 3d ed. (Berlin: Walter de Gruyter, 1977), 194, 206. Cf. Kümmel, "Anklage," 152–55.

80. See Introduction, "Method and Scope of This Work," pp. 4–6.

81. In addition to the commentaries, see H. J. Cadbury, "'We' and 'I' Passages in Luke/Acts," *NTS* 3 (1956–57): 128–32. Cadbury links the "I" of the Prologue (Luke 1:1–4) to the Book of Acts, or at least the latter part, through παρηκολουθηκότι which he understands as to "follow through first-hand experience" (pp. 130–31). The differentiation of the "we" group around Paul from Paul himself in Acts 16:17; 21:18; 28:16 makes good sense with this link of the "I" and "we" (p. 129).

82. Cf. J. Wanke, *Beobachtungen zum Eucharistieverständnis des Lukas auf Grund der lukanischen Mahlberichte,* Erfurter Theologische Schriften 8 (Leipzig: Sankt-Benno Verlag, 1973), 19–24. The Jerusalem meals, Acts 2:42, 46, are, in any case, only summary descriptions.

83. Cf. B. Reicke, "Die Mahlzeit mit Paulus auf den Wellen des Mittelmeers, Act. 27, 33–38," *TZ* 6 (1948): 401–10; and Wanke, *Beobachtungen,* 25–30.

84. Cf., e.g., Acts 16:14–15—Lydia prevails upon Paul and the "we" group to "stay" (μένω) at her house. The story of the meal at the Philippian jailer's house follows in vv. 16–34.

85. Cf. Cadbury, "'We' and 'I' Passages"; and M. Hengel, *Acts and the History of Earliest Christianity*, trans. J. Bowden (Philadelphia: Fortress Press; London: SCM Press, 1979), 66–67.

86. See esp. Part III.A.3, above.

87. For a summary of this development, see above, Part III, "Conclusion," Excursus 3.

88. See above, Part III.D, "The Leaven of the Pharisees-Scribes," pp. 187–88.

89. For historical issues, see, e.g., Hengel, *Acts and the History*, 111–26.

90. Whichever reading is preferred in Acts 11:20, the contrast is still to "Jews" (11:19b: ᾿Ιουδαιοι) which must denote "non-circumcised."

91. On this, see, e.g., B. Reicke, "Der geschichtliche Hintergrund des Apostel-konzils und der Antiochia-Episode, Gal. 2,1–14," in *Studia Paulina*, FS J. de Zwaan (Haarlem: Erven F. Bohn, 1953), 172–87.

92. See, e.g., O. Cullmann, "Die Bedeutung der Zelotenbewegung für das Neue Testament," in *Vorträge und Aufsätze 1925–1962*, ed. and trans. K. Fröhlich (Zurich: Zwingli Verlag, 1966), 292–302; B. Reicke, *The New Testament Era* (Philadelphia: Fortress Press, 1968), 243–49; and M. Hengel, *Die Zeloten: Untersuchungen zur jüdischen Freiheitsbewegung in der Zeit von Herodes I. bis 70 n. Chr.*, AGJU 1, 2d ed. (Leiden: E. J. Brill, 1976), esp. 348–65.

93. In addition to the commentaries, cf., e.g., Reicke, "Hintergrund," 182–87; and Hengel, *Acts and the History*, 119–23.

94. Within the story of Acts, Paul was part of the council that drafted (15:19ff.) and then disseminated the decree among the mission churches (16:14). Therefore the repetition of the decision by James in 21:25 appears to be a "plot device" by which Luke emphasizes the extreme urgency of the situation to which the decree was to be addressed.

95. See this development in Kümmel, "Anklage," 156–59.

96. H. Conzelmann, "Luke's Place in the Development of Early Christianity," in Keck and Martyn, *SLA*, 298–316.

97. See, e.g., W. G. Kümmel's own formulation (*Introduction to the New Testament*, rev. ed. [Nashville: Abingdon Press, 1965], 186): "The most likely assumption . . . is a date for Acts between 80 and 90, but a date between 90 and 100 is not excluded."

98. This atmosphere includes the *one table* of the "breaking of the bread" within the various Christian communities.

99. See esp. Part II, "Luke's Language and Lineage of the Prophets," above; cf. P. F. Feiler, "Jesus the Prophet: The Lucan Portrayal of Jesus as the Prophet like Moses" (diss., Princeton Theological Seminary, 1985), esp. 172–89.

100. For the relatively minor role of the "Davidic" Messiah, see F. F. Bruce, "The Davidic Messiah in Luke-Acts," in *Biblical and Near Eastern Studies*, FS W. S. LaSor, ed. G. A. Tuttle (Grand Rapids: Wm. B. Eerdmans Publishing Co., 1978), 7–17. The Davidic emphasis is restricted to the Nativity Narrative (Luke

1—2) and to the speeches in Acts (mainly Acts 2; 13). Acts 7 is noticeably void of an emphasis on David; instead, he is subsumed by the Mosaic model.

101. For connections of Luke-Acts to Samaria, see, e.g., E. H. Plumptre, "The Samaritan Element in the Gospels and Acts," *The Expositor* 7 (1880): 22–40; J. Bowman, "The Parable of the Good Samaritan," *ExpTim* 59 (1947–48): 151–53; and C. H. H. Scobie, "The Origins and Development of Samaritan Christianity," *NTS* 19 (1972–73): 391–400. For the Samaritans in general, see M. Gaster, *The Samaritans: Their History, Doctrines and Literature* (London: Oxford University Press, 1925); and J. MacDonald, *The Theology of the Samaritans* (London: SCM Press, 1964). For the relation of the Samaritans to the NT in general, see J. MacDonald and A. J. B. Higgins, "The Beginnings of Christianity According to the Samaritans: Introduction, Text, Translation, Notes and Commentary," *NTS* 18 (1971–72): 54–80.

102. E.g., Scharlemann, *Stephen,* 22–51; Gaston, *No Stone on Another: Studies in the Significance of the Fall of Jerusalem in the Synoptic Gospels,* NovTSup 23 (Leiden: E. J. Brill, 1970), 154–61; Scobie, "Origins," 393–96; Spiro, "Samaritan"; for a comprehensive summary, see G. Schneider, *Die Apostelgeschichte,* HTKNT 5 (Freiburg: Herder & Herder, 1980), 1:448–53.

103. See esp. W. A. Meeks, *The Prophet-King: Moses Traditions and the Johannine Christology,* NovTSup 14 (Leiden: E. J. Brill, 1967), 229–30, 249–54, for the relation of the Samaritan *Taheb* to Moses traditions.

104. E.g., Cullmann, *Circle,* 46–49; idem, "Stephanuskreis"; and Scobie, "Origins," 398–400.

105. This verb appears only elsewhere in 1 Pet. 1:18; Titus 2:14.

106. This form is a *hapax legomenon;* but cf. λύτρωσις: Luke 1:68; 2:38; Heb. 9:12.

107. The "sons" of Luke 11:19 may reflect the Stephen-Philip-Seventy(-two) traditionists.

108. Cf. Hengel (*Acts and the History,* 95–98), who links this picture in Acts to an Antioch-Hellenist source. On table fellowship, see L. C. Crockett, "Luke 4:25–27 and Jewish-Gentile Relations in Luke-Acts," *JBL* 88 (1969): 177–83.

109. See further, C. H. H. Scobie, "North and South: Tension and Reconciliation in Biblical History," in *Biblical Studies,* FS W. Barclay, ed. J. R. McKay and J. F. Miller (London: William Collins Sons, 1976), 87–96.

110. Cf. esp. J. Bowman, "The Samaritans and the Book of Deuteronomy," *Glasgow University Oriental Society* 17 (1957–58): 9–18; e.g., "It is not impossible that Deuteronomy was designed for centralization of worship in one sanctuary in the north" (p. 16). For Deuteronomy's link to Northern traditions, see, e.g., E. W. Nicholson, *Deuteronomy and Tradition* (Oxford: Basil Blackwell, 1967), 47–82.

111. Scobie, "North and South," 94. For the universalistic thrust, see N. Q. King, "The 'Universalism' of the Third Gospel," *SE I,* 199–205. For the Gentile mission, see S. G. Wilson, *The Gentiles and the Gentile Mission in Luke-Acts,* SNTSMS 23 (Cambridge: Cambridge University Press, 1973).

112. Cf. Mark 6:53.

113. Notice that Jesus "curses" Galilean cities just as he sends out the Seventy(-two) (Luke 10:13–15).

114. Cf. John 4:20.

115. For the "others" (John 4:38) as referring to the Samaritan mission of the Stephen-Philip group of Acts 6—8, see O. Cullmann, "Samarien und die Anfänge der christlichen Mission: Wer sind die 'ΑΛΛΟΙ von Joh. 4,38" in *Fröhlich, Vorträge und Aufsätze,* 232–40. Our link of the Seventy(-two) with the Stephen-Philip group posits already a mission to parts of Samaria during the ministry and journeying of Jesus to Jerusalem; the perfect tense verbs in John 4:38 would then make more sense to refer on the first level of meaning to disciples who have already "labored" before Jesus sends (4:38—aorist tense) the disciples with him in John 4 to buy food. Our suggestion thus sheds added light on Cullmann's elucidation and sharpens it within the story of the Fourth Gospel. On John 4 and Samaritan links, see also J. Bligh, "Jesus in Samaria," *HeyJ* 3 (1962): 329–46.

116. See above, Part III, "Conclusion," Excursus 3, on *laos* in the travel narrative. That *laos* is never used for the "crowds" of Israel once the journey begins (9:51ff.) fits in well with the suggestion that many of the traditions of the Central Section reflect a nonconformist "Essene" Jewish posture toward the nation as a whole.

117. See above, Part I, "Dissonance of Form from Content," pp. 18–20.

118. See R. H. Charles, ed., *Apocrypha and Pseudepigrapha of the Old Testament,* 2 vols. (Oxford: Clarendon Press, 1913), 2:411; E. Brandenburger, *Himmelfahrt Moses* (Gütersloh: Gerd Mohn, 1976), 59–66; and G. W. E. Nickelsburg, Jr., *Resurrection, Immortality, and Eternal Life in Intertestamental Judaism,* HTS 26 (Cambridge: Harvard University Press, 1972), 43–45.

119. See Mark 8:27 par. Matt. 16:13 with their tradition that the mountain of transfiguration was in the environs of Caesarea-Philippi (probably Mt. Hermon).

120. Cf. Steck, *Israel,* 265–69; Steck's analysis needs to be applied, however, to Deuteronomy. See above, n. 76.

121. See, e.g., J. Neusner, "Qumran and Jerusalem: Two Types of Jewish Fellowship in Ancient Times," in *Contemporary Judaic Fellowship in Theory and in Practice,* ed. J. Neusner (New York: Ktav, 1972), 1–11. For Qumran and Essene meal practice, see, e.g., K. G. Kuhn, "Über den ursprünglichen Sinn des Abendmahls und sein Verhältnis zu den Gemeinschaftsmahlen der Sektenschrift," *EvT* 10 (1950–51): 508–27; G. Graystone, "The Dead Sea Scrolls and the New Testament," *ITQ* 22 (1955), esp. 332–34; J. Daniélou, "La communauté de Qumrân et l'organisation de l' église ancienne," *RHPR* 35 (1955): 104–15; J. van der Ploeg, "The Meals of the Essenes," *JSS* 2 (1957): 163–75; and J. Gnilka, "Das Gemeinschaftsmahl der Essener," *BZ* 5 (1961): 39–55. On Philo's and Josephus's accounts of the Essenes, see M. Black, *The Scrolls and Christian Origins: Studies in the Jewish Background of the N.T.* (New York: Charles Scribner's Sons, 1961), 173–86. See also J. A. Fitzmyer, *The Dead Sea Scrolls: Major Publications and Tools for Study* (Missoula, Mont.: Scholars Press, 1977).

122. See H. N. Richardson, "Some Notes on 1QSa," *JBL* 76 (1957): 108–22; esp. 120–22; and M. Smith, "'God's Begetting the Messiah' in 1QSa," *NTS* 5 (1958–59): 218–24.

123. On messianic notions in Qumran, see, e.g., W. H. Brownlee, "Messianic Motifs of Qumran and the New Testament," *NTS* (1956–57): 12–30, 195–210; K. G. Kuhn, "Die beiden Messias Aarons und Israels," *NTS* 1 (1954–55): 168–79; L. H. Silberman, "The Two 'Messiahs' of the Manual of Discipline," *VT* 5 (1955): 77–82; R. E. Brown, "J. Starcky's Theory of Qumran Messianic Development," *CBQ* 28 (1966): 51–57; and M. de Jonge, "The Use of the Word 'Anointed' in the Time of Jesus," *NovT* 8 (1966): 132–48.

124. See, e.g., H. G. Schönfeld, "Zum Begriff 'Therapeutai' bei Philo von Alexandrian," *RevQ* 3 (1961–62): 219–40; and B. Reicke, "Remarques sur l'histoire de la forme 'Formgeschichte' des textes de Qumran," in *Les manuscrits de la Mer Morte,* ed. M. Simon (Paris: Presses Universitaires de France, 1957), 37–44.

125. For text, M. de Jonge, *Testamenta XII Patriarcharum,* PVTG 1 (Leiden: E. J. Brill, 1964). For recent translation with critical notes, see J. H. Charlesworth, ed., *The Old Testament Pseudepigrapha,* 2 vols. (Garden City, N.Y.: Doubleday & Co., 1983), 1:771–995); and H. F. D. Sparks, ed., *The Apocryphal Old Testament* (Oxford: Clarendon Press, 1984), 505–648. O. Hofius (*Jesu Tischgemeinschaft mit den Sündern,* Calwer Hefte 86 [Stuttgart: Calwer Verlag, 1967], 5–8) points also to *T. Sim.* 6:5; *T. Jud.* 24:1; *T. Isaac.* 7:7; *T. Dan* 5:13; 6:9; *T. Napth.* 8:3; *T. Ash.* 7:3; and *T. Benj.* 10:7–9.

126. See the many references to Jesus' coming in the New Exodus travel narrative (Part III.C).

127. The context is the two Messiahs of Levi and Judah (i.e., a High Priest and King [7:1–3]); cf. the two Messiahs of Qumran and Zech. 6:9–14.

128. Though the disciples of Acts 19:1–7, like those of 8:16, are first baptized "in the name of the Lord Jesus" before Paul then lays his hands on them and they receive the Holy Spirit with signs parallel to those of Pentecost in 2:3ff.

129. See J. Thomas, *Le mouvement baptiste en Palestine et Syrie '150 av. J.-C.—300 ap. J.-C.',* Universitas catholica Lovaniensis 2/28 (Gembloux: Duculot, 1935). For the relation to Samaritanism and early Gnostic groups, see R. Pummer, "The Present State of Samaritan Studies: II, Gnosticism," *JSS* 22 (1977): 27–47. For general surveys of Jewish Christianity and relations to baptist and Samaritan groups, see, e.g., A. F. J. Klijn, "The Study of Jewish Christianity," *NTS* 20 (1973–74): 419–31; A. F. J. Klijn and G. J. Reinink, *Patristic Evidence for Jewish-Christian Sects,* NovTSup 36 (Leiden: E. J. Brill, 1973); and M. Black, "The Patristic Accounts of Jewish Sectarianism," *BJRL* 41 (1958–59): 285–303. For the relation of Samaritan and baptist groups to Qumran, see, e.g., R. McL. Wilson, "Simon, Dositheus and the Dead Sea Scrolls," *ZRGG* 9 (1957): 21–29; and W. H. Brownlee, "A Comparison of the Covenanters of the Dead Sea Scrolls with Pre-Christian Jewish Sects," *BA* 13 (1950): 50–72. On the relation of John the Baptist to the Mandaeans, see, e.g., R. Bultmann, "Die Bedeutung der neuerschlossenen mandäischen und manichäischen Quellen für das Verständnis des Johannesevangeliums," *ZNW* 24 (1925): 100–146; C. H. Dodd, *The Interpretation of the Fourth Gospel* (Cambridge: Cambridge University Press, 1953), 115–30; and K. Rudolph, *Die Mandäer,* 2 vols., FRLANT 56, 57 (Göttingen: Vandenhoeck & Ruprecht, 1960–61), 1:65–80; 2:348–57.

130. Parallels between the Stephen-Philip-Seventy(-two) group and traditions

in the Fourth Gospel include *inter alia:* (1) an anti-official Judaism atmosphere; (2) interest in Samaria; (3) "wonders and signs" and the "signs" of the Fourth Gospel; (4) revelation of Jesus' identity at meals, cf., e.g., John 13—17; (5) Jesus as the fulfiller of the great feasts of Israel; (6) service and servanthood at table (e.g., foot washing, John 13); (7) the "tabernacling glory" of God in Jesus and the universal mission; (8) the Prophet-King (Messiah) like Moses and Northern prophetic traditions; (9) interest in Jesus' disciples "baptizing"; and (10) the "Jews" of John and the anti-Pharisee polemic of the travel narrative.

For the anti-Temple and official cult movement in relation to the NT, in addition to Cullmann *(Circle),* see also, e.g., G. Klinzing, *Die Umdeutung des Kultus in der Qumrangemeinde und im NT,* SUNT 7 (Göttingen: Vandenhoeck & Ruprecht, 1971); B. Gärtner, *The Temple and the Community in Qumran and the New Testament: A Comparative Study in the Temple Symbolism of the Qumran Texts and the New Testament,* SNTSMS 1 (Cambridge: Cambridge University Press, 1965). For the "Jews" and anti-Judean sentiment, see, e.g., W. A. Meeks, "Galilee and Judea in the Fourth Gospel," *JBL* 85 (1966): 159–69; and R. L. Sturch, "The 'ΠΑΤΡΙΣ' of Jesus," *JTS* 28 (1977): 94–96. For Samaritan links to John, see A. M. Johnson, "The Cultural Context of the Gospel of John—A Structural Approach" (diss., University of Pittsburgh, 1978); and G. W. Buchanan, "The Samaritan Origin of the Gospel of John," in *Religions in Antiquity: Essays in Memory of Erwin Ramsdell Goodenough,* ed. J. Neusner (Leiden: E. J. Brill, 1968), 149–75. For "Northern" prophets, see B. P. Robinson, "Christ as a Northern Prophet in St John," *Scr* 17 (1965): 104–8. On parallels of Luke to Hebrews, see W. C. van Unnik, "The 'Book of Acts' the Confirmation of the Gospel," *NovT* 4 (1960): 46–59.

131. In addition to Meeks *(Prophet-King),* see also H. M. Teeple, *The Mosaic Eschatological Prophet,* SBLMS 10 (Missoula, Mont.: Scholars, 1957), esp. 84ff.; O. Cullmann, *The Christology of the New Testament,* trans. S. C. Guthrie and C. A. M. Hall (Philadelphia: Westminster Press, 1959), 13–50; and Steck, *Israel,* 240–49.

132. See the treatments in M. Rese, *Alttestamentliche Motive in der Christologie des Lukas,* SNT 1 (Gütersloh: Gerd Mohn, 1969), 97–104, 111–12, 154–64, 168–71; and G. Voss, *Die Christologie der lukanischen Schriften in Grundzügen,* Stud Neot 2 (Paris: Desclée de Brouwer, 1965), 167–70; see also above, n. 73.

133. See, e.g., Nickelsburg, *Resurrection,* 48–92; and Steck, *Israel,* 254–62. For a broader treatment in the NT and Judaism, see E. Schweizer, *Lordship and Discipleship* (London: SCM Press, 1960), 22–48; and for the Suffering Servant, ibid., 49–55.

134. See, e.g., Steck, *Israel,* 51–53 on Acts 2, 3, and 10.

135. See L. C. Crockett, "The Old Testament in the Gospel of Luke: With Emphasis on the Interpretation of Isaiah 61.1–2" (diss., Brown University, 1966), 280ff.; see also above, Part III.C, n. 274. For Luke's use of Isaiah as a whole, see D. Seccombe, "Luke and Isaiah," *NTS* 27 (1980–81): 252–59; and J. A. Sanders, "Isaiah in Luke," *Int* 36 (1982): 144–55.

136. See, e.g., Nickelsburg, *Resurrection,* 131–80.

137. See, e.g., Bultmann, "Bedeutung."

138. For an interpretation along Johannine christological-eschatological lines, see C. K. Barrett, "Stephen and the Son of Man," in *Apophoreta: Festschrift für Ernst Haenchen* (Berlin: A. Töpelmann, 1964), 32–38.

139. For a summary of opinion and references, see G. Schneider, *Apostelgeschichte,* 1:475 n. 33.

140. Cited by Kümmel, "Anklage," 159. Kümmel admits that Luke (cf. Luke 22:19–20; Acts 20:28) "in no way deletes the atoning significance of the death of Jesus, but does not emphasize it" (p. 159).

141. Conzelmann, *Theology,* 201.

142. Kümmel, "Anklage," 154.

143. Marshall, *Luke,* 803.

144. E.g., Acts 2:23–24, 30–33, 36; 3:13–17, 20–22, 26; 4:10, 33; 7:55–56; 10:39–40; 13:27–38; 17:3, 18, 31–32; 23:6–9; 24:15, 21; 26:23.

145. E.g., 5:18–42; 7:54—8:3; 9:16; 11:19; 14:22; 20:23; 21:11–14, 30–36; cf. 13:50; 15:26; 17:3; see above, Part II, "Luke's Language and Lineage of the Prophets," pp. 51–56.

146. A comparison to Col. 1:24 would seem fruitful. For Peter's speech in Acts 3 incorporating an atoning death into the very logic of the argument, see D. P. Moessner, "Jesus and the 'Wilderness Generation': The Death of the Prophet like Moses According to Luke," in *SBL Seminar Papers, 1982,* ed. K. H. Richards (Chico, Calif.: Scholars Press, 1982), 338–40; idem, "'The Christ Must Suffer,'" 234–47.

147. Hengel (*Acts and the History,* 30–34) suggests that the basic model for Luke's work was the OT "biographical complexes" of Israel's history with, for instance, a "life of Moses" (Exodus-Deuteronomy) followed by the "history of the conquest," etc.

148. C. H. Dodd, "The Fall of Jerusalem and the 'Abomination of Desolation,'" *JRS* 37 (1947): 47–54; B. Reicke, "Synoptic Prophecies on the Destruction of Jerusalem," in *Studies in New Testament and Early Christian Literature,* FS A. P. Wikgren, ed. D. E. Aune, (Leiden: E. J. Brill, 1972), 121–34; D. P. Moessner, "Paul in Acts: Preacher of Eschatological Repentance to Israel," *NTS* 34 (1988): 96–104; and J. A. T. Robinson, *Redating the New Testament* (Philadelphia: Westminster Press; London: SCM Press, 1976), 13–30.

Index I

Biblical and
Other Ancient Literature

(An * in the bold face headings of the text refers to the smaller tradition units (pericopes) within the larger passages. Pericope divisions based on K. Aland, ed., *Synopsis Quattuor Evangeliorum* [Stuttgart: Württembergische Bibelanstalt, 1975]. See also, above, the tables on pp. 131 and 211.)

Index II

Modern Authors